Man's Role
in
Changing the Face of the Earth
Volume 1

Man's Role in Changing the Face of the Earth

International Symposium
Wenner-Gren Foundation for Anthropological Research

Co-Chairmen of the Symposium

CARL O. SAUER   MARSTON BATES   LEWIS MUMFORD

Participants

WILLIAM A. ALBRECHT
HARRY ALPERT
EDGAR ANDERSON
EUGENE AYRES
A. LESLIE BANKS
H. H. BARTLETT
ALAN M. BATEMAN
DAVID I. BLUMENSTOCK
KENNETH BOULDING
HARRISON BROWN
JOHN C. BUGHER
ALBERT E. BURKE
ANDREW H. CLARK
JOHN T. CURTIS
H. C. DARBY
F. FRASER DARLING
CHARLES GALTON DARWIN
JOHN H. DAVIS
JOHN W. DODDS
FRANK E. EGLER
E. ESTYN EVANS
IAGO GALDSTON
CLARENCE J. GLACKEN
ARTUR GLIKSON

PIERRE GOUROU
EDWARD H. GRAHAM
*MICHAEL GRAHAM
GEORGE W. GRAY
ALAN GREGG
E. A. GUTKIND
CHAUNCY D. HARRIS
EMIL W. HAURY
FRITZ M. HEICHELHEIM
J. A. HISLOP
CHARLES B. HITCHCOCK
SOLIMAN HUZAYYIN
EDAVALETH K. JANAKI AMMAL
STEPHEN B. JONES
LESTER E. KLIMM
FRANK H. KNIGHT
HELMUT LANDSBERG
LUNA B. LEOPOLD
*DONALD H. MC LAUGHLIN
JAMES C. MALIN
ALBERT MAYER
*RADHAKAMAL MUKERJEE
ROBERT CUSHMAN MURPHY
*KARL J. NARR
F. S. C. NORTHROP

SAMUEL H. ORDWAY, JR.
FAIRFIELD OSBORN
GOTTFRIED PFEIFER
*RICHARD J. RUSSELL
CHARLES A. SCARLOTT
VINCENT J. SCHAEFER
PAUL B. SEARS
RODERICK SEIDENBERG
J. RUSSELL SMITH
ALEXANDER SPOEHR
H. BURR STEINBACH
OMER C. STEWART
ARTHUR N. STRAHLER
SOL TAX
*PIERRE TEILHARD DE CHARDIN
HAROLD E. THOMAS
WARREN S. THOMPSON
C. W. THORNTHWAITE
JOHN W. TUKEY
EDWARD L. ULLMAN
JOSEPH H. WILLITS
HERMANN VON WISSMANN
KARL A. WITTFOGEL
*ABEL WOLMAN

*Contributors to Symposium as authors of background papers but not in attendance.

Man's Role
in
Changing the Face of the Earth
Volume 1

Edited by

WILLIAM L. THOMAS, Jr.

with the collaboration of

CARL O. SAUER

MARSTON BATES

LEWIS MUMFORD

Published for the

WENNER-GREN FOUNDATION FOR ANTHROPOLOGICAL RESEARCH

and the

NATIONAL SCIENCE FOUNDATION

by

THE UNIVERSITY OF CHICAGO PRESS

CHICAGO AND LONDON

*The INTERNATIONAL SYMPOSIUM ON MAN'S ROLE IN CHANG-
ING THE FACE OF THE EARTH was made possible by funds granted
by the Wenner-Gren Foundation for Anthropological Research, Incorporated, a foundation endowed for scientific, educational, and charitable
purposes. Publication of this volume has been aided by a grant from the
National Science Foundation of the United States. Neither foundation
is the author or publisher of this volume, and is not to be understood
as endorsing, by virtue of its grant, any of the statements made, or views
expressed, herein.*

ISBN: 0-226-79604-3 (Volume 1); 0-226-79605-1 (Volume 2)

Library of Congress Catalog Card Number: 56-5865

THE UNIVERSITY OF CHICAGO PRESS, CHICAGO 60637
The University of Chicago Press, Ltd., London

To

G E O R G E   P.   M A R S H
and to the earliest men who
first used tools and fire;
and to the countless generations between
whose skilful hands and contriving brains
have made a whole planet their home
and provided our subject for study

Foreword

On June 16 of this year it was my privilege, as President of the Wenner-Gren Foundation for Anthropological Research, to extend welcome to the seventy illustrious participants assembled in Princeton, New Jersey, for the International Symposium on "Man's Role in Changing the Face of the Earth." The opening ceremonies, which included addresses of welcome from Dr. C. E. Sunderlin, Deputy Director of the National Science Foundation; Dr. Harold W. Dodds, President of Princeton University; and Dr. Axel L. Wenner-Gren, marked the culmination of nearly three years of planning that made possible the Symposium and this volume.

The Wenner-Gren Foundation, ever since its establishment in 1941, has been uniquely concerned with rendering aid in the advancement of anthropology as the study of man. Over the years, the Foundation's program has developed simultaneously along three broad fronts. First, and largely, it has directly assisted (mostly professional anthropologists) through fellowships and grants-in-aid, publication subsidies, and sponsorship of conferences and seminars and by making possible professional stocktaking, as in the International Symposium on Anthropology held in New York in June, 1952, resulting in the three volumes, *Anthropology Today, An Appraisal of Anthropology Today,* and *International Directory of Anthropological Institutions.* Second, the Foundation has been constantly on the search for new ideas and techniques developed in other fields capable of contributing to solutions of anthropological problems; examples of this are the Foundation's postwar program of loans of field equipment and its pioneer aid in the application of the radioactive carbon theory to the problem of absolute dating in archeology and paleoanthropology. Third, the Foundation has been concerned with broadening the bases of public support of anthropology through dissemination of the results of anthropological research and through diffusion of anthropological theory, methods, and knowledge into other fields of science; examples of this have been the organization and publication of such symposium volumes as *The Science of Man in the World Crisis, Ideological Differences and World Order,* and *Most of the World.*

This Symposium and volume on "Man's Role in Changing the Face of the Earth" reflect the second and third facets of our program. The Foundation has long been aware that one of the ways in which scholars move toward theoretical and conceptual ordering of man's knowledge of himself and his world is by synthesis, transcending the limits of present disciplines or branches of science. The Foundation's purpose through the present undertaking has been to further the recombination and synthesis of available and new knowledge, looking toward the development of a more comprehensive science of man.

The subject of the Symposium was the idea of the Foundation's Assistant Director, Dr. William L. Thomas, Jr., who also acted as organizer and is the editor of this volume. The Foundation is indeed grateful for this opportunity to express publicly its appreciation of the vision and zeal of Dr. Thomas. Grateful thanks are also due to him for his devoted and significant contributions and tireless splendid efforts in his multiple activities in connection with this Symposium. We wish to express, too, our feeling of profound gratitude to the three senior scholars—Professors Carl O. Sauer, Marston Bates, and Lewis Mumford—who so willingly and ably aided the Symposium's development. The co-operative assistance of the National Science Foundation, whose grant-in-aid of publication subsidy made possible this volume, is greatly appreciated.

The Foundation was fortunate to encounter a number of persons with alert, able, and active minds interested in a common problem and invited them to come together that they might benefit by stimulation from one another. In a setting that encouraged men to speak easily with one another, many minds learned what others were thinking. The Symposium, in attempting to survey the state of knowledge of a topic touched only in piecemeal fashion by individual disciplines, provided a focus of interest for persons with different theoretical and descriptive backgrounds. The question explored was: What has been, and is, happening to the earth's surface as a result of man's having been on it for a long time, increasing in numbers and skills unevenly, at different places and times?

The story of mankind may be considered as man's own exploration of the various physical and biological conditions on the earth's surface as a result of the elaboration of human needs, capacities, aspirations, and values. Three interrelated factors are involved: (1) the earth's resources; (2) the numerical pressure of population upon, and sustained by, the resources; and (3) man's differing cultures, or ways of life. Understanding these relationships involves knowledge of values, equipment or artifacts, and of the social organizations by which people group themselves, function, and interpret resources and their use. Cultural development may be viewed as man's growing knowledge of, and control over, forces external to himself. By increasing his range of action, man has intervened more and more in the rest of the organic world. Man's evolutionary dominance seems assured—only he himself can threaten it. Man has supplemented organic evolution with a new method of change—the development of culture, the transmission of organized experience, retained, discarded, or altered by further experience.

The Foundation's interest in calling this Symposium, therefore, is anthropology's own—to keep abreast of all the means at man's disposal to affect deliberately or unconsciously the course of his own evolution; in this case, what man has done, and is doing, to change his physical-biological environment on the earth.

PAUL FEJOS

NEW YORK CITY

Table of Contents

Volume 2
PART II. PROCESS

Introductory

Man's Effects on the Seas and Waters of the Land

Alterations of Climatic Elements

Table of Contents

List of Illustrations

List of Tables

xix

Introductory

About the Symposium
About the People
About the Theme

"Man's Role in Changing the Face of the Earth" is many things. It is part of the historical reality of the earth during its latest phase, which has witnessed the presence of man. It is an idea or theme of which man, conscious of himself and his activities, has become increasingly aware and which has been touched upon in one or another aspect by scores of scholars through the ages. It was an international symposium, organized by the Wenner-Gren Foundation for Anthropological Research, and held at the Princeton Inn, Princeton, New Jersey, June 16–22, 1955. And, lastly, it is this volume, which treats all the above through the writings of fifty-three contributors and a report on the Symposium discussions of the seventy participants.

ABOUT THE SYMPOSIUM

The development of an interdisciplinary symposium with international participation is a study in organized complexity. Active planning began in the fall of 1952, and a full year was spent in research on the theme, in formulating a statement of the significance of the symposium idea, in drafting a tentative program and roster of possible invitees, and in consultation with more than forty scholars in and out of New York City. In October, 1953, the proposal for a symposium was placed before Professor Carl O. Sauer, then Chairman of the Department of Geog-

raphy, University of California, Berkeley, with the request that he serve as Symposium Chairman. We first met for prolonged discussion in Tucson, Arizona, during the annual meeting of the American Anthropological Association in December, 1953. It was agreed that the Symposium's purpose was neither to propose an action program nor to pass resolutions. We did not want it to get lost in elegant verbal acrobatics nor to have it run into the shoals of statistics, except as they might be valid illustrations. The participants were to be selected for their common interest and curiosity about what man has been doing to and with his habitat. To be included was the historical course of action by which man had come to be where he is.

The web of planning and consultation during the winter and spring of 1954 expanded to include sessions with Professors Edgar Anderson, Marston Bates, Stephen Jones, Lewis Mumford, Paul Sears, and Sol Tax. "Round-robin" exchanges of correspondence were voluminous. It was agreed that no effort would be spared in attending to the proper amenities and the comforts of the participants. In seeking to encourage the fullest possible exchange of ideas, there should be a minimum of limitations to communication inherent in group activity. But it was further recognized that the primary objective was not education of the participants

xxi

through interaction of personalities and ideas but publication of a record of the Symposium in a permanent form, so that the ideas expressed might reach a larger audience and be available to scholars in oncoming generations.

Responsibility for thinking toward this primary objective led to outlining not a conference but a volume. As with *Anthropology Today*, which resulted from the 1952 International Symposium on Anthropology, titles for chapters were suggested. The chapters were to be written as factual accounts, inventories, or data papers. Each chapter was to be oriented around a certain body of subject matter, with the primary intent to "brief" or to inform others who are aware of, but not expert in, the field being surveyed. Taken together, these chapters were to provide a common ground of factual data for persons who, in their approaches to the central theme, had come along many different paths not necessarily with previous intersections. Having been written prior to the Symposium, the chapters were to be preprinted and circulated to all participants for study before their departure from their homes. The objective of these background papers was to free the limited Symposium time for full discussion of ideas and to prevent its being bogged down by formal reading of papers heavily weighted with factual data and intended as exchanges of information.

The Symposium itself was to be structured only loosely. A foundation by planning can provide only opportunity and setting. The creativity of a symposium lies in the hands of its participants. Speakers having the floor could talk about what they wished, regardless of what subject might be listed on a printed program. The Symposium was to be thought of principally in terms of the people whom it would be desirable to bring together for a week; secondly in terms of a handful of chairmen for the various half-day discussion sessions; and thirdly in terms of a skeletal framework of session themes that would only roughly sketch in a program. This latter would be a guide for the division of effort among chairmen, within which they would have the fullest latitude for the conduct of their respective sessions.

The function of the background papers for the Symposium was to provide common knowledge to all participants in advance of their gathering together. The Symposium, however, could choose to ignore the papers entirely, discuss them all in detail, or pick and choose as it pleased. The background papers simply were to "be there," without any thought that papers rather than people constitute a symposium. The challenge to the Symposium was to rise above the level of the content of the papers into the realm of ideas—the next higher realm of abstraction, as it were—dealing not with the recitation of facts or with the exchange of anecdotes but with the conjunction of thoughts. The resulting publication was to contain two things: first, the background papers, each authored for an audience of non-specialists by a key scholar at home in his field, and, second, an edited version of the Symposium discussions—a report on the thoughts given expression while the group was assembled.

In March, 1954, Sauer proposed a threefold division for the Symposium—"Retrospect," "Process," and "Prospect" —and suggested that there be three co-chairmen corresponding to each of these views of the Symposium theme. Sauer assumed the task for "Retrospect"; Bates and Mumford accepted his invitations to share the co-chairmanships for "Process" and "Prospect," respectively. Once the general outline of the Symposium had been drawn and a roster of invitees had been developed, the Foundation, on behalf of its Board of Directors, began to extend invitations to participants in early June, 1954. The invitations proposed a meeting in June, 1955, outside of New York City, intended as a gathering of some of the world's best minds in a congenial atmosphere for recorded discussion leading to eventual publication for the benefit of the world of scholarship. Expenses of first-class transportation to and from their homes and a sum for personal expenses, as well as provision for the stay during the Symposium, were to be provided by the Foundation. An appendix to the invitation letter listed the invitees and, by way of introduction, their positions, institutional affiliations or addresses, and the titles and dates of several publications of each.

More than two-thirds of those invited were asked to prepare a background or data paper on a suggested topic, such paper to be submitted not later than March 15, 1955. It was pointed out that papers would be published in full and would be distributed to all participants in advance of the Symposium but would not be read aloud. Also, a copy of the published volume and fifty reprints of his chapter would be furnished each author. An appendix to the invitation letter gave additional details about the background papers. Discussion was invited of an author's views of a better phrasing of the proposed title of his paper. (Twenty-three chapters have been retitled in accordance with their authors' suggestions; three authors eventually wrote on subjects other than those proposed.) As guidance for relating each paper to the Symposium theme, the planning group included a list of subjects that each author might consider for inclusion in the content of his paper. An optimum length of eight thousand words (exclusive of a list of "References") was proposed for the papers. With this limitation, obviously no paper could attempt to summarize existing factual knowledge. Rather, the contributed chapters were to be looked upon as evaluations of the state of knowledge of the topics considered, keeping in mind as a purpose the stimulation of the next generation of research scholars. What are the known problems? What special strategy is called for in planning research? What are the topics and areas principally in urgent need of additional investigation? It was further suggested that, whereas all articles would deal with the qualitative effects of man's working and living in different parts of the world, perhaps some authors would wish to consider the quantitative effects of man on the landscape. How much has man changed the earth's surface? How fast is he changing it? How rapidly can he restore it if his changes have proved unwise or are now considered obsolete and replacement is desired? Perhaps an approach in terms of total amounts and rates of change would produce much more information and insight than would a purely qualitative approach.

Between June, 1954, and March, 1955, ninety-seven invitations were extended, and seventy-six acceptances were received. During the fall of 1954 several memorandums were sent to participants as aids and as reminders of the tasks ahead. In October the place of the Symposium was announced as the Princeton Inn, Princeton, New Jersey, and the dates as June 16–22, 1955; a revised program and roster of participating scholars were included. In November a guide to contributing authors of background papers advised of the format, style for footnotes and bibliography, the inclusion of illustrative material, layout of title page and biographical statement, and manner for ordering author's reprints. In December information was given on the transportation and personal expenses to be furnished each participating scholar.

In December, 1954, through the

award of a grant-for-publication subsidy, the National Science Foundation of the United States joined in the sponsorship of the Symposium. This expression of recognition emphasized the truly broad interest of the Symposium theme for almost all fields of science. Application to the Department of State for designation of the Symposium as an exchange-visitor program in order to facilitate entrance of foreign scholars into the United States was made in December, 1954; notification of such designation and the assignment of serial number P-1974 were received in April, 1955. In May, 1955, a contract was negotiated with the University of Chicago Press for publication of the volume to emanate from the Symposium. Funds received from the National Science Foundation grant were held in a separate account and then transmitted in full to the University of Chicago Press in October, 1955.

The first public announcement of the Symposium meanwhile had appeared in *Science,* on March 11, 1955 (CXXI, No. 3141, 356–57). Other announcements appeared soon after in the British journals *Nature* and *Man.* The first background papers were mailed to all participants in early March; four packages in all were sent by mid-May. Forty-seven of the fifty-three background papers were received by participants for study in advance of the Symposium; four others were distributed upon arrival; the remaining two were reproduced and distributed at Princeton from manuscripts delivered by their authors upon arrival at the Symposium. A special paper on "Princeton and Environs" provided information on travel to Princeton and described the local area and its points of interest. Six scholars who contributed background papers could not attend the Symposium meetings; thus the participants totaled seventy. The Symposium met for six working days, on each of which two three-hour sessions were held. On the evening prior to the Symposium's opening, a dinner in honor of the visiting scholars from outside the United States was attended also by the Symposium co-chairmen and chairmen of the individual half-day discussion sessions. At this pre-Symposium meeting all chairmen had the opportunity to exchange information on the expected nature of their sessions. A briefing was given on the arrangement of the meeting room and on problems of recording, and questions on procedure were answered.

The Symposium program was as follows:

Thursday, June 16

INTRODUCTION

10:15 A.M.   OPENING SESSION: THE SYMPOSIUM THEME

Welcome from the Wenner-Gren Foundation—DR. PAUL FEJOS, President

Welcome from the National Science Foundation—DR. C. E. SUNDERLIN, Deputy Director

Welcome to the Princeton Community—DR. HAROLD W. DODDS, President, Princeton University

Introducing the Symposium Co-Chairmen:

PROFESSOR CARL O. SAUER, University of California
PROFESSOR MARSTON BATES, University of Michigan
PROFESSOR LEWIS MUMFORD, University of Pennsylvania

The Symposium Idea—PROFESSOR SAUER

Remarks of Appreciation—DR. AXEL L. WENNER-GREN

RETROSPECT

1:30 P.M.   MAN'S TENURE OF THE EARTH
              Chairman: F. Fraser Darling

Friday, June 17
9:00 A.M.   SUBSISTENCE ECONOMIES
              Chairman: Alexander Spoehr

2:00 P.M.   COMMERCIAL ECONOMIES
              Chairman: Paul B. Sears

Saturday, June 18
9:00 A.M.   INDUSTRIAL REVOLUTION AND URBAN DOMI-
              NANCE
              Chairman: Kenneth Boulding

PROCESS

2:00 P.M.   TECHNIQUES OF LEARNING: THEIR LIMITATIONS
              AND FIT
              Chairmen: Edgar Anderson *and* Sol Tax

Monday, June 20
9:00 A.M.   CHANGES IN PHYSICAL PHENOMENA
              Chairman: Alan M. Bateman

2:00 P.M.   CHANGES IN BIOLOGICAL PHENOMENA
              Chairman: Marston Bates

PROSPECT

Tuesday, June 21
9:00 A.M.   LIMITS OF THE EARTH: MATERIALS AND
              IDEAS
              Chairmen: Joseph H. Willits *and* Lester E. Klimm

2:00 P.M.   MAN'S SELF-TRANSFORMATION
              Chairman: Lewis Mumford

Wednesday, June 22
9:00 A.M.   THE UNSTABLE EQUILIBRIUM OF MAN IN NA-
              TURE
              Chairman: Harrison Brown

SUMMARY REMARKS

2:00 P.M.   RETROSPECT—Carl O. Sauer
              PROCESS—Marston Bates
              PROSPECT—Lewis Mumford

The Symposium "Program and Calendar of Events" listed the daily program, the background papers (by number, title, and author), a roster of Symposium participants (by name, affiliation, and Symposium role), a floor plan of the Princeton Inn, pertinent information concerning Symposium procedure, information on personal arrangements and local facilities, maps of Princeton and of the Princeton University campus, and a roster of the Foundation's Board of Directors, officers and staff, and the Symposium co-chairmen and staff.

The Symposium meeting room and office, rooms for all participants except those living in the immediate vicinity, and meals were provided for within the Princeton Inn. Extracurricular activities in New York City included a theater program on Saturday night and either a sight-seeing cruise around Manhattan Island or a double-header baseball game on Sunday afternoon. The last evening was devoted to a farewell banquet for all Symposium participants, at which Professor Sauer was presented with a silver tea service and an illuminated scroll signed by all who attended.

Prior to the Symposium meeting all background papers had been edited. An editorial office was established at the Princeton Inn, and, during the week of the meeting, two editorial assistants consulted with the authors of background papers, to discuss such matters as amendments in submitted manuscripts, verification of biographical statements, and signing of consent-to-publish agreements. All Symposium discussion for the full six days was recorded; the full transcript of this recording was prepared in mimeographed form totaling 1,093 pages. Bound copies (in three-volume sets) of this transcript are in the Foundation's office and were presented to each of the three Symposium co-chairmen. The co-chairmen edited their "Summary Remarks" of the closing session on the basis of the mimeographed transcript and a tape recording of their remarks that were provided them. A report of the Symposium discussions, based upon the recorded transcript, was prepared by the editor. Each session chairman was provided a copy of the transcript and of the editor's report of his respective session.

The illustrated background papers and the edited report of the discussions together comprise the contents of this volume. The intended audience for this work is nothing less than the vast numbers of the human kind in the "rest of the world," now and to be, outside of the microcosm of Princeton in June, 1955, when those who shared one another's company provided its substance and gave it birth.

ABOUT THE PEOPLE

Any program of such scope and magnitude as has been described could have been made possible only by the enthusiastic co-operation of a host of individuals.

Whatever value this volume may have stems from the combined efforts of the seventy Symposium participants (listed on pp. ii and 1153–55), the fifty-three contributing authors, the thirteen scholars who chaired various parts of the Symposium discussions, and the three Symposium co-chairmen. After the Symposium, and following return to their homes, the participants wrote to us appreciative letters of thanks. But we of the Foundation know that to act as host is to be but a catalytic agent; the active ingredients in the Symposium reaction were the working participants. We look back with fond memory on having met so many interesting and wonderful people. The reader and editor alike are indebted to them for having provided the content of this volume.

The seventy participants, after having been selected for their qualities as individuals, turned out to have backgrounds or specializations in some twenty-four different conventionally defined disciplines, from anthropology to zoölogy. Broadly classified, about 40 per cent were in the field of earth science, 28 per cent in the biological sciences, 12 per cent in the social sciences and the humanities, and 20 per cent in applied fields (administration, city planning, etc.). Fourteen came from nine countries outside the United States (Canada, England, Scotland, Northern Ireland, Belgium, Germany, Egypt, Israel, and India). Sixty-five per cent were associated with universities; 35 per cent represented private institutions, industry, and government.

In their institutional roles, the Board of Directors of the Wenner-Gren Foundation for Anthropological Research and the National Science Board of the

National Science Foundation are to be thanked for their allocations of funds in support of the Symposium—its organization, meeting, and preparation for publication and its publication, respectively. Dr. Axel L. Wenner-Gren, the Founder, and Dr. Paul Fejos, President of the Wenner-Gren Foundation, together with Dr. C. E. Sunderlin, Deputy Director of the National Science Foundation, participated in the opening ceremonies. Professors John W. Dodds and F. S. C. Northrop, members of the Board of Directors of the Wenner-Gren Foundation, and Dr. Harry Alpert, Program Director for Anthropological and Related Sciences of the National Science Foundation, participated in all Symposium sessions.

We are grateful to Dr. David I. Blumenstock, then of Rutgers University, for preparing the special booklet on "Princeton and Environs," from which every Symposium participant benefited with information in advance of arrival. The Princeton University Library, through the good offices of Dr. William S. Dix, loaned many reference volumes on New Jersey and the Princeton community which were available for consultation by all participants. Dr. Robert Cushman Murphy made memorable one evening at Princeton by presenting color slides and film on "The Guano Islands of Peru."

From the very inception of the planning of the Symposium, the editor has had the secretarial assistance of Mrs. Jean S. Stewart. She is the only person other than the editor who daily has witnessed and tended the transformation of an intangible idea into this massive volume. During the past year, since the arrival of manuscripts of the background papers, she has doubled as editorial assistant. The completion of this volume is a monument in testimony to her faithful and steadfast devotion over the last three and a half years. Assisting during brief stages in the planning phase were Misses Susan Davis and Nancy Silbowitz.

The Symposium staff at Princeton drew in part upon those regularly employed by the Foundation. Miss Alice Uchida (now Mrs. Wasserman) supervised the reception desk and acted as office manager, while Miss Joyce De Podesta and Mrs. Joyce Mendelsohn served as meeting-room attendants and assisted in office duties. Needless to say, behind the scenes, the entire staff of the Foundation contributed directly or indirectly to the development of the Symposium and the realization of its goal.

From June through August, 1955, we were fortunate to have the services of Mr. Frederick J. Simoons, a doctoral candidate in the Department of Geography at the University of California, Berkeley. His co-operative assistance during the course of the meetings was invaluable and his functions many; principally, though, he insured the accuracy of the discussion transcripts by identifying speakers and checking the spelling of proper names, foreign words, and technical phrases. After the Symposium and back at the Foundation's offices, the transcript of all the discussion sessions was corrected before mimeographing by playback of the tape recordings; also, he spent considerable time in library research on the material presented in the section that follows: "About the Theme."

The editorial assistants at Princeton were Mrs. Stewart and Miss Anna M. Pikelis, formerly a Foundation staff member and at that time at the University of Chicago and an editorial assistant for the *American Anthropologist*. Together with the editor, they had previously read and marked all background papers; between them they conferred with all the authors present at Princeton and arranged for the approval of the corrected edited version of the manuscripts to be forwarded to the publisher, the University of Chicago Press.

Miss Nancy Silbowitz spent part of the summer months of 1955 at various libraries in New York City checking and completing bibliographic entries. Mrs. Wasserman, Mrs. Jean Shulman, and Miss Silbowitz have served variously as post-Symposium clerks and secretaries, copyreaders, and proofreaders. The skill of Mr. Felix M. Eger in arranging the microphones and controlling the recording devices insured that faithful and complete tape recordings were made of all remarks presented in the meeting room during all six days of discussion.

Throughout the volume, credits for permission to reproduce certain illustrative material appear immediately beneath the respective illustrations. We are especially indebted to Dr. David Lowenthal, of Vassar College, for the loan of the portrait of George P. Marsh reproduced in Figure 49 and for reading and suggesting corrections and additional remarks to our account of the work of Marsh. In undertaking background reading for the following section, "About the Theme," we have had the assistance in German translation of Mrs. Katherine Klein and Ilona Schenk and in Russian translation of Dr. David Sopher and Mr. Albert E. Burke.

The American Geographical Society has been most helpful in many ways. The end-paper map for this volume originally appeared as an inset on one of the Society's maps in the series "Atlas of Diseases." The equal-area elliptical projection is by William Briesemeister, chief cartographer, with population overlay compiled and drafted by E. D. Weldon. Some 40 of the 180 figures for this volume were redrawn for publication by the Society's cartographic staff. The chart of "Conversion Scales" (p. 1156) originally appeared in *Pioneer Settlement* (Special Publication No. 14), published by the Society in 1934. Two Councilors of the Society, Drs. Lester E. Klimm and Robert Cushman Murphy, and the Director, Mr.

Charles B. Hitchcock, were participants in the Symposium. A review of the Symposium, prepared by Murphy and Hitchcock, appeared in the *Geographical Review*, XLV, No. 4 (October, 1955), 583–86.

ABOUT THE THEME

The intellectual fonts in the modern period in developing the theme, "Man's Role in Changing the Face of the Earth," were the American statesman and scholar George Perkins Marsh and the Russian geographer Alexander Ivanovich Woeikof.[1] It is to these two that many contemporary writers refer and from whom they take their inspiration.

Marsh (1801–82) grew up in the stimulating atmosphere of a nineteenth-century New England family which belonged to the intellectual aristocracy. He carefully observed the changes that men had brought about in the forested hills and valleys of New England and maintained his interest in man's modification of the earth's surface throughout his career of service as a lawyer, member of the Congress of the United States, and minister to Turkey and Italy. In 1864, when he was in his sixties, Marsh set forth his ideas about man's alteration of the earth in his greatest work, *Man and Nature; or, Physical Geography as Modified by Human Action.*[2] He pointed out (p. vii) "the dan-

1. Also variously rendered as Aleksandr Voeykov or Voeĭkov.

2. Prior to his major work, Marsh had in 1847 prepared an address on man's alteration of the landscape, intentional and unintentional, desirable and dangerous ("Address Delivered before the Agricultural Society of Rutland County, September 30, 1847" [Rutland, Vermont, 1848], esp. pp. 17–19). His *Report on the Artificial Propagation of Fish* (Burlington, 1857) and his essay, "Study of Nature" (*Christian Examiner*, LXVIII [January, 1860], 33–62), also dealt largely with this theme. In 1869 and 1872 Marsh brought out Italian

gers of imprudence and the necessity of caution in all operations which, on a large scale, interfere with the spontaneous arrangements of the organic and inorganic world." Further, he suggested (p. 7) "the possibility and the importance of the restoration of the disturbed harmonies and the improvement of waste and exhausted regions."

For Marsh, man was a dynamic force, often irrational in his treatment of the environment. Because of this irrationality, man created a danger to himself that he would destroy his base of subsistence. Marsh decried the environmentalism of many of his contemporaries, who regarded man simply as a passive being acted on by the environment. One of his main objects was to show that, far from being will-less and impotent, man was a free agent "working independently of nature"; it was not the earth that made man, but man who made the earth (Lowenthal, 1953). By understanding the nature of his impact on the environment, man might learn to change the face of the earth in rational, constructive fashion.

Marsh was concerned with man's influence on nature not in an abstract or theoretical sense but in terms of practical changes to improve the lot of mankind. His solution for the problems of Western Europe and the United States was that man should moderate his activities and develop a morality in respect to his use of the earth. He had some very concrete proposals, such as the maintenance of certain proportions of land in forest and the national control of natural resources. Above all, he thought it important to ascertain the probable effects of action before acting.

Marsh's work bears the indelible stamp of his experiences in the forests of the New World and his observations in the scrub and desert regions of the Mediterranean. The largest chapter of *Man and Nature* is entitled "The Woods" and comprises more than one-third of the entire volume. Though man's alteration of the forests in the mid-latitudes thus is extensively treated, Marsh did not touch upon the modification of mid-latitude grasslands, a subject that is receiving considerable attention today.

Another even more noteworthy omission in Marsh's work was his lack of concern with the exhaustion of mineral resources. He considered mining only as it disturbed the beauty of the landscape, not in terms of the depletion of reserves of minerals. Still further, although Marsh was living in a period of booming populations all over the world, his emphasis was on maintaining standards of living in Western Europe and the United States. The specter of overpopulation raised by Malthus finds little place in Marsh's work; it is the injury to the earth by man that dominates his writing.

Like most scholars of the mid-nineteenth century, Marsh's focus in space was on Western civilization and in time on the experiences of the Western world, beginning with classical antiquity. This ethnocentric view was more understandable in Marsh's era, because knowledge of the preclassical world, of the high civilizations of Asia and the New World, and of the strange and distant lands and their peoples and cultures was still limited and unreliable.

Man and Nature, despite its shortcomings, was the first great work of synthesis in the modern period to examine in detail man's alteration of the face of the globe. Marsh's eloquent style and copious footnotes revealed the broad

---

editions of *Man and Nature*, published in Florence and incorporating new material. Based upon the Italian work, a new English-language edition, *The Earth as Modified by Human Action*, was published in 1874. A final edition was published posthumously in 1885, though reprintings occurred at least as late as 1898. All English-language editions had both London and New York imprints.

scope of his reading; his work attracted wide attention at the time. The early conservationists acknowledged their indebtedness to him; every important figure in forestry, both in America and abroad, testified to the impact of Marsh's work. Nevertheless, the period in which he wrote was dominated by an almost unlimited faith in the possibilities of material progress. Those responding to the alarm for the destruction of nature were far fewer than those who were actively engaged in spreading the railroads, producing new agricultural machinery, expanding world commerce, and opening up the grasslands. Interest in Marsh's work was rekindled in this century when man's destructiveness became so evident that it could no longer be ignored and when the problems that Marsh so vividly pictured loomed large before us. [3]

Another important contributor to the theme of man's influence on the earth was Alexander Ivanovich Woeikof (1842–1914), professor of physical geography at the University of St. Petersburg in Russia. Woeikof's writings, which were published in Russian, German, and French, received wider attention on the continent of Europe than did those of Marsh. Moreover, though Woeikof apparently traveled widely, even visiting the United States, there is no indication in his writings that he was familiar with Marsh's work. The chain of influence from Marsh to Woeikof led through Élisée Reclus, the French geographer who corresponded with Marsh while preparing his own great work, *La Terre* (published in New York in 1874 as *A New Physical Geography*), and whose works were cited by Woeikof.

Woeikof considered the surface of the earth to be composed of movable bodies (*corps meubles*) of soil and subsoil, sands and gravels on the land, vegetation, materials suspended in the water or carried by it, dust and sand moved by the wind, and snow. Man influenced the surface of the earth especially through an intermediary—vegetation. In modifying natural vegetation and in replacing wild plants by cultivated plants, man augmented the movable bodies, diminished their quantity, or changed their distribution. Among such activities, Woeikof recognized the important part that fire played as a weapon of man.

Woeikof cited cases of the destruction of vegetation by irrational cattle-grazing, of man-made canyons in the chernozem belt of Russia, and of the destruction of chernozem due to shallow plowing. Woeikof thought that man should strive to achieve a certain harmony both within and in his relation to nature. He found examples of such a harmonious activity of man in the irrigation projects of ancient civilizations, in modern Egypt, in arid states of America, and in Russian Central Asia.

Like Marsh, Woeikof was interested in improving the conditions of human life. Among his interests were land improvement in Russia, the relations between climate and the national economy, the use of water, the problems of sand, irrigation of the Transcaucasian districts, the problems of draining swamps, the problems of colonizing the north, changes in level of rivers, the disappearance of the forest, and the cultivation of new plants in Russia.

Woeikof believed that man had an influence on climate through his modification of vegetation; that is, the deforestation that had gone on so extensively in Russia had affected the temperature of the air, the winds, the rains, and the snows. He considered forests to be desirable and urged the restoration of forests that had been destroyed. The view that forests have a significant effect on

3. For the rediscovery of Marsh see Lewis Mumford's *The Brown Decades: A Study of the Arts in America, 1865–1895* (New York: Harcourt, Brace & Co., 1931).

climate is in disfavor in the Western world today, where climatologists believe that, at best, vegetation influences climate on a local scale and to an insignificant degree. Woeikof was an ardent disciple of the use of irrigation and believed that the control and mastery of the water supply was one of the main tasks man had yet to accomplish.

Like many a contemporary romantic, Woeikof was appalled at the expansion of urban areas. He said (1901, p. 208), "This grouping in cities, under conditions unhealthy to body and mind, this dissociation of man and the earth is proof of a sickly state." This theme—that urban civilization is somehow not good, that urban conditions are unhealthy, and even that cities are parasitic on the countryside—is one that is still very much with us today, though Marsh did not consider it.

The effect of warfare on the landscape was considered by Woeikof too, and he cited examples of the decrease in numbers of sedentary populations and the expansion of forests during times of war.

In dealing with the population problem, Woeikof was apparently interested more in the absolute number of people the world could support than in the limitations of resources and the desirability of developing and maintaining high standards of living. His conclusions about the possibilities of expanding population were optimistic, as would be expected from someone who had experience in the rapidly developing areas of the United States and of Russia. He believed that the direct utilization of the light and the heat of the sun as well as the use of the water of the earth could make possible a tremendous expansion in production. Thus, though Woeikof raised questions regarding the nature and effect of man's past use of the earth, he believed (1901, p. 215) that a rational approach to development of our resources could

lead to "des perspectives de progrès si vaste s'ouvrent devant nous qu'on a peine à les croire possible." Thus he was essentially an optimist with a utilitarian approach, while Marsh, though he took a guardedly optimistic note, was more impressed with the enormous damage done in his native New England and in the Mediterranean lands, where he spent his later life, and recognized the need for more than a utilitarian approach—the fostering in Western man of a love of the earth.

Many of the omissions of Marsh's work are apparent in Woeikof's too: the latter's emphasis was on contemporary and Western societies, with particular attention to Russia rather than on man everywhere and through time; his lack of concern about the depletion of mineral resources was also apparent; and his treatment of the world's population growth was perhaps too optimistic.

In the English-speaking world Marsh had no successor until Nathaniel Southgate Shaler, professor of geology at Harvard University, took up the theme of man's destructive activities in his book *Man and the Earth* (1905). His plea was that of a conservationist, and, like Marsh's *Man and Nature*, his writing had a moral tone (p. 1) that "we may be sure that those who look back upon us and our deeds from the centuries to come will remark upon the manner in which we use our heritage, and theirs, as we are now doing, in the spend-thrift's way, with no care for those to come." Shaler pointed out that primitive man and the lower animals made no drain on the stores of the earth but that, the more advanced the economy becomes, the more destructive it is of animals, plants, and mineral resources. He reported that, since the coming of the Iron Age, the consumption of mineral resources had increased to a frightening degree. Whereas in 1600 there were relatively few substances (mostly precious stones) for which men looked to the underground, now there were several hundred substances which were being used by man.

Shaler suggested that, with increasing consumption, mineral resources would be depleted in the foreseeable future. He observed that there are really only two minerals of absolute importance: iron and copper. While others are useful, they are not essential. In view of the gradually decreasing supply of high-grade iron and copper ores, he concluded that production costs of these ores gradually would rise and that eventually iron ore would be concentrated from rocks, a feat which only today is being spoken of as economically feasible.

Shaler went on to discuss the destruction of soil as a result of agricultural practices and the problems of a rapidly expanding population. However, unlike Woeikof, who was concerned with possible limits of population, Shaler was concerned with the limits of the resource base. Thus he said (p. 13): "In a word, we may estimate that in a historic sense very soon the world will be near its food-producing limit." He concluded that already the planet's resources were taxed to support the people who lived on it. How could a population three times as dense be supported and the fertility of the earth be maintained, he demanded. We should try to prevent soil erosion and restore nutrients to the land that are removed by cultivated plants.

Despite his ominous warning, Shaler thought (p. 19) that there is "every reason to believe that our science is ready for the task and that within two centuries of peaceful endeavor we may prepare the place for it." Shaler's book was concerned with future power sources and the use of coal and oil, which he considered temporary energy sources. But he believed the waters, the winds, and the tides to be the permanent resources of supply of power

and that man would need to develop these resources of power as well as available supplies of solar energy.

Shaler then turned to the possibility of expanding cultivation into the unwon lands of the earth and of reclaiming land from lakes, rivers, and the sea. He examined the resources of the sea and stated his belief that the sea might be made to contribute "far more than it does now to the needs of man."

Shaler urged (p. 228) that we "awaken a sense of the nobility and dignity of the relation man bears to this wonderful planet and the duty that comes therefrom." He went on to point out that, though many consider the universe to be simply an extension of the individual man, there are also many others who believe that the world is essentially related to us and part of us. It was Shaler's hope (p. 229) that man would come to realize that "whatever else he may be, he is the sum of a series of actions linked with all that goes on upon this earth." He thus emphasized (p. 230) the "oneness of nature and intelligence as its master."

But Shaler's approach to the earth, like Marsh's, was more than one of stark utility. He questioned our plans for the earth as a place to live. Do we envisage an earth that is completely covered with men or, as Shaler put it (p. 172), "an intensely humanized earth, so arranged as to afford a living to the largest possible number of men"? It was Shaler's contention that if this is what we do envisage—a completely domesticated earth—we could obtain a fairly accurate impression as to what it might be like by visiting those centers in Holland and England where there are many people and where there is intensive land use. Shaler did recognize (p. 189) that in Holland and England there was "beauty of a high order"; but in a completely domesticated earth, we could expect that beauty would be ordered and that much of the charm of primitive nature would be lost through replacement by artificial, controlled nature. The aesthetic appreciation of the earth was important in Shaler's thinking, and it is involved, at least implicitly, too, in much contemporary thought about the future of man on the earth.

Shaler was not concerned with changes in the biotic community. Moreover, he limited his consideration to Western society during the industrial revolution, ignoring both the previous efforts of man during the long span of human time and the present-day effects of non-industrial peoples on the earth.

Shaler's place of importance in the development of thought about man and nature is that (1) he focused attention on the destruction of mineral resources and gave thoughtful consideration to impending shortages; (2) he feared that resource bases might be insufficient to provide for the very rapidly increasing populations all over the world; and (3) he added the thought that a new human attitude was necessary toward the earth.

In 1915 an article by a young German geologist, Ernst Fischer, was published posthumously, in which he objected to the clear distinction between *Geisteswissenschaften* and *Naturwissenschaften*. He called attention to the neglect in studying the role of man as a geologic agent and presented examples of man's direct activities on the earth's crust and his influence on water bodies, on the plant world, and on the animal world. By learning how to employ the powers of nature, man has been of considerable indirect influence. Small happenings can have widespread, unplanned, and unsuspected effects; the human being is the youngest of the geologic factors.

Other geologists have followed this line of thought. R. L. Sherlock (1922, 1923, 1931) wrote about man as a geologic agent of denudation and accumulation in the physical landscape of Great Britain; he foresaw a period when man's destructiveness would be greatly diminished, a prophecy that has not been borne out by subsequent events. Stanisław Pawłowski (1923) described the lowering of hills and erosion in his native Poland and recognized that man's activities involved changes in the direction of the forces of nature.

During the twentieth century the theme of man's transformation of the earth has been given consideration by geographers of many countries—those from England, France, Austria, Germany, and Italy are cited in the "References" that follow. This literature, to which we are indebted, demonstrates that most human activities advance by virtue of contributions from many different types of individuals, with varying backgrounds, working at different levels. We mention those investigators whose work we know best, fully realizing that other selections could be made. Our concern is with concepts rather than persons—to identify lines of work rather than to attribute credit. If injustices are done—as inevitably they must be—the important interest is not the workers but the work.

In France, Paul Vidal de la Blache, to whom the establishment of modern scientific geography in French university life was largely due, recognized (1913) the great part of man in modifying his basic environment as one of the six distinctive characteristics of geography. Jean Brunhes, a student of Vidal de la Blache, published his *Géographie humaine* in 1910 (revised and enlarged editions in 1912, 1925, and 1934; editions in English in 1920 and 1952). He described and analyzed the many patterns of man's occupancy of the earth as expressed in housing types, in village and town sites, and in changing forms of communication. He discussed man's conquest and adaptation of the vegetable and animal kingdoms by his various agricultural techniques; and he was concerned with man's extraction of minerals. All these matters were examined from a holistic and comparative point of view. Brunhes held (1913, p. 312) that the potency of man in transforming the earth is not due to "superiority in strength, but universality of range" and "synthesis of a series of small achievements." Brunhes pushed the discussion of the influence of man on nature beyond the bounds of Western civilization, to consider man's alterations of the earth by other cultures in a variety of environments from tropical rain forest to desert. Cultural differences were important facts for understanding man's activities on the earth. In the first essay of his posthumous *Problèmes de géographie humaine* (1942) Albert Demangeon laid emphasis on the work of man in modifying his environment by means of communication, artesian wells, the control of rivers, and the evolution of new plants for human food. André Allix in 1948 forcefully stated that it was not the economic motives of "crude interest" that determine man's actions on the earth. Indeed, man has many choices to make, and he chooses according to "traditions and taboos," which are a matter of "rite, breeding, and of sentiment." That to study any subject involving man requires an awareness of man in all his complexity —his attitudes and prejudices—is an idea which follows the teachings of Brunhes.

In England, Marion Isabel Newbigin's textbook, *Man and His Conquest of Nature* (1912), emphasized that man has become almost the master of his fate by the progress of human civilization. Man can live only by destroying the balance of nature, by favoring some animals and plants at the expense of others, by forcing those useless to him to give way to those he needs. But many elements, such as rats, crickets, cockroaches, and weeds, have been favored by man without any intention on his part to do so. Miss Newbigin ac-

knowledged indebtedness to the French geographers for material on which her book was based. P. W. Bryan (1933, p. 372) took the approach that "human activity undertaken to satisfy human desires is the motivating force" in man's changes of the surface of the earth and that man "takes products and utilizes natural surfaces to satisfy those desires." The result is the cultural landscape.

In Italy, Giovanni Negri (1930) examined the general characteristics of human action on vegetation. He agreed that man's action on vegetation is not recent but was important even in Paleolithic Europe and that primitive man with his limited technology was nonetheless effective in changing vegetation. Man, he contended, must be considered the head of a great, complex harmony formed by vegetation and as (p. 216) "the momentum that disturbed the balance." Interestingly, Negri acknowledged the writings of Woeikof and Brunhes but did not mention Marsh, although *Man and Nature* had two Italian editions. Others who considered the theme were E. Migliorini (1936) and Aldo Sestini (1938).

In Germany, Paul Schultze-Naumburg (1928) considered the changes to the surface of the earth by man's cultural work. His volume explored the conflict between economics and ethics; it was a plea for counteraction to thoughtless and unnecessary devastation by a money economy and an exposition of the beauty of cultivated nature. He recognized that only very few places in Germany look the same as they did prior to man's interference. In his Introduction he traced the changes in the German landscape, from the time of Tacitus to the twentieth century, brought about as a result of paths and roads, utilization of the flora, mining of minerals, the water economy, industrial plants and railroads, and buildings of all kinds. He asked whether it is paramount to destroy the beauty of the landscape to step up profit. Is it not in the end to the disadvantage of the general and national well-being?

In 1933 Nikolaus Creutzberg published a pictorial atlas with magnificent illustrations (many of them air views) to show the changes to the surface of the earth caused by man in developing a cultured landscape. Man is living nearly everywhere in a cultured landscape which, during centuries, has been shaped in accordance to his needs, his taste, and his personal peculiarities. The forming of the landscape by man is an artistically unconscious process and therefore reflects the personality of a culture far more than it reflects conscious art. In almost all parts of the earth today, the penetration of machine civilization and the coexistence of forms of original cultures represent the main characteristics of the present cultural landscape.

Edwin Fels, professor of geography and director of the Geographical Institute in the Free University of Berlin, for twenty-five years has consistently developed the theme, as a part of economic geography, of man's influence in transforming the earth. In 1934 he pointed to the work of Sherlock (1922) as having been overlooked in Germany. In his 1935 text he explained that in many works the influence of nature upon man had been considered carefully but that the return consequences of man's actions on nature had not been treated very thoroughly; no German text in economic geography up to 1930 had explored this reciprocal action. His work was to fill this gap. Fels's 1954 volume, *Der wirtschaftende Mensch als Gestalter der Erde,* is a thoroughly revised and enlarged edition of his 1935 work; it comprises Part V of a series on the earth and world economy; and it is the most recent predecessor to the present volume. He considers the transformations of the solid surface of the earth, transformation of water bodies,

man as a shaper of climate, changes of flora, influence on fauna, man in the pattern of nature (population growth and migration, effects on health), and, finally, the economic landscape. Man is inclined by sentiment and habit to consider his earth-transforming force as small in comparison with nature's. This self-underestimation has been justified in the past but is not in the present. However small the physical strength of the individual man may be, it is tremendous when pooled and guided by the human mind. The process has increased extraordinarily rapidly since about 1800, when man entered the machine age and human strength began to multiply through mechanization techniques.

In 1953 David Lowenthal called attention once again to the fact that American geographers have devoted a great deal of attention to the frontier but little to the historical past. George P. Marsh was hailed as the forerunner of historical geography in the United States, and attention was drawn to Marsh's contributions to the subject. Lowenthal (p. 212) brought up the interesting point that, "unlike Thoreau, who also loved nature, but wished to keep it wild, Marsh wanted it tamed; Thoreau appealed to esthetic sentiment, Marsh to economic practicality." Thus attention is focused once again on the premises behind our relations with nature, behind our desires to modify nature and our desires to plan for the future. Shall we have a wild nature or a tamed nature? What is the impact of domestication and civilization on animals and on human beings? What shall man's goals be for his future relations with the earth?

The organized complexity of modern existence is a new phenomenon in man's experience. Considering what has happened in the United States during the last century, one is tempted to ask whether we are living in a moment of great progress or of great aberration in the human adventure.

When George P. Marsh's *Man and Nature* appeared in 1864, President Lincoln was in office by virtue of having received a total of just over two million popular votes; the total annual receipts of the federal government amounted to less than 4 per cent of the current annual *interest* on the public debt; and the urban shift had only begun, for only one-fifth of the population lived in urban places of 2,500 or more. Since then, our population has increased four and a half times, and farm production through mechanization has more than kept pace. There are now annually produced seven and a half times more cotton, five and a half times more wheat, and four and a half times more corn, even though the farm force has increased only slightly in numbers. The cultivated acreage is about what it was in 1920, but there are now some 4,500,-000 tractors at work upon it.

Mechanization, industrialization, urbanization, and transportation have meant the harnessing of energy in fantastic quantities. The United States alone in the last forty years has consumed more minerals and fossil fuels (coal and petroleum) than all mankind used in the previous millenniums of existence. So far in the twentieth century, 70,000 square miles of land in the United States have been absorbed by towns, cities, and urban industrial developments, with another 16,000 square miles covered by artificially impounded water. And service occupations (government, trade, transportation and utilities, finance, etc.) now surpass, in total persons employed, the production occupations (agriculture, manufacturing, construction, mining).

With more people on the earth than at any time in the past, this is really a most extraordinary period in which to be living. Can we, the participants, pull aside enough to read the plot of the spectacle that we are in? Perspective is required to apprehend the uniqueness of the present and the significance of that uniqueness.

Within the last century man has developed the idea that change is continuous and includes himself. Conceptions of fossil man (prior to present man), of biological evolution (in which man is included with all other living phenomena), and of the vast duration of earth history are but a few examples of ideas developed by science and become part of the public consciousness since the mid-nineteenth century. Can the uniqueness of the present be made clearer for those within it by focusing on the role of man in altering the earth's surface, keeping in mind the longevity of the period in which he has been doing so? This Symposium is intended to contribute to such an understanding.

The efforts of small populations of the past have been by no means negligible; their time scale was that of millenniums. The story of man's role in changing the face of the earth begins with the invention of fire-making and the domestication of plants and animals; continues through his trade, warfare, migrations, and the spread of transportation facilities, fields, and settlements; and culminates in the development of modern mining and manufacturing.

Every human group has had to evaluate the potential of the area it inhabits and to organize its life about its environment in terms of available techniques and the values accepted as desirable. The identification, use, and care of resources is in the end a problem of human values and behavior. Cultural differences in techniques and values, and hence in utilization of the physical-biological environment and its conversion into a human habitat, have distinguished one human group from another. The effects of man on the earth are geographically varied and are historically cumulative. Many changes wrought by man have not been destructive; many were unplanned; and many of the results have been unanticipated and have gone undetected.

Man, the ecological dominant on the planet, needs the insights of scholars in nearly all branches of learning to understand what has happened and is happening to the earth under man's impress. This Symposium is a first attempt to provide an integrated basis for such an insight and to demonstrate the capacity of a great number of fields of knowledge to add importantly to our understanding. What the soil scientist, climatologist, geomorphologist, and others are doing are direct contributions to man's understanding of himself. By expressly not setting the study of man and his behavior apart from other fields of knowledge, by recognizing that man is a part, and an active part, of nature and has been so from earliest times, the Symposium theme lays the groundwork for more meaningful formulation of research designs to learn more about what and how environmental factors influence man's development and behavior.

Nature has always contained man, but all the while is being changed by man in the course of his own self-transformation. The dichotomy of man and nature is thus seen as an intellectual device and as such should not be confused with reality; no longer can man's physical-biological environment be treated, except in theory, as "natural."

The most striking symbol of the new scale in time and space that has been brought into being since the time of Marsh is the airplane. The view from the air that it has provided—the ability to look down upon man's work in a new perspective—has been a great stride toward synthesis. The introduction to this volume continues with an analysis of the significance of our new ability to view "Our World from the Air," accompanied by forty-eight striking illustrations.

And with these words by way of introductory, please to begin.

WILLIAM L. THOMAS, JR.

NEW YORK CITY

REFERENCES

ALLIX, ANDRÉ
1948 "Man in Human Geography," *Scottish Geographical Magazine,* LXIV, 1–8.

BRUNHES, JEAN
1913 "The Specific Characteristics and Complex Character of the Subject-Matter of Human Geography," *Scottish Geographical Magazine,* XXIX, 304–22, 358–74.
1925 *La Géographie humaine.* 3d ed. (1st ed., 1910.) Paris: Felix Alcan. 974 pp.
1952 *Human Geography.* Abridged ed. by MME M. JEAN-BRUNHES DELAMARRE and PIERRE DEFFONTAINES; trans. by ERNEST F. ROW. London: George G. Harrap & Co., Ltd. 256 pp.

BRYAN, P. W.
1933 *Man's Adaptation of Nature: Studies of the Cultural Landscape.* New York: Henry Holt & Co. 386 pp.

CREUTZBURG, NIKOLAUS
1933 *Kultur im Spiegel der Landschaft: Das Bild der Erde in seiner Gestaltung durch den Menschen. Ein Bilderatlas.* Leipzig: Bibliographisches Institut. 218 pp.

FELS, EDWIN
1932 "Der Einfluss des Verkehrs auf Naturlandschaft und Lebewelt," pp. 288–94 in *Festschrift für Carl Uhlig.* Öhringen: Verlag der Hohenloheschen Buchhandlung F. Rau. 345 pp.
1934 "Der Mensch als Gestalter der Erdoberfläche: Hinweis auf ein vergessenes Buch," *Petermanns geographische Mitteilungen,* LXXX, No. 2, 50–51.
1935 *Der Mensch als Gestalter der Erde: Ein Beitrag zur allgemeinen*

Wirtschafts- und Verkehrsgeographie. Leipzig: Bibliographisches Institut. 206 pp.

1954 *Der wirtschaftende Mensch als Gestalter der Erde.* Stuttgart: Franckh'sche Verlagshandlung. 258 pp.

FISCHER, ERNST
1915 "Der Mensch als Geologischer Faktor," *Zeitschrift der Deutsches Geologisches Gesellschaft,* LXI, 106–48.

HALTENBERGER, MICHAEL
1937 "Die Technik als umgestaltender Faktor in der geographischen Landschaft," *Comptes-Rendus du Congrès International de Géographie, Varsovie, 1934,* III, 9–15. Warsaw.

LOWENTHAL, DAVID
1953 "George Perkins Marsh and the American Geographical Tradition," *Geographical Review,* XLIII, No. 2, 207–13.

MARSH, GEORGE PERKINS
1864 *Man and Nature; or, Physical Geography as Modified by Human Action.* New York: Scribners; London: Sampson Low. 560 pp. (Two Italian editions, published in Florence, Italy, 1869 and 1872.)
1874 *The Earth as Modified by Human Action: A New Edition of "Man and Nature."* New York: Scribner, Armstrong & Co. 656 pp. (Revised posthumous edition in 1885.)

MIGLIORINI, E.
1936 "L'Uomo come agente che modifica la terra, secondo una recente opera tedesca," *Revista geografica italiana,* XLIII, 36–47.

NEGRI, GIOVANNI
1930 "Caratteri generali dell'azione umana sulla vegetazione," *Atti dello XI Congresso Geografico Italiano, Napoli,* I, 215–33.

NEWBIGIN, MARION ISABEL
1912 *Man and His Conquest of Nature.* London: Adam & Charles Black. 183 pp.

PAWLOWSKI, STANISŁAW
1923 "Zmiany w ukształtowaniu powierzchni ziemi wywołane przez człowieka (Modifications apportées par l'homme à la surface terrestre)," *Przeglad Geograficzny,* IV, 48–64.

SCHULTZE-NAUMBURG, PAUL
1928 *Die Gestaltung der Landschaft durch den Menschen,* Vol. VII. Munich: Georg D. W. Callwey Verlag. 487 pp.

SESTINI, ALDO
1938 "Intorno all'opera dell'uomo come agente modificatore della superficie terrestre," *Revista geografica italiana,* XLV, 231–43.

SHALER, NATHANIEL SOUTHGATE
1905 *Man and the Earth.* New York: Duffield & Co. 240 pp.

SHERLOCK, ROBERT LIONEL
1922 *Man as a Geological Agent: An Account of His Action on Inanimate Nature.* London: H. F. & G. Witherby. 372 pp.
1923 "The Influence of Man as an Agent in Geographical Change," *Geographical Journal,* LXI, No. 4, 258–73.
1931 *Man's Influence on the Earth.* London: Home University Library of Modern Knowledge. 256 pp.

VIDAL DE LA BLACHE, PAUL
1913 "Des Caractères distinctifs de la géographie," *Annales de géographie,* XXII, 289–99.

WOEIKOF (VOEÏKOV), ALEXANDER (ALEKSANDR) IVANOVICH
1901 "De l'Influence de l'homme sur la terre," *Annales de géographie,* X, 97–114, 193–215.
1949 *Vozdeǐstvie cheloveka na prirodu: Izbrannye statʼi* ("Influence of Man upon Nature: Selected Articles"). Edited, with an Introductory Article and Notes, by V. V. POKSHISHEVSKII. Moscow: Gos. izdvo geografich. lit-ry. 254 pp. (In Russian.) (A collection of articles mostly published in the late nineteenth century.)

Our World from the Air: Conflict and Adaptation

E. A. GUTKIND[*]

THE PERENNIAL REVOLUTION

Man and nature are the twin agents of the perennial revolution which shapes and reshapes the face of the earth and the character of man's activities. This struggle, at times violent and sporadic, at others gentle and consistent, but forever demanding a new response to a new challenge, activates the potential energies of man and nature, molding them into a grand pattern of advance or retreat, of creative interaction or disastrous antagonism, and of promise or failure.

The conquest of the air enables mankind for the first time in its history to experience this interaction in all its innumerable ramifications. A new scale in time and space has been added to our mental and material equipment. Before this conquest we were winding our way like worms through narrow passages and seeing only more or less unrelated details. Today we can look at the world with a God's-eye view, take in at a glance the infinite variety of environmental patterns spread over the earth, and appreciate their dynamic relationships. We can see this great variety condensed in time and space and can shed the still-lingering ideas of stable and isolated societies. We can see side by side the different scales in time and space and the tensions arising out of the neighborly proximity of seemingly incompatible transformations of the earth's surface. The whole field of human activities and of nature's gifts and refusals unfolds before our eyes and senses, ranging from the most primitive to the most up-to-date interference with nature, from unconscious, isolated, and small-scale activities to the conscious remaking of the environment in vast parts of the world. All these different stages exist today, and in many parts of the world they overlap.

The airplane has given us the synoptic view. This coincides with the general trend away from the overestimation of the purely analytical approach to numerous problems toward synthesis and unitary ideas. Both analysis and synthesis are needed and should be applied to every problem on equal terms. The advent of the airplane and the air view is, therefore, of symbolic significance. Since the beginning of the scientific revolution, analysis has been paramount. In the ages preceding this event humanity found protection and

* Dr. Gutkind, M.T.P.I., F.R.G.S., Dr.Ing., Dipl.Arch., Member MARS–CIAM, was, after World War I, adviser to the Armistice Commission on Physical Reconstruction, then worked as private architect and town planner. During World War II he was head of the Demographic Survey and Plan, then member of the Control Commission for Germany, in charge of physical planning. His numerous works include: *Revolution of Environment*, 1946; *Our World from the Air: An International Survey of Man and His Environment*, 1952; *Community and Environment: A Discourse on Social Ecology*, 1953; and *The Expanding Environment: The End of Cities, the Rise of Communities*, 1953.

1

guidance in a unifying faith and symbolism—or at least believed that it would find them in these manifestations of its essence as far as it affected its spiritual and mental aspirations. But these guides have lost their power ever since science began systematically to analyze nature and to help to transform the environment on a perpetually widening scale, with growing intensity and at a steadily increasing pace. The revolt against analysis is not new. Goethe was perhaps its most determined and outspoken exponent. In *Die Farbenlehre* he wrote: "A century which relies only on analysis and seems to be afraid of synthesis is not on the right way; for only both together, like breathing in and breathing out, form the essence of science."

It is not mere coincidence that the synoptic view which the airplane offers us emerged as an indispensable instrument of our growing understanding, knowledge, and insight. This change contains a double challenge: It forces us to see the transformations which man has wrought from the earth as a perennial revolution and to experience their dynamic unity as a whole. Without the synoptic view from the air this would be impossible, and without the trend toward unitary ideas we would fail to interpret correctly what we now can see. We are at one of the decisive turning points in the history of humanity comparable to the domestication of animals, the invention of the earliest tools, the foundation of the first cities, and the conception of the heliocentric universe. At this turning point we can look back and take stock of man's past achievements and failures. But we can also perceive the great perspectives in which future generations must make their contributions.

No transformation produces a static and lasting result. Hence our environment is at any moment of human history the product of a perennial revolution, of a continuous process of change. Man's adjustments to his environment are not a series of unrelated stages of development, each more or less accomplished and self-contained entities, but an organic and integrated chain of events. Thus permanency exists only in the uninterrupted *continuity* of change and in the dynamic relations among all aspects of human activities. In other words, permanency without synthesis is a delusion. To these two criteria a third has to be added: the growing scale of the transformations, expanding from small and individual to large and collective operations. This Trinity—permanency of change, synthesis of relations, and the increase of scale—forms the yardstick by which the interaction of man and environment should be judged.

In general, individual efforts are now out of tune, in time and space, with the dynamics of social needs and aspirations. The unity between the individual scale and the totality of the environment has broken down. Something new must be put in its place. The right scale depends on the awareness of relations—of the relations between individual and group, between the functional and personal life, between the man-made landscape and the natural landscape, between all parts of the immediate environment and the wider world around us and, finally, the universe. The old scale has been destroyed, and man as an individual being is cut loose from the totality of the forces which play on the environmental field.

Are these demands not too great or—as the hard-boiled realist will say—too vague? The answer is definitely "No," for in reality they merely repeat the age-old longings of man as a social being, though not as an economic animal. Every primitive tribe was nearer this universal scale than we are today. But we are not a primitive tribe—at least we pretend not to be—and we must, therefore, find a new solution to this eternal problem, the total oneness of re- ations; and with it we must develop a new adaptation to this new scale. The conquest of the air forces us into this adventure. The airplane is the instru- ment which has introduced this new scale as an inescapable reality, bridg- ing the gap between the smallest social un t, the individual human being, and the largest unit, the universe—between, as it were, the social microscope and the social telescope. However, let there be no mistake. This has nothing to do with the mock-heroic flights into space or the megalomaniac idea of launching artificial satellites which would revolve around the earth. The solution lies some- what nearer home and is less expen- sive. It lies within ourselves, but it may cost more effort than to discover the brave new world in the outer spaces of the heavens.

No structure can grow beyond its or- ganic size, for, if it does, it destroys the internal coherence and functional ef- ficiency. Therefore, the results of every human interference with nature should be evaluated with relation to the entire variety of environmental conditions, not to one condition only. Or to put it in another way: If we want to find out the optimum structure of an individual human work and its optimum relation to other works, we must investigate not merely the conditions of the immediate environment in which the work actu- ally takes place but also its relations and reactions to the world at large. We must think not only in terms of proc- esses but also in terms of groups of en- vironments, for this alone can get us out of the rut of daily and narrow routine and ennoble our works beyond mere utilitarian efficiency.

Consequently, the comparative study of man's transformations which the air- plane makes possible opens the way to- ward a re-evaluation of what man has done and what he can do to the earth.

Above all, the widening scale of the re- assessment of the work of previous gen- erations and of the great possibilities which the future holds in store leads us to an increased awareness of the all- embracing unity of mankind and of the absurdity of all spiritual and political frontiers. It makes us aware of the in- escapable fact that only *differences of degree, not of principle, distinguish na- tions.* This is especially evident if we think in terms of generations instead of years. Then the distinction between the uneven development of different civili- zations which today exist side by side shrinks almost to nothing.

No structure can grow beyond its or- ganic size without impairing its coher- ence and efficiency. This is only too painfully obvious when we look down at our cities, towns, villages, and industrial districts. It is not only their unsystem- atic growth and their excessive size but also their amorphous structure in gen- eral and in detail which destroy the dy- namic equilibrium of their functions and, consequently, their productive and bal- anced relations to the surrounding re- gion and the country as a whole. What driving power is behind this lopsided development? It is the same lack of balance which pervades our life in gen- eral. One function—work—is paramount, and all other activities of our functional as well as of our personal life are sub- ordinated to this devouring obsession. Work means industry, and industry means industrial buildings, districts, and countries. This one-sided overes- timation of one function has created the urban deserts, has upset the fertile re- lations between urban and rural life, and has debased human dignity to the level of a soulless machine. The human scale has been lost in the turmoil of an illusory progress toward the "great know-how."

All this can be seen in unerring clar- ity from the air. The landscape which spreads before our eyes and mind is like a seismograph recording the finest oscillations of man's role in changing the face of the earth. On the vast screen of this seismograph of the world the genuinely great revolutions which mark the real turning points in the history of mankind are recorded. In the nomads' tracks through the deserts leading to oases settlements we can still experience the revolution from a migratory to a sedentary way of life. In the contrast between the empty fields of the prairies and the nearest town (Fig. 1) we can still relive the tremendous impact of the urban revolution. In the minute fields of Old China tilled by men as their own living tools (Fig. 2) and in the large fields of the New World (Fig. 3) and Russia worked by tractors the revolution of the machines is still present. In the small and compact village of an African tribe (Fig. 4), in a collective settlement of Israel (Fig. 5), in a walled town of Iran (Fig. 6), and in the sprawling cities of the "progressive" countries (Fig. 7) there is retold the tremendous drama of the social revolution, from closely knit communities

THE URBAN REVOLUTION

Courtesy of the Department of Mines and Resources, Canada

FIG. 1.—Canada, Saskatchewan, Regina. The compact space of the town is cut out from the vastness of the surrounding countryside and separated as a space in its own right, as a rebellious protest against nature. Social proximity within the orbit of the town and social isolation of the outlying farms are the antagonistic results. A new dimension, uncommensurable with nature, has been thrown open to human life, creating a realm of its own in opposition to the country.

to atomized societies, from the coherence and self-sufficiency of clan homogeneity to the fellowship based on elective affinity, and, finally, to the hollow conformity of the uprooted urban multitudes. The great seismograph reveals all these landmarks of the perennial revolution. But only if we can sense the deep unity in the world-wide diversity of the innumerable features which the struggle between man and nature has imprinted on the earth can we hope to understand the intensity and variety, the interdependence, and the true significance of what the past has to teach us. We must work out a new relationship to the external world and conceive it as an ever changing pattern of phenomena and events all intimately connected with one another as an expanding environment abounding in inspiring possibilities. The synoptic view demands the appreciation of the whole nexus of relations in every detail and of the creative potentiality of every detail within the whole. In a more precise way

THE REVOLUTION OF THE MACHINES

FIG. 2.—China, farmland. The small scale of the agricultural landscape of China transformed by the work of millions of peasants as their own living tools is clearly visible in this air view taken from an altitude of 4,500 feet.

this can be expressed once more as the simultaneous need for analysis and synthesis. And for those who are never happy without a new pigeonhole it may be added that something like a new discipline is needed, which for want of a better name might be called "social ecology." This new discipline would include those branches of the social and natural sciences which have a more or less direct bearing upon the role of man in re-forming his habitat.

But there should be no mistake: This does not mean an amorphous new discipline. On the contrary, it means a systematic selection of the really instrumental forces which shape man's social aspirations and transform his environment accordingly. The goal of social ecology is wholeness and not a mere adding-together of innumerable details. This is not the place to enter into a detailed description of the exact meaning, scope, and character of social ecology. This would lead us too far, for in the last instance environment is everything, from the suits we wear to the universe —the whole of the external world. The natural and the man-made environments coalesce, and no clear demarcation line can be drawn between the two. However, we should always remember that we are influenced by an unlimited variety of environmental conditions and that our immediate environment in all its ramifications is itself

THE REVOLUTION OF THE MACHINES

Courtesy of the U.S. Soil Conservation Service

FIG. 3.—United States, Arizona, Pinal County, fields. Many of the original fields have been combined in a geometrical transformation of nature on a large scale and in one continuous sweep for the mechanization of agriculture and the rational use of irrigation.

always part of the greater whole. Ecology, in its original sense, is the study of the relation of animals to their habitat. It deals with "chain reactions" of influences caused by the character and workings of environmental factors and the way in which they affect a particular species and vice versa. These are the same problems which face human civilizations. The main lesson we can learn from animal ecology is the need for studying human communities as a *whole* and in their *total* relationship to their physical and social environment.

These demands are, like all generalizations, open to an easy criticism. But this should not deter us from adapting our thinking to a new and bewildering situation. Admittedly quite a number of cherished ideas and ideals will have to be revised, and even the seemingly unassailable basis of a scientific approach, the analytical and pragmatic method, will have to be re-examined. But our fear of abstract notions or, for that matter, of the deductive method should not stand in the way of finding a new synthesis between science and philosophy, between slow, step-by-step experiments and brilliant, artistic short cuts. For how else can wholeness be achieved than by the unity of the practical and speculative mode of thinking. We may quote in this connection Whitehead, when he says in *Adventures of Ideas:*

THE SOCIAL REVOLUTION

Courtesy of the Agence Economique des Colonies

FIG. 4.—French West Africa, Senegal, Presqu'île du Cap Vert, village of Yof. The compact village is inhabited by Mohammedan fishermen of the same tribe. It consists of a few families, each compound occupied by the same consanguinous group and surrounded by a fence. Social coherence and co-operation bind all inhabitants intimately together in life and work.

Courtesy of Keren Hayesod, Jerusalem

FIG. 5.—Israel, Nahalal. The social and economic structure of this co-operative smallholder's settlement in the Valley of Jezreel is based on four cardinal principles: equal distribution of land, mutual aid, equal work for all, and co-operative purchasing and marketing. The central area is occupied by communal buildings and gardens, while the fields extend behind each farm. The whole is one integrated social and economic unit.

Courtesy of the Oriental Institute, University of Chicago

FIG. 6.—Iran, Bustam. This place of pilgrimage in northern Iran is protected by a fortress wall and surrounded by its fields, forming a compact oasis in the desert plain. The exclusion of the outside world creates social coherence and economic self-sufficiency and co-operation.

In each age of the world distinguished by high activity there will be found at its culmination, some profound cosmological outlook, implicitly accepted, impressing its own type upon current springs of action. This ultimate cosmology is only partly expressed, and the details of such expression issue into derivative specialized questions of secondary generality which conceal a general agreement upon first principles almost too obvious to need expression, and almost too general to be capable of expression. In each period there is a general form of the forms of thought; and, like the air we breathe, such a form is so translucent, and so pervading, and so seemingly necessary, that only by extreme effort can we become aware of it.

It is these "first principles" which we must try to understand, to formulate, and to apply. Then what appeared abstract and vague before will become concrete and precise. If we fail to grasp the particular "form of the forms of thought" which is characteristic of our time, if we fail to sense the translucent atmosphere which pervades our lives, we remain, at best, helpless and confused wanderers on this earth and, at worst, irresponsible tinkers who squander the riches intrusted to them by nature.

To calm the doubts of the eternal realists, we may also cite Kant. Although they may regard him as an utterly impracticable and useless phenomenon in the harsh world of what they call "hard facts," they might yet be induced to ponder over what he says

THE SOCIAL REVOLUTION

Courtesy of the Ministry of Town and Country Planning

FIG. 7.—England, Somerset, Bath. The extremes of two different periods confront each other: culture, masterful restriction and unity, and imaginative town planning, on the one hand; ruthlessness, confusion, and unimaginative "sprawl," on the other. Social disintegration and chaos are the result.

in the *Critique of Judgment:* "We can imagine an intellect which, while it is not discursive like our own but intuitive, proceeds from the general synthesis, from the idea as a whole as such, to the particular, that is from the whole to the parts."[1] A supreme effort is needed to reconcile this new approach with our accustomed methods of transforming our environment. People are afraid of ideas. They prefer the dry facts of daily life. But those who are afraid of ideas lose their meaning in the end. This is perhaps the greatest danger which surrounds this new chapter in the history of mankind. And yet this chapter will be opened not by the many but by the few, as it has always happened in the past. But today the danger is infinitely greater, for the many, united in mediocrity by the pressure of conformity and reduced to the dead level of utter complacency and political immaturity, are far more decisive than ever in times past, because the media of mass communications take hold of their conscience before they are even aware of what is going on. They distrust, moreover, the unusual, the far-reaching, and the defiant passion of the clearsighted rebels. It is so much easier and so much more comforting to rely on what is known, on what can be seen and touched, and to bridge the gap between the old and the new by a flight into romanticism. The responsibility which rests on the few is tremendous. It is a burden of social awareness and scientific integrity, of moral insight and fearless adherence to the highest ethical standards. But there is no need for despondency. On the contrary, there is every reason for a hopeful expectancy and even optimism. In the chain of the perennial revolutions the most important one is still missing: the revolution which will lead to the discovery of man.

1. Author's translation.

This revolution is being carried forward by the double attack of the social and natural sciences. This course has been outlined most brilliantly by Dr. E. D. Adrian in his presidential address to the 1954 meeting of the British Association for the Advancement of Science. He said:

It may be optimistic to think that we should be better off if we had a better understanding of human reactions. . . . But an increased knowledge of how the mind can be influenced could certainly forestall many of the influences which might be used to undermine our integrity. Discoveries about our own nature may disturb our peace of mind, but our own generation has already faced the theories of Freud as our grandfathers faced those of Charles Darwin. There was the same passionate resentment of the idea that our thoughts were more moulded by unconscious forces; but we have recovered our balance and we are not downhearted at finding ourselves less rational than we thought. . . . Now we can look to the many branches of social sciences to make a dispassionate study of what actually happens in our society without regard to what might be expected to happen if we are to believe all we have been told. The picture of human behaviour which the social scientist has to draw is of a system in which the units are men and women. . . . Scientists who work in laboratories have a far easier task in selecting what they should observe and in making measurements and checking theories by experiments. But in spite of our hesitations we can see that there are facts to be found out about our usefulness in society and about our relations with one another and with the group to which we belong. It is too early to be cautious in encouraging these unfamiliar lines of research. We must do what we can to develop the sciences which deal with human behaviour, even though we cannot always see what can come out of them. But human beings, when we consider them as material for the biologist, are not to be thought of as incapable of improvement.

These lofty goals cannot be reached by the accumulation of knowledge alone. Insight and vision are the indispensable counterparts without which pure knowledge remains the doubtful privilege of the ivory towers, now called "laboratories." In the words of two philosophers, Whitehead and Kant, and of a great scientist, Dr. Adrian, the way toward a synthesis of philosophy and science, of the speculative and rational mind, and of the deductive and inductive methods has been charted. The air has been conquered, and with this conquest a new freedom of ideas and insights has been given us. Here lies the field of the new unitary vision which will hold together the innumerable aspects of the dialogue between man and nature. When we look down from the airplane at the earth with an open mind freed from the fetters of preconceived ideas and outworn methods of appreciation, everything falls into a true perspective—even man himself as an integral part of the whole. Man has done tremendous things in his wrestling with nature, but the results are only too often questionable because they lack social responsibility. We can see the general mess he has made of many great opportunities; we can see the decaying ant heaps of our cities, the rural isolation and backwardness in many areas of the world, excluding millions from the main currents of life; we can see the misuse of the natural resources and vast parts of the earth's surface still unused. The new role of man in changing the face of the earth will lead to a different and higher standard of control over his physical environment and, above all, over his social surroundings. This will be the greatest and noblest phase of the perennial revolution, and its outcome will decide whether the social sciences were equal to this occasion—or failed. The leadership in the next stage of transformation belongs to the social sciences. All other sciences must be subordinated to their guidance, for in the realm of learning they represent the moral conscience of mankind. The recent developments are an only too painful reminder that this conscience is not wide awake.

CHAINS OF TRANSFORMATIONS

Our world from the air is a kaleidoscopic jumble of natural and man-made features. And yet in this seemingly inextricable chaos there can be discerned a few trends, a few principles, and a few indications which bind all parts together in one grand pattern of transformations similar in essence and sequence. This veneer, spread by a divine designer over the earth and inlaid with an infinite variety of shapes, materials, and colors, reflects the finest oscillations of man's aspirations and achievements, of his failures and frustrations, and of his understanding but also of his ruthless disregard for nature.

The underlying trends form an indivisible unity in space and time if we apply the right yardstick, that is, a long-term and a large-scale evaluation. Then chains of transformation become visible, and something like an organic and integrated process of development emerges from the ever renewed adaptation of the environment to human needs and of man to his environment.

In broad outlines three principal chains of transformation can be distinguished. The most general is the change in the interaction of man and environment from an "I-Thou" to an "I-It" relationship. The second chain of transformation is more explicit in character; it shows man's reactions to his environment in successive stages, ranging from fear and defense to confidence and aggressiveness and, finally, to growing understanding and responsibility, always guided by the two complementary forces of instinct and reason and resulting in unconscious or conscious control of man's efforts toward systematization.

The third chain represents the widening scale and the changing experience of space, the latter intimately related to the notion of the universe. These three chains of transformation illustrate together and each in its own right the fulfilment of the basic human needs of shelter, food, work, and social intercourse. Consequently, the significance of each chain of transformation should be evaluated in relation to these four basic needs. These three principal chains of transformation and these four basic needs of human nature form an insoluble whole, and, as human nature is everywhere fundamentally the same, they produce in similar conditions also similar results, though for an inexperienced eye these may seem to differ considerably.

There are of course still other possibilities of systematizing the transformations through which the interaction of man and nature has passed and is likely to pass in the future. But those suggested above are, as will be seen, the most comprehensive and the most formative relations between the two contestants.

1. The transformation from an "I-Thou" to an "I-It" relationship is evident in the changing interdependence of man and nature and of group and individual. These two aspects belong together, and the results of this unity and of this change can still be seen today. The layout of tribal villages (Figs. 8 and 9), of old towns in Europe (Figs. 10 and 11) and Asia, the ancestral graves interspersed between the settlements of the living generation in China (Figs. 12 and 13), the pyramids and temples of Egypt, Mexico, and the Far East (Figs. 14 and 15), the rival symbols of church and castle dominating the skyline of medieval towns (Figs. 16 and 17)—all these bear witness to the intimate and direct "I-Thou" relationship between man and nature and man and man. When this relationship became indirect and estranged, when it turned into an "I-It" relationship, disintegrating the symbolic and magical bonds between man and environment and upsetting the oneness of man's functional and personal life, the growing abstractness and the ensuing disunity produced the amorphous character of all modern towns (Fig. 18) and villages and the harsh and purely utilitarian attitude toward nature. Today the transformation from the hesitant and whispered dialogue between man and nature to the aggressive and loud exploitation of nature and from closely knit communities to atomized societies is complete. A juxtaposition of air views of the "I-Thou" and the "I-It" periods reveals at a glance the tremendous impact of this changed state of mind upon all present works of man: The anonymous despotism of modern society has destroyed the organic interdependence of villages and fields and the organic clarity of all places where human beings congregate. The only unity that still exists is a unity of disorder.

If we want to open a new chapter in the history of mankind's relationship to nature, we should try to understand the fundamental character of the change from an "I-Thou" to an "I-It" attitude. How can we rediscover the genuinely creative force which should guide our activities in the future? It is for this reason that we must pause for a consideration of the influences which have brought this transformation about.

We have dealt with these problems in more detail in our *Community and Environment*. On the next few pages we have made use, to a certain extent, of some of the ideas discussed in this work.

As long as man was deeply imbedded in nature and every natural phenomenon had a symbolic significance, the man-environment relationship was more a mutual adaptation than a one-sided conquest of nature by man. The re-

Courtesy of the American Geographical Society, New York

Fig. 8.—Sudan, Bari Village. A closely knit social group occupies the compact and fenced-in space of this village. Here life is immediate, and the traditional huts are part of the landscape. The relationship between man and man and man and nature is intimate and direct. It is an "I-Thou" and reciprocal contact.

Ewing Galloway

Fig. 9.—Belgian Congo, copper-miners' village. Unity through repetition is the characteristic note of this cantonment for the workers in the copper mines. The pathetic attempt to retain something of the indigenous style by putting thatched roofs on the standardized huts is an outward symbol of the helplessness and confusion of an atomized society which has spread its tentacles to this remote part of the world. The workers and their families living in these cells are uprooted and depersonalized beings and trained as human automata. They are estranged from nature and from each other. Life in this regimented agglomeration of huts has lost its immediacy and imposed all the prerequisites of an indirect and impersonal existence, of an "I-It" relationship.

Compagnie Aérienne Française

FIG. 10.—France, Aude, Carcassonne. The ancient part of the town is inclosed by two *enceintes* within which a large number of houses are closely huddled together. The perplexities which threatened to overwhelm medieval man and to disrupt his religious and worldly loyalties drove him into fraternal associations. The shells of the family and the guilds, confraternities, and religious orders enfolded the individual being. The walls were the ever present and bodily manifestations of these all-embracing loyalties. The towns of the Middle Ages were communities in which elected affinities and family bonds were merged into each other and where life was immediate and personal, a perfect "I-Thou" relationship.

FIG. 11.—Anywhere. In these sprawling towns the last vestiges of a community have disappeared. They are hardly anything else than an agglomeration of innumerable and isolated details, of human atoms, and of rows of boxes, called houses, interspersed between industries. It is a total victory of laissez faire insensibility and recklessness over organic growth and even over organized development. Our towns are work-centered power stations of the national state. They are the precursors of the ant state and deliver the vast army of experts. The "I-It" relationship is paramount.

Photo Graf zu Castell

Fig. 12.—China, Kansu, Lanchow, graves. These graves near Lanchow cover many square miles of the plain, although it is only here that the land can be fruitfully cultivated, and are symbols of the impact of the past on the present. The ancestor cult and the general reverence for ancestral graves were stronger even than the pressing need for careful preservation of the soil, which is insufficient for the great number of Chinese peasants. Life in Old China was lived retrospectively, guided by the cult of the dead, which introduced an ever present and powerful element of intimate family coherence and unitedness with the environment within an all-pervading "I-Thou" relationship.

Courtesy of the American Geographical Society, New York

Fig. 13.—Argentina, Buenos Aires, city of the dead. There are worlds between the pious devotion of the peasant of Old China who sacrificed to the dead a valuable part of his barely sufficient soil and the contemporary solution with its rigidly lined-up monuments for the wealthier families and the regimented similarity of the humbler graves. Depersonalization extends to life after death. The dead are cut loose from any direct contact with the living. Impersonal and abstract relations invade even the revered atmosphere of this "city" of the dead.

Courtesy of the Agence Économique des Colonies

FIG. 14.—Indochina, Cambodia, Angkor Wat. The temple lies near the royal city of Angkor Thom within a park surrounded by a moat. Five walls, in ever narrowing rectangles and on rising terraces, encircle the innermost sanctuary, removing it from the mortal ken and yet absorbing the worshipers into its all-embracing holiness. The temple is isolated from the hustle and bustle of the daily life in the near-by town, and yet this isolation is the very source of its emotional appeal to the awareness of the unity of man and the universe and of the individual and the community to which he belongs. Here the "I-Thou" relationship is demonstrated on a grand scale and with the utmost intensity.

Courtesy of the Ministère des Travaux Publics

FIG. 15.—France, Pas-de-Calais, mining town. "Homes and gardens" for the workers living directly above the pit where they work form the basic pattern of this mining town. Two toy churches are inserted into this disingenious and degrading travesty of a town destined for human beings whose only common bond is the identity of their abodes. This rigid layout and the unity by repetition, these unfailing symptoms of massification, are the overt sign of an "I-It" relationship. Although places of worship are included directly in the precincts of the town, apparently as the expression of a "community spirit," they are in reality more isolated from the life of the inhabitants than the isolated temple of Angkor Wat.

FIG. 16.—Spain, Toledo. Church and castle are the rival symbols of the Middle Ages. Here in Toledo, as in many other towns, both dominate the skyline. The houses rise as a compact mass in terraces to the highest plateau. They are "introvert," their rooms arranged around an inner courtyard; only a few windows and doors open onto the streets. The natural features of the site compress the town to a compact unit which, just like the "introvert" houses, forces the whole place into a determined seclusion that increases the personal contact of the inhabitants.

Courtesy of the Ministère des Travaux Publics

FIG. 17.—France, Paris, Billancourt. The industrial district is situated on an island in the Seine. It forms an inseparable unit with the residential quarters. Factory chimneys are the characteristic feature of the skyline. Everywhere they are the symbols of modern society and of its demon, industry. They are the expression of the one-sided preoccupation with work, an attitude which has made the existence of modern man lopsided, destroyed the unity of his personal and functional life, undermined his intimate and personal relations, and produced the dangerous conditions in which a machine-centered managerial revolution can develop.

17

placement of natural features was rather a modification in defense against external dangers than a deliberate attempt at dominating nature in a spirit of aggressiveness. If nature threatened to get out of hand, magic was expected to help. It was an "I-Thou" relationship, with all the ups and downs inherent even in the closest association; and it was also a total relationship in which man was dependent on the universal character of the environment, being himself an integral part of nature and dimly aware that there was nothing which could not influence in one way or another his own existence and his attitude to the surrounding world. Since the scientific revolution, nature has been depersonalized, and the awareness of the total relationship between man and nature has been fading out.

During the first three thousand years of recorded history, man remained deeply imbedded in his natural environment. Nature and man, human and cosmic events, are merged into one, and man's experience is immediate and personal. The symbolic significance of events and phenomena is equated with actual reality. This produces a particular concept of causality and of space and time which establishes between man and the phenomenal world an intimate and reciprocal dependence. The external world is a great "Thou" to early man. He does not search for impersonal laws behind the goings-on of the universe. Consequently, his approach is not analytical.

The world of primitive man is still a living reality today and is still immersed in magic and animism. It is a

TRANSFORMATION FROM AN "I-THOU" TO AN "I-IT" RELATIONSHIP

Compagnie Aérienne Française

FIG. 18.—France, Haute-Garonne, Toulouse. The final result of the misguided "I-It" relationship: the canyon street as the life-artery of urban existence, purposeless, meaningless, joyless, and as the expression of the growing abstractness and the amorphous character of modern cities.

world which has no development as we understand it. Change means a break in the established and reciprocal relationship between man and environment and would destroy the unity between him and the natural phenomena. Two spheres pervade each other: the macrocosm and the microcosm. The effort of primitive man is directed toward a fusion of the two through magical contacts which make the universal and the social space coalesce.

Greek thought is still permeated by an experience of nature which, as Professor Butterfield has expressed it, somewhat controversially, in *The Origins of Modern Science*, "has the door halfway open to spirits," though man's interpretation of the universe has shifted from unquestioning belief to the search for truth. In spite of all progress in logical reasoning and mathematics, the Greek relationship to nature has remained tinged with the conviction that it is an eminently personal world in which one has to find his way. The great "Thou" still lingers on in spite of the brilliant unfolding of individualistic thought and reason. The legacy of the past is still too strong for the Greeks. They have not completely shaken off the fetters of mythical limitations. Macrocosm and microcosm are firmly interwoven, and man symbolizes the general in his individual being. Greek symbolism is very concrete, very direct; it comes to life in visible form, not through complicated analogies. Thus the classical and even the Hellenistic *polis* is the symbolic expression of the ideal structure of society and the only correct form of its synthesis with the supermathematical cosmic order. When created, the *polis* was limited in size and character, and its scale was fixed by human standards. Thus life has not become abstract, and the relations of men to their town remain concrete.

Something similar applies to the towns of Old China. The walls were the most sacred part of the town and were erected first. The town was conceived as a whole from the very beginning, and the space created by the inclosure of the walls was only gradually filled with houses and official buildings. Although quite a number of Chinese towns extend over a large area and their streets and houses seem to form an inextricable mess, they are yet systematic and attuned to the human scale. Life was not deprived of its immediate and personal character. Magical considerations played an important part: The layout of a town was not only based on practical conditions; it was dependent on geomantic rules, as part of the magical ideas which have dominated Chinese thinking from early times. If we look from the air at a Chinese town which has retained its old character, we see the sharp line of the walls inclosing a seemingly chaotic agglomeration of houses in their protecting embrace. The direct and intimate relation between man and nature is still at work.

The burgher of the medieval town was the direct successor of the citizen of the *polis:* The narrow living space of his town was the center where his whole life converged. His spiritual and practical activities were confined to this limited sphere. Family, guilds, religious orders, and confraternities enfolded the individual. The town was a community, a union in the sense of brotherhood.

Christianity tended to break up the magical and taboo links on which blood relationship largely rests in China, India, Japan, and Islamic countries. Elective affinities assumed equal rights with consanguinous relationships. It is this voluntary association which gave a new security and created essential preconditions from which an urban community could grow. Religion was the great "uniter" of medieval life; it guided men into the spirit of genuine communities and made life direct and personal. Work and family life were one and proceeded under the same roof. Man-made and natural environments retained their intimate character, and man still felt that he was the center, like the earth, of the universe. Nature is on a par with man. In the words of Pico della Mirandola, which he puts into the mouth of the Creator when he is speaking to Adam: "In the middle of the world have I placed thee that thou mayst the more easily look about thee and see all that is therein contained."

Since the scientific revolution, the awareness of the total relationship between man and nature has been fading out. Life became gradually more abstract, and the relations between men lost their personal directness. Religious man receded into the shadows of the past, and economic man appeared on the horizon. Group-consciousness weak-

ened, and the interaction of the general and the individual will melted away until it led in the Baroque to the supremacy of a small minority and to the leveling-down of the majority to an inarticulate mass of obedient subjects of the rising state. The strong social and religious bonds which had enveloped and held together the small communities and which had created a unison of individual spontaneity and communal spirit—these bonds were broken, and the way was open to the social disintegration of the present. The new order had a far-reaching effect on the relationship between the places in which men lived, worked, and traded. Family life and business life fell apart. Work became the center around which everything else rotated until it swallowed up the whole of man's thinking and feeling

TRANSFORMATION FROM AN "I-THOU" TO AN "I-IT" RELATIONSHIP

Compania Mexicana Aerofoto

FIG. 19.—Mexico, Guanajuato, Salvatierra. Although the countryside extends far into the town, a genuine and organic relationship between the urban and rural structures is missing. It is difficult to say whether the town or the country is the cause of this lack of systematic unity and dynamic balance between the two settings. The whole complex is a mongrelized paradox with the pretensions of a big city and the purely utilitarian attitude toward nature.

and dictated the cycle of his daily life; until fragmented man, the finished and dangerous product of our time, was the result.

This growing disintegration can be seen in the loss of homogeneity of urban and rural settings (Fig. 19) and in the unrelated attempts at the exploitation of the natural resources. The new "I-It" relationship between man and nature has destroyed the continuity of the intimate and personal contact between man and environment and also the unity of thought linking the everyday events and the immediate environment to the order of the universe. Only about ten generations separate us from the beginning of the scientific revolution. But this short period has created conditions of life which challenge the very essence of our existence. We face the disruptive impact of an "I-It" relationship which extends not only to things but also to persons.

2. The second chain of transformation consists of four stages in man's changing attitude to his environment; all of which can be observed today sometimes in close proximity to one another. The first stage is one of fear and the longing for security—of fear of the unpredictable and unknown forces of nature and of protection against these forces and the hostility of men. Particularly in primitive conditions, careless displacement of the natural features is the result. These activities lead often to collective work and are accompanied by the gradual formation of integrated groups. Man feels himself a part of nature, and cosmic and earthly events are for him inextricably interwoven. His orientations in space and time are concrete, not abstract, concepts. He solves his practical problems in an empirical manner, and his attitude to the external world of things and men is permeated by an "I-Thou" relationship full of symbolic and personal meaning. All this is evident in the works of early and primitive man and can be observed today in the windscreen settlements of the Bushmen, in the pile dwellings of the South Seas and of other parts of the world (Fig. 20), in the careless displacement of the natural conditions for shifting agriculture, in the kraals of the Bantu Negroes (Fig. 21), in the *zadrugas* of Old Bulgaria (Fig. 22), and in many other institutions and works.

The second stage is one of growing self-confidence and increasing observation, leading to a more rational adaptation of the environment to differentiated needs. Elementary protection develops into purposeful reshaping of the environment, and displacement of nature is followed by replacement. The objectives are complex and interrelated and widen in scope and character. Man accepts the challenge of nature as a disciple and re-former, and the "I-Thou" relationship persists, though fashioned by man in a different way, and remolds the interrelationship of individual and group and the appreciation of the cosmic and earthly phenomena correspondingly. During this stage all activities bear the same mark of immediacy and reciprocal adjustment. This is manifest in such works as the rice terraces and fields of China (Fig. 23), in the geomantic adaptation of Chinese towns to environmental conditions (Fig. 24), in the regulation of the rivers and the irrigation of the fields (Fig. 25), and in the social and religious significance of the layout of Indian, African, and other towns, to mention only a few of the innumerable examples.

The third stage which had led to our present situation is one of aggressiveness and conquest. Adjustment to the environment develops into exploitation. The objectives are unlimited and grow in diversity but also in disunity (Fig. 26). With the ruthlessness of a pioneer, man expands his living space, and, with a complete disregard of the danger of a

FIG. 20.—Colombia, Ciénaga Grande, fishing village. The village stands in the Caribbean coastal lowlands, where little habitable ground is available. It is a compact settlement: home and workplace in one and providing economic security and physical protection against the hazards of life in the middle of the swamps fed by the waters of four rivers.

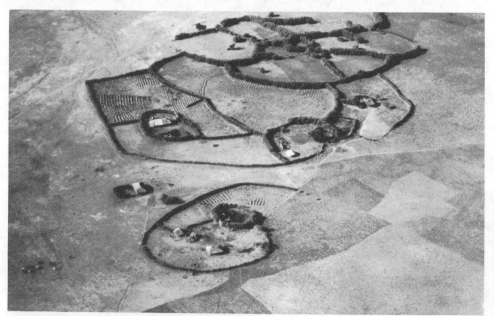

Courtesy of the American Geographical Society, New York

FIG. 21.—British Mandated Territory of Tanganyika, fields behind windbreaks. Security of food supply has been achieved by the protection of the fields behind windbreaks adapted to the terrain and serving as inclosures of the individual kraals.

FIG. 22.—Bulgaria, *zadruga* village. In this loosely grouped village each family farm is surrounded by a low wall. Narrow lanes give access to every single farmstead. The village is built on the *zadruga* principle, a social unit comprising one joint family. Hamlets develop by subdivision of the joint family and by addition of new buildings. In the course of time these hamlets grow into large villages where the *zadruga* units, forming compact groups, can be clearly discerned from the other parts interspersed between them.

CONFIDENCE AND ADJUSTMENT

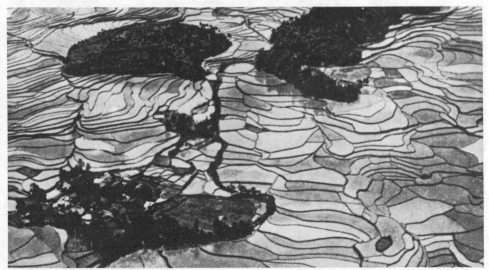

Photo Graf zu Castell

FIG. 23.—China, Hunan, rice terraces. The northern slopes of the mountains separating Kwangtung from Hunan sweep down from a height of 6,000 feet to a gigantic sea of rice fields, above which rise, like islands, hillocks with woods and settlements. Every field can be irrigated and properly drained. The village in the foreground consists of only a few houses covering a minimum of space—no more than can be spared from cultivation.

Photo Graf zu Castell

FIG. 24.—China, Hopeh, Peiping. The "Forbidden City," the emperor's residence, symbolizes the very heart of the Chinese Empire. It is situated right in the center of the outer city, like the yamen, the residence of the representative of the ruler, in any other town. The whole plan is oriented to this center, which, physically and psychologically, is the focal point. The "Forbidden City" is a town within a town. It is perhaps the only architectural work whose actual execution corresponds entirely with the ideal conception. Religious-geomantic considerations play an essential part in the layout of the city in general and in detail.

Courtesy of the Oriental Institute, University of Chicago

Fig. 25.—Iran, Province of Fars, irrigation system. The picture shows the head of an irrigation system developed by an enlightened Buyide prince who during the second half of the tenth century A.D. built the dam to raise the water of the Kur River below its junction with the Pulvar. Ten great wheels raised the water to such a high level that three hundred villages were supplied; each wheel also worked a flour mill. The dam is still in use, and many villages of the Marv Dasht today profit from this old system.

Aggressiveness and Disintegration

Courtesy of the Ministère des Travaux Publics

Fig. 26.—Belgium, Liége. The town of Liége extends along the banks of the Meuse River, including an island which is connected with both banks by numerous bridges. It is an old town with many remarkable buildings, but the modern age, with its ruthless disregard of organic growth, has contributed to its disintegration and unsystematic expansion.

25

Fig. 27.—Somewhere

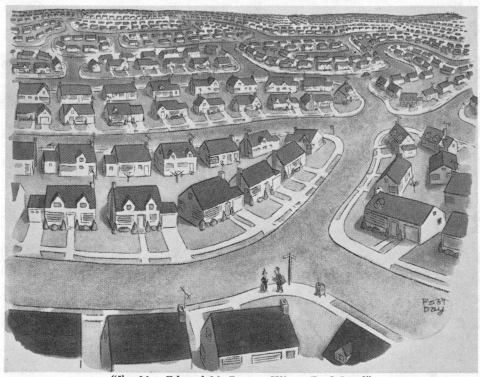

"I'm Mrs. Edward M. Barnes. Where Do I Live?"

Fig. 28.—Anywhere

primarily quantitative expansion, he deludes himself into the role of an omnipotent remaker of his environment (Figs. 27 and 28). Neglect and exploitation of the natural resources, rural isolation and urban expansion, have produced an unexampled disunity of the social and economic structure (Fig. 29). The physical expression of this third stage is evident in practically all works of modern man. They are perhaps the most conspicuous features which meet the eye from the air.

This phase is drawing to a close. The fourth stage of the interaction of man and environment is slowly taking shape. Faintly the outlines of this new epoch are discernible. It will be an age of responsibility and unification (Figs. 30, 31, and 32). Expansive ruthlessness is gradually merging into a careful adjustment to environmental conditions and new possibilities. Man begins to be aware of his real responsibility and of the limitations which the closing frontiers of the world impose upon him. The objectives are gaining in precision, foresight, and co-ordination. Unity in diversity and unification are emerging as the main tasks in the next stage of development in which man must act as a co-ordinator, guided by social awareness and insight into the workings of nature.

3. The third chain of transformation represents the changing experience of space in relation to the conception of the universe and the widening scale of human activities. Through the whole of known history the ideas of space which

AGGRESSIVENESS AND DISINTEGRATION

Courtesy of the Ministère des Travaux Publics

FIG. 29.—France, Pas-de-Calais, coal mine and homes. The inhuman blending of work and living place is part of the mining region in the north of France. The dumps are the most conspicuous landmarks of the exploitation of the natural resources and of the exploitation of the human "material."

man put on the universe were the reflection of his changing attitude toward
the environment and vice versa. And
with these different ideas the scale
widened, and large and comprehensive
operations replaced small and isolated
activities. Roughly three phases can be
distinguished.

a) During the first phase man is the
center of life on earth, and the earth
is the center of the universe, which is
conceived as finite and consisting of
concentric spheres. This is the system

of Aristotle which dominated man's
thought for two thousand years. Similar conceptions, though slightly modified, developed in other parts of the
world. While this lasted, all activities of man were undertaken in the
same spirit: They aimed at stability and
were limited in scope and character.
Nature was experienced as a multitude
of concrete orientations, and, therefore,
a concrete, body-like property was the
essential quality of all human works.
As far as these conceptions still exist

RESPONSIBILITY AND UNIFICATION

Courtesy of the U.S. Soil Conservation Service

FIG. 30.—United States, Texas, Bell County, contour plowing. Creative adaptation to nature
is gaining momentum through the application of scientific knowledge and deeper insight into the
work of nature. A new responsibility toward the soil is emerging. Although different in many
aspects from the streamlined terraces of China, the effects produced are nevertheless similar in
their spirit of close adaptation to nature. In this picture of an individual farm, the upper slopes
are controlled with terracing and strip cropping and the lower slopes with strip cropping alone.
This produces a visual effect which differs from the old field systems as much as does an abstract
from a Renaissance painting.

Courtesy of the U.S. Bureau of Reclamation

Fig. 31.—United States, Arizona, Boulder Dam, the hub of a large region. It is a long way from the earliest regulations of rivers, when a dam served as a protecting screen for the surrounding country, or from the primitive water control of African tribes, to the gigantic modern structures. To mere protection is added generation of power; to the needs of agriculture, those of industry; and to the mimicry with which early works copied natural features, the self-conscious originality of today, beautiful in its simplicity and decisive in its grandeur. The dam is part of the great scheme which is shown on the map (Fig. 32). The electric-power plant supplies hydroelectric power and irrigation water to a large area with a highly developed economy. It is the main source of energy which has enabled Los Angeles and the surrounding region to increase its population to a very considerable degree and at an unprecedented pace.

today, this conformity of the conception of the universal space and of the earthly works of man is unmistakable. This identity is not the result of a deliberate and conscious adaptation of the environment to the ideas of the universal space—such a notion would belong to the dream world of retrospective fabri- cations—but the expression of the latent spiritual forces which unite all thoughts and all works of man in one great scheme. As Whitehead, whose words we repeat in this connection, said, it is the "profound cosmological outlook, implicitly accepted, impressing its own type upon the current springs of ac-

RESPONSIBILITY AND UNIFICATION

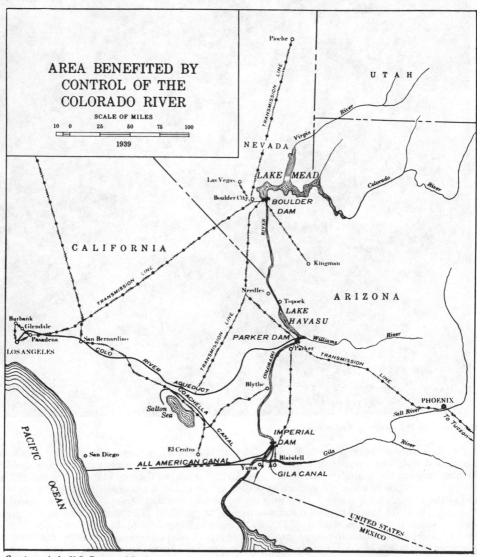

Courtesy of the U.S. Bureau of Reclamation

FIG. 32.—The area benefited by control of the Colorado River

tion." Works which can still be appreciated as evidence of this particular notion of space during this period reveal their characteristic features best from the air, for only then can they show most clearly their limitations and the belief of their creators in the possibility of stable conditions. The erection of fortified walls, protecting and inclosing the great empires of the Incas, the Romans, and the Chinese (Fig. 33), is an outstanding example of this spirit. The towns within these empires, as are also those of the European Middle Ages, though with some modifications, and other parts of the world, are built from outside inward (Fig. 34). They are conceived as limited units for a self-contained and stable life (Figs. 35–39).

b) The heliocentric universe of Copernicus is still finite, terminating in the sphere of the fixed stars, with the sun instead of the earth as the center. A new feeling of space develops, and the relegation of the earth to a secondary role in the universal system engenders tensions which made the ancient conception of the universe meaningless. Man is moved, with the earth, to the periphery. Slowly but irresistibly the whole outlook of man changes. He and his earth lose their central position, and

THE CHANGING SCALE

Fig. 33.—China, the Great Wall. The discovery of the third dimension, the conquest of the air, has made all national frontiers obsolete and their defense senseless. Frontiers have been revealed for what they are in reality—historical incidents. The Great Wall of China is the most expressive manifestation of the faith of a people in protection by walls. It is a grandiose reminder of the past and of the utmost limits to which the security of a national state can be identified with fixed frontiers. The Great Wall, begun about 500 B.C., served as protection against Mongol invaders from the steppes. Its fortlike watchhouses for the soldiers and the numerous towers form, together with the wall itself, a formidable defense system.

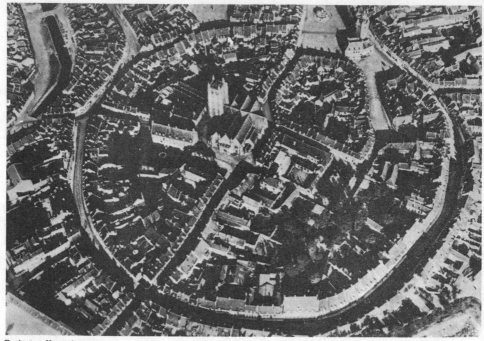

Exclusive News Agency

FIG. 34.—France, French Flanders, Bergues. The pedestrian scale is the standard of measurement. The town was encompassed by a circular wall, now replaced by a road. Gardens are interspersed between the houses. The church occupies the center, while the town hall with the belfry, a watchtower with an alarm bell, stands at the end of the town near the wall.

Courtesy of the Ministère des Travaux Publics

FIG. 35.—France, Gard, Aiguesmortes. The place was founded by St. Louis as one of the fortified towns, the bastides. A single uniform idea inspired the layout, which consists of a rectangular pattern of streets and a central square. This was typical of the Middle Ages wherever a new town was founded as a coherent unit. In return for the plots alloted to them the settlers helped in the building of the walls. Aiguesmortes is not more than 596 yards by 149 yards in extent. It served as a strong-point in a sparsely inhabited region. It is situated in an isolated position in the marshy plain of the Rhone Delta.

Courtesy of the Oriental Institute, University of Chicago

FIG. 36.—Iran, Isfahan, the Maidan-i-Shah. The town was the capital of the kingdom during the period from 1499 to 1736. The maidan, the "King's Square," is dominated by the most impressive structure in the town, the mosque of the shah. Although the circuit of the town extends over 30 miles, this architectural group is clearly the center, surpassing in importance and brilliance the vast mass of other buildings and gardens. The precincts of this complex include the religious center, the mosque, and the secular center, the palace of the king.

Swiss Air Photo

FIG. 37.—Switzerland, Canton of Zürich, Regensberg. The characteristic feature of the small town is the castle. In former times it was the all-important center of social and economic life. The situation on the top of the hill acts as a natural restriction to the size of the town.

Aerofilms, Ltd. K.L.M.

FIG. 38.—Netherlands, Overijssel, Elburg. In this old fortress-town on the shores of the Zuider Zee, each house has preserved its individuality as a clearly defined entity. Life within the town, limited physically by the wall and spiritually by the self-restraint imposed by social and economic bonds, achieved unity in diversity partly because the town never grew beyond pedestrian use and partly by the elimination of everything outside the experience of the community.

FIG. 39.—Italy, Venice, St. Mark's Square. The Square is the center of life in Venice. It is one of the most perfect examples of an open-air festival hall surrounded on three sides by uniform buildings and on the fourth closed by the Church of St. Mark. The *piazzetta,* a smaller square of similar proportions, opens the main square to the waterfront.

he is forced into the acceptance of a totally different view—a view from the periphery toward a new center, the sun. A more dynamic and wider outlook is the result. The compact empires of the first period are superseded by scattered possessions. An outburst of expansion sets in. The towns of Europe begin to expand. The simple walls are replaced by complicated fortifications for defense against long-range firearms (Figs. 40, 41). The perspective view is introduced as an element of town planning (Fig. 42), and the external appearance of the houses gains in importance. The extrovert dwelling place becomes the general rule. A new feeling of space and spaciousness is expressed in all works of man. Of this period we still have numerous examples which bear witness to the tremendous tensions arising out of this new attitude toward life and of thinking and planning on a larger scale.

c) The third phase leads eventually in our time to a conception of space which, like the universe, is unbounded and yet not infinite (Fig. 43), as a sphere is without a boundary and yet is not infinite, for it has a definite size conditioned by its radius. In the same way, the size of the universe depends on its average curvature. The first rudiments of this modern cosmology can be traced back to the Renaissance. Giordano Bruno was the first to assert that the universe has no limits but is infinite, without a creator, for an infinite uni-

THE IMPACT OF COPERNICUS

Aerofilms Ltd. K.L.M.

FIG. 40.—Netherlands, North Holland, Naarden. The fortress stands between the shores of the Zuider Zee and the Naardermeer as a protection of Amsterdam from the west. It is one of the finest examples of Renaissance fortifications. With the appearance of long-range firearms, the simple walls were replaced by a complicated system of bastions and ramparts surrounded by moats. This coincided with a new conception of town planning and especially with the introduction of perspective—the result of the changed conception of the universe originated by Copernicus and Giordano Bruno. In Naarden the church occupies the center, while in Italy the center was mostly reserved for the *piazza d'armi*, the meeting place of the defenders.

verse cannot be created from outside. During this period, from the beginning of the seventeenth century to modern times, the evolution of the feeling of space is more or less identical with a quest for expansion, with the breaking-down of limitations, and with the belief in an almost automatic progress. Today we are face to face with the confused results of this mode of thinking. The limits of expansion have been reached. The earth is fully known. Frontiers and walls as protection are recognized as historical incidents and as useless demonstrations. Our towns are shapeless, flowing over into the country.

At present we are in a particularly dangerous but also particularly formative period of transformation. The old ideas of space are still strong, and the

THE IMPACT OF COPERNICUS

Courtesy of the Ministère des Travaux Publics

FIG. 41.—France, Pyrénées-Orientales, Montlouis. Founded in 1681 by Vauban, the French military engineer, the place exhibits the starlike form which has made his fortifications famous. It stands on a plateau encircled by the deep valley of the Têt River and served as a frontier fortress against Spain. Small fields, owing to the mountainous character of the country and to repeated subdivisions, surround the two villages; one laid out compactly and the other as a roadside settlement.

new conceptions have not yet found a concrete expression. This confused state of mind is visible in all parts of the world. The illusion of infinite spread and the conviction that individual and unrelated actions will produce a coherent whole are fading away. When we look down at the earth and at the results of man's transformations, we may be impressed by the quantitative change—although this should not be overrated—but the qualitative aspects can hardly command the same positive tribute. The general picture is one of disintegration, disorder, and irresponsibility. Only here and there a few beginnings of co-ordination, systematic development, and responsibility can be discovered. The new feeling of space seems so far merely to be a cult of big-

ness. Its true implications still await their consummation in a language of form which grows out of the deep layers of human creativeness.

d) The widening scale of man's transformations suffers from the same and facile deception that bigness is identical with large enterprises. The problem is much more complex and will not be solved by the immature and blind boosters of quantity or by adherence to the dogma that quantity turns into quality, if and when the quantitative increase of change has reached an overwhelming scale.

Moreover, scale, like many other notions, is relative. When we fly from England to Japan, the gradual change of scale is perhaps the most striking impression. Scale is small in the British

The Impact of Copernicus

Fig. 42.—Italy, Rome, St. Peter's Square. The church has been placed at the end of the perspective view which corresponds to the new heliocentric idea of the universe. Like two enormous tentacles, the Colonnades of Bernini encompass the forecourt, linking the ensemble of the church and the gently rising square to the opposite end, where originally a continuation of the perspective layout was planned by Carlo Fontana.

Isles, increases over Europe, grows to large dimensions over Russia, only to decrease again over Japan. This is not exclusively the result of geographical factors, though these play a not entirely negligible role. It is more the outcome of the changing attitude of the inhabitants toward their respective environments. However, the varying scale is manifest in many things which are far removed from the direct and physical influence of the environment. Here are a few examples. For the West European, his garden is a collection of beautiful flowers and plants arranged as pleasingly as possible, or rigidly as the ornamental gardens of Spain or France, or with modest variety as the peasant gardens of Austria and Switzerland. For the Japanese, the garden is a microcosm consciously created out of nature's overwhelming diversity as a "concentrated" nature within a limited space. Or something quite different:

The Impact of the Airplane

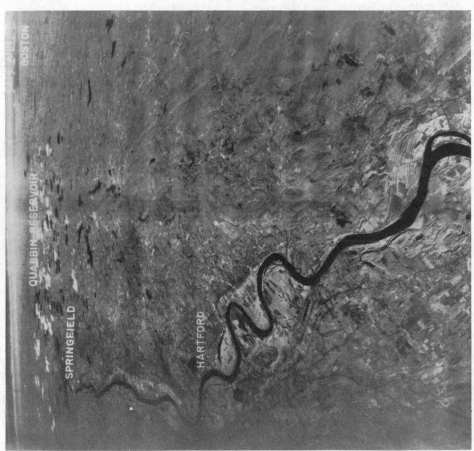

Courtesy of the U.S. Air Force Photo Reconnaissance Laboratories

Fig. 43.—Region between Boston and New York. The scale of the airplane sweeps away boundaries and limitations. Railways, motorcars, and airplanes, all together, if sensibly used and co-ordinated, open up the remotest and almost forgotten parts of the world. The introduction of the helicopter will complete this development. Regional integration on a large scale and physical and, above all, cultural decentralization will result from this tremendous transformation. Within the wide and elastic

The size of the paper on which we write is generally smaller in England than in Middle Europe and Russia, while it is smaller still in Japan. Or the houses: Broadly speaking, they are smaller in England, in general larger in Europe and Russia, but distinctly smaller in Japan. This applies of course only to the indigenous and old buildings, not to the Europeanized monstrosities dotted over the whole route.

What, then, is the correct assessment of scale and its gradually widening character? The answer can be given succinctly. Today we must reconcile two diametrically opposite aspects: the infinitely large and the infinitely small. This means, therefore, not merely an extension but, at the same time, also a limitation in space. The new scale is more than the expression of a transformed environment as such. It is an intellectual adventure into the totality of phenomena and conditions which

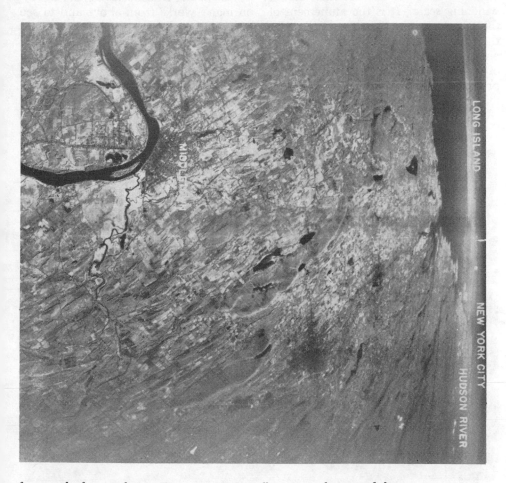

framework of regional unity new communities will come into being, and the oppressive dominance of the big cities will give way to a balanced structure of settlement in which every community will have its rightful place.

The shrinking of the world which the airplane accelerates with every new improvement means the approaching end of the sovereign national states. It opens the way to life-centered communities. It marks the beginning of the end of the work-centered cities and towns.

surround us. As a matter of fact, this has always been so. It is evident in a Zulu kraal, every part of which is within easy walking distance and which can be taken in as a whole at a glance (Fig. 44); in the small fields of Europe (Fig. 45); in the small and compact settlements in oases (Fig. 46); in hilltop towns of Italy, Spain, and Switzerland (Fig. 47); or in medieval towns of Europe and even in the large cities of Old China (Fig. 48).

And what is the characteristic of this widening scale? It is the atunement of the human scale to the universal scale, the simultaneous and willing experience of the infinite, and the acceptance of the safety which the human scale provides. Only if both these scales are joined together on the same level of importance can we hope to regain something of the old unity between the two. Mere bigness crushes the human scale and creates diffidence and finally social disintegration.

It would be a wrong assessment of the significance of the airplane if we regarded it solely as an instrument that brings home most dramatically the shrinking of the globe. This is only one side of this new venture. The airplane enables us for the first time to look down—in the truest sense of the word—on man's works from above and to see them as a still very imperfect attempt at reshaping the natural environment. It imposes upon us forcibly the insigᴛ ificance of what man has done so far to the earth and the challenge of the human scale which we almost lost

THE HUMAN SCALE PRESERVED

Courtesy of the American Geographical Society, New York

Fɪɢ. 44.—British East Africa, Kenya, Kisumu, Kavirondo kraals. The Kavirondo are agriculturists and dairymen. Their area is relatively closely settled, and kraals cover the countryside in unending succession. The cattle pen is sometimes in the center, where it is well protected. The ring fence gives a feeling of limitation and helps to preserve the human scale.

through the childish adoration of the big and yet so inadequate buildings and structures erected by man.

In a recent lecture to the European Management Conference, Ortega y Gasset had the courage to tell this audience of managerial pundits that productivity alone was not identical with the economy of a society but that the economy was intimately connected with the social characer of that society. He argued that the social nexus, in spite of an increase in productivity—he referred only to Europe, but his argument applies, of course, to other countries—has been disintegrating. Since the war there had developed a new social phenomenon which, taken together with the social disintegration in general, was an ominous sign of bewilderment and fear. He called this phenomenon "nationalism turned inward." What he meant by this is that the war marked the end of expansive nationalism and that since its end countries had begun to pay increasing attention to their own national customs and had become consequently more parochial. Instead of fighting each other and admiring the courage of their enemies, they denigrated each other, vilified each other's way of life and institutions, and hated each other more than ever before. And he concluded his argument by suggesting that this "nationalism turned inward" was a sign of the refusal to find a replacement for war. We may add that it is also a symbol of the rivaling forces of nationalism

THE HUMAN SCALE PRESERVED

Fig. 45.—Finland, Gulf of Bothnia, Liminka. Farms are clustered around a church in a small wood; others are widely dispersed over the countryside, and fields are laid out in strips. The physical structure of the whole area is only loosely knit together. In spite of this wide dispersion, the human scale is a living reality expressed in the small fields and in the numerous single farms dotted over the land as an ever present reminder of man as the measure of all things.

Literary Services (Mondiale)

FIG. 46.—Aden Protectorate, The Hadhramaut, Shibam. The town consists of only five hundred houses remarkable for their height: the skyscrapers of the desert. It stands on a slight eminence in the valley. The houses are close together, and there is no further building space. Shibam is a representative example of the intensive use of the small site to which all oases are restricted. The result of this compactness is close social and economic contact, protection against the desert and hostile outsiders, and a feeling of security heightened by the preservation of the human scale.

Courtesy of the Italian Embassy, London

FIG. 47.—Italy, Latium, Montecompatri. The town represents an ideal form of a hilltop settlement focused on the church, which stands right in the center. At the farther end is a palace. The outer street follows the contours of the hill. The whole is an extraordinarily beautiful architectural composition in which everything, man-made works and nature alike, is adapted to human proportions.

Photo Graf zu Castell

FIG. 48.—China, Shensi, Sian. Sian is the provincial capital of Shensi. It is one of the oldest towns of China and has repeatedly been the capital of the Chinese Empire. It is situated on the Wei River. The main arteries lead straight through the town from one gate to the other. Between them is an inextricable maze of lanes and side streets. Chinese towns are laid out mostly on a rectangular ground plan within the inclosure of the walls which were built first in accordance with religious ritual. Gradually the inner space was filled with buildings. The towns of Old China combined growth and organization. They solved this seemingly irreconcilable problem because life, and also such practical works as building, was deeply imbedded in religion and magical symbolism. The bonds of the family and the clan were of primary importance. Especially within the maze of the secondary streets the human scale was preserved, and life retained its immediate and personal character.

and universalism and of the apparent incompatibility between the chores of a daily life-routine within the parochial narrowness of a national state and the latent yearning for universal oneness.

What has this to do with the new scale which the airplane—and the modern means of mass communications—has given us? The answer is plain: The new scale has outrun our political and social comprehension and brought matters to a head. The inverted nationalism is merely an escape, because national frontiers have become meaningless, and yet the unity of the world evades us. This helplessness is a product of fear—but it could also be the very beginning of a new departure, for it can release the forces of self-examination and introspection which are still hidden in the soul of confused and irritated nations.

Ideas are more potent forces than material achievements. They are the real driving power behind our actions. This is the reason why this paper has been written with a strong emphasis on the imponderables which are at work behind the discovery of the third dimension, the conquest of the air, and the reshaping of our environment. It may be expected that this approach is not to the liking of the eternal realists and the hosts of pygmies who call themselves experts. For them, only that counts which can be seen and touched and used directly and practically. For them ideas are thin air, "such stuff as dreams are made of." They will, let us hope, dismiss the tenor of this paper as abstract and almost useless, for they are so preoccupied with their pet subjects that they never see the woods for the trees.

Today the whole world is our unit of thinking and acting. Nothing can develop in isolation, and the transformation in one country produces direct reactions on the physical and social structure of all the others. This awareness is perhaps the greatest triumph of the conquest of the air. It depends exclusively on the spirit in which we take up this challenge, not on our material achievements, whether our independence of the surface of the earth which the airplane has made possible will be a blessing or a curse.

Part I
Retrospect

Man's Tenure of the Earth

Man's Tenure of the Earth

The Agency of Man on the Earth

CARL O. SAUER[*]

THE THEME

As a short title for the present conference we have spoken at times and with hope of a "Marsh Festival," after the statesman-scholar, George Perkins Marsh, who a century ago considered the ways in which the Earth has been modified by human action (Marsh, 1864, 1874). The theme is the capacity of man to alter his natural environment, the manner of his so doing, and the virtue of his actions. It is concerned with historically cumulative effects, with the physical and biologic processes that man sets in motion, inhibits, or deflects, and with the differences in cultural conduct that distinguish one human group from another.

Every human population, at all times, has needed to evaluate the economic potential of its inhabited area, to organize its life about its natural environment in terms of the skills available to it and the values which it accepted. In the cultural *mise en valeur* of the environment, a deformation of the pristine, or prehuman, landscape has been

initiated that has increased with length of occupation, growth in population, and addition of skills. Wherever men live, they have operated to alter the aspect of the Earth, both animate and inanimate, be it to their boon or bane.

The general theme may be described, therefore, in its first outline, as an attempt to set forth the geographic effects, that is, the appropriation of habitat by habit, resulting from the spread of differing cultures to all the *oikoumene* throughout all we know of human time. We need to understand better how man has disturbed and displaced more and more of the organic world, has become in more and more regions the ecologic dominant, and has affected the course of organic evolution. Also how he has worked surficial changes as to terrain, soil, and the waters on the land and how he has drawn upon its minerals. Latterly, at least, his urban activities and concentrations have effected local alterations of the atmosphere. We are trying to examine the processes of terrestrial change he has entrained or originated, and we are attempting to ask, from our several interests and experiences, relevant questions as to cultural behaviors and effects. Thus we come properly also to consider the qualities of his actions as they seem to affect his future well-being. In this proper study of mankind, living out the destiny ascribed in Genesis—"to have dominion over all the earth"—the concern is valid as to whether his organized energies (social behavior) have or should have

[*] Dr. Sauer is Professor of Geography at the University of California, Berkeley, and was chairman of the Department of Geography (1923–54). He is a member of the advisory board of the John Simon Guggenheim Memorial Foundation; was president for 1940 of the Association of American Geographers and is its honorary president (1955–56); and recipient in 1940 of the Charles P. Daly Medal of the American Geographical Society. His publications include: *Aboriginal Population of Northwestern Mexico*, 1935; *Colima of New Spain in the Sixteenth Century*, 1948; and *Agricultural Origins and Dispersals*, 1952.

a quality of concern with regard to his posterity.

ON THE NATURE OF MAN

The primordial condition of man setting our kind apart from other primates involved more than hands, brain, and walking upright. Man owes his success in part to his digestive apparatus, which is equaled by none of his near-kin or by few other similarly omnivorous animals as to the range of potential food which can sustain him on a mixed, vegetarian, or flesh diet. The long, helpless infancy and the dependence through the years of childhood have forged, it would seem, *ab origine* a maternal bond that expresses itself in persistence of family and in formal recognition of kinship, system of kinship being perhaps the first basis of social organization. When humans lost the oestrous cycle is unknown; its weakening and loss is probably a feature of domestication, and it may have occurred early in the history of man, eldest of the domesticated creatures.

Built into the biologic nature of man therefore appear to be qualities tending to maximize geographic expansiveness, vigorous reproduction, and a bent to social development. His extreme food range favored numerical increase; I question, for instance, any assumptions of sporadic or very sparse populations of Paleolithic man in any lands he had occupied. The dominant and continuous role of woman in caring for the family suggests further inferences. Maternal duties prescribed as sedentary a life as possible. Her collecting of food and other primary materials was on the short tether of her dependent offspring. Hers also was the care of what had been collected in excess of immediate need, the problem of storage, hers the direction toward homemaking and furnishing. To the "nature" of woman we may perhaps ascribe an original social grouping, a cluster of kindred households, in which some stayed home to watch over bairns and baggage while others ranged afield. Baby-sitting may be one of the most ancient of human institutions.

Implicit in this interpretation of the nature of man and primordial society, as based on his trend to sedentary life and clustering, are territoriality, the provision of stores against season of lack, and probably a tendency to monogamy. These traits are familiar enough among numerous animals, and there is no reason for denying them to primitive man. Shifts of population imposed by seasons do not mean wandering, homeless habits; nomadism is an advanced and specialized mode of life. Folk who stuffed or starved, who took no heed of the morrow, could not have possessed the Earth or laid the foundations of human culture. To the ancestral folk we may rather ascribe practical-minded economy of effort. Their success in survival and in dispersal into greatly differing habitats tells of ability to derive and communicate sensible judgments from changing circumstances.

The culture of man is herewith considered as in the main a continuum from the beginning; such is its treatment by archeology. The record of artifacts is much greater, more continuous, and begins earlier than do his recovered skeletal remains. Thereby hangs the still-argued question of human evolution, about which divergent views are unreconciled. If culture was transmitted and advanced in time and space as the archeologic record indicates, there would appear to be a linked history of a mankind that includes all the specific and generic hominid classifications of physical anthropology. Man, *sensu latiore*, therefore may conceivably be one large species complex, from archaic to modern forms, always capable of interbreeding and intercommunication. Variation occurred by long geographic isolation, blending usually when different stocks met. The former is accepted; the latter seems assured to some and is rejected by others, the Mount Carmel series of skulls being thus notoriously in dispute.

Neanderthal man, poor fellow, has had a rough time of it. He invented the Mousterian culture, a major advance which appears to have been derived from two anterior culture lines. The Abbé Breuil has credited him with ceremonial cults that show a developed religious belief and spiritual ceremonial (Breuil and Lantier, 1951, chap. xviii). Boyd, in his serologic classification of mankind (1950), the only system available on a genetic basis, has surmised that Neanderthal is ancestral to a Paleo-European race. There is no basis for holding Neanderthal man as mentally inferior or as unable to cope with the late Pleistocene changes of European climate. Yet there remains aversion to admitting him to our ancestry. The sad confusion of physical anthropology is partly the result of its meager knowledge of hereditary factors, but also to *Homo*'s readiness to crossbreed, a trait of his domestication and a break with the conservatism of the instinctive.

We are groping in the obscurity of a dim past; it may be better to consider cultural growth throughout human time as proceeding by invention, borrowing, and blending of learning, rather than by evolution of human brain, until we know more of biological evolution in man. The little that we have of skeletal remains is subject to unreconciled evaluations; the record of his work is less equivocal. The question is not, could Peking man have left the artifacts attributed to him, as has been the subject of debate, but did he, that is, do the bones belong with the tools?

When primordial man began to spread over the Earth, he knew little, but what he had learned was by tested and transmitted experience; he cannot have been fear-ridden but rather, at least in his successful kinds, was venturesome, ready to try out his abilities in new surroundings. More and more he imposed himself on his animal competitors and impressed his mark on the lands he inhabited. Wherever he settled, he came to stay unless the climate changed too adversely or the spreading sea drove him back.

CLIMATIC CHANGES AND THEIR EFFECTS ON MAN

The age of man is also the Ice Age. Man may have witnessed its beginning; we perhaps are still living in an interglacial phase. His growth of learning and his expansion over the Earth have taken place during a geologic period of extreme instability of climates and also of extreme simultaneous climatic contrast. His span has been cast within a period of high environmental tensions. Spreading icecaps caused the ocean to shrink back from the shallow continental margins, their waning to spread the seas over coastal plains. With lowered sea levels, rivers trenched their valley floors below coastal lowlands; as sea level rose, streams flooded and aggraded their valleys. Glacial and Recent time have been governed by some sort of climatic pendulum, varying in amplitude of swing, but affecting land and sea in all latitudes, and life in most areas. The effects have been most felt in the Northern Hemisphere, with its large continental masses, wide plains, high mountain ranges, and broad plateaus. Millions of square miles of land were alternately buried under ice and exposed; here, also, the shallow seas upon the continental shelf spread and shrank most broadly.

This time of recurrent changes of atmosphere, land, and sea gave advantage to plastic, mobile, and prolific organisms, to plants and animals that could colonize newly available bodies of land, that had progeny some of which withstood the stresses of climatic change. The time was favorable for biologic evolution, for mutants suited to a changed environment, for hybrids formed by mingling, as on ecologic frontiers. To this period has been assigned the origin of many annual plant species dependent on heavy seed production for success (Ames, 1939). Adaptive variations in human stocks, aided by sufficiently isolating episodes of Earth history, have also been inferred.[1]

The duration of the Ice Age and of its stages has not been determined. The old guess of a million years over all is still convenient. The four glacial and three interglacial stages may have general validity; there are doubts that they were strictly in phase in all continents. In North America the relations of the several continental icecaps to the phases of Rocky Mountain glaciation, and of the latter to the Pacific mountains, are only inferred, as is the tie-in of pluvial stages in our Southwest. That great lakes and permanent streams existed in many of the present dry lands of the world is certain, that these pluvial phases of intermediate latitudes correspond to glacial ones in high latitudes and altitudes is in considerable part certain, but only in a few cases has a pluvial state been securely tied to a contemporaneous glacial stage. The promising long-range correlation of Pleistocene events by eustatic marine terraces and their dependent alluvial terraces is as yet only well started. Except for northwestern Europe, the calendar of the later geologic past is still very uncertain. The student of farther human time, anxious for an absolute chronology, is at the moment relying widely on the ingenious astronomical calendar of Milankovitch and Zeuner as an acceptable span for the Ice Age as a whole and for its divisions. It is not ac-

ceptable, however, to meteorology and climatology.[2] Slowly and bit by bit only are we likely to see the pieces fall into their proper order; nothing is gained by assurance as to what is insecure.

The newer meteorology is interesting itself in the dynamics of climatic change (Shapley, 1953; Mannerfelt *et al.*, 1949). Changes in the general circulation pattern have been inferred as conveying, in times of glacial advance, more and more frequent masses of moist, relatively warm air into high latitudes and thereby also increasing the amount of cloud cover. The importance now attached to condensation nuclei has directed attention again to the possible significance of volcanic dust. Synoptic climatological data are being examined for partial models in contemporary conditions as conducive to glaciation and deglaciation (Leighly, 1949, pp. 133–34). To the student of the human past, reserve is again indicated in making large climatic reconstructions. Such cautions I should suggest, with reserve also as to my competence to offer them, with regard to the following:

It is misleading to generalize glacial stages as cold and interglacial ones as warm. The developing phases of glaciation probably required relatively warm moist air, and decline may have been by the dominance of cold dry air over the ice margins. The times of climatic change may thus not coincide with the change from glacial advance to deglaciation. We may hazard the inference that developing glaciation is associated with low contrast of regional climates; regression of ice and beginning of an interglacial phase probably are connected (although not in each case) with accentuated contrast or "continentality" of climates. One interglacial did not repeat necessarily the features of another; nor must one glacial phase du-

1. As most recently by Coon, 1953.

2. Shapley, 1953; Willett, 1950; Simpson, G. C., 1934, 1940.

plicate another. We need only note the difference in centers of continental glaciation, of direction of growth of ice lobes, of terminal moraine-building, of structure of till and of fluvioglacial components to see the individuality of climates of glacial stages. In North America, in contrast to Europe, there is very little indication of a periglacial cold zone of tundra and of permafrost in front of the continental icecaps. Questionable also is the loess thesis of dust as whipped up from bare ground and deposited in beds by wind, these surfaces somehow becoming vegetated by a cold steppe plant cover.

The events of the last deglaciation and of the "postglacial" are intelligible as yet only in part. A priori it is reasonable to consider that the contemporary pattern of climates had become more or less established before the last ice retreat began. Lesser later local climatic oscillations have been found but have been improperly extended and exaggerated, however, in archeological literature. In the pollen studies of bogs of northwestern Europe, the term "climatic optimum" was introduced innocently to note a poleward and mountainward extension of moderate proportions for certain plants not occurring at the same time over the entire area. Possibly this expansion of range means that there were sunnier summers and fall seasons, permitting the setting and maturing of seed for such plants somewhat beyond their prior and present range, that is, under more "continental" and less "maritime" weather conditions. This modest and expectable variation of a local climate in the high latitudes and at the changing sea borders of North Atlantic Europe has been construed by some students of prehistory into a sort of climatic golden age, existent at more or less the same time in distant parts of the world, without regard to dynamics or patterns of climates. We might well

be spared such naïvely nominal climatic constructions as have been running riot through interpretations of prehistory and even of historic time.

The appearance or disappearance, increase or decrease, of particular plants and animals may not spell out obligatory climatic change, as has been so freely inferred. Plants differ greatly in rate of dispersal, in pioneering ability, in having routes available for their spread, and in other ways that may enter into an unstable ecologic association, as on the oft-shifted stage of Pleistocene and Recent physiography. The intervention of man and animals has also occurred to disturb the balance. The appearance and fading of pines in an area, characteristic in many bog pollen columns, may tell nothing of climatic change: pines are notorious early colonizers, establishing themselves freely in mineral soils and open situations and yielding to other trees as shading and organic cover of ground increase. Deer thrive on browse; they increase wherever palatable twigs become abundant, in brush lands and with young tree growth; ecologic factors of disturbance other than climate may determine the food available to them and the numbers found in archeologic remains.

The penetration of man to the New World is involved in the question of past and present climates. The origin and growth of the dominant doctrine of a first peopling of the Western Hemisphere in postglacial time is beyond our present objective, but it was not based on valid knowledge of climatic history. The postglacial and present climatic pattern is one of extremes rarely reached or exceeded in the past of the Earth. Passage by land within this time across Siberia, Alaska, and Canada demanded specialized advanced skills in survival under great and long cold comparable to those known to Eskimo and Athabascan, an excessive postulate for many of the primitive peoples of the New World. Relatively mild climates did prevail in high latitudes at times during the Pleistocene. At such times in both directions between Old and New World, massive migrations took place of animals incapable of living on tundras, animals that are attractive game for man. If man was then living in eastern Asia, nothing hindered him from migrating along with such non-boreal mammals. The question is of fundamental interest, because it asks whether man in the New World, within a very few thousand years, achieved independently a culture growth comparable and curiously parallel to that of the Old, which required a much greater span. There is thus also the inference that our more primitive aborigines passed the high latitudes during more genial climes rather than that they lost subsequently numerous useful skills.

FIRE

Speech, tools, and fire are the tripod of culture and have been so, we think, from the beginning. About the hearth, the home and workshop are centered. Space heating under shelter, as a rock overhang, made possible living in inclement climates; cooking made palatable many plant products; industrial innovators experimented with heat treatment of wood, bone, and minerals. About the fireplace, social life took form, and the exchange of ideas was fostered. The availability of fuel has been one of the main factors determining the location of clustered habitation.

Even to Paleolithic man, occupant of the Earth for all but the last 1 or 2 per cent of human time, must be conceded gradual deformation of vegetation by fire. His fuel needs were supplied by dead wood, drifted or fallen, and also by the stripping of bark and bast that caused trees to die and become available as fuel supply. The setting or escape of fire about camp sites cleared away small and young growth, stimulated annual plants, aided in collecting, and became elaborated in time into the fire drive, a formally organized procedure among the cultures of the Upper Paleolithic *grande chasse* and of their New World counterpart.

Inferentially, modern primitive peoples illustrate the ancient practices in all parts of the world. Burning, as a practice facilitating collecting and hunting, by insensible stages became a device to improve the yield of desired animals and plants. Deliberate management of their range by burning to increase food supply is apparent among hunting and collecting peoples, in widely separated areas, but has had little study. Mature woody growth provides less food for man and ground animals than do fire-disturbed sites, with protein-rich young growth and stimulated seed production, accessible at ground levels. Game yields are usually greatest where the vegetation is kept in an immediate state of ecologic succession. With agricultural and pastoral peoples, burning in preparation for planting and for the increase of pasture has been nearly universal until lately.

The gradually cumulative modifications of vegetation may become large as to selection of kind and as to aspect of the plant cover. Pyrophytes include woody monocotyledons, such as palms, which do not depend on a vulnerable cambium tissue, trees insulated by thick corky bark, trees and shrubs able to reproduce by sprouting, and plants with thick, hard-shelled seeds aided in germination by heat. Loss of organic matter on and in the soil may shift advantage to forms that germinate well in mineral soils, as the numerous conifers. Precocity is advantageous. The assemblages consequent upon fires are usually characterized by a reduced number of species, even by the dominance of few and single species. Minor elements in a natural flora, originally mainly confined to accidentally disturbed and exposed situations, such as windfalls and eroding slopes, have opened to them by recurrent burning the chance to spread and multiply. In most cases the shift is from mesophytic to less exacting, more xeric, forms, to those that do not require ample soil moisture and can tolerate at all times full exposure to sun. In the long run the scales are tipped against the great, slowly maturing plants—the trees (a park land of mature trees may be the last stand of what was a complete woodland). Our eastern woodlands, at the time of white settlement, seem largely to have been in process of change to park lands. Early accounts stress the open stands of trees, as indicated by the comment that one could drive a coach from seaboard to the Mississippi River over almost any favoring terrain. The "forest primeval" is exceptional. In the end the success in a land occupied by man of whatever cultural level goes to the annuals and short-lived perennials, able to seed heavily or to reproduce by rhizome and tuber. This grossly drawn sketch may introduce the matter of processes resulting in what is called ecologically a secondary fire association, or subclimax, if it has historical persistence.

The climatic origin of grasslands rests on a poorly founded hypothesis. In the first place, the individual great grasslands extend over long climatic gradients from wet to dry and grade on their driest margins into brush and scrub. Woody growth occurs in them where there are breaks in the general surface, as in the Cross Timbers of our Southwest. Woody plants establish themselves freely in grasslands if fire protection is given: the prairies and steppes are suited to the growth of the trees and shrubs native to adjacent lands but may lack them. An individual grassland may extend across varied parent-materials. Their most common quality is that they are upland plains, having periods of dry weather long enough to dry out the surface of the ground, which accumulate a sufficient amount of burnable matter to feed and spread a fire. Their position and limits are determined by relief; nor do they extend into arid lands or those having a continuously wet ground surface. Fires may sweep indefinitely across a surface of low relief but are checked shortly at barriers of broken terrain, the checking being more abrupt if the barrier is sunk below the general surface. The inference is that origin and preservation of grasslands are due, in the main, to burning and that they are in fact great and, in some cases, ancient cultural features.

In other instances simplified woodlands, such as the pine woods of our Southeast, *palmares* in tropical savannas, are pyrophytic deformations; there are numerous vegetational alternatives other than the formation of grassland by recurrent burning. Wherever primitive man has had the opportunity to turn fire loose on a land, he seems to have done so, from time immemorial; it is only civilized societies that have undertaken to stop fires.

In areas controlled by customary burning, a near-ecologic equilibrium may have been attained, a biotic recombination maintained by similarly repeated human intervention. This is not destructive exploitation. The surface of the ground remains protected by growing cover, the absorption of rain and snow is undiminished, and loss of moisture from ground to atmosphere possibly is reduced. Microclimatic differences between woodland and grassland are established as effect if not as cause, and some are implicit in the Shelter Belt Project.

Our modern civilization demands fire control for the protection of its property. American forestry was begun as a remedy for the devastation by careless lumbering at a time when dreadful holocausts almost automatically followed logging, as in the Great Lakes states. Foresters have made a first principle of fire suppression. Complete protection, however, accumulates tinder year by year; the longer the accumulation, the greater is the fire hazard and the more severe the fire when it results. Stockmen are vociferous about the loss of grazing areas to brush under such protection of the public lands. Here and there, carefully controlled light burning is beginning to find acceptance in range and forest management. It is being applied to long-leaf pine reproduction in Southeastern states and to some extent for grazing in western range management. In effect, the question is now being raised whether well-regulated fires may not have an ecologic role beneficent to modern man, as they did in older days.

PEASANT AND PASTORAL WAYS

The next revolutionary intervention of man in the natural order came as he selected certain plants and animals to be taken under his care, to be reproduced, and to be bred into domesticated forms increasingly dependent on him for survival. Their adaptation to serve human wants runs counter, as a rule, to the processes of natural selection. New lines and processes of organic evolution were entrained, widening the gap between wild and domestic forms. The natural land became deformed, as to biota, surface, and soil, into unstable cultural landscapes.

Conventionally, agricultural origins are placed at the beginning of Neolithic time, but it is obvious that the earliest archeologic record of the Neolithic presents a picture of an accomplished domestication of plants and animals, of peasant and pastoral life re-resembling basic conditions that may still be met in some parts of the Near East.

Three premises as to the origin of agriculture seem to me to be necessary:

(1) That this new mode of life was sedentary and that it arose out of an earlier sedentary society. Under most conditions, and especially among primitive agriculturists, the planted land must be watched over continuously against plant predators. (2) That planting and domestication did not start from hunger but from surplus and leisure. Famine-haunted folk lack the opportunity and incentive for the slow and continuing selection of domesticated forms. Village communities in comfortable circumstances are indicated for such progressive steps. (3) Primitive agriculture is located in woodlands. Even the pioneer American farmer hardly invaded the grasslands until the second quarter of the past century. His fields were clearings won by deadening, usually by girdling, the trees. The larger the trees, the easier the task; brush required grubbing and cutting; sod stopped his advance until he had plows capable of ripping through the matted grass roots. The forest litter he cleaned up by occasional burning; the dead trunks hardly interfered with his planting. The American pioneer learned and followed Indian practices. It is curious that scholars, because they carried into their thinking the tidy fields of the European plowman and the felling of trees by ax, have so often thought that forests repelled agriculture and that open lands invited it.

The oldest form of tillage is by digging, often but usually improperly called "hoe culture." This was the only mode known in the New World, in Negro Africa, and in the Pacific islands. It gave rise, at an advanced level, to the gardens and horticulture of Monsoon Asia and perhaps of the Mediterranean. Its modern tools are spade, fork, and hoe, all derived from ancient forms. In tropical America this form of tillage is known as the *conuco*, in Mexico as the *milpa*, in the latter case a planting of seeds of maize, squash, beans, and perhaps other annuals. The conuco is stocked mainly by root and stem cuttings, a perennial garden plot. Recently, the revival of the Old Norse term "swithe," or "swidden," has been proposed (Izikowitz, 1951, p. 7 n.; Conklin, 1954).

Such a plot begins by deadening tree growth, followed toward the end of a dry period by burning, the ashes serving as quick fertilizer. The cleared space then is well stocked with a diverse assemblage of useful plants, grown as tiers of vegetation if moisture and fertility are adequate. In the maize-beans-squash complex the squash vines spread over the ground, the cornstalks grow tall, and the beans climb up the cornstalks. Thus the ground is well protected by plant cover, with good interception of the falling rain. In each conuco a high diversity of plants may be cared for, ranging from low herbs to shrubs, such as cotton and manioc, to trees entangled with cultivated climbers. The seeming disorder is actually a very full use of light and moisture, an admirable ecologic substitution by man, perhaps equivalent to the natural cover also in the protection given to the surface of the ground. In the tropical conuco an irregular patch is dug into at convenient spots and at almost any time to set out or collect different plants, the planted surface at no time being wholly dug over. Digging roots and replanting may be going on at the same time. Our notions of a harvest season when the whole crop is taken off the field are inapplicable. In the conucos something may be gathered on almost any day through the year. The same plant may yield pot and salad greens, pollen-rich flowers, immature fruit, and ripened fruit; garden and field are one, and numerous domestic uses may be served by each plant. Such multiple population of the tilled space makes possible the highest yields per unit of surface, to which may be added

the comments that this system has developed plants of highest productivity, such as bananas, yams, and manioc, and that food production is by no means the only utility of many such plants.

The planting systems really do not deserve the invidious terms given them, such as "slash and burn" or "shifting agriculture." The abandonment of the planting after a time to the resprouting and reseeding wild woody growth is a form of rotation by which the soil is replenished by nutriments carried up from deep-rooted trees and shrubs, to be spread over the ground as litter. Such use of the land is freed from the limitations imposed on the plowed field by terrain. That it may give good yields on steep and broken slopes is not an argument against the method, which gives much better protection against soil erosion than does any plowing. It is also in these cultures that we find that systems of terracing of slopes have been established.

Some of the faults charged against the system derive from the late impact from our own culture, such as providing axes and machetes by which sprouts and brush may be kept whacked out instead of letting the land rest under regrowth, the replacement of subsistence crops by money crops, the world-wide spurt in population, and the demand for manufactured goods which is designated as rising standard of living. Nor do I claim that under this primitive planting man could go on forever growing his necessities without depleting the soil; but rather that, in its basic procedure and crop assemblages, this system has been most conservative of fertility at high levels of yield; that, being protective and intensive, we might consider it as being fully suited to the physical and cultural conditions of the areas where it exists. Our Western know-how is directed to land use over a short run of years and is not the wisdom of the primitive peasant rooted to his ancestral lands.

Our attitudes toward farming stem from the other ancient trunk whence spring the sowers, reapers, and mowers; the plowmen, dairymen, shepherds, and herdsmen. This is the complex already well represented in the earliest Neolithic sites of the Near East. The interest of this culture is directed especially toward seed production of annuals, cereal grasses in particular. The seedbed is carefully prepared beforehand to minimize weed growth and provide a light cover of well-worked soil in which the small seeds germinate. An evenly worked and smooth surface contrasts with the hit-or-miss piling of earth mounds, "hills" in the American farm vernacular, characteristic of conuco and milpa. Instead of a diversity of plants, the prepared ground receives the seed of one kind. (Western India is a significant exception.) The crop is not further cultivated and stands to maturity, when it is reaped at one time. After the harvest the field may lie fallow until the next season. The tillage implement is the plow, in second place, the harrow, both used to get the field ready for sowing. Seeding traditionally is by broadcasting, harvesting by cutting blades.

Herd animals, meat cattle, sheep, goats, horses, asses, camels, are either original or very early in this system. The keeping of grazing and browsing animals is basic. All of them are milked or have been so in the past. In my estimation milking is an original practice and quality of their domestication and continued to be in many cases their first economic utility; meat and hides, the product of surplus animals only.

The over-all picture is in great contrast to that of the planting cultures: regular, elongated fields minimize turning the animals that pull the plow; fields are cultivated in the off season, in part to keep them free of volunteer growth;

fields are fallowed but not abandoned, the harvest season is crowded into the end of the annual growth period; thereafter, stock is pastured on stubble and fallow; land unsuited or not needed for the plow is used as range on which the stock grazes and browses under watch of herdboys or herdsmen.

This complex spread from its Near Eastern cradle mainly in three directions, changing its character under changed environments and by increase of population.

1. Spreading into the steppes of Eurasia, the culture lost its tillage and became completely pastoral, with true nomadism. This is controversial, but the evidence seems to me to show that all domestication of the herd animals (except for reindeer) was effected by sedentary agriculturists living between India and the Mediterranean and also that the great, single, continuous area in which milking was practiced includes all the nomadic peoples, mainly as a fringe about the milking seed-farmers. It has also been pointed out that nomadic cultures depend on agricultural peoples for some of their needs and, thus lacking a self-contained economy, can hardly have originated independently.

2. The drift of the Celtic, Germanic, and Slavic peoples westward (out of southwestern and western Asia?) through the northern European plain appears to have brought them to their historic seats predominantly as cattle- and horse-raisers. Their movement was into lands of cooler and shorter summers and of higher humidity, in which wheat and barley did poorly. An acceptable thesis is that, in southwestern Asia, rye and probably oats were weed grasses growing in fields of barley and wheat. They were harvested together and not separated by winnowing. In the westward movement of seed farmers across Europe, the weed grains did better and the noble grain less well. The

cooler and wetter the summers, the less wheat and barley did the sower reap and the more of rye and oat seeds, which gradually became domesticated by succeeding where the originally planted kinds failed.

Northwestern and Central Europe appear to be the home of our principal hay and pasture grasses and clovers. As the stock-raising colonists deadened and burned over tracts of woodland, native grasses and clovers spontaneously took possession of the openings. These were held and enlarged by repetition of burning and cutting. Meadow and pasture, from the agricultural beginnings, were more important here than plowland. Even the latter, by pasturing the rye fields and the feeding of oat straw and grain, were part of animal husbandry. Here, as nowhere else, did the common farmer concern himself with producing feed for his stock. He was first a husbandman; he cut hay to store for winter feed and cured it at considerable trouble; he stabled his animals over the inclement season, or stall-fed them through the year; the dunghill provided dressing for field and meadow. House, barn, and stable were fused into one structure. The prosperity of farmstead and village was measured by its livestock rather than by arable land.

The resultant pattern of land use, which carries through from the earliest times, as recovered by archeology in Denmark and northern Germany, was highly conservative of soil fertility. The animal husbandry maintained so effective a ground cover that northern Europe has known very little soil erosion. Animal manure and compost provided adequate return of fertility to the soil. Man pretty well established a closed ecologic cycle. It was probably here that man first undertook to till the heavy soils. Clayey soils, rich in plant food but deficient in drainage, are widespread in the lowlands, partly due to climatic conditions, partly a legacy of the Ice Age. The modern plow with share, moldboard, and colter had either its origin or a major development here for turning real furrows to secure better aeration and drainage. Beneficial in northwestern and Central Europe, it was later to become an instrument of serious loss elsewhere.

3. The spread of sowing and herding cultures westward along both sides of the Mediterranean required no major climatic readjustment. Wheat and barley continued to be the staple grains; sheep and goats were of greater economic importance than cattle and horses. Qualities of the environment that characterized the Near East were accentuated to the west: valleys lie imbedded in mountainous terrain, the uplands are underlain by and developed out of limestone, and, to the south of the Mediterranean, aridity becomes prevalent. The hazard of drought lay ever upon the Near Eastern homeland and on the colonial regions to the west and south. No break between farmer and herdsman is discernible at any time; as the village Arab of today is related to the Bedouin, the environmental specialization may have been present from the beginning: flocks on the mountains and dry lands, fields where moisture sufficed and soil was adequate.

That the lands about the Mediterranean have become worn and frayed by the usage to which they have been subjected has long been recognized, though not much is known as to when and how. The eastern and southern Mediterranean uplands especially are largely of limestone, attractive as to soil fertility but, by their nature, without deep original mantle of soil or showing the usual gradation of subsoil into bedrock and thus are very vulnerable to erosion. The less suited the land was or became to plow cultivation, the greater the shift to pastoral economy. Thus a downslope migration of tillage charac-

terized, in time, the retreating limits of
the fields, and more and more land became range for goats, sheep, and asses.
Repeatedly prolonged droughts must
have speeded the downslope shift, hillside fields suffering most, and with failing vegetation cover becoming more
subject to washing when rains came.

Thus we come again to the question
of climatic change as against attrition
of surface and increased xerophytism of
vegetation by human disturbance and,
in particular, to what is called the
"desertification" of North Africa and
the expansion of the Sahara. A case for
directional change in the pattern of
atmospheric circulation has been inferred from archeology and faunal
changes. I am doubtful that it is a good
case within the time of agricultural and
pastoral occupation. Another view is
that the progressive reduction of plant
cover by man has affected soil and
ground-surface climate unfavorably.
Largely, and possibly wholly, the deterioration of the borders of the dry
lands may have been caused by adverse,
cumulative effects of man's activities.
From archeologic work we need much
more information as to whether human
occupation has been failing in such
areas over a long time, or whether it has
happened at defined intervals, and also
whether, if such intervals are noted,
they may have a cultural rather than
an environmental (climatic) basis.

No protective herbaceous flora became established around the shores of
the Mediterranean on pastures and
meadows as was the case in the north.
Flocks and herds grazed during the
short season of soft, new grass but most
of the year browsed on woody growth.
The more palatable feed was eaten first
and increasingly eliminated; goats and
asses got along on range that had
dropped below the support levels required by more exacting livestock. As
is presently true in the western United
States, each prolonged drought must

have left the range depleted, its carrying capacity reduced, and recovery of
cover less likely. Natural balance between plants and animals is rarely re-
established under such exploitation,
since man will try to save his herd
rather than their range. A large and
long deterioration of the range may
therefore fully account for the poor and
xerophytic flora and fauna without postulating progressive climatic desiccation, for the kinds of life that survive
under overuse of the land are the most
undemanding inhabitants.

Comparative studies of North Africa
and of the American Southwest and
northern Mexico are needed to throw
light on the supposed "desiccation" of
the Old World. We know the dates of
introduction of cattle and sheep to the
American ranges and can determine
rate and kind of change of vegetation
and surface. The present desolate shift-
ing-sand area that lies between the
Hopi villages and the Colorado River
was such good pasture land late in the
eighteenth century that Father Esca-
lante, returning from his canyon exploration, rested his travel-worn animals
there to regain flesh. The effects of
Navaho sheep-herding in little more
than a century and mainly in the last
sixty years are well documented. Lower
California and Sonora are climatic
homologues of the western Sahara.
Against the desolation of the latter, the
lands about the Gulf of California are
a riot of bloom in spring and green
through summer. Their diversity, in
kind and form, of plant and of animal
life is high, and the numbers are large.
When Leo Waibel came from his African studies to Sonora and Arizona, he
remarked: "But your deserts are not
plant deserts." Nor do we have ham-
madas or ergs, though geologic and
meteorologic conditions may be similar.
The principal difference may be that we
have had no millennial, or even cen-
turies-long, overstocking of our arid,

semiarid, and subhumid lands. The scant life and even the rock and sand surfaces of the Old World deserts may record long attrition by man in climatic tension zones.

IMPACT OF CIVILIZATION IN ANTIQUITY AND THE MIDDLE AGES

Have the elder civilizations fallen because their lands deteriorated? Ellsworth Huntington read adverse climatic change into each such failure; at the other extreme, political loss of competence has been asserted as sufficient. Intimate knowledge of historical sources, archeologic sites, biogeography and ecology, and the processes of geomorphology must be fused in patient field studies, so that we may read the changes in habitability through human time for the lands in which civilization first took form.

The rise of civilizations has been accomplished and sustained by the development of powerful and elaborately organized states with a drive to territorial expansion, by commerce in bulk and to distant parts, by monetary economy, and by the growth of cities. Capital cities, port cities by sea and river, and garrison towns drew to themselves population and products from near and far. The ways of the country became subordinated to the demands of the cities, the *citizen* distinct from the *miserabilis plebs*. The containment of community by locally available resources gave way to the introduction of goods, especially foodstuffs, regulated by purchasing, distributing, or taxing power.

Thereby removal of resource from place of origin to place of demand tended to set up growing disturbance of whatever ecologic equilibrium had been maintained by the older rural communities sustained directly within their metes. The economic history of antiquity shows repeated shifts in the areas of supply of raw materials that are not explained by political events but raise unanswered questions as to decline of fertility, destruction of plant cover, and incidence of soil erosion. What, for instance, happened to Arabia Felix, Numidia, Mauretania, to the interior Lusitania that has become the frayed Spanish Extremadura of today? When and at whose hands did the forests disappear that furnished ship and house timbers, wood for burning lime, the charcoal for smelting ores, and urban fuel needs? Are political disasters sufficient to account for the failure of the civilizations that depended on irrigation and drainage engineering? How much of the wide deterioration of Mediterranean and Near Eastern lands came during or after the time of strong political and commercial organization? For ancient and medieval history our knowledge as to what happened to the land remains too largely blank, except for the central and northern European periphery. The written documents, the testimony of the archeologic sites, have not often been interpreted by observation of the physical condition of the locality as it is and comparison with what it was.

The aspect of the Mediterranean landscapes was greatly changed by classical civilization through the introduction of plants out of the East. Victor Hehn first described Italy as wearing a dress of an alien vegetation, and, though he carried the theme of plant introduction out of the East too far, his study (1886) of the Mediterranean lands through antiquity is not only memorable but retains much validity. The westward dispersal of vine, olive, fig, the stone fruits, bread wheat, rice, and many ornamentals and some shade trees was due in part or in whole to the spread of Greco-Roman civilization, to which the Arabs added sugar cane, date palm, cotton, some of the citrus fruits, and other items.

EUROPEAN OVERSEAS COLONIZATION

When European nations ventured forth across the Atlantic, it was to trade or raid, the distinction often determined by the opportunity. In Africa and Asia the European posts and factories pretty well continued in this tradition through the eighteenth century. In the New World the same initial activities soon turned into permanent settlement of Old World forms and stocks. Columbus, searching only for a trade route, started the first overseas empire. Spain stumbled into colonization, and the other nations acquired stakes they hoped might equal the Spanish territorial claim. The Casa de Contratación, or House of Trade, at Seville, the main Atlantic port, became the Spanish colonial office. The conquistadores came not to settle but to make their fortunes and return home, and much the same was true for the earlier adventurers from other nations. Soldiers and adventurers rather than peasants and artisans made up the first arrivals, and few brought their women. Only in New England did settlement begin with a representative assortment of people, and only here were the new communities transplanted from the homeland without great alteration.

The first colony, Santo Domingo, set in large measure the pattern of colonization. It began with trade, including ornaments of gold. The quest for gold brought forced labor and the dying-off of the natives, and this, in turn, slave-hunting and importation of black slaves. Decline of natives brought food shortages and wide abandonment of conucos. Cattle and hogs were pastured on the lately tilled surfaces; and Spaniards, lacking labor to do gold-placering, became stock ranchers. Some turned to cutting dyewoods. Of the numerous European plants introduced to supply accustomed wants, a few, sugar cane, cassia, and ginger, proved moderately profitable for export, and some of the hesitant beginnings became the first tropical plantations. One hope of fortune failing, another was tried; the stumbling into empire was under way by men who had scarcely any vision of founding a new homeland.

What then happened to the lands of the New World in the three colonial centuries? In the first place, the aboriginal populations in contact with Europeans nearly everywhere declined greatly or were extinguished. Especially in the tropical lowlands, with the most notable exception of Yucatán, the natives faded away, and in many cases the land was quickly repossessed by forest growth. The once heavily populous lands of eastern Panama and northwestern Colombia, much of the lowland country of Mexico, both on the Pacific and Gulf sides, became emptied in a very few years, was retaken by jungle and forest, and in considerable part remains such to the present. The highlands of Mexico, of Central America, and of the Andean lands declined in population greatly through the sixteenth and perhaps well through the seventeenth century, with slow, gradual recovery in the eighteenth. The total population, white and other, of the areas under European control was, I think, less at the end of the eighteenth century than at the time of discovery. Only in British and French West Indian islands were dense rural populations built up.

It is hardly an exaggeration to say that the early Europeans supported themselves on Indian fields. An attractive place to live for a European would ordinarily have been such for an Indian. In the Spanish colonies, unlike the English and French, the earlier grants were not of land titles but of Indian communities to serve colonist and crown. In crops and their tillage the colonists of all nations largely used the Indian ways, with the diversion of part of the field crop to animal feed. Only in the Northeast, most of all in our Middle Colonies, were native and European crops fused into a conservative plow-and-animal husbandry, with field rotation, manuring, and marl dressing. The Middle Colonies of the eighteenth century appear to have compared favorably with the best farming practices of western Europe.

Sugar cane, first and foremost of the tropical plantations, as a closely planted giant grass, gave satisfactory protection to the surface of the land. The removal of cane from the land did reduce fertility unless the waste was properly returned to the canefields. The most conservative practices known are from the British islands, where cane waste was fed to cattle kept in pens, and manuring was customary and heavy. Bagasse was of little value as fuel in this period because of the light crushing rollers used for extracting cane juice; thus the colonial sugar mills were heavy wood users, especially for boiling sugar. The exhaustion of wood supply became a serious problem in the island of Haiti within the sixteenth century.

Other plantation crops—tobacco, indigo, cotton, and coffee—held more serious erosion hazards, partly because they were planted in rows and given clean cultivation, partly because they made use of steeper slopes and thinner soils. The worst offender was tobacco, grown on land that was kept bared to the rains and nourished by the wood ashes of burned clearings. Its cultivation met with greatest success in our Upper South, resulted in rapidly shifting clearings because of soil depletion, and caused the first serious soil erosion in our country. Virginia, Maryland, and North Carolina show to the present the damages of tobacco culture of colonial and early post-colonial times. Southern Ohio and eastern Missouri repeated the story before the middle of the nineteenth century.

As had happened in Haiti, sharp decline of native populations brought elsewhere abandonment of cleared and tilled land and thereby opportunity to the stockman. The plants that pioneer in former fields which are left untilled for reasons other than because of decline of fertility include forms, especially annuals, of high palatability, grasses, amaranths, chenopods, and legumes. Such is the main explanation for the quick appearance of stock ranches, of *ganado mayor* and *menor*, in the former Indian agricultural lands all over Spanish America. Cattle, horses, and hogs thrived in tropical lowland as well as in highland areas. Sheep-raising flourished most in early years in the highlands of New Spain and Peru, where Indian population had shrunk. Spanish stock, trespassing upon Indian plantings, both in lowland and in highland, afflicted the natives and depressed their chances of recovery (Simpson, L., 1952). In the wide savannas stockmen took over the native habits of burning.

The Spaniards passed in a few years from the trading and looting of metals to successful prospecting, at which they became so adept that it is still said that the good mines of today are the *antiguas* of colonial working. When mines were abandoned, it was less often due to the working-out of the ore bodies than to inability to cope with water in shafts and to the exhaustion of the necessary fuel and timber. A good illustration has been worked out for Parral in Mexico (West, 1949). Zacatecas, today in the midst of a high sparse grassland, was in colonial times a woodland of oak and pine and, at lower levels, of mesquite. About Andean mines the scant wood was soon exhausted, necessitating recourse to cutting mats of *tola* heath and even the clumps of coarse *ichu* (stipa) grass. Quite commonly the old mining *reales* of North and South America are surrounded by a broad zone of reduced and impoverished vegetation. The effects were increased by the concentration of pack and work animals in the mines, with resultant overpasturing. Similar attrition took place about towns and cities, through timber-cutting, charcoal- and lime-burning, and overpasturing. The first viceroy of New Spain warned his successor in 1546 of the depletion of wood about the city of Mexico.

I have used mainly examples from Spanish America for the colonial times, partly because I am most familiar with this record. However, attrition was more sensible here because of mines and urban concentrations and because, for cultural and climatic reasons, the vegetation cover was less.

LAST FRONTIERS OF SETTLEMENT

The surges of migration of the nineteenth century are family history for many of us. Never before did, and never again may, the white man expand his settlements as in that brief span that began in the later eighteenth century and ended with the first World War. The prelude was in the eighteenth century, not only as a result of the industrial revolution as begun in England, but also in a less heralded agricultural revolution over Western and Central Europe. The spread of potato-growing, the development of beets and turnips as field crops, rotation of fields with clover, innovations in tillage, improved livestock breeds—all joined to raise agricultural production to new levels in western Europe. The new agriculture was brought to our Middle Colonies by a massive immigration of capable European farmers and here further transformed by adding maize to the small grains—clover rotation. Thus was built on both sides of the North Atlantic a balanced animal husbandry of increased yield of human and animal foods. Urban and rural growth alike went into vigorous upswing around the turn of the eighteenth century. The youth of the countryside poured into the rising industrial

cities but also emigrated, especially from Central Europe into Pennsylvania, into Hungarian and Moldavian lands repossessed from the Turks and into South Russia gained from the Tartars. The last *Völkerwanderung* was under way and soon edging onto the grasslands.

The year 1800 brought a new cotton to the world market, previously an obscure annual variant known to us as Mexican Upland cotton, still uncertainly understood as to how it got into our South. Cleaned by the new gin, its profitable production rocketed. The rapidly advancing frontier of cotton-planting was moved westward from Georgia to Texas within the first half of the century. This movement was a more southerly and even greater parallel to the earlier westward drive of the tobacco frontier. Both swept away the woodlands and the Indians, including the farming tribes. The new cotton, like tobacco, a clean cultivated row crop and a cash crop, bared the fields to surface wash, especially in winter. The southern upland soils gradually lost their organic horizons, color, and protection; gullies began to be noted even before the Civil War. Guano and Chilean nitrate and soon southern rock phosphate were applied increasingly to the wasting soils. Eugene Hilgard told the history of cotton in our South tersely and well in the United States Census of 1880. As I write, across from my window stands the building bearing his name and the inscription: TO RESCUE FOR HUMAN SOCIETY THE NATIVE VALUES OF RURAL LIFE. It was in wasting cotton fields that Hilgard learned soil science and thought about a rural society that had become hitched wholly to world commerce. Meantime the mill towns of England, the Continent, and New England grew lustily; with them, machine industries, transport facilities, and the overseas shipment of food.

The next great American frontier may

be conveniently and reasonably dated by the opening of the Erie Canal in 1825, provisioning the cities with grain and meat on both sides of the North Atlantic, first by canal and river, soon followed by the railroad. The earlier frontiers had been pushed from the Atlantic Seaboard to and beyond the Mississippi by the cultivation of tropical plants in extratropical lands, were dominantly monocultural, preferred woodlands, and relied mainly on hand labor. For them the term "plantation culture" was not inapt. The last thrust, from the Mohawk Valley to the Mississippi, was West European as to agricultural system, rural values, settlers, and largely as to crops.

By the time of the Civil War, the first great phase of the northern westward movement had crossed the Missouri River into Kansas and Nebraska. New England spilled over by way of the Great Lakes, especially along the northern fringe of prairies against the North Woods. New York and Baltimore were gateways for the masses of Continental emigrants hurrying to seek new homes beyond the Alleghenies. The migrant streams mingled as they overspread the Mississippi Valley, land of promise unequaled in the history of our kindred. These settlers were fit to the task: they were good husbandmen and artisans. They came to put down their roots, and the gracious country towns, farmsteads, and rural churches still bear witness to the homemaking way of life they brought and kept. At last they had land of their own, and it was good. They took care of their land, and it did well by them; surplus rather than substance of the soil provided the foodstuffs that moved to eastern markets. Steel plows that cut through the sod, east-west railroads, and cheap lumber from the white-pine forests of the Great Lakes unlocked the fertility of the prairies; the first great plowing-up of the grasslands was under way.

Many prairie counties reached their maximum population in less than a generation, many of them before the beginning of the Civil War. The surplus, another youthful generation, moved on farther west or sought fortune in the growing cities. Thus, toward the end of the century the Trans-Missouri grassy plains had been plowed up to and into the lands of drought hazard. Here the Corn Belt husbandry broke down, especially because of the great drought of the early nineties, and the Wheat Belt took form, a monocultural and unbalanced derivative. I well remember parties of landlookers going out from my native Missouri county, first to central Kansas and Nebraska, then to the Red River Valley, and finally even to the Panhandle of Texas and the prairies of Manitoba. The local newspapers "back home" still carry news from these daughter-colonies, and still those who long ago moved west are returned "home" at the last to lie in native soil.

The development of the Middle West did exact its price of natural resources. The white-pine stands of the Great Lakes were destroyed to build the farms and towns of the Corn Belt; the logged-over lands suffered dreadful burning. As husbandry gave way westward to wheat-growing, the land was looked on less as homestead and more as speculation, to be cropped heavily and continuously for grain, without benefit of rotation and manuring, and to be sold at an advantageous price, perhaps to reinvest in new and undepleted land.

The history of the extratropical grasslands elsewhere in the world is much like our own and differs little in period and pace. Southern Russia, the Pampas, Australia, and South Africa repeat largely the history of the American West. The industrial revolution was made possible by the plowing-up of the great non-tropical grasslands of the world. So also was the intensification of agriculture in western Europe, benefiting from the importation of cheap overseas feedstuffs, grains, their by-products of milling (note the term "shipstuff"), oil-seed meals. Food and feed were cheap in and about the centers of industry, partly because the fertility of the new lands of the world was exported to them without reckoning the maintenance of resource.

At the turn of the century serious concern developed about the adequacy of resources for industrial civilization. The conservation movement was born. It originated in the United States, where the depletion of lately virgin lands gave warning that we were drawing recklessly on a diminishing natural capital. It is to be remembered that this awareness came, not to men living in the midst of the industrial and commercial centers of the older country-sides, but to foresters who witnessed devastation about the Great Lakes, to geologists who had worked in the iron and copper ranges of the Great Lakes and prospected the West in pioneer days, to naturalists who lived through the winning of the West.

THE EVER DYNAMIC ECONOMY

As a native of the nineteenth century, I have been an amazed and bewildered witness of the change of tempo that started with the first World War, was given an additional whirl on the second, and still continues to accelerate. The worry of the earlier part of the century was that we might not use our natural resources thriftily; it has given way to easy confidence in the capacities of technologic advance without limit. The natural scientists were and still may be conservation-minded; the physical scientists and engineers today are often of the lineage of Daedalus, inventing ever more daring reorganizations of matter and, in consequence, whether they desire it or not, of social institutions. Social science eyes the attainments of physical science enviously and hopes for similar competence and authority in reordering the world. Progress is the common watchword of our age, its motor-innovating techniques, its objective the ever expanding "dynamic economy," with ever increasing input of energy. Capacity to produce and capacity to consume are the twin spirals of the new age which is to have no end, if war can be eliminated. The measure of progress is "standard of living," a term that the English language has contributed to the vernaculars of the world. An American industrialist says, roundly, that our principal problem now is to accelerate obsolescence, which remark was anticipated at the end of the past century by Eduard Hahn (1900) when he thought that industrialization depended on the production of junk.

Need we ask ourselves whether there still is the problem of limited resources, of an ecologic balance that we disturb or disregard at the peril of the future? Was Wordsworth of the early industrial age farsighted when he said that "getting and spending we lay waste our powers"? Are our newly found powers to transform the world, so successful in the short run of the last years, proper and wise beyond the tenure of those now living? To what end are we committing the world to increasing momentum of change?

The steeply increasing production of late years is due only in part to better recovery, more efficient use of energy, and substitution of abundant for scarce materials. Mainly we have been learning how to deplete more rapidly the resources known to be accessible to us. Must we not admit that very much of what we call production is extraction?

Even the so-called "renewable resources" are not being renewed. Despite better utilization and substitution, timber growth is falling farther behind use and loss, inferior stands and kinds are being exploited, and woodland deterioration is spreading. Much of the world is in a state of wood famine, without known means of remedy or substitution.

Commercial agriculture requires ample working capital and depends in high degree on mechanization and fertilization. A late estimate assigns a fourth of the net income of our farms to the purchase of durable farm equipment. The more farming becomes industry and business, the less remains of the older husbandry in which man lived in balance with his land. We speak with satisfaction of releasing rural population from farm to urban living and count the savings of man-hours in units of farm product and of acres. In some areas the farmer is becoming a town dweller, moving his equipment to the land for brief periods of planting, cultivating, and harvest. Farm garden, orchard, stable, barn, barnyards, and woodlots are disappearing in many parts, the farm families as dependent as their city cousins on grocer, butcher, baker, milkman, and fuel services. Where the farm is in fact capital in land and improvements, requiring bookkeeping on current assets and liabilities, the agriculturist becomes an operator of an outdoor factory of specialized products and is concerned with maximizing the profits of the current year and the next. Increasing need of working capital requires increased monetary returns; this is perhaps all we mean by "intensive" or "scientific" farming, which is in greater and greater degree extractive.

The current agricultural surpluses are not proof that food production has ceased to be a problem or will cease to be the major problem of the world. Our output has been secured at unconsidered costs and risks by the objective of immediate profit, which has replaced the older attitudes of living with the land. The change got under way especially as motors replaced draft animals. Land formerly used for oats and other feed crops became available to grow more corn, soybeans, cotton, and other crops largely sold and shipped. The traditional corn-oats-clover rotation, protective of the surface and maintaining nitrogen balance, began to break down. Soybeans, moderately planted in the twenties and then largely for hay, developed into a major seed crop, aided by heavy governmental benefit payments as soil-building, which they are not. Soil-depleting and soil-exposing crops were given strong impetus in the shift to mechanized farming; less of the better land is used for pasture and hay; less animal and green manure is returned to fields. The fixation of nitrogen by clover has come to be considered too slow; it "pays better" to put the land into corn, beans, and cotton and to apply nitrogen from bag or tank. Dressing the soil with commercial nitrogen makes it possible to plant more closely, thus doubling the number of corn and other plants to the acre at nearly the same tillage cost. Stimulation of plant growth by nitrogen brings increased need of additional phosphorus and potash. In the last ten years the Corn Belt has more or less caught up with the Cotton Belt in the purchase of commercial fertilizer. The more valuable the land, the greater the investment in farm machinery, the more profitable the application of more and more commercial fertilizers.

The so-called row crops, which are the principal cash crops, demand cultivation during much of their period of growth. They give therefore indifferent protection to the surface while growing and almost none after they are harvested. They are ill suited to being followed by a winter cover crop. The organic color is fading from much of our best-grade farm lands. Rains and melting snow float away more and more of the top soil. There is little concern as long as we can plow more deeply and buy more fertilizer. Governmental restriction of acreage for individual crops has been an inducement to apply more fertilizer to the permitted acreage and to plant the rest in uncontrolled but usually also cash crops. Our commercial agriculture, except what remains in animal husbandry such as dairying, is kept expanding by increasing overdraft on the fertility of our soils. Its limits are set by the economically available sources of purchased nitrogen, phosphorus, potassium, and sulfur.

Since Columbus, the spread of European culture has been continuous and cumulative, borne by immediate self-interest, as in mercantilist economy, but sustained also by a sense of civilizing mission redefined from time to time. In the spirit of the present, this mission is to "develop the underdeveloped" parts of the world, material good and spiritual good now having become one. It is our current faith that the ways of the West are the ways that are best for the rest of the world. Our own ever growing needs for raw materials have driven the search for metals and petroleum to the ends of the Earth in order to move them into the stream of world commerce. Some beneficial measure of industry and transport facility thereby accrues to distant places of origin. We also wish to be benefactors by increasing food supply where food is inadequate and by diverting people from rural to industrial life, because such is our way, to which we should like to bring others.

The road we are laying out for the world is paved with good intentions, but do we know where it leads? On the material side we are hastening the depletion of resources. Our programs of agricultural aid pay little attention to native ways and products. Instead of going out to learn what their experiences and preferences are, we go forth to introduce our ways and consider backward what is not according to our pattern. Spade and hoe and mixed plantings are an affront to our faith in progress. We promote mechanization At the least, we hold, others should be taught to use steel plows that turn neat furrows, though we have no idea how long the soil will stay on well-plowed slopes planted to annuals. We want more fields of maize, rice, beans of kinds familiar to us, products amenable to statistical determination and available for commercial distribution. To increase production, we prescribe dressing with commercial fertilizers. In unnoticed contrast to our own experience these are to be applied in large measure to lands of low productivity and perhaps of low effectiveness of fertilizers. Industrialization is recommended to take care of the surplus populations. We present and recommend to the world a blueprint of what works well with us at the moment, heedless that we may be destroying wise and durable native systems of living with the land. The modern industrial mood (I hesitate to add intellectual mood) is insensitive to other ways and values.

For the present, living beyond one's means has become civic virtue, increase of "output" the goal of society. The prophets of a new world by material progress may be stopped by economic limits of physical matter. They may fail because people grow tired of getting and spending as measure and mode of living. They may be checked because men come to fear the requisite growing power of government over the individual and the community. The high moments of history have come not when man was most concerned with the comforts and displays of the flesh but when his spirit was moved to grow in grace. What we need more perhaps is an ethic and aesthetic under which man, practicing the qualities of prudence and moderation, may indeed pass on to posterity a good Earth.

REFERENCES

AMES, OAKES
1939 *Economic Annuals and Human Cultures.* Cambridge, Mass.: Botanical Museum of Harvard University. 153 pp.

BOYD, W. C.
1950 *Genetics and the Races of Man.* Boston: Little, Brown & Co. 453 pp.

BREUIL, HENRI, and LANTIER, RAYMON
1951 *Les Hommes de la pierre ancienne.* Paris: Payot. 334 pp.

CONKLIN, HAROLD C.
1954 "An Ethnoecological Approach to Shifting Agriculture," *Transactions of the New York Academy of Sciences,* Series II, XVII, No. 2, 133–42.

COON, CARLETON
1953 "Climate and Race," pp. 13–34 in SHAPLEY, HARLOW (ed.), *Climatic Change.* Cambridge, Mass.: Harvard University Press. 318 pp.

HAHN, EDUARD
1900 *Wirtschaft der Welt am Ausgang des neunzebuten Jahrhunderts.* Heidelberg: C. Winter. 320 pp.

HEHN, VICTOR
1888 *Wanderings of Plants and Animals from Their First Home.* Ed. JAMES S. STALLYBRASS. London: Swan Sonnenschein & Co. 523 pp.

IZIKOWITZ, KARL GUSTAV
1951 *Lamet: Hill Peasants in French Indochina.* ("Etnologiska Studier," No. 17.) Göteborg: Etnografiska Museet. 375 pp.

LEIGHLY, JOHN B.
1949 "On Continentality and Glaciation," pp. 133–46 in MANNERFELT, CARL M:SON, et al. (eds.), *Glaciers and Climate (Symposium Dedicated to Hans W:son Ahlmann as a Tribute from the Swedish Society for Anthropology and Geography).(Geografiska Annaler,* Vol. XXXI, Häfte 1–4.) 383 pp.

MANNERFELT, CARL M:SON, et al. (eds.)
1949 *Glaciers and Climate (Symposium Dedicated to Hans W:son Ahlmann as a Tribute from the Swedish Society for Anthropology and Geography).(Geografiska Annaler,* Vol. XXXI, Häfte 1–4.) 383 pp.

MARSH, GEORGE P.
1864 *Man and Nature.* New York: Charles Scribner & Co.; London: Sampson, Low & Son. 577 pp.

1874 *The Earth as Modified by Human Action.* New York: Scribner, Armstrong & Co. 656 pp. (2d ed., 1885. New York: C. Scribner's Sons. 629 pp.)

SHAPLEY, HARLOW (ed.)
1953 *Climatic Change.* Cambridge, Mass.: Harvard University Press. 318 pp.

SIMPSON, G. C.
1934 "World Climate during the Quaternary Period," *Quarterly Journal of the Royal Meteorological Society,* LX, No. 257 (October), 425–78.

1940 "Possible Causes of Change in Climate and Their Limitations," *Proceedings of the Linnean Society of London,* CLII, Part II (April), 190–219.

SIMPSON, LESLEY B.
1952 *Exploitation of Land in Central Mexico in the Sixteenth Century.* ("Ibero-Americana," No. 36.) Berkeley: University of California Press. 92 pp.

WEST, ROBERT C.
1949 *The Mining Community in Northern New Spain: The Parral Mining District.* ("Ibero-Americana," No. 30.) Berkeley: University of California Press. 169 pp.

WILLETT, H. C.
1950 "The General Circulation at the Last (Würm) Glacial Maximum," *Geografiska Annaler,* XXXII, Häfte 3–4, 179–87.

Changing Ideas of the Habitable World

CLARENCE J. GLACKEN*

The reason that Attica in former times could support a soldiery exempt from the toil of farming, says Plato in his *Critias*, was that its soil—as is proved by the remnant now left—surpassed all others in fertility. Deluges, however, washed the soil down from the mountains, and it was lost because the land dropped abruptly into the sea. Attica became a "skeleton of a body wasted by disease." Long ago, Plato continues, there were abundant forests in the mountains which provided fodder for the animals and storage for water, which could then issue forth in springs and rivers. "The water was not lost, as it is today, by running off a barren ground to the sea." The extent of these forests, many of which had been cut down, was revealed in the traces still remaining and by the sanctuaries which were situated at the former sources of springs and rivers (Plato, 1929, *Critias* 111, A–D).

Plato reconstructs the prehistory of Attica by showing how the relict soils reveal ancient conditions of the plains and how the relict trees reveal the ancient conditions of the mountains, suggesting that human history was in part the history of environmental changes induced by natural catastrophes and

human activities. Perhaps if this view had found more elaborate expression in the *Laws*, in which Plato discusses the origin and development of society, an awareness of the philosophical implications of man's activities in changing the environment might have at that time entered the main stream of Western thought (1926, iii. 677–86D).

Across the Eurasian continent, Mencius, the Chinese philosopher, described the beautiful trees of the new mountain which were hewn down with axes. When they began growing again, buds and sprouts appeared, and cattle and goats browsed upon them. "To these things is owing the bare and stripped appearance of the mountain, and when people now see it, they think it was never finely wooded. But is this the nature of the mountain?" Few statements have summed up more lucidly than has this question of Mencius the difficulties of distinguishing a natural from a cultural landscape (1933, vi. 1. 8).

In the third century B.C. Eratosthenes described the manner in which the island of Cyprus was made habitable. Formerly its plains could not be used for agriculture because they were covered with forests. Felling trees in order to provide fuel for smelting copper and silver mined there helped to clear the forests, and, "as the sea was now navigated with security and by a large naval force," additional clearings were made for ship timber. These cuttings were not sufficient to clear the forests, and the

* Dr. Glacken is Assistant Professor of Geography at the University of California, Berkeley. An abstract of his doctoral dissertation, "The Idea of the Habitable World," was published in 1952, and his book, *The Great Loochoo: A Study in Okinawan Village Life,* in 1955.

people therefore were allowed to cut down the trees "to hold the land thus cleared as their own property, free from all payments" (Strabo xiv. 6. 5). Eratosthenes thus relates the changes in the landscape to mining, navigation, and governmental land policy.

Early observations such as these failed to inspire men to study the environmental changes made by human cultures as a part of human history. The reason for this failure is not that human modifications of the environment were so inconsequential as to be unworthy of remark but that the emphasis was on human society, its origin, and the manner of its changing through historical time.

THE GOLDEN AGE AND THE IDEA OF CYCLES

In the Greek notion of a past golden age with its "golden race of mortal men," nature which had not felt the intrusions of human art was considered more perfect and fruitful. "The bounteous earth," Hesiod said, "bare first for them of her own will, in plenty and without stint." Similar statements were made centuries later by Lucretius, Varro, and Ovid (Hesiod, 1879, p. 80; Lucretius, 1947, ii. 1155–60; Varro, 1912, ii. 2. 3–4; Ovid *Metam.* i. 101–5). The praise of the fertile soils of the golden age, which did not require cultivation, was probably a reflection of contemporary dissatisfaction with the modest yields obtained by hard work.

The idea of a cycle in the course of history, or in the growth of states and institutions—an analogy derived from the life-cycle of an organism—was in antiquity an alternative conception to the notion of degeneration from a golden age. Epicurus and Lucretius applied the cyclical theory to the earth itself, which in its prime spontaneously yielded crops, vines, fruits, and pastures that now even with toil could not be made to grow. A son should not complain about his father's good luck or rail at heaven because of his old and wilted vines: "nor does he grasp that all things waste away little by little and pass to the grave fordone by age and the lapse of life" (Lucretius, 1947, ii. 1165–74).[1]

Later in the poem, however, Lucretius, following Epicurus, traces the origin of metallurgy to the accidental smelting of ores heated by forest fires which may have been started by lightning, or by men who wished to frighten enemies concealed in the woods, to enlarge their fields or pastures, or to kill the wild animals for profit, for hunting by the use of pitfalls and fire was an earlier development than driving game with dogs into fenced-in glades (*ibid.,* v. 1245–50).

The landscapes of inhabited lands were created by imitating nature; man had learned how to domesticate nature by sowing, grafting, and experimenting with plants. "And day by day they would constrain the woods more and more to retire up the mountains, and to give up the land beneath to tilth" to have meadows, pools, streams, crops, vineyards, and olive orchards (*ibid.,* 1370–75). Lucretius clearly is describing here, in poetical language and without any suggestion of decay and death, the manner in which a people transforms the landscape.

ANOTHER NATURE

The early history of the idea of man as a modifier of his environment is also related to the broader conception, similar to the cyclical theory, of a teleology existent in a single organism or in all nature—a conception fully developed by Aristotle in his discussion of the four causes. The fruit of the tree was inherent in the seed; so was a design implicit

---

1. The author is grateful to the Oxford University Press for permission to quote from *Titi Lucreti Cari De rerum natura,* as translated by Cyril Bailey.

in the living creation. Since man was the highest creature, all nature must have been created for him, an idea which must be one of the oldest of which there is a written record, for it is clearly expressed in ancient Egyptian creation myths (Frankfort *et al.,* 1951, p. 64).

In the idea of a design in nature, as it was developed by the Greeks and their Roman disciples, a pleasant and harmonious relation between man and nature is either expressed or implied, for human art improves the natural advantages of an earth which has been created as a home for man. This idea is discussed by Aristotle (*Politics* i. 8), Cicero, Seneca (1912, iv. 5), and Pliny (1938–52, vii. Pref.), Cicero's exposition being the most detailed. The earth endowed with living nature, said Cicero, is the proper home both for the gods and for man, man taking an active part in the care of nature by cultivating the earth so that its fertility would not be choked with weeds. There is an order of nature existing on earth—which is eternal—an order in which the great variety of organic species is arranged in an ascending scale. Man, as the highest being in the scale, changes nature by using his hands, with which, guided by the intellect, he has created the art of agriculture and the techniques of fishing, animal domestication, mining, clearing, and navigation (Cicero, 1894, *Nature of the Gods* ii. 39, 45, 53).

We are the absolute masters of what the earth produces. We enjoy the mountains and the plains. The rivers are ours. We sow the seed, and plant the trees. We fertilize the earth. . . . We stop, direct, and turn the rivers: in short by our hands we endeavor, by our various operations in this world, to make, as it were, another Nature [*ibid.* 60; cf. 30–67].

The concept of "another," the manmade nature, thus seems a fusion of two elements: the design inherent in nature and the improvements of nature which are interpreted as the effects brought about by human art in fulfilment of the design.

SOIL AND AGRICULTURE

In the technical agricultural writings of antiquity, comments regarding human changes of nature also appear in discussions of land use and of soil fertility. These writings, from Hesiod through Vergil and Pliny, are concerned for the most part with technical details, the Roman writers particularly emphasizing farm management and the cultivation of the olive and the vine. One significant fact about them is the association of soil conservation with agriculture—an association which has persisted in modern, even contemporary, times in discussions regarding population and food supply, in which the chief emphasis has been on the care and fertilization of arable land.

Perhaps the earliest idea is that the soils must be allowed to rest, because cultivation tires them. "Fallow-land," said Hesiod, "is a guardian-from-death-and-ruin, and a soother of children" (1879, p. 99). There is a similar idea in the Old Testament (Exod. 23:10–11; Lev. 25:1–7, 21–22), the Lord commanding that every seventh year be a "sabbath of rest unto the land."

Two Roman writers, Varro and Columella, are significant in this history, because their writings, revealing the influence of Stoic philosophy, dealt with questions which transcended the technical details of agriculture.

Varro said that human life had developed from the original state of nature "when man lived on those things which the virgin earth produced spontaneously"—another reminder of the strength of the idea that soil fertility was characteristic of a golden age. From the state of nature mankind passed through a pastoral stage of gathering and animal domestication followed by the agricultural stage that lasted until the rise of contemporary civilization (1912, ii. 1. 4–5).

This theory and its modern successors diverted attention from the actual historical events, since cultural development presumably took place regardless of the nature of the physical environment. The first serious challenge to this sequence was delayed, as Carl Sauer (1952, p. 20) has said, until Alexander von Humboldt attacked the theory, because pastoral nomadism was not found in the New World. Since Varro's time, however, abstract theories of cultural development have evaded the question of how man was changing his environment as he marched through these stages.

Varro was far more sensible than his latter-day imitators, for he saw an exception to his theory in his own time and in his own country: heads of families have deserted the land for the cities and have imported corn and wine from foreign countries. "And so in that country where the city's founders were shepherds and taught agriculture to their descendants, these descendants have reversed the process, and through covetousness and in despite of laws, have turned corn-land into meadow, not knowing the difference between agriculture and grazing" (1912, ii. Introd.). Agriculture was creative; grazing, extractive. "Grazing cattle do not help to produce what grows on the land; they remove it with their teeth" (*ibid.*).

In his work on agriculture Columella comments approvingly on the opinions of a certain Tremelius that the productivity of land declines rapidly after a clearing; plows break the roots of the plants, and the trees no longer provide organic materials for fertilizer—a sentence reminding one of current discussions of the exhaustion of tropical soils a few years after they have been cleared and cultivated (1941, ii. 1. 6–7). Columella is significant as a thinker, how-

ever, because he objected to the analogy of the earth as a mortal being; his work begins with an attack, probably aimed at the Epicureans and Lucretius, on the popular view that the earth had a life-cycle: "It is not, therefore, because of weariness, as very many have believed, nor because of old age, but manifestly because of our own lack of energy that our cultivated lands yield us a less generous return. For we may reap greater harvests if the earth is quickened again by frequent, timely, and moderate manuring" (*ibid.* 1. 7; cf. i. Pref.).[2] Instead of a philosophy of the earth as a mortal being, the practical Columella substitutes manuring.

The *Natural History* of Pliny gives further evidence of a lively awareness in antiquity of the effects of human activities on the earth. Pliny says, too, that a soil should not be regarded as old in a mortal sense. Soils would last with care, and in cultivating hillsides it was not necessary to denude them if the digging were done skilfully. He also describes how the emptying of a lake in the Larissa district of Thessaly lowered the temperature of the vicinity, causing the olive to disappear and the vines to be frostbitten, how the climate of Aenos on the Maritza became warmer when the river was diverted near it, and how Philippi altered its climate when its land under cultivation was drained (1938–52, xvii. 29–30).

INFLUENCE OF THE PHYSICAL ENVIRONMENT

Another influential body of thought, the theory of the influence of the physical environment on human cultures, owes its origin to the thinkers of antiquity. This literature, both in antiquity and in modern times, has dealt with the influence of climate, soils, and geo-

2. The author is grateful to the Harvard University Press for permission to quote from *On Agriculture*, as translated by Harrison Boyd Ash.

graphical location on individuals and on cultures. Its main outlines may be traced[3] through the Hippocratic writings, Herodotus, Thucydides, Aristotle, Polybius, Pliny, and Vitruvius, although the ancient writers on the whole were far less rigid in their determinism than many thinkers of the eighteenth and nineteenth centuries.

The significance of these theories is that they led to a one-sided preoccupation with environmental influences, largely ignoring the significance of man as an agent in changing the environment; in ancient and modern times both ideas were often expressed by the same writer without any realization of an implied contradiction.

THE BOOK OF GENESIS

Ideas derived from the Old Testament have also been important elements in the formulation of modern conceptions of man's relation to the earth. All beings which existed before the flood were commanded by the Creator to be fruitful and to multiply, man receiving in addition the command to take possession of the earth. After the flood the Lord gave similar commands to Noah and his sons, making a covenant with them that he would not again destroy the living things on earth. Man by divine command assumes a powerful control over nature (Gen. 1:21–22, 27–28; 8:17, 21–22; 9:1–3). The fusion of these Old Testament ideas with the classical and Stoic idea of a design in nature provided a strong stimulus to the seventeenth-century study of living nature in order to find there proofs of the wisdom of God.

The ideas of antiquity which have had the most influence on modern conceptions of the relation of man to the earth were the idea of a design in nature and the various theories of environmental influence. The cyclical idea has been of great importance in the history of social and political thought and in the philosophy of history—Vico and Spengler are modern examples—but does not seem to have had a lasting influence in modern conceptions of man's relation to nature. The agricultural writings were very influential in early modern times but only as a technical literature. The idea of man as a modifier of the earth does not seem to have been transmitted as an idea, probably because it was not well formulated in antiquity and because notices of man's activities were absorbed as descriptions or as elements of well-established ideas.

FELLING OF TREES

Men in early modern times became aware of their power to change nature mostly because they observed the effects of cutting down trees, for comments on the consequences of clearing have been traced to Carolingian times (Maury, 1856, pp. 71–80). Concern over the consequences of deforestation was very marked in the late seventeenth century, as the provisions of Colbert's *Forest Ordinance* (1669) (see Brown, 1883*b*) and the discussions in Evelyn's *Silva* (1664) clearly show. The provisions of the *Forest Ordinance* reveal an awareness of the relation of forest care to such practices as grazing, mast feeding, and the gathering of forest litter. In Evelyn's *Silva* the idea that economic objectives may act at cross-purposes with desirable arrangements in nature is revealed in the discussion of agriculture, industry, and forestry. Evelyn thought the prosperity of the glass-making, iron-smelting, and naval-building industries often was inconsistent with the existence of forests because of the heedless consumption of wood for fuel, resources like woods and iron ore having a capri-

3. See the Hippocratic writings (*Airs, Waters, Places*); Herodotus (*Hist.* ix. 122); Thucydides (*Pelop. War* i. 1); Aristotle (*Pol.* vii. vi. 1–3); Polybius (*Hist.* iv. 19–21); Pliny (*Nat. Hist.* ii. 80); Vitruvius (*On Arch.* i. iv-vi; ii. i).

cious and unfortunate distribution: "But nature has thought fit to produce this wasting Ore more plentifully in wood-land than in any other ground, and to enrich our forests to their own destruction" (1786, II, 265; cf. p. 214 on succession; p. 269). Evelyn's main censure, however, was reserved for the encroachments of agriculture on the forests—for the "disproportionate spread of tillage" (*ibid.*, I, 1–2).

THE WISDOM OF GOD

In the late seventeenth century a grand conception of nature as a divinely created order for the well-being of all life was formulated. It was a time of great interest in philosophy, population theory, botany, geology, and astronomy and of great activity in the drainage of swamps, fens, and bogs. The key ideas in this conception, which is closely related to the idea of a great chain of being whose importance in the history of Western thought has been so profoundly elucidated by Arthur Lovejoy, are fully discussed in John Ray's *The Wisdom of God Manifested in the Works of the Creation* (first edition, 1691) and William Derham's *Physico-theology*. A disciple of Ray, Derham based his work on the Boyle Lectures which he delivered in 1711–12.

Although the conception was closely related to contemporary theological and philosophical thinking, particularly that of the Cambridge Platonists, we must content ourselves here with pointing out several attitudes which were held toward the earth as a habitable planet. (1) Men like Ray and Derham ardently tried to refute the ideas of Thomas Burnet, whose *Sacred Theory of the Earth* contained many unflattering references to the planet as it was constituted after the flood (1753, I, 65). According to Burnet, it was poorly fashioned as a living place for man, and nature was hard and niggardly. Furthermore, the earth was unreasonably tilted

twenty-three and a half degrees from the plane of the ecliptic, there was altogether too much sea, and the haphazard distribution of mountains and valleys could not be compared with the advantages of the smooth-surfaced antediluvian world (*ibid.*, pp. 178–89).

In rebuttal, Ray, Derham, and others of like mind pointed out the great advantages of the earth's tilting on its axis to all life, the inclination being responsible for the seasons and for preventing climatic excess. The sea, far from being superfluous, supplied rain for the land. The hand of a wise Providence was seen also in the washing-down of earth from the mountains to be spread on the meadows, in the running water carrying soil in suspension to nourish plants, and in the winds which moved the clouds in the sky, providing a more "commodius watering." They commented too on the beauties created by the happy distribution of landforms, lakes, and streams on the earth, making life both convenient and enjoyable. (2) The distribution of climates and the production of plants and animals in the various zones were too advantageous to life and too well reasoned to be accepted as fortuitous circumstances. (3) The task of human art was to improve the primeval aspect of the earth through tillage and in other ways. (4) Although the Creator had bestowed great gifts on man, all ranks of being in the world had their place in nature and were not created for man alone. Man in this conception is a mighty but not omnipotent being on earth; he is at the top of the scale, but with responsibilities, for he is a caretaker, or, in the words of Sir Mathew Hale, a steward of God (Ray, 1759, pp. 79–91 *et passim*; Derham, 1798, pp. 60–64 *et passim*).

These thinkers rejected both the idea of the world as a machine and the Baconian view that scientific and religious inquiry should be separate. They saw man living in a world—which he could change and improve—where the order and beauty of nature, manifestations of the Creator's skill and wisdom, could be seen everywhere (Ray, 1759, pp. 31–37; Derham, 1798, pp. 116, 131–32). There was no patience with primitivism: a man, said Ray, would be wanting in sense if he preferred the existence of a Scythian to the polished life and the beautifully tilled fields of Europe (1759, pp. 164–65).

More than a century before Alexander von Humboldt's famous phrases about the unity of nature amid its diversity, these men spoke of a balance and a harmony in nature which had been so wonderfully designed by the Creator.[4] The classical notion of a design in nature, the Old Testament ideas, and the seventeenth-century passion for science had come together and provided the stimulus for the enthusiastic study of living nature.[5]

In the later development of the idea of a harmony in nature, the role of the Creator recedes somewhat, and nature becomes an entity itself—often it is personified—and the idea of man as a being co-operating in the improvement of nature is expanded. In the nineteenth century, especially in the works of Marsh, the idea creeps in that man has failed in his appointed role as a steward of God and that man's vast changes are upsetting the balance and the harmony of nature and are ruining the earth.

INHABITED AND UNINHABITED COUNTRIES

In the stately and eloquent writings of Buffon, which reveal a deep study of the scientific literature of England, man plays a very active role in changing the surface of the earth. Buffon contrasts the appearance of inhabited with uninhabited lands: the anciently inhabited countries have few woods, lakes, or marshes, but they have many heaths and scrub, their mountains are bare, and their soils are less fertile because they lack the organic matter which woods—felled in inhabited countries—supply, and the herbs are browsed. "Men destroy woods, drain marshes and lakes, and in process of time, give an appearance to the surface of the earth totally different from that of uninhabited or newly peopled countries" (Buffon, 1866, I, 38).

The French naturalist also was interested in climatic change brought about by clearing and cited instances from travel accounts of Quebec, Cayenne, and the Guianas. Lands with forests are cold, and, when the forests are cut, the climate becomes warmer. It is more difficult for man to cool than to heat the earth, for it is easier to cut trees in Guiana than to plant them in Arabia (*ibid.*, pp. 45–46, 73; II, 183; 1799, IV, 21–23). In countries which are too small to support polished societies, the surface of the land is more rugged and unequal, and the river channels are more interrupted by cataracts (Buffon, 1866, I, 7).

Buffon stresses the profound effects which man has made in nature by the domestication of animals and plants. The domestication of the dog made man's peaceable possession of the earth possible because it was the means by which wild animals were tracked down, captured, and domesticated. The domestication of animals, in turn, was the basis both of hunting and of agriculture, so that men and animals could multiply; in this manner, an environment was refashioned in the course of time by human art. With the multiplication and dispersal of man and his animals, the days of the wild animals were numbered. "Time fights against them." In words like those Darwin used in the first chapter of the *Origin of*

4. On the balance of animals and a seventeenth-century food chain see Derham, 1798, pp. 257–70; cf. Ray, 1759, pp. 371–75.

5. On Ray's influence see Raven, 1942, pp. 452–76.

Species, Buffon describes the control man has acquired over plants through breeding and artificial selection (*ibid.,* p. 365, essay on the dog; II, 35, on mules; pp. 184–86).

Occasionally, Buffon indignantly criticizes the acts of man, observing, for example, that he would destroy all nature "if by a fecundity superior to his depradations she did not repair the havock he makes" (*ibid.,* I, 392, on carnivorous animals), but in the main Buffon has an optimistic outlook. Like John Ray, he has no patience with the supposed glories of a golden age or with the beauties of a state of nature, but he had praise for nature which had been and would continue to be improved through human art. In the "Epochs of Nature," composed toward the end of a long life, Buffon divides the history of the earth into seven periods, the last of which is called "when the power of man assisted the works of nature." To Buffon, man through his ability to modify nature had now become a force in the evolution of the earth (*ibid.,* II, 184; 1799, IV, 40–41).

The importance of Buffon's thought lay in the recognition of the historical relation between the growth and dispersal of plant, animal, and human populations and the modifications of the earth which this growth and dispersal had brought about both in old settlements and in new colonies.

THE ALPINE TORRENTS

Studies of the torrents of the French and the Austrian Alps undertaken in the late eighteenth and early nineteenth centuries deepened immeasurably the realization of man's power to change the earth. As the century wore on, the field of inquiry had broadened to encompass the relation of human cultures to the forests, climate, soils, and agriculture.

In 1797 a French engineer named Fabre announced that the causes of the sudden and overwhelming Alpine torrents which flooded the farms and settlements of the lowlands were clearing and deforestation in the high Alps. The cutting of trees in the high mountain fastnesses, Fabre said, permitted the formation of torrents which brought about seven kinds of disaster: the ruin of the forests; the erosion of the mountain soils and the consequent destruction of mountain pastures; the ruin of dwellings situated along the streams; the divisions of watercourses in their lower reaches caused by floods; litigation over riparian rights as a consequence of the division of the watercourses; silting of the mouth of streams; and the diminution of the water sources which fed the streams and rivers (extract in Brown, 1880, pp. 55–58).

Fabre's work was the beginning of a long series of French studies, pursued by foresters, engineers, and agronomists, whose work is so intimately associated with the great project of reforestation (*reboisment*) which the French government undertook in the Hautes-Alpes during the nineteenth century (Anonymous, 1911). Fabre's successor, Surell, continued the study, announcing that Alpine torrents appeared when forests disappeared and that they disappeared when forests were restored (extracts in Brown, 1880, pp. 30–47). Similar works on the Austrian Alps, possibly anticipating that of Fabre, appeared about the same time, three of them being published, significantly, in the city of Innsbruck. The Italians also had interested themselves in torrents, control of watercourses, and soil erosion, their interest in these subjects going back at least to Leonardo, who had noted that streams were muddier when they passed through populated districts (*ibid.,* pp. 131–34; Leonardo da Vinci, 1954, p. 310).

The theme running through the specialized studies which appeared in the early-nineteenth-century literature was that clearing, grazing and transhumance, torrents, and shifting agriculture were all parts of the greater problem of Alpine deforestation. Observations made of the levels of Alpine lakes further broadened the inquiry to include study of the relation of deforestation to climate. Horace-Bénedict de Saussure aroused considerable interest when he published, in his *Voyage dans les Alpes,* measurements of the water levels of Lake Neuchâtel, Lake Bienne, and Lake Morat; the French chemist Boussingault studied De Saussure's materials and came to the conclusion that water levels had lowered in modern times owing to the cutting of woods (De Saussure, 1779, I, 324; cf. p. 150).

The prestige and the industry of Alexander von Humboldt also stimulated inquiry into the question, for he had devoted much time to the study of the relation of forest clearance to climatic change, using the lakes both of the New World and of Central Asia as examples. After studying the lake in the valley of Aragua in Venezuela, von Humboldt concluded that the lake level in 1800, the year of his visit, had lowered in recent times and that deforestation, clearing of plains, and the cultivation of indigo were, in addition to evaporation and the dryness of the atmosphere, the causes of the gradual drying-up of the lake. "By felling the trees which cover the tops and sides of mountains," von Humboldt said (1852, II, 9), in a widely quoted sentence, "men in every climate prepare at once two calamities for future generations: want of fuel and scarcity of water."

Twenty-five years later Boussingault visited the same valley in order to see if any changes had occurred since von Humboldt's visit and found that the level of the lake had been rising so fast that people feared the possibility of floods. His explanation for this reversal of conditions was that the country was devastated in the wars of independence, the newly freed slaves had joined the army, agriculture was largely abandoned, and the forest again covered the ground; natural conditions, being easily restored in a tropical environment, had re-established the flow of waters in a region which now approximated virgin conditions (Boussingault, n.d., p. 499).

Alexander von Humboldt's writings are an important landmark in the history of the idea of man as a geographic agent, even though many environmentalistic ideas are scattered throughout his works. Like Mencius and Buffon, von Humboldt had an eye for the distinction between a cultural and a natural landscape. A traveler to Italy, Spain, or the African coasts of the Mediterranean, he said, might "easily be led to adopt the erroneous inference that absence of trees is a characteristic of hot climates." But southern Europe was different at the time of the Pelasgian or Carthaginian colonization; civilization sets bounds to the increase of forests, and the youthfulness of a civilization is proved by the existence of its woods (Humboldt, 1849, p. 232, essay on physiognomy of plants).

Both von Humboldt and Boussingault were influential in promoting scientific investigation of the relation of agriculture and forest clearance to climatic change. Boussingault summarized the results of his investigation of the relation of man's cultural activities to his environment: (1) extensive forest destruction diminishes the amount of running water; (2) the diminution might be owing to less average annual rainfall or more active evaporation or both; (3) the quantity of running water of countries having no agricultural improvement is regular and does not seem to change perceptibly; (4) forests regularize stream flow by impeding evaporation; (5) agriculture in a dry country which lacks forests dissipates an additional portion of running water; and (6) limited clearings of forests cause a diminution of springs (Boussingault, n.d., p. 507).

Early-nineteenth-century American writers also discussed questions relating to the effects of agriculture on the forests; a paper on the subject written by Thomas Jefferson was translated into French by the Abbé Morellet (Becquerel, 1871, p. 408). The early American writers were particularly alarmed at soil exhaustion and soil erosion and suggested many different methods of fertilizing or of plowing to preserve the soils. There was in fact a strong continuity of scientific effort in the United States and in Europe throughout the century with relation to the preservation of soils and of forests (Hough, 1878, pp. 278–79; Van Hise, 1910; McDonald, 1941; Bennett, 1944).

Meanwhile, Carl Fraas had published an influential book on the destruction of the vegetation of Persia, Mesopotamia, Palestine, Egypt, and southern Europe as a result of human activities. Fraas argued that the original vegetation of these regions had been a response to climatic conditions and that man, mostly through deforestation, had changed the vegetation—which was now less useful to him—and also the climate, rejecting explanations of climatic change through purely physical causes (1847, pp. 18–124). Fraas's thesis influenced the eminent German historian Ernst Curtius, whose work on the Peloponnesus stressed the role of man as an agent in changing the environment of the Morea (1851, I, 53–55).

The conclusion of these early-nineteenth-century investigators can be summed up in a sentence: Civilization leads to aridity. These theories of climatic change as a result of human activities both in agriculture and in the forests appeared considerably earlier than those of Prince Kropotkin (1904), Raphael Pumpelly (1908), and Ells-

worth Huntington (1915) that the desiccation of Eurasia and the consequent decline of civilizations were the result of climatic change independent of human agency (cf. Gregory, 1914). Recent writings during the last twenty years on soil erosion, destructive grazing, and the like have in fact returned to earlier views that aridity has been caused by man (e.g., Bennett, 1939; Jacks and Whyte, 1939; Lowdermilk, 1943).

MAN AND PLANTS

Botanists and plant geographers also were discussing the effects of culture on the natural vegetation. The Danish plant geographer Frederick Schouw wrote that nature if uninterfered with would remain about the same throughout time; man, however, could change the vegetation, and his power to do so increased with his cultural advancement. The greatest transformations had taken place in Europe; only the European polar regions and the Alps were relatively unchanged. Perhaps had he lived closer to the Alps, Schouw might have included them as a region of change. Curiously, Schouw did not regard grazing as bringing about significant changes in nature. Although he repeats earlier themes that countries with the oldest civilizations have the fewest woods, his faith in science and technology made him optimistic, for civilization had created natural beauty itself, and a "more profound knowledge of natural forces gives a counterpoise to whatever hurtful effects civilisation brings with it" (1852, p. 238; cf. pp. 15–16, 67, 239).

The German botanist Schleiden stressed the great influence man had exerted in altering the world distribution of vegetation. Plant domestication and plant breeding he considered the most beneficial of man's changes, but man had also been a distributor of weeds; rubbish plants—thorns and thistles—"mark the track which Man has proudly traversed throughout the earth" (1848, p. 306; cf. pp. 299–307).

Around the middle of the century Alphonse de Candolle warned scientists who were interested in the evolution of plants and in their distribution in past geological eras that time was running out. "The increasing activity of man effaces these every day, and it is not one of the lesser merits of our civilization to establish a multitude of facts of which our posterity would no longer have any material visible proof" (1855, p. 1340).

Victor Hehn's celebrated work, *The Wanderings of Plants and Animals* (1888), is unique because he emphasized the power of man and rejected the idea that man caused irreversible changes in nature. It could not be denied that, especially since the age of discovery, "the whole physiognomy of life, labour, and landscape in a country may in the course of centuries be changed under the hand of man." European plants and animals had supplanted those of the New World, but the best illustration was the history of organic nature of Greece and Italy, because the known time span was at least two millenniums (Hehn, 1888, p. 7). In essence, Hehn said that the Mediterranean lands were an indirect creation of the Near Eastern peoples, for, in the Near East, plants and animals had been domesticated and had been diffused through the Mediterranean by man. Hehn had no patience, however, with pessimists like Fraas who saw the exhaustion of the earth as a consequence of human activities and who did not emphasize the possibilities of restoration; the depradations of the goat, deforestation, and soil erosion need not be irreparable. For the same reason he objected to the new agricultural chemistry whose disciples "have already passed sentence on the East and the Mediterranean countries and raised

their lament over the dead" (*ibid.*, p. 23; on exhaustion of culture, pp. 19–30).

The work of Hehn, a philologist, was in that great scholarly tradition of Jones, Adelung, Bopp, Schlegel, Lassen, and Grimm, which was concerned both with comparative linguistics and with the origin of the Aryans. All civilization had been derived from an Eastern cradle, an idea which was summed up in the phrase *ex oriente lux*. Carl Ritter, Arnold Guyot, and George W. F. Hegel used this idea in their interpretation of history as a geographical march from east to west; Hehn applied the idea to environmental change in the Mediterranean.

THE WEAKNESS OF MAN

In the first edition of his *Principles of Geology* (1830–33), Charles Lyell wrote that man must be considered "among the powers of organic nature" which modified the physical geography of the globe. Although these modifications were considerable, they were to Lyell relatively insignificant. "No application, perhaps, of human skill and labour tends so greatly to vary the state of the habitable surface, as that employed in the drainage of lakes and marshes, since not only the *stations* of many animals and plants, but the general climate of a district, may thus be modified" (1830–33, II, 205). Lyell compared the effects of human modifications to those of brute animals, the only anomaly in the intervention of man being that a single species "would exert, by its superior power and universal distribution, an influence equal to that of hundreds of other terrestrial animals." If one inquired whether man, through his direct removing power or indirect changes, tended to lessen or increase the inequalities of the earth's surface, Lyell said, "we shall incline, perhaps, to the opinion that he is a levelling agent" (*ibid.*, p. 207).

The great geologist subsequently

modified his earlier views and no longer maintained that human modifications were similar in kind to brute action. Man in his progressive development increased his power of change through the accumulation of knowledge and could be expected to make even greater changes in the future. Lyell hoped that any man-made modifications would be in harmony with the orderly evolution which he thought had characterized most of the past history of the earth (1872, I, 170–71). The minor role of man as a geological force is in sharp contrast with the violent role many of Lyell's contemporaries found man playing throughout the world, although Lyell himself describes in a vivid passage a man-made gully he observed during his American tour near Milledgeville, Georgia (1849, II, 23–25; cf. I, 344–45).

THE STRENGTH OF MAN

When President Lincoln appointed George Perkins Marsh to be the first American minister to the Kingdom of Italy in 1861, Marsh had already served as American minister to Turkey and on a diplomatic mission to Greece. In the preparation of *Man and Nature, or Physical Geography as Modified by Human Action* (1864), he had at his disposal not only his own observations but the immense accumulation of European materials whose vastness I have only hinted at in the preceding pages.

Marsh rightly said that his work was the first general and extended study of the subject, although he did not, as the title implies, consider the whole earth; the countries of northwestern Europe and of the Mediterranean Basin were his chief examples. His purpose was to indicate "the character and approximately, the extent of the changes produced by human action, . . . the dangers of imprudence and the necessity of caution in all operations, which on a large scale interfere with the sponta-

neous arrangements of the organic or the inorganic world," to make suggestions for "the restoration of disturbed harmonies," and, in a sentence which shows his kinship with the classical, biblical, and seventeenth-century tradition, "incidentally, to illustrate the doctrine that man is, in both kind and degree, a power of a higher order than any other forms of animated life, which, like him, are nourished at the table of bounteous nature" (1864, p. iii). *Man and Nature* may be described as a philosophical treatise documented with technical materials. In his work the technical ideas of men like Evelyn, Fabre, and their successors converge with the seventeenth-century conception of nature as a divinely designed balance and harmony. Marsh attacked the idea that man was a weak geological agent whose power, as Lyell at first thought, is of the same order as brute animals, as well as the environmentalistic ideas, which he ascribed to Ritter, Guyot, and von Humboldt, that human cultures were molded in large part by the physical environment.

Marsh organized his book topically according to "the chronological succession in which man must be supposed to have extended his sway over the different provinces of his material kingdom": first on animal and vegetable life, and then on the woods, the waters, and the sands. The effects of deforestation, however, are given by far the greatest prominence because of the intense preoccupation of the early-nineteenth-century scientists with this subject (*ibid.*, pp. v–vi).

In *Man and Nature* Marsh discussed many themes relating to human cultures and the environments transformed by them: the need of restoring the old lands and of caring for the new in a great era of international migration (*ibid.*, p. 26); the balance of nature, human activities being considered as disturbances of that balance (p. 27);

Alexander von Humboldt (1769–1859)

George Perkins Marsh (1801–82)

Élisée Reclus (1830–1905)

P. Vidal de la Blache (1845–1918)

Fig. 49

the idea that every plant, animal, and human being is a geographical agent, man being destructive, plants—and animals to some extent—being restorative (pp. 57–58); the revolution accomplished by man in plant distributions throughout the world (pp. 59–60); the idea that a domestic animal, like the goat or the camel, is an agent of man in modifying the environment (p. 79); the effects of wars, revolutions, and changes of fashion on physical geography (p. 84); modern agriculture as a feeding and breeding ground for insects and the consequent increase of insect life at the expense of vegetable life, birds, and the smaller quadrupeds (p. 104); the increase in climatic contrasts resulting from deforestation (pp. 153, 210); man's use of fire in clearing and in shifting agriculture (p. 136); the changes resulting from the drainage of bogs, reclamation of polders (chap. iv), and the fixation of sand dunes (chap. v); and the importance of conserving ground water, including proposals for water storage (pp. 449–50).

Marsh was a famous and widely recognized man both in Europe and in America; his works were referred to in the House of Commons in connection with the alarming deforestation of India; he was a recognized authority in America; and he helped compile the irrigation laws of France, Italy, and Spain and to assist the state of California in the development of its irrigation law. Yet his work was submerged in the tide of opinion which saw progress everywhere in the beneficent command which man had attained over nature. While Marsh was writing of the deterioration of the earth as a habitable planet, Herbert Spencer, for example, spoke of the inevitable march of civilization, its population approaching equilibrium as it advanced, until at the end of the evolution the whole world would be cultivated like a garden (1866–67, II, 506–7).

More than twenty years ago Lewis Mumford (1931, pp. 72–78) reminded us of the great contributions of the forgotten American minister to Italy. Marsh brought together materials which had been discussed in Europe for two generations, but his work was no mere compilation. He looked behind the doctrine of man's control over nature through science and technology and emphasized the unplanned, unanticipated, and uncontrolled changes which man had made in his environment, an approach which was responsible for both the pessimism and the urgency of his writings. He did not deny that there was a favorable side to the picture, but restorations had been inconsequential compared with the great accumulation of devastating changes.

Marsh did more than make a plea for conservation; he gave the world a deeper insight into the nature of human history. Our greatest debt to him is that he studied the technical works of European foresters, meteorologists, agronomists, drainage engineers and hydrologists, botanists and plant geographers, and scientific travelers and for the first time placed the results of their investigations where they belonged—in the forefront of human history.

THE WIDE WORLD

The late-nineteenth-century literature is extremely voluminous, and it is possible to give only a few examples which illustrate various points of view regarding the relation of human cultures to environmental change. The studies and observations were world wide, particularly in Europe, the United States, Africa south of the Sahara, China, and India. The great changes which the Europeans were making in the environment of Australia and New Zealand also had been of great interest since Lyell's time.

Baron von Richthofen described the desiccation of the Tarim Basin, a consequence, he thought, of the diversion of water for oasis agriculture resulting in the drying-up of other lands which were then subject to wind erosion, the sand thus blown by the wind ultimately covering the fertile soil of the oases (1877–1912, I, 124–25); he saw a close relation between the deforestation and soil erosion in Shansi Province (*ibid.*, II, 479) and noted the irrigation system of Szechwan (*ibid.*, III, 232–34) and the deforestation of southeastern China (*ibid.*, pp. 414–15).

The French geographer Élisée Reclus, whose nineteen-volume work on the earth and its inhabitants was the most impressive of the nineteenth-century geographical surveys of the world, was torn between a belief in inevitable progress and a pessimism derived in part from Marsh, in part from his own observations. It was difficult to predict the possible course of civilization, for one could be optimistic regarding the impressive land reclamation, as in the Haarlem polder of Holland, but pessimistic regarding the world-wide deforestation and the indifference of minds of a "so-called positive tendency" to changes which man was making in nature (Reclus, 1873, pp. 522–30).

In the late seventies and eighties John Croumbie Brown published a remarkable series of works on forestry which are of great value because they contain extensive extracts of contemporary literature published in out-of-the-way places (see "References," *sub nomine*). Although Brown was interested primarily in the forests, related subjects like shifting agriculture, transhumance, cattle- and sheep-grazing, and the problem of the goat were discussed at length. Equally remarkable was the report which Franklin B. Hough made for the United States Commissioner of Agriculture in 1877, including material on environmental change in the United States and in Europe, with frequent references to the works of von Humboldt, Becquerel, Boussingault, Brown, and Marsh. The works of Brown and Hough—even more than Marsh's—reveal the breadth, variety, and historical depth of the study of environmental change in the nineteenth century.

In the United States, Nathaniel S. Shaler explored many of the themes which Marsh had mentioned. Geologists everywhere, Shaler wrote, recognized changes man had made on the earth, especially in the pursuit of agriculture. "The old view that the earth was firm set and that on it we could build for 'aye' has gone the way of ancient opinions" (1896, p. 328). In his monograph on soils—a landmark in the history of soil concepts—Shaler stressed the importance of maintaining the "tillage values" of a country, for human cultures depend on the soil for their existence and must devise means for its continued preservation. Shaler took many of his illustrations regarding deforestation and soil erosion from both sides of the Atlantic (*ibid.*, pp. 369–71).

Shaler discussed the dependence of civilization on metals and minerals and the problems posed by their accelerated use. Although he gave serious consideration to the possibility of their exhaustion, he had faith in technology and in the power of man to use the falling waters, the winds, and the tides. (The German geologist Fischer also wrote a penetrating analysis [1915] of the effects of civilization on mineral resources.) New resources created by invention would replace exhausted ones; Shaler matter-of-factly predicted the deforestation of the globe by the twenty-third century (1905*b*, p. 31), leaving only a few forests to insure the flow of streams. Man will not disappear from the earth but will master it; his intellect enables him to combat the agents that destroy other forms of organic life. "The limits set to him are not those set by the death of his species, but by the endurance of the earth to the demands his progressive desires make upon it" (1904–5, p. 234).

In 1904 the German geographer Ernst Friedrich tried to give theoretical expression to the great changes which had been made throughout the world—changes which were accelerating because of the expansion of the European peoples. Friedrich distinguished between the simple exploitative economy which did no permanent harm and the characteristic exploitative economy which destroyed so much of the environment that it led to impoverishment of a people. The stages of this economic development were (1) intensive, prolonged, and heedless characteristic exploitation, followed by (2) impoverishment, which in turn led to (3) self-consciousness and awareness of the need for conservation. The need which followed exploitation in the environment of Europe had led to the discovery of soil fertilizers. "We see before our eyes processes going on in the new lands whose completed results may be observed in old Europe" (Friedrich, 1904, p. 72). Exploitative economy (*Raubwirtschaft*), reprehensible as its excesses—apparent in the slaughter of the seal, the bison, the elephant, and the whale—might be from a moral point of view, was the way of progress. Mining, for example, was purely extractive, yet "in many cases we have to seek in mining an explanation for the geographical expansion of mankind on earth" (*ibid.*). *Raubwirtschaft* was temporary, a characteristic of the youth of colonization; the earth gradually would be rationally exploited under the leadership of the European peoples (*ibid.*, p. 95). Friedrich's essay was influential because many of his ideas, which stressed the active force of man, were adopted by the French school of geographers, the possibilists, whose writings

in turn have had a wide influence on twentieth-century concepts of man's relation to his environment.

The Russian geographer and climatologist Alexander Woeikof, whose writings also influenced the French school, thought that the power of man lay in his ability to divide and rule nature; by interfering with vegetation, for example, man permitted the wasting-away of soils by wind and rain. The task of mankind was to control vegetation which held the soil in place, otherwise destruction of soils would lead to the extinction of civilization. Woeikof (1901, pp. 105–6) ascribed the origin of the silt in the Hwang Ho to the activities of man which had induced soil erosion. He thought the great expansion of cities, inclosing man on all sides, contributed to his growing ignorance of the processes of nature (*ibid.*, pp. 207–8). Woeikof was optimistic with qualifications: if the disharmonies were corrected, there were "vast perspectives of progress" ahead (p. 215). There were also the tropical lands between the fifteenth parallels of North and South latitude which could if necessary hold ten billion people (p. 211).

After a century of study of man's activities throughout the world, it is not surprising that a group of French thinkers with interests in geography and history announced the doctrine of possibilism: human cultures were not molded by their environment; environment merely offered various possibilities which different cultures might use in different ways. This doctrine was a fusion of three sets of ideas: (1) the idea of man as a geographic agent, emphasizing, that is, the role of man in changing the physical environment; (2) the significance of historical factors in the development of a culture; and (3) a concept of resources based on the idea of plant and animal associations, derived from the growing science of plant ecology. Possibilism, however, was a weak tea compared with the strong brews of yesteryear.[6]

By the first decade of the twentieth century—scarcely seventy years after Lyell had described man as a weak geological agent—several geologists were calling man the dominant geological force of the planet. Terms like the "psychozoic era," "anthropozoic era," and the "mental era" were used to characterize this new geological period, anticipating Vernadsky's thesis, a generation later, that the world was no longer a biosphere but a noösphere. After reviewing the favorable and alarming aspects of man's power, Chamberlin and Salisbury expressed the newer point of view: "It is to be observed that the mental era has but just begun, and that its effects are increasing with a rapidity quite phenomenal when measured by the slow pace of most geological change" (1904, I, 619; cf. Vernadsky, 1944, pp. 487–88).

ENVIRONMENT AND PROGRESS

This rich and vivid literature concerning environmental change brought about by human cultures was completely ignored by the large majority of the students of man both in the eighteenth and in the nineteenth centuries. How is one to explain this neglect? In the first place, the subject of man's changes of the earth was widely scattered in scientific and technical literature, where the philosophers, moral philosophers, and students of human society would be unlikely to turn for inspiration. In the second place, other ideas, especially environmental determinism and the idea of progress, dominated the thinking of men who wrote history or who attempted a theoretical reconstruction of human development.

Environmental determinism has had an astonishing vitality in modern times,

6. On possibilism see Brunhes, 1920; Febvre, 1925; Vidal de la Blanche, 1926.

especially in the nineteenth century—when one would expect it least—an age of international migration, colonization of new lands, and far-reaching environmental changes throughout the world. There were two general kinds of environmental theory: (1) the older tradition concerned with the influence of such factors as climate, location, and relief which originated in antiquity and was revived in modern times by such thinkers as Bodin, Montesquieu, and Carl Ritter, followed by (2) a more rigid determinism owing to the application of the Darwinian theory to human society. Cultures succeeded in the struggle for existence because of their ability to adapt themselves to limitations enforced by the physical environment. It was the Malthusian theory applied to human society, but in the form which Darwin in the *Origin of Species* had given it by applying Malthus' principle of population to the whole realm of organic nature. The older environmentalism led to an emphasis on geographical factors, influences, and controls, and the newer to an emphasis on the survival value of environmental adaptations. Environmentalism completely overshadowed the idea of man as a geographic agent, and the subject, instead of becoming a vital part of the study of man, was relegated to the technical and scientific literature.

The idea of a progressive cultural development through an ideal series of stages was a dominant one from the eighteenth century until the beginning of World War I. It is true that many writers defined progress in terms of man's increasing control over nature, but this was a control, acquired by a mastery of theoretical science and a knowledge of natural law, which was conscious and purposive in its application. Mankind dutifully marched through the stages of its cultural evolution guided by the philosophers and the schoolmasters. The earth—if it was considered at all—was the stage on which the drama was acted out. The idea that the haphazard, accidental, undesired, unintended, and unforeseen changes which were brought about by man in the pursuit of his economic and social goals might have a place in the histories of civilization and in the study of contemporary peoples was absent from this point of view.

THE LEGACY AND THE PROMISE OF THE PAST

The ancient idea of a unity and design in nature and the Old Testament conception of the role of man on earth provided the basis for the impressive contributions of the seventeenth-century thinkers, like Ray, who gave a fuller meaning to the idea of a balance in nature. The works of French naturalists of the eighteenth century, like Buffon's, von Humboldt's study of plant associations in the different climatic regions of the earth, and Darwin's idea of a web of life, were in the same tradition. Ecological studies since Darwin have in the main adhered to the idea of a balance in nature. Today the concept, a fundamental one in the conservation philosophy, is involved in one of the most important controversies of our time: the influence of world population growth and of theoretical and applied science on the physical geography of the earth. Optimists have faith in the conscious and purposive power of science; pessimists see the destruction of the earth as a consequence of the haphazard and heedless disturbances of the balance of nature.

If human activities, however, are considered—or defined—as interferences with this balance, we assume the existence of a nature which is an abstraction, and we neglect the effects of prehistoric and historic cultures on the natural environment. These effects are historical events, and, if not regarded as such, the study of human cultures, with

their mass of customs and traditions, and the study of physical environments will go their separate ways, and the gap between the two will be bridged with metaphors.

If the problem is regarded as a historical one, we will attain a better understanding of the processes of cultural growth and the processes of nature. The themes mentioned by Buffon, Hehn, and Marsh have been enriched in our times by thinkers who have taken advantage of historical materials. Sauer's emphasis on historical periods like the Neolithic, the age of discovery, and modern industrial times as eras of great environmental change and his stress on the antiquity of human changes in the environment through the use of fire show the importance of studying environmental change throughout history (1938, 1950, 1952). Vavilov's studies (1951) of original areas of plant domestication and his conception of man as a strong force in the evolution of plants create a similar impression. British scholars have linked the study of nature with the study of history, for the British have long been interested in local history and in the changes which long settlement has brought about in their small island. Ritchie's study (1920) of the influence of man on the animal life of Scotland and Sherlock's study (1922) of man as a geological force in England are excellent illustrations of the use of historical materials. In Tansley's history (1939, pp. 147–210) of vegetational change in the British Isles, we see man maintaining or altering the vegetation, sometimes consciously, sometimes unconsciously, to suit the economic demands or the social goals of each historical period.

In this historical essay I have confined the discussion almost exclusively to ideas which have been developed in the Western tradition, because most of them owe their existence to two unique achievements of Western thought: science and critical scholarship. In looking back on the past, it seems that the thinkers of ancient and early modern times saw only the changes that appeared in localities known to them, that those of the eighteenth century realized these changes were world wide, and that the thinkers of the nineteenth recognized both their extent and their cumulative effect, while contemporary thinkers are impressed with the acceleration of change as a consequence of population growth and technological advance.

Today, with all our awareness of the power of man, many thinkers still regard this as a planned and purposefully applied power. The testimony of the past, in all its richness and variety, reminds us that this is a false view. The earth has felt the touch of man in ways which can be understood only by following the devious paths he has taken. The ideas and observations of the past suggest what these paths were—and where they led—and therefore will be a continuing source of new insights into the historical processes which have brought the earth to its present condition.

REFERENCES

ANONYMOUS

1911   *Restauration et conservation des terrains en montagne.* (Ministère de l'Agriculture: Direction Générale des Eaux et Forêts.) 3 vols. Paris: Imprimerie Nationale. (Historical and regional; contains many excellent illustrations.)

BECQUEREL, ANTOINE CÉSAR

1871   "Forests and Their Climatic Influence," *Annual Report of the Smithsonian Institution for the Year 1869,* pp. 394–416. Washington, D.C.: Government Printing Office. (Reviews ideas of climatic change.)

BENNETT, HUGH HAMMOND

1939   *Soil Conservation.* New York and London: McGraw-Hill Book Co. 993 pp.

1944   *Thomas Jefferson, Soil Conservationist.* (U.S. Department of Agriculture Miscellaneous Publications, No. 548.) Washington, D.C.: Government Printing Office. 15 pp.

BOUSSINGAULT, J. B.

N.d.   *Rural Economy, in Its Relations with Chemistry, Physics, and Meteorology; or, Chemistry Applied to Agriculture.* Trans. with an Introduction and Notes, by GEORGE LAW. New York: O. Judd & Co. 507 pp.

BROWN, JOHN CROUMBIE

1877   *Forests and Moisture; or Effects of Forests on Humidity of Climate.* Edinburgh: Oliver & Boyd; London: Simpkin, Marshall & Co. 308 pp.

(All of Brown's works are valuable because of their extensive extracts.)

1878   *Pine Plantations on the Sand-Wastes of France.* Edinburgh: Oliver & Boyd; London: Simpkin, Marshall & Co. 172 pp.

1880   *Reboisment in France: Or Records of the Replanting of the Alps, the Cevennes, and the Pyrenees with Trees, Herbage and Bush, with a View To Arresting and Preventing the Destructive Consequences and Effects of Torrents.* London: Kegan Paul & Co. 351 pp.

1883a   *The Forests of England and the Management of Them in Bye-Gone Times.* Edinburgh: Oliver & Boyd; London: Simpkin, Marshall & Co. 263 pp.

1883b   *French Forest Ordinance of 1669; with Historical Sketch of Previous Treatment of Forests in France.* Edinburgh: Oliver & Boyd; London: Simpkin, Marshall & Co. 180 pp.

1884   *Introduction to the Study of Modern Forest Economy.* Edinburgh: Oliver & Boyd; London: Simpkin, Marshall & Co. and William Rider & Son; Montreal: Dawson Bros. 228 pp.

BRUNHES, JEAN

1920   *Human Geography, an Attempt at a Positive Classification: Principles and Examples.* Trans. from the French by T. C. LE COMPTE; ed. ISAIAH BOWMAN and RICHARD ELwood Dodge. Chicago and New York: Rand McNally & Co. 648 pp. (Many references.)

Buffon, Count de (George Louis le Clerc)
1799 "Époques de la nature," *Histoire générale et particulière*, III, 157–447; IV, 5–164. Paris: F. Dufart.
1866 *A Natural History, General and Particular: Containing the History and Theory of the Earth, a General History of Man, the Brute Creation, Vegetables, Minerals, &c. &c*. Trans. from the French by William Smellie. 2 vols. London: Thomas Kelly & Co. (Volume II [pp. 151–86] contains a partial translation of "Époques de la nature.")

Burnet, Thomas
1753 *The Sacred Theory of the Earth*. 2 vols. Glasgow: R. Urie.

Candolle, Alphonse de
1855 *Géographie botanique raisonnée; ou exposition des faits principaux et des lois concernant la distribution géographique des plantes de l'époque actuelle*. 2 vols. Paris: V. Masson.

Chamberlin, Thomas C., and Salisbury, Rollin D.
1904 *Geology*, Vol. I: *Geologic Processes and Their Results*. New York: Henry Holt & Co. 684 pp.

Cicero
1894 *Tusculan Disputations; Also Treatises on the Nature of the Gods and on the Commonwealth*. Literally Trans. from the Latin, Chiefly by C. D. Yonge. ("Harper's New Classical Library.") New York: Harper & Bros. 466 pp.

Columella, Lucius Junius Moderatus
1941 *On Agriculture*. Trans. from the Latin by Harrison Boyd Ash. ("Loeb Classical Library," Vol. I.) Cambridge, Mass.: Harvard University Press. 461 pp.

Curtius, Ernst
1851 *Peloponnesos: Eine historisch-geographische Beschreibung der Halbinsel*. 2 vols. Gotha: Justus Perthes.

Derham, William
1798 *Physico-theology: Or a Demonstration of the Being and Attributes of God, from His Works of Creation*.

New ed. 2 vols. London: A. Strahan, T. Cadell Jun & W. Davies; Edinburgh: W. Creech. (Valuable notes by the editor.)

Evelyn, John
1786 *Silva: Or a Discourse of Forest Trees, and the Propagation of Timber in His Majesty's Dominions*. New ed. 2 vols. York: A. Ward. (Many references to contemporary materials.)

Febvre, Lucien, in collaboration with Lionel Betaillon
1925 *A Geographical Introduction to History*. Trans. from the French by E. G. Mountford and J. W. Paxton. London: K. Paul, Trench, Trubner & Co.; New York: Alfred A. Knopf. 388 pp.

Fels, Edwin
1935 *Der Mensch als Gestalter der Erde: Ein Beitrag zur allgemeinen Wirtschafts- und Verkehrsgeographie*. Leipzig: Bibliographisches Institut. 206 pp. (Many references; interesting historical introduction.)

Fischer, Ernst
1915 "Der Mensch als geologischer Faktor," *Zeitschrift der Deutsche Geologische Gesellschaft*, LXVII, 106–48. (A remarkable work, including discussions of antiquity of man's role as a geologic agent, mineral exhaustion, and civilization and water.)

Fraas, C.
1847 *Klima und Pflanzenwelt in der Zeit, ein Beitrag zur Geschichte Beider*. Landshut: Verlag von J. G. Wölfle. 137 pp. (Many references to contemporary materials.)

Frankfort, Henri; Frankfort, Mrs. Henri; Wilson, John A.; and Jacobsen, Thorkild
1951 *Before Philosophy: The Intellectual Adventure of Ancient Man*. Harmondsworth: Penguin Books. 275 pp.

Friedrich, Ernst
1904 "Wesen und geographische Verbreitung der 'Raubwirtschaft,'" *Petermanns Mitteilungen*, L, 68–79, 92–95. (Many references to contemporary materials.)

Gregory, J. W.
1914 "Is the Earth Drying Up?" *Geographical Journal*, XLIII, 148–72,

293–318. (Discussion of theories of desiccation; many references.)

HEHN, VICTOR
1888 *The Wanderings of Plants and Animals from Their First Home*. Ed. JAMES S. STALLYBRASS. London: Swan Sonnenschein & Co. 523 pp.
1902 *Kulturpflanzen und Hausthiere in ihrem Übergang aus Asien nach Griechenland und Italien sowie in das Übrige Europa*. 7th ed. Berlin: Gebrüder Bornträger. 651 pp.

HESIOD
1879 *The Works of Hesiod, Callimachus, and Theognis*. Trans. from the Greek by J. BANKS. ("Bohn's Classical Library.") London: George Bell & Sons. 495 pp.

HOUGH, FRANKLIN B.
1878 *Report upon Forestry: Prepared under the Direction of the Commissioner of Agriculture, in Pursuance of an Act of Congress Approved August 15, 1876*. Washington, D.C.: Government Printing Office. 650 pp. (Like Brown's works, an excellent source for nineteenth-century ideas of climatic change and deforestation. Many quotations and extracts.)

HUMBOLDT, ALEXANDER DE, and BONPLAND, A.
1807 *Essai sur la géographie des plantes, accompagné d'un tableau physique des régions équinoxiales*. Paris: F. Schoell. 155 pp.

HUMBOLDT, ALEXANDER VON
1849 *Aspects of Nature in Different Lands and Different Climates; with Scientific Elucidations*. Trans. from the French by MRS. SABINE. Philadelphia: Lea & Blanchard. 475 pp.
1852 *Personal Narrative of Travels to the Equinoctial Regions of America, during the Years 1799–1804*. Trans. and ed. from the French by THOMASINA ROSS. 3 vols. London: Henry G. Bohn.

HUNTINGTON, ELLSWORTH
1915 *Civilization and Climate*. New Haven, Conn.: Yale University Press. 333 pp.

JACKS, G. V., and WHYTE, R. O.
1939 *Vanishing Lands: A World Survey of Soil Erosion*. New York: Doubleday, Doran & Co. 332 pp.

KROPOTKIN, PRINCE
1904 "The Desiccation of Eur-Asia," *Geographical Journal*, XXIII, 722–41.

LEONARDO DA VINCI
1954 *The Notebooks of Leonardo da Vinci*. Arranged, Rendered into English, and Introduced by EDWARD MacCURDY. New York: Georges Braziller & Co. 1,247 pp.

LOVEJOY, ARTHUR O.
1948 *The Great Chain of Being: A Study of the History of an Idea*. (William James Lectures Delivered at Harvard University, 1933.) Cambridge, Mass.: Harvard University Press. 382 pp.

LOWDERMILK, WALTER CLAY
1943 "Lessons from the Old World to the Americas in Land Use," *Annual Report of the Smithsonian Institution, 1943*, pp. 413–27. Washington, D.C.: Government Printing Office.

LUCRETIUS
1947 *Titi Lucreti Cari De rerum natura*. Ed. with Prolegomena, Critical Apparatus, Translation, and Commentary, by CYRIL BAILEY. Oxford: Clarendon Press. 581 pp. (Vol. I contains text and translation.)

LYELL, CHARLES
1830–33 *Principles of Geology, Being an Attempt To Explain the Former Changes of the Earth's Surface, by Reference to Causes Now Operating*. 3 vols. London: J. Murray.
1849 *A Second Visit to the United States of North America*. 2 vols. London: J. Murray.
1872 *Principles of Geology; or, The Modern Changes of the Earth and Its Inhabitants Considered as Illustrative of Geology*. 11th rev. ed. 2 vols. New York: D. Appleton & Co.

McDONALD, ANGUS
1941 *Early American Soil Conservationists*. (U.S. Department of Agriculture Miscellaneous Publications, No. 449.) Washington, D.C.: Government Printing Office. 62 pp. (Full bibliography.)

MARSH, GEORGE P.
1864 *Man and Nature, or Physical*

Geography as Modified by Human Action. New York: Charles Scribner & Co.; London: Sampson, Low & Son. 577 pp. (All of Marsh's works are richly documented.)

1874 *The Earth as Modified by Human Action: A New Edition of "Man and Nature."* New York: Scribner, Armstrong & Co. 656 pp.

1885 *The Earth as Modified by Human Action: A Last Revision of "Man and Nature."* New York: C. Scribner's Sons. 629 pp.

MAURY, ALFRED
1856 *Les Forêts de la France dans l'antiquité et au moyen âge: Nouveaux essais sur leur topographie, leur histoire et la legislation qui les régissait.* Paris: Imprimerie Impériale. 270 pp. (Many references to ancient and medieval sources.)

MENCIUS
1933 *The Four Books: Confucian Analects, The Great Learning, The Doctrine of the Mean, and The Works of Mencius.* Trans. from the Chinese with Notes by JAMES LEGGE. Shanghai: Chinese Book Co. 1,014 pp.

MUMFORD, LEWIS
1931 *The Brown Decades: A Study of the Arts in America, 1865–1895.* New York: Harcourt, Brace & Co. 266 pp.

PLATO
1926 *Laws.* Trans. from the Greek by R. G. BURY. ("Loeb Classical Library.") 2 vols. London: Heinemann; New York: G. P. Putnam's Sons.

1929 *Plato: Timaeus and Critias.* Trans. from the Greek by A. E. TAYLOR. London: Methuen & Co. 133 pp.

PLINY THE ELDER (GAIUS PLINIUS SECUNDUS)
1938–52 *Natural History.* Trans. from the Latin by H. RACKHAM. ("Loeb Classical Library.") Cambridge, Mass.: Harvard University Press. (Vols.I–VI, IX.)

PUMPELLY, RAPHAEL
1908 *Explorations in Turkestan: Expedition of 1904, and Prehistoric Civilizations of Anau: Origins, Growth, and Influence of Environment.* 2 vols. Washington D.C.: Carnegie Institution.

RAVEN, CHARLES E.
1942 *John Ray, Naturalist: His Life and Works.* Cambridge: Cambridge University Press. 502 pp.

RAY, JOHN
1759 *The Wisdom of God Manifested in the Works of the Creation.* 12th ed. corrected. London: John Rivington, John Ward, Joseph Richardson. 405 pp.

RECLUS, ÉLISÉE
1873 *The Ocean, Atmosphere, and Life: Being the Second Series of a Descriptive History of the Life of the Globe.* New York: Harper & Bros. 534 pp.

RICHTHOFEN, FERDINAND FREIHERR VON
1877–1912 *China: Ergebnisse eigener Reisen und darauf gegründeter Studien.* 5 vols. Berlin: D. Reimer.

RITCHIE, JAMES
1920 *The Influence of Man on Animal Life in Scotland: A Study in Faunal Evolution.* Cambridge: Cambridge University Press. 550 pp.

SAUER, CARL O.
1938 "Theme of Plant and Animal Destruction in Economic History," *Journal of Farm Economics,* XX, 765–75.

1950 "Grassland Climax, Fire, and Man," *Journal of Range Management,* III, 16–21.

1952 *Agricultural Origins and Dispersals.* (Bowman Memorial Lectures, Series Two.) New York: American Geographical Society. 110 pp.

SAUSSURE, HORACE-BÉNEDICT DE
1779 *Voyages dans les Alpes, précédés d'un essai sur l'histoire naturelle des environs de Genève.* 2 vols. Neuchâtel: Chez Samuel Fauche Imprimeur et Libraire du Roi.

SCHLEIDEN, M. J.
1848 *The Plant: A Biography.* Trans. from the German by ARTHUR HENFREY. London: Hippolyte Bailliere. 365 pp.

SCHOUW, JOACHIM FREDERIC
1852 *The Earth, Plants, and Man.* Trans. and ed. from the Danish by ARTHUR HENFREY. ("Bohn's Scientific Library.") London: Henry G. Bohn. 402 pp.

SENECA, L. ANNAEUS
1912 *On Benefits.* Trans. from the Latin by AUBREY STEWART. London: George Bell & Sons. 227 pp.

SHALER, NATHANIEL S.
1891 "The Origin and Nature of Soils," *Twelfth Annual Report of the United States Geological Survey, 1890–1891,* Part I: *Geology,* pp. 213–345. Washington, D.C.: Government Printing Office.
1896 "The Economic Aspects of Soil Erosion," *National Geographic Magazine,* VII, 328–30, 368–77.
1904–5 "Earth and Man: An Economic Forecast," *International Quarterly,* X, 227–39.
1905*a* "The Future of Power," *ibid.,* XI, 24–38.
1905*b* "The Exhaustion of the World's Metals," *ibid.,* pp. 230–47.
1912 *Man and the Earth.* New York: Duffield & Co. 240 pp. (Some chapters are reprinted from the *International Quarterly* articles.)

SHERLOCK, ROBERT L.
1922 *Man as a Geological Agent: An Account of His Action on Inanimate Nature.* London: H. F. & G. Witherby. 372 pp.

SPENCER, HERBERT
1866–67 *The Principles of Biology.* 2 vols. New York: D. Appleton & Co.

TANSLEY, A. G.
1939 *The British Islands and Their Vegetation.* Cambridge: Cambridge University Press. 930 pp.

UNWIN, A. H.
N.d. *Goat-grazing and Forestry in Cyprus.* London: Crosby Lockwood & Son. 163 pp. (Contains many extracts regarding goat devastation throughout the world.)

VAN HISE, CHARLES RICHARD
1910 *The Conservation of Natural Resources in the United States.* New York: Macmillan Co. 413 pp.

VARRO, MARCUS T.
1912 *On Farming.* Trans. from the Latin by LLOYD STORR-BEST. London: George Bell & Sons. 375 pp.

VAVILOV, NIKOLAI IVANOVICH
1951 *The Origin, Variation, Immunity and Breeding of Cultivated Plants.* Trans. from the Russian by K. STARR CHESTER. (*Chronica botanica,* Vol. XIII, Nos. 1–6.) Waltham, Mass.: Chronica Botanica Co. 366 pp.

VERNADSKY, W. I.
1944 "Problems of Biogeochemistry. II. The Fundamental Matter-Energy Difference between the Living and the Inert Natural Bodies of the Biosphere," *Transactions of the Connecticut Academy of Arts and Sciences,* XXXV, 483–517.

VIDAL DE LA BLACHE, PAUL
1926 *Principles of Human Geography.* Ed. EMMANUEL DE MARTONNE; trans. from the French by MILLICENT TODD BINGHAM. New York: Henry Holt & Co. 511 pp.

WHITAKER, J. R.
1940 "World View of Destruction and Conservation of Natural Resources," *Annals of the Association of American Geographers,* XXX, 143–62. (Late-nineteenth-century writers.)

WOEIKOF, ALEXANDER
1901 "De l'influence de l'homme sur la terre," *Annales de géographie,* X, 97–114, 193–215. (Excellently documented; includes materials relating to France, Poland, Russia, China.)

Cultural Differences in the Interpretation of Natural Resources

ALEXANDER SPOEHR*

An examination of the interpretation that different peoples have placed on the natural resources on which they depend falls in the more general field of human ecology. The relation of any human population to its natural resources is only part of a more inclusive set of relationships between such a population and its total natural environment. "Human ecology," though variously and often vaguely defined as a field of specific subject matter, emphasizes relationships with the environment and, as Bates (1953) has said, achieves its greatest usefulness as a point of view. The subject of this paper, therefore, is a part of human ecology, and the following remarks will stress a point of view rather than attempt a synthesis of a body of scientific literature.

I am indebted to Carl Sauer for pointing out that the concept "natural resources" is largely derived from our own society's ceaseless attempt at finding new and more intensive uses for the raw materials of nature. It is doubt-

ful that many other societies, most of which are less involved with technological development, think about natural resources in the same way as we do. It is probable that the term itself, with the feeling tones that it carries, is primarily a product of our own industrial civilization. For this reason it is not possible to take the body of ethnographic accounts of different peoples and obtain a clear-cut view as to exactly what interpretation has been placed on their natural resources by non-Western societies in different places and at different times. In ethnographic accounts chapters dealing with such peoples are seldom written quite that way.

In the following review it has been necessary to tie a cross-cultural comparison of the interpretation of natural resources to several rather arbitrarily selected reference points. Three have been chosen and will be examined in turn: (1) natural resources in relation to technology; (2) natural resources in relation to social structure; and (3) natural resources and the interpretation of habitat. Of these three reference points, the first is most restricted in scope. The remaining two involve a progressively wider range of subject matter.

*Dr. Spoehr is Director of the Bernice P. Bishop Museum, Honolulu, Hawaii, a position to which he was appointed in 1953. From 1940 to 1952 he was a member of the staff of the Department of Anthropology, Chicago Natural History Museum. He has conducted anthropological field work among the Indians of the southeastern United States and in the Marshall, Mariana, and Palau island groups of Micronesia. His publications include: *Majuro: A Village in the Marshall Islands*, 1949, and *Saipan: The Ethnology of a War-devastated Island*, 1954.

NATURAL RESOURCES AND TECHNOLOGY

It is a truism that every society must adapt itself to its environment to survive. This adaptation is largely effected through the particular technology that a given society has developed and maintains. Viewed in world perspective and from the vantage point of man's history on earth, the variety of technical systems is very great, ranging from the simple technology of food-collectors such as the Australian aborigines or the Great Basin Indians of North America to the highly complex technology of Western industrial civilization. Various classifications of technologies have been devised, and no attempt will be made here to extend them (Forde, 1934). The point is rather that, regardless of the degree of complexity of a given technology, every technology is necessarily based on a thorough knowledge of the natural resources which are utilized through the working of the technology. A food-collecting technology may be of a very simple order, but the men who practice it must of necessity have a sound empirical knowledge of that sector of the natural environment that provides the food they seek.

This point is made merely to emphasize that so-called "primitive" peoples do not exist in a state of ignorance of the natural world about them. It is true that the knowledge they possess is essentially empirical and that the over-all characteristics of a people's technology tend to direct their interest to those particular resources of nature on which they depend. Thus the population densities of some of the Micronesian atolls are so high in relation to their few square miles of dry-land area that these communities could not possibly survive without the fish resources of the atoll lagoons. A large sector of the technology of these atoll dwellers is comprised of skills and techniques associated with fishing, the building of canoes, and seamanship, which in turn is related to an intimate knowledge of fish species, the habits and relative abundance of various species, whether or not they are poisonous, and similar matters. A given technology, by making possible a particular kind of adaptation, tends to crystallize interest and knowledge around that segment of natural resources on which the technology depends.

Anthropological literature abounds also in examples of different peoples inhabiting the same or very similar habitats but who have made use of different sectors of the resources of their habitat. There may be a high degree of selectivity of particular resources around which the technology is centered. An interesting example can be given from Hawaii. In the days when the Hawaiians had their islands to themselves, they were fishermen and farmers. Their agricultural economy was built particularly on the cultivation of taro, which was grown chiefly in irrigated plots in the bottom-land areas of coastal valleys, usually with very high rainfall. Such a valley, famous in local history, is that of Waipio on the island of Hawaii. It is estimated that at one time from three to four thousand people lived in Waipio. During the nineteenth and twentieth centuries the economy of Hawaii completely changed. With the influx of immigrants from America, Europe, and Asia, the economy of the island of Hawaii changed to large-scale agriculture, centered on sugar cane, coffee, and cattle-raising, for none of which Waipio is suitable. The valley's population today has dwindled to twenty-six persons, and a great part of it has been abandoned. Its soil resources are neglected, for present-day large-scale agricultural technology in use on the island is not suited to them, and they have been by-passed.

The example from Hawaii again illustrates the point that interest in specific natural resources and the uses to which they are put is greatly conditioned by the nature of the technology imposed upon such resources. Technology is in itself a part of man's culture, and the interpretation of specific resources cannot be understood except as a facet of human culture.

To a considerable degree, the interest of our own society in the availability, renewability, and exploitability of natural resources springs from our singular bent toward technological invention. It is true that technological invention has been a potent force throughout man's long history on earth. Yet, viewed against the background of human history, our industrial civilization of the twentieth century has developed in a very short time. One of its characteristics, related, of course, to the growth of science, is its concern with invention. This concern the anthropologist does not find to be shared with all societies. Among many, once an adaptation to a given environment has been made through the medium of a particular technology, the manner of thought imbedded in the culture of these societies may actually militate against the inventive process. One of the best examples is given by Raymond Firth in his outstanding study of the economy of Tikopia, a very isolated small island in the southwestern Pacific. Firth (1939) notes that the material culture and the technology of Tikopia are very closely adjusted to the resources of the island environment. He notes further that the Tikopians are in no way loath to accept trade goods in the form of useful tools. However, the Polynesian people of this small island "have formulated no particular doctrine of technical invention" (*ibid.*, p. 86). Their interest is centered on legendary origins of how they themselves came to be rather than on technological origins and on the technical processes of invention and change.

Although the variety of cultures possessed by non-literate, non-Western societies is so great that the appellation "primitive" is usually a misnomer, it is true that such societies are generally small and tied to a local habitat. Every local habitat imposes certain limitations on a purely local technology. The people of a Pacific atoll must of necessity exist within the limitations of an atoll environment. It is true that as taro-raisers the Marshall Islanders have challenged the natural limitations of their atoll environment by excavating large pits in the coral lime sands of the atoll islets and, by creating humus, through filling these pits with decaying vegetable matter, are able to raise taro. This is a small-scale example of how one society has successfully challenged environmental restrictions. Yet the contrast is great when compared with the manner in which contemporary Western industrial civilization has freed itself from local environmental bonds and through its technology is world wide in scope. Chapple and Coon (1942, p. 249) have pointed out that technologically less complex societies tend to exploit single landscapes, whereas "we . . . live in all environments, not by exploiting single landscapes, separately, but by pooling and redistributing the products of all types of environment." A marked difference in the cultural interpretation of natural resources among different peoples follows from this fact. In small-scale preliterate societies concern with natural resources tends to be local; ours is world wide.

NATURAL RESOURCES AND SOCIAL STRUCTURE

So far we have touched on the relation of resources to technology, which in the last analysis comprises the characteristics of a society's tool system for converting raw materials into finished products. The techniques available to a society, however, are but one facet of its total economy. The latter comprehends also a body of generally accepted concepts regarding the control and use of resources, goods, and productive processes—such as those concepts embodied in the terms "income," "capital," and "rent"—and, in addition, the particular manner in which human beings are organized to carry out activities generally labeled as economic. In this latter category are the particular ways in which the individuals working in a factory or on a farm are organized, or the manner in which the market of a Mexican town is organized. In each case, interpersonal relations tend to fall in definable patterns, into a system of relationships that tends to persist so long as the common end—such as the exchange of goods—is being pursued. This organization of human beings in economic activity is but part of the total social structure of a society. Economic organization is related at many points to other segments of social structure. Thus, the organization of a craft industry carried out in individual households is closely related to the prevailing characteristics of the system of relations among the kinfolk of the various households. A people's kinship system is only in part an aspect of their economy.

This point is made because the use of natural resources is controlled by the nature of social structure in addition to a body of productive techniques alone. One cannot consider the link between natural resources and man merely as a matter of converting raw materials into goods through a given technology in order to house, feed, and clothe so-and-so many people, essential as these facts are.

For purposes of illustration and contrast, the following example from a technologically less complex society may be useful.

To the atoll dwellers of the Marshall Islands the coconut palm, as well as the fish resources of the sea, is a mainstay of life. A relatively simple body of techniques employing hand labor makes possible the use of the coconut for food, for export as copra, and for a variety of other products. However, the control of the coconut palm as a natural resource, the organization of production whereby it is converted into usable goods, and

the distribution of income derived from its production are all linked to Marshallese social structure. The Marshall Islanders retain a feudal-like class system of nobility and commoners. Title to all the land of the atoll nominally rests with the paramount chief. Usufruct rights are apportioned among the lesser chiefs and, in turn, among the commoners. Land is not sold, and our own concepts of ownership of real property are foreign to the system. The commoners cultivate the land, and the nobility receive tribute in the form of produce. Today, a share of cash receipts from the sale of copra is also remitted to the paramount chief as tribute. In addition, land rights are, for the most part, held by lineages of kinfolk who trace descent in the matrilineal line. Each lineage has a head who represents the lineage, and the headship as an office is also passed down in the matrilineal line. Lineages, the class organization, and land tenure are all interrelated elements of a single system. As a result, to the Marshallese, the control and use of land resources are mediated through the particular characteristics of their social structure.

The significance of cultural factors in relation to resources is perhaps most clearly discerned during periods of rapid change. Cultural change is a complex, but not a haphazard, phenomenon. At times it may follow a rigidly defined course that from a biologist's point of view is non-adaptive, in so far as the conservation and use of resources is concerned. An oft-quoted example is found in the cattle-raising peoples of East Africa, among whom cattle are so highly regarded and are so fundamental a basis of status within the community that the greatest resistance to a reduction of herds has been encountered among these people, despite serious depletion of resources (Read, 1938). A somewhat similar case is provided by the resistance of the Navaho to reduction of sheep on their overgrazed ranges.

The purpose of these examples is simply to emphasize that any group "interprets" its natural resources within the framework of its own social structure. The point at which this probably is most apparent is in the organization of production, for it is in production that the manner of control and the use of natural resources are most evident. The initial point in the productive process is the conversion of raw materials into goods. The raw materials are derived from resources in their natural state. If the resources are especially limited, restrictive rights to their use may exist. Our own concepts of "ownership" may be viewed as the conjunction of our own particular social system and limited resources. Yet Western ideas of ownership are by no means universal and are but one example of how an exclusive right may be culturally defined. The Pacific islands provide examples of differently conceived rights to resources, where Western concepts of ownership are not applicable. Yet, among these peoples, rights controlling how resources, particularly land, are to be used and who is entitled to exercise control can also be viewed as the conjunction of social structure and habitat. The case of the Marshallese has been noted. For more extensive analyses of other island societies the reader is referred to Firth (1929, 1939), to Hogbin (1939), and to Herskovits' recent (1952) general review of the problem of ownership and land tenure.

NATURAL RESOURCES AND HABITAT

Natural resources are physically a part of habitat, and habitat is but one aspect of that complex of physical, chemical, and biological processes, with their resultant products, which we call "nature." Modern man has conceptually isolated natural resources as that segment of the physical world that has a present or potential use for the survival and physical well-being of man, to be developed as far as possible through the application of scientific knowledge. Yet natural resources are still a part of nature.

The title of this paper, with its emphasis on the "interpretation" of natural resources, implies a comparison of attitudes held by different peoples toward natural resources. But, to return to a point made earlier, concern for the development of "natural resources" seems largely a facet of modern civilization. What is necessary is an examination, not merely of culturally conditioned attitudes toward natural resources, but of how various peoples have come to regard their relationship with their respective habitats (of which resources are but a part) and indeed with the entire physical universe in which they exist. It is at this point that the most fundamental contrast can be discerned between the Western industrial world and small-scale, often preliterate, societies.

This subject has been explored and presented, in a much more expert fashion than that of which I am capable, by Robert Redfield in his recent book, *The Primitive World and Its Transformations*. It is a subject that anthropologists have long pondered, though few with the breadth of interest displayed by Redfield. His presentation is the point of departure for the following paragraphs.

For the purpose of this essay there are two questions that are particularly relevant: (1) How have men, in different times and places, regarded nature, and hence the habitats in which they dwell? (2) How have these attitudes affected what men feel they should do about conserving and developing their habitats for human use?

In regard to the first question, the initial point to be made is taken from Redfield and the writers that he in turn draws upon. It is that virtually every people regards the universe in some sort of structured cosmology. The degree to which this cosmology is systematized varies enormously. The points of emphasis vary enormously. But everywhere, and since ancient times, man has pondered his relation to the physical facts of the universe and has attempted to see man, nature, and the supernatural in some sort of understandable relation. In this, my feeling from reading the accounts of ethnologists is the same as Redfield's (1953, pp. 105–6)—that preliterate peoples, in regarding the universe, "think of an orderly system originally set running by divine will and thereafter exhibiting its immanent order." Whether the gods do or can interfere in the machine they have set running is either not thought about or perhaps not reported sufficiently by ethnologists. It seems more probable that preliterate peoples tend to regard the universe as operating under irreversible laws, once these are set in motion.

And how is man's place regarded in this scheme? To what degree is he subject also to an order established under supernatural sanction? Here at least most preliterate societies offer a contrast with our own. The contrast is well exemplified in the opening paragraph of Elsdon Best's monograph, *Forest Lore of the Maori*. The contrast is shown both in Best's point of view and in that of the Maori of whom he was writing:

The outlook of the Maori, as in connection with natural phenomena and nature generally, often differed widely from our own; thus he looked upon the far spread forests of his island home as being necessary to his welfare, and also as being of allied origin. This peculiar outlook was based on the strange belief that man, birds, and trees are descended from a common source; their ultimate origin lay with the primal pair, Rangi the Sky Parent and Papa the Earth Mother, though they were actually brought into being by Tane the Fertilizer, one of the seventy offspring of the above-mentioned primal parents [Best, 1942, p. 1].

Man, to many peoples, is not set apart from nature but is part of a single order, combining man, nature, and the gods. When man utilizes the resources of nature, it is within the framework of this system of ideas. Thus, in writing of the lack of interest in technological invention displayed by the island people of Tikopia, Firth notes (1939, p. 88) that the Tikopia are governed by their theory of natural resources, which "may be described briefly as a theory of the human utilization of resources under supernatural control, which governs not only their fertility, but also the social and economic relationships of those who handle them."

Within this essentially stable system, man and nature are not conceptually opposed but are considered as parts of the same thing. The totemic rites of the Australian Karadjeri, whereby the economically and socially important species of plants and animals were believed to be assured of normal increase, reflected a similar manner of thought (Elkin, 1933). When Gayton, writing of the integration of culture and environment effected through economic activity, ceremony, and myth among the Yokuts Indians, states (1946, p. 262) that "men and animals were peers," much the same idea is expressed.

In his consideration of the involvement of man and nature in the thought of preliterate and ancient societies, Redfield notes (1953, p. 104) that the men of these societies did not "confront" nature. For them, "being already in nature, man cannot exactly confront it." Rather, Redfield suggests, the relation is one of mutuality, existing under a moral order that binds man, nature, and the gods in one.

The modern Western world has undergone a major transformation from this orientation. Man has been conceptually separated from nature, and God from both. Speaking of the development of Western thought since classical times, Redfield (pp. 109–10) states:

The subsequent development of a world view in which God and man are both separated from nature, and in which the exploitation of material nature comes to be a prime attitude, may be attributable to our Western world almost entirely and so might be regarded, as Sol Tax has suggested (Tax, 1944), as a particular "cultural invention." By the seventeenth century in European philosophy God was outside the system as its mere clockmaker. To the early American, nature was God's provision for man's exploitation. . . . The contemporary Western world, now imitated by the Orient, tends to regard the relation of man to nature as a relation of man to physical matter in which application of physical science to man's material comfort is man's paramount assignment on earth.

These observations may appear overdrawn to some, but they illustrate what I believe is a fundamental contrast in the thinking of the Western world, as contrasted to preliterate and ancient peoples. It is a contrast that in itself is a least a partial answer to our second question posed earlier—namely, how has this contrasting attitude affected what men feel they should do about developing their habitats for human use? Certainly the tenor of contemporary American thought holds that habitat is something apart from man and is to be manipulated to his advantage. In the world of today, with the ever growing millions of human beings to clothe, feed, and house, this attitude has a very immediate and practical import.

On the other hand, despite the long history of the growth of technology, throughout which some men as far back as the earliest periods of human history must have been concerned with improving tools to develop resources for human use, preliterate societies lack the pervading instrumental attitude toward nature generally characteristic of ourselves. The difference probably accounts for the significance of magic associated with technology, which Malinowski long ago reported for the Trobriand Islands. Among these people, although their full technological skill is called upon in an enterprise, such as gardening, fishing, or voyaging, recourse to magic is had to fill the inevitable gap between the application of human skill and the certainty of success.

The contrasting attitudes of Western and preliterate thought lead to another question. For several decades anthropologists have been attempting to observe the changes that take place in small scale, for the most preliterate, societies, when they come in contact with Western industrial civilization. In so far as the interpretation of natural resources is concerned, is not the contrast just discussed at the root of the change that takes place? I suspect it is. To review all the evidence is beyond the scope of this paper, but I quote an anthropological colleague, John Gillin, comparing the Indian and the Ladino cultures (crystallized out of contact with Spain) of Guatemala:

The principal and fundamental goal of Indian cultures is to effect a peaceful adjustment or adaptation to the universe. In contrast, the main goal of Ladino culture is to effect control of the universe by man. The Indian wishes to come to terms with the universe, the Ladino wishes to dominate it. . . . The Indian attitude is not one of abject submission to natural and supernatural forces. The basic assumptions in Indian cultures, however, do hold that man is in a world which operates according to certain laws or rules ultimately controlled by that part of the universe which we would call the supernatural or unseen, that this general plan of things is ongoing or immutable, that man must learn certain patterns of action and attitude to bring himself into conformity with this scheme of things, and that if he does so he will receive the minimum amount of punishment or misfortune and the maximum rewards of which such a scheme is capable. . . . The Ladino, on the other hand, assumes that the universe, including its supernatural department, can be manipulated by man . . . [Gillin, 1952, p. 196].

The gradual adoption of this attitude could, I believe, be documented from other societies in contact with the West. It seems to have been, for instance, a concomitant of the extension of the copra industry to various islands of the Pacific during the nineteenth and twentieth centuries. The development of the copra industry in the Marshall Islands was almost certainly accompanied by a marked change in attitude toward land, whereby it came to be regarded as a resource to be controlled and manipulated by man to his best advantage, in a fashion comparable to the Ladino point of view described by Gillin. To what degree the extension of this attitude follows the penetration of a money economy into societies such as the Marshallese, together with the growth of trade and a widening in the range of wants, is not clear.

If these contrasting attitudes toward nature, and in consequence toward natural resources, have been correctly described in these paragraphs, I should like to turn to some ramifications in regard to the interpretation of nature by our own society.

To the degree that the Western world is composed of almost completely urbanized individuals, it not merely regards habitat, and consequently natural resources, as an entity that is to be dominated and manipulated by man but tends to relegate the whole matter to a handful of specialists and, in effect, to place nature outside its immediate sphere of concern. Urban man has become so far removed from his biological moorings and so immersed in the immediate problems of urban living that he stands as an "egocentric man in a homocentric world." Despite the millions of Americans who annually visit our national parks each year, it is to be doubted that much change is thereby effected in the basic urban attitude. The aesthetic principles underlying American conservation movements can perhaps best be viewed as a minority reaction to the prevailing urban point of view. Conservation, in the sense of the attempt by the Save-the-Redwoods League to preserve stands of California giant sequoias from extinction, is an effort to protect modern man from himself. Such efforts are not, to my knowledge, found among preliterate peoples living in small communities in close and personal relation to nature. Among most of them, though it is largely unrecorded in the reports of ethnologists, I suspect that the aesthetic appreciation of nature is a common feature of daily life. Yet I should add that most of my own field experience has been in the congenial islands of the Pacific.

If the prevailing mode of thought tends to regard nature as a physical entity apart from man, with the corollary that man's duty is to develop and dominate to the best of his ability the resources of his habitat, there are nevertheless certain countercurrents in contemporary scientific thought that cannot be ignored. These countercurrents are well exemplified by Darwin and Faraday.

Darwin opened our eyes to the functioning of organic nature, and his mode of thought led to discovery of new facts and relationships in the living world. Darwin dealt with man's place in nature and with man as a part of a huge, dynamic biocoenose, of which man was only a small part, actually not very different from the other parts, and subject to the same processes and regularities. In his point of view as to man's integration with the natural world, Darwin might be considered as close to the way in which preliterate peoples regard nature, except for the fundamental difference that the former developed his point of view on the basis of observed reality; the latter, on recourse to the sanction of man-created legend and myth. Darwin left to his successors the concept of man as a part of nature, whatever qualities man may possess that distinguish him from other forms of life.

Faraday, on the other hand, introduced us to inanimate forces which could be made to serve man's needs and wants. He stimulated the invention of new devices and the formation of a great new technology based on the use of natural forces. He also stimulated the creation of a homocentric world, a modern, mechanized, exploiting world of men whose contemplating largely centers about themselves and who attempt to plan, arrange, and administer in their own name. Whereas the heritage of Darwin has provided the fascination of biological revelation, that of Faraday has brought the excitement attending the accomplishment and application of the physical sciences.

In a modern world where men are dedicated to exploiting to the utmost the natural resources of this planet—a dedication that is stimulated by the very numbers of men on earth—the point of view exemplified by Faraday is necessarily uppermost. It could hardly be otherwise. Yet one cannot forget the bearded figure of Darwin watching quietly from the shadows.

REFERENCES

BATES, MARSTON
   1950 *The Nature of Natural History.* New York: Charles Scribner's Sons. 309 pp.
   1953 "Human Ecology," pp. 700–714 in KROEBER, A. L. (Chairman), *Anthropology Today: An Encyclopedic Inventory.* Chicago: University of Chicago Press. 966 pp.
BEST, ELSDON
   1925 *Maori Agriculture.* (Bulletin No. 9.) Wellington, N.Z.: Dominion Museum. 172 pp.
   1942 *Forest Lore of the Maori.* (Bulletin No. 14.) Wellington, N. Z.: Dominion Museum. 503 pp.
BEWS, J. W.
   1935 *Human Ecology.* London: H. Milford. 312 pp.
CHAPPLE, E. D., and COON, C. S.
   1942 *Principles of Anthropology.* New York: Henry Holt & Co. 718 pp.
DARWIN, SIR FRANCIS (ed.)
   1950 *Charles Darwin's Autobiography.* New York: Henry Schuman. 266 pp.
ELKIN, A. P.
   1933 *Studies in Australian Totemism.* ("Oceania Monographs," No. 2.) Sydney. 131 pp.

EVANS-PRITCHARD, E. E.
   1940 *The Nuer: A Description of the Modes of Livelihood and Political Institutions of a Nilotic People.* Oxford: Clarendon Press. 271 pp.
FIRTH, RAYMOND
   1929 *Primitive Economics of the New Zealand Maori.* London: G. Routledge & Sons; New York: E. P. Dutton & Co. 505 pp.
   1939 *Primitive Polynesian Economy.* London: G. Routledge & Sons. 387 pp.
   1946 *Malay Fishermen: Their Peasant Economy.* London: Kegan Paul, Trench, Trubner & Co. 354 pp.
FORDE, C. D.
   1934 *Habitat, Economy and Society: A Geographical Introduction to Ethnology.* London: Methuen & Co.; New York: Harcourt, Brace & Co. 500 pp.
GAYTON, A. H.
   1946 "Culture-Environment Integration: External References in Yokuts Life," *Southwestern Journal of Anthropology,* II, 252–68.
GILLIN, JOHN
   1952 "Ethos and Cultural Aspects of Personality," pp. 193–222 in TAX, SOL

(ed.), *Heritage of Conquest*. Glencoe, Ill.: Free Press. 312 pp.

HERSKOVITS, M. J.
1948   *Man and His Works*. New York: Alfred A. Knopf. 678 pp.
1952   *Economic Anthropology*. New York: Alfred A. Knopf. 547 pp.

HOGBIN, H. I.
1939   *Experiments in Civilization: The Effects of European Culture on a Native Community of the Solomon Islands*. London: G. Routledge & Sons. 268 pp.

KLUCKHOHN, CLYDE, and LEIGHTON, DOROTHEA
1946   *The Navaho*. Cambridge, Mass.: Harvard University Press. 258 pp.

MALINOWSKI, BRONISLAW
1935   *Coral Gardens and Their Magic*. 2 vols. London: Allen & Unwin.

MEAD, MARGARET
1940   *Mountain Arapesh. II. Supernaturalism*. ("Anthropological Papers," Vol. XXXIV, Part III.) New York: American Museum of Natural History.

READ, MARGARET
1938   *Native Standards of Living and African Culture Change*. (Supplement to *Africa*, Vol. XI, No. 3.) 56 pp.

REDFIELD, ROBERT
1953   *The Primitive World and Its Transformations*. Ithaca, N.Y.: Cornell University Press. 185 pp.

SEARS, P. B.
1950   *Charles Darwin: The Naturalist as a Cultural Force*. New York: Charles Scribner's Sons. 124 pp.

SPOEHR, ALEXANDER
1949   *Majuro: A Village in the Marshall Islands*. ("Fieldiana: Anthropology," Vol. XXXIX.) Chicago: Chicago Natural History Museum. 266 pp.

TAX, SOL
1941 "World View and Social Relations in Guatemala," *American Anthropologist*, XLIII, 27–42.
1953 *Penny Capitalism: A Guatemalan Indian Economy*. (Smithsonian Institution, Institute of Social Anthropology, Publication No. 10.) Washington, D.C.: Government Printing Office. 230 pp.

TAX, SOL (ed.)
1952   *Heritage of Conquest: The Ethnology of Middle America*. Glencoe, Ill.: Free Press. 312 pp.

THURNWALD, R.
1932   *Economics in Primitive Communities*. London: Oxford University Press. 314 pp.

The Antiquity and World Expansion of Human Culture

PIERRE TEILHARD DE CHARDIN[*]

PLANETARY NATURE OF MAN: A PRESENTATION OF THE NOÖSPHERE

How and how much does man, by his presence and his activities, transform the face of the earth? As a common background to the various technical answers, dealing with soil conservation, water distribution, city building, etc., we should like to mention and to emphasize a still deeper and more general change which our zoölogical group has brought to the terrestrial world. This change would betray and characterize the presence of man on earth to an observer on Sirius, namely, the progressive expansion of a special layer of thinking and cultured substance all around the globe.

More than a half-century ago the great geologist Suess took a bold and lucky step when, in addition to describing our planet by the classical sequence of concentrical, spherical shells (barysphere, lithosphere, atmosphere, etc.), he decided to add the biosphere, in order to affirm, in a concise and vivid way, that the frail but superactive film of highly complex, self-reproducing matter spread around the world was of decided geological significance and value. Since Suess's times, the notion of a special planetary envelope of organic matter distinct from the inorganic lithosphere has been accepted as a normal basis for the fast-growing structures of geobiology (a new branch of science). But, then, why not take one step more and recognize the fact that, if the appearance of the earth has undergone a major alteration by turning chlorophyll-green or life-warm since the Paleozoic period, an even more revolutionary transformation took place at the end of Tertiary time, when our planet developed the psychically reflexive human surface, for which, together with Professor Édouard Le Roy and Professor Vernadsky, we suggested in the 1920's the name "noösphere"?[1]

Ultimately, neither earth nor man can be fully understood except with regard to the marvelous sheet of humanized and socialized matter, which, despite its incredibly small mass and its incredible thinness, has to be regarded positively as the most sharply individualized and the most specifically distinct of all the planetary units so far recognized.

As a natural introduction to the problem, devoted precisely to the study

* Dr. Teilhard de Chardin's paper appears posthumously. Father Teilhard was Research Associate of the Wenner-Gren Foundation for Anthropological Research at the time of his death on April 10, 1955. During his lifetime he was an adviser to the National Geological Survey of China and a member of the French Academy of Sciences. He was primarily a geologist and vertebrate paleontologist whose interests ultimately led him to the problems concerning the origins of man both in Southeast Asia and in Africa south of the Sahara.

1. From the Greek *noos*, "mind," and *sphaera*, "sphere."

of the relations existing between earth and man in the course of their respective developments, let us therefore summarize the essence of what can be scientifically stated today concerning (1) the historical establishment of the noösphere; (2) the cultural structure; and, finally, (3) the present comportment, as well as the possible future, of mankind considered as a biological whole on a planetary scale.

HISTORICAL DEVELOPMENT OF THE NOÖSPHERE

Scarcely more than a century has elapsed since living man, realizing that he, too, was a product of biological evolution, began to hunt not only for animal fossils but also and predominantly for "fossil man." In spite of intensive research, we are still far from having gained a complete vision of the history of our zoölogical group. Yet, as we consider its main features (Fig. 50), the reconstruction of our past is by now sufficiently advanced to have taken what may be regarded as its *final general shape*. The main lines of the picture gradually have come to light through the joint efforts of prehistory and paleoanthropology.

Most surely, for stringent geological and paleontological reasons, the mysterious phenomenon of initial "hominization" (that is, the mutational emergence in nature of a reflexive, or "self-conscious," type of consciousness) must have taken place, by the end of the Pliocene, within the tropical or subtropical areas of the Old World in which there happened to be concentrated, at the closing of the Tertiary,

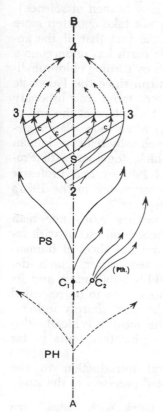

PH = Pre-Hominians (Australopithecines, *Meganthropus,* etc.), branching, diverging

PS = Pre- and para-*sapiens* types of Hominians (Neanderthaloids, Pithecanthropians, etc.), branching, slightly converging

S = *Homo sapiens,* not branching; first expanding, then fast converging

c, c, c = Various cultural units

1 = First emergence of eu-Hominians (critical point, or threshold of reflexion)

2 = Emergence of *Homo sapiens,* and beginning of the formation of the noösphere (through co-reflexion)

$3, 3$ = Division at present, between expansional and compressional phases in the development of the noösphere

$4(?)$ = Upper limit, and critical point of co-reflexion (conjectured)

C_1 = African center of hominization

C_2 = Indo-Malaysian center of hominization (*Pth.* = Pithecanthropians)

AB = Ideal axis of hominization

Approximate time elapsed between *1* and *2,* more than half a million years; between *2* and *3* (Upper Paleolithic, Neolithic, historical times), about fifty thousand years

FIG. 50.—A symbolic expression of the successive phases of hominization

the most advanced representatives of the higher, tail-less chimpanzee- or gorilla-like primates presently included by the zoölogists in the Pongidae family.

What were the number, the physical appearance, and the comportment of these first true Hominians? That, we perhaps shall never know. Owing to the fact that the first stages of any organized system are constitutionally of a fragile structure, the traces of any "beginning" are selectively erased by the passage of time. There is still, and probably there will almost always remain, a blank in our vision of the past at the place occupied by the origins of man, though no more or less, in fact, than in the case of the birth of any other animal species or of any human civilization.

The presence of recognizable para- or pre-Hominians, anatomically comparable with the Pleistocene Australopithecines of Africa recently has been detected as early as the Upper Miocene of Italy (*Oreopithecus bamboli*). But no "eu-Hominians" were likely to have wandered on the surface of the earth before the Basal Pleistocene (Villafranchian), that is, earlier than approximately a million years ago.

In so far as we can guess, the initial hominization must have developed along an extensive west-east South Himalayan belt, ranging from equatorial Africa to Malaysia. But at a very early stage in the process it seems that this elongated "mutational front" was ruptured in the middle; the result of this segmentation was the individualization of two distinct centers of hominization: Center 1, located in Central Africa (C_1, Fig. 50, p. 104), and Center 2 (C_2, Fig. 50, p. 104), located somewhere in Indo-Malaysia.

Zoölogically speaking, Center 1 and Center 2 were remarkably symmetrical in their structures. Each of them shows a core of eu-Hominian type, surrounded by a cluster of para-Hominian forms (Australopithecines of Africa [?], *Meganthropus* of Java, etc.).

But in so far as their evolutive power is concerned, they were in fact of quite different values. Whereas the pithecanthropians (*Pithecanthropus, Sinanthropus, Homo soloensis*) of the Far East never exceeded the dimensions of a marginal branch of humanity, or ever rose above a low anatomical stage comparable with that of Neanderthal man of Middle Pleistocene of Europe, evidence is growing that in the heart of Africa, and nowhere else, there originated what has become the bulk, if not the totality, of modern mankind.

To be sure, bony remains of ancient man still are very scarce in Africa south of the modern Sahara, and so far they consist mostly of the pithecanthropian-like (and relatively late) skulls of Rhodesia and Saldanha. But hidden behind this outer envelope of "neanderthaloid" or "para-*sapiens*" appearance, the presence in Africa of an exceptionally progressive subphylum of proto-*sapiens* type (perhaps actually represented by the modern-looking, yet heavily fossilized, Kanam jaw from Kenya) becomes more and more probable. Without this assumption, it would be extremely difficult either to explain the unique development in the Lower Pleistocene of Africa of a hand-ax culture which is the oldest and the richest of the world or to understand the sudden outburst of "modern man" throughout Eurasia (apparently from south to north) at the dawn of Upper Paleolithic time.

For the greater part of the Pleistocene (that is, during the whole Prelithic[?] and early Paleolithic times), facts force us to admit that man has remained strangely limited, geographically, within the original boundaries of his zoölogical birth. Except for some marked peripheral advance of the hand-ax industry in southwestern Europe and Southeast Asia (as far as Indonesia[?]), the territory occupied by our ancestors some fifty thousand years ago was still substantially the same tropical and subtropical "Pongids belt" on which the first hominization occurred hundreds of thousands of years before at the end of the Pliocene. It is as though, during an enormous span of time, man, still immature, was kept busy by some organic adjustment at the innermost part of himself.

But subsequently, by the end of the Middle Pleistocene, a general movement of populations resulted in a fundamental redistribution of man on the surface of the earth. At that time a definitely modernized type of man, radiating apparently from a Mediterranean base, succeeded for the first time in invading those expanded northern parts of the continents where the Old and the New Worlds come into close contact, or even weld, along a boreal belt. To some extent, Africa, despite its size, had been for millenniums a closed container for man or even a blind corner. Once having reached the vast free spaces, first, of northern Eurasia and, somewhat later, of North America, man, endowed at last both anatomically and culturally with his full expansive force, seems to have progressed quickly, like an irresistible tide, over the newly open land: only a few thousands of years later he had already reached Patagonia!

This was a true "second hominization," indeed: the rise out of Africa and the world-wide spreading of *Homo sapiens,* the "universal man."

As a result of this Upper Paleolithic expansion, Mesolithic man was no longer merely a tropical and subtropical animal. At last he had become what we are now: a pan-terrestrial form of advanced life. But his hold on the earth at this early stage was still most precarious and very loose. And it was to require the continuous and intensive ef-

fort of many more millenniums of agricultural and proto-industrial cultures to fill the gaps and to establish a first satisfactory net of connections between men and men all over the world.

Several hundred thousand years had been spent on the mere *preparation,* mainly in Africa, of a human planetary invasion. Some thirty thousand years more had been required for the actual *occupation* of the extra-African lands. Approximately ten thousand years (that is, the whole combined Neolithic and historical times) were necessary before a preliminary *consolidation* of the human envelope had been realized all around the earth.

But today, after so many eons of hominization, the great accomplishment pursued by life since its first emergence on earth two or three billion years ago is over; namely, the achievement of an unbroken, co-conscious organism, coextensive with the entire area of the globe. Definitely cemented on itself in the course of the last century by the powerful forces of industry and science, the newborn noösphere is now spread right before our eyes and is caught already in the first grip of an irresistible *totalization.*

Before trying to investigate this final phase of the development of the noösphere, let us first analyze the secret of its internal structure in order to discover the deep reasons why man represents so obviously (judging merely from his biological success) a *revolution* in the very process of natural *evolution.*

CULTURAL NATURE OF THE NOÖSPHERE

By human culture, I refer to the manifold process according to which any human population, whenever left to itself, immediately starts spontaneously to arrange itself at a social level into an organized system of ends and means, in which two basic components are always present: First, a material component, or "increase in complexity," which includes both the various types of implements and techniques necessary to the gathering or the production of all kinds of food or supplies and the various rules or laws which provide the best conditions for an optimum birth rate or for a satisfactory circulation of goods and resources within the limits of the population under consideration. Second, a spiritual component, or "increase in consciousness," namely, some particular outlook on the world and life (an approach which is at once philosophical, ethical, aesthetic, and religious), the function of which is to impart a meaning, a direction, and an incentive or stimulus to the material activities and development of the community.

For the many fragments of mankind that have become isolated or have gained their independence in the course of time, just so many tentative technico-mental systems of the world as a whole —that is, just so many *cultures*—have gradually come into existence. This is one of the major lessons taught by the universal history of man, from the earliest known stages until the present time.

Understood thus as a collective answer to the general biological problem of survival and growth, the typically human phenomenon of culture is of course foreshadowed, to some extent, at the prehuman levels of life. In the case of animals, too, the struggle for life leads each different species forcibly toward the discovery of some constructive adjustment between germinal forces of reproduction and multiplication, on the one hand, and quasi-social forces of collective arrangement, on the other.

But whereas, in the case of non-reflexive life, *social* and *germinal* persistently have been unable to combine into a definite and unlimited creative process,[2] in the case of man, on the contrary

(and clearly in some sort of connection with the newly acquired human power of "thinking"), both social and germinal have given rise, by their conjunction, to a decidedly superior type of evolution—a "new evolution" in fact[3]—special to the noösphere and characterized at the same time by a new and more efficient form of invention, by a new and more efficient form of heredity, and by a new and more efficient form of speciation.

A New and More Efficient Form of Invention

Since its earliest beginnings, life has never stopped "inventing" and perfecting new organic contraptions along the most amazing variety of lines. But for a very long time this continuous advance seems to have been achieved much more through a patient expectation and utilization than by a positive pursuit and control of chances. Before man, the evolution of animal life was unquestionably directional and preferential. But in its mechanism it did not show any real *purpose*. Since the appearance of man, however, the living individual being becomes able to *plan*. And this power of planning, when focused on research and when brought socially to the dimensions of a concerted effort for discovery, opens a new era in the development of terrestrial life. Without escaping the general conditions and "servitudes" of every organic substance in the universe, man has introduced, and is gradually expanding at the very core of nature through his collective power of reflexive invention, a new method for arranging matter: no longer the old random arrangement but

2. Either the social is lagging behind in the animal world, or, as it happens for the insects, society chokes the development of the individual.

3. This expression is from George Gaylord Simpson's *The Meaning of Evolution*, 1951.

an active arrangement through *self-evolution*.

A New and More Efficient Form of Heredity

Germinal heredity, so deeply investigated by our modern geneticists, proved to be a marvelous instrument of progress during the earlier, prehuman stages of the development of life. But owing to the very nature of its chromosomic mechanism, germinal heredity is affected, in fact, with a triple basic weakness which makes it unable to insure, if left to itself, any further advance of evolution in the case of such a complicated and fast-changing type of organism as man, especially *collective* man. First, the characters transmitted by genes are by their very nature restricted to a category of rather elementary features; namely, those which control the material arrangement of the cells in the course of embryogenesis. Second, the number of these elementary characters is drastically limited in the germ by the exiguous size of the chromosomes. Third (if we except the possible case of some social instincts among the insects), there is no observable chromosomic transmission to the species of the characters eventually *acquired* by the industrious activity of each individual in the course of its life.

Now, remarkably enough, it is precisely on these three different grounds that a decided improvement becomes manifest in the *cultured* zones of life, in so far as the registration and the transmission of human experience are concerned. Thanks to language, to information, and to education, an unlimited number of unlimitedly complex ideas or techniques accumulate continuously, and organize themselves permanently, in the unlimited capacity of collective human memory.

Thus, duplicating the history of the old *chromosomic heredity*, an incomparably more sensitive and receptive *educational heredity* is now at work in the noösphere. This is precisely the more-needed power to collect the overabundant products and to feed the constantly accelerated progress of a self-evolving process.

A New and More Efficient Form of Speciation

Considered over a sufficiently protracted span of time, every animal population shows a tendency to split, under a statistical effect of genetic mutations, into branching systems of varieties, subspecies, and, ultimately, true, new, specific forms. In the case of man, things proceed in much the same way, except that, as a consequence of the specifically human association between germinal and social, the splitting and branching operation results in the formation of new, *mainly cultural*, instead of new, *mainly anatomical*, types.

Fundamentally, according to my point of view, culturation is nothing but a "hominized" form of speciation. Or to express the same thing differently: *cultural units* are for the noösphere the mere equivalent and the true successors of *zoölogical species* in the biosphere. True successors, we insist. And how much better fitted than their predecessors to satisfy the new requisites of an advanced type of evolution!

Let us briefly dwell on this important point. Considered as an instrument for evolution, zoölogical speciation, in addition to being very much slowed down by the non-inheritance of acquired characters, is seriously handicapped by the fast-increasing estrangement observable between the products of its operation. In the very process of becoming itself, each newly formed zoölogical type becomes more and more separated and isolated from the other surrounding species in the process of its inner development. Growing aloneness, mutual impermeability, and consequent basic incapacity for any sort of interspecific synthesis were the common fate of animal phyla under the "old" regime of evolution.

In contrast, with the rise of self-evolution, not only does the speed of transformation increase rapidly, because of the cumulative transmission of planned inventions, but, and more important, a remarkable capacity emerges among the socialized offsprings of the new evolution for keeping in close inner touch with one another—and even for fusing with one another—in the course of their development. On the one hand, the various human cultural units spread all over the world at a given time never cease (even during the most acute phases of their differentiation) to react mutually on one another at the depth of their individual growth. Whatever may be the degree of their mutual divergence, they still form, when taken together, an unbroken sheet of organized consciousness. And, moreover, on the other hand, they prove able (provided they happen to be sufficiently active and sufficiently compressed on one another) to penetrate, to metamorphose, and to absorb one another into something fundamentally new. This is the well-known process of *acculturation*—a process possibly bound to culminate some day in a complete "mono-culturation" of the human world, but a process, in any case, without which no formation of any continuous human shell would ever have been physically possible on the surface of the earth.

From the preceding analysis of the cultural nature of human expansion one might conclude erroneously that the so-called "noösphere" is nothing more than an uninteresting kind of pseudo- or para-organism, since, according to a widespread opinion, it would be dangerously confusing to identify what is really *natural* and what is simply *cultural* (that is, "artificial") in the world. Here, we confess to touch upon a point

still hotly debated even among anthropologists; namely, to decide whether the word "biological" can or cannot be applied correctly (in a non-allegoric way) to the workings and to the products of human culture. And yet, in our opinion, a decisive and final positive answer to the problem is already forced upon our mind by the three following joint considerations:

1. Whatever may be the ultimate physical nature of psychological awareness, increasing consciousness—traceable by increasing cerebration—is overwhelmingly proved by general paleontology and comparative zoölogy to be a safe and absolute parameter (or index) of biological evolution.

2. Aside from any undue anthropocentrism, but from the inescapable evidence derived from the revolutionary effects of hominization, *reflexive awareness* must be held, not as a mere variety, but as a *superstage* of consciousness.

3. Judging from the very mechanism of its operation, which is ultimately reducible to a process of *co-cerebration* and *co-reflexion,* culturation cannot be regarded as anything less than a direct prolongation of hominization.

Obviously, if they are linked with one another in their natural order, these three successive steps scientifically detected in the terrestrial development of life—(1) direct (or simple) consciousness; (2) reflexion (consciousness raised to its second power; for man, *to know that he knows*); and (3) culture (co-reflexion)—have one, and only one, possible meaning. They show in an unmistakable way by their mere natural sequence that man, through culturation, is not drifting away along some side path and toward some blind corner of the universe but that he is still moving directly along the major axis of cosmic development. From all that we know most certainly from the entire history of the past, culturation, because it biologically expresses a collective advance in reflexion, decidedly is not an inferior or reduced form of evolution but rather represents a supertype. This evidence, far from being of merely speculative interest, turns out to be of the utmost importance, both for our power of vision and for our power of action.

It is of importance for our power of action, of course, because it is tremendously necessary to the security of man and to his sense of values to be sure at last, in his effort to become more human ("ultra-human"), that he is responsible for, and supported by, the main and most central forces of a growing universe. It is important for our power of vision too, because, if the full impact of evolution is actually concentrating at present on the achievement of the noösphere, then we can understand better the terrific energies at work and the incredible potentialities still awaiting us in the process and in the progress of human acculturation.

PRESENT STATUS AND POSSIBLE FUTURE OF THE NOÖSPHERE

A common attitude today, one repeatedly expressed in the statements of highly intellectual and religious people, is that man and mankind are regarded as being a practically stabilized product of evolution and even as a disintegrating and decaying one. Under the influence of science and techniques, man is supposedly not improving but even regressing biologically. Hence "progress" is a myth and an illusion. In many quarters this is the new and fashionable way of thinking "realistically."

For anyone who is aware of the basic evolutive significance of any *increase of consciousness through complexity* inside the noösphere, such a pessimistic view of the present status of the world is so incredibly wrong scientifically, and at the same time so dangerously depressing psychologically, that we believe that the time has come to react against

it openly and vigorously. And this can best be done, it seems to us, by presenting a more objective and more comforting interpretation of the major crisis which we have been going through since the beginning of the twentieth century.

Something very deep and very wide is certainly taking place, these days, at the core of the humanized zones of the planet. But *what?* To this question the only satisfactory answer, in our opinion, is as follows.

Up to a very recent date the phenomenon of "hominization," because it was continuing (for perhaps about a million years) to operate on a relatively unpopulated world, was predominantly a process of *expansional and diverging* directions. Just as in any given animal species the main rule of life is to propagate and to differentiate at a maximum, so the chief occupation of man during this first period was to invade all the free parts of the earth and, at the same time, to attempt every possible form of cultural arrangement.

At present, however (that is, for less than a century!), owing to the coincidence of a sharp demographic jump with an incredible progress in intercommunication, the development of mankind has suddenly become *compressional and converging* in its direction.[4] The movement has completely reversed its phase, with the result that, under a tremendous and incoercible *rapprochement* and compression of both human bodies and human minds, co-arrangement and co-reflexion are now rising toward astronomical values at the interior of the noösphere. Even if humanity is not becoming either better or happier in the course of the process,

4. Very much in the same way as a pulsation entering a globe through the lower pole would first expand, up to the level of the equator, and then, in moving farther on toward the upper pole of the sphere, would become more and more compressed (cf. Fig. 50, p. 104).

it is today forced, more than ever, in its entirety and under two irresistible factors (that is, by the double curvature of our rounded mother-planet and of our converging minds) to move toward unheard-of and unimaginable degrees of organized complexity and of reflexive consciousness.

To become ultra-reflexive (that is, "ultra-human") by reaching some stage of mono-culturation—or else to resign and to die on the way—this, aside from any temperamental or philosophical considerations, must on purely scientific grounds be regarded as the biological fate of man.

For conventional and conservative reasons we dislike, and we try to weaken, the growing evidence that, judged by the best standards of biological evolution, our species is still far from being zoölogically mature. Instead of closing our eyes to the stupendous technico-mental acceleration of anthropogenesis in our modern times, why not rather try to face the situation and to guess how far the process is likely to carry us and how it is going to end eventually?

Whenever we speculate on the future of civilization, we generally assume that, except for the unlikely case of some physical, physiological, or psychological accident of planetary dimensions, man will survive practically unchanged as long as the earth will supply him with a sufficiency of food and energy. But, in our opinion, we should consider another idea that is both more interesting and more probable; namely, that the whole human adventure, in so far as it turns out to represent *a fast-converging process*, is bound to end some day, not by exhaustion from *external* causes, but climactically for *internal* reasons, just because *there is* a critical upper limit (or threshold) to the planetary development of co-reflexion.

If we follow this line of thought to the end, we are led to the suspicion that every "thinking planet" in the universe (like a psychical nova) must culminate sooner or later, through protracted inner maturation, in some implosive concentration of its cultural noösphere. And this specific event should possibly coincide with some escape of the fully "co-reflected" parts of the *Weltstoff* outside and beyond the apparent boundaries of time and space. Strangely enough, such a wild hypothesis of a transhuman universe conforms perfectly to the general pattern of a physical world in which absolutely nothing can grow indefinitely without meeting ultimately some critical level of emergence and transformation. From the inflexible point of view of energetics, the process fulfils, we believe, a condition *sine qua non* for the steady continuation of human effort during the next million years toward an ever greater culture and acculturation.

So far, man has accepted blindly (just as the industrial workers of a century ago) the pushing-ahead of the terrestrial development of life, without asking himself whether it was a paying game to play at being Atlas. But this phase of instinctive co-operation is decidedly over. The time can be foreseen when the human drive for climbing always higher toward consciousness through complexity will die out, unless it is stimulated by growing scientific evidence that, through ever intensified hominization, we are really moving *somewhere* and *forever*.

That some definite Everest should really be there ahead of us, behind the clouds, an Everest from which there is no return to the plain; that through a stubborn confluence of our minds and hearts we should eventually succeed in breaking the barrier of darkness and mutual exteriority which still separates life as we know it from some higher and more stable form of knowledge and unanimity; and to become actually and acutely conscious of the imperative craving of our deepest ego for some definitely *irreversible* type of achieve-ment—might well be, we venture to say, the next step which man will take (very soon, perhaps) in the process of his co-reflexive self-evolution.

REFERENCES

BLUM, HAROLD F.
1951 *Time's Arrow and Evolution.* Princeton, N.J.: Princeton University Press. 222 pp.

BOYD, WILLIAM C.
1950 *Genetics and the Races of Man.* Boston: Little, Brown & Co. 453 pp.

BRIDGMAN, P. W.
1949 "The Potential Intelligent Society of the Future," pp. 229–50 in NORTHROP, F. S. C. (ed.), *Ideological Differences and World Order.* New Haven, Conn.: Yale University Press. 486 pp.

DARWIN, CHARLES GALTON
1953 *The Next Million Years.* New York: Doubleday & Co. 210 pp.

HUXLEY, JULIAN S.
1953 *Evolution in Action.* New York: Harper & Bros. 177 pp.

NEEDHAM, JOSEPH
1943 *Time, the Refreshing River.* New York: Macmillan Co. 280 pp.

REDFIELD, ROBERT
1953 *The Primitive World and Its Transformations.* Ithaca, N.Y.: Cornell University Press. 183 pp.

SEIDENBERG, RODERICK
1950 *Post-historic Man.* Chapel Hill: University of North Carolina Press. 246 pp.

SIMPSON, GEORGE GAYLORD
1951 *The Meaning of Evolution.* ("New American Library.") Rev. ed. New York: Mentor Books. 192 pp.

TEILHARD DE CHARDIN, PIERRE
1951 "La Structure phylétique du groupe humain," *Annales de paléontologie,* XXXVII, 77–106.

WHITE, LESLIE
1949 *The Science of Culture.* New York: Farrar & Straus. 444 pp.

WIENER, NORBERT
1954 *The Human Use of Human Beings: Cybernetics and Society.* Boston: Houghton Mifflin Co. 199 pp.

Through the Corridors of Time

Through the Corridors of Time

Fire as the First Great Force Employed by Man[1]

OMER C. STEWART[*]

EVIDENCE FROM ARCHEOLOGY
AND ETHNOLOGY

Use of fire and manufactured implements of stone are the cultural achievements recorded in ancient strata of the earth as indicators of the beginning of humanity. Language, stone tools, and control of fire probably distinguished mankind from other primates by the beginning of the Pleistocene, which we might place at one million years ago. The actual evidence for the use of fire by the first humans is as scarce and indefinite as the evidence of the origin of man himself.

The oldest hearths geologically were those discovered about 1920 by J. Reid Moir near Ipswich, England (Osborn, 1927). Some doubt about them has persisted, and may increase, owing to the fact that Moir attributed the hearths to Piltdown man of recent infamy. On the other hand, the rostrocarinates of Moir, assigned to the preglacial age of England, have gained acceptance in spite of the abandonment of the notion of "Eolithic age" and "Pliocene man" in Continental Europe. The paucity of fireplaces from open sites of early Pleistocene age limits the direct evidence of the date of man's first control of fire but does not subtract from the value of fire as a diagnostic trait for human origins.

Cave sites offer more certain data on the control of fire by man, because there is little chance of ash or charcoal from lightning fires entering caves. A layer of ash in an open site could be attributed to fires of a non-human agency. It might be assumed that lightning has occurred for millions of years and that vegetation could have been ignited during all the eons that it has existed on the earth's surface. The recognition of such a possibility does not establish the fact that vegetation has been burned during all its history. Geologists have identified little wood ash or partly burned wood in pre-Pleistocene deposits (Plummer, 1912b, p. 7), and its presence in Pleistocene strata is usually accepted by geologists and paleontologists, as well as by archeologists, as evidence of human occupation. Thus, notwithstanding the admitted possibility of forest fires set by lightning in prehuman times, the failure to find much evidence of pre-Pleistocene vegetation burning permits us to minimize its role. Lightning fires were presumably of importance in the early Pleistocene, however, since they provide the most rea-

---

[*] Dr. Stewart is Professor of Anthropology at the University of Colorado, Boulder, Colorado, and from 1952 to 1954 was chairman of the Department of Social Sciences (Anthropology, Economics, Political Science, and Sociology). In 1940–41 he was a Post-doctoral Fellow of the Social Science Research Council. His publications include: *The Northern Paiute Bands*, 1939; *Culture Elements Distribution: XVIII—Ute, Southern Paiute*, 1942; and *Ute Peyotism*, 1948.

1. Research on which this paper is based has been supported by grants from the University of Colorado Graduate School Committee on Research and Creative Work.

sonable source for man's knowledge of fire. With fire, as with all aspects of Paleolithic and even Neolithic culture, however, we are dependent largely upon imagination and pure logic to explain ultimate origins.

The cause of prehuman fires and the source of man's first knowledge of fire may be considered together. Evidence with which to substantiate theories of such origins is about as plentiful for us as it was for Aeschylus when he wrote *Prometheus Bound* about 470 B.C. (Osborn, 1927, pp. 16–17). In seeking to explain the origin of fire as a tool of man, I recognize my kinship with aboriginal mythmakers as well as with the scientific optimists of a century ago who expected to learn of cultural beginnings from surviving Stone Age peoples. We continue to speculate nevertheless. In 1926 Hough in his monograph *Fire as an Agent in Human Culture* stated (p. 5) that "natural ignitions may be divided into volcanic, chemical, electrical, frictional due to earth movements, and frictional on wood."

Of the natural agencies which start fires, only volcanoes and lightning are frequently observed igniting vegetation. Molten lava could have served as a recurrent source of fire in the vicinity of the proper types of active volcanoes.

If volcanoes were the only source of new fire by fire-using people otherwise unable to make fire, however, great sections of the world would have remained unoccupied.

Lightning is at present much more nearly universal than volcanoes. Fires started by lightning are widespread over the earth and occur regularly. Although we can imagine lightning as a fundamental factor in man's initiation into the mysteries of fire, its relative importance throughout human history must be carefully evaluated and will be considered at some length later in this paper.

The chemical agent for natural ignition proposed by Hough (*ibid.*) is spontaneous combustion of seams of coal and coal dust. Burning seams of coal possibly spontaneously ignited in prehistoric times are reported for New Zealand, the Mackenzie River, and Borneo. Other examples of burning coal in West Virginia and Russia are of questionable natural origin. However, the world distribution of exposed seams of coal which might have become lighted by spontaneous combustion or by friction is too limited to have helped teach many ancient men the usefulness of fire. Spontaneous combustion may have occurred in the marshes of Louisiana in prehuman times, according to the botanist Roland M. Harper (1943, p. 32) and to Viosca (1931).

Equally difficult to verify is the theory that flames may have resulted from dead branches being rubbed together by winds. Hough (1926, p. 7) quotes this observation made by François Bernier in Kashmir in 1663: "Some of the trees were scorched and burnt, either blasted by the thunderbolt, or, according to the traditions of the peasantry, set on fire in the heat of summer by rubbing against each other when agitated by fierce, burning winds." Also unverified is the belief that sparks from contact of boulders falling on rocks may have ignited fires (Chipp, 1926, p. 228).

Whatever may have been its start, fire must have been known to man and have been controlled by him before he learned to manufacture it. The discovery of a method to ignite vegetable matter looms as one of humanity's greatest acts. Yet, before that momentous event, hominids may well have guarded and transported fire for hundreds of thousands of years. *Australopithecus prometheus* of South Africa now stands up to proclaim that a small-brained ape-man had the ability to tend fire. Professor Raymond Dart (1948) of the University of the Witwatersrand has declared that this peculiar primate, intermediate between apes and man, kept fire in his caves. Few anthropologists are willing to accept the proposition that this small-brained man-ape could have controlled fire, and the evidence Dart used to justify naming his fossil *prometheus* has been carefully scrutinized and generally rejected. However, Dart and his few supporters confidently expect additional evidence confirming use of fire by *Australopithecus* to be discovered soon.

Although exciting because of its morphology, *Australopithecus* is not generally accepted as the most ancient hominid fossil geologically. The *Australopithecus* deposits have been assigned to such diverse periods as Upper Pliocene and Middle Pleistocene. Most geological opinion seems to favor the more recent date. The geologic dating of *Australopithecus* is as disputed as the question of his tool-using and fire-making. Nevertheless, *Australopithecus* may yet prove to be the progenitor of mankind and force us to admit that half a brain was enough to get fires started and to push us forever onto the hominid sidetrack.

Sinanthropus pekinensis is the earliest man known to have controlled fire. Extensive excavations at Choukoutien, near Peking, brought to light fifteen individual skulls and skull fragments which indicate a human type much nearer to modern man than *Australopithecus*. In the cave with the hundreds of pieces of fossilized bones of human type were crudely chipped stone tools and large quantities of solidified wood ash, charcoal, seeds, animal bones, and other material distinct from the rocks of the limestone caves. There is no doubt that Peking man tended the fire in his cave home and must have carried it with him when he moved abroad.

The deposits in the Choukoutien cave have been variously assigned to late Middle, early Middle, and Lower Pleis-

tocene. *Sinanthropus* has been placed from a quarter- to a half-million years ago. In any event, man's use of fire as a powerful tool capable of tremendous influence on his environment has continued for at least a quarter-million years.

As important as the fact of the first control of fire is for our thesis, we are forced to reason by analogy with modern aborigines to get some idea of what happened during most of the time of human occupation of and influence upon the earth. The few bits of archeological evidence, outside of ashes in cave dwellings, of primitive man's role in changing his geographic environment come from Upper Paleolithic and Neolithic times, not more than twenty-five thousand years ago, and will be mentioned later. The difficult problem we face is to reconstruct man's use of fire outside his family hearth during the hundreds of thousands of years of his development from the protoanthropic stage of *Sinanthropus* and *Pithecanthropus* to his appearance as *Homo sapiens*. During those millenniums this new primate moved out from his natural habitat in the tropical rain forests and came to occupy virtually all the earth. Use of fire was certainly essential for man's life away from the tropics, and it may have played an important role wherever he settled. Domestic fires, however, are pertinent for consideration only as they may have had wider influence. Although our archeological evidence of most ancient fires comes from the rock shelters and caves occupied by man from the time of *Sinanthropus*, it is reasonable to suppose that campfires were made during hunting trips away from caves and during migrations. It is fair to assume that man has used fire from the time he gained control over it, much as it has been used by the culturally most primitive aborigines up to the present.

Since modern aborigines carry hot

coals, punk, and slow matches, so that they can make fire to prepare meals during the day and at temporary overnight stops, I assume this practice has been customary since man acquired the use of fire. Hough (1926, pp. 3–4) recorded means of carrying fire from areas as scattered as New Guinea, the Mississippi Valley, Patagonia, Arizona, Australia, and China. It was probably universal among natives who had only the simple hand fire drill with which to manufacture fire. Almost all tribes of western North America, listed in the Culture Element Distribution survey of the University of California (Kroeber, 1939), reported carrying some sort of slow match, so that they could easily start a campfire while away from home.

As humans spread out from the tropical zone, within which they were by nature equipped to live without artificial protection or supplementary heat, preservation and transportation of fire must have been a major concern for the entire group. Before the manufacture of fire was discovered, and even when the simple fire drill or fire saw was used to ignite new fire, there must have been much more thought and energy given to preserving fire than to extinguishing it. Indians of western America reported lighting bushes and trees, so that the roots would become ignited and yet burn very slowly underground for days or weeks, in order that a light could be obtained if necessary without using the fire drill.

Would earliest man traveling with fire across the countryside carefully extinguish each campfire? More likely, would he not put on a big log and bank his fire to preserve it against the chance of his return, even though he carried a spark in a horn or carried a bark slow match? If an accident occurred and the portable spark were put out, it would be comforting to know that logs or roots had been left burning and that a return trip might find a glowing spark.

Reason suggests that the first fire users, while migrating or hunting far from home base, intentionally left campfires burning and whenever possible tried to leave them smoldering slowly, so that they might burn for days. The analogy with modern natives supports this reasoned conclusion. Europeans, as well as Indians from Alaska, California, Kansas, and Virginia, have been reported leaving campfires unextinguished. In a very extensive search of the literature I discovered almost no reference that natives anywhere carefully extinguished fires.

This brings me to my first important deduction about the beginning of fire as a factor of significance in modifying the surface of the earth. Everywhere that man traveled, he made campfires and left them to ignite any and all the vegetation in the vicinity. Campfires of a sparse population might not do much igniting in many regions. In flat country which dried out at certain seasons and where strong winds occurred with the drought, a few abandoned campfires might influence the vegetation of a large area. It is my opinion that native peoples have rarely been careful to extinguish their campfires when made in the open country and that primitive hunting and gathering peoples from the time they acquired fire have allowed their fires to ignite the landscape, because it did not occur to them to protect the vegetation from fire.

We may project back to the beginning of human culture other historically known burning practices which would have extensive effect on the landscape. In fact, except for the use of fire in connection with agriculture and grazing, all the reasons given by modern natives for setting vegetation on fire may also have motivated our most remote ancestors. Wild animals and plants now existing, with few exceptions, are those with which man has competed and to which he has adjusted during his entire history. We may assume that the interrelationships of life-forms have been in general fairly uniform during the last million years. Local variations of tremendous proportions have indeed occurred, like the glacial advances. Even the glaciers, however, were relatively restricted, and beyond their limits man lived with the animals and plants we know. Hunting and gathering folk hundreds of thousands of years ago may be presumed to have developed many of the techniques for exploiting the natural environments which people at the hunting level of culture still employ.

Not only did ancient man abandon his campfires to ignite vegetation but he probably deliberately started conflagrations which swept over the country. In ancient times, as in recent ones, thick forests and dense jungles of brush offered very little use to the hunter or collector. On the contrary, narrow trails through tangled and heavy growth were dangerous because of the concealment provided to human, as well as animal, enemies. Whenever possible, aborigines have set fire to jungles and thick woods in order to "open them up." Widely spaced trees and clear meadows and plains offer better and safer hunting.

Klamath Indians in forested southern Oregon and Pomo Indians in the redwood country of northern California complained to me that modern forestry, which allows brush and trees to grow rank and uncontrolled, was depriving the Indians of much hunting territory. The Klamath Indian said: "Now I just hear the deer running through the brush at places we used to kill many deer. When the brush got as thick as it is now, we would burn it off." There are many other references to intentional burning to thin or remove brush and trees in order to improve visibility for hunting and to facilitate travel. Clearing to get an advantage for hunting would also reduce the danger from enemies.

Aubréville, in his exhaustive work (1949, p. 323) on the forests and savannas of French Equatorial Africa, also concluded that aborigines would have burned for the advantages afforded by open woods and plains. Werner in British Central Africa observed (1906, pp. 9–12) that, "where there are no trees or bushes, the grass is usually tall . . . and has to be burned off at the end of every dry season—otherwise it would become an impenetrable jungle." Werner noted that brush fires were set purposely "or accidentally by some travellers' campfire," and he added:

These fires have from the earliest ages formed one of the characteristic features of African travel. One of the oldest records of exploration [from about 500 B.C.]—the *Periplus* of Hanno—describes them, ". . . by day we saw nothing but woods, but by night we saw many fires burning . . . going along four days, we saw by night the land full of flame and in the midst was a lofty fire, greater than the rest and seemed to touch the stars."

Historic aborigines tell us of a number of other reasons for broadcast burning which may also have motivated primeval man. To rouse or drive game during hunting was the reason most frequently recorded over the world. A hundred different Indian groups of North America as well as natives of South America, Africa, Tasmania, Australia, New Guinea, China, and Turkestan set fire to drive game. Birket-Smith (1929) believes Europeans have used fire for hunting since Solutrean times, or during the last fifteen thousand years. Sauer (1944) and Eiseley (1954) interpret the evidence of late Pleistocene man in America to mean that fire drives were used here ten to twenty thousand years ago. Lucretius (1908, p. 212) in 55 B.C. assumed that the practice was very ancient and had, possibly, contributed to the discovery of smelting thousands of years before his time. It seems reasonable to assume that fire as an aid to hunting would have been used with greater frequency as one extended further and further into the past. In the most ancient times the weapons, traps, and other hunting tools would be less efficient. In other words, during the Lower Paleolithic for approximately nine hundred thousand years, while the hunting tools consisted only of sharpened sticks and the stone fist ax or *coup de poing,* fire would have been a relatively greater aid to hunting than in the Neolithic, when the bow and arrow were perfected. Fire also would be used in the collection of various insects, like crickets, whenever they were used as food.

Burning of grasslands and forests to improve pasture for game has been widely reported. This practice includes burning off year-old dry stocks in order to make new growth available, burning to produce greener and more tender grass, burning to remove brush and trees, and burning to speed the appearance of new grass in the spring. To improve pasture has been given as the reason for setting fire to vegetation by hunting peoples from the Atlantic to the Pacific in the United States, as well as in Argentina, Manchuria, and South Africa.

It has long been realized that even the poorest hunting and gathering peoples who appeared to be on the lowest level of material culture had a very thorough knowledge of the characteristics of the wild plants in their homelands. Aborigines not only knew growth patterns and the geographic conditions favored by each plant species; they were well aware also of various means to assist different plants in the struggle with other plants. That they understood the value of fire as a tool to procure and maintain the yield of certain wild plants they desired has been much in evidence. This knowledge was displayed,

as noted above, through deliberate burning to improve grazing conditions for game. In addition, throughout the western United States, Indians from about fifty tribes reported intentional broadcast burning in order to increase the yield of seeds of wild grasses and weeds which were collected for food. Several forest-dwelling tribes, among them the Iroquois and Powhatan of the Atlantic seaboard, the Kwakiutl of British Columbia, and several California tribes, as well as the Yahgan of Tierra del Fuego, burned woods and bushes to improve the berry harvest. Fire has also been widely used to make vegetable food more available, as when forest litter was ignited to uncover acorns or nuts. Furthermore, fire has been used to aid growth of tobacco and to produce willows for basketry weaving.

The practical motivations for incendiarism listed above would lead to repeated and regular application of flame to vegetation. The benefits obtained during recent years could have been obtained equally well hundreds of thousands of years ago. Although there is no way to determine at what period in human history natives applied the torch for which reason, there is, nevertheless, no basis for thinking that any one of the motives so far listed is of recent origin. All of them have probably influenced mankind to set fires since the beginning of humanity.

Of less general applicability and of more specialized use is the setting of vegetation on fire as an act of war. It is logical to suppose that small populations at war would have readily recognized that fire could be a weapon. The first men to see the value of flame to rouse or drive game would quite certainly have realized that the same tool could be helpful to flush an enemy from dry brush or grass.

Herodotus in 447 B.C. (1936, p. 240) provides the earliest apparent documentation of the scorched-earth method of defense on the Russian grasslands. When the Scythians retreated before the army of Darius, they left "the whole country bare of forage . . . destroying all that grew on the ground." Lucretius (1908, p. 212) also mentions fire as an implement of war. American Indians from the prairies of the United States, the pampas of Argentina, and the grasslands of California report using fire as a weapon. It was even a practice of the Papuans of New Guinea.

In addition to the references which specify the reasons for intentional broadcast burning, there are a number of sources which state simply that such fires occurred in particular areas. There are records of natives firing the vegetation for unspecified reasons for nearly all the separate states of the United States. Similar reports of incendiarism for undetermined reasons have come from Mexico, the Antilles, Argentina, Brazil, Venezuela, India, China, Ceylon, Sumatra, Lapland, Sweden, Russia, and Africa. I must believe, with Sauer (1952), Hough (1926), Shantz (1947), and Kuhnholtz-Lordat (1939), that aborigines the world over since time immemorial have set vegetation on fire. In recognizing that the preagricultural populations of the world had good and sufficient reasons for clearing lands and also had the means to do so, we add many thousands of years to the period that man has been an important ecological factor on the earth.

I am aware that some scholars appear reluctant to grant that the hunters and collectors had any influence on the geographic environment. Clark (1952, pp. 91–92), introducing his chapter on Neolithic farming in Europe, asserted that prior to clearing by the early agriculturalists Europe was covered by a great primeval forest. Clark (*ibid.*, p. 94) draws his conclusion from the increase in herb pollen and charcoal at the Neolithic level of Danish peat bogs analyzed by Iversen. The fact that there were significant amounts of both charcoal and herb pollen and that the amounts fluctuated markedly before the Neolithic should have suggested that intentional burning preceded the Neolithic farmers. It is true, of course, that damp forests of pre-Neolithic times could not be ignited easily. However, Stefansson (1913, p. 10) tells of intentional burning of forests by American Indians to improve hunting in the subarctic coniferous forest of the lower Mackenzie River, and Seifriz (1934, p. 307) gives an account of Lapps burning their pine forests, indicating that hunters may go to great trouble to burn moist forests at those rare and irregular periods when the forests would carry fire.

It seems certain that forest-burning expanded in Europe during Neolithic times, as indicated by the amount of the charcoal and herb pollen in the Neolithic peat deposits. A sharp rise in population was made possible by improved and stabilized food supply resulting from the introduction of farming and herding. Agriculturalists with good axes, whether made of stone or steel, and with the milpa or slash-and-burn system of land preparation, would surely clear more damp forest than would hunters. Notwithstanding the increase of open lands in Europe brought about by cultivation, fire as a tool without agriculture should not be minimized. Whether in Europe, Africa, Asia, or the Americas, the record is clear that burning for hunting preceded as well as accompanied the use of fire with agriculture and grazing. It is not always clear which is the strongest motivation —hunting, agriculture, or herding— where there is a mixed economy. The importance of the agricultural motive is clear and dominant in the moist northern forests and the tropical rain forests, where cutting of some brush and trees and stripping the bark from others are necessary to allow the area to become dry enough to burn. Where broadcast wild fires are impossible, the work of opening a section is justified only where a crop can be grown in the fertilizing ash. Extreme tropical rain forests, however, have been removed initially for planting but have been maintained in grass by annual burning. Tansley and Chipp (1926), Aubréville (1949), and Kuhnholtz-Lordat (1939) abundantly document this sequence for historic peoples and project its occurrence into the distant past. Clark (1952, p. 95) briefly summarizes the relationship of plants to prehistoric burning in Europe and concludes that extensive meadows, grasslands, and heaths were formed with the aid of fire during the Neolithic. Some grasslands have continued until the present and are only now being returned to forest. The generalization that all primitive hoe-and-dibble planters the world over used fire as a tool in cultivation seems justified.

Gordon M. Day (1953) carefully and thoroughly documented vegetation burning by Iroquois and Algonkin Indians to clear fields for agriculture and to open forests for hunting in New England at the time of European discovery. All the aboriginal maize farmers of the eastern United States employed similar methods. Furthermore, the Maya of Yucatan were forced to move their towns, according to Hough (1926, p. 67) and Lundell (1934, p. 265), after milpa cultivation had degraded the soil and established sod in place of trees. The New Zealand grasslands, although ancient and pre-European, are now attributed to the old Maori custom of clearing forests for planting with the aid of fire. Repeated burning maintains grass on ancient fields (Allen, 1937, p. 27). The same process was observed in 1952 on Guadalcanal. Annual fires maintained grass on old fields, while new fields were acquired by cutting and burning forests (Johnson, personal com-

munication). I have received personal reports of similar practices leading to comparable results in New Guinea, Alor, and Sumatra, and I have found in the literature references to the same customs in South America, Africa, Madagascar, China, Ceylon, and Indochina.

Some antiquity for the slash-and-burn agriculture in Korea is implied by its being designated by special terms: *hwajon* (Japanese: *kaden*) for the fire field, and *hwajommin* (Japanese: *kadenmin*) for the fire-field farmer. In 1944 Grajdanzev (p. 95) wrote of Korea that *kaden* "consists of the burning of grasses and bushes in the forest area and planting cereals or potatoes there for a few seasons and then moving to another place when the fertility of the ground has been exhausted." Over 100,-000 acres were said to have been cultivated in 1938 by *kadenmin*, who constituted 2.4 per cent of Korean farmers (*ibid.*, p. 109).

There are numerous examples of the passage of land from cultivation into pasture and thereafter of the maintenance of the grazing area by fire. Several scholars tell of the renewal of the heath by burning after the brush grows beyond a certain height. Young shoots provide better feed for cattle, sheep, and goats.

In 1931 the American geographer Ellen Churchill Semple presented an excellent summary of the role of fire and grazing in the deforestation of the Mediterranean. I quote Dr. Semple's classic study at some length (pp. 290–91):

Denudation of the forests made such inroads upon the wood supply of Italy that by the fifth century Roman architectural technique had become modified to meet the growing scarcity and increased price of wood.

Clearing for tillage land and the legitimate consumption of wood as lumber were only part of the process of destruction.

The long dry summers and the resinous character of Mediterranean *maqui* shrubs made forest fires frequent and disastrous, while the high winds of the hot season fanned the flames. Such fires were a commonplace event in ancient Palestine. Isaiah describes one in a metaphorical passage: "It shall devour the briers and thorns, and shall kindle in the thickets of the forest, and they shall mount up like the lifting up of smoke." Homer knows the effect of protracted drought and strong summer winds upon such a conflagration. "Through deep glens rageth fierce fire on some parched mountain side and the deep forest beneath, and the wind, driving it, whirleth everywhere the flame. . . ."

Fires were often started, either intentionally or accidentally, by the herdsmen who ranged the mountain forests with their sheep and goats in the dry season. Burning improved the pasturage, because the ashes temporarily enriched the soil, and the abundant shoots from the old roots furnished better fodder. The forests once destroyed were hard to restore.

Dr. Semple could have used also quotations from Lucretius (1908, p. 213) and Vergil (1947, pp. 14, 51).

Burning to improve grazing was also reported for the steppes of the lower Volga during a trip in spring of 1794 by Pallas (1803, p. 115, with footnote): "The nights, however, still continue cold, and we saw fire on the steppe, at a considerable distance. . . . The steppes are frequently fired, either by the negligence of travellers, or willfully by the herdsmen, in order to forward the crops of grass."

Kuhnholtz-Lordat (1939, pp. 191–241) devoted a fifty-page section of his book *La Terre incendiée* to "Fire and Herding." He discovered that fire was used as a tool to help prepare pastures in Madagascar, French North Africa (by Berbers), South Africa, Rhodesia, the Congo, France, Switzerland, the Malay Peninsula, the Balkans, and other lands of the Mediterranean.

All the reasons for burning over the landscape already enumerated, except for farming and herding, could have existed generally during all the history of man. I have considered also the practices of ancient animal and plant husbandry, in so far as these used fire as a tool, but I wish to emphasize that most of the motivations of the primitive hunters and gatherers continued to activate some of the simple agriculturists as well as the modern farmers, mechanics, doctors, and other specialists of all kinds who hunt as a sport.

Dr. Marion Kingston, professor of English at the University of Colorado, wrote me that "the deer burn still comprises a thick chapter in the Maine poacher's handbook." Kuhnholtz-Lordat (1939, pp. 245–47) also wrote of the importance of the use of fire in hunting by those who have agriculture and herds. This is true in tropical Africa, Indochina, Madagascar, the Baltic, and America.

The most ancient reasons for burning persist and are joined to the motives of the planter and the herder. With the domestication of plants and animals, commencing about 8000 B.C., all the known motives for using fire as a tool were operative. From the earlier hunting stage the change was very slight in some instances, as with the shift from preparing pasture for wild game to doing so for domestic herds. The sample of archeological and ethnological evidence presented seems sufficient to sustain the opinion that man has set fire to the landscape during his entire history. It may be worth while, nevertheless, to review some of the botanical material which supports and bolsters the above opinion. Although the anthropological and botanical data combine and strengthen the structure of evidence of man's influence on his geographic environment, plant distributions and other knowledge gained from botany appear more complete and more certain in some respects.

THE EVIDENCE FROM BOTANY

Botanical evidence for the antiquity and universality of burning falls into three general categories. (1) Exact dating of burns by means of fire scars and tree-ring analysis is possible and provocative in a few localities. (2) Some studies in plant succession indicate clearly and immediately that the normal plant succession of the area has been disturbed. Many species are known as *pyrophytes* (Kuhnholtz-Lordat, 1939, pp. 31–34) or fire plants and indicate frequent burning-over. (3) Related to plant succession but more complicated in analysis is a comparison of plant potential from an analysis of soil, moisture, temperature, etc., with the actual plant cover. This is of particular importance where very extensive regions, such as the American prairies and plains, the Argentine pampas, the Russian steppes, and the African sudan and veld, present an appearance of being entirely natural and climatically determined.

To discover the impact of man and his cultural tools on nature from a study of plant cover, it is always necessary to weigh man's potential against similar effects which could be produced by other means, such as by lightning. Whenever we find botanical evidence that an area has been burned over, there is always the question whether the fire was from natural or from human cause. American botanists, plant ecologists, and geographers as a group appear to favor the idea that all prehistoric fires were due to natural causes, and, by so doing, they greatly minimize human influence. I know of no study of lightning-caused fires which permits such a conclusion to be drawn with confidence.

In the tree rings and fire scars of giant sequoias is the history of their survival against regular attacks by flames throughout their entire lives of two thousand years. Were these fires set by Indians or lightning? There is no sure answer. Yet, in the Sierra Nevada, where the sequoias are located, authenticated lightning fires occur annually by the hundreds and could certainly account for all the scars made during the last two millenniums. However, redwoods of the Coast Range of northern California and lightning statistics for that region tell a very different story. Fritz (1932, pp. 2–3) wrote that fires ignited by lightning are extremely rare.

Analysis of burned tissue and growth rings shows that forests in Oregon (Keen, 1940, p. 498) and in Pennsylvania (Lutz, 1930, pp. 1–29) were also repeatedly subjected to fire during the last thousand years. Relatively few lightning fires are recorded for Pennsylvania; it would seem that the majority of the scars in these forests were from man-made fire. Within the time limits imposed by the trees themselves, the record of the trees may be interpreted to mean that Indians certainly caused fires for about two thousand years. Moreover, if hunters and gatherers in California and Pennsylvania are certainly known to have used fire as a tool for two thousand years, there is no reason not to suppose that the practice has been carried on for many more thousands of years.

From regions widely distributed over the world come reports of ancient and extensive burning, as evidenced by the types of plants growing under various particular climatic conditions. Let me first cite the material for the southern pine area of the United States. Shantz and Zon (1924, p. 14 and their Fig. 2) designated the region "Longleaf-Loblolly-Slash Pines (Southeastern Pine Forest)" and wrote that this forest, which is like that of the drought-resistant western yellow pine, occurs where there is heavy precipitation, because of the sandy soil and evaporation.

The first Europeans in the area reported game drives by means of fire and also reported that some open prairies, such as the Shenandoah Valley, became tree-covered as soon as burning was curtailed (Maxwell, 1910). Weaver and Clements (1929, p. 512) wrote of the area as follows: "The extent of this great pine belt has naturally led to the assumption that it is climax in nature, but its ecological character, as well as actual successional studies at widely separated points, leaves little or no doubt that it is essentially a fire subclimax."

H. H. Chapman, of Yale University, directed extensive observations and experiments for about thirty years and established beyond doubt that the longleaf pine forest was dependent upon fire for its very existence. Early in the thirties Chapman (1932a, p. 603) wrote that "if complete fire protection must be enforced . . . the long-leaf pine will disappear as a species." Later he proposed (1950a, 1950b) that the longleaf pine had made a fundamental genetic, probably evolutionary, adjustment to fire. The longleaf can survive being defoliated several times and still quickly produce a remarkably large and healthy tree. Chapman thought lightning fires responsible for the genetic adjustment, but there are too few cases of lightning starting fires in the southeastern pine forest for that natural agent to have stimulated special adaptation. In this area lightning almost inevitably occurs with rain, which extinguishes any fire due to lightning strikes. Harper (1943, p. 32) suggested spontaneous combustion as the natural agent in antiquity, which over the millenniums maintained the pine forest in a hardwood area.

If ten to twenty-five thousand years would suffice for the genetic adjustment of the southern pines, the adjustment could be due to man-made fires. The Vero and Melbourne, Florida, sites, at which human skeletons were found in association with mastodon bones, suggest that the southeastern section of the United States has been inhabited by man as long as any in the New World. If it were thought that a longer time—say, a hundred thousand years—was required for evolutionary development of longleaf pine peculiarities, I believe this evidence could be taken as support for placing man's occupancy of the New World in the third interglacial.

Daubenmire (1947, pp. 331–34) lists a number of other fire plants, including the lodgepole pine, which are encouraged and multiplied by fire. Troup (1926, pp. 308–9) wrote that Burmese teak forests need fire to exist, and Gorrie (1935) reported that the cheer pine of the Himalayas was likewise dependent upon fire for survival. There are other examples of extensive forests, such as the Douglas fir of the Pacific Coast of the northwestern United States, which appear to be subclimax, and possibly dependent upon fire, in an area where lightning fires are almost unknown.

In summary, the botanical evidence just outlined leaves little doubt that fire has played a decisive role on the landscape during many thousands of years. And it seems reasonable to believe with Braun-Blanquet (1932, p. 278) that human rather than atmospheric agents were responsible:

> While prairie and forest fires may occasionally be caused by lightning, that is the exception rather than the rule. In 90 out of 100 cases they are caused by man, either willfully or accidentally. Contrary to the opinion of some American investigators, therefore, fire is to be classed among the anthropogenous factors.

Additional botanical analysis as an aid to understanding man's primeval influence on the face of the earth may be introduced by a quotation from Farmer (1953, pp. 115–17):

"The savanna is one of the most widespread landscapes of Africa. . . . It results from the tropical climate with a moderate amount of rainfall and a long spell of drought." Many of us were brought up at school to believe this statement from M. E. Hardy's *Geography of Plants* (Oxford, 1920). But few would now agree that African savanna, at least in its present aspect, is a true climax vegetation, and the same might be said of other tropical grasslands, such as the *llanos* and *campos* of South America and the *cogonales* of the Philippines. The conviction has grown that such grasslands, as we see them today, are wholly or partly man-made, the product of shifting cultivation and periodic burning. Savanna, in this view, is a fire-climax. . . . A careful study . . . is C. H. Holmes's valuable and well illustrated paper "The Grass, Fern, and Savannah Lands of Ceylon.". . . Holmes analyzes the climate of Ceylon and concludes that the climax vegetation of all seven present types [of Ceylon vegetation] is a closed forest . . . all seven types as they stand today are secondary, the result of clearing, burning, cultivation, and thereafter, periodic burning.

Troup (1926, p. 310) would add the grasslands of India to the list of those made by man.

Even though the human cause of tropical wet grassland may be established beyond doubt, the question of the prairies and plains of the temperate zone is still challenging. These are the world's greatest continuous areas of pure grass. Their size and the fact that they have been in all historic time essentially uniform and unchanged lead almost inevitably to the conclusion that they are climatically and geographically determined. Many scientists who have studied them have been steadfast in their belief that the extensive grasslands of Argentina, Russia, and North America resulted solely from the response of vegetation to precipitation, evaporation, temperature, and soil. The American prairies have been the home, training ground, and object of mature

research for the leading plant ecologists of the United States. For over fifty years botanists, geographers, ecologists, geologists, and other scientists attached to the large and respected state universities of Nebraska, Illinois, Indiana, Kansas, Iowa, Wisconsin, Ohio, Minnesota, and Missouri have studied the prairies. World-famous scholars, such as F. E. Clements, B. Shimek, and J. E. Weaver, have spent their lives analyzing the vegetation of American prairies and plains and have maintained their belief that the peculiar purity of plant cover over the whole area resulted from the fact that grass was its climax vegetation. Weaver's recent book, *North American Prairie* (1954), which presents the essence of his own forty years of research and the results obtained by many of his colleagues and students may well serve as an example of the views of American plant ecologists. According to Weaver (1954, p. 21), "climax prairie is the outcome of thousands of years of sorting out of species and adaptations to the soil and climate." Fire as a factor is dismissed with a few passing references.

Weaver (1954, p. 273) summarized his three-page section on "Effects of Burning" partly by quoting the Minnesota geographer Borchert (1950) as follows:

Fire is less destructive to grasses than to woody vegetation and it may sometimes benefit prairie where debris has accumulated over several years. This undoubtedly occurred where fires were set by lightning. The prairie and indeed the entire area of North American Grassland at time of settlement consisted of a climax vegetation, the extent of which was controlled by climate. Fire was only one of the many environmental factors. The grasses produced large amounts of dead, dry, inflammable material. Lightning often started fires. "Thus the Grassland climates favor fire, just as they favor grass whether there are fires or not. . . . Fire, if not primitive man, himself, would simply have been one part of the ecological complex of a region with the climate of the Grassland. . . . Also, the precipitation pattern of eastern America during major drought years can explain why the influence of fire was restricted to the grassland. The climate of the forests generally did not favor burning" (Borchert, 1950, pp. 38–39). After extended study of the climate of Central North America, Borchert concludes: "The geographical pattern of postulated postglacial fluctuation of the Grassland fits the facts of the recorded climate. The pattern of the Grassland at the time of white settlement also fits those facts. The patterns, themselves, suggest very strongly that they were, in the words of an earlier author, dictated by the master hand of climate."

It is the very stability and size of the temperate grasslands which make them of special value for evaluating man's influence on his environment. If the evidence would allow for a strong presumption that the great mid-latitude plains and prairies had been dependent on man's fire for their existence, then we could give much more weight to fire as the first tool with which man changed his geographic environment. Both the extent and the uniformity of the herbaceous plant cover would require a tremendous time period to achieve. And, if the temperate as well as tropical grasslands should be attributed to man, we must say that it was the hunters and gatherers, in ages before agriculture and herding, who produced such profound and permanent modification of the landscape. I believe there is considerable evidence for such a conclusion notwithstanding the contrary opinions of the many American ecologists and geographers.

There is, of course, room for differences of opinion even when the same raw data are evaluated. For example, the experiments conducted by Clements, Weaver, and Hanson (1929), cited by Weaver (1954, p. 189), demonstrated that shrubs could and did invade prairie sod. To Weaver, however, they showed only how slow such an invasion would be. There is involved here a difference of time-and-space perspective. An advance of forest onto prairie of a few feet a year may be interpreted to allow forests to replace grass only if viewed as continuing thousands of years. Not all studies confirm such a slow rate of invasion into tall-grass prairie: Chavennes (1941, p. 80) discovered that there had been a decrease of 60 per cent of Wisconsin prairie in the twenty-five years from 1829 to 1854, owing to the invasion of trees and brush following the cessation of fires and preceding cultivation. Gleason (1932, pp. 80–82) wrote of Illinois that "barrens were converted into forests as by magic when fires that had maintained them were stopped." Gleason went on to say that forests advanced into Illinois grasslands one to two miles in thirty years and also that northwestern Illinois and southwestern Wisconsin, now heavily forested where not cultivated, was 80–90 per cent prairie grassland when first visited by Europeans. And elsewhere (1913, p. 181) he wrote that "prairie fires have been the deciding factor in determining the distribution of forests in the Middle West."

Whereas Weaver (1954, p. 190) minimized the "extension of forest into prairie" by saying it "occurred in a limited manner following settlement and the cessation of prairie fires," there is abundant evidence to show that brush and trees, if given a chance, would invade virtually all the tall-grass moist prairie. The Kentucky barrens and the prairies of Ohio, Michigan, and Indiana have all been invaded by woods. The 75,000,000 acres of grassland of Texas and neighboring states have become covered with mesquite jungles. Sagebrush and juniper have invaded parts of the drier grasslands from the west, and aspen forests have crept hundreds of miles into the northern prairie as a prelude to pine.

We cannot judge from observations whether forest would eventually spread over all the grasslands, because there does not yet exist an opportunity for a fair and free competition between prairie grass and weeds, on the one hand, and brush and trees, on the other. Cultivation, overgrazing, and mowing interfere. Also, fires still sweep over vast sections of the prairie and plains so frequently that they are declared the greatest barrier to the establishment of forests and shelter belts in the Midwest. However, the fact that throughout the tall-grass prairie planted groves of many species have flourished and have reproduced seedlings during moist years and, furthermore, have survived the most severe and prolonged period of drought in the 1930's suggests that there is no climatic barrier to forests in the area. Also the success, at the driest western edge of the tall-grass prairie, of the Shelter Belt Project, made up of 16,000 miles of tree plantings extending from Canada to Texas, shows that soil and moisture are sufficient for tree growth (Anonymous, 1942, p. 456).

The Nebraska National Forest was planted in the sand hills at the driest extreme of the prairie zone in 1903, but a prairie fire spread into the planted area in 1910, destroying most of the trees. Replanted in 1911 and protected by firebreaks, the 20,000 acres of conifers have developed mature trees and true forest conditions where natural reproduction is taking place (Davis, 1951). The firebreaks have stopped several large outside grass fires from spreading into the planted area, but there is no mention of lightning igniting the forest itself.

Let us consider this question of lightning on the North American grasslands. Weaver (1954, p. 273), as quoted above, repeats an assertion frequently made that "lightning often started fires" on the prairies. I have found no evidence that lightning ignited vegetation on the plains and prairies at times and places to cause widespread grass fires. Lightning increases with elevation, and most of the fires it starts in plant cover are in the Rocky Mountains and the Sierra Nevada–Cascade ranges of western America. Even in the forests of the Wichita Mountains of Oklahoma, only twenty-six fires in four years were attributed to lightning. Plummer (1912a), in the monograph entitled *Lightning in Relation to Forest Fires*, stated that there are very few records of fires being started on the plains and prairies, and even then he is not really explicit. In fact, I have been able to discover no authentic record of any grass fire ever being ignited by lightning. This agrees with the experience of Gleason (1913, p. 176), the famous plant geographer, already quoted, who wrote that he could find "no record of a prairie fire produced by lightning."

Borchert's misconception, apparently accepted by Weaver in 1954, that in aboriginal times "the influence of fire was restricted to the grassland," may be passed over without further comment, since the record for Indian burning of all woodlands of the eastern United States is so complete (Maxwell, 1910; Day, 1953; Chapman, 1932, 1944, 1947, 1950). Another point made by Borchert (1950, pp. 38–39) and cited by Weaver is frequently found in publications of American plant ecologists. I refer to the idea that fire and primitive man as influences on the physical environment can be passed over by the simple statement that they were "one part of the ecological complex of a region." If the geographers and ecologists really acted on this expressed view, how different might be their conclusions! Unfortunately, this statement of principle is as far as they go. Whereas rainfall, snowfall, evaporation, wind, frost, temperature, etc., are measured, correlated, analyzed, and charted for each month and for many years, and these are applied to each plant and then to plant complexes, fire is treated only in a passing reference. Borchert (1950) himself gave "The Effect of Fire" one paragraph of a half-page length in his thirty-nine-page article on the climate of the American grassland. I found no other record, measurement, or analysis of the effects of fire in the dozens of Vestal's publications. Stating the principle that fire should be treated as any other part of the natural environment is not enough. It should in fact be treated and studied as fully as other ecological factors.

It is the record of vegetation burning by American Indians throughout the hemisphere from Alaska to Tierra del Fuego and from coast to coast which has led me to consider fire an ancient and powerful force in the hand of man in America. Archeology supports the opinion that fire was employed to drive game on the plains by America's first inhabitants and has been so used to the present. The American grasslands were regularly and frequently burned over at the time of European discovery and exploration.

In summarizing the effect of fire on the North American grassland, it seems reasonable to assume that, since the moist prairies can support true forests and the dry plains can support xeric brush and scattered trees, and since the trees are capable of invading the sod, some non-geographic force is critical for the formation and maintenance of grasslands in America. Fires set by man have been present for thousands of years, and lightning-set fires have been rare. Burning by primitive peoples may thus be considered a determining factor.

Although the matter has been debated for the last century, a number of scientists have preceded me in this conclusion: Marsh (1864), Christy (1892), Cook (1908), Gleason (1913, 1932), Sauer (1920, 1952), and Humphrey (1953), to name a few. Schmieder (1927) came to the same conclusion regarding the pampas of Argentina, and it appears that the evidence regarding the Russian steppes would justify a similar view. For example, Pallas (1803) saw several grass fires and implied that they occurred regularly; Mirov (1935) and Vyssotsky (1935) reported the success of shelter-belt planting on the steppes. The data on grasslands of the tropical and temperate zones of the world support the view that they have been formed and have undoubtedly been maintained by man by means of fire. The implication that man used fire as a tool in remote prehistoric times is strong.

The unrestricted burning of vegetation appears to be a universal culture trait among historic primitive peoples and therefore was probably employed by our remote ancestors. Archeology indicates that extensive areas of the Old and New Worlds were being burned over ten thousand years ago. It is logical to assume that some of the reasons which motivated historic and Neolithic men would also have motivated our remote ancestors to set vegetation on fire. One may conclude that fire has been used by man to influence his geographic environment during his entire career as a human. Furthermore, it is impossible to understand clearly the distribution and history of vegetation of the earth's land surfaces without careful consideration of fire as a universal factor influencing the plant geography of the world.

REFERENCES

ALLEN, H. H.
1937 "Origin and Distribution of the Naturalized Plants of New Zealand," *Proceedings of the Linnean Society of London*, CL, Part I, 25–47.

ANONYMOUS
1942 "Record Survival Made by Shelterbelt Trees," *Journal of Forestry*, XL, No. 6, 456.

AUBRÉVILLE, A.
1949 *Climats, forêts et désertification de l'Afrique tropicale.* Paris: Société d'Éditions Géographiques, Maritimes et Coloniales. 351 pp.

BIRKET-SMITH, KAJ
1929 *The Caribou Eskimos: Report of the Fifth Thule Expedition 1921–1924*, Vol. V, Part II. Copenhagen: Gyldendal. 419 pp.

BORCHERT, JOHN R.
1950 "The Climate of the Central North American Grassland," *Annals of the Association of American Geographers*, XL, No. 1, 1–39.

BRAUN-BLANQUET, J.
1932 *Plant Sociology.* New York: McGraw-Hill Book Co. 439 pp.

CHAPMAN, H. H.
1932*a* "Some Further Relations of Fire to Longleaf Pine," *Journal of Forestry*, XXX, No. 5, 602–5.
1932*b* "Is the Longleaf Type a Climax?" *Ecology*, XIII, 328–34.
1944 "Fire and Pines," *American Forests*, L, 62–63, 91–93.
1947 "Natural Areas," *Ecology*, XXVIII, 193–94.
1950*a* "Lightning in the Longleaf," *American Forests*, LVI, No. 1, 10–12.
1950*b* "An Unknown Pioneer in Prescribed Burning in Burma," *Journal of Forestry*, XLVIII, No. 2, 131–32.

CHAVENNES, ELIZABETH
1941 "Written Records of Forest Succession," *Scientific Monthly*, LIII (July), 76–77.

CHIPP, T. F.
1926 "Aims and Methods of Study of Tropical Countries, with Special Reference to West Africa," pp. 194–237 in TANSLEY, A. G., and CHIPP, T. F. (eds.), *Aims and Methods in the Study of Vegetation.* London:

British Empire Vegetation Committee and the Crown Agents for the Colonies. 383 pp.

CHRISTY, MILLER
1892 "Why Are the Prairies Treeless?" *Proceedings of the Royal Geographical Society and Monthly Record of Geography*, XIV, 78–100. London.

CLARK, J. G. D.
1945 "Farmers and Forests in Neolithic Europe," *Antiquity*, XIX, No. 74, 57–71.
1952 *Prehistoric Europe, the Economic Basis.* London: Methuen & Co. 349 pp.

CLEMENTS, FREDERIC E.; WEAVER, JOHN E.; and HANSON, HERBERT C.
1929 *Plant Competition.* (Publication No. 398.) Washington, D.C.: Carnegie Institution. 340 pp.

COOK, O. F.
1908 *Change of Vegetation on the South Texas Prairies.* (Bureau of Plant Industries Circular No. 14.) Washington, D.C.: U.S. Department of Agriculture. 7 pp.

DART, R. A.
1948 "The Makapansgat Proto-human *Australopithecus prometheus*," *American Journal of Physical Anthropology*, VI, 259.

DAUBENMIRE, R. F.
1947 *Plants and Environment.* New York: John Wiley & Sons. 424 pp.

DAVIS, WILFRED S.
1951 "Nebraska Firebreaks," *Fire Control Notes*, XII, No. 1, 40–46. Washington, D.C.: U.S. Department of Agriculture Forest Service.

DAY, GORDON M.
1953 "The Indian as an Ecological Factor in the Northeastern Forest," *Ecology*, XXXIV, 329–46.

EISELEY, LOREN C.
1954 "Man the Fire-maker," *Scientific American*, CXCI, 52–57.

FARMER, B. H.
1953 "Tropical Grasslands of Ceylon," *Geographical Review*, XLIII, No. 1, 115–17.

FLANNERY, REGINA
1939 *An Analysis of Coastal Algonquian Culture.* ("Anthropological Se-

ries," No. 7.) Washington, D.C.:
Catholic University of America Press.
219 pp.

FRIEDERICI, G.
1925 *Der Charakter der Entdeckung
und Eroberung Amerikas durch die
Europäer.* 3 vols. Stuttgart: Gotha.
1930 "Der Grad der Durchdringbar-
keit Nordamerikas im Zeitalter der
Entdeckungen und ersten Durchfor-
schung des Kontinents durch die Europäer," *Petermanns geographische
Mitteilungen,* CCIX, 223–26.

FRITZ, EMANUEL
1932 *The Role of Fire in the Redwood Region.* (Circular No. 323.)
Berkeley: University of California
Agriculture Extension Service. 22 pp.

GLEASON, HENRY ALLEN
1913 "The Relation of Forest Distribution and Prairie Fires to the Middle
West," *Torreya,* XIII, 173–81.
1932 "The Vegetational History of the
Middle West," *Annals of the Association of American Geographers,* XII,
39–85.

GORRIE, R. MACLAGAN
1935 "Protective Burning in Himalayan Pine," *Journal of Forestry,*
XXXVIII, 807–11.

GRAJDANZEV, ANDREW J.
1944 *Modern Korea.* New York: John
Day Co. 330 pp.

HARPER, ROLAND M.
1943 *Forests of Alabama.* (Monograph No. 10.) University, Ala.: Geologic Survey of Alabama. 230 pp.

HERODOTUS
1936 *History.* Trans. GEORGE RAW-
LINSON; ed. MANUEL KOMROFF. New
York: Tudor Publishing Co. 544 pp.

HOLMES, C. H.
1951 *The Grass, Fern, and Savannah
Lands of Ceylon: Their Nature and
Ecological Significance.* (Institute
Paper No. 28.) Oxford: University
of Oxford Imperial Forestry Institute.
95 pp.

HOUGH, WALTER
1926 *Fire as an Agent in Human Culture.* (Bulletin No. 139.) Washington, D.C.: United States National
Museum. 270 pp.

HUMPHREY, R. R.
1953 "The Desert Grassland, Past and
Present," *Journal of Range Management,* VI, 159–64.

KEEN, F. P.
1940 "Longevity of Ponderosa Pine,"
Journal of Forestry, XXXVIII, 597–
98.

KROEBER, A. L.
1939 "Culture Element Distributions,
XI: Tribes Surveyed," *University of
California Anthropological Records,*
I, No. 7, 435–40.

KUHNHOLTZ-LORDAT, G.
1939 *La Terre incendiée.* Nîmes,
France: Éditions de la Maison Cairée
Ateliers Bruguier. 361 pp.

LUCRETIUS
1908 *On the Nature of the Universe.*
Trans. from the Latin by H. A. J
MUNRO. London: George Bell & Sons.
267 pp.

LUNDELL, CYRUS LONGWORTH
1934 *Preliminary Sketch of the Phyto-
geography of the Yucatan Peninsula.*
(Publication No. 436.) Washington,
D.C.: Carnegie Institution. 355 pp.

LUTZ, H. J.
1930 "The Vegetation of Heart's Content: A Virgin Forest in Northwestern Pennsylvania," *Ecology,* XI, 1–29.

MARSH, G. P.
1864 *Man and Nature.* New York:
C. Scribner & Co. 560 pp.

MAXWELL, HU
1910 "The Use and Abuse of Forests
by the Virginia Indians," *William and
Mary College Historical Magazine,*
XIX, 86–104.

MIROV, N. T.
1935 "Two Centuries of Afforestation
and Shelterbelt Planting on the Russian Steppes," *Journal of Forestry,*
XXXIII, 971–73.

MOIR, J. REID
1919 *Pre-Palaeolithic Man.* Ipswich:
W. E. Harrison; London: Simpkin,
Marshall, Hamilton, Kent & Co. 67
pp.

OSBORN, HENRY FAIRFIELD
1927 *Man Rises to Parnassus.* Princeton, N.J.: Princeton University Press.
216 pp.

PALLAS, P. S.
1803 *Travels through the Southern
Provinces of the Russian Empire in*

the Years 1793 and 1794. 2 vols. London: A. Strahan.

PLUMMER, FRED G.
1912a *Lightning in Relation to Forest Fires.* (Bulletin No. 111.) Washington, D.C.: U.S. Department of Agriculture Forest Service. 39 pp.
1912b *Forest Fires.* (Bulletin No. 117.) Washington, D.C.: U.S. Department of Agriculture Forest Service. 39 pp.

SAUER, CARL O.
1920 *Geography of the Ozark Highland of Missouri.* Chicago: University of Chicago Press (for the Geographical Society of Chicago). 245 pp.
1927 *Geography of the Pennyroyal.* ("Kentucky Geological Survey," Series VI, Vol. XXV.) Frankfort. 299 pp.
1944 "A Geographic Sketch of Early Man in America," *Geographical Review,* XXXIV, 529–73.
1947 "Early Relations of Man to Plants," *ibid.,* XXXVII, 1–25.
1950 "Grassland Climax, Fire, and Man," *Journal of Range Management,* III, 16–22.
1952 *Agricultural Origins and Dispersals.* (Bowman Memorial Lectures, Series Two.) New York: American Geographical Society. 110 pp.

SCHMIEDER, O.
1927 "The Pampa," *University of California Publications in Geography,* II, No. 8, 255–70.

SEIFRIZ, WILLIAM
1934 "The Plant Life of Russian Lapland," *Ecology,* XV, 306–18.

SEMPLE, ELLEN CHURCHILL
1931 *The Geography of the Mediterranean Region.* New York: Henry Holt & Co. 737 pp.

SHANTZ, H. L.
1947 *The Use of Fire as a Tool in the Management of the Brush Ranges of California.* Sacramento: California State Board of Forestry. 156 pp.

SHANTZ, H. L., and ZON, RAPHAEL
1924 *Atlas of American Agriculture: Natural Vegetation.* Washington, D.C.: U.S. Department of Agriculture. 29 pp.

SHIMEK, B.
1911 "The Prairies," *Contributions from the Laboratories of Natural History,* VI, No. 2, 169–224. (Bulletin No. 35.) State University of Iowa.

STEFANSSON, VILHJALMUR
1913 *My Life with the Eskimo.* New York: Macmillan Co. 538 pp.

STEWART, O. C.
1943 "Notes on Pomo Ethnogeography," *University of California Publications in American Archeology and Ethnology,* XL, 29–62.
1951 "Burning and Natural Vegetation in the United States," *Geographical Review,* XLI, 317–20.
1953 "Why the Great Plains Are Treeless," *Colorado Quarterly,* II, 40–50. Boulder.
1954 "The Forgotten Side of Ethnogeography," pp. 221–48 in SPENCER, R. (ed.), *Methods and Perspectives in Anthropology: Essays in Honor of Wilson D. Wallis.* Minneapolis: University of Minnesota Press. 323 pp.

STOECKELER, JOSEPH H.
1945 "Narrow Shelterbelts for the Southern Great Plains," *Soil Conservation,* XI, No. 1, 16–20. Washington, D.C.: U.S. Department of Agriculture.

TANSLEY, A. G., and CHIPP, T. F. (eds.)
1926 *Aims and Methods in the Study of Vegetation.* London: British Empire Vegetation Committee and the Crown Agents for the Colonies. 383 pp.

TROUP, R. S.
1926 "Problems of Forest Ecology in India," pp. 283–313 in TANSLEY, A. G., and CHIPP, T. F. (eds.), *Aims and Methods of the Study of Vegetation.* London: British Empire Vegetation Committee and the Crown Agents for the Colonies. 383 pp.

VERGIL
1947 *Georgics.* Trans. from the Latin by C. DAY LEWIS. New York: Oxford University Press. 83 pp.

VIOSCA, PERCY, JR.
1931 "Spontaneous Combustion in the Marshes of Southern Louisiana," *Ecology,* XII, 439–42.

Vyssotsky, G. N.
1935 "Shelterbelt in the Steppes of Russia," *Journal of Forestry*, XXXIII, 781–88.

Weaver, J. E.
1954 *North American Prairie*. Lincoln, Neb.: Johnsen Publishing Co. 348 pp.

Weaver, J. E., and Clements, F. E.
1929 *Plant Ecology*. New York: Mc-Graw-Hill Book Co. 601 pp.

Werner, A.
1906 *The Natives of British Central Africa*. London: A. Constable. 303 pp.

Early Food-producing Populations

KARL J. NARR[*]

Man's contest with external nature is expressed in two different ways: *adaptation* to and *changing* of a given environment. Adaptation may be a matter of organic evolution as well as of intellectual power. To meet the rigors of a cold climate, for instance, some animals developed a coat of hair as the result of a change in the germ plasm. But man can adapt himself to life in the same environment by inventing and making coats. Creative spiritual actions thus form an exclusively human way of adaptation, man's compensation for his relatively poorly endowed body being his superior intellect, which brought forth the typical human phenomenon of culture. In the course of history man created new industries and new economies that have furthered the increase of his species. With growth of population and addition of skills, he did not confine himself to mere adaptation but changed more and more of the surrounding world until he became in many regions the ecologic dominant. Man also affected the course of organic evolution, in particular, when he began to control his food supply by cultivating plants and breeding animals, finally displacing both from their original biome and habitat, either subsequently transforming an environment by that artificial exotic invasion or previously preparing the new area for the reception of the exotic plants and/or animals in question. Thus the growing intensity of new economies answering the want for food exhibits a logical relation to man's increasing role in changing the face of the earth.

[*] Dr. Narr is Scientific Assistant at the Seminar für Ur- und Frühgeschichte of the Georg-August University at Göttingen, Germany. Primarily a prehistorian, he focuses his research on problems which concern the synthesis of archeological work with geological, environmental, anthropological, and ethnological studies. His publications include contributions to the international manual, *Historia mundi:* "Das höhere Jägertum: Jüngere Jagd- und Sammelstufe" ("Developed Hunting: the Later Stage of Hunting and Gathering") and "Hirten, Pflanzer, Bauern: Produktionsstufe" ("Herdsmen, Plant Cultivators, and Peasants: The Stage of Food Production"), 1952–53; and "Formengruppen und Kulturkreise im europäischen Paläolithikum: Stand und Aufgaben der Altsteinzeitforschung" ("Form Complexes and Culture Areas in the European Paleolithic: State and Tasks of Researches into the Old Stone Age"), 1954. His book, *Das rheinische Jungpaläolithikum: Zugleich ein Beitrag zur Chronologie der späten Altsteinzeit Mittel- und Westeuropas* ("The Rhenish Upper Paleolithic: A Contribution to the Chronology of the Upper Paleolithic of Middle and Western Europe"), is in press.

PRELUDE: COLLECTORS AND HUNTER-FISHERS

Among populations whose economy is confined to mere hunting and gathering, adaptation to the environment evidently plays a far greater part than change. Variations of climate and the appearance and disappearance, increase and decrease, of particular plants and animals are able to stimulate new demands which can be appeased only by the invention of new methods of hunting and new weapons and implements.

134

This has already been conjectured for some groups as early as the Lower Paleolithic (Narr, 1953*b*). On the other hand, cultures of this simple kind, once adapted to a particular biome, showed a general tendency to cling to the latter. This, too, is almost certainly true for the earliest times, but the rich evidence of the Upper Paleolithic provides examples which can be far better demonstrated than those from the poorly documented Lower Paleolithic. Thus we see, for instance, that the East Gravettian mammoth hunters extended the limits of their area of distribution with the progressing loess steppe in full glacial times (but apparently avoided the completely treeless loess tundra—a phenomenon that might be explained by requirement of wood for fire and, perhaps, for the construction of the well-known semisubterranean dwellings). Also, we see that the West Magdalenian hunters of reindeer, horse, and red deer preferred life in the park tundra and followed the pioneering pines and birches (and the animals attached to this environment) when they entered the plains of northwestern Germany and the Netherlands at the end of the Ice Age (Narr, 1954). Nevertheless, a certain amount of new, though eventually minor, adaptations were required. The plains north of the German and Belgian central range of mountains completely lack the caves and rock shelters which facilitated the life of the Magdalenian hunters in their Franco-Cantabrian homeland. Huts and tents (like those fortunately discovered by Rust [1948, 1951] in northern Germany and the Netherlands) must have played a far greater part and been of different type, perhaps, than those in southwestern France and northern Spain. To be sure, the attachment of certain cultures to a particular environment must not be overestimated or made a general and unconditional rule. Regarding the early spread of mankind over the whole *oiku-*

mene, we can postulate that Paleolithic man was able to overcome the barriers of nature. But we need not insist on that problem. The critical question for our theme is whether, or to what degree, the activities of hunting and gathering populations altered or did not alter the aspect of the earth.

There can be no doubt that early hunting and food-gathering people possessed certain means of altering their environment. At first thought, one may be tempted to consider hunters specialized in a distinct species of animals as having disturbed the ecologic equilibrium by diminishing the number of their prey, until finally destroying the hunters' very base of sustenance. (See also Darling, pp. 778–87.) But it is very improbable that even Upper Paleolithic and Mesolithic man killed more game with his still-primitive weapons than could be replenished by annual increase under normal ecologic conditions. Moreover, it may be thought that prehistoric hunters preserved game to a certain degree, as many of our primitive contemporaries also do. Among recent hunting populations it is a general rule not to kill more game than is needed, and, frequently, this is sanctioned by ethical codes and religious beliefs.

Certainly there was also a tendency toward the making of clearings of a sort by collectors and hunters of the Old and Middle Stone Age. Around their more or less temporary camps, shrubs, brushes, and small trees needed for the construction of windbreaks and huts and as fuel were removed. Clearing an area caused changes of vegetation around the camps, such as the stimulation of chenopods, by the accumulation of organic refuse. This has been demonstrated for the northern Mesolithic by pollen analytical work (Iversen, 1941), but similar processes can be supposed for other times and regions. (See also Sears, p. 475.) To be sure, the way of life of shifting hunters and collectors prevented permanent changes. Moreover, they affected but small patches.

If one could have flown over northern Europe in Mesolithic times, it is doubtful whether more than an occasional wisp of smoke from some campfire, or maybe a small cluster of huts or shelters by a river bank or an old lake bed, would have advertised the presence of man: in all essentials the forest would have stretched unbroken, save only by mountain, swamp and water, to the margins of the sea [Clark, 1952, pp. 91–92].

Indeed, the damp forests of Mesolithic northern Europe could not be ignited easily. But what about less dense, coniferous woods, park tundras, and savannas, especially in plains, with dry seasons or in periods of a generally drier climate? Under such conditions, campfires which had been left unwatched or fire drives, which almost certainly must have been practiced during the Old Stone Age (Soergel, 1922), or even the setting of fires to burn off the brushwood could have done extensive work in clearing the forests. Fortunately, this is no mere deduction. During the Allerødian climatic period the flatlands north of the German and Belgian central range of mountains were occupied by forests of pines and birches. At the very end of that period, in the transitional so-called "Usselo horizon," when the climate again was becoming colder and drier, the existence of great forest fires is documented by rather thick layers of charcoal and even carbonized trunks, at several sites in the Netherlands and in northern Germany. These strata frequently contain artifacts, fireplaces, and other refuse of the camps of late Magdalenian hunters. The best-explored sites are Usselo, Twente (as yet unpublished excavations by Hijszeler; see also Schwabedissen, 1954),[1] and Rissen near Hamburg (Schwabedissen, 1951, 1954). There is no proof, of course, that it was Paleolithic man who, either by carelessness or to improve hunting and the berry harvest (e.g., Stewart, pp. 118–24, 125), set fire to the forests. But the possibility, or even probability, thereof cannot be denied. With this restriction in mind, we may suppose that the sudden decrease of pines and birches which marks the beginning of the colder and drier Later Dryas period is due partially to the activities of man. We may suppose that comparable phenomena would also be revealed in other periods and regions, for instance, in the French "Paradise of Early Man," if similar conditions of preservation had prevailed there (or, perhaps, if excavations were not so exclusively confined to the easily discoverable and most promising cave sites).

NEOLITHIC AGRICULTURE AND PASTORALISM

Adhering to the approved advice of Aristotle that the essentials of a phenomenon are best understood if one tries to explore their rise from the very beginnings, we first should inquire about the *origins of food production* and its bearing on changes of environment. Alas! The state of our knowledge does not permit such an inquiry, for the question of agricultural and pastoral origins is still controversial. One theory favors the view that, from a common cradle of mixed farming, which is to be located in the lands of the Fertile Crescent, the new food-producing economy spread in different directions. One of these led into the steppes of Eurasia, where the culture was altered into a completely pastoral and nomadic one—a process which was furthered by environmental factors. A second theory hinges on different origins of plant cultivation and stock-raising, respectively. Spreading into the other continents of

1. From economical and environmental points of view the site of Usselo is especially interesting because of the great amount of crowberries found there.

the Old World, the two economies met each other and intermingled in the region of the Fertile Crescent or adjacent countries, thus giving rise to mixed farming.

A few years ago the author tried to evaluate the different arguments (Narr, 1953a). In the meantime fresh evidence and new reconsiderations have been brought forward in favor of both theories (Jettmar, 1953, 1954; Pohlhausen, 1954a, 1954b). On the whole, however, the evidence available today does not permit a definite decision. No doubt the archeological record proves that mixed farming (full agriculture combined with stock-raising) was already in existence at the latest by the fifth millennium B.C. (Some sites between northern Iran and Nubia seem to hint that transhumance may have been an early, or perhaps the earliest, form of mixed farming.) But the archeological record still is very meager or nonexistent for the centers of full nomadic pastoralism and semiagriculture (in the sense of Hatt in Curwen and Hatt, 1953), respectively. (Moreover, nomadic herdsmen, living in tents and using implements of perishable material, are less likely to leave recognizable traces than full agriculturists; roots and tuberous plants cultivated by semiagriculturists will be found among cultural refuse only under exceptionally favorable conditions of preservation.)

On completely theoretical foundations we can establish several levels of food production based upon the relation of the respective domesticated plants and/or animals to the original environment.

STAGE 1.—*Domesticated plants and animals remain within the biome and habitat of their wild ancestors.* The newly found capacity to domesticate certain kinds of animals spread over parts, or the whole, of the region of natural distribution of the species in question but did not surpass the ecologic limits of the species. Examples: The tame reindeer inhabits only the same regions as its wild cousins do or did. Several plants of primitive agriculture in the southern woodlands remained therein.

STAGE 2.—*Man brings domesticated plants and animals out of their original biome and habitat.* This can be done in two different ways:

SUBSTAGE 2a.—*Plants and animals are transplanted into, and accustomed to, a new environment.* The new area subsequently is altered by the effects of that exotic invasion. Examples: Selection of more resistant sorts of cultivated plants can allow the introduction of cultivation into regions where agriculture hitherto had been impossible. Man also was capable of moving domesticated animals into habitats devoid of their wild ancestors. Goats are brought from the mountainous countries into valleys and plains and sheep from the slopes of high hills. Grazing pressure (and protection against predators) may then alter the ecosystem of the newly occupied area.

SUBSTAGE 2b.—*Plants and animals are transplanted into an artificially prepared area.* The environment has previously been adjusted to the exotic invaders. Examples: Woodland is cleared to suit it for the sowing of grains and thus is transformed into a kind of artificial steppe. Brush and trees are removed by burning, to promote or make possible growth of grass and herbs, thereby improving pasture for animals originally adapted (or accustomed by man) to grassland.

The above classification shows an intensification of change in the physical-biological environment by the activities of man. Perhaps it should be stressed that it is only a classification of phenomena which must not be mistaken for an established historic sequence. While it undoubtedly contains elements of a true evolutionary sequence, nevertheless this cannot be taken as a decision a priori but has to be established by careful historical inquiry for each separate case. Confusion of a theoretical evolutionary system (like that constructed by H. L. Morgan and E. B. Tylor, which even today is not yet overcome completely) with a historical sequence of cultural and economic levels has caused trouble enough. *Vestigia terrent!*

Consequently, it is our task, as culture historian, to examine whether the historic changing of the face of the earth by early food-producing populations affords a picture which can be related to the above classification. As already indicated, this is as yet impossible to do completely. At present we can but select some examples from times and regions where the state of research provides sufficient evidence. But even that is practically impossible for the earliest decisive periods of food-producing economies. Mixed farming, for instance, was practiced very early in the valleys of the Nile, the Euphrates, and the Tigris. Yet the oldest sites where mixed farming, probably transhumance, can be affirmed are not situated near the banks of these great rivers, as has been believed previously, but rather on some of the adjacent plains and foothills. In the streamlands of the Fertile Crescent the face of the earth was deeply changed by the irrigation activities of man, yet it cannot even be decided whether or not irrigation began to be practiced by some rather early communities of farmers during the fifth millennium B.C. Was irrigation eventually the "Response" to the menacing "Challenge" of the encroaching desert (expressed in layers of drift sand in the refuse of occupation sites, such as the Faiyûm and Merimde)? Or was it invented only in connection with the "Urban Revolution" of the late fourth or early third millennium B.C.?

Examples which give a satisfactory picture of the economic system of an early food-producing population and its bearing on changes of the environment can be selected only from the better explored regions of Europe. But such regions are far removed in space and time from the supposed cradle, or cradles, of plant cultivation and stock-raising. Nevertheless, it seems more useful to consider some food-producing populations of the European Neolithic than to lose our way in a labyrinth of mere theoretical deductions.

Danubian Farmers of the Early Neolithic: Clearance in the Wooded Loess Lands of Middle Europe

The so-called "Danubian" culture represents the earliest definitely known farming population in Middle Europe. To be sure, the name "Danubian" is somewhat misleading, for the bulk of Danubian sites lies north of the Danube, stretching from Hungary into the southern fringes of the northern German plains and from the Vistula to Belgium (and by a few spurs even into the region of Paris). The term "Danubian" customarily is used in a wide sense to include some rather different Neolithic groups of Central Europe and the Balkans. But here it will be used only in the strict sense of *Bandkeramik* (as defined by Milojčić, 1951, and roughly corresponding to the "Danubian I" of Childe, 1950*a*). Though the Danubian is related to some early Neolithic groups of Hungary and the Balkans, this relation is almost exclusively confined to rather general economic elements, namely, similar cereals and domesticated animals. The typological elements, in particular the ceramics, show quite distinct patterns. The Danubian, therefore, may best be classified as a civilization that, by its basic economic traits, ultimately comes from the great "oriental drift" (Schachermeyr, 1954) but which also has developed many elements of its own (perhaps by action of an indigenous pre-Neolithic substratum as yet practically unknown). This justifies our speaking of a quite distinct and particular culture, the origin of which lies in Moravia, Bohemia, and the adjacent parts of central Germany.

The absolute age of the Danubian is still controversial. There is convincing archeological evidence that the closing stage of its older part is contemporaneous with the Starčewo III—Vinča A horizons of the Balkanic sequence, which, in their turn, by correlation with Mediterranean groups, can be dated in the older centuries of the third millennium B.C., perhaps stretching to the middle of the latter (Milojčić, 1949, 1951). The beginning of the Danubian is a crucial question, for we cannot say with certainty whether it parallels the older levels within the "oriental drift" or of what age these are. Natural science seems to favor a rather early date, perhaps around 4000 B.C.[2] As yet we cannot state much more than that the commencement of the Danubian can be placed somewhere between the closing of the fifth and the beginning of the third millennium B.C. The Later Danubian lasted until its replacement by other Neolithic cultures within the centuries around 2000 B.C.

The archeological record of the Danubian consists mainly of domestic sites. This is a happy circumstance for our theme, because it provides us with a sufficiently complete picture of the general way of life of that ancient farming population (Buttler, 1938; Childe, 1950a; Tackenberg, 1953; Danthine, 1954). The Danubian economy was

based on the cultivation of barley, one-grained wheat (*Einkorn*), emmer, at least in some regions, and, perhaps, bread wheat,[3] beans, peas, lentils, and flax. Stock-breeding was apparently practiced on a rather small scale, for only relatively few bones of dogs, oxen, sheep, and pigs turn up in the settlement refuse. The Danubian peasants preferred the well-drained and fertile loess soils, which are exceptionally easy to work (see the instructive map of Clark, 1952, p. 96). Moreover, in some regions they seem to have selected particular kinds of loess. In the northern Rhineland, for instance, Danubian set-

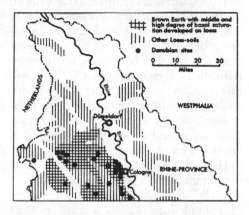

Fig. 51.—Soils and Neolithic sites in the northern Rhineland, showing the Danubian. (After Tackenberg and Mückenhausen.)

tlements (as well as those of the peasants of the late Bronze Age) are restricted to the southern parts of the loess region, where the loess layers are less thick than in the northern parts (Steeger, 1932; Uslar, 1951) and where the brown earth (centuries earlier and more intensely tilled) shows a higher degree of basal saturation (Mückenhausen, 1952). (See Fig. 51.)

It is quite unlikely that the Danubian peasants knew the plow. Because of the lack of corresponding traces on the

2. Radiocarbon datings suggest a date within the centuries around 4000 B.C.; but, as this method is still in its infancy, one has to be careful not to infer too much from its results. Pollen-analysis examinations show an amount of grain pollen, which has to be ascribed to Danubian grain cultivation, in the middle of the Atlantic period. The Atlantic period has been dated by indirect correlation with varve series as between about 5500 and 2500 B.C. (Munthe, 1940) or about 4600 and 2000 B.C. (Florin, 1944), respectively.

3. Emmer is reported from the Rhineland and Belgium; bread wheat, from Poland (Childe, 1950a, p. 97).

tools in question, it must be denied that rather clumsy axes and other stone implements were used as plowshares, as has been suggested by some authors. We must suppose that the agricultural technique of the Danubians was a kind of hoe cultivation, though the implements for tilling the soil are still unknown, with the possible exception of kinds of perforated "maceheads" which, in reality, may have been used as charging stones for digging sticks. The Danubian hoes seem to have been made of wood,[4] since the so-called "flat hoes" and "shoe-last celts" of stone were almost certainly not used for cultivation but as carpenters' implements (Rieth, 1949–50). Carpentry played a great part in the life of the Danubian peasants, because they lived in great rectangular wooden buildings, up to more than 40 meters in length (Paret, 1946; Stieren, 1951), which were grouped together in villages surrounded by palisades. The quest for wood of a Danubian community must have covered a considerable area.

Hoe cultivators who, by lack of a corresponding degree of stock-breeding, did not have a sufficient resource of animal dung almost certainly must have practiced shifting cultivation. When, after a few easy crops, the available ground within easy reach had been exploited, the Danubians passed on to fresh grounds not too far distant. Eventually, after this procedure occurred several times, and the soil of the earlier sites had regenerated sufficiently, the people returned to their old dwelling places, or these areas were occupied by a kindred group. There is convincing evidence that the famous settlement of Köln-Lindenthal near Cologne was abandoned and resettled at least seven times within a period of a few hundred

4. Among recent primitive hoe cultivators also, the use of tilling implements of stone is almost unknown (Hoeltker, 1947; for one of the rare exceptions see Purse-Stanek, 1953).

years (Sangmeister, 1951; Buttler and Haberey, 1936).

The loess lands were once hailed as an open corridor through the hostile forest. This view is rather incompatible with the great need for wood among the Danubians. Moreover, the general picture of the Central European vegetation in Atlantic times shows that the loess soils supported a friendly, mixed-oak forest. This is also verified by the examination of soil profiles (Tüxen, 1931; Garnett, 1945; Schwarz, 1948). This forest must have allowed a growth of foliage in addition to the fattening acorns on which cattle and swine could feed. The assumption of settlement in wooded countries implies a deduction which is most important for our theme, namely, that the Danubian peasants cleared the forests. "Slash and burn" (Brandwirtschaft) is the method which could easily have been practiced by Neolithic man. Recent experiments have shown that extensive clearings could have been made with Neolithic stone tools and that felled mixed-oak forests could successfully have been burned even while the wood was still green. Moreover, these experiments demonstrate that cereals grew luxuriantly in the burned area, in contrast to an unburned one (P., E., 1954). Thus, at first, small patches and, gradually, greater parts of the Central European woodland were transformed into a kind of artificial steppe. To be sure, this procedure slackened by the shifting of settlements, which allowed the forest to regenerate without serious depredations of grazing animals. On the other hand, the newly regenerated plots may have remained attractive, compared with the original virgin forests. Because of the probably long duration of the Danubian culture and the shifting of settlements, the density of the Danubian population may not have been so great as one is tempted to assume when regarding the densely dotted distribution maps. But our knowledge of sites certainly reflects only a small part of the true settlement. The pressure of population on the desirable loess soils in the closing stages of Danubian civilization may indeed have been great enough to permit J. G. D. Clark to say (1952, p. 97) that "new communities have continually hived off from the old ones, so that ultimately the point was reached when clearance outstripped the capacity of the woodlands to regenerate themselves."

The Loess Lands of Northwestern Europe: The Problem of the Campignian (Hunter-Collectors or Clearing Farmers[?])

A very interesting problem is posed in the loess lands of France and Belgium. The westernmost compact Danubian province is formed by the settlements in the Belgian Hesbaye, where penetration seems to have been rather short and late. The Belgian Danubian ("Omalien"), which shows close affinities to the Rhenish styles of Plaidt and Cologne, corresponds only to the later stages (III–IV, and perhaps II, of the sequence at Köln-Lindenthal near Cologne) and, therefore, is to be placed within the centuries around the middle and before the end of the third millennium B.C. Only a scanty offshoot is represented by a few finds in the loess regions of northwestern France. The same country is occupied by a very interesting, though highly problematic, civilization, namely, the Campignian. The bulk of the typical Campignian (the "facies d'habitation" of the "Campignien classique" of Nougier, 1950), lies in northwestern France, where the Danubian is very poorly represented, whereas in Belgium only a few sites attest the presence of the Campignian (Fig. 52, p. 142).

The Campignian is known mainly through its industry of chipped (not polished!) silex with predominance of picks and tranchets. Its typological relations to the Mesolithic forest cultures of northern Germany, the Baltic lands, and Scandinavia are so close that it almost certainly is to be interpreted as a genetic connection. There is as yet no convincing and well-established third group which could claim to be the common ancestor of both, but this may be partially due to a certain lack of archeological research in some of the countries in question. Nevertheless, on the evidence available today, one may be justified in trying to derive the one from the other: the Campignian from the northern Mesolithic forest cultures, or vice versa. This latter possibility has been denied by some historians, because some aspects of the Campignian industry occur only in the later stages of the northern sequence[5] (Oldesloe-Gudenaa and Ertebölle), which belong to the Atlantic climatic period of the postglacial. In the northern woodland cultures these can be derived from the older stages, whereas a possible comparable ancestor is completely lacking in the Campignian region. However, it is very troubling that no continental group is known which might establish a sufficiently direct link between both. The "Præ-Campignian" of Nougier (1950) has, at least partially, to be taken cautiously, for its sites are very doubtful or, as in the case of the Belgian sites in the vicinity of Aubel, represent a lateral (and late) offshoot. On the other hand, the Mesolithic forest cultures extended to England by the only possible way—over land which today is covered by the North Sea (Schwabedissen, 1952). This land route must still have been in existence at the beginning of the Atlantic period. (Its submergence may have pushed people from the North Sea land to the east and

5. See also the review of Nougier's book (1950) by Schwabedissen, 1952.

southwest, respectively.) The distribution of the typical Campignian gives the impression, in fact, of a bridgehead attached to the English Channel (see the map of Nougier, 1950, p. 541, where the "Præ-Campignian" has to be held in question). Moreover, the typical Campignian shows close affinities to the Mesolithic cultures of England in Atlantic times, in particular, the Lower Halstow group.

The question of the age of the Campignian is intimately linked with its origins. If the typological and genetic connection with the northern forest cultures is taken for granted, one conse-

quently has to assume the beginning of the Atlantic period as a *terminus post quem* for the Campignian development, say, a date about the middle of the sixth or fifth millennium B.C.[6] On the other hand, the later stage of the Campignian (the "Post-Campignian" of Nougier, 1950) shows admixtures of the "Western Neolithic" ("Neolithic lacustre" or "Robenhausien," of an antiquated terminology still used by some

6. The middle of the Atlantic period has been dated at 5500 and 2500 B.C. (Munthe, 1940) and 4600 and 1950 B.C. (Florin, 1944) by indirect correlation with varve series. See also n. 2, p. 139.

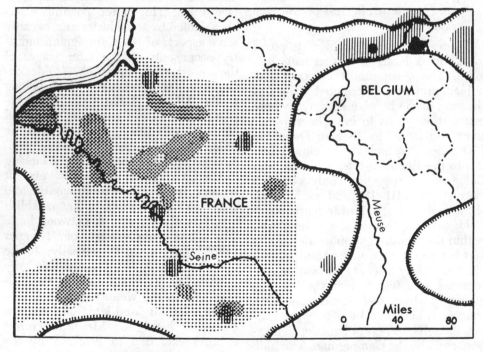

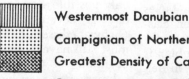

Westernmost Danubian

Campignian of Northern France

Greatest Density of Campignian sites

● Campignian sites in Belgium

〰〰〰 Approximate limits of loess

FIG. 52.—Loess lands of northwestern Europe, showing Danubian and Campignian. (After Buttler, Destexhe-Jamotte, Hamal-Nandrin, and Nougier, with additions.)

authors) and ultimately merged with the latter, giving rise to some special technical facies. Thus the introduction of the "Western Neolithic," which has to be placed in the centuries around 2000 B.C., provides us with a *terminus ante quem*. In Belgium the "Western Neolithic" is later than the Danubian. The Campignian's being closely connected in time with the "Western Neolithic" but showing no marked influences of the Danubian[7] prompts some Belgian prehistorians to place it into a supposed lag of time between the Danubian and the "Western Neolithic" (Destexhe-Jamotte, 1953; Philippe, 1953). That might be true for Belgium, where the pure Campignian is very rare, but does not exclude a greater, though as yet not exactly determined, age of the latter in the other parts of its area of distribution, namely, in northwestern France, where the Danubian, for the most part, is very poorly represented. Because of the general chronological position of both cultures, a partial contemporaneousness of the Campignian and Danubian seems highly probable, though it must be admitted that archeologically verified connections are extremely scanty and by no means cogent.[8]

The Campignians are considered by many authors to be a plant-cultivating population even in the early stages of that civilization. An extreme theory regards them as "the first to put their seal on the landscape, which is henceforth 'humanized,' . . . the founders of [the] Western rural life, . . . the first peasants of the West" (Nougier, 1950, p. 534). If this point of view is granted, one has to assume that the Campignians were the first to clear the forests on the French loess lands (there being no reasonable evidence that eventually these countries were not wooded in Atlantic times). No doubt, the Campignian stone tools were fitted to deal with trees and wood, though the polished ax is superior to the chipped ax.

If one takes the Mesolithic peoples of the northern woodlands who were hunter-collectors and fishers attached to the postglacial forest as the probable ancestors of the Campignian, at once the question rises whence the assumed peasant life of the "typical" Campignian took its origins. Did those early Campignians themselves invent a food-producing culture of their own, or did they learn it from an already existing farming population with which they may have been in contact? In the latter respect one might think of the Danubians, as do Stokar (1942, p. 11) and Corbeil (1949).

But, first of all, we must ask whether the assumption of peasant life of the "typical" Campignians is really substantiated. Finds of some grinding stones and a few bones of dogs, cattle, and pigs form the only direct evidence. Even if the context with the "typical" Campignian implements of the sites in question is proved, that does not demon-

7. However, one could ask whether several Campignian picks which, by their general shape and, in particular, by their cross-section (but not by technique and material!), closely resemble the Danubian "shoe-last celts" (e.g., Nougier, 1950, Fig. 35) are not possibly signs which indicate that a foreign principle of form was taken over by indigenous workers using their old technique and accustomed material. A parallel may be demonstrated by "mace-heads" of Campignian tradition, which also seem to copy those of true Neolithic civilizations by applying the inherited technique of chipping flint to the borrowed form (Nougier, 1949, 1950).

8. Picks with a triangular and subtriangular cross-section also turned up in some domestic sites of the Danubian and the "Western Neolithic" (Hamal-Nandrin and Servais, 1928). A formidable pick has also been found at Köln-Lindenthal in a pit of the Later Danubian (Buttler and Haberey, 1936, Pl. 69, 14). However, this form occurs also in the "Western Neolithic" of Campignian tradition, though an overlap in time of the latter with the Danubian is as yet unproved but not unreasonable, since these groups preferred different soils.

strate that these "early" Campignians themselves practiced farming and stock-breeding. The findings are too sporadic to rule out the possibility, or even probability, that they belong to a relatively late occurrence which already had undergone influences by penetration of true Neolithic peasants. (The same is valid also for the whole question of the Campignian ceramics.) Moreover, isolated finds of that kind, within a culture that lived in the neighborhood of (or even overlapped spatially and chronologically) a well-established farming population (such as the Danubians), can also be explained in terms of symbiosis and barter or like possibilities.

Furthermore, it has been argued that a kind of indirect evidence is given by the predilection for loess soils, which, by this theory, are regarded as open "prairies" inviting the early plant-cultivators (Nougier, 1950). But that new infusion of the old theory of a natural late postglacial steppe heath (*Steppenheidetheorie*) is certainly not in conformity with modern views of the vegetational picture of postglacial, in particular, "Atlantic," Europe. Therefore we must ask ourselves whether the "typical" Campignians were not a mere hunting and collecting population (as the people of the northern Mesolithic were, too) who preferred the loess soils because they supported a wooded country of a kind that facilitated their habitual way of life as hunter-collectors attached to a like environment (Forde, 1930; Philippe, 1953).

Thus, the Campignian problem, though of no great direct value for our theme, may stand here as a warning that one must not conclude too much from general, though sometimes attractive, views. Even though the ecologic conditions of an area are well explored, one cannot deduce the economy of its former inhabitants from a densely dotted distribution map. The economic

state of a prehistoric population can be established only by sufficient excavations of a kind still lacking for the French Campignian. To study the result of man's activities on the environment, we first have to gain a sufficient conception of these activities themselves. Only then can we hope to understand what happened to a certain environment, even if there is no direct evidence.

"Pastoral Farmers" of the Late Neolithic and Early Bronze Age: The Growth of the Heath

Precious direct evidence for changes of the environment is provided by pollen analysis. An already well-known example is that of Neolithic Denmark, where Iversen (1941) concluded that "(1) connected with settlement there was extensive forest-clearing; (2) trees were felled (by stone axe); (3) extensive scrubby pasture sprang up immediately after forest-clearing; (4) burned areas were sown with cereals; (5) settlements were of short duration and new areas were colonized as soon as the forest regenerated" (P., E., 1954, p. 9). It is the same general scheme which also could be supposed for the Danubian. The Danubian example has been used here because it is much older and, therefore, nearer to the origins of food production than the Neolithic of northern Germany and southern Scandinavia. However, in the "Northern Neolithic" cattle-breeding and grazing pressure played an important part in contrast to the Danubian. Consequently, in the north, and especially on poorer, sandier soils, the temporary clearings of shifting agriculturists quickly became more permanent than on the loess soils of Central Europe (Clark, 1952, p. 97). But the final breakdown of forest regeneration seems to have been completed by the action of some late Neolithic populations. These exhibit so many common traits, in particular corded ware and battle-axes, that they are conveniently treated together as "Battle-ax" cultures, and their emergence is to be explained by immigration rather than by local differentiation. Their distribution stretches from the Pontic steppe to western Germany. In reality, they fall into a series of local and regional groups, such as, for instance, the "Saxo-Thuringian Corded-ware" and the "Sepatate Grave II" cultures of northern Germany and Jutland. On the western fringes these—in particular, the northern group—intermingled with the "Bell-beaker" culture coming from the Iberian Peninsula and formed, together with interacting local substrata, the different "Beaker" cultures of the Rhineland, the Netherlands, and England. These late Neolithic "melting pots" formed the foundations for the Bronze Age populations of the regions in question. Of course the newly arrived techniques of the Bronze Age transformed the picture of civilization, but in some regions it can be observed that the Bronze Age people erected principally the same great burial mounds, and their settlement is restricted to the same parts of the land as before (Marschall *et al.*, 1954; Beck, 1951).

Unfortunately, the different "Corded-ware" and "Beaker" cultures are better known from graves than from settlements, which renders more difficult the reconstruction of their economic systems. Nevertheless, it can be supposed that stock-raising played so great a part that one may speak of "pastoral farmers" (*Weidebauern;* see Tackenberg, 1953, 1954). On the other hand, it would be an unjustified exaggeration to speak of mere "nomadic herdsmen." The cemeteries are too extensive to belong to nomads, and a sort of cultivation is proved by grain imprints on pottery (Childe, 1950a). On the whole, the life of the "Battle-ax" people of Central Europe seems to have been sedentary,[9]

though shifting more easily than that of other Neolithic groups and with parts of its population leading the life of herdsmen. Because of like circumstances, we may expect that the "Battle-ax" folk bred pigs only on a very small scale and preferred animals which were more easily driven, such as cattle, sheep, and horses. Bones and crania of horses turn up rather frequently among the grave goods, particularly in the younger stages of that civilization. We may infer that "Battle-ax" people, as do most of the known horse-breeders, observed a certain ritual attitude with reference to the horse. Therefrom, we may deduce that they did not feed upon horses (except for rare ritual purposes) and needed other beasts for substantial meat provisions. Among most of the known horse-breeders, sheep play a great part in this respect. That is precisely the situation which is revealed by some domestic sites of the "Battle-ax" culture in its eastern area of distribution and which, because of the great uniformity of some basic common traits of that culture, may serve as an analogy to the groups farther west. A marked predominance of sheep is shown, exceeding the number of horses, oxen, goats, and the very few pigs.

Many groups of the "Battle-ax" culture preferred the poorer and sandier soils less favorable for agriculture than the loess of Central Europe or the younger moraines of the north (Fig. 53). The great expansion of the "Battle-ax" culture occurred in a time of slightly more humid climate, within the generally drier subboreal period of the postglacial (Overbeck, 1939, 1950). These soils were less densely wooded, but, nevertheless, clearings were neces-

9. Great rectangular buildings at Succase and Tolkemit (West Prussia) point in the same direction (Ehrlich, 1936) but are perhaps to be ascribed to the interaction of an older substratum of the local mixed culture (*Haff-Küsten-Kultur*).

sary to prepare the ground for agriculture and pasture. Though the exact method is not known, we may suppose, on the basis of the known general technical level of the late Neolithic populations, that fire played an important part in their activities. The process of making permanent the temporary clearings was doubtless enhanced by the depredations of grazing animals of the "Battle-ax" culture to a higher degree than among the Danubians. Sheep, if locally concentrated, can provide a grazing pressure which exceeds even that of cattle.

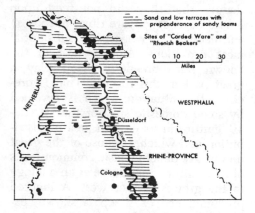

Fig. 53.—Soils and Neolithic sites in the northern Rhineland, showing "corded ware" and "Rhenish beakers." (After Tackenberg and Mückenhausen, simplified.)

"Corded-ware–Battle-ax" people penetrated into northern Germany and southern Scandinavia earlier than into the western margins of the great "Battle-ax" province. Perhaps this may explain the observation that, in Jutland, Schleswig-Holstein, and northwestern Germany, clearance and depredation already during Neolithic time seem to have outstripped the capacity of the forests to regenerate themselves, whereas in parts of the Netherlands and the Rhineland this occurred only at the beginning of the Bronze Age (Shwantes, 1939; Giffen, 1930; Marschall *et al.*,

1954; Clark, 1952).[10] The heath has occupied great areas as a result of the activities of man, who, by extensive stock-raising and, eventually also, by intentional burning off the shrubs and seedlings, prevented the regeneration of the forests.

CONCLUSIONS AND PERSPECTIVE

The scarcity of evidence available today makes it very dangerous to infer too much from those examples which tell us the story of man's changing the face of the earth. Nevertheless, one may state that the research of the last two decades has shown that the early food-producers of the Neolithic practiced clearing on far greater a scale than had been hitherto believed. On the other hand, one has to be careful not to exaggerate this result. Neolithic man, too, went the way of less resistance, and there were obstacles which he did not overcome. There are regions, even some of fertile and easily workable soil, which prehistoric man apparently avoided. The small country called "Bergisches Land," which lies east of the Rhine between the Ruhr and the Sieg, on the windward side of a mountain range and, at least in times of prevailing western winds, was always more humid and densely wooded than its counterparts west of the Rhine, was not occupied by the Danubians. Only in the beginning of the somewhat drier subboreal period did it have scanty traces of settlement. The late Neolithic "Battle-ax" and "Beaker" cultures also avoided this region, except for a small western margin, and it remained unoccupied until the period of great clear-

10. In the latter areas the Neolithic burial mounds were made of sand, whereas those of the Bronze Age were commonly built from heath sods. Bronze Age finds are relatively rare in the Rhineland, but, as yet, it cannot be decided whether this is due to progressive deterioration of the habitat caused by a not markedly nomadic pastoralism. (See also Darling, p. 780.)

ances in the Middle Ages (Marschall *et al.*, 1954; Uslar, 1950–51).

Moreover, it seems that some of the observable changes of the environment are but partially due to the activities of man, who, in some cases, only furthered the effects of an ecologic crisis. Such may be the case for the forest fires of the late Allerød, which were followed by the reintroduction of tundra during the drier and colder Later Dryas period. This must not be overlooked even in the case of the well-known clearances at the beginning of the "Northern Neolithic," which coincide with the commencement of the somewhat drier subboreal period and the retreat of the mixed-oak forest. Man's action in that case seems to have been furthered by environmental changes through forces independent of man, who, nevertheless, profited thereby.

All this is apt to inhibit our making general deductions about the historic process. But the above examples allow us to make some conclusions on the archeological work that is needed to explore that process. Splendid results have been obtained where the basic economy of a culture is known and the original environment, as well as its changes caused by man, are verified by pollen analysis or like methods (e.g., Iversen's research [1941] into the "Northern Neolithic"). Where the economy of a culture (e.g., the Danubian) is known by sufficient excavations of domestic sites and the environment can be reconstructed in its general traits, we can also infer the changes which may have occurred. Where the economy can be deduced only from grave goods (e.g., Western battle-ax groups), the results are less assured. But even approximate conclusions are quite impossible if the economy of a culture (e.g., Campignian) cannot be identified with sufficient assurance.

To be sure, there is another condition besides the demand for carefully excavated domestic sites, namely, a well-defined distribution of the culture in question, expressed in densely dotted maps. Only this can give exact information on the relations between archeologically explored complexes and the geographical and environmental factors. But this aim can hardly be fulfilled by archeological expeditions only. Cooperation of local inhabitants with archeologists is required, and this, in turn, calls for a certain degree of education and consciousness of, and fondness for, the history of one's own country and people. For this reason we remain skeptical about the quick growth in our knowledge of just those regions which are especially interesting because they are the supposed cradle or cradles of origin of food production.

REFERENCES

ANONYMOUS
1948 "The Culture Sequence in the Northern Stone Age Revised after Twelve Years' Research," *University of London, Institute of Archaeology, Annual Report,* IV (1946–47), 46–60.

BECK, HANS
1951 "Zur vor- und frühgeschichtlichen Besiedlung Südwestfalens," *Westfalen,* XXIX, No. 1, 9–26.

BRAIDWOOD, ROBERT J.
1950 "Jarmo: A Village of Early Farmers in Iraq," *Antiquity,* XXIV, No. 96, 189–95.

BUTTLER, WERNER
1931 *Die Bandkeramik in ihrem nordwestlichsten Verbreitungsgebiet.* Marburg an der Lahn: N.G. Elwertsche Verlagsbuchhandlung. 87 pp. (See also the shorter original version in *19. Bericht der Römisch-Germanischen Kommission 1929* [1930], pp. 146–200.)
1938 *Der donauländische und der westische Kulturkreis der jüngeren Steinzeit.* ("Handbuch der Urgeschichte Deutschlands," Band 2.)

Berlin and Leipzig: Walter de Gruyter & Co. 108 pp.

BUTTLER, WERNER, and HABEREY, WALDEMAR
1936 *Die bandkeramische Ansiedlung bei Köln-Lindenthal.* ("Römisch-Germanische Forschungen," Band 11.) Berlin and Leipzig: Walter de Gruyter & Co. 178 pp.

CASTILLO, ALBERTO DEL
1947 "El Neoeneolítico," pp. 487–714 in MENÉNDEZ PIDAL, RAMÓN (ed.), *Historia de España*, Vol. I: *España prehistórica*. Madrid: Espasa-Calpe, S.A. 896 pp.

CHILDE, V. GORDON
1950a *The Dawn of European Civilisation*. 5th ed. London: Routledge & Kegan Paul. 362 pp.
1950b *Prehistoric Migrations in Europe*. Oslo: H. Aschehoug & Co. (W. Nygaard). 249 pp.
1954 *New Light on the Most Ancient East*. London: Routledge & Kegan Paul. 255 pp.

CLARK, J. G. D.
1952 *Prehistoric Europe: The Economic Basis*. London: Methuen & Co. 349 pp.

COON, CARLETON S.
1951 *Cave Explorations in Iran 1949*. ("Museum Monographs.") Philadelphia: University Museum. 80 pp.

CORBEIL, JEAN
1949 "La Civilisation d'Ertebölle et les origines du Campignien," *Bulletin de la Société Préhistorique Française*, XLVI, Nos. 3–4, 102–10.

CURWEN, CECIL E., and HATT, GUDMUND
1953 *Plough and Pasture: The Early History of Farming*. New York: Henry Schuman. 329 pp.

DANTHINE, HÉLÈNE
1954 "Le 'Danubien,'" *Bulletin de la Société Préhistorique Française*, LI, No. 8, 82–84.

DESTEXHE-JAMOTTE, J.
1952 "Le Gisement Campignien de Latinne (Province de Liège)," *Bulletin de la Société Royale Belge d'Études Géologiques et Archéologiques "Les Chercheurs de la Wallonie,"* XV, 145–57.

EHRLICH, BRUNO
1936 "Bericht Succase, Kr. Elbing,"

Nachrichtenblatt für Deutsche Vorzeit, XII, 206–9.

FIRBAS, FRANZ
1949 *Spät- und nacheiszeitliche Waldgeschichte Mitteleuropas nördlich der Alpen*, Vol. I: *Allgemeine Waldgeschichte*, Jena: Gustav Fischer. 480 pp.

FLORIN, ST.
1944 "Havstrandens förskjutningar och bebyggels-eutvecklingen i östra Mellansverige under senkvartär tid," *Geologiska Föreningens Förhandlingar*, LXVI, 551–634.

FORDE, DARYLL
1930 "Early Cultures of Atlantic Europe," *American Anthropologist*, XXXII, 19–100.

GARNETT, A.
1945 "The Loess Regions of Central Europe in Prehistoric Times," *Geographical Journal*, CVI, 132–43.

GIFFEN, A. E. VAN
1930 *Die Bauart der Einzelgräber*. (*Mannus-Bibliothek*, Vol. XLIV–XLV.) Leipzig: Curt Kabitzsch. 208 pp.

HAMAL-NANDRIN, J., and SERVAIS, J.
1928 "Instruments à section triangulaire," *Bulletin de la Société Préhistorique Française*, XXV, No. 12, 28–38.

HANČAR, FRANZ
1937 *Urgeschichte Kaukasiens von den Anfängen seiner Besiedlung bis in die Zeit seiner frühen Metallurgie*. ("Bücher zur Ur- und Frühgeschichte," Vol. VI.) Vienna: Anton Schroll. 448 pp.

HERMANNS, MATHIAS
1949 *Die Nomaden von Tibet: Ursprung und Entwicklung der Viehzucht*. Vienna: Herold Verlag. 325 pp.

HOELTKER, GEORG
1947 "Steinerne Ackerbaugeräte," *Internationales Archiv für Ethnographie*, XVI, Nos. 4–6, 77–156.

IVERSEN, JOH.
1941 "Landnam i Danmarks Stenalder, En pollenanlytisk Undersøgelse over det første Landbrugs Indvirkning paa Vegetationsudviklingen," *Danmarks Geologiske Undersøgelse*, II, No. 66, 7–68.

JETTMAR, KARL
1953 "Neue Beiträge zur Entwicklungsgeschichte der Viehzucht," *Wiener völkerkundliche Mitteilungen,* I, No. 2, 1–14.
1954 "Les plus anciennes civilisations d'éleveurs des steppes d'Asie Centrale," *Cahiers d'histoire mondiale,* I, No. 4, 760–83.

LAVIOSA-ZAMBOTTI, PIA
1943 *Le Più antiche culture agricole Europee.* Milan-Messina: Giuseppe Principato. 514 pp.
1947 *Origini e diffusione della civiltà.* ("Pubblicazzione dell'Istituto di Ricerche Preistoriche e Archeologiche presso la Società Archeologica," Comense 1.) Milan: Dott. Carlo Marzorati. 509 pp.

MARIËN, M. E.
1952 *Oud-België van de eerste landbouwers tot de komst van Caesar.* Antwerp: De Sikkel. 527 pp.

MARSCHALL, ARTHUR; NARR, KARL J.; and USLAR, RAFAEL VON
1954 *Die vor- und frühgeschichtliche Besiedlung des Bergischen Landes.* (3. Beiheft der "Bonner Jahrbücher.") Neustadt an der Aisch: Ph. C. W. Schmidt. 272 pp. (Also *Zeitschrift des Bergischen Geschichtsvereins,* Vol. LXXIII.)

MENGHIN, OSWALD
1931 *Weltgeschichte der Steinzeit.* Vienna: Anton Schroll & Co. 648 pp.

MILOJČIĆ, VLADIMIR
1949 *Chronologie der jüngeren Steinzeit Mittel und Südosteuropas.* Berlin: Gebr. Mann. 137 pp.
1951 "Die Siedlungsgrenzen und Zeitstellung der Bandkeramik im Osten und Südosten Europas," *Bericht den Römisch-Germanischen Kommission,* XXXIII (1943–50), 110–24.

MÜCKENHAUSEN, E.
1952 "Die Böden des linken Niederrheins," *Der Niederrhein (Zeitschrift für Heimatpflege und Wandern),* XIX, Nos. 3–4 (Krefeld), 72–77.

MUNTHE, H.
1940 *Om nordens, främst Baltikums, senkvartära utveckling och stenåldersbebyggelse.* ("Kungliga Svenska Vetenkaps akademiens Handlingar,"

Series III, Vol. XIX, No. 1.) Stockholm. 242 pp.

NARR, KARL J.
1952 "Das höhere Jägertum: Jüngere Jagd- und Sammelstufe," pp. 502–22 in VALJAVEC, F. (ed.), *Historia mundi: Ein Handbuch der Weltgeschichte in Zehn Bänden,* Vol. I: *Frühe Menschheit.* Bern: A. Francke; Munich: Leo Lehnen. 560 pp.
1953a "Hirten, Pflanzer, Bauern: Produktionsstufe," pp. 66–100 in VALJAVEC, F. (ed.), *Historia Mundi: Ein Handbuch der Weltgeschichte in Zehn Bänden,* Vol. II: *Grundlagen und Entfaltung der ältesten Hochkulturen.* Bern: A. Francke; Munich: Leo Lehnen. 655 pp.
1953b "Zur Frage altpaläolithischer Kulturkreise," *Anthropos,* XLVIII, Nos. 5–6, 773–94.
1954 "Formengruppen und Kulturkreise im europäischen Paläolithikum: Stand und Aufgaben der Altsteinzeitforschung," *Bericht der Römisch-Germanischen Kommission,* XXXIV (1951–53), 1–40.

NOUGIER, LOUIS-RENÉ
1949 "La Répartition géographique des casse-têtes discoides," *Bulletin de la Société Préhistorique Française,* XLVI, 428–33.
1950 *Les Civilisations Campigniennes en Europe occidentale.* Le Mans: Ch. Monnoyer. 571 pp.

OVERBECK, FRITZ
1939 *Die Moore Niedersachsens in geologisch-botanischer Betrachtung.* ("Wirtschaftswissenschaftliche. Gesellschaft zum Studium Niedersachsens," Reihe A, Vol. LII.) 54 pp.
1950 "Neue pollenanalytisch-stratigraphische Untersuchungen zum Pflug von Walle," *Nachrichten aus Niedersachsens Urgeschichte,* XIX, 3–30.

P., E.
1954 "A Report on the Conference Held in London, 9th to 11th April, 1954, 'Prehistoric Agriculture,'" *Archaeological News Letter,* V, No. 1, 8–14.

PARET, OSCAR
1946 *Das neue Bild der Vorgeschich-*

te. Stuttgart: August Schröder. 225 pp.

PHILIPPE, JOSEPH
1953 "Le Campignien occidental et les gisements des environs d'Aubel (Province de Liège)," pp. 165–84 in SOCIÉTÉ ROYALE BELGE D'ANTHROPOLOGIE ET DE PRÉHISTOIRE (ed.), *Mélanges en hommage au professeur Hamal-Nandrin.* Brussels: Imprimerie Administrative. 216 pp.

PITTIONI, RICHARD
1950 *Beiträge zur Geschichte des Keramikums in Afrika und im Nahen Osten: Prähistorische Forschungen,* Vol. II. Horn-Vienna: Ferdinand Berger. 50 pp.

POHLHAUSEN, HENN
1954a *Das Wanderhirtentum und seine Vorstufen: Eine ethnographisch-geographische Studie zur Entwicklung der Eingeborenenwirtschaft: Kulturgeschichtliche Forschungen,* Vol. IV. Braunschweig: Albert Limbach. 176 pp.
1954b *Nachweisbare Spuren des Wanderhirtentums in der südkaspischen Mittelsteinzeit.* Lund: Berlingska Boktryckeriet. 15 pp.

PURSE-STANEK, ERIKA
1953 "Stone Implements and Their Use in the Agriculture of Taiwan," *Wiener völkerkundliche Mitteilungen,* I, No. 2, 22–31.

RIETH, ADOLF
1949–50 "Geschliffene bandkeramische Steingeräte zur Holtzbearbeitung," *Prähistorische Zeitschrift,* XXXIV–XXXV, Part I, 230–32.

RUST, ALFRED
1948 "Jungpaläolithische Wohnanlagen bei Hamburg," *Hammaburg, vor- und frühgeschichtliche Forschungen aus dem niederelbischen Raum,* I, 33–38.
1951 "Über die Kulturentwicklung des endglazialen Jungpaläolithikums in Nordwesteuropa," pp. 48–58 in KERSTEN, KARL (ed.), *Festschrift für Gustav Schwantes.* Neumünster: Karl Wachholtz. 233 pp.

SANGMEISTER, EDWARD
1951 "Zum Charakter der bandkeramischen Siedlung," *Bericht der*

RÖMISCH-GERMANISCHEN Kommission, XXXIII (1943–50), 89–109.

SAUER, CARL O.
1952 *Agricultural Origins and Dispersals.* (Bowman Memorial Lectures, Series Two.) New York: American Geographical Society. 110 pp.

SCHACHERMEYR, FRITZ
1954 "Die vorderasiatische Kulturtrift," *Saeculum: Jahrbuch für Universalgeschichte,* V, No. 3, 268–91.

SCHWABEDISSEN, HERMANN
1951 "Das Magdalénien im nordwesteuropäischen Flachland," *Eiszeitalter und Gegenwart,* I, 152–65.
1952a "Zur Besiedlung des Nordseeraums in der älteren und mittleren Steinzeit," pp. 59–77 in KERSTEN, KARL (ed.), *Festschrift für Gustav Schwantes.* Neumünster: Karl Wachholtz. 233 pp.
1952b Review of L. R. NOUGIER, *Les Civilisations Campigniennes en Europe occidentale, Germania,* XXX, 399–405.
1954 *Die Federmesser-Gruppen des nordwesteuropäischen Flachlandes: Zur Ausbreitung des Spät-Magdalénien.* ("Offa-Bücher," N.F., Vol. IX.) Neumünster: Karl Wachholtz. 104 pp.

SCHWANTES, GUSTAV
1939 *Die Vorgeschichte Schleswig-Holsteins (Stein- und Bronzezeit).* Neumünster: Karl Wachholtz. 589 pp.

SCHWARZ, KLAUS
1948 "Lagen die Siedlungen der linearbandkeramischen Kultur Mitteldeutschlands in waldfreien oder bewaldeten Landschaften," pp. 1–28 in SCHWARZ, KLAUS (ed.), *Strena praehistorica.* Halle an der Saale: Max Niemeyer. 253 pp.

SOERGEL, W.
1922 *Die Jagd der Vorzeit.* Jena: Gustav Fischer. 149 pp.

STEEGER, ALBERT
1932 "Studien zur Siedlungsgeschichte des Niederrheinischen Tieflandes," *Rheinische Vierteljahrsblätter,* II, 278–95.

STIEREN, AUGUST
1951 "Bandkeramische Grossbauten bei Bochum und ihre Parallelen in

Mitteleuropa," *Bericht der Römisch-Germanischen Kommission,* XXXIII (1943–50), 61–88.

STOKAR, WALTER VON
1942 "Phylogenie und Vorgeschichts-forschung," *Praehistorische Zeitschrift,* XXXII–XXXIII (1941–42), 3–15.

TACKENBERG, KURT
1953 "Die jüngere Steinzeit Europas: Das Neolithikum," pp. 11–65 in VALJAVEC, F. (ed.), *Historia mundi,* Vol. II. Bern: A. Francke; Munich: Leo Lehnen. 655 pp.
1954 *Fundkarten zur Vorgeschichte der Rheinprovinz.* (Beiheft 2 der "Bonner Jahrbücher.") Bonn: Rudolf Habelt. 107 pp.

TÜXEN, REINHOLD
1931 "Die Grundlagen der Urland-schaftsforschung," *Nachrichten aus Niedersachsens Urgeschichte,* V, 59–96.

USLAR, RAFAEL VON
1950–51 "Zur vor- und frühgeschicht-lichen Besiedlung des Bergischen Landes," *Rheinische Vierteljahrsblätter,* XV–XVI, 8–18.
1951 "Zur vorgeschichtlichen Besiedlung des Niederrheins," *Niederrheinisches Jahrbuch,* III, 54–56.

ZEUNER, F. E.
1951 "A Postglacial Period of Dry Summers Expressed in Soils, and Its Archaeological Date," *University of London, Institute of Archaeology, Annual Report,* VII (1949–50), 46–53.

The Hydraulic Civilizations

KARL A. WITTFOGEL[*]

THE HYDRAULIC AND THE
URBAN REVOLUTION

A great deal has recently been said about the "urban revolution"—a process of differentiation that split an originally village-centered agrarian society into an urban and a rural sector: town and village. The distinction between town and village considerably interested certain classical economists (Smith, 1937, pp. 373 ff.), including Marx (1953, pp. 381, 382 ff.; 1919, I, 317; III, Part I, 318). Properly employed, it opens up important sociohistorical vistas.

However, those who use it today, either as part of a general developmental scheme or as a means for juxtaposing urban and rural ("folk") culture, tend to disregard two essential methodological precautions. Stress on the revolutionary character of the rise of the town one-sidedly accents what at the most is only one among several features of cultural change. For instance, Childe, who is eager to accustom his readers to the idea of revolution (1952, p. 19), thus promotes historical views that are highly problematic. And his unqualified emphasis on urbanization as a developmental feature bulwarks the thesis of a general evolution in agrarian civilization that is manifestly false. This thesis, which culminates in the concept of a unilinear and necessarily progressive development of society, clearly contradicts the facts of history. It also contradicts the views of the classical economists, who with varying consistency recognized that the higher agrarian civilizations of the "Orient" and their urban and rural conditions followed a pattern of development decidedly unlike that of the West.

A juxtaposition of rural and urban institutions will promote our analysis of agrarian history to the extent to which we realize that there are at least two major types of rural-urban agrarian civilizations—hydraulic and non-hydraulic—and that the primitive farmers who started on an agrohydraulic course initiated a revolution that, structurally and for a whole epoch, split the higher civilizations into two different parts. Prior to the urban revolution and with extraordinary consequences, the fate of agricultural man was profoundly shaped by what may be suitably called the "hydraulic revolution."

[*] Dr. Wittfogel is Professor of Chinese History, University of Washington, Seattle, and Director of the Chinese History Project, co-sponsored by the University of Washington and Columbia University. He is author of *Wirtschaft und Gesellschaft Chinas*, 1931, and co-author, with Fêng Chia-shêng, of *History of Chinese Society, Liao (907–1125)*, 1949. A recently completed book, *Oriental Despotism and Hydraulic Society* is scheduled for publication in 1956.

MAJOR EFFECTS OF THE HY-
DRAULIC REVOLUTION

Hydraulic Agriculture

The peculiarities of agrohydraulic civilization become apparent as soon as we realize the role that the management of water has played in the subsistence economy of certain agrarian societies.

To be sure, water is no more essential to agriculture than several other basic factors, such as temperature, the lay of the land, the fertility of the soil, and the character of the cultivable plants. But water is specific in that, among the manipulative essentials, it is the only element which tends to agglomerate in bulk (Wittfogel, 1956, chap. ii). In its agriculturally most precious occurrence —as the water of rivers and large streams in arid or semiarid regions—it therefore defied the small-scale approach which, under preindustrial conditions, was so effective in the treatment of soil and plants. In order to bring fertility to large water-deficient areas by the management of substantial sources of water supply, man had to create large-scale enterprises that usually were operated by the government. The emergence of big productive water works (for irrigation) was frequently accompanied by the emergence of big protective water works (for flood control), and at times the latter even surpassed the former in magnitude and urgency. I suggest that this type of agrarian economy be called "hydraulic agriculture" to distinguish it from rainfall farming and hydroagriculture.

It is customary to apply the term "rainfall agriculture" to a situation in which a favorable climate permits cultivation on the basis of natural precipitation. The term "hydroagriculture" may be applied to a situation in which the members of a farming community resort to irrigation but, because of the scarcity and fragmentation of the available moisture, to irrigation on a small scale only. The term "hydraulic agriculture" may be applied to a situation in which the dimension of the available water supply leads to the creation of large productive and protective water works that are managed by the government.

Institutional Essence of Hydraulic Civilization

Irrigation was practiced in parts of Greece to compensate for the deficiencies of a semiarid climate and in Japan for the cultivation of an aquatic plant— rice. But in both countries a broken terrain permitted the growth of only small irrigation works, which could be handled without government direction. This fact has had far-reaching sociohistorical consequences. Japan established a simple variant of the same feudal society which, in a more complex form, emerged in medieval Europe (Wittfogel, 1956, chap. x). And Greece, prior to the Hellenistic period, developed aristocratic and democratic ways of life. In each case hydroagriculture encouraged the evolution of a multicentered society, an institutional conformation that assumed great significance in the rainfall-based civilizations of feudal Europe.

The contrast between this development and that of the agrohydraulic world is striking. Where agriculture required substantial and centralized works of water control, the representatives of the government monopolized political power and societal leadership, and they dominated their country's economy. By preventing the growth of strong competitive forces, such as a feudal knighthood, an autonomous church, or self-governing guild cities, they were able to make themselves the sole masters of their society. It is this combination of a hydraulic agriculture, a hydraulic government, and a single-centered society that constitutes the institutional essence of hydraulic civilization.

Differentiations

Within the orbit of hydraulic civilization immense cultural differences occur; but this essay cannot elaborate on them.

An inquiry dealing with man's impact upon his natural environment may content itself with discussing certain subdivisions of the general institutional order that concern this man-nature relation.

Development in political structure is most consequential when the primitive governments of hydraulic tribes, managed largely by part-time functionaries, evolve into statelike organizations, managed by a body of full-time officials. The hydraulic state provides more comprehensive opportunities for imposing hydraulic installations upon the natural environment, but it also gives the men of the state apparatus the opportunity to neglect water works which will benefit the people, in order to build huge palaces and tombs and process precious organic and inorganic materials which will benefit the rulers.

Development in the patterns of property may lead from a predominance of state control over land and over professional handicraft and trade (simple hydraulic society) to a configuration in which mobile property in industry and trade is largely private, while land remains government controlled (semicomplex hydraulic society), or to a configuration in which private property in land is also widespread (complex hydraulic society). The rise of a semicomplex hydraulic order tends to differentiate the individual producer's interaction with nature; and it furthers the processes of locomotion which overcome difficulties of space and terrain. The rise of private property in land (tenancy as well as ownership) tends to stimulate careful agriculture. The intensive farmers of the ancient Near East were mainly tenants of public (state and temple) lands or of private estates. In China the transition to private landownership evoked the comment that the peasants worked less carefully on the public fields than on their own land (Lü, 1936, ch. 17). Chinese peasant farming, which for over two thousand years has been based on private property of land, represents perhaps the most advanced form of intensive agriculture prior to the machine age.

Development in the spatial expansion of the hydraulic state is equally consequential. It is a historical fact that certain non-hydraulic *constructional* patterns and the major *organizational* and *acquisitive* patterns of hydraulic ("Oriental") despotism advanced far beyond the area of hydraulic economy proper. In "loose" hydraulic civilizations, such as China, India, and pre-Spanish Mexico, the monopolistic state apparatus controlled wide areas that had no comprehensive water works and in some cases not even small-scale irrigation.

This aspect was readily accepted by earlier analysts of "Asiatic" society, from the classical economists to Max Weber. But little effort has been made to explain the underlying mechanics of power. Still less analytic attention has been given to the fact that, either through a breakoff from a hydraulic regime proper (later Byzantium) or through institutional transfer (Mongol and post-Mongol Russia and probably Maya society), there may be governments which fulfil few or no agrohydraulic functions but which utilize the organizational methods of hydraulic despotism (such as record-keeping, census-taking, centralized armies, a state system of post and intelligence) as well as its acquisitive methods (such as general labor service, general and heavy taxation, and periodic confiscations) and its legal and political methods (such as fragmentative laws of inheritance and the suppression of independent political organizations) to keep private property weak and the non-bureaucratic forces of society politically impotent.

In fact, so strong were the devices of hydraulic statecraft and social control that they operated successfully in "marginal" areas without those large-scale water works which persisted in the hydraulic core areas and which apparently were an essential feature in the genesis of all historically relevant agrarian monopoly despotisms. From the standpoint of man's relation to man, the institutional periphery of the hydraulic world has been important in that it enormously widened the range of this despotic order. From the standpoint of man's relation to nature, it has been important in that, like the hydraulic core area, it frustrated the development of a big mechanized industry—the most profound recent change in man's attitude toward his natural environment.

MAN AND NATURE IN HYDRAULIC CIVILIZATION

Having considered the institutional setting of hydraulic civilization, we are now ready to contemplate more closely the specific relations between man and nature within it. These relations involve a peculiar system of mass labor in one segment of the economic order and a peculiar system of intensive work in another.

Government-directed Preparatory Operations: Division of Labor and Co-operation, Bureaucracy, Astronomical and Mathematical Sciences

Hydraulic civilization came into being not through a technological but through an organizational revolution. Its rise necessitated the establishment of a new system of division of labor and co-operation.

Economic historians, when dealing with this matter, frequently assert that until recent times agriculture, in contrast to industry, involved little division of labor and no significant co-operation (Seligman, 1914, p. 350; Sombart, 1927, II, 825 ff.; Marshall, 1946, p. 290; for pioneer formulations see Smith, 1937, p. 6; and Marx, 1919, I, 300, 322 ff.). By and large, this view is justified with regard to the conditions of non-hydraulic farming. But it does not fit the operational pattern of hydraulic agriculture. A major separation between "preparatory labor" (for this term see Mill, 1909, p. 31) and production proper is held to have occurred first in the industrial revolution. Actually, it took place much earlier and on an enormous scale in the hydraulic revolution.

Comprehensive preparatory activities were necessary to make cultivation either possible (in arid areas) or safe and rewarding (in semiarid areas) or specific (in humid areas suitable for the growth of aquatic plants, such as rice and wet taro). The difference between this type of preparatory labor and the preparatory labor employed in modern industry is obvious. In industry preparatory labor provides the ultimate producer with raw material, with auxiliary material (e.g., coal for fuel and oil for lubrication), and also with special tools (machinery). In hydraulic economy preparatory labor consisted essentially in the gathering, conducting, and distributing of one auxiliary material—water. In modern industry the workers who engage in preparatory activities, such as mining, the making of machinery, etc., tend to work full time at their various jobs. In agrohydraulic economy division of labor proceeded differently. The great mass of the men who made and maintained the canals and dikes and who watched for floods did not do so full time and for the greater part of the year but part time and for as short a period as possible. In their overwhelming majority they were farmers, and the very authorities who mobilized them for hydraulic and other *corvée* duties were eager to have them return in good time to their villages to attend properly to the cultivation of their fields.

Thus, like modern industry, hydraulic agriculture involves significant division of labor; but, unlike modern industry, it involves no significant division of laborers. And while the organizers of preparatory work in industry endeavor to achieve their purpose with as small a labor force as possible, the organizers of the hydraulic *corvée* are interested in mobilizing as large a labor force as circumstances permit.

In hydraulic tribes, such as the Suk and Chagga of East Africa and the Pueblo Indians of New Mexico, all able-bodied males participated as a matter of course in the ditch work. In small, state-centered hydraulic civilizations, such as Bali and the early Mesopotamian and Indian city-states, the same mobilization pattern seems to have been customary (Wittfogel, 1956, chap. ii). A list of canal workers in ancient Lagash includes one corviable person from each commoner family (Schneider, 1920, pp. 108 ff.). In an irrigation conflict which, according to a pious legend, led to the Buddha's personal interference, the whole laboring population of the towns involved is said to have engaged in the hydraulic work (Anonymous, n.d., *Jātakam*, p. 441). Even clusters of territorial states may, at times, have gathered their combined populations to execute a big hydraulic task. This appears to have been the case in the Mexican federation prior to the arrival of the Spaniards. And it may have been a recurring trend in countries such as Egypt, where all villages depended on one huge source of irrigation water and where, therefore, their labor forces could be called up, either simultaneously or in shifts, to dig, dam, and watch for floods (Wittfogel, 1956, chap. ii).

In larger hydraulic civilizations varying regional conditions suggested varying patterns of state-directed *corvée* labor, but its mass character remained unchanged. The underlying mobilization principle is drastically formulated by a historian of Mogul economy, Pant (1930, p. 70): "The King by his *firman* (order) could collect any number of men he liked. There was no limit to his massing of labourers, save the number of people in his Empire." Pant was speaking of Mogul India, but his statement is valid for all analogous periods and countries. In hydraulic economy man extended his power over the arid, the semiarid, and certain humid parts of the globe through a government-directed division of labor and a mode of co-operation not practiced in agrarian civilizations of the non-hydraulic type.

The development of such a work pattern meant more than the agglomeration of large numbers of men. To have many persons co-operate periodically and effectively, there had to be planning, record-keeping, communication, and supervision. There had to be organization in depth. And above the tribal level this involved permanent offices and officials to man them—bureaucrats.

Of course, there were scribes in the city-states of ancient Greece and Rome and on the manorial estates, at the courts, and in the church centers of medieval Europe. But there was no national managerial network. In the great Oriental civilizations a hydraulic bureaucracy (*Wasserbau-Bureaukratie* [Weber, 1921–22, p. 117]) emerged together with the new type of organization in depth.

It was in these same Oriental (hydraulic) civilizations that man, in seeking a more rational approach to nature, laid the foundations for several sciences: astronomy, algebra, and geometry. Significantly, Greek mathematics and astronomy drew their early inspiration from the Oriental Near East, and they reached their climax under Euclid, Heron, and Ptolemy, not in Greece, but in one of the foremost centers of hydraulic culture—Egypt (Wittfogel, 1931, p. 682).

To be sure, neither the bureaucratic nor the scientific possibilities of hydraulic civilization were always exhausted. Some simpler hydraulic civilizations did not advance far. But the major hydraulic centers created elaborate administrations, and their astronomical and mathematical accomplishments were impressive. Thus any attempt to define hydraulic man's relation to nature must also consider the organizational (bureaucratic) and the scientific aspects of hydraulic economy.

Irrigation Farming with Intensive Labor and Special Operations of Tillage

Government management of the great hydraulic works is supplemented by intensive farming based on irrigation. As stated above, irrigation farming also occurs in certain non-hydraulic societies, and to this extent the subsequent statements have validity beyond the borders of hydraulic civilization. But, while irrigation farming occurs occasionally in the non-hydraulic agricultural world, it is essential in the core areas of hydraulic civilization.

Irrigation demands a treatment of soil and water that is not customary in rainfall farming. The typical irrigation peasant has (1) to dig and re-dig ditches and furrows; (2) to terrace the land if it is uneven; (3) to raise the moisture if the level of the water supply is below the surface of the fields; and (4) to regulate the flow of the water from the source to the goal, directing its ultimate application to the crop. Tasks (1) and (4) are essential to all irrigation farming proper (inundation farming requires damming rather than ditching). Task (3) is also a frequent one, for, except at the time of high floods, the level of water tends to lie below that of the cultivated fields.

The type and amount of work involved in these operations become clear when we contrast the labor budget of an Oriental irrigation farmer with that of a rainfall farmer of medieval Europe. The medieval peasant usually plowed his field once or twice, then he sowed

(Parain, 1942, p. 142; cf. Maitland, 1921, pp. 398 ff.; Lamprecht, 1886, p. 557), and he harvested his crop at the end of the season. As a rule he spent no time watering.

The irrigation farmer, who, of course, plows, sows, and harvests, is in addition burdened with a number of other chores. In regions like Egypt, which depended mainly on inundation, these activities were insignificant, yet such regions were not very numerous. In others, such as ancient Mesopotamia, inundation was supplemented by canal irrigation. In this case a considerable amount of time was devoted to the watering of the fields (Meissner, 1920, pp. 192, 194). In modern India the husbandmen of a Punjab village spend much time irrigating their crops, wheat receiving three to four waterings in January, February, and March during more than twenty days. This work period is the most time-consuming item listed in the year's agricultural calendar (Singh, 1928, pp. 33–36, 38). Sugar cane is an old Indian crop, requiring a great deal of water. In certain Deccan villages favoring its cultivation, the total cost of plowing, harrowing, planting, harvesting, and related operations is about 97 rupees as against 157 rupees for watering (Mann and Kanitkar, 1920, p. 86). In a South Gujarat village, studied by Mukhtyar (1930, p. 96), watering is by far the heaviest expense item in the labor budget of the grower of sugar cane.

Concerning Chinese traditional irrigation economy, Buck has provided us with valuable numerical data. In 1923, 152 farms in Pinghsiang (in present Hopeh Province) grew wheat as their main crop. Of the time devoted to this crop, the peasant spent 10.2 per cent in plowing, 1.7 per cent in harrowing, 9.2 per cent in harvesting, or altogether 21.1 per cent, as against 58.5 per cent in irrigating (Buck, 1930, p. 306). In 1924 two groups of farmers in Kiangsu Province spent 21 and 25.1 per cent, respectively, in plowing, harrowing, and harvesting their main rice crop, as against 18.1 and 39.6 per cent in its irrigation (*ibid.*, p. 310). As may be expected, the labor budgets show great variation in detail, but they all reveal that the amount of work involved in watering operations is commonly far in excess of the combined operations of a non-irrigation farmer.

Repeated preparatory tillage—plowing or hoeing—was also undertaken by the rainfall farmers of feudal Europe (Cole and Mathews, 1938, pp. 324 ff.). But it was primarily on the manorial domain that the fields were "worked" three or four times, while the "poor peasants could often only work their land once to the detriment of the yield" (Parain, 1942, p. 141; cf. Lamprecht, 1886, p. 557).

Except for some cutting of thistles (Parain, 1942, pp. 144 ff.; Kulischer, 1928, p. 160), intertillage was then, as now, technically impossible for grain crops, because, under conditions of rainfall farming, these "can be grown satisfactorily and most economically by planting them in solid stands so that they cover all the ground equally." As a rule, they are today "given no tillage while they are growing" (Cole and Mathews, 1938, p. 327).

Plants grown in rows are easily approached and easily cultivated. But the most important of these, corn and potatoes, appeared in Europe only after the discovery of America, and even after the sixteenth century their economic importance remained definitely secondary to that of the cereals. In the West the modern dry farmer still hesitates to cultivate grain crops in rows. After an early harrowing he frequently lets nature take its course (Widtsoe, 1913, pp. 163 ff.).

Irrigation agriculture requires a row-like arrangement of the seeds not only for crops such as corn and potatoes but also for cereals. Plants can be watered by ditches only if proper space for the distributing furrows is provided. The layout of the fields differs in accordance with economic experience, crops, and terrain, but all patterns aim at making the plants accessible to the irrigation farmer, who may work the soil and the crop as thoroughly as he wishes.

Intensive techniques are not limited to the period between sowing and harvesting. Frequently the soil is plowed or harrowed several times before the sowing. Nor are these techniques limited to the fields for which irrigation water is available. In semiarid areas (under conditions of full aridity cultivation ends where the water supply ends) the farmers are eager to grow not only crops which they can water but also crops which may mature without the benefit of irrigation.

Chinese farmers in the province of Kiangsu who had sufficient water for two main crops only, rice and vegetables, used to grow wheat and barley without irrigation. However, they treated the last two as intensively as the first two. Of all labor devoted to wheat, intertillage accounted for over 20 per cent; in the case of barley, it accounted for almost 33 per cent; and in the case of kaoliang, which in some parts of Hopeh is grown without irrigation, it accounted for more than 40 per cent (Buck, 1930, p. 306).

In India certain Deccan villages grow their main cereal crop, *bajri*, also without irrigation. But, like the irrigated cereals, it is planted in rows and intensively cultivated. It gets one plowing and four harrowings before sowing and further treatment after sowing (Mann and Kanitkar, 1920, pp. 72 ff.).

The good Aztec farmer made beds for his corn, pulverized the soil, and kept his crop free of weeds (Sahagun, 1938, p. 39). He irrigated whenever this was possible, but he obviously was expected to farm intensively under any circumstances. The Mayan peasants of Yucatán, who did not water their crops, weeded them as carefully as did the inhabitants of the highland regions in which irrigation farming was customary.

Thus, as the political patterns of hydraulic civilization spread far beyond the areas of hydraulic economy, so the techniques of irrigation farming spread far beyond the irrigated fields. These techniques established an agronomical relation among man, soil, and plants that, in terms of a given amount of land, was much more rewarding than the agriculture of preindustrial Europe. Early in the twentieth century a European agronomist found the Indian peasants, who by and large followed their traditional pattern of cultivation, quite as good as the average modern British farmer and in some respects better (Anonymous, 1909, p. 6). The father of organic chemistry, Justus von Liebig, in comparing nineteenth-century German agriculture with contemporary Chinese farming, viewed the former as the procedure of "a child compared to that of a mature and experienced man" (Liebig, 1878, p. 453).

Demographic Consequences

In some ways Liebig's statement touches upon problems that lie outside the concern of the biochemist. But he was quite right in noting the greater refinement—and better results—of hydraulic agriculture as practiced in China. Whatever its deficiencies, this method of farming produced great quantities of food on a given acreage, and it permitted the individual peasant to support his family on a very small farmstead. For this reason the areas of intensive hydraulic farming came to support extremely dense populations.

In preconquest America relatively small hydraulic regions comprised about 75 per cent of America's total population (Kroeber, 1939, p. 166; Ro-

senblat, 1945, pp. 188 ff., 202 ff.; Kubler, 1946, p. 339; for a considerably higher estimate of the population of the Inca Empire see Rowe, 1946, p. 185). Beloch's classical estimates (1886, p. 507) for the time of Augustus assume a much greater density for the Asian provinces of the Roman Empire (thirty persons per square kilometer) than for the European provinces (ten persons per square kilometer). The contrast becomes even more spectacular when we juxtapose his figures for Augustan Greece (eleven) and Italy (twenty-four) with those of Egypt (one hundred and seventy-nine). More recent studies (Premerstein, 1936, p. 56; Rostovtzeff, 1941, II, 1138; III, 1605) suggest a still higher figure for Egypt, namely, about two hundred and eighty persons per square kilometer.

The population distribution in contemporary Han China was not unlike that of the Roman Empire. The old Chinese territories of the north seem to have been as densely populated as Rome's eastern provinces, while the hydraulic core areas of the Han world showed demographic trends similar to those of their western counterparts, Egypt and Babylonia (Lao, 1935, pp. 216 ff.).

The dimension of the Oriental cities expresses both the productivity of hydraulic agriculture and the acquisitive power of its administrative centers. While, in classical days, Athens may have had 120,000 inhabitants, Corinth 70,000, and the majority of all Greek cities between 5,000 and 10,000 persons (Beloch, 1886, p. 478), Hellenistic Ephesus may have harbored 225,000 people (*ibid.*, p. 231), Antioch 500,000 (*ibid.*, p. 479; Kahrstedt, 1924, p. 663; Rostovtzeff, 1941, I, 498), Seleuceia 600,000 (Beloch, 1886, p. 479; Rostovtzeff, 1941, I, 498; II, 1140), and Alexandria at the end of the Hellenistic period the same number (Rostovtzeff, 1941, II, 1139 ff.). The recently published "gerusia acts" lead Rostovtzeff (*ibid.*, p. 1139; cf. Premerstein, 1936, p. 56) to conclude that for A.D. 37 the total population of the Egyptian capital "must be estimated at one million at least."

It is also illuminating to compare these figures with estimates for metropolitan populations in pre-Spanish America and feudal Europe. Prevailing expert opinion credits Cuzco with 200,-000 and Mexico City with 300,000 inhabitants (Rosenblat, 1945, pp. 205, 191). Some cities of Moorish Spain may have housed several hundred thousand persons, and the capital, Cordova, at its peak, a million (Wittfogel, 1956, chap. vi; cf. also al-Makkari, 1840, pp. 214 ff.). In contrast, in the fourteenth century the most populous city north of the Alps seems to have had 35,000 inhabitants (London), while other major English cities comprised 11,000 (York), 9,500 (Bristol), or between 7,000 and 5,000 persons (Rogers, 1884, p. 117). At the beginning of the fifteenth century the foremost city of the Hanseatic League, Lübeck, had 22,300 inhabitants and Frankfurt 10,000. Other big German towns of this century sheltered between 20,000 and 10,000 persons, Leipzig 4,000 and Dresden 3,200 (Büchner, 1922, p. 382).

Chinese census data have been discussed at length. What should be remembered is that these data were compiled primarily for fiscal reasons. Since tax payments had to agree with the announced population, the census records tended to represent not the actual but the admitted population, that is, the lowest figures the regional officials dared to submit (Wittfogel and Fêng, 1949, p. 53). Weak regimes got understatements, and tougher and more effective governments more realistic accounts. Two decades ago Buck, on the basis of a comprehensive rural survey, obtained population figures about 23 per cent higher than the official data.

He hesitated to press his findings, but he stated that, if his higher figures were used, "the total would be over 600 million" (1937, p. 363). The first census taken by the new Communist government claims a total mainland population of almost 600 million persons.

Much more could be said on this subject. But the just-cited data fit with our other information on Oriental demography. Obviously, the hydraulic way of life permitted an accumulation of rural and urban populations which, though paralleled in a few non-hydraulic territories of small-scale irrigation, such as Japan, has not been matched by the higher agrarian civilizations based on rainfall farming.

DIMENSIONS OF HYDRAULIC CIVILIZATION IN TIME, SPACE, AND MANPOWER

According to conservative estimates, hydraulic civilizations took shape in the ancient Near East not later than the fourth millennium B.C., and they persisted until very recent times. It may therefore be said safely that in this area hydraulic civilization endured for about five millenniums.

The great hydraulic civilizations of India and China maintained themselves for some three or four millenniums. And recent archeological finds suggest that in certain areas of the Western Hemisphere, such as Peru, hydraulic civilizations may have existed at least since the first millennium B.C., that is, for more than two millenniums prior to the arrival of the Spaniards.

Neither ancient Greece nor feudal Europe nor Japan can equal these figures. Greek agrarian civilization seems to have lasted for a millennium until Hellenistic despotism put an end to its non-Oriental pattern. The societies of feudal Europe and Japan had an even shorter duration.

The core areas and the margins of the hydraulic civilizations covered the greater part of western, southern, and eastern Asia. The Hellenistic regimes, the Orientalized Roman Empire, the Arab conquests of Spain and Sicily, and the Byzantine, Turkish, and Russian expansions imposed Orientally despotic regimes on large areas of Europe.

In Africa north of the Sahara, a hydraulic way of life prevailed for millenniums. A thousand years ago it seems to have spread temporarily from Lake Tanganyika and Kenya to Rhodesia (Huntingford, 1933, pp. 153, 159 ff.; Wilson, 1932, pp. 252 ff.; Hall and Neal, 1904, pp. 356 ff.; Randall-MacIver, 1906, pp. 12 ff.). In recent times it was observed among the Chagga and a few other tribes of central East Africa.

Hydraulic agriculture and government persisted in some major Pacific islands, such as Hawaii. In pre-Columbian America hydraulic developments spread beyond the Rio Grande in the north. In the Meso-American highlands and in the lowlands of Yucatán, clusters of loose and marginal hydraulic civilizations emerged. And in the south hydraulic expansion reached its maximum on the eve of the Spanish conquest. Early in the sixteenth century the Inca Empire stretched from Peru to Ecuador in the north and to Bolivia and Chile in the west and south. It co-ordinated practically all important centers of higher agrarian development in South America. Clearly, hydraulic civilizations covered a vastly larger proportion of the surface of the globe than all other significant agrarian civilizations taken together.

The demographic dimension of the hydraulic world has already been indicated. According to our present information, it would seem that, prior to the commercial and industrial revolution, the majority of all human beings lived within the orbit of hydraulic civilization.

COSTS AND PERSPECTIVES OF HYDRAULIC CIVILIZATION

Manifestly, then, this civilization was an eminently successful "going concern." It stimulated organization in depth. It gave birth to certain sciences. And it refined farming and handicraft. Yet, in terms of human affairs, it was as costly as it was tenacious. While such scientific aids to counting and measuring as astronomy and mathematics emerged, these developments eventually stalled, and the experimental sciences never gained significance. Masses of men were co-ordinated for public works and warfare, but the patterns of integration were crude, and they improved little throughout the centuries. Farming techniques were subtle, but from the standpoint of the main protagonist, the peasant, their one-sidedly labor-intensive development was frustrating. Hydraulic agriculture made the cultivator till his fields with a minimum of labor-saving tools and animals and with a maximum of human labor. Being politically without influence, the hydraulic farmer maintained a man-nature relation that involved unending drudgery on a socially and culturally depressing level.

Aristotle's vision of a society of free men based on the advance of the mechanical arts is increasingly being realized in the multicentered industrial societies of the West. It never materialized in hydraulic society. For reasons inherent in this institutional conformation, the masters of hydraulic civilization succeeded in perpetuating the economic and technological order which was the *raison d'être* for their existence.

The stationary character of the great Oriental civilizations was noted incisively in the eighteenth and nineteenth centuries, when the expanding commercial and industrial societies of the West began to loosen up what had previously seemed to be an indestructible societal edifice. The Western impact on man-nature relations in the countries of Oriental despotism was as varied as the forms in which it occurred. No fair-minded observer will deny its destructive aspects. But he will also point to the positive and non-totalitarian innovations that not infrequently accompanied it. And he will submit that, even in its most predatory and aggressive manifestations, Western colonialism, which today is subsiding, is more superficial than the new totalitarian colonialism, which is spreading so rapidly.

Hydraulic ("Oriental") civilization has been in transition for generations. It continues to change in a global situation dominated, on the one hand, by the forces of the totalitarian revolution and, on the other hand, by the forces of the multicentered Western world, in which the growth of an increasingly open society is enhanced by the democratic version of a second industrial revolution. The future of hydraulic civilization and of man's relation to nature and man everywhere ultimately depends on the relative strength of these two competing revolutions.

REFERENCES

ANONYMOUS
1909   *Imperial Gazetteer of India,* Vol. III. Oxford: Clarendon Press. 520 pp.
N.d.   *Jātakam: Das Buch der Erzählungen aus früheren Existenzen Buddhas,* Vol. V. Trans. by JULIUS DUTOIT. Munich: Oskar Schloss. 608 pp.

BELOCH, JULIUS
1886   *Die Bevölkerung der griechisch-römischen Welt.* Leipzig: Duncker & Humblot. 520 pp.

BUCK, JOHN LOSSING
1930   *Chinese Farm Economy.* Nanking: University of Nanking; Chicago: University of Chicago Press. 476 pp.
1937   *Land Utilization in China.* Chicago: University of Chicago Press. 494 pp.

BÜCHER, KARL
1922   *Die Entstehung der Volkswirtschaft,* Vol. I. Tübingen: H. Laupp. 475 pp.

CHILDE, V. GORDON
1952   *Man Makes Himself.* New York: Mentor Books. 192 pp.

COLE, JOHN S., and MATHEWS, O. R.
1938   "Tillage," pp. 321–28 in U.S. DEPARTMENT OF AGRICULTURE, *Soils and Men: Yearbook of Agriculture.* Washington, D.C.: Government Printing Office. 1232 pp.

HALL, RICHARD NICKLIN, and NEAL, W. S.
1904   *The Ancient Ruins of Rhodesia.* London: Methuen & Co. 404 pp.

HUNTINGFORD, G. W. B.
1933   "The Azanian Civilization of Kenya," *Antiquity,* VII, No. 26, 153–65.

KAHRSTEDT, ULRICH
1924   "Die Bevölkerung des Altertums," *Handwörterbuch der Staatswissenschaften,* II, 655–70. 4th ed. Jena.

KROEBER, A. L.
1939   *Cultural and Natural Areas of Native North America.* Berkeley: University of California Press. 242 pp.

KUBLER, GEORGE
1946   "The Quechua in the Colonial World," pp. 331–410 in STEWARD, JULIAN H. (ed.), *Handbook of South American Indians,* Vol. II. (Smithsonian Institution, Bureau of American Ethnology, Bulletin No. 143.) Washington, D.C.: Government Printing Office. 976 pp.

KULISCHER, JOSEF
1928   *Allgemeine Wirtschaftsgeschichte des Mittelalters und der Neuzeit,* Vol. I: *Das Mittelalter.* Munich and Berlin: R. Oldenbourgh. 351 pp.

LAMPRECHT, KARL G.
1886   *Deutsches Wirtschaftsleben im Mittelalter: Untersuchungen über die Entwicklung der materiellen Kultur des platten Landes auf Grund der Quellen zunächst des Mosellandes,* Vol. I, No. 1. Leipzig: Alphons Dürr. 663 pp.

LAO KAN
1935   "Liang Han chün-kuo mien-chi chih ku-chi chi k'ou-shu tsêng-chien

chih t'ui-ts'ê," *Academia sinica*, V, No. 2, 215–40. Peking.

LIEBIG, JUSTUS VON
1878 *Chemische Briefe*. 6th ed. Leipzig and Heidelberg: Carl Winters. 479 pp.
[LÜ]
1936 *Lü-shih ch'un-ch'iu* ("Mr. Lü's Spring and Autumn Annals"), in *Ssŭ-pu Pei-yao*. Chung-hua ed. Shanghai. 770 pp.

MAITLAND, FREDERIC WILLIAM
1921 *Domesday Book and Beyond*. Cambridge: Cambridge University Press. 527 pp.

AL-MAKKARI, AHMED IBN MOHAMMED
1840 *The History of the Mohammedan Dynasties in Spain: extracted from the "Nafhu-t-tíb min Ghosni-l-Andalusi-r-rattíb wa Táríkh Lisánu-d-dín Ibni-l-khattíb*," Vol. I. Trans. from the Arabic by PASCUAL DE GAYANGOS Y ARCE. London: Oriental Translation Fund. 548 pp.

MANN, HAROLD H., and KANITKAR, N. V.
1920 *Land and Labour in a Deccan Village*. ("University of Bombay Economic Series," No. III.) London and Bombay: H. Milford and Oxford University Press. 182 pp.

MARSHALL, ALFRED
1946 *Principles of Economics*. London: Macmillan & Co. 871 pp.

MARX, KARL
1919 *Das Kapital*, Vols. I and III, Part I. Hamburg. Otto Meissner. 739+ 448 pp.
1953 *Grundrisse der Kritik der politischen Oekonomie (Rohentwurf)*. Berlin: Dietz. 1,102 pp.

MEISSNER, BRUNO
1920 *Babylonien und Assyrien*, Vol. I. Heidelberg: Carl Winters. 466 pp.

MILL, JOHN STUART
1909 *Principles of Political Economy*. London and New York: Longmans, Green & Co. 1,013 pp.

MUKHTYAR, G. C.
1930 *Life and Labour in a South Gujarat Village*. Ed. C. N. VAKIL. London and New York: Longmans, Green & Co. 304 pp.

PANT, D.
1930 *The Commercial Policy of the*

Moguls. Bombay: D. B. Taraporevala Sons & Co. 281 pp.

PARAIN, CHARLES
1942 "The Evolution of Agricultural Technique," pp. 118–68 in CLAPHAM, J. H. and POWER, E, (eds.), *Cambridge Economic History*, Vol. 1. 2 vols. Cambridge: Cambridge University Press.

PREMERSTEIN, ANTON VON
1936 *Alexandrinische Geronten vor Kaiser Gajus*. ("Mitteilungen der Papyrussammlung der Giessener Universitätsbibliothek," Monograph V.) Giessen. 71 pp.

RANDALL-MACIVER, DAVID
1906 *Mediaeval Rhodesia*. London and New York: Macmillan & Co. 106 pp.

ROGERS, JAMES E. THOROLD
1884 *Six Centuries of Work and Wages*. New York: G. P. Putnam's Sons. 591 pp.

ROSENBLAT, ÁNGEL
1945 *La Población indígena de América desde 1492 hasta la actualidad*. Buenos Aires: Institución Cultural Española. 295 pp.

ROSTOVTZEFF, M.
1941 *The Social and Economic History of the Hellenistic World*. 3 vols. Oxford: Clarendon Press. 1,779 pp.

ROWE, JOHN HOWLAND
1946 "Inca Culture at the Time of the Spanish Conquest," pp. 183–330 in STEWARD, JULIAN H. (ed.), *Handbook of South American Indians*, Vol. II. (Smithsonian Institution, Bureau of American Ethnology, Bulletin No. 143.) Washington, D.C.: Government Printing Office. 976 pp.

SAHAGUN, BERNARDINO DE
1938 *Historia general de las cosas de Nueva España*, Vol. III. Mexico, D.F.: Pedro Robredo. 390 pp.

SCHNEIDER, ANNA
1920 *Die Anfänge der Kulturwirtschaft: Die sumerische Tempelstadt*. Essen: G. D. Baedeker. 120 pp.

SELIGMAN, EDWIN R. A.
1914 *Principles of Economics*. New York and London: Longmans, Green & Co. 711 pp.

SINGH, SARDAR GIAN
1928 *An Economic Survey of Gaggar*

Bhana, a Village in the Amritsar District of the Punjab. (Board of Economic Inquiry, Punjab, Conducted by . . . under the Supervision of M. KING . . . [Rural Section Publication No. 16], "Punjab Village Survey," Vol. I.) Lahore. 235 pp.

SMITH, ADAM
1937 *An Inquiry into the Nature and Causes of the Wealth of Nations.* New York: Modern Library. 976 pp.

SOMBART, WERNER
1927 *Das Wirtschaftsleben im Zeitalter des Hochkapitalismus.* 2 vols. Munich and Leipzig: Duncker & Humblot. 1,064 pp.

WEBER, MAX
1921–22 *Wirtschaft und Gesellschaft: Grundriss der Sozialökonomik.* 2 vols. Tübingen: J. C. B. Mohr. 840 pp.

WIDTSOE, JOHN A
1913 *Dry-Farming: A System of Agriculture for Countries under a Low Rainfall.* New York: Macmillan Co. 445 pp.

WILSON, G. E. H.
1932 "The Ancient Civilization of the Rift Valley," *Man,* XXXII, No. 298, 250–57.

WITTFOGEL, KARL A.
1931 *Wirtschaft und Gesellschaft Chinas.* Leipzig: C. L. Hirschfeld. 768 pp.
1956 *Oriental Despotism and Hydraulic Society.* (In press.)

WITTFOGEL, KARL A., and FÊNG CHIA-SHÊNG
1949 *History of Chinese Society, Liao (907–1125).* (*Transactions of the American Philosophical Society,* Vol. XXXVI.) New York: Macmillan Co. 752 pp.

Effects of Classical Antiquity on the Land

FRITZ M. HEICHELHEIM*

THE THEMA

This survey is concerned with Greco-Roman civilization from about 1100 B.C. to A.D. 565 as far as it influenced the over-all geophysical structure of the Mediterranean lands and their neighboring regions. We exclude from our inquiry the Minoan, Mycenaean, Helladic, and the Italian prehistoric third and second millenniums B.C. Italy was an essential part of prehistoric western Europe during this time, and Greece was not essentially different in social and economic conditions from the contemporary ancient Oriental Bronze Age civilizations as far as we are able at present to ascertain such matters.

Similarly, the Byzantine development from the death of Justinian I in A.D. 565 to the Turkish conquest of Constantinople in A.D. 1453 has closer affinities, on the whole, with the contemporary medieval Western, medieval Islamic, and medieval Russian structural alterations in social and economic pat-

terns and technical know-how than it has with the ages of Pericles, Cicero, and Tribonianus. Two rather unique and violent population and language changes appear near the beginning and the end of classical antiquity as we define it. About 1100 B.C. the incipient Iron Age led to Indo-European, Semitic, and other migrations and to language changes of great intensity from Britain to India, probably surpassing in historic importance and revolutionary impact the much-discussed and powerful Germanic, Slav, Arabic, and related migrations before and after A.D. 565.

In addition, a terrible plague, from A.D. 542 or so, depopulated the world from Wales to Central Asia, eliminating for good the genes of between one-third and one-half of the population groups and races of classical antiquity proper. Under these circumstances, it is not surprising that, after A.D. 565, Latin and Greek ceased to be living languages, giving way to the Romance, Germanic, Celtic, and Western Slav languages and literatures of the medieval West and to Middle Greek, Slavic, Armenian, Syriac, Coptic, Persian, and especially Arabic literary development in the medieval East.

FROM *ca.* 1100 TO *ca.* 560 B.C.

The world of the early Iron Age, after the Dorian, Italic, and the many other migrations of this period had come to an end, looked essentially different from that of the ancient Oriental Bronze Age. The new Iron Age villages, from India to Spain and Britain, maintained politi-

* Dr. Heichelheim is Assistant Professor in Greek and Roman History at the University of Toronto, Canada; Honorary Full Professor for Ancient Economic History at Hochschule Giessen, Westdeutsche Bundesrepublik; and Secretary of the Joint Papyrus Project of Toronto University and University Library Giessen. His works include: *Wirtschaftliche Schwankungen der Zeit von Alexander bis Augustus*, 1929; *Wirtschaftsgeschichte des Altertums* (2 vols.), 1939 (soon to be published in English); "Roman Syria," in T. Frank, *An Economic Survey of Ancient Rome*, Vol. IV, 1938; and "Roemische und byzantinische Sozial- und Wirtschaftsgeschichte," *Historia mundi*, Vol. IV, 1955.

cal autonomy, or even independence, and a higher standard of technical civilization for the lower classes (i.e., for at least 90 per cent of the world population) than the ancient Oriental Bronze Age cities had been able to offer. The invention of the iron plowshare alone, not to speak of numerous other improved or novel agricultural iron tools, brought about an agricultural revolution, for the wooden prehistoric and ancient Oriental plowshares could be worked only in so-called "light soils."

When the heavy soils, the most fertile of our globe, were taken under the plow for the first time in human history, enormous population increases outside of Egypt, Babylonia, and other territories of "hydraulic" civilizations were the consequence. Similarly, owing to new Iron Age techniques, mining production throughout the world was intensified considerably. Greece, about 800 B.C. or so, gradually began to take the lead in improving the potentialities of the new Iron Age civilizations. First, a new type of city settlement developed, the Greek *polis,* originally mainly an agrarian settlement of aristocrats, their dependents and retainers, some craftsmen, merchants, small farmers, and priests.

Thereafter the Greek colonization movement planted such Hellenic *poleis* in large numbers from Naucratis in Egypt and the Cyrenaica to the Crimea and the Taman Peninsula of southern Russia and from Poseidion and the Karatepe of the "Danuna" on the Syrian coast to the shores of the Iberian Peninsula. Everywhere, with the help of iron plowshares and the other new agricultural tools, the heavy soils were opened to the growing of grain. The Hellenic vineyard and olive plantations on hilly terraces and viticulture on high trees were introduced; some forests were transformed into more open park landscapes for aesthetic reasons; fishing and piracy intensified. The agricul-

tural plants and animals of Greece, especially vines, olives, certain grain species, certain breeds of dogs, donkeys, horses, bees, horned cattle, sheep, pigs, goats, spread to all new Greek settlements and those of neighboring natives, as far as the climate from Spain to Syria and from North Africa to southern Russia permitted. In exchange, new domestic breeds were brought to Greece from abroad. The domestic fowl in its advance from India and the Orient reached the Greek settlements during the eighth century B.C.

The Etruscans, a proto-Indo-European nation, whose upper class hailed from northwestern Asia Minor and originally from the Caucasus, founded semiagricultural towns (similar to those of the Greeks) in the Toscana and Latium, among them Rome (probably between 650 and 575 B.C.). Greeks and Etruscans were soon imitated by the so-called *oppida* of the native Italic tribes.

During the last decades of the eighth century B.C., Phoenician and Greek inventors in shipbuilding intensified Mediterranean communications. Phalanx infantry, a pattern of battle formation and armament which had originally been brought by the Assyrians to their Phrygian and Lydian allies, finally spread to the Greek motherland from southwestern Asia Minor. This tactic, adapted by the Greeks, gradually made the small, free Hellenic infantryman more important politically and strategically than the horsed aristocrat of the preceding centuries.

The Greek invention of the coin, near 650 B.C., first being struck in electrum, then in silver and gold, and the subsequent rise of early Greek coin economy revolutionized capital investment in agriculture, mining, craftsman's workshops, trade, and banking operations. The output of Corinthian, Attic, and other pottery for export throughout the Mediterranean area was stimulated and greatly increased. The issues of small silver denominations, which began in Aegina and Corinth slightly before 600 B.C., made possible small savings and, especially, domestic trade without clumsy and wasteful barter operations. By these means, the hardworking and thrifty mass of free Greek *polis* citizens gradually was made independent in their economic aims from their ruling aristocratic families. The Greek phalanx and the Greek coin economy became, in fact, the main forces which stimulated the nascent Greek democracy and small farming.

FROM *ca.* 560 TO 333 B.C.

The earlier structural revolution of Hellenic town and agricultural societies was imitated intensively by non-Greeks from the time of King Croesus of Lydia. The Greeks themselves advanced to a period of classical refinement in all spheres of human life, especially by introducing the principles of reason, logic, and the analysis of cause and effect into all suitable patterns of human activity. The capital which could be invested by society in changing the appearance of cities and countryside increased, mainly because of the creation of world currencies, such as the Attic silver money, which was accepted from Spain to India, but also owing to professional bankers, nautical loans, and *Giro* transfers in bookkeeping that made their appearance in Greece and Babylonia.

The prices of agricultural products rose not only in Hellas between the sixth and the fourth centuries B.C. but also in Babylonia, an indication of increased demand from growing city populations in West and East. The Greek *poleis* of the period were characterized by scientific and rational town building and town planning and by well-made harbor and dock buildings, aqueducts, roads, light-fires, and large workshops of craftsmen with some division of labor (*ergasterion*). We even find the Athenian *deigma*, a clearing-house and exchange for samples of import goods, or the Athenian agora, a permanent and large market with stands for the traders in accordance with their goods. Agorai of this kind were to be the models for the similarly organized bazaars of the Hellenistic-Roman era and those of the Oriental Middle East in our own time. Even artificial harbor basins were excavated. Sailing ships were as quick then as they were until A.D. 1500 or so.

As recent excavations in Austria have made certain, the Celtic inhabitants of the Alps invented the horseshoe about 400 B.C., gradually to be accepted in western Europe during the following centuries as an assistance to overland transport. Earlier, this revolutionary transport invention enabled Celtic cavalry to annihilate a Roman army on the Allia, to sack Rome in 387 B.C., and to annihilate the cavalry and phalanx of Macedonia in 278 B.C. The carefully excavated silver mines of Laurium in Attica and the contemporary Attic inscriptions which are concerned with this mining district are witnesses to numerous technical and economic improvements and well-thought-out legal provisions in this important field of primary production.

Agriculture in Greek *polis* territory also was made more logical and more rational. The use of manure in various forms and of special seeds and breeds of animals, the timing of plowing, seeding, and harvesting, the administration of and the bookkeeping for small and large agricultural estates were treated as a fine art and, during the fourth century B.C., stimulated mankind's first scientific agricultural treatises. Three-field crop rotation, which was generally made use of during the Hellenistic age, appears to be alluded to, in a much-discussed inscriptional rent contract from Euboea, as early as the fourth century B.C.

In Italy, Roman colonization began systematically and permanently during the second quarter of the fourth century B.C. In its gradual advance it revolutionized agriculture throughout the peninsula. As early as the sixth and fifth centuries B.C., the wet, but fertile, soils near the mouth of the Tiber and throughout central Italy had been drained and opened for intensive agriculture, especially with the help of the so-called *cuniculi*. The cat, originally only a domesticated animal of Egypt, appeared then in Etruria also, to spread into Greece and over the whole world during the following period.

The structural changes in the Greek *polis* territories of the period would not have been possible without an enormous increase in the number of slaves for agricultural, industrial, and mining employment. Slavery, however, with the exception of mining and a few other fields of labor, was still comparatively humane. Free men were permitted to take residence wherever they wished, to go to law on their own responsibility, and to work as long and in whatever field of activity they wished, and they were protected against seizure as property. As Professor Westermann proved in an illuminating analysis of Delphic inscriptions (1943), the Greek master could give his slaves three of the "four freedoms" without legally freeing them. Even Roman slavery was still rather patriarchal. Freed slaves of Roman masters could expect their children to be treated as full citizens. Only during the subsequent period and under the influence of a strict interpretation of Roman law was slavery to become that scourge of mankind which was to destroy the happiness and even the lives of millions between 201 and 31 B.C. and to menace the population structure of classical antiquity.

FROM 333 TO 31 B.C.

Alexander the Great established Macedonian government and Hellenic influence as far to the east as the Indus region and present-day Chinese Turkestan. The Ganges region in India was subjected temporarily by Indo-Bactrian kings of Greek descent after 200 B.C. or so. Ptolemaic kings of the third century B.C. had occupied Zanzibar, parts of the coasts of East Africa and southern Arabia, and parts of the Sudan. The seaway to India had been discovered in 117–116 B.C. with the help of the monsoon. Finally, Rome began to conquer and colonize Spain (from 209 B.C. onward), North Africa (from 146 B.C. onward), the central and northern Balkan Peninsula (from 229 B.C. onward), and Gaul (from 125 B.C. onward). By these means was the geographical and anthropogeographical structural revolution, characteristic of early Greco-Roman development, intensified over a comparatively large part of the earth.

A central region of refined civilization (from Babylonia to Italy and Sicily) was surrounded by a larger, outer zone (from the Ganges to the Atlantic) of assimilated barbarian kingdoms, Greek colonial states, and Roman outer provinces and subject allies, in which there were islands of *polis* economy or Roman municipal settlements from which the know-how of Hellenistic and Roman agriculture was gradually appropriated by the native villagers. This was not a period of capital growth pure and simple; there also were considerable capital destruction and waste of capital, owing mainly to the Roman wars of conquest after 201 B.C., the civil wars, the slave-hunting, and the exploitation which characterized Roman provincial administration from 201 to 31 B.C.

World currencies like the "Attic" currency of Alexander the Great and most of his successors, the "Phoenician" currency of the Ptolemies, and, finally, the "Attic" Roman denarius and its many subject currencies made capital transfers easy. The first two coin issues were trimetallic, gold, silver, and bronze being comparatively well adjusted to one another, a pattern of refinement reached by Rome as late as the time of Julius Caesar. For the surprisingly modern capital-investing and generally economic planning of the Hellenistic empires in town, agricultural, and mining production, we have very instructive evidence from the kingdom of Syracuse, from Ptolemaic Egypt (with the largest banking organization of antiquity), from the Seleucid Empire, and from the Hellenistic India of the Arthashastra of Kautilya.

During the third century B.C. much capital was brought to the Middle East, where the interest rate for capital investments was at least three times as high as in the Greek motherland. The capital destruction during the two subsequent centuries of Roman supremacy was cushioned by new colonization and town foundations in Italy and the West. In addition, a new type of money appeared, the bill of exchange, payable to any bearer, quite possibly rejuvenated and Hellenized from unknown ancient Oriental survivals of the cuneiform bearer instruments of the second millennium B.C. Three such documents are known from Ptolemaic Egypt during the second and first centuries B.C. (*Strassburg Ostraka* 510; *Papiri di Regale Università di Milano I*, No. 25 and especially *Papyrus Rylands Library IV*, No. 580); a number of much-discussed references about capital transfer transactions in Plautus and Cicero now have to be reinterpreted in the light of this new evidence.

Planned colonization, general economic planning, world currencies, and the novel bills of exchange made possible a changed appearance of the cities and even more of the countryside from Spain and Gaul to India and Turkestan. The coastal cities, especially in the Mediterranean area, came under the influence of an intensive foreign trade, with cheap mass products, an intensi-

fied market and domestic trade, and comparatively large workshops, with, in some cases, as many as three hundred or so employees and slaves, which often produced for trade over large distances. Campanian bronze vessels and iron tools of the period are found in Scandinavia, for instance, and Mediterranean textiles in Mongolia. Port, dock, and harbor buildings, well-constructed light-fires, *deigmata*, permanent markets for trade and political assemblies, aqueducts, splendid private buildings of the rich, and the use of bricks and concrete for the dwellings of the poor characterized this brilliant and often well-planned Greco-Roman town development, the center of which moved from Greece and the Middle East to Italy during the second century B.C.

From the late fourth century B.C. onward, improved caravan routes in the Middle East and especially the famous network of Roman military roads made the still rather expensive overland communications of the world of classical antiquity more profitable than before. Hellenistic and Roman agriculture from Spain and Gaul to India owed much to Greek, Carthaginian, and, eventually, Roman agricultural science, but perhaps even more to Greek applied mathematics. Not only the Archimedian screw but also the *sakye*, and practically all other irrigation machines and devices which we now call typically Oriental, were, in fact, invented during the third century B.C. as a consequence of Hellenistic progress in mathematics. The *norag*, a new threshing device, was similarly useful, as were improved plows, sickles, and other agricultural tools.

Enormous territories, from the Middle East and North Africa to India and, perhaps, China, which could not be irrigated by the few already ancient Oriental devices for canals and irrigation, now were opened for agriculture and destined to remain in cultivation, on the whole, up to the present day. Mathematically improved water mills, wine and olive-oil presses, and other such devices had a similar importance for the agricultural production of Roman Italy and the Roman provinces from North Africa to the Rhine.

In addition, the agricultural plants and domesticated animal breeds of the whole enormous region from India to Spain and Gaul were now gradually exchanged, as far as the local climate permitted. Cotton came to Egypt, to Babylonia, and even occasionally to Aegean Greece. Apricot trees, lemon trees, melons, Asiatic cattle, and Egyptian cats, ducks, and geese appeared in Greece and Italy. Italy received, in addition, sesame, several clover species, nut, cherry, peach, certain plum, certain fig, quince, almond, chestnut, walnut, and other fruit and nut trees, cypresses, radish, flax, and beetroot. Still more important were the improvements of the period in breeding scientifically or importing superior breeds of horses, donkeys, camels, horned cattle, sheep, goats, pigs, dogs, cats, chickens, ducks, geese, pigeons, pheasants, peacocks, rabbits (from Spain), bees, and even outlandish fish and oysters, special vines, date and fig trees, olive plants, and grain varieties from everywhere in the world where climatic and market conditions made this possible.

Even China participated in this exchange of animals and plants to a smaller extent, receiving, during this period and that of the Roman principate, bloodstock horses, lucerne clover, vines, walnut seeds, pomegranates, peas, certain cucumbers and onions, coriander, and other plants and animals in exchange for the apricot tree, perhaps the peach tree, and goldfish. The reason for these revolutionary changes in the agricultural pattern of the countryside from the Atlantic to the Yellow Sea was that a change-over from subsistence to

market farming characterized enormous territories of the globe during the Hellenistic age and that of the Roman Republic.

Wherever market economy had become profitable, the small and almost self-sufficient peasant estates of earlier centuries were on the retreat. In Egypt, Sicily, Hellenistic India, and large provinces of the Seleucid kingdom, economic agricultural planning by the state bureaucracy treated, to a very far degree, the small and the (not much freer) large agricultural units of the regions in question as subordinated economic entities of a centrally organized, provincial state agriculture. In those regions of the Carthaginian Empire, of Italy, and of the Roman provinces where the new agricultural market economy was profitable, large independent slave estates, the much-discussed latifundia, took the place of numerous small, free peasant homesteads. In both groups of territories scientific, rational agriculture was promoted and was expounded simultaneously in textbooks like those of Theophrastus, the Carthaginian Mago, and the Latins Cato and Varro.

Agricultural tools, agricultural methods (manure, two crops in one year, three-field crop rotation, summer and winter grazing of cattle, vegetable production, wine and olive production, and much more), estate and territorial planning, training of especially qualified servants, and the building of complementary estate workshops for products of craftsmanship were carefully adapted to the most recent and most profitable textbook advices. Destructive tendencies were not wholly missing during this period. The population of the Mediterranean area decreased between 201 and 31 B.C., owing to the Roman wars of conquest, civil wars, social revolutions, and slave-hunting. In Greece and Egypt a reduction of the area under agriculture and of the size of village and town settlements appears from archeological excavations. This temporary loss was more than made good by the population growth and colonial activity in the *imperium Romanum* of the first and second centuries A.D.

The fertility potential of the soil was, however, rarely endangered in classical antiquity. The plows and other agricultural tools of the period were not strong enough to cause what we now call soil destruction. A visit to any museum where Greco-Roman agricultural instruments are preserved will bear this out. In Greece proper and in similar hilly and mountainous subtropical regions which were conquered by Rome and depopulated by slave-hunting, the hillsides, which were steep but still suitable for vineyards, olive plants, vegetable gardens, or modest fruit trees, became barren wasteland. These artificial terraces, which had replaced forest and undergrowth during the Bronze and especially the earlier Iron ages, were no longer protected by the farmer's watchfulness against rain, which gradually washed away the small amount of subsoil held in place by human endeavors.

Malaria was introduced into Sicily during the fourth century B.C. and into Italy during the Second Punic War, in both cases by Carthaginian soldiers from North Africa. Thereafter, this endemic disease of the Apennine Peninsula is the probable reason why the Maremma of Etruria and the Pontine marshes in the Romagna were abandoned by peasant homesteaders from the early second century B.C. onward. However, the main part of Italy, with the exception of these and some other fertile fenlands, was not seriously affected before the Middle Ages by this much-discussed scourge of mankind. Neither did the latifundia, as we know now for certain, destroy the natural soil fertility of any part of Italy, although

damage from overgrazing on estates devoted to cattle-breeding would have been imaginable in theory.

That this is so can be proved irrefutably, to our surprise, in opposition to majority opinions of modern experts, with the help of the aerial survey of practically the whole of Italy taken during World War II by the Royal Air Force of Great Britain; the negatives of this strategic survey are now preserved in Oxford and are accessible to interested scholars. According to these air photographs, the fertility and the extent of the originally cultivated agricultural soil, even in now desolate Apulia, were never impaired in antiquity.

There appear in these photographs evidences of the primitive round huts of the pre-Roman natives of the Bronze and Iron ages. The numerous ditches and walls of the agricultural *centuriatio* of the simultaneously Roman military and agricultural *coloniae*, in the times of the so-called Second and Third Samnite Wars, can be outlined. The second century B.C., the time of the changeover from subsistence to market farming in many parts of Italy, brought into being larger units of land, yet practically all the earlier peasant plots remained in cultivation under old and new owners. Even during the thirteen or so centuries of the periods of the Roman principate, the late Roman Empire, and the earlier Middle Ages, Apulia and other now desolate regions of southern Italy and Sicily remained fertile peasant country. The British air photographs, supporting trial excavations, and documents forgotten in Italian archives until a few years ago have now irrefutably made obvious this conclusion. Spanish destructive methods of sheep-breeding after A.D. 1300, and not Roman or early medieval agricultural mismanagement and maladministration, are the real cause for the present emptiness of many regions of the southern Italian country-side.

The period of the Roman principate from Augustus to Carinus is Janus-faced. The enormous Empire territory, from the Wall of Hadrian in Britain to the Euphrates and from the Sahara, the first Nile cataract, Aden, and Zanzibar to the eastern banks of the Rhine, the southern banks of the Danube, the Carpathians of modern Romania, and the regions to the north, east, and west of the Black Sea, was filled with more city settlements than ever before, far into the third century A.D. On the other hand, as early as the reign of Emperor Hadrian these cities began to shrink in size and population, a gradual process which was accelerated during the troubles of the third century A.D., to the point when hundreds, if not thousands, of such town settlements had to be abandoned forever.

The intellectuals of the period were proud of the splendor, the standard of life, and the civilization which manifested itself in the cities of the Roman Empire. They did not realize that the permanent structural changes of their age were to be found not in the cities but in the despised agricultural sector of the Roman world, where more than 90 per cent of the inhabitants of the Roman Empire found employment and livelihood. The reason for the striking and unintentional shrinking of the cities was that the capital and labor potential at the disposal of the Roman Empire authorities for urbanizing their world was totally insufficient.

The Roman silver and gold currency, which Augustus finally reorganized, and its subsidiary provincial currencies were sadly depleted during the three centuries from Augustus to Carinus as a consequence of the generally passive trade balance of the Empire. Contemporary authors and numerous Roman coin hoards from northern Germany, Scandinavia, southern Russia, Scotland, Ireland, southern Arabia, Iran, the Russian Caucasus, western Siberia, and especially India bear witness to this. From Augustus to Marcus Aurelius, the ratio of copper to silver was stabilized at 1:56 or so; that of silver to gold fluctuated between 1:12 and 1:9 or so. In the fourth century A.D., on the other hand, we find a ratio of copper to silver of 1:125; of silver to gold fluctuating at between 1:14 and 1:18. According to these figures, much more than half of the silver and much more than two-thirds of the gold which had circulated in Roman territory during the reign of Augustus had left the Mediterranean world, mainly during the time from Nero to Carinus.

The canals, roads, harbor works, and docks which were constructed from Britain to the Euphrates during the first, second, and even the troubled third centuries A.D. were very numerous. Many of them were never destroyed or could be restored easily, proving to be very useful in maintaining the standards of the mainly agricultural and the nascent town economies of the early Middle Ages. Nevertheless, these means of communication were not sufficiently numerous and not sufficiently well planned to maintain free trade, with cheap mass products, between the town communities of the Empire from Britain to the Euphrates in the same intensity as had been characteristic for the centuries from *ca.* 560 to 31 B.C. As early as about A.D. 100 most of the colonized Roman provinces in the east and west and even much smaller subdivisions of some Roman provinces had become practically self-sufficient economic units as far as the production and trade of cheap mass products were concerned.

From the reign of Emperor Hadrian onward, interprovincial free trade was largely restricted, owing to the unbeatable local competition in cheap goods, to the valuable and luxury products, and to government transports, for which captains and merchants had to be bound to their professions for an increasing number of cheap goods. For government transports overland the *cursus publicus,* the imperial government's permanent courier and transport service over the Roman road system, became such a terrible burden, owing to its increased use by the army and the bureaucracy, that settlements close to imperial relay stations were abandoned occasionally. On the other hand, trade inside of the more or less recently urbanized provinces, like Britain, Gaul, much of Spain and North Africa, the Alpine and Danubian provinces, eastern Asia Minor, and the province of Arabia, reached a relative intensity which, on the whole, was to be permanent and was never again to decline to pre-Roman and prehistoric levels, even under the impact of the most destructive migration waves of the early Middle Ages.

Local trade inside of and between the old and new villages of the Empire reached a similar intensity, which was to remain permanent in post-Roman times. During the second and third centuries A.D. the local trade and especially professional banking throughout the shrinking town settlements became so unprofitable, however, that the government authorities had to bind many such specialized traders and bankers to their professions to maintain all essential services for army, court, and Empire administration and to uphold, for the troubled town populations, at least an appearance of the intensity of local trade and banking transactions which had been characteristic of the Empire towns of the first century A.D.

As a consequence of the gradual strengthening of the new provinces and the efflorescence of the agricultural districts everywhere in the Empire, the considerable know-how of Hellenistic-Roman craftsmanship spread to all new towns and to villages and estates in the countryside from Britain to Arabia. The colonization efforts, which filled the Empire with towns, villages, country villas, and the redoubtable *limes* fortifications, signal systems, and strategic roads, which protected the peaceful settlers against foreign enemies, would not have been possible without concrete and the brickworks which sprang up throughout the provinces. More than that, new inventions, mostly connected with technical methods of using air for economic purposes, made Greco-Roman craftsmanship more efficient than ever.

Improved bellows not only made mining safer but led eventually to the production of true steel for the first time in human technical history, probably about the third century A.D. Windmills in suitable regions supplemented the earlier water mills, from the first or second centuries A.D. More important still was the invention of glass-blowing between 40 and 30 B.C., which occurred on the Mediterranean coast of either Egypt or Syria-Palestine. Cast glass had been known from the third millennium B.C., but its production costs had been too high to permit inexpensive use for non-luxury purposes. Henceforth, vessels made of cheap blown glass were to be found also in the village huts of the poor.

Glass sarcophagi and especially glass windows were used by the upper and even the middle classes of the Empire. Roman administration and proper town life would not have been possible in Britain, on both sides of the Rhine, and on the Danube without the imperial administrators and the well-to-do being protected against the Central European winter by glass windows, which permitted office work and reading at all times of the year. A completely novel industry of glass-making sprang up during the first century of the principate, mainly concentrated in Cologne, some other cities of Gaul, Rome and other Italian towns, Alexandria, Antioch, and several smaller cities of Syria and Asia Minor, achieving a permanent and most important contribution of classical antiquity to the well-being of medieval and modern mankind.

In the newly colonized and urbanized territories of the Roman Empire, the Hellenistic-Roman know-how in craftsmanship had been appropriated first by the city settlements, as is only natural. When these shrank in size again during the second and third centuries A.D., the government had, in the more ancient centers of civilization and in trade and banking, to bind many professional workers to their jobs to prevent endangering the safety of the Roman armies and the imperial administration. What happened simultaneously in the countryside was, however, of far greater historic importance than this process of decay in the cities.

Throughout the Empire the large estates which worked for foreign and local markets gradually expanded their own workshops for those crafts whose production was profitable and suitable for their economic pattern. The competition from the sale of the surplus of these estate workshops in near-by free markets endangered the livelihood of many city craftsmen throughout the Empire from the second century A.D. onward and induced many insufficiently employed town-dwelling craftsmen to take service on countryside estates. Through such newcomers the simple villagers, freeborn or slaveborn, were gradually instructed in all technical inventions and devices of classical antiquity which were apt to improve the peasant's standard of life and income.

The beauty of Samian and other pottery, of bronze, iron, steel, and glass tools, and some technical niceties of earlier mechanical devices were sacrificed to local cheap production by village and estate craftsmen. As a result,

however, the average villager throughout the Empire of the Roman principate had more technical comfort at his disposal than had the Athenian *polis* proletarian during the period from the Persian Wars to Pericles or than had the Roman city proletarian at the time of the Gracchan brothers. More important still, the difference between the standards of life of a small and dependent farmer in the countryside of the Empire of the Roman principate and that of the contemporary city proletarian had become negligible, except if in Rome, Alexandria, Antioch, and two or three other famous centers which were well cared for by the government.

This process was intensified by the agricultural changes of the period, which took place, in regional variation, during different decades of the first, second, and third centuries A.D. With the help of the fully developed methods of Greco-Roman agricultural science and technique, large new territories were permanently taken into cultivation. In England the fertile fenlands of East Anglia were drained, and the Fosse and other still existing canals were constructed to transport grain from these and other imperial and private estates to the garrisons and camp followers in northern England and the Scottish Lowlands. Vineyards producing local and world-famous beverages were to be characteristic of the hilly countryside of Gaul and the Rhineland for all the future. The regions on both sides of the Danube were similarly opened up. In Holland the sea was brought under control as never before with the help of well-planned ditches and drainage systems. In the fenlands of East Anglia the Roman drainage works and many Romano-British villages survived beyond the time of Roman occupation, to be given up readily under the earlier and later Anglo-Saxon kings and, anyway, before the *Domesday Book* was compiled. In Holland the Roman ditches and canals were preserved and kept in good order by the Salian Franks but were unable to withstand the rising water levels of the early Middle Ages.

In regions bordering the deserts of North Africa and the Middle East, methods of agriculture were used which were successfully imitated by French colonizers in Algeria, Tunisia, and Morocco during the nineteenth and twentieth centuries. In these semiarid regions with slight soil moisture, olive plantations were kept alive for two or three years by transporting water from afar to new plantations. Once the roots of the olive plants reached the subsurface water, the very desert became habitable and profitable agricultural soil. In Egypt careful Roman flood-control measures and new irrigation canals made productive again those territories of the Nile country which had been given up as desert or marshlands during the last two centuries of Ptolemaic rule. In Transjordania, the Negev, and the Syrian Desert regions numerous new cisterns and irrigation systems preserved the life-giving water of heavy rainfalls for years and, exactly as at present again in the state of Israel, made settlements possible everywhere. The small Roman province of Mesopotamia, which was of the highest strategic importance, was most thoroughly colonized during the third century A.D. Here and in Britain urban decline was delayed up to the fifth century A.D.; in Roman Arabia, even into the sixth century A.D. In Italy and elsewhere there occurred a novel wheeled plow.

The agricultural plants and domestic animals which had been adapted to the countries from Babylonia and Syria to Italy during the preceding period were now used everywhere in the Roman Empire, as far as the climate permitted, first on large estates and on agricultural soil annexed to the new town settlements and thereafter by the simple villagers. The slave estates of the preceding period vanished, however, as early as the period of Augustus and his immediate successors. The *pax Romana*, which the world owed to the first princeps, made slave-hunting of the earlier profitable *en gros* pattern impossible, and the numbers of cheap slaves from victorious campaigns of conquest were reduced to a trickle. In consequence, the market price of slaves soon rose so high that to employ menial agricultural slaves in large numbers became unprofitable.

Only rump estates, therefore, were cultivated scientifically with the help of a comparatively small number of unfree agricultural and household servants and a library containing the main agricultural textbooks of the past and present. The largest part of the latifundia of the republican centuries and of their successors in the provinces were instead farmed out to small peasants, in modern times all usually called *coloni*. They had to pay a contractual rent and took over some contractual work on the main estate. They received some technical agricultural advice from the experts on the main estate, and were gradually offered contracts on imperial and private estates which covered not only the lifetime of an individual farmer but even those of his sons and grandsons.

Furthermore, it was now profitable for many estate owners and imperial estates to free experienced agricultural slaves, permit them to marry, and to provide them contractually with land as *coloni*. Germanic and Eastern prisoners of war were similarly settled on imperial and private estate soil, although with some police supervision and without the legal protection given to Roman citizens and provincials in good standing. On many of the plots of the *coloni*, subsistence farming more or less gradually replaced market farming again, but without the agricultural production potential and the technical comfort of the Roman Empire peasantry, relapsing to pre-Hellenic, pre-Roman, or prehistoric levels.

Owing to the troubles of the third century A.D., the latifundia of the time of the principate, with their rump estates and *coloni,* often changed over from imperial administration or from a rich city-dwelling owner to proper *patrocinia.* Army officers retired to such estates as their permanent abode, maintained mercenary, private guard units (*bucellarii*), and protected their lands and those of their *coloni* not only against foreign invaders and inimical and friendly army units appearing in their region but also against visits from the imperial tax-collectors. Gradually, numerous free villagers, unbearably oppressed by plundering soldiers and the tax-collectors, voluntarily ceded their lands to owners of neighboring *patrocinia,* to be protected as *coloni.* The *patrocinium* owners, as a rule, knew how to use their influence at the imperial court and, with the provincial administration, to obtain permission to collect all taxes from their *coloni* directly and to pay no more than a fixed lump sum from the whole *patrocinium* territory into the imperial treasury.

The native barbarians everywhere outside of the Empire's frontiers, with the exception of the inhabitants of the Parthian kingdom, had so far been completely unable to transplant and adapt to their own needs the pattern of the Greco-Roman city settlements without becoming Roman allies. The new Empire peasantry, however, with their semiscientific technical know-how, village craftsmanship, and use of a wide variety of agricultural tools, plants, and domesticated animals, could be imitated more easily, especially as prisoners of war from all neighboring barbarian countries had been trained as *coloni* in Roman agricultural production by Roman masters. It is not surprising under these circumstances that, from the

second century A.D., agriculture in Ireland, Scotland, free Germany, Scandinavia, eastern Europe, and western Siberia began to include the tools, plants, animals, and technical methods of classical antiquity.

The coasts of East and West Africa, the Sudan, Abyssinia, the more backward regions of the Middle East, the Arabian Peninsula, and Iran had been subject to similar trends from the third century B.C. and continued their agricultural refinement with stronger intensity than before. This is borne out by the results of excavations and by the thousands of technical words which are early intruders from Latin and Greek into practically all languages of Europe, North Africa, and western Asia and are connected with Greco-Roman agriculture and simple craftsmanship. A revolution of village life and village production began in a territory many times larger than the Roman Empire. Gradually, in this way, the agricultural foundations for the Western, Islamic, and Russian medieval civilizations were laid.

The population of the Roman Empire under the principate at the time of Augustus amounted to between fifty and seventy millions, an estimate which has been accepted tentatively by the overwhelming majority of experts. The shrinking of the city settlements (with the exceptions mentioned on p. 175). almost everywhere throughout the Roman Empire during the third century A.D. has led many scholars to the assumption that this was a period of considerable population decrease, similar to that which has been guessed for those late Roman centuries during which comparably troubled conditions prevailed, especially in Gaul, Britain, Spain, and North Africa. Unfortunately, our sources do not permit absolutely certain conclusions to this difficult question.

Excavations show that, different from the urban development, the number of peasant plots and villages certainly did not decrease during the third century A.D., as Germanic and other prisoners of war replaced in large numbers possible losses from the serious civil wars and foreign invasions of this period. In addition, the Greco-Roman practice of exposing newborn babies to die was virtually discontinued wherever the population masses turned to Christianity. Therefore, it seems rather likely that the population of the Roman Empire, if it did not increase, at least held its own during the third century A.D., as the late Professor Delbrueck maintained (1921) from mainly strategic considerations. Recent research by Professor Kahrstedt (1954), on the population numbers on estates which had taken the place of some small earlier *poleis* in Greece proper, leads to similar conclusions for the second and third centuries A.D., as far as the province of Achaia is concerned. At any rate, the Roman Empire seems to have gained in the agricultural sector at least as much during the third century A.D. as it lost in the town settlements.

FROM A.D. 284 TO 565

The late Roman period, from our point of view, cannot be classified as a time of outright decline. It is true that the great Emperor Diocletian and his successors, during the fourth and fifth centuries A.D., were able only to strengthen and maintain city life in their dominions by asking for very serious sacrifices from practically all inhabitants of the Roman Empire. The help of extensive and permanent state assistance given to most towns of the Empire and state control over the agricultural sector upheld a minimum for Empire defense and civilized Empire administration. In the subsequent eastern Roman Empire, however, city life recovered and came into its own again as early as the fifth and sixth centuries A.D. Constantinople and other eastern Roman town centers continued to increase in size.

Even in territories, like Britain, which were lost to the Empire, money economy and local money trade remained to a noticeable extent, at least regionally. Our museums today include the so-called *minimi* and *minimissimi*, tiny bronze coins issued by local, and probably private, mints for small shopping transactions of the population after the Roman administration had left Britain in the early fifth century A.D. and all Roman mints had closed down. Diocletian and Constantine the Great, early in our period, were able to create a gold currency, that of the solidus, or the later bezant, which was essential for trade transactions of the world from Scotland and Scandinavia to India and from Russia to Abyssinia for more than a full millennium and which was not adulterated or diminished in weight for almost a thousand years.

For bills of exchange, known for the later part of the period from Alexander to Augustus, we cannot prove, on the basis of present evidence, that they survived into the earlier or later centuries of the time of the principate. Since the fifth century A.D., however, bearer documents are mentioned again in the Talmuds, Iranian, Arabic, and Byzantine sources, indicating a rejuvenation of money and town economy in the eastern Mediterranean area. These late Roman and Oriental bearer documents are the models for the bills of exchange in Latin, which initiated medieval conditions in this field in Frankish western Europe.

Foreign trade in cheap mass products was almost exclusively organized by the Roman state during the first two centuries of the period but gradually stood again on its own feet in the eastern Roman Empire from the fifth and sixth centuries A.D. onward. Only to the west of Constantinople, in the same period, was local city trade and banking on the downgrade. Trade in luxury products increased in intensity during the late Roman period in the west and east, and new products, like Asiatic and Mediterranean silk, supplemented the earlier valuable products. Naval transport conditions and overland transport on most Roman roads were inferior only in times of war to those of the second and third centuries A.D. Overland transport was even improved during the Byzantine centuries when the originally Chinese inventions of saddle and stirrup gradually became known in the eastern Mediterranean area and subsequently farther west. Many technical peculiarities of Greco-Roman craftsmanship came more and more to be used in villages. Special skills which were not profitable in the agricultural sector were kept alive and often improved in the famous imperial factories, mainly of Constantinople, where privileged craftsmen worked for the requirements of the imperial court, the army and navy, the administration, and occasionally private buyers.

Neither were technical inventions and new professions of craftsmen missing. Better steel was now made. The earliest chemical formulas preserved on papyrus are known from the early fourth century A.D. The first reference to Greek fire, a potent mixture of unburned chalk, petrol, and saltpeter, belongs to approximately A.D. 500. An independent silk weavers' craft began to develop after A.D. 552–53. Numerous craftsmen of various professions were resident on the soil of the *patrocinia* and worked for local needs. More important, still, was a completely novel, late Roman type of economic unit which combined many professions of craftsmanship with agriculture.

In Egypt of the early fourth century A.D., monasteries sprang up in which manual labor was considered to be a religious duty. In large Egyptian units

of this kind, like the "White Monastery," there were more craftsmen at work in a co-ordinated manner than in any Greek *ergasterion* or Roman *fabrica* of earlier centuries. As far as agriculture was concerned, such monasteries had access to all Greek and Latin works on agricultural science or related subjects, either in the original or in translations into an oriental language of the Middle East. These monasteries proved especially able in making desert lands or, from the sixth century A.D. onward in the West, forest, fen, and other waste lands as fertile as the climate and the agricultural knowledge of their time permitted. Many monasteries even specialized in this backbreaking work of agricultural colonization.

It is well known that, after tentative experiments in Italy, the Provence, Spain, and North Africa, the Benedictine monasteries of the sixth century A.D. finally found the pattern by which this originally Egyptian form of religious community life could become an integral stimulus for the western Middle Ages. They prevented any real collapse of civilization in the countryside and even the earliest cities, any far-reaching agricultural deterioration even in troubled times, or any permanent abandonment of potentially fertile soil. Here, in this and in many other fields of activity, it is obvious that late Roman agriculture was as active and open to improvements as in earlier ages, in spite of all the difficulties and troubles of the time of migrations in West and East.

The silkworm and the specialized, intensive cultivation of the mulberry plant were introduced into the eastern Roman Empire from Central Asia in A.D. 553 or so. New types of cucumber, better breeds of dogs, "Arabic" horses, camels, and hunting birds were produced, and the number and specialization of agricultural tools further increased. The inherited agricultural textbooks were supplemented by new works and by more or less modernized and embellished translations. Modern authors often have expressed severe judgments about late Roman agricultural conditions, because serfdom of the originally free *coloni*, which had begun during the third century A.D., became practically universal during the fourth and the early fifth centuries A.D., swallowing up most of the free villagers also.

But one usually forgets that this development was only temporary as far as the eastern Roman Empire was concerned. Feudalism was suppressed to a very marked degree, and the binding of the peasant to an estate was lifted or mitigated from the sixth century A.D. onward, a change which was strongly supported by the Christian church. In the seventh century A.D., Byzantine peasantry was organized, as a rule, into military (*themata*) and civilian villages and was practically free again. The beginnings of this structural change of great world historic importance appear as early as the sixth century A.D., in the papyrus evidence from Egypt, in Chalcedonian and monophysitic church authors of the sixth and early seventh centuries A.D., and in the much-discussed agricultural reform legislation of Pope Gregory the Great.

Only the West, under Visigothic, Frankish, Burgundian, and Lombard rule, remained dedicated to peasant serfdom for political reasons during these centuries. But, even so, the population of the countryside certainly did not, as a rule, decrease, nor was soil fertility undermined. In the Frankish, Burgundian, and Alemannic territories and in Anglo-Saxon Britain, modern excavations have revealed numerous Germanic villages on the soil of earlier imperial and private Roman estates, evidence of numerous families making a living where only a small agricultural and administrative staff of servants had dwelt before. Recently discovered Latin documents from Vandalic North Africa show that life was certainly not as much disturbed as Latin and Greek authors report for this area.

In Italy air photography has proved that, whatever damage Ostrogoths, Lombards, and Byzantine generals may have done to agriculture in the fifth and sixth centuries A.D., during temporary warlike operations, was repaired quickly, the Benedictine monasteries even improving regionally on the earlier state of affairs. Egyptian agriculture, as Professor Johnson recently has pointed out (Johnson and West, 1949), and likewise the agriculture of Syria and Palestine do not seem to have suffered at all, except from temporary Persian invasions. Transjordania and other semidesert territories of the Roman Middle East flourished more than ever, especially as these regions were a favorite haunt of eremites and monasteries and experienced, in addition, an enormous population increase from Arabic immigrants. This occurred long before Islam, a migration movement which was especially intensified after a dam break of Marib in A.D. 450, and the final collapse of the artificial irrigation system of southern Arabia between A.D. 542 and 570 diminished enormously the agricultural productivity of southern Arabia.

Asia Minor and the Greek-speaking, southern part of the Balkan Peninsula were made the center of the eastern Roman Empire during this period and experienced in consequence a sizable increase in their town and village populations. The political weakness of the late Roman Empire in the east and west and the final loss of Italy, the western Roman provinces, the Roman Middle East, and the North Balkan regions was not caused by a permanent economic decline of the Empire structure or a population decrease. The main reason for this far-reaching political change was that the *imperium Romanum,* and also the Persian kingdom, had ceased to be the only civilized territories of the world outside of India and China.

The technical methods and the essentials of Greco-Roman civilization in their Christian reformulation were taken over during the last period of classical antiquity by practically the whole of Europe, large parts of western and Central Asia, East Africa, and Arabia. As a result, the military superiority of the Roman army was undermined, and Empire defense became more difficult and often impossible.

Finally, new civilizations arose in what is now the Islamic Middle East, in Abyssinia, in the Romance, Germanic, Celtic, and Western Slavic-speaking West, and in eastern Europe. These daughter-civilizations were, in the course of time, to surpass by far their Greco-Roman mother-civilization, albeit bringing, during their later history, soil destruction to more than one region which had flourished during classical antiquity.

REFERENCES

Where no special references are given below, the problems touched upon in this survey have been discussed in detail in:

HEICHELHEIM, FRITZ M.
1939 *Wirtschaftsgeschichte des Altertums,* Vols. I and II. Leiden: Sijthoff. 1240 pp.

Of general surveys not mentioned in the pertinent notes of the above work, see especially:

ANONYMOUS
1924–39 *Cambridge Ancient History.* 12 vols. Cambridge: Cambridge University Press.

BENGTSON, HERMANN
1950 *Griechische Geschichte von den Anfängen bis in die römische Kaiserzeit.* ("Handbuch der Altertumswissenschaft," Vol. III, No. 4.) Munich: Beck. 592 pp.

BURY, JOHN B., and MEIGGS, RUSSEL
1951 *A History of Greece to the Death of Alexander the Great.* 3d ed. London: Macmillan & Co. 926 pp.

CARY, MAX
1954 *A History of Rome Down to the Reign of Constantine.* 2d ed. London: Macmillan & Co. 820 pp.

FRANK, TENNEY
1933–40 *An Economic Survey of Ancient Rome.* 5 vols. Baltimore: Johns Hopkins University Press.

MICHELL, H.
1940 *The Economics of Ancient Greece.* Cambridge: Cambridge University Press. 416 pp.

OSTROGORSKY, GEORG
1940 *Geschichte des byzantinischen Staats.* ("Handbuch der Altertumswissenschaft," Vol. XII, Nos. 1–2.) Munich: Beck. 448 pp.

PREAUX, CLAIRE
1939 *L'Economie royale des Lagides.* Brussels: Fondation Reine Élisabeth. 646 pp.

ROSTOVTZEFF, MICHAEL
1951 *The Social and Economic History of the Hellenistic World.* 3 vols. Oxford: Clarendon Press. 1780 pp.

STEIN, ERNST
1928 *Geschichte des spaetroemischen Reiches.* Vienna: Seidel. 592 pp.
1949 *Histoire du Bas Empire.* Paris and Brussels: Desclée de Brouwer. 900 pp.

REFERENCES ON SPECIAL PROBLEMS

AGRICULTURE OF BYZANTINE EGYPT
AND VANDALIC AFRICA

COURTALS, CH.; LESCHI, L.; PERAT, CH.; and SAUMAGNE, CH.
1952 *Tablettes Albertini: Actes privés*
de l'époque vandale (fin du Ve siècle), Vols. I and II. Paris: Arts et métiers graphiques. 344 pp.

JOHNSON, ALLAN CH., and WEST, LOUIS C.
1949 *Byzantine Egypt.* ("Princeton

University Studies in Papyrology," No. 6.) Princeton, N.J.: Princeton University Press. 344 pp.

AIR PHOTOGRAPHS OF ITALY

BRADFORD, JOHN

1947 "A Technique for the Study of Centuriation," *Antiquity*, XXI, 197–204.

1949 "Buried Landscapes in Southern Italy," *ibid.*, XXIII, 65–72.

1950 "The Apulia Expedition: An Interim Report," *ibid.*, XXIV, 84–95.

1955 *Ancient Landscapes in Europe and Asia: Studies in Archaeology and Photography.* Oxford: Oxford University Press. 164 pp.

BEGINNINGS OF COINAGE

ROBINSON, E. S. G.

1951 "The Coins from the Ephesian Artemision Reconsidered," *Journal of Hellenic Studies*, LXXI, 156–67.

COINAGE IN POST-ROMAN BRITAIN

SUTHERLAND, C. H. V.

1938 "Minimi, Radiate and Diademed," *Transactions of the International Numismatic Congress, 1936*, pp. 252–61. London: Quaritch.

1950 "The Canterbury Minimissimi Again," *Numismatic Chronicle*, 6th ser., IX, 242–44.

DATE OF THE FOUNDING OF ROME

GJERSTADT, EINAR

1952a "Stratigraphic Excavations in the Forum Romanum," *Antiquity*, XXVI, 60–64.

1952b "Scavi stratigrafici nel Foro Romano e problemi ad essi relativi," *Bulletino di Commissione Archeologica Communale di Roma*, LXXIII, 13–29.

HORSESHOE IN PREMEDIEVAL TIMES

HELL, MAX

1950 "Keltische Hufeisen aus Salzburg," *Archaeologia Austriaca*, VII, 92–95.

1953 "Weitere keltische Hufeisen aus Salzburg und Umgebung," *ibid.*, XII, 44–49.

MONASTERIES

HEICHELHEIM, FRITZ M.

1955a "Art Domaene," in KLAUSER, H. (ed.), *Reallexikon für Antike und Christentum*, Vol. III. 3 vols. Stuttgart: Hiersemann Verlag.

1955b "Roemische Sozial- und Wirtschaftsgeschichte," in VALJAVEC, F. (ed.), *Historia mundi: Ein Handbuch der Weltgeschichte in Zehn Bänden*, Vol. IV. Bern: A. Franke; Munich: Leo Lehnen.

PHALANX

STIER, HANS ERICH

1950 "Probleme der frühgriechischen Geschichte und Kultur," *Historia*, I, 195–230.

PLANNING ECONOMY OF THE HELLENISTIC MONARCHIES FROM INDIA TO SICILY

HEICHELHEIM, FRITZ M.

1938 "New Light on the Influence of Hellenistic Financial Administration in the Near East and India," *Economic History*, February, pp. 1–12.

1953 "The Wilbour Papyrus," *Historia*, II, 129–35.

POPULATION OF THE ROMAN EMPIRE UNDER THE PRINCIPATE AND DOMINATE

BOAK, ARTHUR E. A.

1955 *Manpower Shortage and the Fall of the Roman Empire in the West.* Ann Arbor: University of Michigan Press. 164 pp.

DELBRUECK, HANS

1921 *Geschichte der Kriegskunst*, Vol. II. 3d ed. Berlin: Stilke. 508 pp.

KAHRSTEDT, ULRICH

1954 *Das wirtschaftliche Gesicht Griechenlands in der Kaiserzeit.* ("Dissertationes Bernenses," Vol. I, No. 7.) Bern: A. Francke. 296 pp.

SLAVERY IN CLASSICAL GREECE

WESTERMANN, WILLIAM L.

1943 "Slavery and the Elements of Freedom in Ancient Greece," *Quarterly Bulletin of the Polish Institute of*

Arts and Sciences in America, January, pp. 1–16.

1955   *The Slave Systems of Greek and Roman Antiquity.* ("Memoirs of the American Philosophical Society," Vol. XL.) Philadelphia. 180 pp.

SOUTH ARABIAN IRRIGATION COLLAPSE

GROHMANN, ADOLF

1930   In PAULY-WISSOWA, *Realencyklopaedie der klassischen Altertumswissenschaft,* XIV, 1736–44. Stuttgart: Metzler. 2,584 pp.

The Clearing of the Woodland in Europe

H. C. DARBY[*]

Perhaps the greatest single factor in the evolution of the European landscapes has been the clearing of the wood that once clothed almost the entire continent. The presence of woodland, and the effort to use it or subdue it, has been a constant motif throughout the history of successive centuries; and the struggle has left a mark, often upon the form and intensity of human settlement, and always upon the general character of the landscape. The attack, begun in prehistoric times, has been continued from innumerable centers, and, little by little, as population has grown, the wood has given way to pasture and to arable land. But the clearing has not been a continuous or sustained process, for at times the forest has reasserted itself and crept back. Nor has the clearing been complete, for substantial tracts of wood still remain. But the net result has been ever more open space; and man, driven by economic motives, and as if relenting at the success of his attack, is now seeking to stay, or at any rate to regulate, the clearing and to place the care of forests upon a rational basis. "The woods"—their de-

struction and its consequences and the need for a policy of conservation—was one of the main themes of George P. Marsh's *Man and Nature*, which first appeared in 1864.

Broadly speaking, the clearing has had its own characteristics in each of the three regions of European history—Southern Europe, Central and Western Europe, and Eastern Europe. Although this division into three is not very precise, it is a convenient one. In Southern Europe, under Mediterranean conditions of climate and soil, the forest was open in character and was composed largely of evergreen oaks and pines. Once cleared, it showed less regenerative power than did the forests to the north; already by classical times much of it seems to have disappeared, leaving behind scrub and, in places, bare surfaces exposed to soil erosion. In the second region, in Western and Central Europe, the temperate forest zone is dominated by the oak, mixed with a variety of other deciduous trees, including the beech, but giving way to conifers on the higher ground. It was not until the Middle Ages that the main outlines of the clearing of this dense woodland were sketched, and the story of that clearing is relatively much better documented than the story elsewhere in Europe. The third region is that of Eastern Europe, with which the north may be linked. The mixed forest of Central Europe stretched into this region, but without the beech, which may be regarded as an indicator of the

[*] Dr. Darby is Professor of Geography in the University of London and Head of the Department of Geography at University College, London. He is a member of the Royal Commission on Historical Monuments (England). He edited *An Historical Geography of England before A.D. 1800*, 1936, and his publications include: *The Medieval Fenland*, 1940; *The Draining of the Fens*, 1940; and *The Domesday Geography of Eastern England*, 1952.

contrast between peninsular and continental Europe (Fig. 54). In the south lie the steppes which, if they ever bore forests (and they may well have), must have been cleared in preclassical times. In the north lies the coniferous belt where agriculture is restricted and where man's impression has been relatively slight.

FIG. 54.—Europe: limits of certain trees

THE MEDITERRANEAN LANDS

Classical Times

The difference between the climate of the Mediterranean Basin and that of the rest of Europe is striking. The rainfall of the three summer months (June, July, August) rarely exceeds six inches, and in many areas it is less than two. The northward limit of the olive follows very closely that of truly Mediterranean conditions (Fig. 54). As a result of this climate, the characteristic Mediterranean forest grows in open formation and is largely evergreen in character; it comprises such species as the Aleppo pine and various kinds of evergreen oak, particularly the holm oak and the valonia oak. To what extent the Mediterranean lowlands were originally covered by forest is uncertain, but it is clear that there was, and is, much local variation, with gradations northward into the dense deciduous woodlands of Central and Western Europe and south-

ward into the scatter of solitary, thorny, and spiny shrubs of steppe and desert. In the mountainous areas within the basin, the characteristic open forest gives way to a wood cover that resembles that to the north; here are the beech, the Spanish chestnut, and species of deciduous oak, and these, in turn, merge higher up into various kinds of fir mixed with, or dominated by, the black pine. This is so in the Pyrenees, the Alps, the Apennines, and the Balkan Mountains. The same succession in varying degrees is encountered in the higher parts of Sicily, the Peloponnesus, Crete, and Cyprus.

Classical writers provide abundant indications of the existence of wood (Semple, 1931). Homer, maybe as early as the ninth century B.C., spoke of "wooded Samothrace," of "wooded Zacynthos," of the "tall pines and oaks" of Sicily, and of other "wooded country." He told how Sarpedon fell in battle "as falls an oak or silver poplar, or a slim pine tree, that on the hills the shipwrights fell with whetted axes, to be timber for shipbuilding." And he described the noise of battle as "the din of woodcutters in the glades of a mountain." In another metaphor he compared the press of battle with the consequences of fire in this land of parched summers: "Through deep glens the fierce fire rages on some parched mountain-side, and the deep forest burns, and the driving wind whirls the flame every way."[1] Thucydides also knew of the consequences of forest fires and wrote of "spontaneous conflagrations sometimes known to occur through the wind rubbing the branches of a mountain forest together."[2] Once destroyed, whether by chance fire or by the hand

1. The references from Homer are as follows: *Iliad* xiii. 13; xvi. 482–84; xvi. 643–46; xx. 490–92 (see also x. 154–57; xxi. 340–49); *Odyssey* i. 246; ix. 186 (see also xiii. 243–46; xiv. 1–2).

2. Thucydides *History of the Peloponnesian War* ii. 77.

of man, the forest could regenerate itself only with difficulty, for the new growth found an implacable enemy in the goat. By the fifth century B.C. the destructive nibble of the goat up the mountainsides was already well advanced. Plato in the *Critias* provides us with a theory of the consequences of the destruction of wood. Not long since, he wrote, the soil of Attica was deep and carried "much forest-land." But its trees had disappeared, some to provide rafters for the roofs of Athenian buildings; and, as he wrote, Attica was a naked upland: "What now remains compared with what then existed is like the skeleton of a sick man, all the fat and soft earth having been wasted away, and only the bare framework of the land being left."[3]

But, although Attica was thus laid bare by the fifth century B.C., much of Greece, and indeed of the whole basin of the Mediterranean, was still well wooded. It was Theophrastus, who, in the following century, wrote the *Enquiry into Plants,* which provides us with considerable information about the forests of his time. He referred to the forests of the plains, but it is about the more important forests of the uplands that he gave us most detail. It was they that best produced "serviceable timber"; the trees, he wrote, "that grow on the level parts of the mountains are specially fair and vigorous; next to these come those which grow on the lower parts and in the hollows; while those that grow on the heights are of the poorest quality," presumably because of their stunted nature. He repeatedly referred to the timber of many parts of Greece and of western Crete. Beyond Greece, he noted the fir and pine of Latium and southern Italy, but he added that these were "said to be nothing to the trees of Corsica." Various species of trees were discussed and their suitability noted for shipbuilding and for housebuilding—for

rafters and beams, for yardarms, masts and keels, for making charcoal, and for "the carpenter's various purposes."[4]

In the centuries that followed, a variety of other classical authors fill out the picture of the Mediterranean forests, giving details about this locality or that. Strabo, in his *Geography,* at the beginning of the Christian Era, showed that the woods of many Mediterranean uplands still survived in abundance. In the west, the mountains of southeastern Spain were described as "covered with thick woods and gigantic trees," and these furnished timber for shipbuilding as well as other forest products, such as pitch and kermes berries. In the north the Spanish slopes of the Pyrenees were likewise "covered with forests containing numerous kinds of trees and evergreens," which yielded excellent hams (equal to those of the Cantabrians), presumably from the swine that fed in their shade. Marseilles was famous for shipbuilding; and, eastward, in the hinterland of Genoa, the Ligurian Mountains furnished "plenty of wood for the construction of ships." In the Po Basin the woods contained "such an abundance of mast, that Rome was principally supplied from the swine fed there"; the pitch works were "amazing," and so were the large casks produced for wine. The central Apennines and the hills of Etruria provided wood for the "ceaseless building" that went on in the Eternal City itself. In the southern Apennines the Sila Mountains yielded "fine trees" and the excellent pitch that was noted by many writers. Across the Straits of Messina, in Sicily, there were "woods and plantations of all kinds."[5] The Alps and Corsica, although Strabo

3. Plato *Critias* 111BC.

4. The references are from Theophrastus *Enquiry into Plants* Books iii, iv, and v, *passim.*

5. The references from Strabo's *Geography* are as follows: 3. 4. 2; 3. 2. 6; 3. 4. 11; 4. 1. 5; 4. 6. 2; 5. 1. 12; 5. 2. 5; 5. 3. 7; 6. 1. 9.

does not say so, were also prominent lumber regions at this time.[6]

Strabo's references to the forests of the eastern Mediterranean Basin are not so numerous, but he tells a story of Cyprus that may well have exemplified what had also happened elsewhere:

Eratosthenes says that anciently the plains abounded with timber, and were covered with forests, which prevented cultivation; the mines were of some service towards clearing the surface, for trees were cut down to smelt the copper and silver. Besides this, timber was required for the construction of fleets, as the sea was now navigated with security and by a large naval force; but when even these means were insufficient to check the growth of timber in the forests, permission was given to such as were able and inclined, to cut down the trees and to hold the land thus cleared as their own property, free from all payments.

Yet, even in Strabo's time, the western promontory of Acamus was covered by "a large forest." That the Macedonian forests were still in existence is evident from Strabo's references to "dockyards for shipbuilding" along the northern coast of the Aegean; Crete, too, could still be described as wooded.[7] That the Peloponnesus was also well wooded at this time we may assume from the fact that Pausanias' *Description of Greece,* written in the second century A.D., refers to trees (cypress, oak, and pine) on the plains as well as in the higher mountain regions. It was the same to the north of the Gulf of Corinth and in Boeotia.[8]

The general impression left by these and other classical authors is that the Mediterranean lands were then more densely wooded than they are today but that already there had been considerable clearing and that the extensive forests which remained were for the most part in the mountainous areas. Toward the end of the classical period, in the economic crisis that befell the Roman Empire during the third and fourth centuries, the progress of clearing was halted. What is more, land that had once been tilled became derelict and overgrown. Lactantius, writing in about A.D. 300, said tersely: "The fields were neglected; cultivated land became forest" (Koebner, 1941, p. 24). By the end of the fourth century, in 395, large tracts of the once-fertile province of Campania, for example, were derelict, and this even before the war bands of the Goths and Vandals had set foot in the peninsula of Italy.[9]

Postclassical Times

It is difficult to construct, even in outline, a narrative of the vicissitudes of clearing in postclassical times. The conditions were so varied, and the record is incomplete; but the general facts are not in doubt (George, 1933; Parain, 1936; Turrill, 1929). When the Mediterranean region emerged from the confusion of the barbarian impact, we see men at work once more cutting down trees to satisfy the demands of agriculture, pasture, and industry and also for a variety of miscellaneous purposes.

In medieval Italy, for example, the cultivated area was extended slowly and laboriously, partly by diking and draining but also by clearing forest, and landowners encouraged such pioneering by offering favorable terms (Caggese, 1907–8, I, 157 ff.; II, 216 ff.). Not only were the lands of existing communities extended but new communities were founded in the wilderness by both lay and ecclesiastical land-

6. Pliny *Natural History* 16. 15, 16, 18, 29; 13. 15, 16.

7. The references from Strabo's *Geography* are as follows: 14. 6. 5; 14. 6. 2; Frags. 33 and 36; 10. 4. 4.

8. Pausanias *Description of Greece* **5. 6.** 4; 7. 26. 10; 8. 1. 6; 8. 11. 1; 8. 12. 1; 8. 38. 5; 8. 54. 5; 9. 24. 5; 10. 38. 9.

9. J. B. Bury (ed.), *Edward Gibbon's The History of the Decline and Fall of the Roman Empire* (London: Methuen & Co., 1897), II, 194.

lords. In this way was the fruitfulness of such places as inland Tuscany created.

The wood found an enemy not only in the cultivator but in the pastoralist. The practice of transhumance, so common in Mediterranean lands, meant that destruction by animals was extended over wide areas. In Spain the powerful organization of the Mesta, which controlled the large-scale annual migrations of Castilian flocks, was able to safeguard pasturage at the expense of the woodland; and, wrote Klein (1920, p. 307), "there can be no doubt that the Castilian forests suffered severely from the regular visits of the millions of migrating sheep." Various conservation measures adopted in the thirteenth century seem to have had some effect, but sixteenth-century descriptions contrast the naked desolation of Castile with the dense forests of the northern coast (*ibid.*, p. 321). In varying degrees, woodland elsewhere also suffered from the moving flocks and their shepherds. It was the same in Mediterranean France, in the hill country of the Apennines, and throughout the Balkans. Patsch gives instances (1922, pp. 23–26) of the deliberate destruction of forests and brushwood to provide new pasture throughout the Balkans. The havoc wrought by grazing lay not only in its destruction but also in its prevention of new growth. Even much of the bare karstlands were once wooded and could be made to carry trees once more if grazing animals were excluded.

Industry also took a heavy toll. The demands of tanning and of charcoal-making were important locally, and Patsch (*ibid.*, p. 28) has shown how destructive were the efforts of charcoal-burners in Herzegovina. The silver and copper mines of Serbia and Bosnia, the silver and quicksilver of Guadalcanal and Almaden in southern Spain, the iron of the Basque provinces, the iron

and the alum of the Italian Peninsula—all needed much timber. The coming of the railway brought new demands for its own purposes and also facilitated the transport of sawn timber elsewhere. But the greatest of the wood-devouring industries in the Mediterranean area may well have been shipbuilding. The medieval fleets of the Byzantine Empire, of Venice, Genoa, and other Italian maritime states, and of Catalonia were launched at the expense of the Mediterranean forest. The Venetian Republic might once have held "the gorgeous east in fee," but part of the price of this sovereignty was the bareness of the Adriatic coastlands; and during the fifteenth and sixteenth centuries Venice had to face the problem of diminishing timber supplies (Lane, 1934, p. 217; Turrill, 1929, p. 197). Along the eastern Adriatic shore was the city-republic of Ragusa, which has given us the word "argosy"; shipbuilding here was always an important industry, and its grand fleet denuded the forests of the mountains behind and of the islands near by. One of the complaints in her last dispute with Venice in 1754 was that the Venetians had illegally cut down wood in Ragusan territory (Villari, 1904, p. 328). Farther south timber was also being cut at this time, and Lord Broughton, who traveled here with Lord Byron, noted that "the woods of Albania, before the French revolution, furnished Toulon with timber for ship-building."[10] It was the same elsewhere in the Mediterranean area. Even Spain, in the days of the Armada, looked as far away as the Baltic for suitable timber (Albion, 1926, p. 183).

Warfare, both regular and irregular, increased the pace of destruction. Peter

10. J. C. Hobhouse (Baron Broughton), *A Journey through Albania, and Other Provinces of Turkey in Europe and Asia, to Constantinople, during the Years 1809 and 1810* (London: James Cawthorn, 1813), p. 74.

Mundy, in 1620, observed that "whole woods" of pine trees in western Bosnia were "cutt downe to the ground, To prevent Theeves that usually lurked amonge them."[11] During the Turkish wars of the 1870's and 1880's great stretches of timber were also felled, for strategic reasons, along the Bulgarian and Serbian frontiers.[12] At the other end of the Mediterranean, in Spain, much wood disappeared during the wars of the reconquest from the Moslems (Cánovas del Castillo, 1910, p. 43); and then again, during the Peninsular and Carlist wars, the woods that sheltered rebels and brigands were destroyed.

Much wood has also been cut for building, for fuel, and for a hundred and one domestic purposes. A frequent method of felling trees, in the Balkan Peninsula at any rate, was to make a fire at the base of a tree and burn through the trunk. It is not surprising that accidental forest fires were common in such a dry land. W. M. Leake, for example, recorded an accidental fire in southern Cephalonia: "The bare stems are now," he wrote in 1835, "conspicuous monuments of the misfortune."[13] It was not the first forest fire in Cephalonia, and such blackened monuments were also to be found in other places. Conifers were a source of resin, tar, and pitch, and Leake encountered an example of destructive exploitation in central Greece—"a forest which seems as if it would not long exist, as the greater part of the trees are in a process of destruction for the purpose of collecting their resin to make pitch"; hacked and wounded over a number of years, the trees could not survive.[14] In

11. *The Travels of Peter Mundy, in Europe and Asia, 1608–1667* (Cambridge: Hakluyt Society, 1907), I, 84.

12. A. Stead, *Servia by the Servians* (London: Heinemann, 1909), p. 255.

13. *Travels in Northern Greece* (London: J. Rodwell, 1835), III, 59.

14. *Ibid.,* II, 380.

the growth that followed the destruction of a pine forest, the beech with its dense shade frequently gained at the expense of the conifers; stumps of conifers are recorded in beech forests in the Shar Planina region on the Serbian-Albanian border. Or, again, Mount Pelion in Thessaly carried conifers in classical times, but they have been largely replaced by beech and oak (Turrill, 1929, p. 195).

The result of this interference, human and animal, coupled with the dry climate and the poor soil, is that much of the Mediterranean lands are covered by seminatural brushwood communities. The names given to this scrub in all its variations are many—*garrigue, maquis, macchie, matorral, monte bajo, phrygana*—and among its constituents are such aromatic shrubs as lavender, myrtle, rosemary, and thyme. The deciduous brushwood of the higher Balkan interior is known by the Serbian name of *shiblyak*. Varied by dwarf evergreens, this scrub is encountered from Portugal to the Dardanelles, and, with its associated pastures, it is the grazing ground of sheep and goats. Where the soil is thin or otherwise unfavorable, the vegetation becomes even more open, and bare rock appears between the stunted shrubs. The menace of soil erosion broods over the whole area. The development of state forest services and of programs of afforestation in the Mediterranean countries is the answer to this challenge, but the difficulties presented by the legacy of bare surfaces are formidable.

CENTRAL AND WESTERN EUROPE

Prehistoric and Roman Times

It has long been recognized that the heavier impervious soils carried great stretches of wood at the dawn of prehistory in Central and Western Europe; and it was thought, until recently, that the lighter soils, on the other hand, were open and treeless. Penck suggested that, for example, Neolithic settlements were concentrated in loess country because it may have been as free from forest "as the prairies of the North American West" (1887, pp. 437–41). This was the thesis developed by Gradmann in a succession of publications (e.g., 1898, 1901, 1906, 1931). He believed that these early communities were almost incapable of clearing woodland and that, as a corollary, the areas which they colonized must have been forest-free, or, at any rate, only lightly forested. This open character he attributed to a dry climatic phase during the subboreal period (between about 2500 and 500 B.C.) that followed an earlier forest phase; it was the spread of steppe-heath conditions over the loess and other light soils that, according to this view, gave the Neolithic farmers their opportunity. It was a view that was widely accepted (e.g., by Hoops, 1905, p. 99).

But the development of the technique of pollen analysis (Godwin, 1934) brought with it the realization that even the lightest soils were not devoid of wood when farming first began and that, for example, so-called "natural heath" had its origin in the clearing of its wood by Neolithic farmers (Godwin, 1944b). The pollen of forest trees in many localities is abruptly replaced by that of other vegetation, and the light soils are revealed not as treeless steppes but as areas of vigorous tree growth (Tüxen, 1931; Garnett, 1945). Even the dry Alföld of the Hungarian plain, noted for its steppelike character in Europe, is said to have been originally wooded (De Soó, 1929, p. 335), although others have thought this view an exaggeration (Rungaldier, 1943, p. 55). Schott (1952, p. 266) likewise thinks that it is an exaggeration to attribute all the heaths along the coast of northwestern Germany to human interference; he believes that, in any case, they would have been formed on the poorest land as a result of a gradual deterioration of the soil.

We must then envisage the primitive landscape of Central and Western Europe as covered by a mantle of forest, broken only where the Alps, the Carpathians, and a few other mountains rose above the tree line, and where occasional stretches of country, for one reason or another, were too sterile or too marshy. It was a broad-leaved forest, where oak generally predominated, but mixed with such other trees as elm, beech, and lime, and with an undergrowth of hazel. In its shade lived some Mesolithic hunters and food-gatherers, opening up small areas for their dwellings, using tree trunks for boats, and finding in the forest both fruit and game (Childe, 1931).

With the advent of agriculture in Neolithic times, the wood in places was cleared partly by the ax and partly by fire. There is abundant evidence of the use of the flint or stone ax in Neolithic times, and modern experiment has shown that trees can be cut down relatively easily with these implements; a polished ax is superior to a chipped ax (Nietsch, 1939, p. 70). Flint mines supplied the material for the axes, and widespread trade contacts disseminated it. Grenier instanced (1930, p. 29) the large number of broken polished axes found when the wood around the spring of Bonnefontaine in Lorraine was cleared; it seems that the spring had attracted settlers who destroyed the wood around it and cultivated the land. In a later age the forest re-established itself, only to be cleared once more to reveal evidence of the earlier effort. The other method of clearing was by fire. Iversen found, in the bog of Ordrup in Denmark, a marked and widespread layer of charcoal at the level where forest pollen abruptly decreased; burning seems to have been followed by cultivation, for it is at this level that the pollen of cereals and of weeds appears. Here, suggests Iversen (1941), is an example of *Brandwirtschaft* and of forest clearance by Neolithic farmers.

Once a wood was cleared, whether by the ax or by fire, grazing by domestic animals must have done much to hinder or prevent regeneration.

Grenier regarded the great achievements of the Neolithic age as "the domestication of animals, the invention of agriculture, and the conquest of land under forest" (1930, p. 28). But we must not think of wholesale and necessarily permanent destruction of large tracts of wood; the stumps, for example, may well have remained for long, as they did in some clearings of a much later age (see below). "What in reality we have to envisage," writes Clark, "is the temporary clearance of restricted areas carried out in successive stretches of forest, many of which re-established themselves as the farmers and their stock moved elsewhere" (1945, p. 67; cf. 1944 and 1947).

During the succeeding prehistoric ages of bronze and iron there was some extension of the areas of settlement, but on the whole such extensions were few, and development seems to have been toward a more intensive utilization of the area already occupied (Gradmann, 1901, p. 374). This is seen, for example, from the maps accompanying Fox's study (1923) of the Cambridge region. Nor is this difficult to explain, for it was not until the close of prehistoric times that the farmer possessed a heavy, wheeled plow with which he could attack the heavier and ill-drained soils. The clay lands, therefore, continued for long in the shade of their dense woods. Certainly at the dawn of history Europe was covered with immense forests. In the first century before our era, the so-called "Hercynian Forest" of the classical authors stretched eastward from the Rhine for a vast distance. Caesar tells of men who had journeyed through it for two months without reaching an end, and other writers commented upon its somber solitude.[15] Yet it seems clear that this forest was not as continuous nor as formidable as some classical allusions suggest, and we hear of clearings and of unforested areas and of the movement of troops through the forest itself (Dopsch, 1937, pp. 30–32). Still, the woodlands of *Germania* were very extensive, and within the Roman Empire, in Gaul and Britain, there were also large wooded tracts. In Britain a good deal of clearing took place locally, but "there is nothing to suggest a wholesale and general destruction" (Fox, 1923, p. 225), and the same is true of Gaul (Jullian, 1920, p. 179).

The Middle Ages (to A.D. 1500)

During the barbarian invasions it is difficult to perceive what happened to the Roman clearings. Documents of the time speak of deserted lands, *vastinae* or *solitudines;* and, although this impression may have been exaggerated (Dopsch, 1937, p. 92), it seems clear that the woods crept back over many neglected fields (Boissonnade, 1927, pp. 24–30). With the advent of more settled times, the attack upon the woodland was begun in earnest and was to gather force with the centuries. Behind the clash of warfare and the noise of political affairs the work of clearing went on in relative silence; but, if the details are obscure, we are, at any rate, able to judge by the results. The circumstances varied from place to place —an isolated clearing here; an enlargement of an existing field there; an inclosure for pasture in another place; maybe the throwing-off of a hamlet elsewhere. Sometimes a clearing was made by a single settler with the permission of his lord, to whom he paid a rent. At other times it was made by a large group of peasants who joined together for the purpose and incorporated the new arable within the regime and economy of their existing field system. But we know all too little of the details.

An echo of this activity in England

15. Caesar *Gallic War* 6. 25.

comes to us from the Anglo-Saxon poet who described the plowman as the "grey enemy of the wood";[16] and we can obtain some indication of the progress made over the span of six centuries or so (A.D. 450–1086) from the evidence of place names and from the statistics of the *Domesday Book*. The earlier evidence is becoming clear through the work of the English Place-Name Society. The distribution of different types of names in the county of Middlesex, for example, provides a revealing supplement to any deductions from surface geology (Gover *et al.*, 1942). Upon the light gravel and loamy soils of the south of the county, names which do not indicate wood are common (e.g., those ending in "-ham" and "-cote"). They belong to the early phase of the Saxon settlement upon fertile land already open. The wood names, later in date, lie on the intractable London clay to the north. In the extreme northeast there are scarcely any names, for here was a great expanse of unsettled woodland, the memory of which is preserved today in the name of Enfield Chase. The contrast between the distribution of the two groups of names is striking (Fig. 55). The northern woodland, within easy reach of London, could still be described in the twelfth century as "a great forest with wooded glades and lairs of wild beasts, deer both red and fallow, wild boars and bulls" (Stenton *et al.*, 1934, p. 27).

The effects of Anglo-Saxon and Scandinavian pioneering upon the landscape of England were summed up in the Domesday Inquest of 1086 (Darby, 1950). One of the questions asked by the Domesday commissioners was, "How much wood?" The form of the answers varied in different parts of the country. Occasionally, they merely stated that there was enough wood for

fuel, or for repairing the houses, or for making and mending the fences. But, normally, the amount of wood was indicated in one of two ways: either by areal or linear dimensions or in terms of the swine that fed upon the acorns or beech mast. The woodland of Middlesex was measured by the latter method, and Figure 55 shows that some of its villages had wood for as many as two thousand swine; the feeding of swine has always been a great feature of the European forests (Fig. 56*a*). When the Domesday evidence for all England has been assembled, we shall be able to perceive a number of still heavily wooded tracts (Darby, 1952). But, although clearing was taking place generally, the forest was always ready to assert itself. Land devastated by raiding or by the march of armies soon became overgrown, and on the unsettled Welsh border of England we occasionally hear of plowland that had relapsed into woodland (Darby and Terrett, 1954, p. 85).

It is clear that in post-Domesday times, as in earlier years, throughout the length and breadth of the countryside, the ax was at work cutting down the trees, and the pick was at work grubbing up the roots. Bennett (1937, p. 51) has described the role of the clearing in the life of a medieval village: "For a family burdened with more children than their shares in the common fields would warrant such assart land was a godsend. Here they could utilise their spare labour, and produce something to help fill the many hungry mouths at home." The records of every English county tell their own story of this spreading cultivation, and much of the work must have escaped mention in any document. Some memorial of this activity exists today in the form of field names dating from post-Domesday times, and Middle English elements such as "stubbing" (place where trees have been stubbed) are common. Other

16. R. K. Gordon (ed.), *Anglo-Saxon Poetry* (London: Everyman's Library [J. M. Dent & Sons], 1954), p. 295.

names, to be found alike in early documents and on modern maps, are "sarts" from "assarts," "intak" or "intake," and "stokking," a "stump clearing"; a name such as "Brindley," on the other hand, means "clearing (*leah*) caused by fire (*brende*)," and "Brentwood" is "burnt wood." Nor must we forget that the need for arable land was not the only demand upon woodland. Timber for the building of bridges, castles, and cathedrals, for scaffolding as well as for the fabric; wood for the making of utensils

and for a hundred and one purposes about a house or farm; and charcoal for the iron forges and for other industrial activity—all took their toll (Darby, 1951).

On the Continent there was even greater scope for the pioneer, and, in the centuries after the breakup of the Roman Empire, we begin to discern the early attack in progress. The Salian Franks in the fourth and fifth centuries avoided the great *Silva Carbonnaria*, the Charcoal-burners' Forest, on what

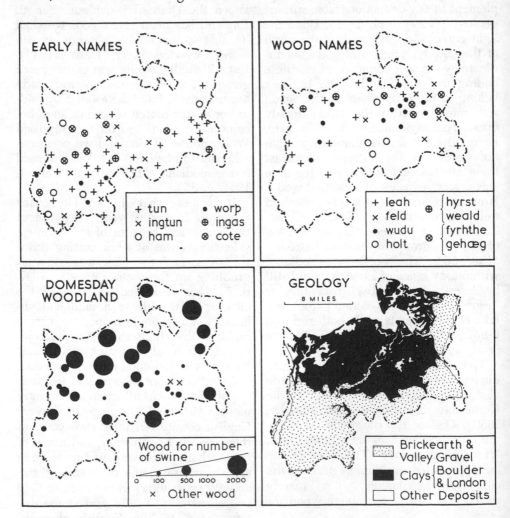

Fig. 55.—The woodland of Middlesex. (After Gover *et al.*, 1942; Darby and Campbell, in press.)

is now the unwooded plain of southern Brabant, and then began to occupy it in the sixth and seventh centuries (Des Marez, 1926). Elsewhere, we see the newcomers in the Empire making clearings (*Bifänge*), not only on overgrown deserted lands, but in the hitherto undisturbed forests (Dopsch, 1937, pp. 99, 116, 151). By the time of Charlemagne (*ca.* A.D. 800), much had been accomplished; one of his decrees bade his agents, "whenever they found capable men, to give them wood to clear." From widely separate places come indications of the retreat of the wood, and even parts of the great forests (such as that of the Ardennes) were already beginning to lose their primeval charac-

ter. Before A.D. 800 the valleys of the Odenwald, between the Neckar and the Main, were not much cultivated, but shortly afterward there were many clearings in them, and the so-called "forest village" (*Waldhufendorf*) appeared here at an early date (Koebner, 1941, pp. 45–46). Its form differed fundamentally from that of the traditional nucleated village surrounded by "open fields" with intermixed strips. The houses were laid out in a single or double row, usually along a valley bottom, and behind each house stretched its land in a long, narrow belt reaching back into the wood (Niemeier, 1949).

But clearing was not universal, and already in the relatively long-settled

Fig. 56a.—Swine feeding in the wood. (From British Museum, MS Tiberius, B. V, Part I, folio 7; the manuscript comes from the eleventh century A.D.)

Fig. 56b.—Cutting wood. (From British Museum, MS Tiberius, B. V, Part I, folio 6; the manuscript comes from the eleventh century A.D.)

lands of the west a conflict of interests can be observed. Set against the advantage of colonization were the interests of the chase and the wish to preserve forests as hunting parks; the game laws and the penalties for infringement of forest rights were often severe. Also, the wood itself was not without value. It provided timber and fuel, pasture and fruit; and a lord's interest frequently lay in denying his peasants the freedom to destroy it. Licenses were exacted to pasture swine, to fell timber, and to till the cleared land, and a great array of rights to control the use of the forest grew. When the Count of Vendôme found unauthorized clearings in his woods, he had the houses destroyed and the crops cleared away, and the monk who recorded this did so with approval. Thus was progress governed "by the varying balance between a peasantry growing by natural increase and the restrictive policies of its feudal lords" (Koebner, 1941, p. 69).

But the time was soon to be when lords were not so insistent upon their forest rights. From about 1050 onward, for some two hundred years or so, came the great heroic period of reclamation, "l'âge des grands défrichements" of the French writers. The outline has been sketched by Bloch (1931, pp. 1–20), and Flach has shown the earlier pioneers replacing forests by villages (1893, pp. 145 ff.). There are also older accounts of the French forests (Maury, 1850, 1866, 1867), and many detailed studies fill in the picture for this or that locality (e.g., Campagne, 1912; Sclafert, 1926). Among those who took the lead in organizing the new effort were the religious houses. The older Benedictine monasteries had pioneered in the mountains of the Dauphiné and on the plains of the Ile de France and elsewhere; and they were followed in the twelfth century by new monastic orders, above all, by the Cistercians. Their rule laid stress upon manual labor and especially

upon work in the field; they sought the wilderness and became the great farmers of the Middle Ages, and they were to find that solitude was but a poor defender of poverty. By the end of the twelfth century the Cistercian houses alone numbered five hundred, and this figure was to reach seven hundred and fifty in the fifteenth century. Countless other monasteries also took part. Nor were laymen, lords and peasants alike, slow to share in the rewards of this new and peaceful crusade.

There was a widespread extension of the arable land of existing villages, and new fields were brought into being alongside the old. In other places the expansion took the form of subsidiary hamlets and isolated homesteads. Modern topographical maps often indicate how scattered settlements were spread through the forest in small clearings. That the assart (from the French *essarter*, "to grub up," or "to clear") had come to have a definite place in manorial economy is abundantly clear from monastic and other documents. The obituary of Albericus Cornu, who had been a canon of Notre-Dame de Paris, tells us, for example, how he had improved the abbey estates; the woods had "for long been so useless that they were a burden rather than a source of income," and Albericus had been able to free them from the forest jurisdiction of the Count of Champagne and other lords and turn them into arable land (Koebner, 1941, p. 77).

Clearing was also promoted by the establishment of entirely new settlements. Village colonies were organized to bring the near-by waste or forest under cultivation. The *villes neuves* of northern France, the *bourgs* of the west (Koebner, 1941, pp. 71–72), and *bastides* and *sauvetés* of the south (Arqué, 1948; Ourliac, 1949) housed *hospites*, or colonists, who came to invade the waste. The form of many of these settlements reminds us of the *Waldhufen* village of Germany. The names of some of them were taken from the woods upon which they encroached; the names of others include an element such as *sart;* yet other names also tell us something of their story. In the wooded countryside of Puisaye, between the Loire and the Yonne, we find, side by side, a Jerusalem, a Jericho, a Nazareth, and a Bethlehem, which reflect the Crusading age in which they were born (Bloch, 1931, p. 11).

It was the same elsewhere in Western Europe. We hear of clearing operations, of *hospites* and of *villae novae,* in Flanders, Hainault, and Brabant; and French names that end in "-sart" and Flemish names that end in "-rode" indicate the success of the attack (Duvivier, 1859). To the east, the monasteries of the Rhineland endowed with ample lands were no less active. They and their daughter-abbeys between the Rhine and the Elbe were breaking into the woods and heaths of Saxony and Thuringia. Place names that end in "-wald" ("wood") and "-holz" ("grove") indicate the former character of the countryside, and those that end in "-rode" ("grubbed up"), "-schwend" ("burned") and "-hau" ("cut down") bear witness to the clearing (Schlüter, 1952, pp. 23–35). Conditions varied from place to place, but the net result of the Great Reclamation, or *Urbarmachung,* was to change the economy and the appearance of considerable stretches in the broad lowlands and the Alpine zone alike. Upland massifs such as the Harz, the Eifel, the Westerwald, the Thuringian Forest, and the Black Forest were coming to look like great wooded islands in a sea of cultivation; but even their shades were not undisturbed. The copper- and silver-bearing lead ores of the once-wooded Rammelsberg in the Harz were perhaps the most famous metal deposits, but the working both of these metals and of iron, to-

gether with the activity of the charcoal-burner, was widespread (Nef, 1952, p. 435). Moreover, agriculture was being extended in the valleys of these uplands, and the changes can be summed up in the words of Caesarius of Prüm, set in the wooded Eifel. Writing in 1222, and referring to the previous century, he said: "During this long space of time many forests were felled, villages founded, mills erected, taxes ordained, vines planted, and an infinite amount of land reduced to agriculture" (Thompson, 1928a, p. 758).

Great though the efforts in the long-settled regions of Western Europe and the Rhineland were, it was to the east, in the heart of Central Europe, that the most spectacular changes took place. The lands abandoned by the Teutonic peoples as they moved into the Roman provinces had been occupied by the Slavs, who migrated westward across the Vistula and the Oder and southward across the Danube. By about A.D. 600 the frontier between the German and Slav worlds had become roughly the line of the Elbe-Saale in the north, while southward it ran across the Alps toward the head of the Adriatic (Fig. 57). After an interval, and following the setbacks of border warfare, the Germans began to advance southeastward in the tenth century and northeastward across the European plain after about 1100. It was, wrote Lamprecht (1893, p. 349), the great deed of the German people in the Middle Ages. In all its complexity, it has attracted an enormous literature.[17] The advance took place under the impetus of economic and missionary motives, and there arose a contrast between the old western feudal Germany and the new eastern colonial Germany. Analogy has been drawn between this advance and the expansion of the American people west-

17. For some convenient reviews see Aubin, 1041; Kötzschke and Ebert, 1937; and Thompson, 1928b.

ward from the Atlantic seaboard. What the new west meant to young America in the nineteenth century, the new east meant to Germany in the Middle Ages (Thompson, 1928*b*, pp. xviii, 523). Although historical analogies are often misleading, this comparison does emphasize the colonial character of much of medieval Germany. Some parallels between clearing in the Old and New Worlds have also been drawn by Schott (1935).

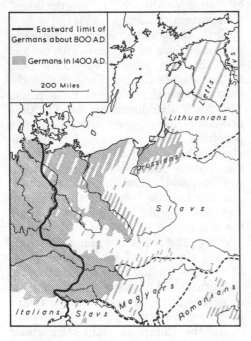

Fig. 57.—German colonization eastward. (After W. R. Shepherd, *Historical Atlas* [3d ed.; London: University of London Press, 1924], Pl. 80.)

The surface of the northern German plain is covered almost everywhere with deposits laid down by the great ice sheets which spread out from Scandinavia in Quaternary times. Much of the clay is hummocky, and on its ill-drained surface lay marsh and shallow lakes of curious shape; many of the river valleys were also marshy. Elsewhere, stretches of infertile sand and gravel, derived from the glacial de-

posits, formed a type of country known as geest; the landscape that confronted the German colonists was one of wood, marsh, and heath. The wood, or a great deal of it, fell before the ax of the pioneer, and both place names and the *Waldhufen* village testify to the clearing activity. The settlers came from the older parts of Germany, "with horses and oxen, with ploughs and waggons," to transform the countrysides of what are now Mecklenburg, Pomerania, Brandenburg, and Silesia (Thompson, 1928*b*, p. 501). About 1100, we hear, for example, of Count Wiprecht of Groitzsch, to the south of Leipzig between the Saale and the Elbe, bringing colonists from the west to clear his forests (Koebner, 1941, p. 81). Later in the century the ruler of Meissen was settling colonists in the frontier forests of the Erzgebirge (Aubin, 1941, p. 366). Some words of Helmold of Holstein, whose "Chronicle" describes the pioneering life of the time, illustrate not only the vicissitudes of the frontier struggle but also the recuperative power of the forest. Speaking of an earlier Saxon advance and retreat, he said: "There still remain many evidences of that former occupation, especially in the forest which extends from the city of Lütjenburg through the mighty tracts of Schleswig, in whose vast and almost impenetrable solitudes yet may be descried the furrows which once marked out the plowlands" (Thompson, 1928*b*, p. 491). But even as Helmold wrote (*ca.* 1170), the plow was soon to move over the ground once more.

Alongside the clearing of the wood went other transformations. The German colonists with their axes were accompanied and followed by Dutch, Flemish, and Frisians who embanked streams and drained marshes. Into the dry soils of part of the geest they cut irrigation canals, and they gave their name to the district of Fläming that lies to the east of Magdeburg. The changes were urban as well as rural. The dates of the founding of the cities of northern Germany mark the success of the advance. Behind the achievement of the Hanseatic cities in the fourteenth and fifteenth centuries lay a background of some generations of colonial struggle.

By the end of the thirteenth century the advance had spent itself. Poland was penetrated by German colonists and civilization, but only to a limited degree. Yet in the forests and waste of two outlying eastern areas, German missionary zeal and colonizing impulse had found fruitful fields of activity. Early in the thirteenth century the military order of the Brethren of the Sword had planted the country around the Gulf of Riga with German fortified towns; it was, wrote a chronicler of the time, a land of fertile fields and abundant pasture, but with much wood (*ibid.*, p. 526). Later in the century, between this northern outpost and the homeland, a second military order, the Teutonic Knights, more thoroughly occupied the woodland (Schlüter, 1920). It was the last chapter in the history of medieval colonization by the Germans in the north. The consequences were fateful for the affairs of Europe, because this new area of activity, later known as East Prussia, was separated from the main body of German settlement by what was to be called "the Polish Corridor" (Fig. 57).

The activity in northern Germany had been paralleled to the south. In the eastern Alps, the rise of Austria, founded as an outpost against the Magyars in the tenth century, was accompanied by an advance of German-speaking peoples comparable to that across the northern plain, but the information is more scanty. The advance took place partly down the Danube and partly southward into the lands of the southern Slavs. Not only the main valleys, but the side valleys as well, were cleared for tillage below and pasturage

above. Beyond the main frontier of German speech, isolated German settlements appeared as islands in Slav or Magyar territory. One of the characteristic features of the mountain belt as a whole was its mining activity. If the amounts appear small to us and the technology primitive, we must consider them in the context of their time. German mining camps grew into towns on the slopes of the Erzgebirge (Ore Mountains), in the Sudeten Mountains, in Bohemia itself, eastward in Slovakia, southward in Styria, Carinthia, and Carniola, and beyond in Bosnia and Serbia. Still farther east lie the mountains of Transylvania. Its Latin name indicates its forested nature, and its Magyar name, "Edily," comes from *erdö* ("forest"). To these mountains came Germans from the Rhineland, mostly in the twelfth century, at the invitation of the early Magyar kings, to fell the frontier forests and to become farmers and miners; the many place names that end in "-hau" form some memorial to their clearing. Nef, who has discussed the importance of mining in medieval Europe, writes (1952, p. 472) of the demands made upon wood for pit props, for building, for fuel, and for charcoal.

But, in recording the importance of the eastward movement of the German-speaking peoples, we must not forget the work of the Slavonic peoples themselves. Even in Germanized areas, such as Mecklenburg, Slavonic lords and peasants may have been responsible for much clearing (Power, 1932, p. 725). Slav place-name elements, such as *drewa* ("wood") and *trebynja* ("clearing") form memorials of their activity (Trautmann, 1948–49, II, 37, 89). Beyond, in Poland, Bohemia, and elsewhere, they founded new villages and reclaimed the wilderness, sometimes under German law, sometimes under Slavonic. Settlements of a *Waldhufen* type are to be found in the uplands of southern Poland (De Martonne, 1931, p.

629). In Bohemia there are over three hundred place names that include the element *lhota,* and there are eighty more in Moravia. The word, roughly speaking, means "freedom," and it was used in this connection to denote the exemptions from render that were sometimes granted to settlements made on empty or waste land. Its widespread distribution may be taken as some index of the transforming activity of the Czechs. The word in the form of *léhota* occurs more than forty times in Slovakia farther east, but there it seems to have been associated with German law (Aubin, 1941, pp. 395–96). In this area other place-name elements, such as *kopanice, lazy,* and *paseky,* specifically indicate clearing (Deffontaines, 1932, p. 57). Here, the activity was smaller in amount and maybe later in time, but the phenomenon was fundamentally the same.

This great expansive movement of clearing during the Middle Ages did not continue uninterruptedly into modern times. In places it slowed down; in others it ceased; in yet other places the frontiers of cultivation even retreated. Certainly over most of central and western Europe agrarian effort had passed its maximum by 1300, and the great age of expanding arable land was succeeded in the fourteenth and fifteenth centuries by one of stagnation and contraction. During the hundred years between 1350 and 1450, the decline was especially marked. The causes of this recession are obscure and involved, and among the agencies invoked to explain it are the destruction of war, great pestilences, falling prices, and a basic decline in population (Postan, 1952, pp. 191–216). Abandoned holdings and depopulated or deserted villages were to be found not only in the "old lands" of the south and west but also in Mecklenburg, Pomerania, Brandenburg, and Prussia. In the south and west of Germany the acreage of these *Wüstungen* has been placed as high as one-half of

the area once cultivated; the statistical mode for Germany as a whole has been placed at 25 per cent. These figures probably overemphasize the contraction, because some abandoned holdings may represent no more than temporary withdrawals or changes in the use of land; but, when all reservations are made, the facts are striking enough (Pohlendt, 1950). To what extent the woods advanced upon the untilled fields and unused pastures we cannot say, but there is no doubt that they did in many places, and traces of cultivation are to be found in wooded areas even today. The abandonment took place at various dates, but, says Mortensen (1951, p. 359), in the main it is clearly a medieval phenomenon. Figure 58 shows the oscillation in the area around Hofgeismar in the upper Weser Basin (Jäger, 1951); and, more recently, Jäger has also shown (1954) how many large forests in Germany have come into being since the Middle Ages. From such evidence as this we must not assume that the area under cultivation was at one time greater than it is today, because the phenomenon may in part be due to the more complete separation of forest and farm land. But more investigation is needed before we can be clear about these matters (Mortensen, 1951, p. 359).

The ravages of war and pillage bore particularly hard upon some localities. The cultivated land that had been brought into being in Bohemia was very adversely affected by the Hussite Wars (1419–36), and it has been estimated that one-sixth of the population either perished or left the country. In the west, France suffered grievously during the Hundred Years' War (1337–1453). Thomas Basin, bishop of Lisieux, writing about 1440, described the vast extent of uncultivated land between the Somme and the Loire all "overgrown with brambles and bushes" (Boissonnade, 1927, p. 316). Population fell in places to one-half, even to one-third, of its former level. Some of the accounts may have been exaggerated, but there is no doubt about the widespread desolation and about the growth of wood on the untilled fields (Waddington, 1930). In the southwest, in Saintogne, between the Charente and the Dordogne, for a long time people said that "the forests came back to France with the English."

Modern Times (*after A.D. 1500*)

The clearing that had taken place in the Middle Ages, epic though it was, still left Western and Central Europe with abundant tracts of wood. But soon, in the sixteenth century, in many places there were complaints about a shortage of timber, and the shortage developed into a problem that occupied the attention of statesmen and publicists for many centuries. It was not only that the woods were becoming smaller but that the demand for timber was growing greater. There had been signs toward the end of the fifteenth century that the recession in the economic life of the late Middle Ages was merging into recovery and into a new prosperity that

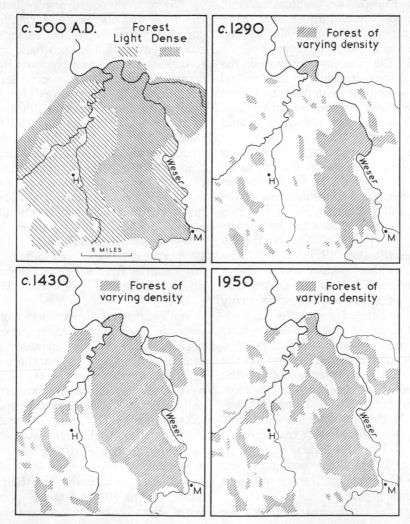

Fig. 58.—Woodland in the area around Hofgeismar in the upper Weser Basin. *H* = Hofgeismar, *M* = Münden. (After Jäger, 1951.)

brought with it an ever increasing appetite for wood.

The pace of industrial life was quickening. Glassworks and soapworks, for example, needed more and more wood ash. The production of tin, lead, copper, iron, and coal depended upon timber for pit props and charcoal for fuel; the salt industry in the Tyrol and elsewhere also needed wood for evaporating the brine. It was perhaps the iron industry that made the greatest single demand, and, particularly in the wooded valleys of the upland blocks of France and Central Europe, an endless series of small metal establishments were to be found, often run by men who divided their labors between the forge and the field. As the clearing progressed, the huts of the charcoal-burners moved from one locality to another, and there appeared new mounds of small logs, covered with clay to prevent too rapid a combustion.

The fears of a shortage of timber in England can be seen in a commission of 1548 to inquire into the destruction of wood in the ironmaking area of the Weald. But neither its report nor successive Acts of Parliament in the sixteenth century were able to stay the destruction (Straker, 1931, p. 109). The solution to the problem was to find a substitute, and it is not surprising that during the seventeenth century many treatises suggested the use of coal instead of charcoal. It was about the year 1709 that Abraham Darby first smelted ore with coke in Shropshire, and by the middle of the eighteenth century the use of coal for smelting had become common in England. Here, as elsewhere, the growth of the iron and steel industry was linked with coal and not wood, and names such as "Forge Wood" and "Furnace Wood" recall, on modern English maps, the activities and changes of a past age.

The problem was less acute on the Continent, where there was more wood and less industry, and it was not until well into the nineteenth century that smelting with coke became established. But that the problem was not absent here can be seen from a French proposal of 1715 to limit the number of forges; late in the eighteenth century, as in earlier times, we hear of numerous small potteries, glassworks, and forges scattered through the forests of France (Brunhes and Deffontaines, 1926, p. 354; Dion, 1938). In Germany, as late as 1848, Banfield could write (1846–48, II, 65) of the wooded district between the Ruhr and the Sieg: "A rotation of coppice or underwood, cut down every sixteen years, affords both bark for the numerous tanners and charcoal for the metallurgists; and both occupations alternate with the care of small farms belonging to these small manufacturers, as the rye is admitted into the forest rotation the year after the underwood is cut down." This forest-field rotation was known as *Reutbergwirtschaft,* as opposed to the more permanent *Brandwirtschaft,* and it was a feature of many parts of Germany (Schmitthenner, 1923). It has left a memory in the place names of some districts (Mutton, 1938, p. 119); and, even today, there are localities from which it has not entirely disappeared (Fickeler, 1954, p. 27).

With the overseas expansion of Europe, the need for timber for shipbuilding was also greatly increased. The growth of England's mercantile marine and the development of the English navy from the Tudor age onward depended upon an adequate supply of oaks for the hulls of ships; fir trees, for masts, together with such "naval stores" as pitch and tar, were imported from Baltic lands. The Dutch wars of the seventeenth century, the maritime wars of the eighteenth, and the Napoleonic Wars were a heavy and continuous drain upon English oak, and English seamen were only too conscious of their difficulties. Samuel Pepys, employed at the Admiralty, could only write, "God knows where materials can be had" (Albion, 1926, p. ix). English timber never recovered from the strain of the wars with France, and English ships came to rely more and more upon the pine and oak of the New World and the teak of India.

foreign, colonial, commercial, and forest policies as well."

The rise of the Dutch navy was even more dependent upon the Baltic trade; the timber and "naval stores" of these northern lands were as important to sea power in the seventeenth and eighteenth centuries as heavy industry was to be in more modern times. It was certainly so in France. Richelieu and especially Colbert, in the seventeenth cen-

Fig. 59.—Agricultural improvement. (From Andrews, 1853.)

In the meantime, the Admiralty, in its alarm over the timber shortage, consulted the newly formed Royal Society, which in turn asked John Evelyn to report upon the problem. The result was the appearance in 1664 of Evelyn's *Sylva: A Discourse of Forest Trees*, and in the years that followed there were various intermittent attempts at planting. The influence of the timber shortage appeared in many ways, wrote Albion (1926, p. vii), "not only in the Navy itself, but in international law, in naval architecture, and in England's

tury, aimed at the creation of a French navy. Colbert instituted dockyards and naval schools and reorganized the naval service. In 1669 came the famous "Ordonnance des eaux et forêts," which stated that no wood should be cleared without authority; but, as in England, these regulations soon ceased to be observed.

The timber problem remained acute for the navies of Europe until March 9, 1862. It was on that day that the Battle of Hampton Roads in the American Civil War demonstrated the superiority of the iron-clad ship (Albion, 1926, pp. 408–9). The end of the era of wooden ships had come suddenly, and it left a permanent mark upon the countrysides of Europe.

There was yet another and continuing demand upon wood. Although the pioneer age of *défrichement* and *Urbarmachung* was over, agriculture still con-

but it continued and was even accelerated by an edict of 1766, which exempted newly cleared land from taxation for fifteen years (Debien, 1952, p. 45). In mountainous districts, such as the Alps (Blache, 1923) and the Ardennes (Liouville, 1897), temporary clearings for cultivation continued to be made by burning, and the ash fertilized

CENTRAL EUROPE

FOREST *c.*900

100 Miles

Fig. 60.—Central Europe: forest *ca.* 900. (After Schlüter, 1952.)

tinued to expand at the expense of the forest in this locality or that. It was certainly so in England, as much evidence after 1500, and even after 1800, testifies (Darby, 1951, pp. 78–79). Figure 59, from G. H. Andrews' *Modern Husbandry* of 1853, shows the cutting-down of trees and the tile-draining of the clay soils that had nourished them. It was the same in France. Widespread felling had disquieted the agricultural writer Bernard Palissy in the sixteenth century,

the soil. In other places, too, upland communities of herdsmen, eager for pasturage, regarded trees as their enemies; and their successors have been left to inherit a legacy of soil erosion and inundation (Rabot, 1905, p. 207).

Eastward, in the German realm, the Thirty Years' War (1618–48) left a staggering legacy of devastation. Conservative estimates say that at least one-third of the population perished, but to what extent the forest crept back over the untilled fields we cannot say. Anyway, there was recovery, and German agricultural chemistry was greatly to distinguish itself. But immense stretches of forest continued into the twentieth century; they amounted to over thirty million acres, and about one-half of this was on the large estates of private owners. The plain of Poland had also still remained. In the twentieth century about 18 per cent of Belgium was wooded, 19 per cent of France, 27 per cent of Germany, and 23 per cent of Poland. Southward, the figures rose to 37 per cent for Austria, 33 per cent for Czechoslovakia, and 29 per cent each for Yugoslavia and Bulgaria, and 28 per cent for Rumania. For Hungary, with

CENTRAL
EUROPE

FOREST c.1900

100 Miles

Fig. 61.—Central Europe: forest *ca.* 1900. (After Schlüter, 1952.)

been far from cleared, while to the south the clearings and the woodland industries of the Slovakian highlands (Deffontaines, 1932) and the Carpathians recalled those of the upland regions of the west. Looking at Central and Western Europe as a whole in the nineteenth and twentieth centuries, the surprising thing is that, despite the varied demands upon wood and the long centuries of exploitation, so much its plains, the figure fell to 11 per cent (Dietrich, 1928).

The contrast between Figures 60 and 61 shows the net result of clearing as opposed to regeneration and replanting over the thousand years between A.D. 900 and 1900 (Schlüter, 1952). Much of the existing forest bears the mark of long exploitation and differs considerably from the natural forest that would cover almost the whole area had there been no interference by man. The most striking evidence of this interference has been the steady increase during the nineteenth and twentieth centuries in the percentage of conifers. Since about the middle of the nineteenth century, various national forest policies have resulted in the formation of state forest services. To varying degrees, the management of forested areas has been put upon a scientific basis; reasoned programs of felling have been organized, and new methods of seed selection and regeneration have been devised. One feature of the new policies has been the concentration upon soft woods, reflecting the changing demand from fuel to timber and pulpwood. The Scotch fir, the larch, the spruce, and new varieties of fir from abroad—the silver fir and the Douglas fir, for example—are giving a new value to poor hillsides and infertile stretches of sand and gravel. Large areas of heath in northwestern Germany and of sand dunes along the Baltic coast have been planted with conifers. In Belgium extensive planting has altered the appearance of the barren Kempenland (Monkhouse, 1949, p. 93). In Britain the sandy waste of the Breckland has also taken on a new look (Clarke *et al.*, 1938). But perhaps the most striking change has been on the Landes in southwestern France. At the end of the eighteenth century there were only a few scattered maritime pines and some dwarf oaks on this dreary expanse of marsh, gravel, and shifting sand. But the scene has been transformed, by draining and planting, into a vast forest covering some two million acres and forming a conspicuous feature of the woodland map of France (Fig. 62). The trees are mostly maritime pines, and they yield resin, pit props, and a variety of constructional timber (Larroquette, 1924). These are only a few examples of the recent transformations of the European landscape. But great though such changes have

been, they are localized. Could the Roman legionaries tramp the countryside once more, they would be reminded only rarely of the dense shades they had encountered when they left the Mediterranean lands to build an empire.

EASTERN AND NORTHERN EUROPE

From south to north the great vegetation belts of European Russia in historical times have been the steppes, the mixed forest, and the coniferous forest, together with the transitional zones between them (Fig. 63).

The Steppes

Traveler after traveler has described the vast treeless plain of the steppes, and historians have emphasized its role as an open corridor along which nomadic peoples, with their herds, traveled westward from central Asia. But in classical times there was certainly some wood along the lower courses of the rivers that flow into the Black Sea. Herodotus, for example, wrote of "the forest country" along the lower Dnieper. Neumann (1855, pp. 74–99) came to the conclusion that there were substantial stretches of woodland here, but his ideas have been thought by some to be exaggerated (Minns, 1913, p. 1). Looking back beyond the classical age into prehistory, Taliev thought that the grass steppe had been formed on the site of destroyed forest, but, added Keller (1927, p. 232), "this view has not been generally accepted." Since then, Leimbach, in a survey of the Russian literature (1948, p. 255), has thought it "very likely that the Ukraine in the same way as the Hungarian Puszta was once mainly forest land," while Wilhelmy, in another survey (1950, p. 31), is not in agreement. We must await further elucidation of the problem, but it may not be without significance that Keller pointed out (1927, p. 228) that, in the transitional zone between steppe and forest, "the forest often occupies areas which are apparently identical in conditions of soil and land relief with other areas which are occupied by steppe vegetation. And clear evidence of the advance of forest on steppe is not lacking. . . . In the northern parts of the forest-steppe zone this advance is very marked. Burial mounds, which were unamong the woods, and with projections of woodland southward, especially along the river valleys; but the wooded tracts have grown fewer and smaller, "until nowadays the steppe lands begin farther north than they once did." Kiev, founded in the ninth century, by tradition lay "amongst forests" where now is

FIG. 62.—France: forest *ca.* 1920. (After *Atlas de France*, 1935, Pl. 38 [Paris: Comité National de Géographie].)

doubtedly made in open steppe, are now covered with trees."

But, while the forest may have advanced in places, it is clear that the transitional forest steppe as a whole has been greatly cleared with the advance of colonization southward from the seventeenth century onward. Both steppe and forest have mingled and contested here, with islands of steppe open steppe (Kluchevsky, 1911–31, V, 233, 241).

The Mixed Forest

The homeland of the Slavs in the early centuries of the Christian Era seems to have lain between the Carpathian Mountains and the middle and upper Dnieper. From this base, according to some scholars, they advanced not only westward and southward but also northward and northeastward into the valleys and plains of the upper Volga and its tributaries. Here, in the mixed oak forest, they seem to have met with but little resistance from the sparse Finno-Ugrian population. There is much

est near the river Sheksna (Davies, 1952, p. 119). Some memory of the great woodland through which they passed is preserved in the name of the city of Bryansk. It is difficult to obtain a clear picture of this great epoch of colonization, so silent was it. But in the

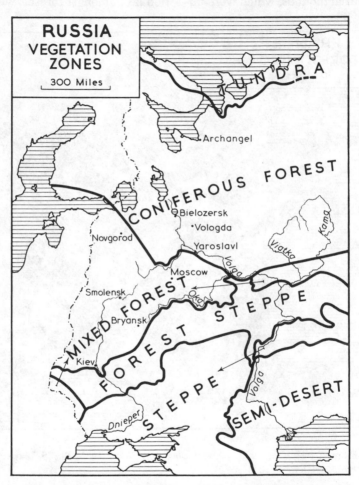

FIG. 63.—Russia: vegetation zones. (After Keller, 1927.)

that is controversial about these matters (Paszkiewicz, 1954, p. 255), but it is clear that the agriculture of the area was primitive, apparently migratory, and supplemented by trapping and by the honey of wild bees. From the third and fourth centuries comes evidence of a slash-and-burn husbandry in the for-

eleventh and twelfth centuries we hear of new settlements and new principalities in the land between the Volga and the Oka, and some of the princes embarked upon a policy of deliberately attracting new settlers and took pride in the success of their colonization (Kluchevsky, 1911–31, I, 196 ff.).

Moscow itself was first mentioned in 1147 and by the end of the Middle Ages was to establish its control over the other Volga-Oka principalities. The mixed-forest country between the Volga and the Oka has been called the "Ile de France" of Russia, the cradle of the Russian state; and the wedge of colonization, set between the inhospitable north and the insecure steppe, was not only to develop and fill out with the centuries, as forest hamlets and villages were established (Eck, 1933, pp. 55, 275), but also to improve its agriculture. The temporary cultivation of burned clearings gave way by the sixteenth century to more intensive cultivation on a two- or three-field basis, as in the West. Yet the Russians were much slower in clearing the wilderness than the trans-Elbean Germans who moved into the lands of the western Slavs, and the retreat of the wood was more gradual. "Indeed, eighteenth-century Muscovy would have struck a Western European traveller journeying from Smolensk to Moscow as one huge forest, and the towns and villages in it as mere clearings." But the clearing was to continue until the forest land of central Russia became "a mere dwindling reminiscence of the past, and preserved as a luxury" (Kluchevsky, 1911–31, V, 244–45). It had supplied fuel and building material, it had supported a whole range of small-scale forest industries, and it had yielded its soil for agriculture.

The Coniferous Forest

To the north, beyond the upper Volga, the growing season becomes shorter, and the soil more infertile; the mixed forest gives way to the coniferous forest which still covers the greater part of the countryside. The dominant trees are the spruce and the pine, the former on clay, the latter on sand, and everywhere these are mingled with peat moors. It was thinly peopled by Finnish and Lapp tribes and provided an enormous reservoir of fur—sable, marten, fox, and, of lesser value, bear, squirrel, and otter. Fur led the traders northward and eastward along the great rivers linked one to another by portages. It was an economy that anticipated that of the *coureurs de bois* of French Canada. The great part of the trade of this hinterland found an outlet at Novgorod in the west, a Hanse center and a market of renown in medieval Europe; its main commodity was fur, but forest products—tar, pitch, potash, and wax— were also among its exports.

Not only traders but missionaries came north to these trans-Volgan lands. Between 1340 and 1440, especially, there was a great development of monasticism, and the monks sought the untamed wilderness. Bielozersk, founded in 1397, and many other houses, together with their daughter-foundations, became agrarian colonies. We hear of black, impassable, and untilled forests, of the hewing of trees, of newly plowed fields, and of fresh villages and hamlets (Kluchevsky, 1911–31, II, 151 ff.). The opening of the White Sea route from the west by Elizabethan Adventurers in 1533 greatly increased the importance of these northern lands. By this time, the subjection of Novgorod in 1478 had brought her rough trading empire within the sphere of Muscovy, and the new gains of the sixteenth century were to fall to Moscow. Hakluyt's account of the Adventurers' journey from Archangel to Moscow speaks of the very large forests of fir trees, the wooden houses, the flax and hemp, and the great quantity and variety of furs, and it is a description that was echoed by later writers.[18] The effects of the new contact were soon evident. Small settlements developed into prosperous towns between Moscow and

18. Richard Hakluyt, *The Principal Navigations* (London: Everyman's Library [J. M. Dent & Sons], 1907), I, 254, 278–79.

the White Sea, and Yaroslavl, Vologda, and other centers added to the consumption of timber. The pace of exploitation increased as factories for boiling tar, burning potash, and making rope were established; the tanning industry was developed; the salt industry, too, was important. There were also grants of land, in the Kama area in the 1560's, for example, with power to settle immigrants upon them (*ibid.*, p. 224). Metallurgical industries and mining were developed, especially from the time of Peter the Great in the eighteenth century, and they consumed timber both in the coniferous and in the mixed-forest zone. A whole range of traditional forest industries continued to grow, often with considerable specialization between village and village (Roudski and Shafranov, 1893, p. 334).

But we must not endow this northern settlement with an intensity it did not possess. The crops were mostly rye and oats, flax and hemp, and much of the agriculture was primitive. A Russian account from as late as the end of the nineteenth century is interesting because of the light it throws upon earlier practices elsewhere:

> The forest-field system means an alternation of agriculture with more or less lasting periods of forest-growing between. Properly speaking, the forest-field system of economy as practised in most parts of the north and north-east districts of Russia, cannot be called a system of economy in the strict sense of the term, because, in most cases, the felling of trees and the clearing of woods for the cultivation of grain, and afterwards, for the re-growing of trees, are practised without any definite plan. This is one of the simplest forms of primitive economy, and in which field-cultivation is of second-rate importance, as portions of improved land, in most cases, are quite insignificant in comparison with the forests among which they are dispersed [Ermolov, 1893, pp. 64–65].

We hear, too, of the burning of trees and undergrowth in connection with the cultivation (Semenov, 1893, p. 82). Manninen has also described (1932, pp. 245, 274–75) the agriculture of the Finno-Ugrian peoples as involving the felling and burning of successive tracts of forest; the rich ash resulted in a yield some three to four times that from ordinary plowland. Frequently, as among the Votyaks of the Volga-Kama region, the tree stumps were left in the ground and the soil tilled between them.

That this was an immemorial practice among the Finnish peoples we may suppose from a passage in the *Kalevala* epic where the voice of the aged Väinämöinen is said to halt "like the hoe among the pine roots."[19] Traces of this primitive agriculture have also survived among the Baltic Finns. Mead's study of land clearance in Finland shows that "burning might be rotational or casual," and he instances an example of rotational burning in eastern Finland in 1781. The trees were felled in the first year and fired in the second year. Four to six years of crop then followed, often amid the tree stumps, after which the land relapsed to scrub and wood for a span of twenty to thirty years. "Where rotational burning occurred, four cycles in a century was the average. In a hundred years, therefore, the burnt-over land experienced twenty years under grain, perhaps twelve under rough pasture and sixty-eight as woodland grazing" (Mead, 1953, p. 46). Since the eighteenth century, and particularly since the middle of the nineteenth, the practice has declined as methods of agriculture have improved and the value of forests has increased (Figs. 64 and 65). It still occurs, but only occasionally and with caution. On the forests that remain (70 per cent in Finland), it has left a mark, for the first trees to appear on burned-over areas

19. *Kalevala: Or, The Land of Heroes,* trans. W. F. Kirby (London: Everyman's Library [J. M. Dent & Sons], 1907), I, 248.

FIG. 64.—Firing the woodland. (From Mead, 1953; sketches made by Magnus von Wright, 1883.)

FIG. 65.—Plowing the fired land. (From Mead, 1953; sketches made by Magnus von Wright, 1883.)

are birch and alder, not conifers or hardwoods.

Across the Baltic Sea, in Sweden, rotational burning was also found, and it has recently been studied by Montelius, who says (1953) there is no doubt that it has been practiced "since prehistoric times." Medieval evidence indicates the cultivation of rye and turnips in forest clearings over large parts of the country. The practice was greatly stimulated by the immigration of Finns during the sixteenth and seventeenth centuries, and the result was a conflict with mining companies interested in wood for miners and in charcoal for foundries and forges. Attempts made to limit burning in the mining districts resulted in a compromise by which the heavy tree trunks were used for charcoal, the tops and branches burned. With changing economic conditions, the habit gradually disappeared, and the last crop of rye grown on burned forest land was har-

vested in 1918. In the meantime, the demands of the important iron industry upon wood for charcoal greatly increased from 1830 to 1885; but, with the introduction of coke, it declined, and "in a few years the role of charcoal in the Swedish steel industry will be very insignificant" (Arpi, 1953, p. 27).

On the forest map of Europe today, the coniferous belt stands out strikingly (Heske and Torunsky, 1951——), and the demands of the twentieth century for lumber and for pulpwood have given it a new importance. The great extent of standing wood does not imply a lack of human interference. Much, perhaps most, of it has been logged over at least once, and forest fires have wrought havoc (Streyffert, 1934, p. 4). Much, too, has come under the care of forestry services. Not as dramatically as elsewhere in Europe, but quite unmistakably, the northern forest bears witness to the transforming hand of man.

REFERENCES

Albion, R. G.
 1926 *Forests and Sea-power.* Cambridge, Mass.: Harvard University Press. 485 pp.
Andrews, G. H.
 1853 *Modern Husbandry: A Practical and Scientific Treatise on Agriculture.* London: Nathaniel Cooke. 404 pp.
Arpi, G.
 1953 "The Supply with Charcoal of the Swedish Iron Industry from 1830 to 1950," *Geografiska Annaler,* XXXV, 11–27.
Arqué, P.
 1948 "La Conquête du sol en Périgord méridional," pp. 13–26 in *France méridionale et pays ibériques: Mélanges géographiques offerts en hommage à M. Daniel Faucher.* 2 vols. Toulouse: Éditions Toulousaines de l'Ingénieur. 685 pp.
Aubin, H.
 1941 "The Lands East of the Elbe and German Colonisation Eastwards," pp. 361–97 in Clapham, J. H., and

Power, E. (eds.), *The Cambridge Economic History of Europe,* Vol. I. Cambridge: Cambridge University Press. 650 pp.
Banfield, T. C.
 1846–48 *Industry of the Rhine.* 2 vols. London: Charles Knight & Co. 244 + 252 pp.
Bennett, H. S.
 1937 *Life on the English Manor.* Cambridge: Cambridge University Press. 364 pp. (Reprinted 1938, 1948.)
Blache, J.
 1923 "L'Essartage, ancienne pratique culturale dans les Alpes dauphinoises," *Revue de géographie alpine,* XI, 553–75
Bloch, Marc
 1931 *Les Caractères originaux de l'histoire rurale française.* Oslo. 261 pp. (Reprinted 1952. Paris: Armand Colin.)
Boissonnade, P.
 1927 *Life and Work in Medieval Eu-*

rope. London: Kegan Paul, Trench, Trubner & Co. 395 pp.

BROWN, J. C.

1884 *Forests and Forestry of Northern Russia and the Lands Beyond.* Edinburgh: Oliver & Boyd. 279 pp.

BRUNHES, J., and DEFFONTAINES, P.

1926 "Arbres et forêts: Types et sites d'activités humaines liées à la forêt," pp. 337–62 (chap. xxvi) in *Géographie humaine de la France*, Vol. II. Paris: Société de l'Hístoire National. 652 pp.

BUFFAULT, P.

1937*a* "Les Forêts de l'Europe pendant le moyen âge," *Revue des eaux et forêts*, LXXIV, 140–50.

1937*b* "Le Déboisement: Ses causes, ses consequences," *ibid.*, pp. 432–41, 506–18.

CAGGESE, R.

1907–8 *Classi e comuni rurali nel medio evo italiano.* 2 vols. Florence: Tipografia Galileiana. 405 + 392 pp.

CAMPAGNE, A. J. P.

1912 *Les Forêts pyrénéenes: Évolution à travers les âges. État et rendement actuels. Avenir économique.* Paris: Laveur. 190 pp.

CÁNOVAS DEL CASTILLO, A.

1910 *Historia de la decadencia de España.* Madrid: Liberia Gutenberg de José Ruiz. 761 pp.

CAVAILLÈS, H.

1905 "La Question forestière en Espagne," *Annales de géographie*, V, 318–31.

CHILDE, V. GORDON

1931 "The Forest Cultures of Northern Europe: A Study in Evolution and Diffusion," *Journal of the Royal Anthropological Institute of Great Britain and Ireland*, LXI, 325–48.

CLARK, J. G. D.

1944 "Man and Nature in Prehistory, with Special Reference to Neolithic Settlement in Northern Europe," *University of London Institute of Archaeology, Occasional Paper*, No. 6, pp. 20–28.

1945 "Farmers and Forests in Neolithic Europe," *Antiquity*, XIX, 57–71.

1947 "Forest Clearance and Prehistoric Clearing," *Economic History Review*, XVII, 45–51.

1952 "Farming: Clearance and Cultivation," pp. 91–107 (chap. iv) in *Prehistoric Europe: The Economic Basis.* Cambridge: Cambridge University Press. 349 pp.

CLARKE, R. R.; MACDONALD, J.; and WATT, A. S.

1938 "The Breckland," pp. 208–29 (chap. xv) in DARBY, H. C. (ed.), *The Cambridge Region.* Cambridge: Cambridge University Press. 234 pp.

DARBY, H. C.

1936 "Colonisation," pp. 178–89 in DARBY, H. C. (ed.), *An Historical Geography of England before A.D. 1800.* Cambridge: Cambridge University Press. 566 pp. (Reprinted 1948, 1951.)

1950 "Domesday Woodland," *Economic History Review*, 2d ser., III, 21–43.

1951 "The Clearing of the English Woodlands," *Geography*, XXXVI, 71–83.

1952 *The Domesday Geography of Eastern England.* Cambridge: Cambridge University Press. 400 pp.

DARBY, H. C., and TERRETT, I. B. (eds.)

1954 *The Domesday Geography of Midland England.* Cambridge: Cambridge University Press. 482 pp.

DAVIES, R. W.

1952 "Russia in the Early Middle Ages," *Economic History Review*, 2d ser., V, 116–27.

DEBIEN, G.

1952 *En Haut-Poitou: Défricheurs au travail, XVᵉ–XVIIIᵉ siècles.* Paris: Armand Colin. 93 pp.

DEFFONTAINES, P.

1932 *La Vie forestière en Slovaquie.* Paris: Travaux Publiés par l'Institut d'Études Slaves. 94 pp.

1933 *L'Homme et la forêt.* Paris: Gallimard. 188 pp.

DES MAREZ, G.

1926 *Le Problème de la colonisation franque et du régime agraire en Belgique.* Brussels: Académie Royale de Belgique. 191 pp.

DIETRICH, B. F. A.
1928 "European Forests and Their Utilization," *Economic Geography*, IV, 140–58.

DION, R.
1938 "Usines et forêts: Conséquences de l'ancien emploi du bois comme combustible industriel," *Revue des eaux et forêts*, LXXVI, 771–82.

DOPSCH, A.
1937 *The Economic and Social Foundations of European Civilization*. London: Kegan Paul, Trench, Trubner & Co. 404 pp.

DUVIVIER, C.
1859 "*Hospites:* Défrichements en Europe et spécialement dans nos contrées aux XIe, XIIe et XIIIe siècles," *Revue d'histoire et d'archéologie*, I, 74–90, 131–75.

ECK, A.
1933 *Le Moyen Âge russe*. Paris: Maison du Livre Étranger. 574 pp.

ERMOLOV, A. S.
1893 "Systems of Agriculture and Field Rotation," pp. 62–73 (chap. iv) in CRAWFORD, J. M. (ed.), *The Industries of Russia*, Vol. III. St. Petersburg: Department of Agriculture, Ministry of Crown Domains. 488 pp.

FERNOW, B. E.
1911 *A Brief History of Forestry: In Europe, the United States and Other Countries*. Toronto: University of Toronto Press. 506 pp.

FICKELER, P.
1954 "Das Siegerland," *Erdkunde*, VIII, 15–81.

FLACH, J.
1893 "Les Villages créés dans les forêts et sur les terres désertes," pp. 139–57 (chap. xii) in *Les Origines de l'ancienne France*, Vol. II. Paris: Librairie du Recueil Général des Lois et des Arrêts. 584 pp.

FOX, SIR CYRIL
1923 *The Archaeology of the Cambridge Region*. Cambridge: Cambridge University Press. 360 pp. (2d ed., 1949.)

GARNETT, A.
1945 "The Loess Regions of Central Europe in Prehistoric Times," *Geographical Journal*, CVI, 132–43.

GEORGE, P.
1933 "Anciennes et nouvelles forêts en région méditerranéenne," *Les Etudes Rhodaniennes*, IX, 85–120.

GOBLET, F. (COUNT D'ALVIELLA)
1927 *Histoire des bois et forêts de Belgique. ... Des Origines à la fin du régime autrichen*. 3 vols. Paris: Paul Lechevaliers; Brussels: Maurice Lamertin. 491 + 351 + 140 pp.

GODWIN, H.
1934 "Pollen Analysis: An Outline of the Problems and Potentialities of the Method," *New Phytologist*, XXXIII, 278–305, 325–58.
1944a "Neolithic Forest Clearance," *Nature*, CLIII, 511.
1944b "Age and Origin of the 'Breckland' Heaths of East Anglia," *ibid.*, CLIV, 6.

GOVER, J. E. B.; MAWER, A.; and STENTON, F. M.
1942 *The Place-Names of Middlesex*. Cambridge: Cambridge University Press. 237 pp.

GRADMANN, ROBERT
1898 *Das Pflanzenleben der schwäbischen Alb*. Tübingen: Schnürlen. 376 pp. (2d ed., 1900; 3d ed., 1936; 4th ed., 1952.)
1901 "Das mitteleuropäische Landschaftsbild nach seiner geschichtlichen Entwicklung," *Geographische Zeitschrift*, VII, 361–77, 435–47.
1906 "Beziehungen zwischen Pflanzengeographie und Siedlungsgeschichte," *ibid.*, XII, 305–25.
1931 *Süddeutschland*. 2 vols. Stuttgart: J. Engelhorns Nachf. 215 + 553 pp.

GRENIER, ALBERT
1930 "Aux origines de l'économie rurale: La conquête du sol français," *Annales d'histoire économique et sociale*, Deuxième année, pp. 26–47.

HESKE, FRANZ, and TORUNSKY, RICHARD (eds.)
1951—— *Weltforstatlas; World Forestry Atlas; Atlas des forêts du monde; Atlas forestal del mundo*. Hamburg and Reinbeck: Zentralinstitut für Forst-

und Holzwirtschaft. (In course of publication.)

Hoops, J.
1905 *Waldbäume und Kulturpflanzen im germanischen Altertum.* Strasbourg: Verlag von Karl J. Trübner. 689 pp.

Hornstein, Felix von
1951 *Wald und Mensch: Waldgeschichte des Alpenvorlandes Deutschlands Österreichs und der Schweiz.* Ravensburg: Otto Maier Verlag. 282 pp.

Iversen, J.
1941 *Landnam i Danmarks Stenalder* ("Land Occupation in Denmark's Stone Age"). ("Danmarks geologiske Undersøgelse," Series II, No. 66.) Copenhagen. 68 pp. (For a review see Godwin, 1944a.)
1949 *The Influence of Prehistoric Man on Vegetation.* ("Danmarks geologiske Undersøgelse," Series IV, Vol. III, No. 6.) Copenhagen. 25 pp.

Jäger, H.
1951 *Die Entwicklung der Kulturlandschaft im Kreise Hofgeismar.* ("Göttinger geographische Abhandlungen," No. 8.) Göttingen. 114 pp.
1954 "Zur Entstehung der heutigen grossen Forsten in Deutschland," *Berichte zur deutschen Landeskunde,* XIII, 156–71.

Jullian, C.
1920 *Histoire de la Gaule,* Vol. V: *La Civilisation gallo-romaine.* Paris: Librairie Hachette. 381 pp.

Keller, B. A.
1927 "Distribution of Vegetation on the Plains of European Russia," *Journal of Ecology,* XV, 189–233.

Klein, J.
1920 *The Mesta: A Study in Spanish Economic History, 1273–1836.* Cambridge, Mass.: Harvard University Press. 444 pp.

Kluchevsky, V. O.
1911–31 *A History of Russia.* 5 vols. London: J. M. Dent & Sons. 373 + 326 + 380 + 382 + 338 pp.

Knüll, B.
1903 *Historische Geographie Deutsch-*

lands im Mittelalter. Breslau: Ferdinand Hirt. 240 pp.

Koebner, R.
1941 "The Settlement and Colonisation of Europe," pp. 1–88 (chap. i) in Clapham, J. H., and Power, E. (eds.), *The Cambridge Economic History of Europe,* Vol. I. Cambridge: Cambridge University Press. 650 pp.

Kötzschke, R., and Ebert, W.
1937 *Geschichte der ostdeutschen Kolonisation.* Leipzig: Bibliographisches Institut. 251 pp.

Kretschmer, K.
1904 *Historische Geographie von Mitteleuropa.* Munich: R. Oldenbourg. 650 pp.

Lamprecht, K.
1893 *Deutsche Geschichte,* Vol. III. Berlin: R. Gaertners Verlagsbuchhandlung. 488 pp.

Lane, F. C.
1934 "The Timber Supplies," pp. 217–33 (chap. xii) in *Venetian Ships and Shipbuilders of the Renaissance.* Baltimore: Johns Hopkins Press. 285 pp.

Larroquette, A.
1924 *Les Landes de Gascogne et la forêt landaise: Aperçu physique et étude de transformation économique.* Mont-de-Marsan: Imprimerie Dupeyron. 404 pp.

Leimbach, W.
1948 "Zur Waldsteppenfrage in der Sowjetunion," *Erdkunde,* II, 238–56.

Liouville, E.
1897 "Les Taillis des Ardennes," *Revue des eaux et forêts,* XXXVI, 257–67.

Lodijensky, N.
1901 "The Forests of Russia," pp. 316–24 (chap. xxv) in Lodijensky, J. N. (ed.), *Russia: Its Industries and Trade.* Glasgow: Hay Nisbet & Co. 324 pp.

Lorenzi, A.
1918–19 "L'Uomo e le foreste," *Rivista geografica italiana,* XXV, 141–65, 213–42; XXVI, 47–57.

Mager, F.
1930 *Entwicklungsgeschichte der Kulturlandschaft des Herzogtums Schles-*

wig in historischer Zeit. Breslau: Ferdinand Hirt. 523 pp.

MANNINEN, I.
1932 *Die finnisch-ugrischen Völker*. Leipzig: Otto Harrassowitz. 384 pp.

MARSH, G. P.
1864 "The Woods," pp. 128–329 (chap. iii) in *Man and Nature: Or, Physical Geography as Modified by Human Action*. London: Sampson Low, Son & Marston. 560 pp.
1874 "The Woods," pp. 148–397 (chap. iii) in *The Earth as Modified by Human Action* (new ed. of *Man and Nature*). New York: Scribner, Armstrong & Co. 656 pp.

MARTONNE, E. DE
1931 *Géographie universelle: Europe centrale*. 2 vols. Paris: Armand Colin. 845 pp.

MAURY, L. F. A.
1850 *Histoire des grandes forêts de la Gaule et de l'ancienne France*. Paris: A. Leleux. 328 pp.
1866 *Les Forêts de la France dans l'antiquité et au moyen âge*. Paris: Imprimerie Impériale. 270 pp.
1867 *Les Forêts de la Gaule et de l'ancienne France*. Paris: Ladrange. 501 pp.

MAZOYER, L.
1932 "Exploitation forestière et conflits sociaux en Franche-Comté, à la fin de l'ancien régime," *Annales d'histoire économique et sociale*, Quatrième année, pp. 339–58.

MEAD, W. R.
1953 *Farming in Finland*. London: Athlone Press. 248 pp.

MINNS, E. H.
1913 *Scythians and Greeks*. Cambridge: Cambridge University Press. 720 pp.

MONKHOUSE, F. J.
1949 *The Belgian Kempenland*. Liverpool: University of Liverpool Press. 252 pp.

MONTELIUS, S.
1953 "The Burning of Forest Land for the Cultivation of Crops," *Geografiska Annaler*, XXXV, 41–54.

MORTENSEN, H.
1951 "Neue Beobachtungen über Wüs-

tungs-Bandfluren und ihre Bedeutung für die mittelalterliche deutsche Kulturlandschaft," *Berichte zur deutschen Landeskunde*, X, 341–61.

MORTENSEN, H., and SCHARLAU, K.
1949 "Der siedlungskundliche Wert der Kartierung von Wüstungsfluren," *Nachrichten der Akademie der Wissenschaften in Göttingen, Philosophisch-historische Klasse, 1949*, pp. 303–31.

MUTTON, A. F. M.
1938 "Place-Names and the History of Settlement in South-west Germany," *Geography*, XXIII, 113–19.

NEF, J. U.
1952 "Mining and Metallurgy in Medieval Civilisation," pp. 429–92 (chap. vii) in POSTAN, M., and RICH, E. (eds.), *The Cambridge Economic History of Europe*, Vol. II. Cambridge: Cambridge University Press. 604 pp.

NEUMANN, K.
1855 *Die Hellenen im Skythenlande*. Berlin: Verlag Georg Reimer. 578 pp.

NIEMEIER, G.
1949 "Frühformen der Waldhufen," *Petermanns geographische Mitteilungen*, XCIII, 14–27.

NIETSCH, H.
1939 *Wald und Siedlung im vorgeschichtlichen Mitteleuropa*. Leipzig: Mannus-Bücherei. 254 pp.

OURLIAC, P.
1949 "Les Villages de la région Toulousaine au XIIe siècle," *Annales: Économies, sociétés, civilisations*, Quatrième année, pp. 268–77.

PARAIN, C.
1936 *La Méditerranée: Les hommes et leurs travaux*. Paris: Gallimard. 225 pp.

PASZKIEWICZ, H.
1954 *The Origin of Russia*. London: Allen & Unwin. 556 pp.

PATSCH, C.
1922 *Historische Wanderungen im Karst und an der Adria*. Vienna: Verlag des Forschungsinstitutes für Osten und Orient. 170 pp.

PENCK, ALBRECHT
1887 "Das deutsche Reich," pp. 115–596 in KIRCHOFF, A. (ed.), *Länder-*

kunde des Erdteils Europa, Vol. II: *Unser Wissen von der Erde,* Part I. Vienna: F. Tempsky.

POHLENDT, H.
1950 *Die Verbreitung der mittelalterlichen Wüstungen in Deutschland.* ("Göttinger geographische Abhandlungen," No. 3.) Göttingen. 86 pp.

POSTAN, M.
1952 "The Trade of Medieval Europe: The North," pp. 119–256 (chap. iv) in POSTAN, M., and RICH, E. (eds.), *The Cambridge Economic History of Europe,* Vol. II. Cambridge: Cambridge University Press. 604 pp.

POWER, E.
1932 "Peasant Life and Rural Conditions (c. 1100 to c. 1500)," pp. 716–50 in TANNER, J. R., et al., *The Cambridge Medieval History,* Vol. VII. Cambridge: Cambridge University Press. 1073 pp.

RABOT, C.
1905 "Le Déboisement dans la vallée d'Aspe et son influence sur le régime des cours d'eau," *La Géographie,* XI, 207–8.

ROUDSKI, A. F., and SHAFRANOV, N. I.
1893 "Forestry," pp. 311–52 (chap. xv) in CRAWFORD, J. M. (ed.), *The Industries of Russia,* Vol. III. St. Petersburg: Department of Agriculture, Ministry of Crown Domains. 488 pp.

RUNGALDIER, R.
1943 *Natur- und Kulturlandschaft zwischen Donau und Theiss.* ("Abhandlungen der Geographischen Gesellschaft in Wien," Vol. XIV, No. 4.) 127 pp.

SCHLÜTER, O.
1920 "Wald, Sumpf und Siedelungsland in Altpreussen vor der Ordenszeit," *Geographischer Anzeiger,* XXI, 245–49.
1952 *Die Siedlungsräume Mitteleuropas in frühgeschichtlicher Zeit,* Part I. ("Forschungen zur Deutschen Landeskunde," Vol. LXIII.) Hamburg. 47 pp.

SCHMITTHENNER, H.
1923 "Die Reutbergwirtschaft in

Deutschland," *Geographische Zeitschrift,* XXIX, 115–27.

SCHOTT, CARL
1935 "Urlandschaft und Rodung: Vergleichende Betrachtungen aus Europa und Kanada," *Zeitschrift der Gesellschaft für Erdkunde zur Berlin,* pp. 81–102.
1952 "Das Heideproblem in Schleswig-Holstein," *Verhandlungen des Deutschen Geographentages,* XXVIII, 259–68.

SCLAFERT, T.
1926 *Le Haut-Dauphiné au moyen âge.* Paris: Société anonyme du recueil Sirey. 765 pp.
1933 "A propos du déboisement des Alpes du Sud," *Annales de géographie,* XLII, 266–77, 350–60.
1934 "A propos du déboisement des Alpes du Sud: Le Rôle des troupeaux," *ibid.,* XLIII, 126–45.

SEMENOV, D. P.
1893 "Cultivation of the Soil," pp. 74–92 (chap. v) in CRAWFORD, J. M. (ed.), *The Industries of Russia,* Vol. III. St. Petersburg: Department of Agriculture, Ministry of Crown Domains. 488 pp.

SEMPLE, E. C.
1931 "Ancient Mediterranean Forests and the Lumber Trade," pp. 261–96 (chap. xi) in *The Geography of the Mediterranean Region: Its Relation to Ancient History.* New York: Henry Holt & Co. 737 pp.

SOÓ, R. DE
1929 "Die Vegetation und die Entstehung der ungarischen Puszta," *Journal of Ecology,* XVII, 329–50.

STENTON, F. M.; BUTLER, H. E.; HONEYBOURNE, M. B.; and DAVIS, E. JEFFRIES
1934 *Norman London: An Essay.* ("Historical Association Leaflets," Nos. 93–94.) London. 40 pp.

STRAKER, E.
1931 *Wealden Iron.* London: G. Bell & Sons. 487 pp.

STREYFFERT, T.
1934 "Softwood Resources of Europe," *Economic Geography,* X, 1–13.

THOMPSON, J. W.
1928a *An Economic and Social History*

of the Middle Ages (300–1300). New York: Century Co. 900 pp.

1928b *Feudal Germany.* Chicago: University of Chicago Press. 710 pp.

TRAUTMANN, R.

1948–49 *Die Elb- und Ostseeslavischen Ortsnamen.* 2 vols. ("Abhandlungen der Deutschen Akademie der Wissenschaften zu Berlin, Philosophisch-historische Klasse, 1947," Nos. 4 and 7.) Berlin. 187 and 119 pp.

TÜXEN, R.

1931 "Die Grundlagen der Urlandschaftsforschung: Ein Beitrag zur Erforschung der Geschichte der anthropogenen Beeinflussung der Vegetation Mitteleuropas," *Nachrichten aus Niedersachsens Urgeschichte,* No. 5, pp. 59–105.

TURRILL, W. B.

1929 "The Influence of Man on the Flora and Vegetation," pp. 189–239 (chap. x) in *The Plant-Life of the Balkan Peninsula.* Oxford: Clarendon Press. 490 pp.

VILLARI, L.

1904 *The Republic of Ragusa.* London: J. M. Dent & Co. 424 pp.

WADDINGTON, C. H.

1930 "Note sur la dépopulation des campagnes gâtinaises pendant la guerre de cent ans et leur reconstruction économique," *Annales de la Société Historique et Archéologique du Gâtinais,* XXXIX, 164–78.

WILCOX, H. A.

1933 *The Woodlands and Marshlands of England.* Liverpool: University of Liverpool Press. 55 pp.

WILHELMY, H.

1950 "Das Alter der Schwarzerde und der Steppen Mittel- und Osteuropas," *Erdkunde,* IV, 5–34.

ZON, R.

1920 "Forests and Human Progress," *Geographical Review,* X, 139–66.

ZON, R., and SPARHAWK, W. N.

1923 "The Forest Situation in Europe," pp. 72–349 (chap. ii) in *Forest Resources of the World.* 2 vols. New York: McGraw-Hill Book Co. 997 pp.

The Ecology of Peasant Life in Western Europe

E. ESTYN EVANS*

In 1944 there appeared a remarkable monograph on *Cereals in Great Britain and Ireland in Prehistoric and Early Historic Times* by two Danish scientists, Knud Jessen and Hans Helbaek. It is important as an original work on an obscure subject, but what makes it remarkable is the fact that it was published in Copenhagen, in English, during the Nazi occupation of Denmark. The maintenance of a modernized peasantry and the correlated enlightened outlook on education surely stand vindicated in the outstanding contributions made by Danish archeologists and paleobotanists to our knowledge of the evolution of European agriculture. It is no accident that Scandinavian scholars have pioneered in the study of agrarian history. Brøgger indeed has claimed that, to approach any understanding of early cultures, it is necessary to work back from the present, "to know something of life along the coast and at sea, in the forests and amid the mountains, on the land, the fields, the pastures, the hinterland and the mountain farms"

* Dr. Evans is Professor of Geography and Head of the department and former Dean of the Faculty of Arts in Queen's University, Belfast. He was Tallman Visiting Professor of Geography and Anthropology at Bowdoin College, Brunswick, Maine, in 1948–49. He has conducted many excavations on prehistoric sites in Ireland. His publications include: *Irish Heritage*, 1942; *Mourne Country*, 1951; and *Lyles Hill: A Late Neolithic Site in County Antrim*, 1953.

(1940, p. 166). Equally it may be asserted that a full understanding of peasant societies, as they have survived until yesterday, is impossible without a knowledge of their origins and of their painful but fateful adaptation to the difficult western European environments of forests, mountains, moorlands, clouds, and seas.

The roots of our folk life strike deep into the past, and the conventional documentary tools of the historian cannot reach down to them. But a Marc Bloch can read the runes of old field boundaries carved on the landscape as archeological documents and can glimpse the truth that, when the Middle Ages began, "l'agriculture était déjà, sur notre sol, chose millénaire" (Bloch, 1931, p. 1). Rural prehistory, says Bloch, dominates rural history. In Britain, as in Scandinavia, a great deal of research on prehistoric geography and archeology is in progress, and the co-operation of workers in several related sciences is proving fruitful. There are many gaps in the evidence—dark ages in time and dark areas in space—but in the course of some three decades much new light has been thrown on the origins of the peasantries of Western Europe. We have had, too, illuminating statistical studies of their present-day economies, but the ordinary laws of economics do not apply to traditional subsistence farming, and statistics cannot measure the values of rural living. They have come down to us from the past. I am therefore concerned with the patterns of rural life and landscape as they came to take shape and with their mutual relationships.

For our purpose Western Europe is taken to be the insular and peninsular ends of the Continent, north of the Mediterranean lands of summer drought and south of the cold coniferous forest, which lie open to the climatic influences of the Atlantic Ocean and to the impact of sea-borne cultures. Our region makes easy contact with the head of the Adriatic Sea by way of the Alpine passes leading from the upper Danube Basin. The transition to northeastern Europe is defined by a cultural watershed which runs approximately along the fourteenth east meridian and leaves western Sweden, with most of Norway, on the Atlantic cultural slope. Erixon has summarized the evidence (1938a) for these western European connections in Scandinavia, which is derived from such diverse material as archeology, peasant furnishings, house types, oaten bread, the two-wheeled cart, back baskets, and wooden shoes.

In middle Europe, between the Baltic Sea and the eastern Alps, the interpenetration of East and West—of upland and plain, of oceanic and continental climates, with their counterparts in the archeological record and in the historic conflicts of German and Slav—makes the definition of a frontier an insoluble problem for geographer and statesman alike. But our eastern limit lies somewhere within the transition zone of Mackinder (1944), between his "Marginal Lands" and "Heartland"; and we have chosen a line from Stettin to Trieste, which is effectively the present political divide between East and West (Fig. 66). It will be seen from the map that our line runs parallel to the January isotherm of 0° C., which defines the North Atlantic Gulf of winter warmth and marks the divide between areas having on the average at least one month of the year frozen, and those on the west, where January is normally a green month. In the extreme west the farthest peninsulas and islands of Ireland, southern England, and France lie on the warm side of the January isotherm of 6° C., the approximate zero of plant growth; and these favored evergreen ends of Western Europe are the homes of such milky breeds of cattle as the Kerry, the Jersey, and the Guernsey. Western Europe knows neither prolonged summer drought nor, as a rule, lengthy winter frost; in this equable climate soil erosion, save on steep slopes, is not a serious problem, and farming life has been continuous through the centuries. Rather it is the accumulation of waterlogged peats that has upset the ecologic balance of farming communities along the Atlantic seaboard.

Western Europe as thus defined, facing the Atlantic along thousands of miles of drowned coasts from Trondheim Fjord to the mouth of the Douro, belongs in the main to a single ecological zone, that of the temperate deciduous forest, broken only by the Scandinavian fjeld and its fringe of boreal forest and by the mountain islands of the High Alps and Pyrenees. If to these inhospitable regions we add the broken Caledonian and Hercynian uplands and certain areas of high precipitation or impoverished soils, we can distinguish two major types of environment within Western Europe, which we may term, following Fleure (1919), "regions of difficulty" and "regions of effort." They are marked on Figure 66, together with patches of fertile loessic soil which offered a relatively favorable habitat for early farming and which, linking with more extensive deposits in the middle Danube Basin and southeastern Europe, served repeatedly as avenues along which colonists and adventurers invaded the west. Our map marks also

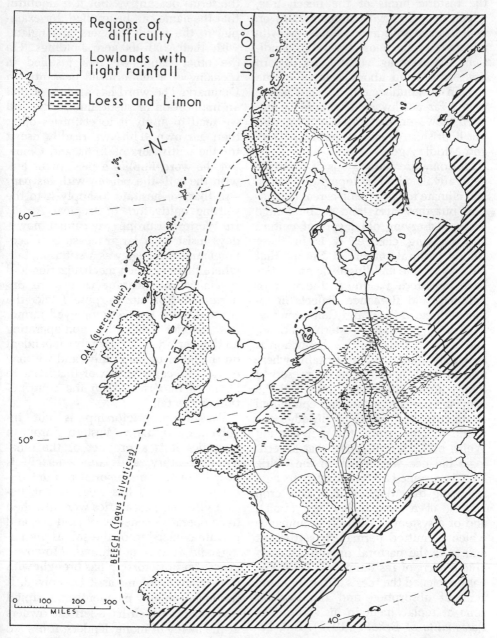

FIG. 66.—Some environmental factors in the rural life of Western Europe. Continental and Mediterranean regions are hatched. The map distinguishes between regions of difficulty having high relief and/or high rainfall and lowland areas. It also shows the distribution of loessic soils. The continuous line is the January isotherm of 0° C. Broken lines show the historic limits of the oak and the beech.

the historic limits of the beech tree, which flourishes with summer rains on well-drained soils and provides us with an index of the most favorable conditions for early agriculture. Its eastern limit runs from about Danzig to the Balkan Mountains, and it is not native to the far northwest. It should be noticed, however, that the beech tree did not flourish in Denmark until the Dark and Middle Ages.

Not only are the regions of difficulty generally ill suited by topography, soils, and climate to large-scale cereal cultivation but they also tend to be refuge areas, conserving old layers of culture and resisting change. It is in these cloudy pastoral corners of Europe that old ways of life and linguistic minorities have persisted: Basque in the western Pyrenees, old Romance dialects in remote Alpine valleys, and Celtic tongues in Brittany, Wales, western Scotland, and western Ireland. The distinction is strikingly illustrated in Britain, where upland and lowland have preserved their cultural differences and where the English language, which has conquered continents, has failed to dislodge the Celtic tongue from the neighboring Welsh hills. Here it seems that an ecologic balance was struck in the Celtic Iron Age, some two thousand years ago, following the adoption of a new crop (oats), of a new technology (iron), and of a system of cattle transhumance which permitted permanent settlement and gave the pastoral uplands remarkable powers of resistance. Sir Cyril Fox has developed the thesis of the highland zone of absorption and the lowland zone of replacement in his study, *The Personality of Britain* (1947). But, before we resume the question of origins and regional differentiation, we must ask ourselves what we mean by a peasantry.

WHAT IS A PEASANTRY?

We may find peasant values persisting among farmers who would resent the term "peasantry," but it is doubtful that the name can be applied, for example, to the family farmers of England with their 100–300-acre holdings. On the other hand, we feel justified in speaking of a modernized peasantry in Denmark. The word has always carried an implication of rustic inferiority, and we tend to apply it to countries other than our own. Thus we readily use it for the cultivators of India and China. Yet the word implies a permanent link with the soil—the *paysan* with his *pays* —so that we hesitate to apply it to the shifting cultivators of tropical Africa. In Western Europe we cannot nowadays insist on a large measure of economic self-sufficiency as a criterion, but, where there is much mechanization and specialization, peasant values are undermined. For our purpose I take the peasant to be the self-employed farmer (as distinct from the non-operating landowner) who is largely dependent on the labor of his family; and we may expect the contribution of this labor to be more important than the contribution of capital.

Peasant proprietorship is not involved, for in many Western European countries it is a product of the nineteenth century, and landownership is no part of the immemorial peasant tradition. In fact, it has weakened it, because the old peasantries were attached to co-operative schemes of land use, and private ownership of the soil as we understand it was not found. Moreover, peasant proprietorship has brought with it as many problems as it has solved. It has meant money payments and capital investments which have left the owners at the mercy of moneylenders; it has led to inflated land values and acute land hunger where, as in Ireland, it is impossible to rent land save for short periods; and it has in some cases left the peasants without leaders.

The significant fact is that in most regions of Western Europe, in upland

and lowland, it is the small family farm of from 5 to 50 acres that predominates. More than half the Danish farms, for example, are under 25 acres. A considerable but decreasing number of holdings is less than 2½ acres (1 hectare) in size, and these derive as a rule from successive subdivisions among joint heirs, a process which, though now discouraged or prohibited in most countries, has left as a legacy not only diminutive properties but also the serious problem of fragmentation or *parcellement*. Some Swiss holdings of under a hectare are split into over fifty scattered pieces, and there are worse cases on record from pre-famine Ireland. It has happened in Brittany, even recently, that minute fragments of a square yard or so, too small and too remote to be worth cultivating and growing only thistles, are yet prized and jealously guarded. Moreover, a high proportion of good land is wasted in balks or fences, and a farmer may walk hundreds of miles each year merely in moving from one field to another. Fragmentation is one of the pathological problems of peasant farming which has been or is being solved in most parts of Western Europe but which is still the norm in southern Asia. Behind it we see the passion for equal shares of the precious soil as something to be handed down from one generation to another. It is this attachment to the land that gives a peasantry its strength and continuity—an attachment deepened by the devotion of daily work and seasonal festival and by the traditional use of home-grown foods and of local materials for tools, crafts, clothing, and housing. The quality of peasant craftsmanship resides in its ecological fitness, in the use of local products for local needs. The peasant, in continuous touch with the whole cycle of production, can sense the wholeness of life and derive therefrom satisfaction and self-confidence.

Reacting from the specialization and artificial values of urban life, many writers have idealized the untutored folkways of the peasant. We have become accustomed to uncritical eulogies from intellectuals who have never endured the toil of the fields and see only the gay festivals which mark its periodic breaks. More sinister is the political exploitation of peasant attitudes: of large families encouraged to supply the armed forces and of holdings recklessly multiplied to provide votes from "forty-shilling freeholders" in eighteenth-century Ireland. We have witnessed in our own day the consequences of a political philosophy in which peasant worship was prominent, and we recall Hitler's phrase, "Germany must be a peasant people" (Yates, 1940, p. 449). Under the mystical Nazi conception of "blood and soil," the peasant farm was to become "the cradle of the race," a symbol of supposed racial purity. But it also became the means of achieving strategic self-sufficiency in essential foods. Rural festivals were prostituted for political ends, and the peasant urge for progeny was exploited to increase the German birth rate. Nationalistic fervor was bolstered by extravagant claims for the Nordic center as an originator of prehistoric cultures. Since this Nordic center involves Danish territory, it is refreshing to recall the contemporary interest of Danish scientists in the Western European heritage.

There are, as I hope to show, significant differences in peasant values between our regions of difficulty and of effort, as well as between different countries with their varying experiences, but we may conclude this section by considering some attitudes and customs which were, until recently, universal. A very widespread feature is the extensive part played by women in the care of animals, especially cattle and their milk products, and in some field operations. Presumably the earliest cultivators, using the digging stick or stone hoe, were women. In the west of Ireland, potatoes grown in ridges are planted by women and children with a kind of digging stick—a dibble—and on the margin of our region, in Norrland, it is the housewife who has charge of the sowing of crops (Erixon, 1938*b*, p. 288).

Since sons and daughters are helpers from an early age, there is an economic urge for children, especially for sons, to inherit the land; and it must be remembered that, according to one calculation, it was necessary down to the eighteenth century for the average rural wife to bear six children in order to maintain the population. However much the position has changed in some countries, through delayed marriage or family limitation, it remains true that, immemorially, peasant families were large. There are many hints that the fertility of the family was magically connected with the fertility of the soil —that a birth each spring was lucky, an encouragement to the crops and animals to produce a like increase. Devotion to symbols of fertility was a powerful motive force, and its transference, in part, to the worship of the Virgin Mary was a source of inspiration to the medieval world.

Moreover, the peasant festivals which rounded off the seasons of the year have been more or less taken over by Christianity. In Celtic tradition the first day of each quarter, February, May, August, and November, is of great significance. The first of May and the first of November are, in rural Ireland, for example, family festivals, half-pagan, half-Christian; and even in towns they have become the gale days, the times when rents are paid. Traditionally they mark the completion of sowing and harvest and also the beginning and end of the season when the cattle were away on the hill pastures. Behind many of the May Day and Halloween customs there lies the idea of sympathetic magic per-formed to insure good luck for another season. But they were also times when taboos were lifted and a good deal of license was permitted, serving as emotional outlets to ease the strain of periods of intense activity. Similarly, the festivals of midsummer and midwinter were both breaks in routine and occasions for the practice of magic associated with water (cf. Midsummer Day, the Feast of St. John the Baptist, June 24) and with fires, intended perhaps to assist the sun in its turning.

The ceremonies of the last sheaf, whether or not we accept the animistic theories of Mannhardt and Frazer and see in them fertility cults, came to be associated with the fear of being last and acted as a means of insuring the due completion of necessary tasks. Many of the rites of spring are looked on as omens and linked in the peasant mind with the necessity of beginning a new phase of work propitiously. The start of plowing and sowing and the gatherings for sheep-shearing and for the movements of livestock have also been times of ceremony, celebrated by feasting, singing, and dancing. In this way a wonderful wealth of folk tunes and folk songs has been bequeathed to us, handed down from one generation to another. The unlettered peasant often has an amazing memory and remarkable faculties of speech and rhetoric, and these qualities tend to be most marked in regions of difficulty. Poverty, indeed, may be a safeguard of quality in other ways; for example, our most highly prized cheeses come from the poor districts. Where there is little meat to spare, soups and stews have somehow to be made tasty, and, if a certain amount of dirt is involved, may there not be virtue in trace elements and wisdom in the Irish saying that "clean meat never fattened a pig"?

Folklore, proverbs, riddles, children's games, songs, dances, and an astonishingly rich oral literature are the heritage of Europe's peasantries, linking them with the cultivators of other parts of the Old World. Craft knowledge was similarly handed down from father to son, and its secrets cannot be found in books. (Handicrafts, however, are less developed in Western than in Eastern Europe, where towns are fewer and where winter cold limits outdoor work.) The extreme diffusionist view, that peasantries originate nothing, cannot be sustained, yet it is clear that they owe a great deal to ideas filtering down from other social classes. The self-contained community must always have been rare, and from early times no peasantry was entirely independent of external control. Periodic and annual fairs are a very old feature associated with pagan sites and seasons and later with religious centers and saints' days. They were a factor in the growth of towns, which became centers of government and administration as well as of exchange, and, as towns grew, their demand for an agricultural surplus affected in various ways the life of the countryside. The parallel growth of urban industries also profoundly affected rural life, both by flooding the countryside with machine-made goods and by depriving it of the craftsmen who brought to it a healthy variety of work and experience. "The drift from the land" is both a cause and a symptom of rising material civilization (Ashby, 1939). Yet there is general agreement that the rural tradition is an indispensable element in society, a source of vitality and continuity, conserving social values which urbanism tends to destroy. The problem is to preserve these values while increasing the efficiency of farming and the standards of rural living. Our views will be more hopeful if we realize the immemorial antiquity of peasant life.

PREHISTORIC ORIGINS

Farming communities had already reached the southern and eastern approaches to Western Europe before the end of the third millennium B.C. Danubians from the east seem to have been the first to enter the region, but the earliest farmers to reach Britain (about 2000 B.C.) were colonists from western Mediterranean lands who by that time had also pushed eastward from France into Switzerland and Lombardy and crossed the Rhine into the Elbe and Bavaria, where they settled in the fertile loessic areas previously occupied by farmers from the east (Childe, 1950, p. 88). There is evidence that from the beginning the westerners were more concerned with stock-raising than were the Danubians, and mixed farming was to become, as it still remains, the cornerstone of western European agriculture. Their western Neolithic pottery is characterized by its burnished, round-bottomed forms, significantly imitative of leather vessels. Already in the early centuries of the second millennium well-defined regional cultures were taking shape, distinguished by such traits as their pottery styles (Cortaillod, Michelsberg, Windmill Hill, etc.; see Fig. 67); and they occupy geographical areas which have had well-marked personalities in historic times. The differentiation of Western Europe into human regions is thus a fact of great antiquity, and the environmental conditions which colored the original Neolithic occupation of each region call for careful study if we are to comprehend the sources of regional consciousness and the persistent patterns of regional culture. We must also take into account the acculturation of local Mesolithic communities with their immensely old traditions. An inheritance from these deeper layers seems to be the survival of a pre-instrumental pentatonic scale in the haunting folk tunes of northwestern Europe, from Ireland to Finland. As we peer into the prehistoric twilight, we become aware of powerful forces which have shaped peasant life and persist in some

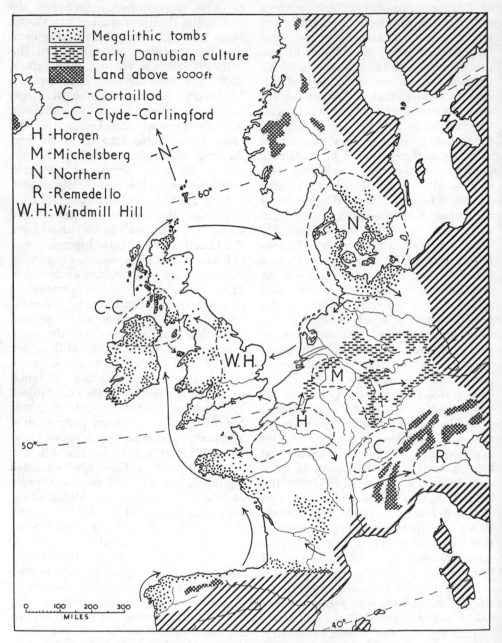

Legend:
- :::: Megalithic tombs
- ≡≡≡ Early Danubian culture
- ▓▓▓ Land above 5000ft
- C - Cortaillod
- C-C - Clyde-Carlingford
- H - Horgen
- M - Michelsberg
- N - Northern
- R - Remedello
- W.H.- Windmill Hill

FIG. 67.—Late Neolithic culture areas in Western Europe (2000–1500 B.C.). The somewhat earlier First Danubian culture is marked in short bars; note its association with areas of loess. The distribution of megalithic tombs betrays coastwise diffusion. Arrows indicate directions of movement.

measure to this day, for the immobile peasantries provide the only unbroken human link with the past, maintaining social and religious as well as physical and economic ties with the soil. We begin to see the megaliths of the outer coast lands (Fig. 67) not as mute memorials of a forgotten civilization but as an integral part of the heritage of Western Europe. We need not be surprised at Sydow's claim (1948, p. 242) to have found folk tales "at least four thousand years old" in areas of megalithic culture. The natural and cultivated environment and the tools of early farmers took on a spiritual significance which is echoed in the folk practices of Ireland and Brittany, for example, to this day.

The polished stone ax has long been recognized as the index of Neolithic culture; we now see it as the hallmark of forest farmers, much as the steel ax was the symbol of the North American pioneers. Petrological studies have revealed the care with which Neolithic farmers sought the most suitable lithic materials and the extensive trade that took place in stone axes. For instance, certain bluestone axes found throughout the British Isles came from a small exposure of porcellanite on Tievebulliagh, County Antrim—so small, indeed, that it escaped the notice of the Geological Survey of Ireland and has only recently been rediscovered by archeological detection (Jope, 1952). Forest clearance was necessary almost everywhere, for the only considerable breaks in the forest were areas of bare rock or of soils so poor that they would not have supported the earliest cereal crops, wheat and barley.

The speed with which colonists spread through Western Europe, avoiding only the marshes, heavy clays, and barren mountains, is explained by their migratory slash-and-burn economy (*Brandwirtschaft*). The subboreal climate of the Neolithic and Bronze ages is believed to have been drier and more favorable to clearance by fire than the earlier Atlantic or the later Sub-Atlantic phases. We need not suppose that all the timber was felled; ring-barking would have sufficed for the larger trees. In Denmark layers of oak charcoal have been observed in some of the bogs, occupying horizons poor in tree pollens —indicating forest clearance—but rich in the pollens of grasses, cereals, and weeds, especially the telltale ribwort plantain (*Plantago lanceolata*). Regeneration of the forest in the form of scrub is attested by the predominance of birch, alder, and hazel pollens in the succeeding layer of peat (Iversen, 1949, p. 12). In Ireland, too, hazel, birch, thorn, and other forest weeds increase at about the same time as the first herbaceous and cereal pollens appear in the bogs, and on the same horizon there is a marked decline in the amount of elm pollen (Mitchell, 1953). It has been suggested that the reduction of the elm, relative to the oak—a reduction which has been observed in Neolithic horizons throughout northwestern Europe—may be explained by the use of the bark and branches of the elm as cattle fodder. The oak, on the other hand, would have been treasured for its hog-fattening mast. We know that, apart from the dog, cattle and swine were the earliest domesticated animals in Europe; and Sauer (1952, p. 37), developing Menghin's views, has postulated a pre-Indo-European pig cult which spread north from the western Mediterranean. The virtual absence of the pig from the Neolithic village of Skara Brae, Orkney (Childe, 1931, p. 203), may be correlated with the northern limit of the oak forest (Fig. 66) and with the surviving traces of an ancient pig taboo in the Scottish Highlands.

While livestock was clearly of great economic importance, nomadic herding societies could have found no place in Neolithic Europe. Forested country, poor in grasses and encumbered with dead branches, would have provided little grazing. Clark has shown (1952, p. 117) that sheep, which require extensive grazing grounds, become important only as the Bronze Age passes into the early Iron Age. The evidence points to small co-operating communities of farmers, presumably kin groups occupying clusters of from ten to twenty houses, who cleared successive patches of forest over a fairly extensive area round about and sent out daughter-colonies to repeat the process. Their well-built houses and finely finished pottery certainly imply fixed if temporary settlement; and the enormous quantities of ritually broken pots offered at megaliths—yielding to the excavator tens of thousands of sherds on some sites—show that occupation must have continued for a generation or two at least. With pottery, we note in passing, came the stockpot and the first stews, broths, and soups, which have remained a part of peasant diet; there is always something in the pot, even if only—in Highland Britain—stewed tea. Note also the good quality of Neolithic pottery, inherited from Mediterranean cultures, and the progressive deterioration of the potter's art through the Bronze Age—in Ireland until the end of the Middle Ages—which is partly to be explained by an increasing dependence on livestock as pastures and bogs replaced forests.

We must not assume that dramatic environmental change is proof of a change of climate. In Ireland the growth of heather and the initiation of blanket bog in upland areas cleared and farmed by Neolithic settlers followed land use which was intensive enough to bring about the podzolization of the soil. Scores of megaliths now buried in the Irish bogs testify to a deterioration of the environment, which has been too readily attributed solely to climatic change (Fig. 68a). Recent investigations suggest that far more weight should be given to ecologic factors, to the disturbances brought about by forest clearance, by leaching of the exposed soil, rapid runoff, blocked drainage, and the redistribution of surface water (Mitchell, 1953). But the clearing of forest also let in the winds. I doubt that cereals could be successfully harvested in many areas without the assistance of the wind: the equinoctial gales are the very life of corn harvest in the west.

PLOWS AND FIELDS

It has been claimed that the light plow, the *ard,* had reached the western Baltic from the Mediterranean region before the end of the Neolithic period (Erixon, 1938a, p. 137), and marks of furrows have been observed underneath barrows of the Bronze Age in Jutland and Holland (Clark, 1952, p. 99). The oldest identified field systems in Western Europe, however, date from the late Bronze Age, after 1000 B.C.; but, since they tend to survive only in marginal areas of poor soil where they have not been obliterated by later fields, it is possible that permanent settlement and true peasantries go back to the second millennium. The plots are squarish, as in the Celtic field system brought to southern Britain by invading urn-field peoples (Fig. 68b), and they were presumably cross-plowed with the *ard* in Mediterranean fashion. Danish fields of the "Celtic Iron Age" have been investigated by Hatt, who finds evidence to suggest (1939, p. 11) that there were both single farms individually owned and clustered hamlets with fields subdivided by inheritance. He thinks that, from the irregular sizes of the plots, they did not change hands periodically, though we know that this was traditional in many open-field schemes, especially in regions of difficulty. Nor do we know whether the single farms imply social distinctions, as is suggested by

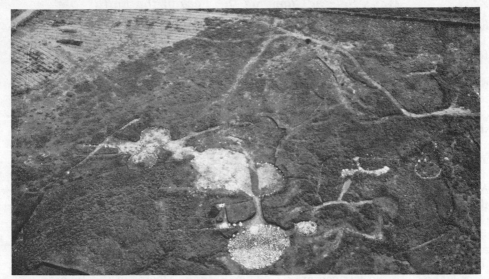

a

b

FIG. 68.—Archeological evidence

a) In Ireland and elsewhere in northwestern Europe peat-cutting has revealed many ancient sites under the bogs. This air photograph shows a complex of megalithic circles and alignments after archeological excavation had been undertaken following the removal of up to 6 feet of peat for fuel. The site is at Beaghmore, County Tyrone, Northern Ireland, on a plateau of pre-Cambrian rocks at a height of 600 feet. The leached sandy soil under the peat shows white inside the circles. Stone walls and causeways, probably associated with prehistoric fields, pass under and are older than some of the megalithic structures. The basal peats contain the pollens of weeds such as ribwort plantain (*Plantago lanceolata*) and dock (*Rubex*) and among tree pollens a high proportion of hazel. The upper peats show a complete dominance of heather pollens.

Old lazy beds visible at top left betray recent outfield cultivation—after an interval of some thirty-five hundred years—on land from which the peat had previously been removed. They probably date from the nineteenth century. Heather is again invading the cultivated land.

b) Circular settlement site (*top center*) and associated "Celtic fields" near Grassington, Yorkshire, underlying the present-day field pattern.

field evidence and by the Irish Law Texts for Dark Age Ireland. Certainly, for most of Western Europe, the archeological evidence points to a concentration of economic and political power, by the early Iron Age, in the hands of conquering herders; already in the Hallstatt phase splendid horse trappings and long cavalry swords tell of mounted leaders who foreshadow the military aristocrats of the Middle Ages. And the introduction of urbanism under Rome was preceded by an approximation to city life and specialized professions in the La Tène culture, developed in the region north of the Alps under the stimulus of Mediterranean contacts after 500 b.c. In the last centuries b.c., La Tène war chariots carried the Celtic conquerors over nearly all parts of Western Europe (Childe, 1950, p. 230).

The improved plow, with colter and moldboard to cut and turn the furrow slice, is also the product of the pre-Roman Iron Age and was designed for the cultivation of the deep heavy soils now being cleared of their mixed-oak forests with axes of iron. With it came a new type of cultivated landscape and a new order of rural living and social stratification evolving in time into the feudal system and the historic kingdoms of Western Europe. The heavy plow, sooner or later fitted with wheels, had reached southern England in pre-Roman times, and it was to spread to most of the lowland areas of Western Europe (Fig. 66, p. 219), leaving the light plow and the older order to the upland regions of difficulty, whose thin, stony soils and uneven terrain were unsuited to the new plow. We may accept the view that the cumbersome moldboard plow pulled by large teams of oxen brought with it not only the long furrow (furlong) and the acre strip but also co-aration and an increasing measure of co-operation and fixed routine in field operations. It helped to stabilize settlement by the accumulation of

heavy gear and by its association with the system of open-field strip farming in (normally) three great fields, whose fertility was maintained by regular fallows and by stubble grazing and manuring. Moreover, while the light plow brought from the south had been adequate for Mediterranean soils, which tend to have their minerals concentrated at the surface by evaporation, the heavy plow was needed to renew the fertility of the leached soils of Atlantic Europe by bringing the plant nutrients from deeper layers to the surface. Archeological and botanical research in Ireland has thrown a suggestive light on this question. At Lagore, in County Meath—in the favored metropolitan lowland adjacent to the east coast—land previously cultivated by the light plow and overgrown with heather shows a marked reduction of heath vegetation after the introduction of the heavy plow about the seventh century a.d. (Mitchell, 1951, p. 201).

Once the accumulated fertility of the deep forest soils of the lowlands had been opened up to permanent settlement, the uplands, which had shown a precocious development in the Neolithic and Bronze ages, suffered a relative decline. They were faced with a crisis. Not only was there less demand for tools made of their hard stone and of their copper and tin but they were affected by a rapid growth of blanket bog about the time when the Bronze Age was passing into the early Iron Age. We have seen that the bogs were initiated in some areas by podzolization of the soil following cultivation, and theories of a general Sub-Atlantic climatic deterioration, though apparently well established for Scandinavia, need reconsideration. In Ireland the field evidence points to an increase in pastoral activities, above all in cattle and dairying; and upland areas which had been inhabited in earlier times came to be utilized by lowland settlers as summer grazing grounds under a system of transhumance. Wooden utensils, carved, turned, or stave-built, replace the abundant pottery of the Neolithic and Bronze ages. In Norway haymaking and barn-building seem to have become established practices with the early Iron Age. Records and traditions of the Celtic fringe tell of inclosures—even if temporary—from early times, and we can correlate this both with the need to protect the growing crops from grazing animals and with the folding of stock to enrich limited patches of land.

The three-field system was ill adapted to these regions of difficulty. Instead, there was evolved a scheme better fitted to the extensive rough grazing and the limited areas of fairly good soil on deltaic fans and fluvial or marine terraces. It relied on the old practice of shifting cultivation for the outlying areas of rough grazing, and supplemented this with more or less permanent cultivation of the carefully selected home fields (the infield of Scotland and Ireland; *terres chaudes* of Brittany) enriched by manure accumulated each winter in single-roomed long houses which were both homes and byres. To it the name "infield-outfield" is given; in Scotland, where its recent survivals have been most fully studied, it is also known as runrig (Handley, 1953). The field plots were small and resembled in shape those of the Bronze Age, and they were cultivated either with the plow or, for the tough-skinned outfield, with the foot plow, breast plow, or spade. We shall see that the social system that went with it was familistic, based on the kin group, which is perhaps the oldest form of human society.

Outfield cultivation is not entirely a thing of the past (Fig. 69a); it survives among the marginal mountains of Ireland and Switzerland, and in parts of Sweden the Neolithic method of clearing forest by fire persists to this day.

"Paring and burning" or *denshiring* (from "Devonshire") was a widespread practice in Highland Britain in the eighteenth century, and it was largely by this method of breaking in rough hill pastures that the rapidly expanding population of western Ireland was supported on the potato in the century preceding the Great Famine of 1845. Monoculture brought a terrible revenge. In France the outfield system was characteristic of the interior of Brittany, the Ardennes, the Vosges, Lorraine, the Jura, the Alps, the Pyrenees, and the Central Plateau (Bloch, 1931, p. 28). We find traces of it also in the Asturias and in Galicia. Most of the land thus broken in piece by piece to temporary cultivation before relapsing to rough grazing was coarse pasture, heather, or scrub (in Brittany chiefly gorse, which was harvested as a crop), but in the High Vosges it was forest country. Outfield farming is also known to have been customary in some of the less fertile parts of the Western European lowlands.

Infield cultivation was more restricted in distribution and characterized especially the Atlantic coast lands (rundale or changedale in Ireland, *rhandiroedd* [share lands] in Wales, *aarkast* [annual change] in Norway). As the names imply, the infield was an open field whose plots—on soils of varying quality —were periodically redistributed. They were held by joint tenants who were members of a co-operating kin group living in a more or less clustered settlement of small farmhouses situated, as a rule, on the uphill side of the open field (Fig. 69b). The Irish clachan was often placed at the infertile apex of a deltaic fan, the slope facilitating the washing and carrying-down of the accumulated manure, human as well as animal. (It is an interesting detail that for this purpose the women went with the cows, the men with the horses.) The peasants not only shared the infield and the out-

S. T. Carleton   *a*

V. B. Proudfoot   *b*

Fig. 69.—Infield and outfield in Ireland

a) Spade-dug lazy beds in outfield, Achill Island, now reverting to heather and encroaching peat. The ridges run downslope and may be beveled toward the sun, as in center of the picture. They probably date from the nineteenth century.

b) Ashleam, Achill Island. The linear hamlet, strung out between infield (*below*) and outfield (*above*), is typical of many areas along the Atlantic coasts. It goes with a modified form of run-dale, without periodic redistribution. The infield has here been "striped" to give each farm its own land, but subdivision has persisted so that small plots and scattered holdings are reappearing. The outfield is now used for rough grazing only.

field but enjoyed rights of common grazing and peat-cutting, for peat bogs, instead of the forests which they replaced, came to supply fuel. Along the Atlantic coasts sea wrack and shellsand have traditionally been utilized, in complicated systems and rituals of distribution, to supplement supplies of animal fertilizers (Evans, 1951, chap. xv). This scheme seems to have taken its historic shape after the introduction of oats, which have a short growing season and take less out of the soil than wheat. Not only are they food for cattle but they became the vehicle of "an ovenless, thin-bread, open-hearth complex" which is part of the peasant culture of Celtic Europe. Free of winter crops, the infield could be grazed and manured by live-stock for half the year (traditionally, from the end of October to the end of April; for the other half of the year they were away in the hills), and it grew crops of oats, varied occasionally with barley, beans, flax, or rye, more or less without rest. It is possible that this scheme was taking shape before the adoption of oats; it has been claimed that, in Denmark, wheat was spring-sown from Neolithic times onward, down to the thirteenth century A.D. (Steensberg, 1952, p. 302).

The pattern of life in areas of infield-outfield cultivation was pastoral and patriarchal, familistic and flexible, relatively independent but linked with a "tribal" or clan system. It stands in contrast both to the three-field scheme of the richer lowlands with its heavy, ordered routine and to the classical Mediterranean two-field system of southern France. Historians have generally assumed that the single farms with their inclosed fields are original forms of settlement and land use in Celtic lands, but it is necessary to add that prejudices against "primitive communism" have colored some statements. The truth seems to be that single farms are the mark of conquerors who were more literary and have left written records, while the history of the peasants is traced only in the archeological record. It seems that both open fields and single farms have existed side by side in historic times, and we know from nineteenth-century records that a single farm might become a complex joint holding in two or three generations (Fig. 70). But I think that the co-operating kin group must be of high antiquity. The Welsh evidence strongly suggests that the open fields and clustered settlements originated in prehistoric times among mixed-arable farmers who later became the bondmen of pastoral overlords (Jones, 1953). These, in early medieval times, lived as large households under one roof. The Irish homesteads (the raths or forts), of which the remains of over thirty thousand can still be seen among the Irish fields, would be the Gaelic equivalent, the houses of the better classes of free-men. The bondmen would be the descendants of the prehistoric pioneers. Together they all fell victims to later landlords, but in the end they have won their freedom as the peasant proprietors of modern Ireland. Folklore and ethnology support this view, but we find very little evidence concerning the underdogs in the Irish Law Texts, since they relate to the upper classes. Documentary evidence by itself is thus misleading. What has archeology to say?

The techniques of archeological field work have made such rapid progress in recent years that we may expect much new light on field systems and methods of prehistoric cultivation, but we cannot yet say when settlements became permanent. I believe that the adoption of ridge cultivation was an important advance. The narrow ridges on which Irish potatoes are traditionally planted (Fig. 69a) were adapted from the wider ridges on which oats were sown. Their preparation required much

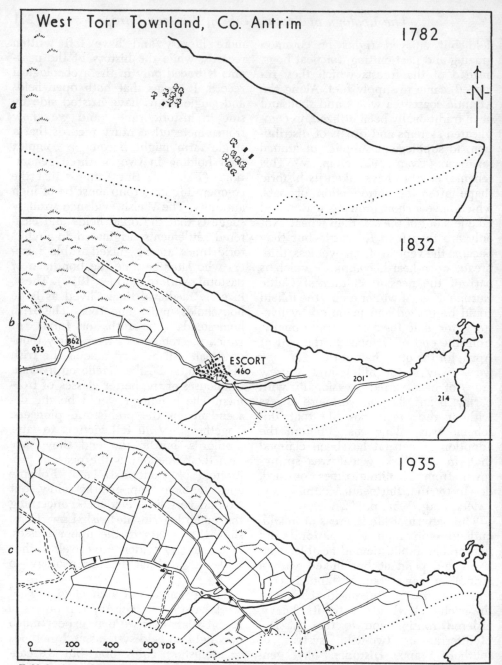

West Torr Townland, Co. Antrim

1782

1832

ESCORT
460
935   862
201
214

1935

0   200   400   600 YDS

Fig. 70.—Part of the townland of West Torr, County Antrim, Northern Ireland, showing settlement in the eighteenth, nineteenth, and twentieth centuries.

a) Carrivegarive quarterland (West Torr Townland) from an estate map, *ca.* 1782. If this map is to be trusted, there were at most three farms in the quarterland at that time, presumably established in the outfield of the "town" (cluster) of Torr which is marked on William Petty's map (The Down Survey, *ca.* 1655).

b) The first Ordnance Survey map (1832) shows a cluster with its open field round about, the result of joint inheritance. Heights in feet.

c) Ordnance Survey map, 1935. The townland is now one of scattered farms and inclosed fields which have taken in much of the old outfield.

hard labor and "mannering" with spade, rake, and shovel and usually meant co-operation. As made in the outfield, the ridges depended on efficient sod-cutting implements and are therefore not likely to predate the early Iron Age. Similarly, I think that the great expansion of cultivation and population in the Irish "potato age" depended on the steel-edged spade, which is still hand-forged in hundreds of shapes to suit local conditions and techniques and which gave the Irish peasant his strong back and his reputation as a navvy. Even today spades are sometimes employed on old grassland which is said to be "too tough for the plow."

Ridge cultivation was the answer to the problem of the rapid loss of fertility involved in the shallow tillage of the pioneer farmers, and I suggest it was a factor in that new ecological adjustment in regions of difficulty—the Celtic synthesis—to which I have referred. The Irish "lazy bed" will illustrate one variety of spade ridge. It is so called because the sod under the ridge is left intact, and the layer of decaying grasses on which the potato sets are placed not only provides humus in the right place but prevents the plant nutrients in the covering manure and soil from being washed down. Moreover, the sods and earth pared and dug from the intervening furrows raise the bed above the water table, while the furrows themselves act as open drains and are also dug deep enough to break the iron pan and thus give improved soil drainage. Old ridges are to be seen almost everywhere in Ireland and Scotland, and there are traces of spade ridges in many other parts of Highland Britain, in Norway, and in Switzerland. The high-backed plow ridges of many lowland areas of open-field cultivation, typically in the clay lands, served a similar purpose.

CROPS AND ANIMALS

To the primary Neolithic crops and animals—wheat and barley, cattle and pigs—others were added in later prehistoric times. The subject has been so recently treated (Clark, 1952; Helbaek, 1953; Zeuner, 1954) that we may confine ourselves to some ecologic aspects. The fact that wheat thrived in northwestern Europe in the second millennium B.C. in areas where it will hardly ripen today has been adduced as evidence of the dry subboreal climate. Yet, in Ireland, bogs and alder were spreading during some phases of the period. The abundant remains of domesticated plants and animals recovered during the last century from the Swiss lake dwellings, which included in one case piles of manure with layers of litter and droppings of cows, sheep, pigs, and goats, have since been supplemented by evidence obtained from many sources. The dominant Neolithic cereal was emmer (*Triticum dicoccum*), which is still grown in a few isolated corners of our region. Barley became far more important than wheat during the Bronze Age, after the disturbances which broke up the Neolithic cultures, and it has been suggested that it was beer which gave the migrant Beaker folk their characteristic drinking vessels and their spirituous ascendancy. Rye and oats, beginning their careers as weeds among the older cereals, became established as secondary cultivated plants, it is claimed, when the Sub-Atlantic climatic deterioration deprived the wetter regions of their wheat. This correlation is too simple to be true. Vital ecologic changes followed the destruction of forests, and, since many of the weeds which found congenial pioneer habitats in the clearings were boreal or tundra species such as the birch, their invasion of the lowlands might easily be interpreted as proving climatic change. At any rate, both oats and rye are first recorded in Britain in the early Iron

Age, and the former was to become in time the "corn" of the highland zone, food for man and beast. The adoption of oats confirmed the Atlantic coast lands in their pastoral ways. Rye took root in the old massifs of mid-Europe and on the sandy moraines of the Baltic lands. It was these same areas that welcomed the potato in the eighteenth century, with immense social consequences for Ireland and Germany in particular (Salaman, 1949). It may be surmised that oats and rye brought changes of a similar order in the life of the marginal lands of Western Europe in late prehistoric times.

VILLAGE AND HAMLET

Meitzen's monumental work (*Siedelung und Agrarwesen*, 1895) attempted to explain field and settlement patterns in Western Europe by reference to historically attested peoples. Regional studies and archeological research have shown that the facts are more complex, and, though much is confused, it is at least clear that no single theory will suffice to explain them. An ecological approach which considers the interrelations of cultures and environments seems to be necessary, but it must allow for the inheritance of traditions from earlier phases of adjustment. We need intensive studies, before it is too late, of the dialects and traditional dresses, the crafts, oral traditions, folklore, and folk music of our peasantries—work in which Swedish scholars have pioneered —but we also need systematic, anthropological surveys of peasant communities as functioning entities.

In the present-day rural landscapes of Western Europe the contrast between the villages of the plain with their strip fields and the scattered farms of the Atlantic coast lands with their hedged fields, even if rarely so sharp as that shown in the air photographs (Fig. 71), is nevertheless striking. And the attitudes of the folk who live and work in them are correspondingly different. The English village has lost many of its old functions and has changed its social structure, but there can be little doubt that it bred a disciplined tradition of self-government and a respect for law and order which, to the Irishman, appear to be the mark of simple minds. Its favorite game, a figure of fun to the Irish, is the flanneled ritual of cricket with "gentlemen and players" in friendly rivalry on village greens. It is a pleasant theory that the twenty-two yards of the cricket pitch owe their origin to the chain-wide furlong strips of the open fields.

In the pastoral uplands loyalties are to kin rather than to community. The Irishman's inherent lawlessness and independence spring from this attachment. The countryman likes to have personal relations with those who govern him, and the outside world should be capable of being manipulated on a personal basis. It is all-important to "know the right people." "Friendship" keeps its original meaning of blood relationship, and the claims of friendship may be stronger than the claims of abstract justice. Civic virtues are poorly developed; the country towns are small and for the most part no more than three or four centuries old. With the breakdown of the clan system and the substitution of a money economy and alien landlords, the pastoral peasantries lost their leaders; they have remained suspicious of the borrowed trappings of representative government.

Taking Western Europe as a whole, the villages of the plains, unless deliberately broken up, as happened in Denmark, have retained their form as nucleated settlements. The little hamlets of the uplands, however, have almost entirely given way to scattered farms since the late eighteenth century. Sometimes the change was made by agreement with the landlord, and sometimes it was enforced; but, on the

a

b

Fig. 71.—Contrasting patterns of land use and settlement in the European plain and the highland zone.

a) The village of Uetterath, Münster, Westphalia, showing open-strip cultivation and limited *parcellement*. It was estimated in 1943 that between a quarter and a third of the arable land of Western Europe was still held in scattered parcels. The landscape is loessic.

b) Inclosed landscape with hedged fields and scattered farms, County Tyrone, Northern Ireland. Glacial drumlin topography. Near the center is the site of a Dark Age rath on top of a drumlin, surrounded on one side by traces of concentric inclosures. A modern farm lies alongside the original homestead site. The average field size is about two acres.

whole, save for instances of pathologically complex *parcellement*, it was a peaceful process which left little trace in records or acts of Parliament. The hamlets were merely clusters of farms, with no public buildings, no church, shops, or other attractions; and, once the advantages of permanent inclosure were seen, the little houses were abandoned. For a pastoral people there are obvious advantages to living in the midst of the fields, with the animals close at hand; and the compact farm, either squarish or ladder-like in plan, according to the terrain, has become the standard holding of upland Britain and Ireland. The fields are small, and, while most are laid down to grass—for hay is the main crop—the plow is "taken round the farm" periodically. Thus the outfield method, improved by the sowing of grass and clover mixtures and by the laying of drains, evolved into the system of fairly long leys which is well adapted to humid climates where overcultivation leads to leaching and souring of the soil. We know from records of Cistercian granges in eastern Scotland that grass parks for alternate husbandry were inclosed as early as the fifteenth century, but the system did not become general until after the adoption of root crops. In the transformation of an open countryside with clustered houses into an inclosed land with scattered farms, the improved iron swing plow (i.e., without wheels), introduced into Scotland about the year 1765 by James Small, played an important part. It was pulled by two horses in place of the large ox teams required for the crude wooden plow, and it was well adapted to the small fields of the uplands, much as the *ard* had been to the little Celtic fields whose shapes they reproduce. Small's plow was speedily adopted throughout northwestern Europe from Norway to Ireland.

THE PAST IN THE PEASANT

I have drawn many of my examples and illustrations from that part of Western Europe with which I am most familiar, and if I now confine myself to Ireland it is because, in addition, this peripheral island provides abundant material for the study of archaic survivals among a peasant people (Arensberg and Kimball, 1940; Evans, 1942; Mogey, 1947). Despite the industrialization of the northeast and the drive toward economic self-sufficiency in the Republic, well over half the population remains rural, dwelling for the most part on farms averaging 25–30 acres. The lowing of kine and the bellowing of bulls echo through the folklore and legendary histories of the Celtic world. True to tradition in this land of grass, oats, and cattle, the consumption of milk and dairy products per head of population is the highest in the world: 1,439 pounds in 1953 (if we are to believe the astonishing statistics issued by the United States Department of Agriculure). For the Irishman, "meat" means beef. The pig, "the gentleman" that once paid the rent, is also a gentleman in his lineage, and he thrives on the by-products of the dairy.

To this day in isolated spots the breeding of cattle and the making of butter are hedged around with taboos and lucky omens which have to do with flowers and shrubs. It is noteworthy that they are the plants which followed in the footsteps of the pioneer farmers —the shrubs of forest clearings, the flowers of the fields, and the weeds of cultivation. There is great virtue in the golden "Mayflowers," in the hazel twig, the rowan branch, and, above all, in the flowering May tree—the hawthorn—to which offerings of milk were once made. Summer is welcomed on May Eve by ceremonies of decking with flowers the house, byres, middens, and springs which are thus linked in a golden chain of fertility, for the flowers chosen—

marigolds, primroses, and gorse—are golden-yellow, the color of fresh butter. Clearly there is in this an element of sympathetic magic. Thus the dandelion, which is blessed with both a golden head and a milky stem, is "the plant of Bride," associated with the favorite Irish saint who was a milkmaid, protector of cows, and successor of a pagan goddess. Birch twigs and green rushes fashioned into crosses are used in rites celebrating St. Bridget's Day on the first of February, the beginning of spring. The solitary thorn tree (the fairy or gentry thorn) is regarded with such superstitious reverence that I have seen a tractor plow carefully avoiding its roots, and there are parts of the country where the only trees left are fairy thorns, whose creamy white blossoms are both a sign that damaging frosts are over and a bounteous promise of a full flow of milk. I see in the strength of these beliefs a measure of the intimate associations between early man and his immediate surroundings, but do they not also reflect his efforts to ward off the evils of diminishing returns which followed the use of Mediterranean tools and crops in an Atlantic environment? Like the bogs which grew over many of the first farmlands, the timeless peasant mind holds the past in its depths.

The complex mosaic of peasant beliefs is also colored by lingering fertility rites associated with the great stone monuments which remain as visible reminders of man's early efforts. There are traces of an old belief that the fairies are the spirits of the dead waiting to be reborn, haunting old burial places. In the early nineteenth century it was written of County Clare: "If a woman proves barren, a visit with her husband to one of the megaliths certainly cures her." Some of the games formerly played at wakes for the dead were frankly pagan, involving, for example, symbolism derived from boat-building, which recalls the rock carvings of sacred vessels (associated with fertility cults) found on Bronze Age sites along the coast of Norway. One might refer to many other examples of survivals, such as the process of match-making and the fixing of the dowry, involving negotiations which clearly reveal the values of rural life. There is little room for romantic love or divorce—the luxuries of a landless society—in a community which measures wealth in terms of land and livestock.

Surveying the present cultural landscape, we see a countryside parceled out into isolated farms which have won their freedom but have lost their self-sufficiency and their local leaders. When farming began, the land was forested from coast to coast; in ecological terms it is the peasantry which now forms a closed association over the face of the land. The craftsmen, the petty kings, and the landlords have gone. It is an egalitarian society, and its most prized virtue is "modesty." It is difficult not to conform in a naked countryside where one's neighbors are always watchful. The drive for increased output and mechanization means that fewer people are required on the land. Families are dying out or moving out of the marginal areas, and it is those with initiative who move first. But a peasantry which has endured for so long and survived so many vicissitudes and technological changes will, I believe, still preserve some of the values it has kept through the centuries.

REFERENCES

ARENSBERG, C. M., and KIMBALL, S. T.
1940 *Family and Community in Ireland.* Cambridge, Mass.: Harvard University Press. 322 pp.

ASHBY, A. W.
1939 "The Effects of Urban Growth on the Countryside," *Sociological Review,* XXXI, No. 4, 345–69.

BLOCH, MARC
1931   Les Caractères originaux de l'histoire rurale française. ("Institutt for sammenlignende Kulturforskning," Series B, Vol. XIX [Oslo, 1928].) Paris: Société d'Édition les Belles-Lettres. 261 pp.

BRØGGER, A. W.
1940   "From the Stone Age to the Motor Age," Antiquity, XIV, No. 54 (June), 163–81.

CHILDE, V. GORDON
1931   Skara Brae: A Pictish Village in Orkney. London: Kegan Paul. 208 pp.
1947   The Dawn of European Civilization, 4th ed. (1st ed. 1925.) London: Kegan Paul. 362 pp.
1950   Prehistoric Migrations in Europe. ("Institutt for sammenlignende Kulturforskning," Series A, Vol. XX.) Oslo. 248 pp.

CLARK, J. G. D.
1945   "Farmers and Forests in Neolithic Europe," Antiquity, XIX, No. 74 (June), 57–71.
1947   "Forest Clearance and Prehistoric Farming," Economic History Review, XVII, 45–51.
1952.   Prehistoric Europe: The Economic Basis. London: Methuen & Co. 349 pp.

COLLIER, A.
1953   The Crofting Problem. Cambridge: Cambridge University Press. 191 pp.

DUIGNAN, M.
1944   "Irish Agriculture in Early Historic Times," Journal of the Royal Society of Antiquaries of Ireland, LXXIV, No. 3, 124–45. Dublin.

ERIXON, SIGURD
1938a   "West European Connections and Culture Relations," Folk-Liv, II, 137–72. Stockholm.
1938b   "Regional European Ethnology," ibid., III, 263–94. Stockholm.

EVANS, E. ESTYN
1940   "Transhumance in Europe," Geography, XXV, No. 4, 172–80.
1942   Irish Heritage. Dundalk, Ireland: Dundalgan Press. 190 pp.
1951   Mourne Country: Landscape and Life in South Down. Dundalk, Ireland: Dundalgan Press. 226 pp.

FLEURE, H. J.
1919   "Human Regions," Scottish Geographical Magazine, XXXV, No. 3, 94–105.
1937   "What Is a Peasantry?" Bulletin of the John Rylands Library, XXI, No. 2, 1–19. Manchester.
1943   "Peasants in Europe," Geography, XXVIII, No. 2, 55–61.
1948   "Land Use and Liberty," ibid., XXXIII, No. 4, 167–75.

FOX, SIR CYRIL
1947   The Personality of Britain. 4th ed. Cardiff: National Museum of Wales. 74 pp.

GODWIN, H.
1940   "Pollen Analysis and Forest History of England and Wales," New Phytologist, XXXIX, 370–400. Cambridge.

HANDLEY, J. E.
1953   Scottish Farming in the Eighteenth Century. London: Faber & Faber. 314 pp.

HATT, GUDMUND
1939   "The Ownership of Cultivated Land," Det Kongelige Danske Videnskabernes Selskab: Historiske-filologiske Meddelelser, XXVI, No. 6, 1–22. Copenhagen.

HELBAEK, H.
1953   "Archaeology and Agricultural Botany," University of London, Institute of Archaeology, Ninth Annual Report, pp. 44–59.

IVERSEN, J.
1949   The Influence of Prehistoric Man on Vegetation. ("Danmarks geologiske Undersøgelse," Series IV, Vol. III, No. 6.) Copenhagen. 29 pp.

JESSEN, KNUD, and HELBAEK, HANS
1944   Cereals in Great Britain and Ireland in Prehistoric and Early Historic Times. ("Det Kongelige Danske Videnskabernes Selskab: Biologiske Skrifter," Vol. III, No. 2.) Copenhagen. 68 pp.

JONES, G. R. J.
1953   "Some Mediaeval Rural Settlements in North Wales," Institute of British Geographers, Transactions and Papers, No. 19, pp. 51–72.

JOPE, E. M.
1952   "The Porcellanite Axes of the

North of Ireland: Tievebulliagh and Rathlin," *Ulster Journal of Archaeology*, XV, 31–60. Belfast.

MACKINDER, H. J.
1944 *Democratic Ideals and Reality.* 4th ed. (1st ed. 1919.) West Drayton, Middlesex: Penguin Books. 155 pp.

MEDICI, SENATOR G., et al.
1950 "Diagnosis and Pathology of Peasant Farming," pp. 18–63 in MAXTON, J. P. (ed.), *Proceedings of the Seventh International Conference of Agricultural Economists.* London: Oxford University Press. 372 pp.

MITCHELL, G. F.
1951 "Studies in Irish Quaternary Deposits, No. 7," *Proceedings of the Royal Irish Academy*, LIII, B II, 113–206. Dublin.
1953 "Vegetational Environmental Studies," *Advancement of Science*, IX, No. 36, 430–32. London.

MOGEY, J. M.
1947 *Rural Life in Northern Ireland.* London: Oxford University Press. 240 pp.

ORWIN, C. S. and C. S.
1938 *The Open Fields.* Oxford: Clarendon Press. 332 pp.

PIGGOTT, STUART
1954 *The Neolithic Cultures of the British Isles.* Cambridge: Cambridge University Press. 420 pp.

REES, ALWYN D.
1950 *Life in a Welsh Countryside.* Cardiff: University of Wales Press. 188 pp.

SALAMAN, R. N.
1949 *The History and Social Influence of the Potato.* Cambridge: Cambridge University Press. 685 pp.

SAUER, CARL O.
1952 *Agricultural Origins and Dispersals.* (Bowman Memorial Lectures, Series Two.) New York: American Geographical Society. 110 pp.

SINGER, C.; HOLMYARD, E. J.; and HALL, A. R. (eds.)
1954 *A History of Technology*, Vol. I: *From Early Times to Fall of Ancient Empires.* Oxford: Clarendon Press. 827 pp.

STEENBERG, A.
1952 *Bondehuse og Vandmøller: Farms and Watermills in Denmark through Two Thousand Years.* ("The National Museum's Third Department: Researches into Village Archaeology," Vol. I.) Copenhagen: National Museum. 325 pp.

SYDOW, C. W. VON
1948 *Selected Papers in Folklore.* Copenhagen: Rosenkilde & Bagger. 257 pp.

YATES, P. L.
1940 *Food Production in Western Europe.* London: Longmans & Co. 572 pp.

ZEUNER, F. E.
1954 "Cultivation of Plants," pp. 353–75 in SINGER, C., et al. (eds.), *A History of Technology*, Vol. I: *From Early Times to Fall of Ancient Empires.* Oxford: Clarendon Press. 827 pp.

The Quality of Peasant Living in Central Europe

GOTTFRIED PFEIFER[*]

INTRODUCTION

To pose the "quality of peasant living" as a problem related to man's role in changing the face of the earth presupposes that a special "man-made landscape" originated in Central Europe, produced not merely by agricultural activities but by the prolonged action of peasant living upon the soil. The proposed theme emphasizes the "quale" of such peasant living and not solely the peasant landscape. Discussion is weighted toward this factor, with its historical, social, and economic implications, which created certain forms and features on the face of the earth. Nature, as the more passive partner in the evolutionary drama, has had to be passed over briefly.

It is in the nature of peasantry that it has its own history, only slightly touched by strife and warfare among major political powers. Only cata-

strophic movements that uproot all fundaments, like the French Revolution or the wars and revolutions of our times, which devastate not only the lands but also the peoples and their social structures, annihilate historical peasantries. On the other hand, the molding of influences working in the social and economic spheres to alter the quale of peasant living may not heed political frontiers. Thus, for our discussion of questions pertaining to cultural geography, political boundaries—past or present—may appear as factors but do not serve as boundaries of the first order.

Central Europe, in our definition, overlaps with the eastern fringe of Western Europe (cf. Evans, Fig. 66, p. 219). I include the drainage area of the Rhine in the west and the upper reaches of the Danube in the south. The eastern boundaries are less easily defined, owing to wide spacing of natural gradation and a complex history (Sinnhuber, 1954). Our discussion is here confined to the area where the peasants speak a German dialect and have a common history.

Between 48° and 52° N., the climate of Central Europe is moderate, of the northern, cooler variety. The growing season is in the summer, while the ground in winter is left dormant. The range of crops adaptable to the climate is limited but includes small grains and certain root crops, among the latter no-

[*] Dr. Pfeifer is Professor and Head of the Department of Geography, University of Heidelberg, Germany. In 1950 he traveled with Professor Waibel as a guest of the Conselho Nacional de Geografia, Rio de Janeiro, Brazil. He has been a visiting professor at the University of Georgia, Athens (1952), and at the University of Minnesota, Minneapolis (1953). His works include: *Das Siedlungsbild der Landschaft Angeln*, 1928; *Die räumliche Gliederung der Landwirtschaft im nördlichen Kalifornien*, 1936; "Sonora und Sinaloa, Beiträge zur Kulturgeographie des N.W. Mexico," 1939; "Die Ernährungswirtschaft der Erde," 1948; and "Die kulturgeographische Stellung Brasilien in des Neuen Welt (I)," 1952.

tably the Andean potato.[1] Between the oceanic and mild Western Europe and the great expanse of continental eastern Europe, the zones of climatic gradation follow from the northwest to the southeast. Topographic relief is moderate in most parts with respect to altitude and inclination of slope, but topography interacts with climate sufficiently to bring about decided regional variations.

Soil fertility is moderate, generally speaking. Sandy parent-materials are liable to podzolization in the northwest. In lee positions of the middle upland and mountain belt, and in basins with warmer climate, soils of substeppe-like quality occur, notably on loesses and limestones. The soils in the central upland belt and the escarpment landscape of southern Germany are conditioned more by great petrographic variety of parent-material than by climatic gradation.

Tilling of the soil in Central Europe (though not so old as early high civilizations) dates back to at least Neolithic times (cf. Evans, pp. 223 ff.), yet in the course of more than five thousand years and considerable historic turbulence the peasantry has maintained continuous productivity of the land. Although the expanse of agriculturally used territory changed considerably in historic times, emphasis has been placed upon increased productivity and intensification of use. At the same time one of the most surprising features of the Central European landscape is that forests have been preserved to such an extent. They still cover more than 25 per cent of the total surface, and the watersheds are still sufficiently protected. The pleasing mixture of forests and open, cultivated land has led geographers to speak of a "harmonious landscape" (Gradmann, 1924, p. 30), which contrasts with some parts of western and southern European scenery. In spite of shifts in area between wilderness and cultivated land, the impression is of stability rather than of catastrophic change.

Although the mild nature of Central Europe threatens the peasant with fewer climatic hazards than those which occur in many other parts of the world, nevertheless peasant management of the land and peasant attitudes and institutions have to be credited for such stability through many centuries. Central Europe exhibits no extensive areas of soil erosion, nor have sizable areas completely passed out of production. We know that the land of European peasantry has not entirely been spared of various forms of land misuse, but recuperative powers have outbalanced the detrimental processes. In Central Europe, as in many parts of the world, the peasant areas of quality are not the ones where the conservationist is most needed.

The economic results of Central European peasant agriculture bespeak surprising adaptability, which has maintained a high degree of self-sufficiency of the population (for Germany, conventionally rated at 80 per cent). The harvest yields have increased—though they have not attained the very highest returns in a statistical average—and Central European agriculture has led that of other countries for nearly all crops grown. Yet it must not be overlooked that, for many decades, Central European farmers have enjoyed tariffs which, unlike some of the smaller countries, protected them from the full force of impact of the free world market.

Central European peasant society bears many affinities and similarities with that of Western Europe, but the

1. Grapes thrive and produce wine of commercial quality in the more favored parts, and the *"Weingärtner"* is decidedly an important subtype of the Central European peasant. The American will miss the soybean, which it has been impossible as yet to add to the Central European range of crops. Maize also is of minor, though increasing, importance.

distribution of sizes of holdings is somewhat different, and tenantry is far less important. This will be easily recognized by comparing Figures 72 and 73. Most conspicuous is the contrast in Central Europe between an area of very small farms, on the average, in the southwest, and an area of formerly large estates in the northeast. Tiny holdings and true latifundia occur, yet neither characterizes Central Europe as a whole. Like Western Europe, true peasant sizes of holdings prevail. Property structure points toward ownership of the soil (Fig. 73), in contrast with wide areas of Western Europe. Nine-tenths of the total utilized surface is in the hands of owners; one-tenth is held by tenants, though local variations are important.

Today, the Central European peasantry, like the rest of the world, feels the changes wrought by industrialization and urbanization. Rural depopulation, scarcity of labor, mechanization, traditional methods, and unfavorable price relations, as well as changes in modes of life and living standards, affect the countryside. The old peasant structures are shaken with uneasiness and a sense of approaching revolutionary alterations. It is our task to save what has been best in historic peasantry, lest we lose a fundamental basis of our society as it has grown through time.

CHARACTERISTICS OF PEASANTS AND PEASANT SOCIETY

Social Traditions

Who are peasants and why do we speak of a special "peasant" way of living? The English and German languages conform, in so far as the term denotes in both more than just a person occupied in agriculture (cf. Evans, p. 220). To be a peasant is to have a definite estate, in the historical sense of the term—to belong to the "*Bauernstand*" (Riehl, 1851, pp. 33 ff.). One does not choose to be a peasant. One is born into peasantry. Peasantry does not derive its quality alone from the character of its economy but refers to the mode of life of a social group of traditional standing. After the great melting of medieval society in the fire of the French Revolution, peasantry and nobility retained longest the medieval quality of an estate and declined to become a class. Riehl (*ibid.*) characterized both nobility and peasantry as the forces for stability (*Kräfte der Beharrung*), contrasted to the forces for mobility (*Kräfte der Bewegung*) of the third and fourth estates (*Bürgertum* and *Arbeitertum*). Nobility, just as peasantry, has retained its rooting in the soil in Central Europe more than in many other parts of Europe. The fate of peasantry has been tied up with nobility for better or worse over a long period. We cannot understand the landscape unless we also recognize the influences of tradition and social institutions created by man, for these influences became the means by which the patterns of land distribution were established.

The peasant was born on the land inherited from ancestors as the son of a peasant. Birth determined one's status not only in a scale of wealth but frequently also in a rural hierarchy of graded rights and social status. The fully righted peasant—the "*Vollerbe*," as he was called in northwestern Germany —was born as such, just as was the lower man, the "*Kätner*," "*Seldner*," or whatever his particular character may have been. The accident of being a second son might spell non-participation in inheritance and even descent to lower social status, for the desire to keep the family landholding together led to majorates or minorates (*Anerbenrecht, geschlossene Hofübergabe*). The custom of dividing land among sons into equal parts (*Realerbteilung*), prevalent today notably in southwest-

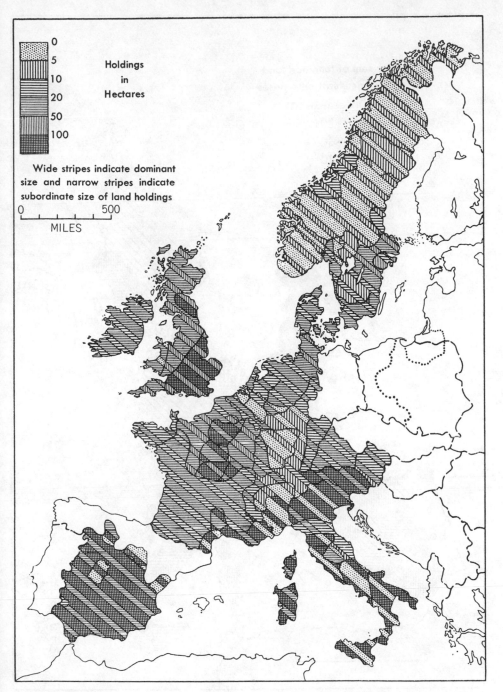

Fig. 72.—Distribution of sizes of land in agricultural enterprises in Western Europe and parts of Central Europe. (After Abel, 1955.)

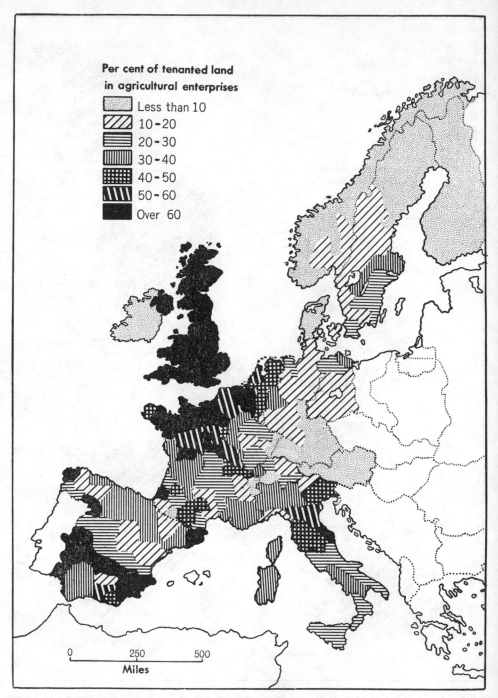

Per cent of tenanted land
in agricultural enterprises

Less than 10
10–20
20–30
30–40
40–50
50–60
Over 60

0   250   500

Miles

Fig. 73.—Distribution of tenantry in Western Europe and parts of Central Europe. (After Abel, 1955, and Huppertz, 1935.)

ern Germany, seems to be of more recent origin, developed under the influence of urban practices and the reception of Roman law. There, the peasant holdings tend to suffer *parcellement;* the older social orders dwindle; families rise and sink with the change of generations; the mobility of real estate increases; and something of the aboriginal quality of peasant life is lost.

The traditional customs of antecedents and neighbors determined behavior very rigidly. Food habits, modes of clothing, wooing and mating, worship and burial, material and ideal scales of values, even religious convictions, conformed to one's neighbors. Whether the settlement structure consisted of single farmsteads, hamlets, or villages, the peasant always found himself deeply rooted in communal bondage that was older than he himself. Family, neighborhood (*Nachbarschaften*), manorial relationships (*grundherrschaftliche Bindungen*), the single farmstead rural communities (*Bauernschaft*), or the modern forms of community (*Gemeinde*), and even political units made up of several estates (*Gutsbezirk*), framed his individual and social existence. Within such narrow but meaningful spheres, he carried on his contribution to public life. In spite of manor, serfdom, or other forms of bondage, the peasant exerted some kind of self-administration, by traditional and carefully watched laws and customs. Such laws and customs were set down in written texts as so-called "*Weistümer,*" "*Dorfwillküren,*" and "*Dorfbeliebungen.*" Peasantry arose hesitantly and with difficulty, from thinking in the realm of family and community, to acknowledge the modern state. The peasant wars (*Bauernkriege*) of the fifteenth and sixteenth centuries were caused largely by resentment to the rising state authority that tried to penetrate the countryside with new laws and regulations.

It is of extreme geographic importance to take cognizance of the fact that the rural scene is broken into small, areal units which are not merely expressions of natural sites, patterns, or artificial groupings for administrative or statistical purposes. The peasant way of living expresses itself on the land by the impress of groups acting on their respective areas. The home of the peasant is part of a traditional settlement structure; his fields are parts of a communal area, and frequently he participates in rights of usufruct on land held in common. "*Dorf,*" "*Flur,*" "*Allmende,*" "*Gemarkung,*" and "*Gemeinde,*" to use some German terms, are social and spatial institutions by which peasantry stamps its activity on the face of the earth.

The good peasant takes honor and pride in his work. To work and to live are still identical, the idea of limited hours of working being alien to his thinking. He feels a responsibility toward the land, as part of the duties bestowed upon him by the Lord. His economic spirit (*Wirtschaftsgeist*) is largely directed by considerations about the farmstead (*Hof*) rather than toward profit-making in a monetary sense; to think in terms of the market has not been foreign to him, dating to medieval times. But we should not glorify him as altruistic; avarice is one of his vices. Abel (1935) has endeavored to exemplify how business cycles have exerted strong influences upon rural life. Riehl (1859, pp. 233, 237–39) has given a vivid description of the cattle-raising peasant in the marshes, who bears himself like a "baron," and of the grain peasant in the fertile plain (*Börde*), who frequents the casino. However, truly conservative and frequently archaic refuges of traditional peasant life still may be found—on a lonely farmstead in the Low German heath, in a mountain hamlet, or even in villages not touched by strong currents of trade and communications, although the influences of the modern age tend to dissolve more and more of such islands.

Structure of Rural Society[2]

The basis of an individual peasant enterprise is the family. The family-size farm is the peasant holding par excellence. This definition does not prohibit the employment of hired hands (*Gesinde*), for such traditionally belonged to the family. They stemmed from the neighborhood, usually the same village, if not from the same family tree. The hired hand might have been born into his status, just as his peasant employer inherited status and property from his ancestors. The earliest Germanic societies of historical record were composed not solely of free peasants of equal rights and of a few leading families; a substratum of lesser order, varying in status from true slavery to bonded freedom (*Hintersassen*) and attached to individual peasants or the whole community, also inhabited the countryside. We may scarcely conceive of the peasant landscape of Central Europe having been created without such lower ranks in the rural society, who were usually shut off from usufruct of the common lands (*Allmende*). The breakup of such graded hierarchies of rural social structure, accompanying the downfall of medieval order, has been one of the major achievements of the last two centuries. The lower orders were personally freed

2. See the excellent article "Agrarverfassung" in *Handwörterbuch des Grenz- und Auslanddeutschtum*, edited by C. Petersen, O. Scheel, P. H. Ruth, and H. Schwalm (Breslau: F. Hirt, 1933), I, 23–70, especially the parts written by R. Kötzschke, K. Weimann, and S. Ipsen, pp. 23–52. The English reader may resort to the *Encyclopaedia of the Social Sciences*, edited by E. R. A. Seligman and A. Johnson (New York: Macmillan Co.), especially the articles, "Manorial System" by R. Kötzschke, IX, 97–102, and "Peasantry" by C. V. Dietze, XI–XII, 48–52, and related articles quoted there.

(like peasants of bondage) and given some land, which frequently was taken from the common lands, a process which increased the number of smallest holdings. Their homes filled the open spaces in the villages or were scattered along the borders of the communal territory.[3]

During the eighteenth century, governments endeavored to better the conditions of the lower rural orders by attempting to furnish the lower ranks with sufficient land to bring them close to family self-sufficiency—to bring them into *Ackernahrung*. In the *Ackernahrung*, denoting the smallest unit of family subsistence farming, was the man who was forced to seek additional work to make a living for his family and who did not properly belong to the full category of peasant. He belonged to the rural society, which had always been stratified, but he may have been classed as "*Tagelöhner*," "*Heuerling*," rural "*Handwerker*," or, under modern conditions, "*Arbeiter-Bauer*" and "*Pendler*," according to occupation or local term.

Family size, enterprise, and self-sufficiency have always been stressed as essential characteristics of peasantry. But production for the market and specialization of production by no means destroyed peasant quality. In fact, for as far back as we are able to trace rural economy historically, we must infer that peasants produced surpluses which went either into channels of the manorial system or, later, to urban populations. The *capitulare de villis* of Charles the Great embodied provisions concerning the grain trade. Livestock-raising, grape-growing, dye-weed production, etc., provided an early basis for specialization. It must be admitted, though, that such commercial specialization tended to prepare inroads for city ways not akin to, and not developed out of, primeval peasant life. Subtypes of peasantry evolved, but the up-

3. See Pfeifer, 1928, Part V, pp. 95–107.

per limit of rural structure was the estate (*Gut*). *Gut* is a large, rural enterprise where management and field work are carried out by different persons. Socially, the owner does not belong to the peasant estate.

Just as there was a lower order, there was also an upper stratum of landed aristocracy in rural society. The growth of the manorial system (*Grundherrschaft*), recognizable since Merovingian times, created the typical structure of medieval rural society. Extensive, but usually widely scattered, holdings and rights over peasants in bondage came into the hands of lords (*Grundherren*), either worldly or ecclesiastical. The manorial court (*curia*; Ger.: *Salhof*) was the center of the organization, and the *villicus* attended to the production on the manorial land (*Salland, demesne*) and of the dependent peasants (*Grundholden*). The *Grundherrschaft* has come to be reckoned more and more as the most important institution in medieval rural society and economy. Manorial ties (*Grundherrschaftliche Bindungen*) strongly controlled the development of settlement patterns, property order in the fields (*Flurverfassung*), the rights in the common lands (*Allmende* and *Markungen*), the laws of inheritance, the spreading and colonizing of new lands, and the fate of the forests. The decline of the manorial system was of equal importance and went in two directions: conversion of rights and delivery of work (*Frondienste*) and produce into cash income (*Rentengrundherrschaft*); or to consolidation for production in large enterprises (*Gutswirtschaft*) worked by peasants held in serfdom (*Gutsuntertanigkeit, Leibeigenschaft*). The former course was taken largely in the German southwest; the latter, in the northeast.

In the estate economy (*Gutswirtschaft*) the owner does not work the soil with his own hands. He supervises the enterprise or intrusts it to a manager, and it is connected with considerably larger holdings (Figs. 72 and 74). The separation of ownership and management does not always imply the development of true absentee ownership. It is characteristic for the larger areas of the *Gutswirtschaft* in Central Europe that a land-seated aristocracy remained and strikingly influenced the composition of the rural society. Other, more modern, capitalistic forms of *Gutswirtschaften* that developed later during the nineteenth and twentieth centuries were connected with the investment of urban and industrial capital in real estate. Absentee owners developed large-scale production, especially in strongly commercialized forms of agriculture like the sugar-beet production in the *Börden* of central Germany. In such areas manager-operated farms and tenantry attain greater proportions.

Regional Variety in Sizes of Property Holdings

The simple term "peasantry" will not be sufficient to cover the variability of the rural landscape. Maps of the distributions of property size (Figs. 72 and 74) serve for a first orientation. Several characteristic major areas are easily discernible. The one major area—now historic—where large-scale property with *Gutswirtschaften* has predominated is northeastern Germany, where the majority of holdings are larger than those typically held by peasants. In western and southern Germany such large holdings are infrequent. Along the North Sea coast more than 50 per cent of the surface is in large peasant holdings, the regions of the large farms or estates (*Hof-Bauer* or *Gutsbauer*). Medium-sized peasant holdings (5–20 hectares) prevail in southwestern Germany, in the Black Forest, in eastern Württemberg, Bavaria, Franconia, in the Kölner Bucht, Westphalia without

Münsterland, and southwestern Hannover and Saxony.

The larger part of southwestern Germany, notably the loess-covered *Gäulandschaften,* large areas in the *Rheinische Schiefergebirge,* in Hesse and Thuringia, is dominated by small holdings of less than 5 hectares. Conse-

is penetrated by industrial communities (*Gewerblichen Gemeinden*), workers' dormitory settlements (*Arbeiterwohngemeinden*), mixed workers, part-time farmers, and peasants (*Arbeiter-Bauerngemeinden*) (Hesse, 1949). Even more mottled would be a map showing the *parcellement* of property with re-

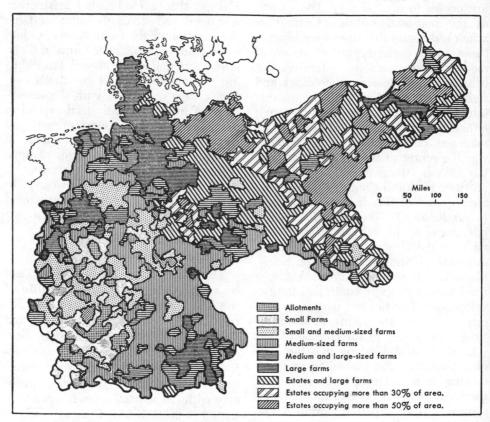

FIG. 74.—Distribution of sizes of rural holdings in parts of Central Europe (Germany within the boundaries of 1939). (After Huppertz, 1935.)

quently, the whole range of the peasant order is different. For example, the limit for owner-managed land (*Gutsbetriebe*) is low, commonly set at merely 75 hectares; and in the Kreis Ettlingen, in Baden, more than 92 per cent of all holdings are parceled out in tiny holdings below the limit of true peasant holdings (Fig. 75). A social map of southwestern Germany presents a very mottled aspect. The whole countryside

spect to the distribution of tiny plots over the *Flur*. Weingarten in Baden, a typical example, is a village of 6,000–7,000 inhabitants, with 1,700 hectares of field and some 100 hectares of woodland atomized into 14,000 parcels! This certainly is a morbid structure. It is here that consolidation of the holdings and rearrangement of the pattern of rural settlement are most urgently needed but meet almost insurmountable difficulties. It has been estimated that 7,000,000 hectares still wait for the process of rearrangement of the land (*Flurbereinigung*) in Germany (Bundesrepublik)!

PLOW AGRICULTURE IN CENTRAL EUROPE

Central European peasant agriculture is a branch of the larger Old World culture complex of plow agriculture (in the sense of Hahn, 1909, 1914), which is the parent-form of modern agriculture. For some aspects of its prehistoric development see Evans (pp. 223 ff.). Our purpose is to analyze some of its traits with regard to the way in which Central European peasantry took roots on the surface of the earth.

The Role of Animal Husbandry

The essential feature of plow agriculture, in contrast to other forms of cultivating the soil (planting stick, hoe, and Eastern Asiatic agriculture), is the integration of animal husbandry with plant production. It involves not merely a juxtaposition of both types of production (as in some parts of Africa, for instance); it is a genuine wedding, where-

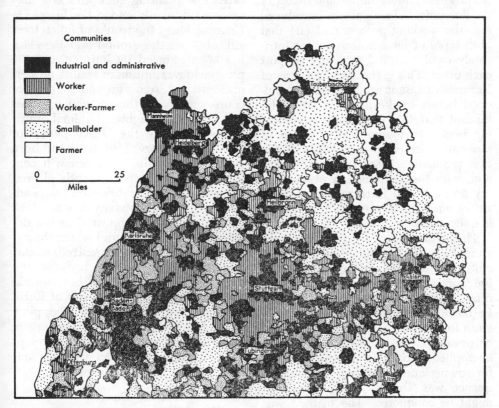

FIG. 75.—Social types of rural communities, northern Württemberg-Baden, Germany. (After Hesse, 1949.)

by one branch supports the other. The animals are not only an object *of* production but also an important factor *in* production; the cultivated land serves not only for direct human use but also for the maintenance of livestock. Ask the peasant why he keeps so many animals, and he may answer, "Because I have so much land of such-and-such quality." Ask him why he plants his fields in a particular system, and he may reply, "For I have so many animals." The animals of importance are cattle, horses, and swine. They are used for food (meat and milk), for raw materials (hides, wool, leather), for work (drawing, carrying, and riding), and—very important—for manure to maintain the stability of soil fertility. For our purpose it is most important that (1) the domesticated animal was introduced into the working process and (2) that both types of land utilization are intricately combined and mutually support each other. This is the standard type of European peasant economy as it developed before medieval times. It is significant that this productive interlocking begins to loosen with the end of peasantry: in colonial agriculture the two productive lines frequently part, and, with the introduction of machinery and artificial fertilizers, the necessity of inner coherence of both branches is questioned.

The consequence of making the work animal a factor in production permitted cultivation of an expanded area. In this, the work animal proved to be the genuine forefather of modern machinery. In fact, plow agriculture contained a germ for further technology, in that the harnessed power of the animal was to be applied, in time, to other implements for sowing and harvesting. The consequence was always that larger areas might be conquered. The method was particularly adapted to the small grains, which are sown broadcast, but less to root crops, which must be planted and cultivated during the growing season.

The introduction of root crops—one of the major improvements of European agriculture during later medieval times—had far-reaching consequences. The animal and the plow brought the man out to the field as the chief agricultural worker and released the women, so prominent in hoe agriculture, for home-

work. However, that the women historically served as a labor reserve was proved when root crops appeared in the plow system. The planting of root crops and the cultivation with the hoe during the summer are jobs for women. Men will never beat women in digging roots and potatoes in harvest time![4]

The use of animal and plow in breaking the ground called for a clean surface. The planting stick and hoe may successfully work among the litter of a clearing where the trunks of fallen trees still obstruct the ground and the slash has been reduced by burning, but the plow achieves optimum results on permanently cleared ground. This, of course, refers to the plow in its final development. Lighter, animal-drawn implements, like the *"Hakenpflug,"* or the *"Zoche,"* served in slash-and-burn economy.[5] But the exception will confirm the rule. The permanently cleared fields, to a considerable extent dependent in size on the capacity of man, work animal, and plow, appeared as the determining entities around which the agricultural system was organized, as distinguished from garden beds or the plots of planting-stick and hoe cultivation. Many important features of European peasant life, such as the plow team and field patterns (long strip, etc.), have been related to the development of plow types and working animals (oxen, cows, or horses).

Fallowing and the Danger of Erosion

The capacity to cultivate larger fields enabled the plowman to break more ground than used annually for production. Fallowing, in the true sense of the

4. The whole subject of women in Central European agriculture as a reserve labor force is worthy of study. It has been estimated that they perform about 50 per cent of the work.

5. For such forest-field rotation connected with burning, various terms are used, e.g., *Nordischer Brandrodungsbau, Reutbergwirtschaft,* or *Haubergwirtschaft.*

agriculturist, made its appearance. Following, as opposed to shifting cultivation, is a feature of high importance, for it allows the land to rest and recover some of its spent fertility without reverting to wilderness. Fallow lands are ready for planting early in spring of the next year and are a great help where climate shortens the seasons (*jachère climatique, Höhenbrache, Brache in hohen Breiten*). Cultivated fallow land will absorb precipitation without giving it back by plant transpiration when handled by dry-farming methods (*jachère de secheresse*). Such climatic fallowing greatly favored the spread of the plow complex to otherwise unsuited climatic areas. The summer fallow, where fenced in, served as additional pasture, especially for the smaller animals.

Fallowing practices were equally important from the economic point of view. They provided another subject for common counsel (*Flurzwang*) and folkways among the peasants. They were the means for adapting the field system to the economic situation. With increasing distances from markets, fallowing was advocated as a labor-saving device. Regular fallowing determined the order of the most important early field systems: the two-field and the three-field systems. But fallow land also introduced a cleaned and cultivated reserve field, upon which new crops entered the system with growing intensity. Black fallowing changed to green fallowing. Root crops and potatoes covered the former fallow land in the improved three-field system. The loss in meager pasture was outweighed by the gain in fodder production of forage crops.

But clean fallow points to some dangers implicit in plowing. The plow breaks the total area, and all protective plant cover is removed. A clean surface lies bare to the erosive action of strong rainfall or sweeping, dry winds. The early sprouting of a dense carpet of winter-sown small grains may alleviate the danger of soil erosion, but where plow agriculture is applied in more dangerous climatic regions to crops taken over from hoe agriculture, as happened so widely with maize or cotton in the New World, dangerous soil erosion ensues.

The plow is inferior to the hoe or the planting stick on steep slopes. Plowed, inclined slopes are also endangered by soil erosion, especially when the furrows run down the slope. But peasant agriculturists early found remedies. The slopes were preferred, for reason of fresher soil and better natural drainage. By handling the plow skilfully along the contour lines, the peasant succeeded in building up low terraces, which, in time, were fastened by hedges or stones. The arrangement of property plots along isohypses anticipated, in effect, modern scientific contour farming. Some of these terraces are supposed to date back to the Bronze Age. Contour plowing and strip cropping (promoted by the structure of property division on the *Flur*) are common and old traditional features of the peasant landscape. Furthermore, by plowing the furrows together, the peasant could build up ridged fields ("ridge and furrow" [*Hochäcker*]) where low, damp ground made drainage advisable.

Certain conservational and reclamation practices are of long standing and may account for the absence of serious features of soil erosion. But it has not been avoided altogether. In fact, archival evidence (Jäger, 1951), as well as field evidence (e.g., Hempel, 1954*a*, 1954*b*), reveals that soil erosion left considerable scars locally and at certain times on the surface. Some of the excessive alluvial sediments, which have raised the surface, for example, around an early medieval church (*Grünsfeldhausen*) by 3 meters, may correspond to soil erosion following new clearings. The bases of stone walls in the Kocher

Valley, running downhill, today stand a meter above the cultivated plots in between. The matter of historic denudation due to soil erosion may not yet be ready for quantitative and regional discussion, for the preservation of periglacial soil features has been proved over wide areas. At any rate, the peasant landscape of today may again be suffering locally from soil erosion, but, *in toto,* it is blissfully absent in comparison with other parts of Europe or overseas areas of plow and hoe agriculture. How much this is due to careful action by the peasants is not known quantitatively, though it is known that peasant folkways call for recovery of soil when washed downhill by rain, and the peasants in the steep, terraced vineyards carry the soil up the slopes in baskets on their backs even today.

The permanently cleared fields, perhaps improved by ridging or slope-terracing, made for stability in the spatial arrangement of the landscape and tended to fix fields and settlements to the spot. It is not yet well known what importance forms of slash-and-burn agriculture, perhaps with shifting of fields and villages, had in prehistoric agriculture. Where we find such methods of forest-field rotation with burning (*Hau-Bergwirtschaft*), as in Siegerland, in the Moselle area (Schmithüsen, 1934), or in parts of the Black Forest or of Bayrischen Wald, evidence points to development in medieval times rather than to preservation from prehistoric times.

The Role of the Pasture

Pastures and meadows were important special areas that served to maintain the staple types of land utilization supplementary to or alternatively to crop production.

The pasture in historic peasant agriculture has changed through time from primarily natural pasture (woodland, degenerated woodland with grass and shrubbery, heath, "*Hutungen*") to predominantly artificial pasture (permanent, or alternating with field use, "*Feldgraswirtschaft,*" "*Koppelwirtschaft*"). From pastures held in common (*Allmende, Markungen*), the trend was to pastures as individual property. The pasture added to the plowed field a unit of land utilization highly adaptable to varying natural, economic, and social situations. Like fallowing, it helped to maintain peasant agriculture when field crops were restricted or had failed. Shifting emphasis on plant and livestock production made possible the triumph of plow agriculture.

It has been increasingly apparent that utilization of forests for pasturing promoted and guided the early penetration of forested Central Europe (Nietsch, 1939). Contrary to earlier concepts that the forest was inimical to the primitive Neolithic settler, it is now held that certain types of forest (notably more open, mixed, deciduous types, bearing fruit and suitable·for fattening swine) had been indispensable. The rough, high-mountain uplands were opened for pasture in medieval times. In the poor heath countries of northwestern Germany a wide circle of semi-wildland pasture spread around the small, oldest permanent fields (*Esche*), which were fertilized by heath-bedding enriched by the manure from winter stables.[6] Infield and outfield systems were developed in the varied forms of field grass, where crops alternated with grassland. Maritime areas, not well suited to grain production, were developed highly by means of intensive pasturing. It is beyond our purpose to discuss the relationship of pasturing to changing economic conditions. The meadow as the land for hay production

6. *Eschland* was manured with *Plaggen,* i.e., clumps of heath that had been used as bedding in sheep stables. A special soil type resulted, the *Plaggenboden* (Niemeier and Taschenmacher, 1939).

opened the low-lying, damp bottoms along the brooks and rivers and thus added a new ecologic type to the system of land utilization in the plow economy.

Combined System of Plant Production and Animal Husbandry

The alternation of cropland and fallow, pasture and meadow, spatially in adaptation to ecological or economic situations or rotationally in varying proportions and time sequences, gives a high degree of flexibility to plow agriculture as practiced by Central European peasantry. This, in turn, leads to a wide range of regional variations in peasant life and economy.

The value of hoe and planting-stick agriculture rests with the care devoted to the individual plant and the possibility of raising many varieties in combination on one plot (see Sauer, p. 57). The achievements of plow agriculture come with intricate systems of land utilization, combinations, and rotational systems of plant production and animal husbandry. Several mixed plants on one field are not unknown (mixed grains for fodder), though this is the exception. The deductive schemes of von Thünen (Figs. 76a and 76b) and Aereboe (Fig. 77) serve as examples of the flexibility of plow agriculture in relation to changing market and climatic conditions.[7]

Equally important was the internal improvement of production based upon the plant-animal combination. The animals furnished manure to fertilize the fields as soon as stables for animals increased in importance. As the manure pile proverbially is a matter of pride to the good peasant, it also was the mainstay of traditional plow agriculture in Central Europe.[8]

The extension of fields at the expense of common pasture land and the closing of the forests for pasturing promoted the stabling of the animals. It is extremely important that the necessity to turn attention to forage crops to make up for loss of open-air pasture proved beneficial for field crops as well. The increase of hoe and forage crops, notably leguminous plants, led to new, improved rotations (e.g., the "Norfolk" system). "Green manuring" appeared as a practice that steadily improved up to present times. Such improved field practices seem to have originated first in Flanders and the lower Rhine area, as well as in Italy. Attempts at scientific field rotation aspire to proper alternation of crops with regard to both high economic yield and maintenance of soil fertility. The introduction of artificial fertilizers has somewhat lessened the emphasis on manuring. Today, advisers advocate bringing cattle out into the open air. New paddocks (*Koppeln*), sometimes held in common, make their appearance around settlements or outer fringes of fields.

It is not our aim to exhaust the lore of land management and field practices. Our endeavor has been to outline some characteristic qualities of plow agriculture as developed among Central European peasantry and to point out its high degree of flexibility and adaptability that may account for its surprising stability. How such agricultural systems have been realized within the social patterns of the peasant landscape remains to be outlined.

STRUCTURE OF THE PEASANT ECONOMIC LANDSCAPE

Two basic factors determine the structure of the peasant economic land-

7. Cf. Brinkmann, 1913; Beschorner, 1923; Waibel, 1933; Krzymowski, 1914; Otremba, 1953; Müller-Wille, 1936, 1938a, 1941, 1952, 1955.

8. The development of manuring practices and intensity is worth studying. In the eighteenth century many regions in Europe did not practice manuring in a satisfactory way. The early great agricultural scientists of the eighteenth and nineteenth centuries greatly helped to bring the lore of manuring to perfection and to spread knowledge of its use gradually over the countryside.

scape: (1) the individual family holding is the smallest unit and (2) many such holdings unite to form a community within an area.

The Family Holdings

The home of the peasant family and the center of activity is the *Bauernhaus* or, in its larger and functionally compound form, the *Bauernhof*. The construction of the house and the layout of the farm (*Hof*) determine more than anything else the regional aspect of the settlements. The distribution of such house forms is frequently independent of settlement patterns.[9]

9. For various explanations of development of the structure of the peasant economic landscape see Pessler, 1907–8; Schier, 1932; Schilli, 1953; and Ellenberg, 1937, 1941.

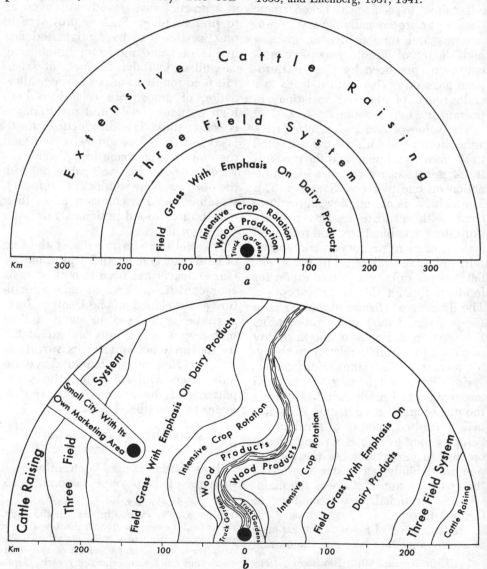

FIG. 76.—Arrangement of agricultural systems based upon the plow. (After von Thünen, 1826; the scale in kilometers has been added by Waibel, 1933.) *a*, the rings of an isolated state; *b*, the above as modified by a navigable river.

The historic term for the peasant holding belonging to the *Bauernhaus* or *Bauernhof* is the "*Hufe.*"[10] The *Hufe* (Lat.: *mansus*), as the basis of existence, combined individual property (*Sondereigentum*) with rights of usufruct in common holdings and social standing. All attempts to discover standard quantitative measures have come to naught, for the size of the *Hufe* varied in time and region. The *Hufe* is the peculiar form by which the principle of

10. *Hufe* (Lat.: *mansus;* Ger.: *hova, hoba, huoba,* etc.) denotes in most general meaning the basis for peasant existence, i.e., land and all material and juridical belongings. *Hufe* was

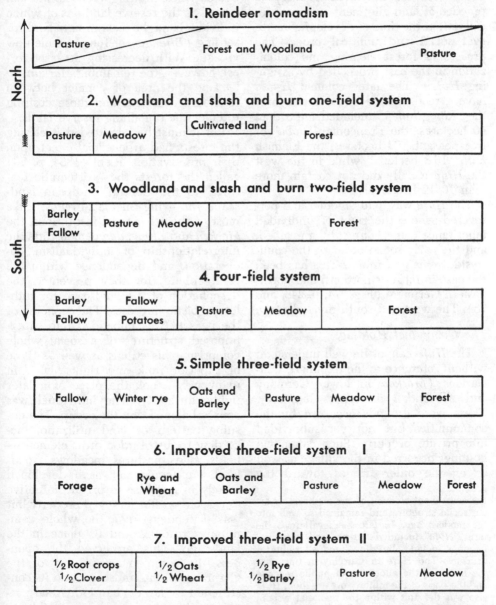

FIG. 77.—Influence of climate on types of land utilization and field systems. (After Aereboe, 1920.)

individual property was integrated into co-operative communal life and, beyond this, into the whole network of medieval social pattern. The *Hufe* encompassed *Hof* fields and participation in use of the common lands. The origin of the *Hufe* dates back to the times of first occupation, which occurred by families and in groups. It remained the accepted practice of land allotment and rural social unit at the time of developing medieval social and political order. The process of forest clearing and colonization in the east proceeded by assigning *Hufen*. The later colonial *Hufen* have a recognizable basis of measure: the *"Königshufen"* included more than 40 hectares; the Franconian *"hoba"* of free peasants, 24 hectares; the Flemish *Hufe*, 16.8 hectares, while in the west the *Hufe* usually did not contain more than 10–12 hectares.

The *Hufe* was held together and persevered where the right of undivided inheritance (*Anerbenrechte*) prevailed, and the early social order of the countryside remained intact. This has been the case in most of northern and northeastern Germany (Figs. 74, p. 248, and 78). The west and south divided early.

The Communal Holdings

The *Hufe* cannot be well understood without reference to the free-mark associations (*Marken* in lower Germany and *Allmenden* in upper Germany). These were grounds occupied by the communities but not yet subdivided into private property. Such communal holdings occurred in the village as well as on the outer fringes toward the

great woods. Around the administration of the *Marken* and *Allmenden* developed a good deal of peasant self-government and jurisdiction. The rights and terms of utilization were determined by peasant regulations concerning pasture, wood and timber supply, gathering of litter for stable-bedding, bee pastures, hunting, etc. The *Marken* served as the reserve land out of which individuals might reclaim new land for settling (*Bifänge*) or found whole new villages. With decreasing areas of forest, however, the remaining *Markungen* became the area of conflict between territorial overlords and those desiring to enter the remaining reserve lands.

But it must be admitted that closing the forests had a beneficial effect upon their preservation. Riehl (1854, p. 26) called the forests the "aristocratic features" in the Central European landscape, the living "medieval relics." Like most of the other rural institutions, the *Marken* and *Allmenden* demonstrate the interrelationship of individualism, co-operation, and dependence within the rural sphere, for they prevented the despoliation of the landscape for ruthless, egoistic purposes. The economy of the peasant was imbedded into superimposed structures of a social whole comprising his equals as well as those of superior rank and rights, who, in many ways, took the place of a later public authority. The individual was counterbalanced by the group. The ensuing pattern of land utilization according to distribution of its elements—fields, roads, pastures, meadows, woodland, etc.—could not have developed merely in response to private initiative as exerted within surveyed property but was dependent upon the whole community structure and its place in the landscape. This preserved the openness, the common accessibility of the German peasant landscape, and its construction by larger than individual patterns, which still make it possible to

---

the constituent element of the medieval agrarian social structure and remained so well into the modern age. In late medieval times the term *"Hufe"* included the peasant's total belongings in land, buildings, and all rights of usufruct. The *Hufe* in Carolingian time was the basis for the allotment of public revenue and the basis of the military organization. *Hufe* also was the unit within the manorial system, the basis for all burdens, tithes, work, etc.

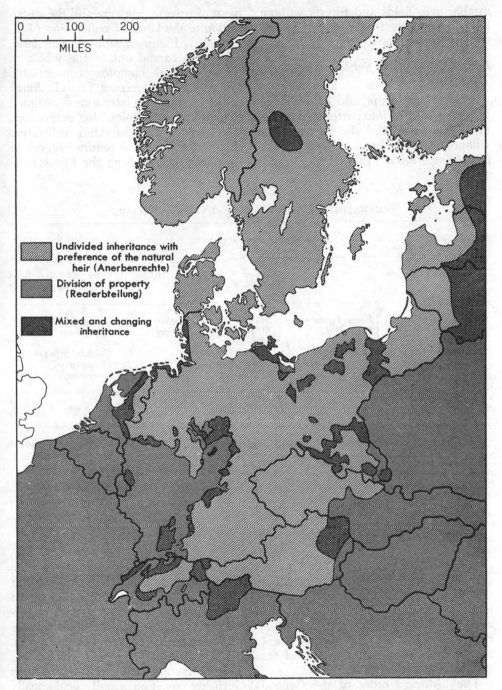

FIG. 78.—Types of legal inheritance in Central Europe, *Anerbenrechte* and *Realerbteilung*. (After Huppertz, 1935.)

ramble over fields and forests without being constantly impeded by fencing and danger of trespassing.

Regional Variety in Settlement Patterns

Haus or Hof, Hufe, and Allmende or Markungen fitted into patterns of settlement that comprised the forms of the villages, hamlets, etc., as well as the pertaining Fluren (Table 1).

ment of private property and the distribution of the kinds of cultivation (Kulturarten). Fields, meadows, woodland, etc., were carved out of the whole of the ecological complex appropriated during the land seizure (Landnahme) of the group or—in later times—assigned to a group by the colonizing authorities. The major units of land utilization therefore followed as nature suggested: the meadowland along the brooks; the

TABLE 1*

SCHEMATIC ORDER OF SETTLEMENT AND *Flur* PATTERNS

I. SETTLEMENT PATTERNS

Number of Houses	1	2, 4, 8	16,	32, 64< (no fixed upper limit)
Irregular 　Without formal 　order	Single farmstead (*Einzelhof*)	Hamlet (*Weiler*) (*Drubbel*)	Small village (*Dorf*)	Large closed village (*Haufendorf*)
Regular 　With rational 　order	Line villages Forest villages Marsh villages	Small villages 　with greens (*Rundling*)		Colonial villages (*Strassendorf*) (*Angerdorf*, etc.)

II. *Flur* PATTERNS

Irregular 　Without formal 　order	Compact, contiguous pattern (*Einödflur*)	Aggregate of blocks (*Blockgemengeflur*)		Aggregate of strips (*Streifengemengeflur*)
Regular 　With rational 　order	*Wald-*, *Marsh-*, *Hufenflur*			*Gewannfluren*

* Source: Hömberg, 1935.

Older concepts have correlated settlement patterns with ethnic or tribal distributions in the time of early settlement (Meitzen, 1882). While Meitzen saw old primary differentiations, it is now agreed that changes in subsequent economic and social history are of far greater importance.[11]

The historical order of the Central European *Flur* determined the arrange-

11. Steinbach, 1927, 1937; Hömberg, 1935; Mortensen, 1945, 1946–47, 1955; and many others.

fields to the drier, easily plowable soils; the woodlands to the steeper parts of the terrain or to the farther fringes of the communal area. The pattern of distribution of individual property was subordinated to such larger groupings.

The pattern on the plowable land is of greatest interest. In northwestern Germany we find small, ecologically conditioned localities that rise slightly above the ground. These were used as the oldest plots of plowable land and have apparently determined the location of settlements since prehistoric times (Niemeier, 1938, 1944a, 1944b). They were called *"Esch"* and were owned only by peasants in possession of the full rights of their estate. These fully righted peasants (*Erben*) joined for working the *Esch* into so-called *"Eschgenossenschaften,"* from which the social substratum was excluded. In its most extreme form, the *Esch* was

During earlier medieval times new settlements of fully righted peasants developed on either single farmsteads (*Einzelhöfe*) or in small, loosely textured groupings (*Drubbels*). Later, those cottagers (*Kötter*) without the full rights of the peasant were furnished plots from the *Markungen*. Suitable land also was individually appropriated in blocklike fashion, as the so-called

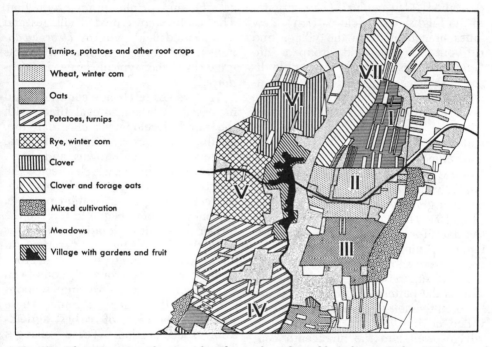

Turnips, potatoes and other root crops

Wheat, winter corn

Oats

Potatoes, turnips

Rye, winter corn

Clover

Clover and forage oats

Mixed cultivation

Meadows

Village with gardens and fruit

FIG. 79.—The economic utilization of a *Flur* in the Odenwald. (After F. Tichy, 1954; part of unpublished field map.)
A seven-field system is practiced in a common rotation, proceeding in seven *Zelgen:* I–VII. Crops rotate in sequence from one to seven. Lands not in seven-year rotation are newly cleared and managed independently.

managed in a one-field system, which, year after year, served for the production of rye (Müller-Wille, 1939, 1942, 1944a, 1944b). This *Esch* pattern was surrounded by extensive areas of low-lying lands, heath, or bogs (*Markungen*), where pasturing was the normal activity (Fig. 79). In the outfield small plots for minor crops might alternate with long years of heath or bogs. Burning was practiced on the bogs before the land was put under cultivation.

"Kämpe," in which the upper and lower strata of the society participated. In the eighteenth and nineteenth centuries the *Markungen* were divided as a result of an era of reform.

The arrangement differed in southern and western Germany. In the older settled areas—the basins, the loesslands, or corresponding landscapes—the closed village (*Haufendorf*) prevailed. The area of the fields increased early at the expense of the outer circle of woodland area (*Allmende*) by additions of plots of land called "*Gewanne.*" In the fully developed arrangement the *Gewanne* determined the distribution of the single, small strips into which individual peasant holdings were subdivided. These small strips of the *Hufe* appeared parceled out over the entire plowed area and also over the meadowland, giving rise to the famous, frequently described "*Gewannflur*" (like virgates in the English open-field pattern). Few lanes branch off from the village and run out into the field grouped into *Gewanne*. It is obviously impossible directly to reach each single plot. A common order is necessary to work the fields, and this probably appeared along with the three-field system. The *Gewanne* were grouped into "*Zelgen*" (sometimes called "*Ösche*" and equivalent to the open-field pattern in England), which served as field units for summer grain, winter grain, and fallow (Fig. 80). The rights of trespassing and the dates for plowing, fencing, harvesting, or opening of stubble fields for pasturing were subject to common regulation and supervised by village officials. This is the pattern of community-regulated cultivation (*Flurzwang*) that prevailed on the fields of many *Gewann* villages well into the nineteenth century. Open-field practices (*zelgengebundene Bewirtschaftung*) may still be observed in many parts of western Germany (Figs. 81 and 83 [p. 269]). This system conditioned the historic complex of the peasant landscape in the regions of earliest occupation in southern and western Germany.

EVOLUTION OF PEASANT INSTITUTIONS AND PEASANT LANDSCAPE

Full appreciation and understanding of Central European peasant institutions and peasant landscape call for brief reference to the evolutionary stages. Northern Germany preserved old patterns, owing to less intensive cultural historic movements and its peculiar social and ecological structure. Southern Germany underwent a succession of important changes. The catchwords denoting the trends are: increase of population; increase of plowed land in distributed individual plots at the expense of common land (*Allmende*); early, almost universal, spreading of the manorial system (*Grundherrschaft*); and surplus grain production. The results were crowded villages and complicated field patterns (*Vergewannung*). The earlier, smaller settlements grew into the typical large *Haufendörfer*.

The process of change continued and increased in late medieval times with the rapid development of urban life. Southern and western Germany became densely dotted with towns and cities, the mere presence of which affected the countryside. Market conditions improved, making specialization possible. A money economy began to replace the former autarchical situation, as well as methods of exchange or taxations in kind, in the countryside. Numerous small towns grew crowded, notably in the important wine-growing sections and along the routes of trade. These were also the areas of earliest agricultural specialization. These changes brought city ways to the country—market dependence, free mobility of real estate, declining conservatism—to create in the extreme what Riehl (1869, pp. 181–216) has aptly called "*Bauernland mit Bürgerrechten.*" The growth of towns and cities also affected the settlement pattern of the countryside by attracting labor. Many a village with accompanying fields was embodied into urban areas, and the peasants became burghers, frequently quite willingly, to improve their legal status (*Stadtluft macht frei,* "town air does away with bondage"), while in the countryside (*Luft macht eigen,* "Country air puts into bondage") bondage often pre-

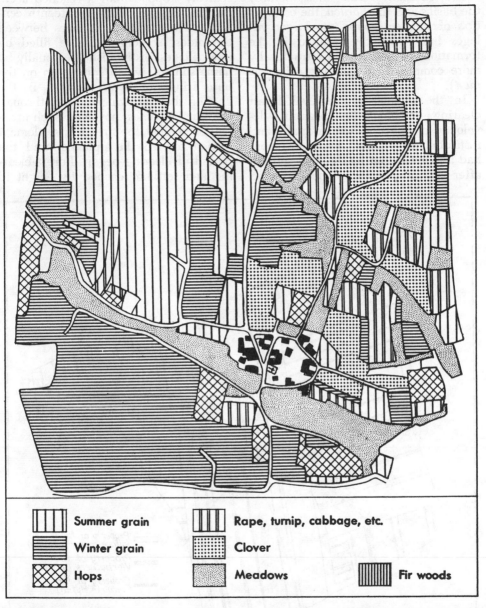

⦀ Summer grain	‖‖‖ Rape, turnip, cabbage, etc.
▤ Winter grain	▦ Clover
▧ Hops	⠿ Meadows
	⦀ Fir woods

Fig. 80.—Field pattern and economic organization of a small, closed hamlet in Lower Bavaria. (After Fuchs, in Otremba, 1953.)

The field is imperfectly distributed among the peasants in relation to contiguity of area. Three *Zelgen* are still recognizable, although frequent exceptions occur along the fringes in connection with the field lanes. Hops, being a crop that keeps the ground more permanently, does not fit into three-field rotation. Plots with hops, therefore, are not included in the *Zelgen* system. All hop lands are directly accessible from field lanes.

vailed. In many fertile areas, notably the basins and the *Börden,* the contraction of smaller groups into larger villages has repeatedly resulted in the formation of larger but structurally more complex field patterns (*Flurformen*).

In the regions of medieval forest clearing and colonization, peasantry developed under conditions formally and institutionally different. Such movement had already begun by the final settling after the migration of peoples and scarcely stopped until it reached a climax at the end of the fourteenth century. At first the open spaces between the oldest settlements were filled by new villages, distinguishable usually by name suffixes, which sprang up on the outer fringes of the *Markungen.* By the end of the Merovingian and through Carolingian times, however, such areas had been filled, the stream of settlement turned toward the uplands, and the period of clearing began. Forest clearing and settling reached its height in

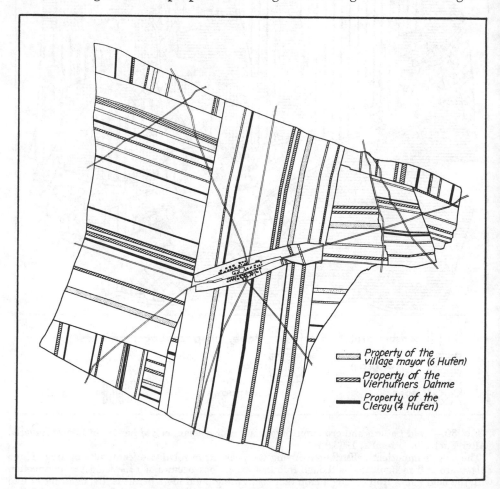

FIG. 81.—A typical eastern colonial village and its *Flur.* (After Krenzlin, 1954.)

The type represented is a somewhat narrow *Angerdorf.* The individual holdings are distributed in long, very narrow strips. The whole *Flur* is divided into three major blocks and several minor ones. This corresponds to the simplified *Gewannflur* type in the colonial east. The three larger *Gewanne* seem to coincide with the three *Zelgen* of the three-field system.

the twelfth to thirteenth centuries. Then suddenly the stream dried up, and, within a few decades, a reversal took place. Many settlements that had been founded a generation before were abandoned, and the forest recovered ground. The reasons for, and quantitative importance of, this period of sudden desertion of the settlements (*Wüstungen*) are even yet not fully understood (cf. Darby, pp. 198–99).[12]

Because of differences in time and geographical habitat, these later peasant settlements began under differing circumstances; their divergence widened with further evolution. The tilling of the settled land had begun under the changed historical milieu of the Merovingian and Carolingian world. In the Germania Romana, in what was later eastern France including the Basin of Paris, a process of culture contact had brought important amalgamations of Nordic Germanic and Mediterranean culture inheritance. The birth of the medieval *Grundherrschaft* and intense political and jurisdictional reorganization took place at that time. The free, open spaces had disappeared, having been either settled or taken over by legal claims of the king and the lords of the *Grundherrschaften*. Squatting did not entirely vanish, but the typical forest clearing was done upon ground pertaining to the king's domain or to some big *Grundherrschaft*. The forms that developed differed as well, as may be taken from Figures 82 and 83 (p. 269). Most important was the development of formally regulated patterns.

In the Black Forest, in the Odenwald, in the eastern *Mittelgebirge*, as well as in the forests of the northern lowlands, forest-line villages (*Waldhufendörfer*) appeared. Each settler re-

ceived a *Hufe* in an elongated strip running from the valley bottom to the top of the ridge. This pattern combined important features of single farmstead settlement with village community coherence.

Distance from the old regions of a few kilometers meant a great deal in later evolution. Such new forest lands were cherished ground for ambitious aristocracy to carve out territory by settling. The interlacing of manorial holdings and jurisdictional rights within one village were less than in the old areas. Under stronger manorial influence, the *Hof* structure remained more intact. Some of the parts of the central Black Forest are still today an island of undivided inherited right (*Anerbenrecht, Höferecht*) within the southwestern realm of equally divided inheritance rights (*Realerbteilung*). The influence of the new town integration into the former rural pattern of the old land was less felt. Market relations were impeded by distance and terrain. The higher altitude prevented the growing of grain, with its accompanying three-field system and subdivision (*Vergetreidung*). Rotation of grassland alternating with plowed land (*Feldgraswirtschaft*) and emphasis on livestock determined the agricultural system. Work in the forests or mines and on handicrafts (textiles, glassmaking, mechanical crafts) supplemented life when the soil and climate failed to support the population. Though late in origin, the peasantry of the forest clearing was the preserver of folklore, costumes, and old-fashioned peasant qualities and habits. Such regions have proved very attractive for tourism as well as for authors of peasant novels.

The neat regional juxtaposition to the older areas is characteristic for southern and some parts of central Germany, with its nicely configurated landscape, though not so much so in northern Germany. The Saxon territory is

12. Recently there has been a revival of interest by geographers and agricultural historians. Field research (by Mortensen, Scharlau, Jäger, and others), as well as work in archives (by Jäger) and on the complex of economic history (by Abel), is in progress.

very old *Volksland,* having been occupied centuries earlier, before Franks and Alemannic tribes founded their new areas following conquest from the Romans. Medieval settlements arose in the intervening spaces between the old Saxon nuclei. The *Grundherrschaft* arrived later but maintained itself in older forms. Urban life was less densely intercalated than in the south and west. The maritime climate allowed emphasis on the growing of grain (*Vergetreidung*)

only along the inner continental fringes. The boundary of the three-field system with *Gewannflur* and *Flurzwang* followed decidedly a climatically and edaphically conditioned line to the north and northwest, where other systems with stronger emphasis upon livestock and green land were combined with the very old *Esch* type, one-field system, or very extensive ways of utilizing heath and bogs (Müller-Wille, 1938a, 1941; Pfeifer and Schüttler,

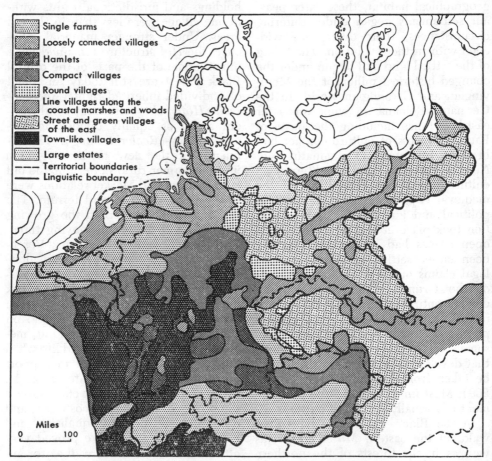

Legend:
- Single farms
- Loosely connected villages
- Hamlets
- Compact villages
- Round villages
- Line villages along the coastal marshes and woods
- Street and green villages of the east
- Town-like villages
- Large estates
- --- Territorial boundaries
- — Linguistic boundary

Miles
0   100

FIG. 82.—Distribution of types of settlement forms in Central Europe. (After Huppertz, 1935.)

Two major regions stand out rather clearly: western Germany, settled since the migrations of people, and eastern Germany, settled since the medieval colonial movement. Western Germany breaks down into the loosely grouped, smaller settlements of the northwest; planned patterns along the North Sea coastal marshes; irregular, compact patterns in the west and southwest. Eastern Germany contains large estates along the coastal regions; compact, planned villages farther inland; planned patterns in the mountain uplands and along reclaimed alluvial bottom lands.

1941). Only in certain areas did *Hagen-hufendörfer* develop, practically identical with forest-line villages (*Wald-hufendörfer*); they also were allocated upon manorial territory.

The zone of North Sea marshes, with Frisian and Saxon population, produced many forms of settlement. Reclamation and diking occurred during the phase of medieval colonization. It was brought to the eastern section by skilful people from Flanders and the Low Countries (A.D. 1106, near Bremen), along with a marsh village (*Marsch-hufendorf*) resembling closely the *Waldhufendorf*. The isolated marshes for a long time sustained a high degree of peasant independence. Proximity to the sea early brought commerce to the countryside; Frisian traders were among the earliest reported. Sheep-raising suggested early wool trade. Later, coastal shipping brought contact with the rising markets in the crowded Western countries. Grain, butter, and meat were exported by peasants who were shipowners as well. This type of economy fostered a lively spirit of trade and commerce among the people. The very even qualities of the soil suggested its commercial use as well. Quite in contrast to the upland (*Geest*), equally divided inheritance (*Realerbteilung*) is found today in many parts of the marshes.

A third region of peasant development is the east. Bavarian peasantry settled in the Tirols, Carinthia, and Styria and laid the foundations for the Austrian march between the eighth and tenth centuries. The great period of eastern colonization began in the tenth century, when the area east of the Elbe was added to the old German *Volksland* in the Old German Empire (*Altreich*). It was a mass movement of people into new lands contiguous to the homeland, in which peasants and nobility from most of the older sections participated. Warlike and peaceful diplomatic relations with the Slavs opened the way for the settlers, who were guided and directed by the nobility. "*Locatores*" spotted the places for new settlements and recruited people from back home. Not until the settling of the American continent was there a peasant movement of similar proportions.

The patterns of settlement were truly colonial. They were derived from traditional forms in the west but were adjusted to practices and experiences in the new environment. The unit of allotment remained the *Hufe,* but in its later concept as a measurable quantity of individual property. *Locatores,* functionaries of lower jurisdiction, and nobility received larger allotments (from 2 to 4 *Hufen*). The closed form of village settlement furnished the normal standard. The *Höfe* were regularly arranged on both sides of rectangular or almond-shaped "greens" (Fig. 81, p. 262). Special types were the *Rundlinge* and the *Wald-* or *Hagenhufendörfer.*

The *Flur* was normally laid out in the three-field system, which was the leading field system of the time. The *Hufen* property was subdivided in a few long strips, in numbers accordant with the larger subdivisions of the *Flur.* In a generalized way it may be said that the *Gewanne* and *Zelgen* coincided here more closely than in the west (Fig. 81, p. 262). The allotment of *Markungen* and *Allmenden* was insignificant in comparison with the old land.

The relations of colonial settlement patterns lately have been carefully investigated with regard to ethnical, ecological, and economic facts (Krenzlin, 1952). The variety is greater than is usually supposed, and—as in the west—the factors of change and succeeding development had greater importance. Changing field systems had considerable influence on the further evolution of the *Flur.* The east attracted the western peasants, not only in their quest for new soil, but also because it offered improved social conditions. Rights were improved, and the drive to new social conditions suggests comparison with the American West. Terms of tenantry were better defined, and the manorial burdens were less. The political aspect was decidedly of larger scale. The *Grundherrschaften* also were closed, compact holdings, in which manorial and jurisdictional rights could be more efficiently applied.

The truly colonial character of the movement subsided when the stream of peasants from the west dwindled by the fourteenth century. The great period of desertion (*Wüstungen*) touched the east as well. Wars and epidemics (the Black Death) decimated the population; even re-migration to the west may have taken place, at least locally. The nobility felt the loss of income when *Hufen* lay deserted. A good deal of former peasant land changed over into the hands of aristocracy as abandoned homes (*Heimfall*). Thus began a tendency to larger agricultural enterprises among the nobility, a factor of greatest importance for the peasantry in the east.

By the fifteenth and sixteenth centuries, with the growing markets in Western Europe and the development of shipping from the Hanseatic cities along the Baltic coast, a real opportunity opened for large-scale grain production. A similar market development in England also greatly influenced the countryside there. Nobility began actively to enlarge the land around the court. *Hufen* without heirs reverted to the *Grundherrschaft;* epidemics, feuds, and wars helped to reclaim peasant land; and obstinate peasants were evicted. But, contrary to similar actions by the English nobility, who went in for grazing, the eastern German barons turned to grain-growing; they needed the hands and consequently bound the evicted peasants to the ground as serfs to secure the necessary labor force. The large estate (*demesne*) enterprises

(*Gutswirtschaft*) on latifundias were born and were followed by systems of bondage (*Leibeigenschaft*) and serfdom under jurisdictional authority of the feudal overlord (*Gutsuntertänigkeit*). It was the abuse of medieval manorial rights, which included also jurisdictional rights, that in time made conditions so vicious. While peasant villages degenerated until only little hamlets (*Gutsweiler*) remained, estates and subsidiary farms (*Gutshof* and *Vorwerke*) for outlying fields grew.

The fate of the peasantry largely depended upon the relations between nobility and *Landesherrschaft*. The stronger monarchies, like Prussia, earlier had tendencies to protect the peasant against the inroads of nobility (in Prussia, edict of 1709). But in Mecklenburg and Swedish Pomerania, which were strongly dominated by aristocracy, the process of peasant eviction (*Bauernlegen*) had greatest consequences. By the end of the eighteenth century, nearly two-thirds of the whole country was in latifundia.

Tragically enough, the so-called "reform movements" of the eighteenth and nineteenth centuries brought the greatest amount of peasant land into the hands of the nobility. In Prussia, peasants enjoyed a certain protection after 1709, and the domainal peasants were free. By the famous edict promulgated by the Freiherrn von Stein in 1807 all peasants were made free, and hereditary serfdom (*Erbuntertänigkeit*) was abolished. In 1811 all material and personal obligations of the peasants were theoretically removed. But, during 1808–10, the application of proclamations for reforms had largely canceled the earlier intentions. The large owners received emoluments for the liberation of their peasants amounting to one-third of the peasant land and, in some cases, even one-half. In this way, the nobility received 1,200,000 hectares in Prussia.

The old order had given a certain

protection, in a patriarchal way, for weak peasants. Such was no longer the case; consequently, many, if not most, of the smaller people were forced off the land or degenerated into landless day workers (*Tagelöhner*) near the lowest minimum of existence. The situation was most extreme in Mecklenburg. *Leibeigenschaft* was lifted here in 1820, but, with it, all rights of the people on the land. Nobility acquired, consequently, as much as 80–90 per cent of the total area (Fig. 74, p. 248). By the time the revolutionary movements of the middle of the nineteenth century stimulated legislation to improve conditions, it was too late. Industry attracted the poorer rural population and offered new occupations, and the large estates began to feel the scarcity of hands. The way out—to import Polish harvesters (*polnische Schnitter*)—did not improve social conditions in the countryside. Protective tariffs helped maintain this unhappy structure until the end of World War II.

The revolutionary change in eastern German land reform after 1945 may be gathered from a few figures (Abel, 1951, p. 178) on changes in property structure in the eastern German Democratic Republic (1939, 1946) as compared to West Germany (1949). In size of holdings the east has become similar to the west, as the accompanying tabulation

HECTARES	EAST GERMANY (PER CENT) 1939	1946	WEST GERMANY (PER CENT) 1949
0–5	9.1	9.7	20.5
5–20	31.7	53.4	43.6
20–50	22.5	24.0	23.4
50–100	8.4	7.7	6.3
100 and over	28.3	5.2	5.8

shows, but the unfortunate circumstances of the reform and the continuing pressure with "plans" and productive quotas (*Solls*) has not allowed the growth of happy conditions.

But such conditions did not charac-

terize the whole east until 1945. Healthy peasant structures had survived in many parts of eastern Prussia (notably within the old diocese Ermeland), Pomerania (back from the coast), Brandenburg (notably the lands reclaimed by Frederick the Great along the Oder and Warta), Silesia (outside the truly latifundia sections), and Saxony. In the east the right of undivided inheritance (*Anerbenrecht*) predominated, and the property structure was better preserved. *Parcellement* never attained such vicious consequences as in the southwest. The influence of the towns on the countryside was less than in the west. In fact, many small towns had a strong rustic flavor. Eastern peasantry retained a more truly traditional, rural character. If there is a peasantry in the world in which something of the pioneer qualities of the nineteenth century is still alive, it is in the eastern peasantry.

CONCLUSIONS

The problems of peasantry have been only touched upon but by no means covered. What I have endeavored to demonstrate is that peasantry in Central Europe developed in time and differentiated itself in area. Changing historic situations have left stratifications which vary from region to region. Peasantry is old as an estate (*Stand*), but many of its institutions are of recent origin. It is necessary to discriminate carefully between conditions that are truly old and those that have evolved during a long, sometimes complicated, history.

There remains to add a few remarks about some of the historical developments which I have not been able to cover. The great crisis in medieval development is the period of abandonment of villages (*Wüstungen*), which led to a settlement structure which was the basis for developments in the new era after 1500. The importance of this period with regard to the distribution of open land and forests has been evaluated in the *"Göttinger Schule"* (Mortensen, 1951; Scharlau, 1938, 1943; Jäger, 1951).

But later forces continued to shape the fate of peasantry. In the fifteenth and sixteenth centuries the modern state began to appear; its influences at first were frequently resented by the peasantry. The supervision of the forests was enforced, and the state gradually became the great forest proprietor. The developing state administration requested numerous innovations in law and taxation, which were felt especially in the many small territories of the southwest, where the personal bondage of the newly forming political dependencies (*Untertänigkeits-Verhältnisse*) was rather rigid. Here unrest prevailed, and finally the peasant wars of 1524–25 flared up.

On the other hand, it must be agreed that the *Landesherren* placed a protecting arm over the peasants against inroads from the nobility. Rising ideas of mercantilism brought new interest in the productiveness of the land and in an increase of population. The growing market economy also affected the countryside and stimulated the tendency toward specialization.

The sixteenth century, but even more the seventeenth and eighteenth centuries, saw great changes in some sections with respect to the pattern of settlement. In the Algäu and somewhat later in Schleswig-Holstein, movements began among the peasants, and were favored by the *Landesherren*, to separate the *Allmenden* and to establish properties. In the Algäu and later in northern Schleswig, villages disbanded, and single farmsteads replaced the former agglomerations.

The reforms affected the whole traditional way of peasant living and social order. With the *Gemarkungen* and *Allmenden*, the old social order of the countryside dwindled. It was no longer possible to maintain divisions of social rank and right among the rural classes. The eighteenth century also saw the start of liberation and modernization of the peasant society, which, in a way, led to a certain atomization. Where, formerly, almost indelible material bonds had supported the older order, now individual rights and properties dominated the scene. But the forces of tradition remained valid in strongly profiled areas, such as Lower Saxony.

The movement of separation or inclosure (*Verkoppelung*) spread over the greater part of the nineteenth century. In Hannover, an order of King George III in 1786 remained without much success. Later ordinances followed in lower Germany in 1802, 1824–25, and 1842. In southern Germany there were laws of land rearrangement (*Flurbereinigung*) in 1856 and 1862; in the Rhineland, not until 1888. But in many sections *Flurbereinigung* has not yet made such progress. With the nineteenth century, agriculture already was a subject for historic retrospective—partly for mere scientific interest, partly as the aboriginal image of national social character.

Today peasantry in Germany is again confronted with most severe problems. The industrialization of Germany has definitely diminished the importance of agriculture from the state's point of view. Autarchic interests, with a view to conditions in time of war, have supported protective tariff policies that gave an artificial climate to peasant economy. But the growing discrepancies between rural living conditions and urban industrial standards, as well as between rural wages and industrial wages, have created a latent labor crisis, especially felt under boom conditions as of today. The grotesque situation has arisen that the importation has been planned of seven thousand Italian agricultural workers into southern Germany —into areas of the smallest average peasant holdings, where part-time farming not connected with latifundia but with undersized rural property is abundant!

during the last few years; it is a sight to see the young peasant, with a companion on the rear seat who may carry a scythe, fly up the rough field lanes on a motorbike!

Figure 83 summarizes the most important facts and portrays the distribution of the major social regions of peas-

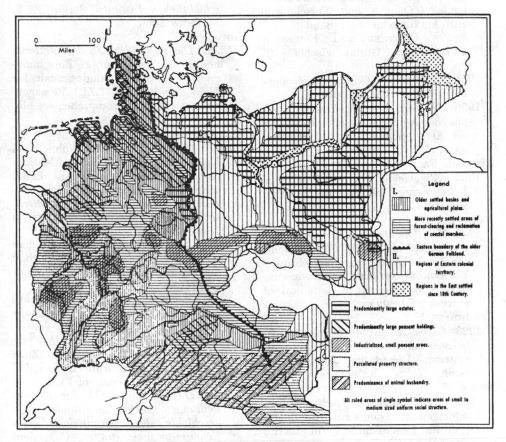

Fig. 83.—The areal differentiation of peasantry in Central Europe, according to size of holding and age of settlement. (After Otremba, 1942.)

The growing labor scarcity hastens the pace of mechanization. But many technical problems—let alone those of education and knowledge—await solution before we may say that adaptation of the tractor to the small-scale farm has been an all-round success. The increase of motorization has been amazing

antry, period of settling and size of property determining the construction of the map (Otremba, 1942). We can easily recognize the regions repeatedly distinguished in this paper: the northwest, the southwest, and the east beyond the line separating old land and colonial area.

REFERENCES

ABEL, W.

1935 *Agrarkrisen und Agrarkonjunktur in Mitteleuropa vom 13. bis zum 19. Jahrhundert.* Berlin: Paul Parey. 179 pp.

1943 *Die Wüstungen des ausgehenden Mittelalters: Ein Beitrag zur Siedlungs- und Agrargeschichte Deutschlands.* ("Quellen und Forschungen zur Agrargeschichte," Band I, ed. FRANZ GÜNTHER and FRIEDRICH LÜTGE. Jena: Gustav Fischer. 165 pp.

1951 *Agrarpolitik.* Göttingen: Vandenboeck & Ruprecht. 419 pp.

1955 "Schichten und Zonen europäischer Agrarverfassung," *Zeitschrift für Agrargeschichte und Agrarsoziologie,* III, No. 1, 1–18.

AEREBOE, FR.

1920 *Allgemeine landwirtschaftliche Betriebslehre.* 5th ed. Berlin: Paul Parey. 697 pp.

ANONYMOUS

1941–55 *Berichte zur Deutschen Landeskunde,* Vols. I–XIV. (Zentralarchiv für Landeskunde von Deutschland.) Ed. BUNDESANSTALT FÜR LANDESKUNDE. (A comprehensive periodical of current publications.)

BESCHOMER, F.

1923 "Zur Geographie der haupsächlichsten landwirtschaftlichen Betriebssysteme." Dissertation, University of Bonn.

BOBEK, H.

1952 *Südwestdeutsche Studien.* ("Forschungen zur deutschen Bundesanstalt für Landeskunde," Vol. LXII.) Remagen. 67 pp.

BRINKMANN, TH.

1913 "Über landwirtschaftliche Betriebssysteme," *Fühlings landwirtschaftliche Zeitung,* LXII, 184–214.

CREDNER, W.

1938 "Über Kartierung landwirtschaftlicher Nutzflächen," *Zeitschrift für Erdkunde,* VI, 229–36.

1943 "Die deutsche Agrarlandschaft im Kartenbild," *Sitzungsberichte europäischer Geographen,* pp. 177–201. Leipzig.

DÖRRIES, H.

1940 "Siedlungs- und Bevölkerungsgeographie (1908–1938)," *Geographisches Jahrbuch,* LV, No. 1, 3–380.

EBERT, W.

1937 "Ländliche Siedelformen im deutschen Osten," in KÖTZSCHKE, R. VON (ed.), *Auftrage des landesgeschichtlichen Instituts.* Berlin: E. S. Mittler & Sohn.

EHEMANN, K.

1953 *Das Bauernhaus in der Wetterau und im SW. Vogelsberg.* ("Forschungen zur deutschen Bundesanstalt für Landeskunde," Vol. LXI.) Remagen. 150 pp. (Contains comprehensive bibliography.)

ELLENBERG, H.

1937 "Über bäuerliche Wohn- und Siedlungsweise in Nordwestdeutschland in ihrer Beziehung zur Landschaft insbesondere zur Pflanzendecke," *Mitteilungen der floristisch-soziologischen Arbeitsgemeinschaft in Niedersachsen,* No. 3. Hannover.

1941 "Deutsche Bauernhauslandschaften als Ausdruck von Natur, Wirtschaft und Volkstum," *Geographische Zeitschrift,* XLVII, 72–85.

1954 "Steppenheide und Waldweide," *Erdkunde (Archiv für wissenschaftliche Geographie),* VIII, 188–94.

ENGEL, F.

1934 "Deutsche und slawische Züge in der Dobbertiner Kulturlandschaft." Dissertation, University of Kiel.

1949 *Das Rodungsrecht der Hagensiedlungen: Quellen zur Entwicklungsgeschichte der spätmittelalterlichen Kolonisationsbewegung.* ("Quellenhefte zur Niedersächsischen Geschichte," No. 3.) Hildesheim.

ERNST, V.

1926 *Die Entstehung des deutschen Grundeigentums.* Stuttgart: W. Kohlhammer. 146 pp.

FICKELER, P.

1954 "Das Siegerland als Beispiel wirtschaftsgeschichtlicher und wirtschaftsgeographischer Harmonie," *Erdkunde (Archiv für wissenschaftliche Geographie),* VIII, 15–51. (Contains illustrations of *Haubergwirtschaft.*)

FIRBAS, FR.
1949 *Spät- und nacheiszeitliche Wald-geschichte Mitteleuropas nördlich der Alpen,* Vol. I: *Allgemeine Waldge-schichte.* Jena: Gustav Fischer. 480 pp. (Modern synthesis, balanced ap-praisal of the controversial views of Gradmann and Nietsch in the light of postglacial vegetational develop-ment.)

GRADMANN, R.
1901 "Das mitteleuropäische Land-schaftsbild nach seiner geschichtli-chen Entwicklung," *Geographische Zeitschrift,* VII, Nos. 3–4, 361–77, 435–47.
1906 "Beziehungen zwischen Pflanzen-geographie und Siedlungsgeschichte," *ibid.,* XII, 305–25.
1924 *Das harmonische Landschafts-bild.* (Zeitschrift der Gesellschaft für Erdkunde Berlin.) 130 pp.
1928 "Die Arbeitsweise der Siedlungs-geographie in ihrer Anwendung auf das Frankenland," *Zeitschrift für Bayerische Landesgeschichte,* I, 316–57.
1931 *Süddeutschland.* 2 vols. Stutt-gart: J. Engelhorns. 215+553 pp.
1933 "Die Steppenheide-theorie," *Ge-ographische Zeitschrift,* XXXIX, No. 5, 265–78.
1936 "Vorgeschichtliche Landwirt-schaft und Besiedlung," *ibid.,* XLII, Nos. 9–10, 378–86.
1942 "Hackbau und Kulturpflanzen," *Deutsches Archiv für Landes und Volksforschung,* VI, 107–13.
1943 "Siedlungsformen als Geschichts-quelle und als historisches Problem," *Zeitschrift für Württembergische Landesgeschichte,* VII, 25–56.

HAHN, E.
1909 *Die Entstehung der Pflugkultur.* Heidelberg: Carl Winter. 192 pp.
1914 *Von der Hacke zum Pflug.* ("Wis-senschaft und Bildung," Vol. CXXVII.) Leipzig: Quelle & Meyer. 121 pp. (2d ed., 1919.)

HANSSEN, G.
1861 *Die Aufhebung der Leibeigen-schaft und die Umgestaltung des gutsherrlich-bäuerlichen Verhältnisses überhaupt in den Herzogtümern Schleswig-Holstein.* St. Petersburg: Eggers. 195 pp.
1875 "Zur Geschichte der norddeut-schen Gutswirtschaft, seit dem Ende des 16. Jahrhundert," *Journal für Landwirtschaft.* Göttingen.

HARTKE, W., and WESTERMANN, E.
1940 "Zur Geographie der Vererbung der bäuerlichen Liegenschaften in Deutschland bis zum Erlass des Reichserbhofgesetzes," *Petermanns geographische Mitteilungen,* LXXXVI, No. 1, 16–19.

HAUSRATH, H.
1911 *Pflanzengeographische Wandlun-gen der Deutschen Landschaft.* ("Wis-senschaft und Hypothese," Vol. XIII.) Leipzig and Berlin: B. G. Teubner. 274 pp.

HELBOK, A.
1925 "Der germanische Ursprung des oberdeutschen Bauernhauses," pp. 273–92 in *Ottenthal Festschrift Shlernschriften.* Innsbruck and Mu-nich: Wagner.
1929 "Die Formenlandschaft des deutschen Bauernhauses," *Württem-bergische Monatschrift.*
1932 "Über vorzeitliche und heutige Haustypenlandschaften," *Zeitschrift für Volkskunde* (N.S.), II, 223–34. Berlin and Leipzig.
1937–38 *Grundlagen der Volksge-schichte Deutschlands und Frank-reichs.* 2 vols. Berlin: Walter de Gruy-ter & Co. 564+565 pp.
1938 *Deutsche Siedlung: Wesen, Aus-breitung, Sinn.* Halle: Niemeyer. 228 pp.

HEMPEL, L.
1954a "Beispiele von Bodenerosions-karten im niedersächsischen Bergland sowie Bemerkungen über Berück-sichtigung der Erosionsschäden bei der Bodenschätzung," *Neues Archiv für Niedersachsen,* pp. 140–43.
1954b "Die Entstehung einiger an-thropogenbedingter Oberflächenfor-men und ihre Ähnlichkeit mit natür-lichen Formen," pp. 119–26 in *Er-gebnisse und Probleme moderner geo-graphischer Forschungen, Hans Mor-tensen zu seinem 60. Geburtstage.* ("Abhandlungen der Akademie für Raumforschung und Landesplanung,"

Vol. XXVIII.) Bremen-Horn: W. Dorn. 332 pp.

HESSE, P.
1949 *Grundprobleme der Agrarverfassung: dargestellt am Beispiel der Gemeindetypen und Produktionszonen von Württemberg-Hohenzollern und Baden.* Stuttgart: W. Kohlhammer. 284 pp.

HÖMBERG, A.
1935 *Die Entstehung der westdeutschen Flurformen: Blockgemengflur, Streifenflur, Gewannflur.* With a Foreword by WALTHER VOGEL. Berlin. 64 pp.
1938 *Grundfragen der deutschen Siedlungsforschung.* ("Veröffentlichungen aus dem Seminar für Staatenkunde und historische Geographie an der Universität Berlin," Vol. VI.) Berlin.

HUPPERTZ, B.
1939 *Räume und Schichten bäuerlicher Kulturformen in Deutschland.* Bonn: L. Röhrscheid. 315 pp.

HUTTENLOCHER, F.
1937 "Zusammenhänge zwischen ländlichen Siedlungsarten und geschichtlichen Wirtschaftsweisen im südwestdeutschen Raum," *Zeitschrift für Landesgeschichte,* I, 88–121. Württemberg.

JÄGER, H.
1951 *Die Entwicklung der Kulturlandschaft im Kreise Hofgeismar.* ("Göttingen geographische Abhandlungen," No. 8.) Göttingen: Hans Mortensen. 114 pp.

JESSEN, J.
1922 "Die Entstehung und Entwicklung der Gutswirtschaft bis zum Beginn der Agrarreformen," *Zeitschrift der Gesellschaft für Schleswig-Holsteinische Geschichte,* XLI, 1–206.

KÄUBLER, R.
1938 "Junggeschichtliche Veränderungen des Landschaftsbildes im mittelsächsischen Lössgebiet," *Wissenschaftliche Veröffentlichungen des Deutschen Museums für Landerkunde* (N.S.), V, 71–91.

KNAPP, G. F.
1887 *Die Bauernbefreiung und der Ursprung der Landarbeiter in den* *älteren Teilen Preussens,* Vols. I and II. Leipzig: Duncker & Humblot. 352 +473 pp.

KÖTZSCHKE, R.
1942 "Die Siedelformen des deutschen Nordosten und Sudosten in volks- und sozialgeschichtlicher Bedeutung," *Deutsche Ostforschung,* I, 362–90. Leipzig.
1953 *Ländliche Siedlung und Agrarwesen in Sachsen.* ("Forschungen zur deutschen Bundesanstalt für Landeskunde," Vol. LXXVII.) 236 pp. Remagen.

KOTHE, H.
1953 "Völkerkundliches zur Frage der neolithischen Anbauformen in Europa," pp. 28–74 in KOTHE, H., and OTTO, K. H. (eds.), *Ethnographisch-archäologische Forschungen.* Berlin: Deutscher Verlag der Wissenschaften. 126 pp.

KREBS, N.
1937 *Atlas des deutschen Lebensraumes in Mitteleuropa.* ("Auftrage der Preussischen Akademie der Wissenschaften.") Leipzig: Bibliographisches Institut. (Not completed. The most detailed set of maps on the physical basis and some of the related historical and economic facts.)

KRENZLIN, A.
1940 "Probleme der neueren nord-ostdeutschen und ostmitteldeutschen Flurformenforschung," *Deutsches Archiv für Landes- und Volksforschung,* IV, 547–69.
1952 *Dorf, Feld und Wirtschaft im Gebiet der grossen Täler: und Platten östlich der Elbe.* ("Forschungen zur deutschen Landeskunde," Vol. LXX.) Remagen: Verlag des Amtes für Landeskunde. 144 pp.

KRZYMOWSKI, R.
1914 *Die landwirtschaftlichen Wirtschaftsysteme Elsass Lothringens.* Gebweiler. 477 pp.
1951 *Geschichte der deutschen Landwirtschaft (bis zum Ausbruch des zweiten Weltkrieges 1939) under besonderer Berücksichtigung der technischen Entwicklung der Landwirtschaft.* 2d ed. Stuttgart: E. Ulmer. 372 pp.

KUHN, W.
1953 *Hecken, Terrassen und Boden-zerstörung im hohen Vogelsberg.* ("Rhein-Mainische Forschungen," Vol. XXXIX.) 54 pp.
KURON, H.
1941 "Die Bodenerosion und ihre Bekampfung in Deutschland," *Der Kulturtechniker,* Vol. XLIV.
LEISTER, I.
1952 *Rittersitz und adliges Gut in Holstein und Schleswig.* ("Schriften des Geographischen Instituts der Universität Kiel," Vol. XIV, No. 2.) 157 pp.
LÖW, K.
1940 "Ackerterrassen im Vogelsberg," *Zeitschrift für Erdkunde,* VIII, 488–90.
LÜTGE, FR.
1937 *Die Agrarverfassung des frühen Mittelalters in Mitteldeutschen Raum, vornehmlich in der Karolinger Zeit.* Jena: Gustav Fischer. 570 pp.
1949 *Die Bayrische Grundherrschaft, Untersuchungen über die Agrarverfassung Altbayerns im 16–18. Jahrhundert.* Stuttgart: Piscator Verlag. 187 pp.
MAGER, F.
1937 *Entwicklungsgeschichte der Kulturlandschaft des Herzogtums Schleswig in historischer Zeit.* 2 vols. Breslau: F. Hirt (Vol. I); Kiel: Verlag Heimat & Erde (Vol. II).
1955 *Geschichte des Bauerntums und der Bodenkultur im Lande Mecklenburg.* ("Veröffentlichungen der Historischen Kommission," Vol. I.) Deutsche Akademie der Wissenschaften Berlin: Berlin Akademie Verlag. 580 pp. (Mager published many books and articles on the historical development of landscapes.)
MARTINY, R.
1926 *Hof und Dorf in Altwestfalen: Das westfälische Streusiedlungsproblem.* ("Forschungen zur deutschen Landes- und Volkskunde," Vol. XXIV, No. 5.) 66 pp.
MEITZEN, A.
1895 *Siedlung und Agrarwesen der Westgermanen und Ostgermanen, der Kelten, Römer, Finnen und Slaven.* 3 vols. and atlas. Berlin: W. Hertz.

MEYNEN, E. (ed.)
1949 "Bibliographien und Handbücher zur deutschen Landeskunde (1920–1945)," *Geographisches Taschenbuch* (*Bearbeitet im Amt für Landeskunde*), pp. 98–105.
MORGEN, H., and SIEVERS, A.
1941 "Die natürlichen Grundlagen der ländlichen Besitzverfassung," *Berichte zur Raumforschung und Raumordnung,* V, No. 8, 368–77.
MORTENSEN, H.
1945 "Beiträge der Ostforschung zur nordwestdeutschen Siedlungs- und Flurforschung," *Nachrichten der Akademie der Wissenschaften in Göttingen, Philosophisch-historische Klasse,* pp. 12–14.
1946–47a "Fragen der nordwestdeutschen Siedlungs- und Flurforschung im Licht der Ostforschung," *Nachrichten der Akademie der Wissenschaften in Göttingen, Philosophisch-historische Klasse,* pp. 37–59.
1946–47b "Zur Entstehung der deutschen Dorfformen, insbesondere des Waldhufendorfes," *Nachrichten der Akademie der Wissenschaften in Göttingen, Philosophisch-historische Klasse,* pp. 76–80.
1951 "Neuere Beobachtungen über Wüstungs-Bandfluren und ihre Bedeutung für die mittelalterliche deutsche Kulturlandschaft," *Berichte zur deutschen Landeskunde,* X, 341–61.
1955 "Zur Entstehung der Gewannflur," *Zeitschrift für Agrargeschichte und Agrarsoziologie,* VII, No. 1, 30–48.
MÜLLER-WILLE, W.
1936 *Die Ackerfluren im Landesteil Birkenfeld und ihre Wandlungen seit dem 17. und 18. Jahrhundert.* (Beiträge zur Landeskunde der Rheinlande.) 2d ser. Bonn: L. Röhrscheid. 129 pp.
1938a "Der Feldbau in Westfalen im 19. Jahrhundert," *Westfälische Forschungen,* I, No. 3, 302–25.
1938b "Der Niederwald im rheinischen Schiefergebirge," *ibid.,* pp. 51–86.
1939 "Haus- und Gehöftformen im

Mitteleuropa," *Geographische Zeitschrift*, XLII, 121–38.

1941 "Zu Systematik der Feldsysteme in Norddeutschland," *Zeitschrift für Erdkunde*, IX, Nos. 1–2, 40–43.

1942 "Das rheinische Schiefergebirge und seine kulturgeographische Stellung: Besiedlung, Siedelformen, Haus und Hofanlagen," *Deutsches Archiv für Landes- und Volksforschung*, VI, 537–91.

1944a "Langstreifenflur und Drubbel: Ein Beitrag zur Siedlungsgeographie Westgermaniens," *ibid.*, VIII, 9–44.

1944b "Die Hagenhufendörfer in Schaumburg-Lippe," *Petermanns geographische Mitteilungen*, IX, Nos. 9–10, 245–47.

1952 *Westfalen: Landschaftliche Ordnung und Bindung eines Landes.* Münster: Aschendorff. 384 pp.

1955 "Agrarbäuerliche Landschaftstypen in Nordwestdeutschland," *Deutscher Geographentag*, XXIX, 179–86. Wiesbaden.

MUNZINGER, H.

1936 "Die Flurbereinigung in Süddeutschland, ihre Geschichte und ihr Stand am 1. Januar. 1935," *Berichte über Landwirtschaft* (N.S.), Vol. CXXIII. Berlin.

NIEHAUS, H.

1933 "Agricultural Conditions and Regions in Germany," *Geographical Review*, XXIII, No. 1, 23–47.

NIEMEIER, G.

1938a "Eschprobleme in Nordwestdeutschland und den östlichen Niederlanden," pp. 27–40 in *Travaux de la Section V, Paysage géographique, Comptes-rendus du Congrès International de Géographie*, Vol. II. Leiden: E. J. Brill. 615 pp.

1938b "Bäuerliche Wohnweise in ihrer Beziehung zur Landschaft und Volkstum," *Geographische Zeitschrift*, XLIV, No. 4, 139–46.

1939 "Die Altersbestimmung der Plaggenböden als kulturgeographisches Problem," *Geographische Anzeiger*, XL, Nos. 9–10, 237–45.

1944 "Gewannfluren," *Petermanns geographische Mitteilungen*, XC, Nos. 3–4, 57–74.

1949 "Frühformen der Waldhufen," *ibid.*, XCIII, 14–27.

NIEMEIER, G., and TASCHENMACHER, W.

1939 "Plaggenböden: Beiträge zur Genetik und Typologie," *Westfälische Forschungen*, II, 29–64.

NIETSCH, H.

1927 "Mitteleuropäischer Urwald," *Zeitschrift der Gesellschaft für Erdkunde Berlin*, pp. 1–16.

1935 *Steppenheide oder Eichenwald: Eine urlandschaftskundliche Untersuchung zum Verständnis der vorgeschichtlichen Siedlung in Mitteleuropa.* Weimar. 81 pp.

1939 *Wald und Siedlung im vorgeschichtlichen Mitteleuropa*, Vol. LXIV. Leipzig: Mannus Bücherei. 254 pp.

OBST, E., and SPREITZER, H.

1939 "Wege und Ergebnisse der Flurforschung im Gebiet der grossen Haufendörfer, *Petermanns geographische Mitteilungen*, LXXXV, No. 1, 1–19.

OTREMBA, E.

1938 *Das Problem der Ackernahrung, untersucht an ausgewählten Beispielen des nördlichen Rhein-Maingebietes.* ("Rhein- Mainische Forschungen," No. 19.) Frankfurt on the Main: H. L. Brönner. 116 pp.

1942 "Die Gliederung der ländlichen Kulturlandschaft in Deutschland," *Zeitschrift für Erdkunde*, X, 513–30.

1951 "Die Entwicklungsgeschichte der Flurformen im oberdeutschen Altsiedellande," *Berichte zur deutschen Landeskunde*, IX, No. 2, 363–82.

1953 *Allgemeine Agrar- und Industriegeographie.* Stuttgart: Frank'sche Verlagsbuchhandlung. 341 pp.

PESSLER, W.

1908 "Die Haustypengebiete im Deutschen Reich," *Deutsche Erde*, VII, 14–22, 45–52.

PFEIFER, G.

1928 *Das Siedlungsbild der Landschaft Angeln.* ("Veröffentlichungen der Schleswig-Holsteinischen Universitätsgesellschaft," No. 17.) Breslau: F. Hirt. 167 pp.

1939–46 "Wirtschaftsgeographie," pp. 175–204 in WISSMANN, H. VON, *Naturforschung und Medizin in Deutsch-*

land, Vol. XLIV: *Geographie*, Part IV. Wiesbaden: Dieterich'sche Verlagsbuchhandlung. 220 pp.

PFEIFER, G., and SCHÜTTLER, A.
1941 "Die kleinräumige Kartierung landwirtschaftlicher Nutzflächen und ihre kulturgeographische Bedeutung," *Petermanns geographische Mitteilungen*, LXXXVII, No. 5, 153–67.

RIEHL, W. H.
1851 "Die bürgerliche Gesellschaft," in *Die Naturgeschichte des Volkes als Grundlage einer deutschen Sozial-Politik*, Vol. II. Stuttgart: J. G. Cotta. 486 pp.
1854 "Land und Leute," in *Die Naturgeschichte des Volkes als Grundlage einer deutschen Sozial-Politik*, Vol. I. Stuttgart and Augsburg: J. G. Cotta. 329 pp.
1857 *Die Pfälzer: Ein rheinisches Volksbild.* Stuttgart and Augsburg: J. G. Cotta. 315 pp. (1st ed., 1857; 3d ed., 1907.)
1859 *Culturstudien aus drei Jahrhunderten.* Stuttgart: J. G. Cotta'feher Verlag. 407 pp.
1869 *Wanderbuch.* Stuttgart: J. G. Cotta. 379 pp.

RIEPENHAUSEN, H.
1938 *Die bäuerliche Siedlung des Ravensberger Landes bis 1770.* ("Arbeiten der geographischen Kommission, Provinzial Institut für Westfälische Landes- und Volkskunde," No. 1.) Münster. 144 pp.

ROSHOP, U.
1932 *Die Entwicklung der ländlichen Siedlungs- und Flurbildes der Grafschaft Diepholz: Eine siedlungsgeographische Studie.* ("Quellen und Darstellungen zur Geschichte Niedersachsens," Vol. XXXIX.) Hildesheim and Leipzig. 104 pp.

SCHARLAU, K.
1933 *Beiträge zur geographischen Betrachtung der Wüstungen* ("Badische geographische Abhandlungen," Vol. X.) Freiburg in Breslau and Heidelberg: Selbstverlag Geographische Institut. 46 pp.
1938 "Zu Frage des Begriffs Wüstung," *Geographischer Anzeiger*, XXXIX, No. 11, 247–52.

1941 *Siedlung und Landschaft im Knüllgebiet: Ein Beitrag zu den kulturgeographischen Problemen Hessens.* ("Forschungen zur deutschen Landeskunde," Vol. XXXVII.) Leipzig: S. Hirzel. 335 pp.
1943 "Die Wüstungen des ausgehenden Mittelalters," *Petermanns geographische Mitteilungen*, LXXXIX, Nos. 9–10, 271–74.
1954 "Die Bedeutung der Pollenanalyse für das Freiland-Wald problem unter besonderer Berücksichtigung der Altlandschaften im hessischen Bergland," *Berichte zur deutschen Landeskunde*, XIII, No. 1, 10–32.

SCHIER, B.
1932 *Hauslandschaften und Kulturbewegungen im östlichen Mitteleuropa.* Reichenberg: F. Kraus. 456 pp.

SCHILLI, H.
1953 *Das Schwarzwaldhaus.* Stuttgart: W. Kohlhammer. 302 pp. (Contains comprehensive bibliography.)

SCHLENGER, H.
1951 "Forschungsprobleme der modernen Siedlungskunde," *Blätter für deutsche Landesgeschichte*, LXXXVIII, 41–72.

SCHLÜTER, O.
1911–13 "Deutsches Siedlungswesen," *Reallexikon der germanischen Altertumskunde*, I, 402–39. Straszburg.
1952 *Die Siedlungsräume Mitteleuropas in frühgeschichtlicher Zeit*, Vol. I: *Einführung in die Methodik der Altlandsforschung.* ("Forschungen zur deutschen Landeskunde," Vol. LXIII.) Hamburg: Atlantik Verlag; Remagen: Paulist und Verlag des Amtes für Landeskunde. 47 pp.
1953 *Die Siedlungsräume Mitteleuropas in frühgeschichtlicher Zeit*, Vol. II: *Erklarung und Begrundung der Darstellung*, Part I: *Das südliche und nordwestliche Mitteleuropa.* ("Forschungen zur deutschen Landeskunde," Vol. LXXIV.) Remagen: Verlag der Bundesanstalt für Landeskunde. 240 pp. (The latest and most comprehensive discussion of pertinent questions by the master of historic geography in Germany. Well-balanced résumé of divergent opinions. Map and bibliography.)

SCHMITHÜSEN, J.
1934 *Der Niederwald des linksrhei-nischen Schiefergebirges.* ("Beiträge zur Landeskunde der Rheinlande," Series II, No. 4.) Bonn: L. Röhrscheid. 106 pp.
1940 *Das luxemburger Land: Landes-natur, Volkstum und bäuerliche Wirt-schaft.* ("Forschungen zur deutschen Landeskunde," Vol. XXXIV.) Leipzig: S. Hirzel. 431 pp.

SCHMITT, O.
1952 *Grundlagen und Verbreitung der Bodenzerstörung im Rhein-Mainge-biet mit einer Untersuchung über Bo-denzerstörung durch Starkregen im Vorspessart.* ("Rhein-Mainische For-schungen," No. 33.) Frankfurt on the Main: M. W. Kramer. 130 pp.

SCHMITTHENNER, H.
1923 "Die Reutbergwirtschaft in Deutschland," *Geographische Zeit-schrift,* XXIX, 115–27.

SCHREPFER, H.
1938 "Zur Geographie des ländlichen Hausbaus in Süddeutschland," *Zeit-schrift für Erdkunde,* VI, No. 1, 236–46.

SCHRÖDER, K. H.
1941 *Die Flurformen in Württemberg und Hohenzollern.* Tübingen: F. Rau. 71 pp.

SCHÜTTLER, A.
1939 *Die Kulturgeographie der mittel-devonischen Eifelkaklgebiete,* Series III, No. 4. Bonn: L. Röhrscheid. 197 pp.

SCHULTZE, J. H.
1951–52 "Über das Verhältnis von De-nudation und Bodenerosion," *Die Erde,* III, 220–33.
1952 *Die Bodenerosion in Thüringen: Wesen, Stärke und Abwehrmöglich-keiten.* ("Petermanns geographische Mitteilungen, Ergänzungs," No. 247.) Gotha: Justus Perthes. 186 pp.

SERING, M.
1908 *Erbrecht und Agrarverfassung in Schleswig-Holstein auf geschichtlicher Grundlage.* ("Die Vererbung des länd-lichen Grundbesitzes im Königreich Preussen," Vol. II, No. 2.) Berlin: E. S. Mitler & Sohn. 588 pp.
1934 *Deutsche Agrarpolitik auf ge-schichtlicher und landeskundlicher*

Grundlage. Leipzig: H. Buske. 194 pp.

SICK, W. D.
1951–52 "Die Vereinödung im nörd-lichen Bodenseegebiet," *Württem-bergische Jahrbücher für Statistik und Landeskunde.*

SIEVERS, A.
1942 "Zu Geographie der landwirt-schaftlichen Betriebsgrössen. I. Eine vergleichende Betrachtung nordost-deutscher Diluviallandschaft," *Berich-te zur Raumforschung und Raumord-nung,* VI, Nos. 4–5, 114–26. Heidel-berg and Berlin.
1944 "Schriftum zur Landwirtschafts-geographie: Ein Überblick über das letzte Jahrzehnt," *ibid.,* XI, 1–63. Leipzig.

SINNHUBER, K.
1954 "Central Europe, Mitteleuropa, Europe Centrale: An Analysis of a Geographical Term," *Transactions and Papers of the Institute of British Geographers,* Publication No. 20, pp. 15–39.

STEINBACH, FR.
1926 *Studien zur westdeutschen Stammes- und Volksgeschichte.* ("Schriften des Instituts für Grenz- und Auslandsdeutschtum, Marburg," Vol. V.) Jena. 180 pp.
1927 "Gewanndorf und Einzelhof," pp. 44–61 in *Historische Aufsätze: Festschrift für A. Schulte.* Düsseldorf: L. Schwann.
1931 "Das Bauernhaus der westdeut-schen Grenzlande," *Rheinische Vier-teljahrsblätter,* I, 26–47.
1937 "Geschichtliche Siedlungsformen in der Rheinprovinz: Aufgaben der Siedlungsgeschichte in der Rhein-provinz," *Zeitschrift des Rheinische Vereins für Denkmalspflege und Heimatkunde,* XXX, 19 ff.

THÜNEN, J. H. VON
1826 *Der isolierte Staat in Beziehung auf Landwirtschaft und National-ökonomie.* Rostock. (Vol. I, 1842, 391 pp.; Vol. II, No. 1, 1850, 285 pp.; Vol. II, No. 2, 1863, 444 pp.)

TRIER, J.
1938 "Das Gefüge des bäuerlichen Hauses im deutschen Nordwesten," *Westfälische Forschungen,* Vol. I.

TÜXEN, R.

1931 "Die Grundlagen der Urlandschaftsforschung: Ein Beitrag zur Erforschung der Geschichte der anthropogenen Beeinflussung der Vegetation Mitteleuropas," *Nachrichten aus Niedersachsens Urgeschichte*, No. 5, pp. 59–105. (With Nietsch and Schott, criticized the classical Gradmann theory and initiated a new phase in the discussion.)

WAIBEL, L.

1933 *Probleme der Landwirtschaftsgeographie*. Breslau: F. Hirt. 94 pp.

WERTH, E.

1954 *Grabstock, Hacke, Pflug*. Ludwigsburg: E. Ulmer. 435 pp.

WITTICH, W.

1896 *Die Grundherrschaft im nordwestlichen Deutschland*. 2 vols. Leipzig: Duncker & Humblot. 461+143 pp.

WÜHRER, K.

1935 *Beiträge zur ältesten Agrargeschichte des germanischen Norden*. Jena: Gustav Fischer. 152 pp.

On the Role of Nature and Man in Changing the Face of the Dry Belt of Asia

HERMANN von WISSMANN*

In Collaboration with H. POECH,† G. SMOLLA,‡ *and* F. KUSSMAUL§

Three subcontinents, green with forest, are divided from one another by the vast desert belt of the Old World: Africa south of the Sahara, Monsoon Asia, and Europe, including Siberia and the Mediterranean lands. The desert barrier as well as the frost line, the utmost limit of frost, which is (in more continental regions) the margin of the tropics (Wissmann, 1948; Coon, 1953), have probably been responsible for dividing humanity during parts of the Quaternary age, so that racial units could develop to some extent in isolation. Did this take place in one, perhaps in the long penultimate interglacial period?

CHANGES OF CLIMATE AND VEGETATION

According to its atmospheric circulation, the Dry Belt can be divided into a trade-wind section from the Atlantic coast to Arabia and a continental or "central" section from southern Russia and Iran to Mongolia. If we follow the thesis of Büdel (1952, 1953), the aridity of the trade-wind section probably was less intense during the last Ice Age, especially on the polar, but also on the equatorial, side. According to him, the steppe vegetation then replaced the semidesert vegetation of today.[1] So the Sahara and the desert of Arabia would have been not quite so effective barriers against human migrations during cold (glacial) periods as they are at present and were during parts of interglacial periods (compare below).

It is different in the continental section of the Dry Belt, that is, in Inner Asia. In this belt, as a whole, humidity

* Dr. von Wissmann is Professor of Geography and head of the department at the University of Tübingen, Germany. He is a corresponding member of the Akademie der Wissenschaften und Literatur in Mainz, the Akademie der Wissenschaften in Vienna, and the Akademie für Naturforscher (Leopoldina) in Halle. Of the latter he is recipient of the Carus Medal. He is recipient of the Carl Ritter Medal of the Gesellschaft für Erdkunde zu Berlin. He was professor of geography of the National Central University of China in Nanking from 1931 to 1937 and was on the staff of the Academia Sinica. He has made expeditions to different parts of China, especially Yunnan, as well as to southern Arabia (1927, 1931, 1939).

† Dr. Hella Poech is an anthropologist of the school of R. Poech, Vienna, at present living in Sumbawa, Indonesia.

‡ Dr. G. Smolla is Dozent and the scientific assistant in the Department of Prehistory, University of Tübingen.

§ Dr. F. Kussmaul is a curator of the Linden-Museum of Ethnology in Stuttgart.

1. The thesis maintained by Penck (1913), Klute (1930), Wissmann (1952), Willett (1953), and others, that during the last Ice Age the humid tropics were narrower in the west of the continents and the dry trade-wind belts shifted toward the equator, seems to be wrong. Flohn's considerations (1952, 1953) on atmospheric circulation during the last Ice Age should be compared here. They support Büdel's thesis in the trade-wind zone (1949, 1952, 1953).

was not much different from that of to-day.[2] It was somewhat lower in Central Europe and Hungary (Poser, 1948; Büdel, 1949; Wilhelmy, 1950; Frenzel and Troll, 1952), as well as in China (Wissmann, 1938). In both cases this lower humidity certainly depended on the eustatic regression of the seas (the North Sea, the seas round the British Isles, the Adriatic Sea, the Yellow Sea, and the East and the South China seas). By this regression the land masses became rounded off and more extensive than they are now. Thus Europe and China became more continental. Bobek (1953–54) supposes that even Turan was a little more arid than today, in spite of its terminal lakes being enlarged. According to his experience in Iran, he concludes that, in this country, precipitation was equal or even less than at present, so that, owing to lower temperatures, humidity was but slightly higher. Therefore, while vegetation was much the same as today (not taking the lowering of timber line into consideration), the runoff was stronger, and the terminal lakes showed higher levels, owing to reduced evaporation. The climate was more fluvial but not more pluvial (*ibid.*). Louis (1938, 1939) came to similar conclusions for the interior of Asia Minor, as did Picard (1938) for Syria.[3] According to Zeuner (1953), India had drier periods but no moister ones in the Upper Pleistocene and showed about the same distribution of humidity during the last glaciation as it does today.

In Figure 84 a synopsis is given of the vegetation in northern Eurasia during the last glaciation. This figure is based on Büdel's map (1949; Hack, 1953) for Europe, on my map (Wissmann, 1938)

for China, and on Frenzel and Troll's map (1952) for the U.S.S.R. area. The latter utilizes extensive Russian literature. Figure 84 differs strongly from that of Frenzel and Troll as regards the extent of glaciation in northeastern and central Asia, following the results of my studies on the snow line of Asia at present and in the Ice Ages (1956, MS). For Syria the map is based on Gradmann (1934, 1943) and Picard (1938); for Asia Minor, on Louis (1939); and for Persia and its surroundings, on Bobek (1951, 1952, 1953–54). The source material is of unequal value; the map represents a preliminary attempt. However, when compared with a map of the present climate or vegetation, it shows clearly that the boundaries of the thermal zones, especially the timber line, were displaced over much greater distances than the boundaries of the humidity zones, for example, the border of arable steppe and desert steppe, or the transition between forest and wooded steppe. After all, it is evident that the last Ice Age area of the Dry Belt of Inner Asia and its contours were much like those of the present day, while the area of the tundra and the northern timber line underwent a very striking change. The present large coniferous forest belt of Europe and western Siberia was more or less removed. It nearly disappeared by the swift advance of the tundra toward the wooded steppe margin, which remained almost in its original position. In the west of the continent, forest was reduced to the

2. Because of the reduction in temperature, evaporation was reduced and, by this, precipitation. Humidity is precipitation minus evaporation (evapotranspiration). In the continental Dry Belt precipitation, as well as evaporation, must have been much lower than at present (Klute, 1951).

3. However, Wright (1951) concludes, from geomorphologic reasons (accelerated stream deposition associated with eustatic low sea level), that there was a moister period at the time of the Paleolithic (last Ice Age) site of Ksar 'Akil on the slope of Lebanon toward the Mediterranean Sea. Yet, accelerated stream deposition here may better be explained by the fact that solifluction was spread in the higher slopes. According to Bobek (1953–54), the lower line of extension of solifluction was depressed 700 meters (2,300 feet) in Iran in this period.

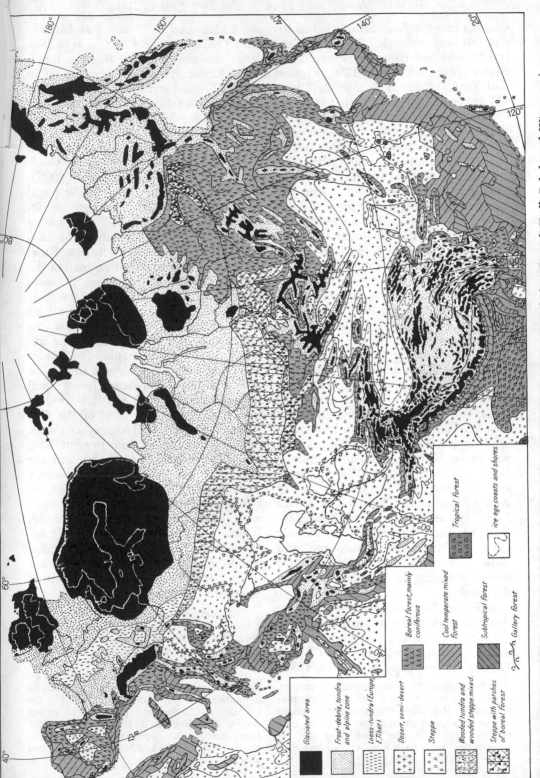

FIG. 84.—The vegetation of Eurasia, except its south, during the last Ice Age. (After Frenzel, Troll, Bobek, and Wissmann.)

Legend:

- Glaciated area
- Frost-debris, tundra and alpine zone
- Loess-tundra (Europe E.Tibet)
- Desert, semi-desert
- Steppe
- Wooded tundra and wooded steppe mixed.
- Steppe with patches of boreal forest
- Boreal forest, mainly coniferous
- Cool temperate mixed forest
- Subtropical forest
- Gallery forest
- Tropical forest
- ice age coasts and shores

Mediterranean belt. In Monsoon Asia, however, its area did not become much smaller than it is now, except in the utmost northeast and around the fog-bound Sea of Okhotsk.[4]

The snow line was lowered about 1,200 meters in western Europe and the northwestern Alps as well as in monsoonal eastern and southeastern Tibet, and about 1,000 meters on the western front of the Pamirs. But it was lowered only 300 meters[5] and even less in central Tibet; so glaciation was not much more extensive there than today, in contrast with the Himalayas, which were strongly glaciated, with the glaciers of the main valleys coming down into the forest.[6]

Perennially frozen subsoil now covering Siberia east of the Yenisei, the U.S.S.R. Far East, and northeastern Mongolia, and strong inversions of winter (and night) temperatures in the lowlands and basins, which are now found in those regions (Flohn, 1947), were then spread as far as western Germany, Hungary (Poser, 1947; Weischet, 1954), and probably to large parts of central Asia.[7]

Temperatures seem to have been about 5°– 7° C. lower than at present as a global mean during the culmination of the last Ice Age (correspondence with Flohn; cf. Bobek, 1953–54). But in postglacial periods they were about 2° C. higher during the "Thermal Maximum," about 5500–2500 B.C., which is the middle phase of a period, which was warmer than before and after

("Postglaziale Wärmezeit") and extended from about 6800 B.C. to about 800 B.C. (Firbas, 1949; Smolla, 1953). For the climate of this warm period in northern Eurasia, three recent papers, including maps, are of importance: Neistadt on Russia (1953), Frenzel on northern Eurasia (1955), and Bobek on Iran (1953–54). The position of the northern timber line was shifted approximately 200–500 kilometers northward of this line today, so that mostly there was but a narrow rim of tundra, including wooded tundra, on the peninsular parts of the Arctic coasts of northern Russia and of the Far East of the U.S.S.R. In the mountains of Central Europe, especially in the Alps, as well as in the Karakoram Mountains (Visser, 1935), the timber line was located at least 400 meters higher than it is today.

In comparison with the temperature curve of climate, the fluctuations of humidity seem to have been comparatively small also in postglacial periods, and, therefore, they are much more difficult to establish. They often seem to run inversely in two zones adjacent to each other. It seems that the Thermal Maximum was a global phenomenon, just as was the last Ice Age and its last culmination, which has to be dated about 13000–9000 B.C. For the Thermal Maximum (5000–2500 B.C.), Bobek's considerations (1953–54) come to the conclusion that the climate of Iran and the Fertile Crescent was somewhat more arid than it is now. This, however, does

---

4. The area lost to the steppe in China and Manchuria was balanced by the area gained because of the eustatic regression of the Yellow Sea and the East and the South China seas.

5. These values for the snow-line depression are the differences between the last Ice Age snow line and the present one.

6. It seems that the southern rim of the High Himalayas has been lifted several hundred meters by tilting and probably overthrusting since the last Ice Age.

7. It probably is not accurate to speak of *the* culmination of the last Ice Age, for this long period had different culminating points. As in the United States (Flint, 1953), where the frontal moraines of the last Ice Age belong to an earlier substage in the more continental region west of the Mississippi than in the more oceanic East, new investigations of Graul (1956) show that, along the northern front of the Alps, the more one proceeds from the continental east to the oceanic west, the more the frontal moraines belong to younger substages.

not mean that precipitation must have been necessarily lower at that time.[8]

When reconstructing a previous climate, one has always to take into consideration that the effects of precipitation, evapotranspiration, and the duration of annual humid and arid periods are bound to be proportionally different for the discharge of rivers, for the rising and sinking of levels of terminal lakes, for river load, river-grading, and pediment slope than they are for the boundaries of the different graduations of vegetation and soil between forest and desert. We should also remember that a higher amount of precipitation is needed to obtain the same index of humidity in a warm climate than is needed in a cool climate. Pollen diagrams and a careful study of fossil soils are of decisive importance for a reconstruction of former climatic and vegetational conditions.

It has been our concern to show that the shifting of temperature belts between the culmination of the last Ice Age and the Thermal Maximum stretched over much greater distances than the shifting of humidity zones and that the fluctuations of humidity were relatively small, at least in the continental part of the Dry Belt. Thin populations of hunters and even those of steppe farmers, who were more livestock-breeders than agriculturalists (cf. below), could easily adapt themselves by means of migrations over short distances to such a small shifting of humidity zones. A crowded population engaged in rain agriculture without much irrigation, as, for example, in northwestern China, is always the worst off. A change of humidity (aridity) in Inner Asia, in the amounts known, cannot be made solely responsible for such migrations as are known in history, which ranged over enormous distances and even crossed the continent.

Pollen diagrams may mislead. In the subtropical and temperate belt the shaded slopes have a vegetation of the adjacent moister zone; a pollen diagram here may represent this "aclimatical"

8. The period of the Thermal Maximum (between *ca.* 5500 and 2500 B.C.) seems to have been somewhat more humid than today in the east of the United States and in Western and Central Europe, but also in Egypt (Deevey, 1953; Huzayyin, 1941, and the next chapter; Firbas, 1949). It seems, however, to have been somewhat more arid in Turan (Tolstow, 1953), with southern winds prevailing then, and in Iran (Bobek, 1953–54), including the borders of Mesopotamia. Bobek gives a list of the sites of this period and their present approximate precipitation. Wright gives a sketch map and description (1952) of the agricultural site of Jarmo of the fifth millennium in the foothills of northeastern Mesopotamia, excavated by Braidwood. Wright suggests that there was a period drier than before and after then. His argument applies the geomorphological hypothesis of Bryan (1941). The period of the site was one of dissection. But the dependence of river-grading upon climate is a very complex problem (Bobek, 1953–54). It is questionable whether Bryan's hypothesis is appropriate here. Wright estimates the present annual rainfall of Jarmo at about 16 inches (400 mm.), i.e., about 3 inches (80 mm.) more than on the marginal line of potential rain agriculture (Bobek's estimate is 500 mm.). The location of the Jarmo site shows that it could not have had irrigation. As the temperatures in that period must have been about 2° C. warmer, and, therefore, evaporation stronger, it seems that precipitation was not less than today. The same amount of precipitation in a warmer climate, however, would mean a lower degree of humidity.

Tolstow (1953) states that in the middle phase of the third millennium, the climate of the Amu Darya Delta into Lake Aral became cooler and moister. Until that time, he states, southern winds had prevailed, while northern winds have prevailed since.

The sudden "deterioration" of climate in Central and northern Europe about 800 B.C., with decrease of temperature and increase of rainfall, was most probably contemporary with a decrease of rainfall in the Mediterranean area, including Hungary (cf. Smolla, 1953).

In southern Russia the climate of the first stage of the warm period ("boreal," *ca.* 6500–5000 B.C.) was probably about as arid as in the last Ice Age and somewhat more arid than at present. It became more humid after the beginning of the Thermal Maximum (Gerasimov, 1946; Neistadt, 1953; Frenzel, 1955).

vegetation. Besides, pollen is spread over far distances. On the other hand, forest vegetation with a dry season, as well as a wooded steppe vegetation, will often be transformed into grassland by fire, especially in a period of more advanced hunters and of planters, farmers, and cattle-breeders (Sauer, 1952, pp. 15, 100).

HERDING STEPPE FARMERS AND IRRI-
GATING FARMERS CONQUER
THE DRY BELT

In his book *Agricultural Origins and Dispersals* (1952) Sauer comes to the conclusion that in all probability the seat of the origin of planting (not of sowing) and of the domestic animals belonging to the human settlements, especially the dog, pig, and fowl (not herd animals), was situated in the moist tropics, on the riverbanks and coasts of southern Asia around the Bay of Bengal. Sauer looked for the progenitors in an unspecialized, sedentary fishing folk, with water communications, who, in addition, hunted and collected waterside plants. Werth arrives at similar results (1954) by a different method. My concise attempt (1946) to interpret the changes of significance for man of the subcontinental geographical units of the Old World, while not entirely free of misjudgments, arrived at similar conclusions.

It is a lucky coincidence that two scholars of the younger generation who have been engaged in research at Tübingen furnished me with extremely valuable contributions to the present theme. G. Smolla, a prehistorian, dealt (1955) in a cautious, judicious, and responsible way with the beginning of several important Neolithic traits of culture in the Old World. He included an examination of the questions concerning the beginning of the cultivation of plants and the domestication of animals. F. Kussmaul, a historical ethnologist, gave (1953) enlightening contributions

to our knowledge of the early history of the Inner Asiatic nomadic horsemen.

Smolla placed at my disposal some provisional results of his comprehensive research as follows:

The importance which C. Sauer attached to coastal fishermen and mussel-collectors for the origin and spread of planting gains even more in probability when considered in combination with archeological, climatological, and ethnological phenomena. Shell mounds (kitchen middens), with their world-wide distribution, seem to have been in many places destroyed either by the surf during the eustatic drowning of coasts of the postglacial age of increasing temperatures or by the tectonic sinking of coastal areas. The result is that those areas of shell mounds remaining must represent only a fraction of their former extent and distribution. At a time when only hunters and food-gatherers lived in the hinterland of the coast, these coastal peoples enjoyed a certain cultural ascendancy, since an assured supply of the basic foodstuffs allowed them fixed residence and relatively high population density.[9]

This old stratum of fishermen and mussel-collectors was important not only for the origin of planting but also, to a large extent, for the swift spread of several culture traits (from what can be gathered from prehistorical research), such as household animals (cf. Sauer), e.g., the dog and, to a lesser extent, the pig, but, above all, of ground stone axes and, later on, pottery.

The region of origin of tuber-planting in humid southern Asia, postulated by Sauer and others, cannot yet be proved archeologically. There has hardly, of course, been any intensive research in this direction, and

9. However, since the time when there were tribes in the hinterland with a productive food economy, the coastal inhabitants were mostly culturally amalgamated with the inland tribes. These later specialized fishing peoples may not, therefore, be lumped together with the fishermen and mussel-gatherers of the earlier period. Only at a few places, where the hinterland was unfavorable for a productive type of farming, could some rather poor survivals of this older stratum maintain themselves. This fact explains why they have scarcely been considered by ethnologists.

the remains of such cultivation would have to be searched for mostly under later delta deposits of rivers, in so far as they have not completely disappeared due to eustatic rising of the sea level. If there were not quite extraordinary conditions for their preservation—which are, in fact, difficult to imagine in tropical forest areas—the only survival of the culture of such planters was their stone industry, which probably was of a very primitive kind. The lack of archeological proof for these earliest planter tribes does not, therefore, speak against their former existence. Ethnographers, anthropologists and human geographers, botanists, and zoölogists should attempt to examine this question anew. The archeologist can maintain only that no discoveries are against such an argument and that, by using it, several phenomena become understandable which before were inexplicable.

The beginnings of this early science of planting may then be assumed to have been approximately at the time of the last culmination of the last glacial period, parallel to the western European Magdalenian (*ca.* 13000–9000 B.C.). The spread of these cultural phenomena, which developed from this region over vast areas, must, therefore, have taken place shortly before and during the postglacial Thermal Maximum, above all, in the seventh to fifth millenniums B.C. This spread must have been particularly swift among the coastal fishermen and mussel-gatherers. The further extension of planting into faraway zones lasted, of course, many thousands of years more.

The fact that the coastal belt from India, over southern Arabia, to East Africa, with its dry climate, and thence along the banks of the Nile must have been an early road for migration, not merely a passage along which new cultural "inventions" and goods were disseminated, results from the new anthropological research by Poech (MS), evaluating, among other materials, that of our expeditions in southern Arabia. She recognizes that two races, the Gondid and the Aethiopid, which both belong to the large family of "Europid" races, are to be found in India as well

as in southern Arabia and in parts of East and North Africa.

Especially of importance here is the distribution of the Gondid race. It is dominant and numerous in parts of central India. But people of the Gondid race are also frequent in southern Arabia, Nubia (Barabra), and Egypt (cf. Fig. 85). On the Nubian Nile (Koro sho), a population of this race can be traced back as far as the Old Empire. Among the Egyptian sculptures of this period, we find clerks and officials of the Gondid race. Even the Berbers of northwestern Africa include elements of it. In all regions of their distributions

H. Poech

FIG. 85.—Three women of the Gondid race *From left to right:* Tunisia, Yemen Highland, central India.

the people of the Gondid race belong to a busy agricultural population.[10]

It has to be emphasized that the above-mentioned races are only two out

10. As this race was not distinctly defined by von Eickstedt (1931–32), we give a description by Poech:

"According to south Arabian material, the people of the Gondid race show markedly Europid forms, with a total lack of prognathy. They have a slender and strong body with smooth and rounded forms. Their skin is of a light brown color. Their eyes are dark brown. The rich and wavy hair is black. Men have their hair floating down to the shoulder. The outline of the face, which is more or less broad, is oval. Their cheeks are full and rounded. Noses are narrow, straight, high, and of medium length. Their tips are pointed. The integumental upper lip is concave, and the mouth is not very big. The lips are rather thick. The vertical height of the lower jaw is short. The contours of the lower jaw converge in a more or less acute angle. In profile, the chin protrudes, softly rounded. The smooth features of the Gondid face may be of a gentle beauty."

of a rather great number of races sorted out by Poech in southern Arabia. As a matter of fact, most of the other races of this country are also found in other parts of the Middle East and Europe.

We go on to follow the exposition of Smolla:

The domestication of sheep and goats and the cultivation of grain were probably begun in the wooded steppe and steppe areas of northwestern India and the adjoining western Asiatic mountain regions during the sixth millennium B.C. at the very latest. For several reasons it is probable that the impulse which stimulated the transition to these new forms of production came from tuber-planting. Naturally enough, this cannot at the moment be proved archeologically. It is, however, possible that the cultivation of several small-seeded cereals, which we comprehend under the term "millet," forms the point of transition between tuber-planting and cereal-crop farming. Perhaps the round-butted ax (*Walzenbeil*), which serves as a connecting link between India and northern China, belonged originally to such a period of early millet farming in the wooded steppe regions of northern and western China.[11]

Forms of cereal farming combined with the herding of sheep and goats, and then of cattle, which seem to have been domesticated somewhat later, spread quickly over parts of the Old World. Beside rainfall agriculture, elementary types of irrigation and oasis economy were known at a very early period from Iran to Syria. This can be deduced from the fact that Jericho and other early agricultural sites show a

11. "Another question arises: Was it the case, perhaps, that in this early period a stream of culture proceeded westward from China through the natural oases of what later became the silk road, finally arriving as far as Central Europe, spreading the round-butted ax, and perhaps also *Panicum miliaceum* (proso millet), *Fagopyrum* (buckwheat), and *Setaria italica* (foxtail millet)? (For later movements from east to west of a fishing and hunting population through the northern belt of wooded steppe and through the taiga forest belt at the beginning of the second millennium B.C. see Jettmar, 1954*b*)."

marked desert climate and certainly cannot have had any rain agriculture as shown by their early excavated periods.

The ancient civilizations of the Near East—western Iran, northern Mesopotamia, Syria, Palestine, and Egypt—derived from this farming and herding culture. About 3000 B.C., with the invention of writing, they were completely developed. Among the first Sumerian characters we find a portrayal of the plow, the first known document of this tool. Since the townlike settlements, temple buildings, etc., began at an earlier date, the beginning of civilization (*Hochkultur*) will have to be dated back to the start of the fourth millennium B.C. In Jericho an early stratum has been discovered in which pottery was still unknown, yet which had already developed into a large type of settlement, surrounded by a town wall. Therefore, the lower strata of the southwestern Asiatic tells already represent early forms of the beginning of a civilization which led to the invention of the plow and of highly developed systems of irrigation.

This earliest phase of civilization obviously exerted its influence over a wide area, for it would be difficult to understand a large part of the development of the Neolithic on the Balkan Peninsula and in Central Europe, were we not to consider influences from this phase.

Geographically, this rise, spread, and development of cultures, which invented ways to put plants and animals into their service, may be hypothetically summarized approximately as follows.

In large parts of the Old World there was an early sedentary unspecialized fishing folk with varied occupations and a hinterland of roaming collectors and hunters. It spread along coasts and riverbanks, partly by means of primitive vessels. In the regions inhabited by such a fishing population, in humid tropical southern Asia, the planting of tubers and the domestication of dogs and pigs originated during the period of approximately 13000–9000 B.C. This unspecialized fishing population living along the widespread ribbons of coasts and river-banks passed on the spark of the new "inventions" of planting and domestication. At first, the monsoonal forests of southeastern Asia were penetrated. In areas which were seasonally inundated, taro root was planted and, at a later stage, rice. Then, in transitional areas between these monsoonal forests and the wooded steppes of India, of Burma, and of western and northern China, the sowing and cropping of small-seeded grains of the wooded steppe (i.e., of the so-called "millets") seem to have begun. This meant a penetration of a food-producing culture and economy into drier regions, into wooded and other arable steppes, and, by this, an increasing density of population in these regions. Then, somewhere among hunters of the Indo-Iranian border ranges, the breeding of sheep and goats was "invented." It is an open question whether an impulse came from those early food-producing and domesticating populations of the riverside, tropical forest, and steppe with which we just have dealt. But it is plausible that there really was some stimulus from this source.

Then, among tribes growing millets and herding sheep and goats, somewhere between Turan and Syria, grasses with larger seeds were cultivated for the first time, with grains which it was possible to store (i.e., wheat and barley). Yet, the high mountains of eastern and western Iran, which are surrounded by tillable steppes, are divided from one another by a broad zone with almost no land fit for rain agriculture, even in the mountains, which are lower than those to the east and west. But this intermediate zone was rich in natural oases along the foot of its mountains. Therefore, it is probable that a primitive kind of irrigation (which enabled storage) was already carried out at the time when wheat and barley were first sown. For in a period which was drier than today (Bobek, 1953–54) rain agriculture without irrigation could not have easily crossed this dry zone. The same population may also have begun to domesticate wild cattle, not in the driest regions, as cattle are not suited to the desert steppe, but in wooded land around the forest margin of the mountains. Thus Iran and its surroundings fostered a farming, herding, and hunting people, for which a light pedocal soil, easily prepared, is convenient. Such types of soil can be found in open country of steppe and wooded steppe, or in light forest, as well as in natural oases of the desert, where irrigation may easily be carried out.

Two main ways of living could branch off from this stage of culture. One, based on irrigation and the storage of grains, led to larger settlements with brick buildings and, further, to the founding of the earliest form of civilization (cf. Wittfogel, p. 152 above). In the other mode of life, herding was, besides hunting, at least as important as grain-growing. Between the light forest and the margin of arable steppe, especially in the wooded steppes, this way of life of a herding farmer or farming herdsman spread far over large parts of the Dry Belt and its surroundings of light forest, becoming more pastoral here, more agricultural there, according to the vegetational circumstances. In most cases, it seems, there was no sharp tribal separation between agriculturalist and herdsman. Cain and Abel were brothers. We may call this a "steppe-farming" culture and economy. Besides these two branches of farming, a herding nomadism with sheep (and goats) not only may have branched off from steppe farming but also seems to have spread independently from its earliest source (cf. Jettmar, 1954b; Kussmaul, 1952–53).

Along the coasts from India westward and along the Mediterranean coasts as far as the Atlantic Ocean, all of which are drier than those of monsoonal southern Asia, the old culture of fishing peoples, impregnated with the cultural achievements of the tuber-planters and breeders of household animals, was combined in various ways with the other "producing," no longer "collecting," cultures developed in the Dry Belt, which we mentioned above. In tropical Africa a new selecting and molding of these elements took place under climatic, vegetational, racial, and spatial circumstances different from those in Asia. Yemen and Abyssinia be-

(black in Fig. 86). This middle belt stretches from Morocco and Spain to northern China. It is in this belt—from desert to semihumid climate—that natural oases and irrigation became, and still are, of the greatest importance, especially along the foot of mountain chains (cf. Gradmann, 1934). Toward the east this belt becomes ever narrower. In Kansu there is only one chain of oases. But, at its eastern end, it bulges out, forming the wooded steppes of northern China. In the west it is in-

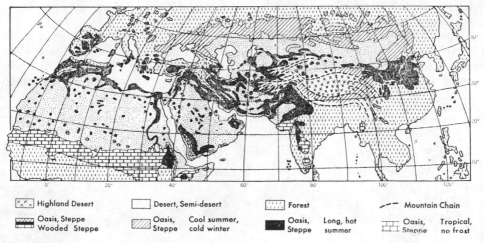

Highland Desert   Desert, Semi-desert   Forest   Mountain Chain
Oasis, Steppe Wooded Steppe   Oasis, Steppe Cool summer, cold winter   Oasis, Steppe Long, hot summer   Oasis, Steppe Tropical, no frost

H. von Wissmann

Fig. 86.—Oases and steppe regions of the Dry Belt of the Old World, classified according to their thermal conditions.

came a secondary nucleus, where cultivation and domestication began of new plants and animals, such as the donkey and probably the tall tropical millets (perhaps sorghum, most probably *Pennisetum*).

The Dry Belt of the Old World, over which farming and herding spread, can be divided into three temperature belts (Fig. 86).

The region between southern Turan and Syria, in which the growing of large-grained cereals and the breeding of herd animals took its origin, lies in the center of the *middle belt*, a region of long, hot summers and short winters

dented, in a lucky way, as we may say, with the Mediterranean coasts and light forests.

West of Yemen and Abyssinia the *southern belt* of tropical steppe of the Sudan has conditions of its own kind but not dissimilar to those of peninsular India.

The *northern belt* of steppes (cf. Fig. 86) runs from Manchuria and northern Mongolia to Kazakhstan, southern Russia, and Rumania. In Hungary and Central Europe it ebbs away in dispersed islands of wooded steppe surrounded by oak and hornbeam forest. Like the other two belts, this belt must have made excellent hunting ground too. Yet, for primitive agricultural people used to winter crops, the climate of this northern belt becomes more severe from west to east. In this direction winters become harder and longer, and the snow cover gets thinner and scarcer, until finally the belt ends in the region of perennially frozen subsoil. In the whole of this northern belt, summers are too cool in the west and too short in the east to yield good, or several, crops sufficient to make intensive and laborious irrigation worthwhile. The milder winters of the westernmost wooded steppes of this belt, however, as well as the light oak forest on the loessal soil of Central Europe, which is easily tilled, favored the spreading there of winter cereals from southwestern Asia. The

"Danubian" culture (*Bandkeramiker*), in which agriculture was important or even predominant, seems to have already reached Germany in the fourth millennium B.C., when the temperature was about 2° C. warmer than it is today.

As to the question of the spreading of herding and agriculture into the steppes of the northern belt, from the middle of the third millennium to about 2000 B.C., Russian archeology has collected much material by excavation, which has been dealt with carefully by Jettmar (1945b, 1954c; cf. Fig. 89, p. 298).

In the Amur region the short summers are hot and must have been even somewhat hotter in those periods. Therefore, one might suppose that proso

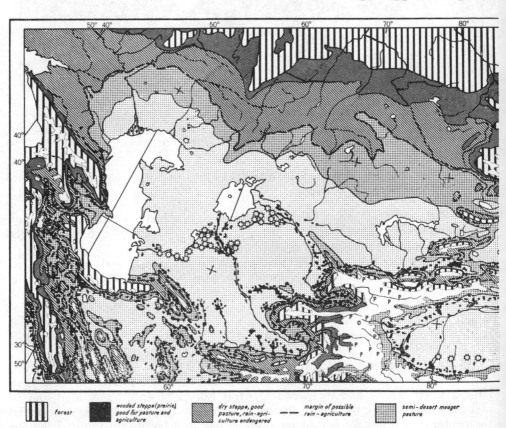

| |||| forest | ▨ wooded steppe (prairie) good for pasture and agriculture | ▨ dry steppe, good pasture, rain-agriculture endangered | – – – margin of possible rain-agriculture | ▦ semi-desert meager pasture |

FIG. 87.—The zones of vegetation and

millet and buckwheat as summer crops came to the Amur area from the south before herding came in. But up to now no evidence of that kind has been discovered.

Figure 87 shows the zones of vegetation of the continental part of the Dry Belt running from southern Russia to Manchuria. Between dense forest vegetation and full desert there are three zones to be distinguished: (1) the wooded steppe, which is good for agriculture and pasture; (2) the open steppe, which is good pasture and is still arable (where, however, rain agriculture is endangered by dry years); and (3) the desert steppe or semidesert with meager pasture. It is probable that, in regions where the third of these zones is broad, an independent shep-

herd nomadism was preserved or branched off from the steppe-farming economy (with sheep and goats in the southern and central belts [Fig. 86, p. 287], and with sheep only in the northern belt). But it appears that such a nomadic shepherd folk always lived an impoverished life compared with the farming and herding tribes of the moister zones or of regions interspersed with oases.[12] Good pasture is found in the Tien Shan, in the Pamirs, and especially in eastern and southern Tibet above the cereal line. But it must be remembered that this line was several hundred meters, perhaps 400 meters, higher than today. (Painted pottery was

12. Such tribes may be only partly nomadic, a part of the tribes being agricultural, a part ranging as shepherds ("Teil-Nomadismus").

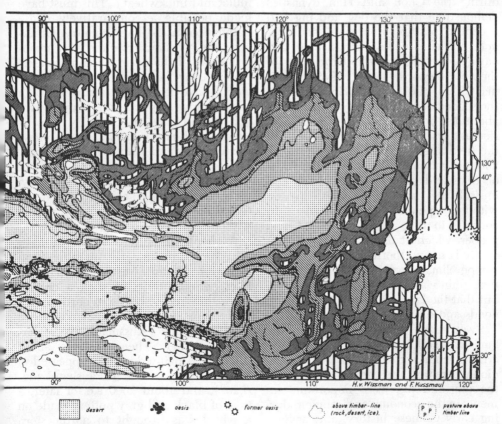

desert	oasis	former oasis	above timber-line (rock, desert, ice).	pasture above timber line

H. v. Wissman and F. Kussmaul

he oases of the Dry Belt of Inner Asia

found near the Ch'ing-hai [Kuku Nor].) Nevertheless, a shepherd culture can be clearly distinguished at the beginning of the northeastern Tibetan culture (Hermanns, 1949; Kussmaul, 1953).

Figures 84, 86, and 87 show clearly that China north of the Hwai River is the easternmost outpost of the middle steppe belt with long hot summers. These long summers mean that two crops can be grown in one year on the same field if water is sufficiently available. In Manchuria the summers are too short for this. Southern China, with its moist subtropical forest and its net of navigable rivers, is broadly connected with the forests of southern Asia, the cradle of planting and of the breeding of household animals, according to Sauer. Descriptions of southern China during the Chou and Han dynasties demonstrate that the dog and pig had a central position in the religious beliefs of many tribes, and fishing and navigation were important for many of them (Eberhard, 1942a, 1942c). Ssŭ-ma Ch'ien, the Chinese Herodotus, in the second century B.C. wrote as follows about the forested south: "People eat rice and make a soup of fish. They till the field after burning, or cultivate by flood-irrigation(?). Thanks to the fruits of trees and plants and to snails and mussels they have sufficient to live on without depending on merchants." In contrast to this, he states that China proper, which at that time was still restricted to northern China with its steppe climate, was densely populated, that grain was grown and stored there, but that the land was often harassed by floods and droughts.

Even in the primitive culture of the Suchen, who lived in the forests of eastern Manchuria, that is, north of the region where taro and yams can be grown, the dog and pig were important elements in the economy and religion, during early Chinese history, and navigation was developed (Eberhard, 1942a;

Kussmaul, 1953). All this supports the thesis of Sauer—that food-producing and domesticating of household animals had its origin in the monsoonal forests of southern Asia. Jettmar, using recent Russian and Swedish literature, shows (1954a) that at the beginning of the second millennium B.C. there must have already been a kind of traffic carried on by a fishing and hunting population, connecting Manchuria with the river net of the forests of Siberia and Russia even as far as Gotland in the Baltic Sea.

Our hypothesis has been already mentioned that, as in India, so in northern China, the growing of "millets" allowed the food-producing economy to leave the forests and enter the wooded steppes (proso, foxtail, and barnyard millet and buckwheat). This must have made possible a comparatively dense population in the loess country. Otherwise, the invasions from the west, mainly by way of the narrow chain of oases, which later became the "silk road," would have led to the formation of a prevailingly Inner Asian people, language, and race in China, which, of course, did *not* happen. The Chinese of the Chou and Han dynasties would, for instance, have drunk milk. It is not surprising that, up to the present day, no archeological traces have been detected of such a millet-growing people without pottery and cattle.

A shepherd culture seems to have been spread by an early migration from the west to northwestern China. For later periods, traits of such a culture are mainly recognizable in northeastern Tibet, especially in its grasslands above the timber line (Kussmaul, 1953; Hermanns, 1949). Then, perhaps about 2300 B.C., a painted pottery appeared in northwestern China ("Panshan-Yangshao"), and about 2000 B.C. or later, a type of black and gray pottery made on a wheel was brought to northeastern China ("Lungshan"). The latter was still contemporary with late phases of the painted pottery of more westerly parts of northern China.[13] The appearance of both these types of pottery must represent at least two invasions along the narrow chain of oases in Sinkiang and Kansu. The invading populations derived their culture from much earlier periods in Iran and its surroundings. The first probably brought cattle, wheat, and irrigation, as well as certain lunar and chthonic beliefs to northern China (Kussmaul, 1953). All this was superimposed upon the culture of the old millet-growing population, who were related to the peoples of the forest in race, language, habits, and belief.

In my opinion the work of Kussmaul (1953) has strongly confirmed the interpretation that the beginning of the Shang Dynasty, about 1500 B.C., signifies an invasion of a people of Aryo-Iranian culture through the narrow central Asian chain of oases. Kussmaul can prove this statement mainly by a new arrangement of the extensive and important ethnological material in old Chinese literature compiled by Eberhard (1942a, 1942b, 1942c). Though Eberhard formerly opposed this interpretation, which had been a supposition of many scholars before (cf. Bishop, 1932), he has informed us that he now shares Kussmaul's opinion. In the cultural complex brought by the Shang to China, the horse, the war chariot, and bronze were of special importance, as well as the belief in the Indo-Aryan god of sun and heaven. This and the old chthonic belief united to form a dualistic creed. Mythology and tradition show this distinctly. The Chou, who appeared in northwestern China

about 1200 B.C., in the west of the Shang empire, and replaced the Shang about 1050 B.C., augmented and intensified the Aryo-Iranian cultural elements in Chinese civilization.

Although it would fit into the framework of our general thesis, we cannot, in this paper, follow the spread in many directions of the Indo-Europeans ("Aryans") and of the war-chariot tradition, out of the western part of the Inner Asiatic Dry Belt (Childe, 1926). But we must state that these Indo-Europeans, as far as they had not become oasis farmers, were what we have called steppe farmers above. As these were herdsmen, hunters, and farmers at the same time (though they may have included groups which led only one of these ways of life), they probably displayed more "nomadic" traits during their migrations and invasions. Nevertheless, it is most misleading to call them nomads. It is clearly recognizable, for instance, that the Aryans entering India and probably destroying the Harappa civilization were steppe farmers.

Excavations in the Shang capital in China have revealed that a fully developed pictographic script was used as early as 1300 B.C. In addition, the Shang empire shows many other civilizational elements which must have been stimulated from the early town civilizations of southwestern Asia or northwestern India (e.g., its priest kingdom). However, although the culture of the Shang was mainly Indo-Iranian, it cannot have been a steppe-farming culture. The Tarim Basin and its approaches to China, which were the only way of access to China from the west, are so dry that they cannot and could not support a steppe-farming population. Yet oases could be developed there because of the rivers coming from the high surrounding mountains. So the Shang, as well as the "Lungshan" and "Panshan-Yangshao" people, must have been irrigating oasis farmers when intruding

13. The date of "Panshan" given here is intermediate between that of Jettmar (1954a, 1954b, 1954c) and that of Loehr (1952). The dates of Jettmar are adapted to a new chronological arrangement of A. P. Okladnikov, who at present is the best expert of the archeology of Siberia.

into China. We do not know which of them brought the stimuli of script, priest kingdom, and other attributes of civilization.[14]

At the beginning of the Chou Dynasty the southern frontier of the feudal empire ran almost exactly along the margin between wooded steppe and forest (Wissmann, 1940).

EQUESTRIAN NOMADIZATION[15]

The herding and hunting culture of the northern steppe belt in the second millennium B.C. was, even in its eastern section, not without agricultural elements. At first the share of agriculture may have been but a small one, difficult to evaluate. But by and by it must have become quite essential. At least since the middle third of the second millennium B.C., we may call the whole wooded-steppe zone of this belt a zone of steppe farmers (Kussmaul, 1953). The farther east we go, the more this status holds true, as we shall see. We learn from Kussmaul that such steppe farming, with large herds on a vast area, offers the best conditions for a social gradation, of kinships, warlike nobility, and dynastic leadership, just as we find among the war-chariot people and most Indo-Europeans. Hančar (1951, 1954) has reconstructed some of the essential mental, spiritual, and economic characteristics of these steppe-farming communities of western Inner Asia.

The first peoples to find out that horse-riding was of great advantage in wartime and the first who developed the art of fighting on horseback were probably not the herding farmers of the open steppe but tribes of mountain basins, especially of Transcaucasia and of northwestern Iran (Jettmar, 1954c). In such mountainous countries, partly

covered with forests, the war chariot must have been of little use, but fighting on horseback must have been an excellent way of defense. These peoples cannot be called nomads, since they did not abandon farming and sedentary life.[16]

The first peoples of the steppe and wooded steppe to become horse-riding nomads seem to have been the "North Iranians" (e.g., the Scythians) and their neighbors (Rostowzew, 1931; Hančar, 1951). It seems that they lived between the rivers Volga and Irtysh. Until that time they had been leading the life of steppe farmers. Some hunting tribes, living farther north, also were included in the new movement. Once aware of the great superiority of fighting on horseback over the older ways of fighting, especially by war chariots, they gave up sedentary life entirely and specialized in the breeding of herd animals, especially horses. They became the first horse-riding nomads and the first to break into the neighboring countries, disseminating terror and panic among all sedentary populations. When we use the word "nomad," we usually think of this equestrian type.[17]

The distinct social and economic gradation of the steppe farmers of the rough northern wooded steppe was favorable to the formation of leaders of high political and military ability. This

14. Heine-Geldern assumes (1950) that writing arrived in China with the "Lungshan" culture (*ca.* 2000 B.C.).

15. Cf. Figs. 87 and 88.

16. The Medes and Persians of about 1000 B.C. probably have to be included here. Even in later times they did not abandon their three main knightly ideals: horse-riding, archery, and love of truth.

17. It has not been very long that equestrian nomadization has been clearly recognized and described. Jettmar and Kussmaul arrived at the same conclusion more or less at the same time, Jettmar, by making full use of recent Russian excavations, Kussmaul, mainly by utilizing the rich ethnological material of old Chinese literature, especially its compilation by Eberhard (1942a, 1942b, 1942c). Kussmaul arranged the characteristic attributes of the tribal cultures, as they had been described by the Chinese, into genetic groups according to modern ethnological methods.

was of essential importance during the period of nomadization. When a strong nomadic horde had been established, the warmer climate and the oasis civilization of the south, known to some of the men by mercenary services, as well as the milder climate of the open plains of the west, attracted their invasions. (That the climate became rather suddenly colder in the eighth century B.C. perhaps was a stimulus too.) Eastward, along the foot of the Altai Mountains and through the gap of Dzungaria, nomadization worked like a chain reaction of explosions. The poorer farmers and hunters probably were forced to join the "aristocracy" of horse-breeders, so that a new nomadic horde organization was brought about which grew by raiding, sacking, killing, and enslaving other populations, especially other hordes of horsemen, and by winning over vassals by disseminating fear.

Kussmaul shows in his work and map (1953, our Fig. 88) that the spread of equestrian nomadization began with the North Iranians, especially the Scythians, and was followed by the Wusun, whose home seems to have been central and eastern Tien Shan. We may suppose that during that period herdsmen, hunters, and farmers of the open steppes surrounding Mongolia were forced to take up nomadic life. It is possible that the pressure of the Wusun against the population of the oasis chain of present western Kansu caused the last invasion of farmers into China, especially the "Jung," which led to the breakdown of the dynasty of the western Chou (770 B.C.).

The first nomadization to be traced in Chinese reports is that of the Hsiung-nu. The Huns, as they were called later on in Europe, were neither Iranians nor "Proto-Turks." (According to Ligeti [1950–51], the Hsiung-nu language seems to stand isolated or to be related to that of the Yenisei Ostyaks.) In their habitat between ancient China and the Mongolian Desert, the Hsiung-nu took over en bloc a considerable group of elements of the culture of the nomadic North Iranians. During centuries of fierce wars, in which the Chinese defended themselves against the Hsiung-nu and built the Great Wall, the Chinese again took over a part of these elements, for example, iron, cavalry, trousers, and the concept of heaven as a tent. Other traits of the life of the Hsiung-nu, however, prove not only their former dependence on China but also their cultural relation to the non-nomadic primitive tribes of eastern Manchuria.

Figure 88 does not deal with the growth of more or less short-lived nomadic empires and with their conquests in the Dry Belt. It does not deal with their pressure on agrarian and urban China, which sometimes became vassal or even partly subdued (and even marginally transformed into pasture). Nevertheless, China was growing, during long periods of defense, retreat, and counterattack, although it was, in its north, a land of wooded-steppe climate, attractive for nomads. Into the forests of the south it was growing mainly by its civilizational superiority. Furthermore, Figure 88 does not deal with those tremendous migrations and invasions into the west, during which the Dry Belt served as a corridor through which the invaders broke into the countries of old oasis civilization in southwestern Asia or into the beginnings of forest civilization in medieval Central and Western Europe (Grousset, 1948, 1954; Spuler, 1950).

All these movements destroyed what had been left of steppe farming in the plains of the steppe. The hilly and mountainous countries surrounding Mongolia, however, with a pattern or mosaic of steppe, meadow, and forest (and sometimes of pasture above the timber line), and the marginal parts of the forest belt became areas of retreat and regeneration of a population which made its living by hunting, cattle-breeding, and farming (Lattimore, 1938). That the population of farmers must have been quite numerous and dense before the period of nomadization in some areas of the wooded steppe is shown, for instance, by the ruins of a wall of defense 650 kilometers long. This wall cuts off the northeastern corner of the steppes of Mongolia, running from west to east near the Gan River Valley (Plaetschke, 1939, pp. 132 ff.). The Gan River is an eastern tributary of the Argun.

We can see from Figure 88 how, again and again in such hilly and mountainous border regions of the eastern part of the great Dry Belt, new nuclei sprang up among hunting, herding, and farming groups, who led a simple life under hard conditions. In these we find some able man, endowed with the gifts of leadership, who organized a complex horde by raiding, robbing, and winning vassals. Here the name of a tribe or kinship, more or less unknown before, became the name of a growing power and sometimes even that of a vast empire. By some lucky chance, a "Secret History of the Mongols" has been preserved (Haenisch, 1948): a story of the life of Genghis Khan, of the origin of his kinship, and of how he founded the Mongol empire. It was written by a Mongol in A.D. 1240 as a plain, firsthand report. In the time of Genghis Khan's forefathers his semisedentary clan in the Kentei Mountains did not own many horses, cattle, and sheep. There

Margin of forest toward wooded steppe   Pasture above timber-line

F. Kussmaul

Fig. 88.—The spreading of explosive outsets of horse-riding nomadism, with feudal state-building. The previous population had a food-producing economy of farming,

was little agriculture. Wild vegetables were collected. Hunting on horseback was very important. The neighbors in the open steppes outside the mountains, however, were true horse-riding nomads with large herds. Many of these had become saturated by raiding and addicted to the luxuries with which they had become familiar during their raids. From hiding places in the valleys and forests of the Kentei Mountains, the incipient clan of Genghis Khan began a life of robbery among the rich nomads of the plains. Their booty consisted of horses, cattle and sheep, women, children, and servants. Thus the clan turned entirely nomadic, steadily growing by the acquisition of new vassals, many of them of foreign blood, an association taking its name from the leader's kin-

ship, growing in strength according to the looting ability of the leader. Finally, well-known tribes and peoples of Mongolia lost their independence as well as their name and merged with the new great "Mongol" unit.

Kussmaul (1953, n.d.) shows that such a region on the margin of the Dry Belt of Mongolia hardly ever repeated the formation of a new and powerful nomadic aggregation if it had once before been the cradle of such a fast nomadization. The whole procedure, as we see it in Figure 88, worked like a chain reaction of explosions running from west to east and from south to north, rooting out steppe farming and continually regenerating equestrian nomadism, that terrible scourge of rural and urban communities of Eurasia,

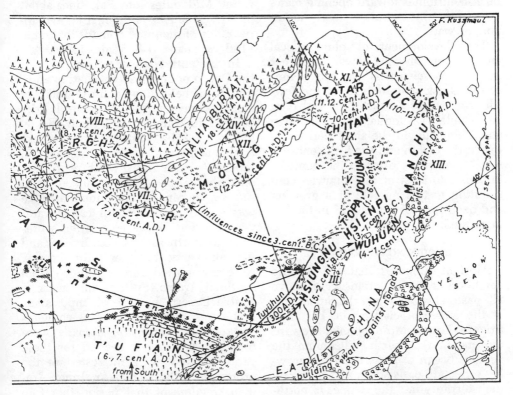

⚬⚬⚬ *Margin of arable steppe toward semi-desert*   ⚬⚬⚬ *Oasis regions*

herding, and hunting, mainly in the wooded steppes. The Roman numerals show the succession of these outsets. The dates are approximate.

which in itself was a cul-de-sac phenomenon.

We cannot say whether the destruction the mounted nomads carried into the countries in and around the Dry Belt, especially into the original cradle of civilization in southwestern Asia, is balanced by the contribution of nomadic states to the interchange of materials and ideas between these surrounding countries. All we see is that the empty spaces of the Dry Belt were terribly enlarged by the plague of nomadic migrations, which annihilated steppe-farming communities and reduced and weakened oasis civilization (Gradmann, 1943). We do not know to what extent suffering is necessary to save from degeneration and decay that which is sound and good in man's mind and how far it contributes toward opening man's eyes so that he can understand the import of wars.

The development of philosophical and religious thought toward a higher stage of consciousness, the appearance of the Greek philosophers, of the Jewish prophets, of Zoroaster, of Mahāvīra and Gautama Buddha, and of Lao-tzu and Confucius, in the short period between the eighth and the fifth centuries B.C.,[18] took place prior to the nomadic inroads into most of the countries contributing to this miracle of a growing and deepening of the "logos" in the human mind.

BEDOUIN NOMADIZATION

Albright supposes that the Semitic neighbors of the Sumerians were, above all, pastoral tribes when the Sumerians, at the outset of civilization, began to irrigate Lower Mesopotamia. Toward the end of the fourth millennium the Semites began to press upon the growing sedentary oasis states and to extend their territory into the steppes of northern Mesopotamia, before Semites became rulers in the oasis countries. Then, toward the end of the third millennium, there was a strong pressure of pastoral tribes on the whole Fertile Crescent, and the sedentary population decreased and lost much of its territory (climatic influence?). But by 1900 B.C. a reversal had set in. The Amoritic "nomads" (compare the migration of Abraham) possessed neither horses nor camels. But they had donkeys to carry loads. Hunting and robbing the harvest were important. They had to travel and attack on foot. This made complete crossings of the desert (except in spring) and rapid expeditions impossible. In summer they had either to depend on oases or other settled areas or to live in tillable regions of the Fertile Crescent. Albright shows that the inroad of camel-riding Midianites into Palestine, about or after 1100 B.C., is the first known appearance of mounted nomads in Arabia (Judges, chaps. 6–8; Walz, 1951).[19]

In the tenth century B.C. the story of the Queen of Sheba shows that, in addition to camel-riding, a busy traffic of camel caravans had been fully developed in competition with traffic by sea, with Saba (Sheba) in southern Arabia as its center. From the Assyrian reports (eighth and seventh centuries) on tributes of Arabian queens and princes, we can also conclude that there was a strong traffic with camel caravans crossing Arabia (e.g., from southwest to northeast). Even Indian and African wares, together with incense, were transported and exchanged from southern Arabia. Springs and wells of Arabia Deserta became of importance, first as resting places, then as commercial centers. Since the nomads were breeding the camels needed for these caravans, they were interested in the profits from the traffic. An Inner Arabian kingdom of that period therefore

---

18. Cf. Menghin (1937, p. 612), Wissmann (1946), and especially Jaspers (1949).

19. We cannot deal here with the late introduction of camel-riding and of mounted nomadism into Africa.

cannot be compared with a nomadic state of Inner Asia. Commercial oases or town centers played an important role. Taima, for instance, had its own script. The nomadic clans lived separately and, probably, rather independently, having their own rules of revenge and blood feud. Caskel (1953) demonstrates that a Bedouin nomadism comparable with the equestrian nomadism of Inner Asia is first found in the steppes and deserts between Syria and Mesopotamia and that it began to spread to the south in the second and third centuries A.D. The constant wars between Rome and Persia, the decay of the feudalized southern Arabian kingdoms and of their caravan trade, and the decline of overland traffic gave rise to great insecurity, which spread in Arabia from north to south (cf. Wissmann, 1953, Wissmann and Höfner, 1952). The nomads now form tribal organizations. The heads of these are *primi inter pares*. Their position depends on their wealth in good riding camels and their ability to raid and loot and to persuade their comrades and allies. This resembles what has been related above about the Mongols.

Yet it differs in some points of view (Bobek, 1943, 1948). Although the famous dam which watered the oasis of Marib (Saba) broke down, there still remained in Arabia a framework of impoverished oases, with townsmen, and peasants living in bondage. And there were still the *qabā'il*, the highland farmers in their fortified dwellings in Yemen and Oman, where feudalism led to an extreme dissipation of power and even to anarchy, as well as to tribal organizations similar to those of the barbarized camel-nomads, the Bedouins. These *bedu* we all know from the excellent descriptions of Doughty (1936) and Oppenheim (1939–52).

Mecca at first was a place of Bedouin religion and trade. Without the *bedu* and the *qabīli*, as well as the townsman

and the fellah, the rise *and* the stability of the Islamic empire cannot be imagined.

THE SPREADING OF CULTURES IN EURASIA: A SUMMARY

In order to summarize and visualize our view of the spreading of planting and animal-breeding cultures in Eurasia, I drew Figure 89, which in parts is to a high degree hypothetical. Seen as a whole, the most ingenious line of development seems to run from the moist tropical forest around the Bay of Bengal (tuber-planting, pig- and dog-breeding) to the steppes of northwestern India (millets?) and the mountains and their foothills of eastern Iran (goats, sheep, large-grain cereals), then to the dry girdle of central Iran (oasis irrigation), the highlands of western Iran (cattle, steppe farming), and the river oases of Mesopotamia (rising of civilization, of *Hochkultur*). The later development of human genius spread into the forest again, in Europe, as well as in China and India. Greece, Shantung, and Magadha lie on the margins of the forest.

Each of these steps of development sends out a wave of spreading, which often combines with other waves or is overtaken by later ones. For the progression of these waves, the coasts, the vegetational belts, and the chains of natural oases are of (unequal) importance. The spreading of tuber-planting and pig- and dog-breeding, closely connected with fishing, were unhindered along the coasts of Indonesia and the coasts and rivers of eastern Asia. North of Korea the tubers had to be left behind because of the cool climate. Branches merged into the taiga boreal forest along the northern Asiatic rivers. On the dry coasts of the Arabian Sea the spreading of this oldest producing culture had to join with later waves on its way by southern Iran and southern

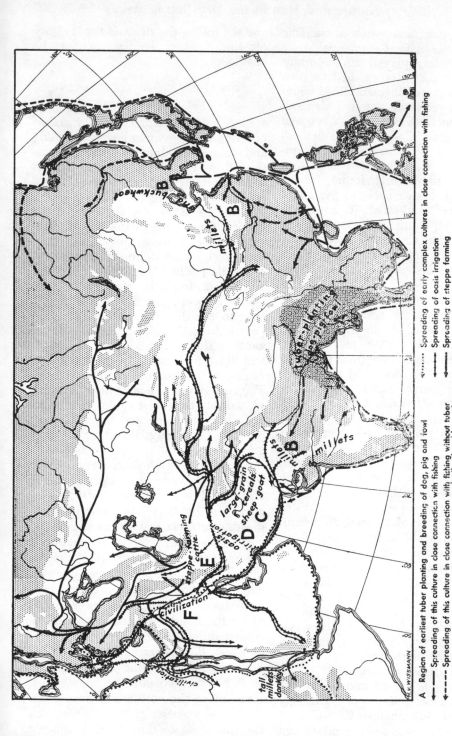

A Region of earliest tuber planting and breeding of dog, pig and fowl
— Spreading of this culture in close connection with fishing
--- Spreading of this culture in close connection with fishing
B Millet as first seed plant in wooded steppe planting in colder regions
C Beginning of sowing large-grain cereals and of breeding sheep and goats
D Beginning of oasis irrigation
E Beginning of cattle breeding and steppe farming

······ Spreading of earliest complex cultures in close connection with fishing
→ Spreading of oasis irrigation
⇢ Spreading of steppe farming
F Beginning of civilization
⟿ Spreading of civilization
☐ Wooded steppe and desert
Forest

FIG. 89.—The development of food-producing man and his conquest of Asia (partly hypothetical)

Arabia to Africa. Early cultures based on fishing and shipping also reached the Mediterranean coasts (by the Nile and perhaps the Euphrates) and thence even the Atlantic Ocean and the North Sea. Chains of natural oases led irrigating agriculture to Turan and the Tarim Basin and finally to northern China. This wave was perhaps caught up on its way by traits of full civilization. Steppe farming found its way very early to Asia Minor and southeastern Europe. Then it adjusted itself to the forests which surround the islands of steppe in Central Europe. From Rumania, as well as from the Tien Shan Mountains, steppe farming conquered the northern belt of the steppes.

REFERENCES

ALBRIGHT, W. F.
1946a *Archaeology and the Religion of Israel.* Baltimore: Johns Hopkins Press. 238 pp.
1946b *From the Stone Age to Christianity.* 2d ed. Baltimore: Johns Hopkins Press. 495 pp.
1949–50 "Zur Zähmung des Kamels," *Zeitschrift für die alttestamentliche Wissenschaft,* LXII, 315. Berlin.

ALTHEIM, F.
1947–48 *Weltgeschichte Asiens im griechischen Zeitalter.* 2 vols. Halle an der Saale: Niemeyer. 412 + 262 pp.

BISHOP, C. W.
1932 "The Rise of Civilization in China with Reference to Its Geographical Aspects," *Geographical Review,* XXII, 617–31. (Cf. XII [1922], 19–41.)

BOBEK, H.
1943 "Der Orient als sozialer Lebensraum." MS. 101 pp.
1948 "Stellung und Bedeutung der Sozialgeographie," *Erdkunde,* II, 118–25.
1951 *Die natürlichen Wälder und Gehölzfluren Irans.* ("Bonner Geographische Abhandlungen," No. 8.) Bonn: Geographisches Institut der Universität. 62 pp.
1952 "Beiträge zur klima-ökologischen Gliederung Irans," *Erdkunde,* VI, 65–84.
1953–54 "Klima und Landschaft Irans in vor- und frühgeschichtlicher Zeit," *Geographischer Jahresbericht aus Österreich,* XXV, 1–42.

BRAIDWOOD, R. J.
1952 *The Near East and the Foundations of Civilization.* (Condon Lec-

tures, No. 5.) Eugene, Ore.: Oregon State System of Higher Education. 43 pp.

BRYAN, K.
1941 "Pre-Columbian Agriculture in the Southwest as Conditioned by Periods of Alluviation," *Annals of the Association of American Geographers,* XXXI, 219–42.

BÜDEL, J.
1949 "Die räumliche und zeitliche Gliederung des Eiszeitalters," *Die Naturwissenschaften,* XXXVI, 105–12, 133–39.
1952 "Bericht über klima-morphologische und Eiszeit-Forschungen in Nieder-Afrika," *Erdkunde,* VI, 104–32.
1953 "Die 'periglazial'-morphologischen Wirkungen des Eiszeitklimas auf der ganzen Erde," *ibid.,* VII, 249–66.

CASKEL, W.
1953 *Die Bedeutung der Beduinen in der Geschichte der Araber.* ("Arbeitsgemeinschaft für Forschung des Landes Nordrhein-Westfalen, Geisteswissenschaften," No. 8.) Cologne and Opladen: Westdeutscher Verlag. 35 pp.

CHILDE, V. G.
1926 *The Aryans: A Study of Indo-European Origins.* London: Kegan Paul, Trench, Trubner & Co.; New York: Alfred A. Knopf. 221 pp.

COON, C. S.
1953 "Climate and Race," pp. 13–34 in SHAPLEY, H. (ed.), *Climatic Change.* Cambridge, Mass.: Harvard University Press. 318 pp.

DEEVEY, E. S.
1949 "Biogeography of the Pleisto-

cene. Part I. Europe and North America," *Bulletin of the Geological Society of America*, LX, 1315–1416.
1953 "Paleolimnology and Climate," pp. 273–318 in SHAPLEY, H. (ed.), *Climatic Change*. Cambridge, Mass.: Harvard University Press. 318 pp. (Rich in references.)

DOUGHTY, C. M.
1936 *Travels in Arabia Deserta*. New ed. London: Jonathan Cape. 612 pp.

EBERHARD, W.
1942a *Kultur und Siedlung der Randvölker Chinas*. (Supplement to *T'oung Pao*, Vol. XXXVI.) Leiden: Brill. 506 pp.
1942b *Lokalkulturen im Alten China*, Part I: *Die Lokalkulturen des Nordens und Westens*. (Supplement to *T'oung Pao*, Vol. XXXVII.) Leiden: Brill. 447 pp.
1942c *Lokalkulturen im Alten China*, Part II: *Die Lokalkulturen des Südens und Ostens*. ("Monumenta Serica," Monograph III.) Peking: Catholic University; Leiden: Brill. 588 pp.

EICKSTEDT, E. VON
1931–32 "Der Zentral-Dekkan und die Rassengliederung Indiens," *Anthropologischer Anzeiger*, VIII, 89–103. Stuttgart.

FIRBAS, F.
1949 *Spät- und nacheiszeitliche Waldgeschichte Mitteleuropas nördlich der Alpen*, Vol. I: *Allgemeine Waldgeschichte*. Jena: Fischer. 480 pp.

FLINT, R. F.
1953 "Evidence from Glacial Geology as to Climatic Variations," pp. 165–78 in SHAPLEY, H. (ed.), *Climatic Change*. Cambridge, Mass.: Harvard University Press. 318 pp.

FLOHN, H.
1947 "Zum Klima der freien Atmosphäre über Sibirien. II. Die regionale winterliche Inversion," *Meteorologische Rundschau*, I, 75–79.
1952 "Allgemeine atmosphärische Zirkulation und Paläoklimatologie," *Geologische Rundschau*, XL, 153–78.
1953 "Studien über die atmosphärische Zirkulation in der letzten Eiszeit," *Erdkunde*, VII, 266–75.

FRANKE, O.
1930 *Geschichte des chinesischen Reiches*, Vol. I. Berlin and Leipzig: De Gruyter. 431 pp.

FRENZEL, B.
1955 "Die Vegetationszonen Nordeurasiens während der postglazialen Wärmezeit," *Erdkunde*, IX, 40–53.

FRENZEL, B., and TROLL, C.
1952 "Die Vegetationszonen des nördlichen Eurasiens während der letzten Eiszeit," *Eiszeitalter und Gegenwart*, II, 154–67 (with map).

GERASIMOV, I. P.
1946 "Ancient Soil and Eluvial Formations and Their Significance for the Paleogeography of the Quaternary Period," *Surveys of the Geographical Institute of the Academy of Science of USSR*, Vol. XXXVII. Moscow and Leningrad. (In Russian.)

GRADMANN, R.
1934 *Die Steppen des Morgenlandes in ihrer Bedeutung für die Geschichte der menschlichen Gesittung*. ("Geographische Abhandlungen," Series III, No. 6.) Stuttgart: Engelhorn's Nachf. 66 pp.
1943 "Blüte und Niedergang des Orients in geographischer Betrachtung." MS. Tübingen.

GRAUL, H.
1956 "Sind die äusseren Jungendmoränen im Alpenvorland gleich alt?" *Eiszeitalter und Gegenwart*, Vol. VII. Öhringen, Württemberg: F. Rau. (In press.)

GROUSSET, R.
1948 *L'Empire des steppes*. 2d ed. Paris: Payot. 639 pp.
1954 "Die Steppenreiche," pp. 359–90 in RANDA, A. (ed.), *Handbuch der Weltgeschichte*, Vol. I. Olten and Freiburg im Breisgau: O. Walter. 1,159 pp.

HACK, J. T.
1953 "Geologic Evidence of Late Pleistocene Climates," pp. 179–88 in SHAPLEY, H. (ed.), *Climatic Change*, Cambridge, Mass.: Harvard University Press. 318 pp.

HAENISCH, R.
1948 *Die geheime Geschichte der*

Mongolen. 2d ed. Leipzig: Otto Harrassowitz. 190 pp.

HANČAR, F.
1951 "Probleme und Ergebnisse der neuen russischen Urgeschichtsforschung," 33. *Bericht der Römisch-Germanischen Kommission, 1943–50,* pp. 25–60. Berlin.
1954 "Der eurasische Raum: Das Steppenneolithikum," pp. 146–53 in RANDA, A. (ed.), *Handbuch der Weltgeschichte,* Vol. I. Olten and Freiburg im Breisgau: O. Walter. 1,159 pp.

HEINE-GELDERN, R. VON
1950 "China, die Ostkaspische Kultur und die Herkunft der Schrift," *Paideuma,* IV, 51–92.

HERMANNS, M.
1949 *Die Nomaden von Tibet.* Vienna: Herold. 325 pp.

HERRMANN, A.
1935 *Historical and Commercial Atlas of China.* ("Harvard-Yenching Institute Monographic Series," Vol. I.) Cambridge, Mass.: Harvard University Press. 112 pp.

HUZAYYIN, S. A.
1941 *The Place of Egypt in Prehistory.* ("Mémoires Présentés à l'Institut d'Égypte," Vol. XLIII.) Cairo: L'Institut Français d'Archéologie. 474 pp.

JASPERS, K.
1949 *Vom Ursprung und Ziel der Geschichte.* Munich: R. Piper & Co. 349 pp.

JETTMAR, K.
1954a "Mongolide Schädel in der Frühbronzezeit Mittel- und Nordeuropas?" *Archiv für Völkerkunde,* IX, 8–20.
1954b "Les plus anciennes civilisations d'éleveurs des steppes d'Asie centrale," *Cahier d'histoire mondiale,* I, No. 4 (April), 760–83.
1954c "Urgeschichte: China; Entstehung des Reiternomadentums," pp. 342–48 in RANDA, A. (ed.), *Handbuch der Weltgeschichte,* Vol. I. Olten and Freiburg im Breisgau: O. Walter. 1,159 pp.

KLUTE, F.
1930 "Die Verschiebung der Klimagürtel der letzten Eiszeit," *Petermanns geographische Mitteilungen,* Supplement, CCIX, 166–82. Gotha. (*Hermann Wagner Gedächtnisschrift.*)
1951 "Das Klima Europas während der Würmeiszeit und die Änderung bis zur Jetztzeit," *Erdkunde,* V, 273–83.

KUSSMAUL, F.
1952–53 "Frühe Nomadenkultur in Innerasien," *Tribus: Jahrbuch des Linden-Museums, Stuttgart, 1952 und 1953,* pp. 305–60.
1953 "Zur Frühgeschichte des innerasiatischen Reiternomadentums." Dissertation. Tübingen. (Typewritten.)
N.d. "Einige Bemerkungen zur geheimen Geschichte der Mongolen." MS. 22 pp.

LATTIMORE, O.
1938 "The Geographical Factor in Mongol History," *Geographical Journal,* XCI, 1–20.

LAWRENCE, T. E.
1935 *Seven Pillars of Wisdom.* Garden City, N.Y.: Doubleday, Doran & Co. 672 pp.

LIGETI, L.
1950–51 "Mots de civilisation de Haute Asie en transcription chinoise," *Acta Orientalia Academiae Scientiarum Hungaricae,* I, 141–88. Budapest: Magyar Tudományos Academia.

LOEHR, M.
1952 "Zur Ur- und Vorgeschichte Chinas," *Saeculum,* III, 15–55. Freiburg im Breisgau and Munich.

LOUIS, H.
1938 "Eiszeitliche Seen in Anatolien," *Zeitschrift der Gesellschaft für Erdkunde zu Berlin,* pp. 267–85.
1939 *Das natürliche Pflanzenkleid Anatoliens.* ("Geographische Abhandlungen," Series III, No. 12.) Stuttgart: Engelhorn's Nachf. 132 pp.

LUNDHOLM, B.
1947 *Abstammung und Domestikation des Hauspferdes.* ("Zoologiska Bidrag från Uppsala," Vol. XXVII.) Uppsala: Almquist & Wiksells Boktryckeri AB. 287 pp.

MENGHIN, O.
1937 *Weltgeschichte der Steinzeit.* Vienna: Anton Schroll & Co. 648 pp.

NARR, K. J.
1952 "Das höhere Jägertum: Jüngere Jagd- und Sammelstufe," pp. 502–24 in VALJAVEC, F. (ed.), *Historia mundi*, Vol. I. Munich: L. Lehner. 560 pp.

NEISTADT, M. I.
1953 "Palaeogeography of the Natural Zones of the European Part of USSR in Postglacial Time," *Records of the Academy of Sciences, USSR, Geographical Series*, I, 32–48. (In Russian.)

OPPENHEIM, MAX VON
1939–52 *Die Beduinen*, in collaboration with ERICH BRAUNLICH and WERNER CASKEL. 3 vols. Leipzig and Wiesbaden: Otto Harrassowitz. 447 + 447 + 495 pp.

PENCK, A.
1913 "Die Formen der Landoberfläche und Verschiebungen der Klimagürtel," *Sitzungsberichte der Königlich Preussischen Akademie der Wissenschaften*, pp. 77–97. Berlin.

PICARD, L.
1938 "Über Fauna, Flora und Klima des Pleistozäns Palästina-Syriens," pp. 287–91 in GÖTZINGER, G. (ed.), *Verhandlungen der III. Internationalen Quartär–Konferenz, 1936*. Vienna: Geologische Landesanstalt. 393 pp.

PLAETSCHKE, B.
1939 "Landschaftliche Wesenszüge der östlichen Gobi," *Wissenschaftliche Veröffentlichungen des Deutschen Museums für Länderkunde Leipzig* (N.S.), VII, 103–48.

POSER, H.
1947 "Dauerfrostboden und Temperaturverhältnisse während der Würmeiszeit im nicht vereisten Mittel- und Westeuropa," *Die Naturwissenschaften*, XXXIV, 1 ff.
1948 "Boden- und Klimaverhältnisse in Mitteleuropa während der Würmeiszeit," *Erdkunde*, II, 43–68.

ROSTOWZEW, M.
1931 *Scythien und der Bosporus*, Vol. I. Berlin: Hans Schoetz & Co. 651 pp.

SAUER, CARL O.
1952 *Agricultural Origins and Dispersals*. (Bowman Memorial Lectures, Series Two.) New York: American Geographical Society. 110 pp.

SMOLLA, G.
1953 "Der Klimasturz um 800 v. Chr. und seine Bedeutung für die Kulturentwicklung in Südwestdeutschland," pp. 168–86 in KIMMIG, W. (ed.), *Festschrift für P. Goessler*. Stuttgart: W. Kohlhammer. 221 pp.
1955 "Bemerkungen zur Frage nach der Herausbildung neolithischer Kulturerscheinungen." MS. 334 pp.

SPULER, B.
1950 "Geschichte Mittelasiens," pp. 309–60 in WALDSCHMIDT, E. (ed.), *Geschichte Asiens*. Munich: Bruckmann. 767 pp.

TOLSTOW, S. P.
1953 *Auf den Spuren der altchoresmischen Kultur*. (14. Beiheft zur "Sowjetwissenschaft.") Berlin: Kultur & Fortschritt. 362 pp.

VISSER, C. and J.
1935–38 *Wissenschaftliche Ergebnisse der Niederländischen Expedition in den Karakorum und die angrenzenden Gebiete in den Jahren 1922, 1925, und 1929/30*. 2 vols. Leiden: Brill. 499 + 216 pp. (with maps).

VLADIMIRTSOV, G.
1948 *Le Régime social des Mongols: Le féodalisme nomade*, trans. M. CARSOV. ("Bibliothèque d'Études," Vol. LII.) Paris: Publications du Musée Quimet. 291 pp.

WALZ, R.
1951–54 "Zum Problem des Zeitpunktes der Domestikation der altweltlichen Cameliden," *Zeitschrift der Deutschen Morgenländischen Gesellschaft*, CI, 29–51; CIV, 45–87.

WEISCHET, W.
1954 "Die gegenwärtige Kenntnis vom Klima in Mitteleuropa beim Maximum der letzten Vereisung," *Mitteilungen der Geographischen Gesellschaft in München*, XXXIX, 95–116.

WERTH, E.
1954 *Grabstock, Hacke und Pflug*. Ludwigsburg: Eugen Ulmer. 434 pp.

WILHELMY, H.
1950 "Das Alter der Schwarzerde und die Steppen Mittel- und Osteuropas," *Erdkunde*, IV, 5–34.

WILLETT, H. C.
1953 "Atmospheric and Oceanic Circulation as Factors in Glacial-Interglacial Changes of Climate," pp. 51–71 in SHAPLEY, H. (ed.), *Climatic Change*. Cambridge, Mass.: Harvard University Press. 318 pp.

WISSMANN, H. VON
1938 "Über Lössbildung und Würmeiszeit in China," *Geographische Zeitschrift*, XLIV, 202–20.
1939 "Die Klima- und Vegetationsgebiete Eurasiens," *Zeitschrift der Gesellschaft für Erdkunde zu Berlin*, pp. 1–14, and map.
1940 "Südwest-Kiangsu, der Wuhu-Taihu-Kanal und das Problem des Yangdse-Deltas," *Wissenschaftliche Veröffentlichung des Deutschen Museums für Länderkunde Leipzig* (N.S.), No. 8, pp. 61–131.
1942 "Stellung und Bedeutungswandel des Orients in den Lebensräumen der Alten Welt," *Zeitschrift der Gesellschaft für Erdkunde zu Berlin*, pp. 353–68.
1946 "Die Entwicklungsräume des Menschen," *Universitas*, I, 313–31 (I), 445–64 (II).
1948 "Pflanzenklimatische Grenzen der warmen Tropen," *Erdkunde*, II, 81–92 (with 2 maps).
1952 "Discussion on the Climate of the Dry Belt of Eurasia in the Last Ice Age after H. Wilhelmy's Paper on 'Die eiszeitliche Verschiebung der Klima- und Vegetationszonen in Süd-

amerika,'" *Tagungsbericht und wissenschaftliche Abhandlungen zum Deutschen Geographentag Frankfurt a.M. 1951*, XXVIII, 305 ff. Remagen.
1953 "Geographische Grundlagen und Frühzeit der Geschichte Südarabiens," *Saeculum*, IV, 61–114. Freiburg im Breisgau and Munich.
1956 "Die Vergletscherung und Schneegrenze von Hochasien. I. Die heutige Vergletscherung und Schneegrenze," *Akademie der Wissenschaften und Literatur, Abhandlung der Naturwissenschaftlichen Klasse*. Mainz. (In press.)

WISSMANN, H. VON, and HÖFNER, M.
1952 *Beiträge zur historischen Geographie des vorislamischen Südarabien*. ("Akademie der Wissenschaften und Literatur, Abhandlung der Geistes- und Sozialwissenschaftlichen Klasse," No. 4.) Mainz. 165 pp., 12 pl., map. (Also published in *Jahrgang, 1952*, pp. 221–385.)

WRIGHT, H. E., JR.
1951 "Geologic Setting of Ksar 'Akil, a Palaeolithic Site in Lebanon," *Journal of Near Eastern Studies*, X, 112–22.
1952 "The Geological Setting of Four Prehistoric Sites in Northeastern Iraq," *Bulletin of the American Schools of Oriental Research*, CXXVIII, 11–24.

ZEUNER, F. E.
1953 "Das Problem der Pluvialzeiten," *Geologische Rundschau*, XLI, 242–53.

Changes in Climate, Vegetation, and Human Adjustment in the Saharo-Arabian Belt with Special Reference to Africa

SOLIMAN HUZAYYIN*

THE SAHARO-ARABIAN BELT: DEFINITION, SPACE RELATIONS, AND SCOPE OF STUDY

The Saharo-Arabian belt of desert and semidesert has played a crucial part in the story of man on the earth. Perhaps in no other major belt was the interaction of *man* and *milieu* more oscillating in nature, and yet uniform in pattern, than in this area. The story of human activity in these deserts and semisteppes is characterized by its immense length. It goes back into the remote past of prehistory and paleogeography. Indeed, the intricacies of human adjustment and changes in nature in this area cannot be properly understood or deeply appreciated in the light of a study limited to the present-day geography. We must go back deep into paleogeographical stages at least to the beginnings of the so-called "Pluvial Period," when man was still in his early stages of exploiting natural resources

* Dr. Huzayyin is Professor of Geography at the University of Cairo, Egypt. After graduation from Cairo in 1929, he did postgraduate work in England, France, and Austria in 1930–35. He then carried out field work in southwestern Arabia in 1936 and in the Nile Valley and the Egyptian deserts since 1937. His publications include: *Some Contributions of the Arabs to Geography*, 1932; *The Place of Egypt in Prehistory*, 1941; *Arabia and the Far East*, 1942; and "Physiographic History of the River Nile," 1953.

and roaming over this wide belt. In such a study of paleogeography and paleoclimatology it is necessary to cover the whole area of the Saharo-Arabian belt as a geographical unit. The great rift of the Red Sea represented no real divide in the strict geographical sense. Conditions along each of its banks were practically the same, both in the past and in the present. Also, human intercourse and drifts of population were possible across both ends of the Red Sea. The Isthmus of Suez was a natural corridor for migrations and contacts in both directions. Movements of population, as well as drifts of culture and thought, were possible both along valleys dissecting the high mountains of southern Sinai and along the northern coastal plain. This latter has always received adequate Mediterranean rainfall and was also fitted with natural water reservoirs in the form of sand dunes from whose cores underground water seeped to intervening wells and waterholes. The Bab el Mandeb never represented a barrier between the highlands and semiarid plateaus along both its sides. Natural conditions on both sides of the Red Sea were so identical in southwestern Asia and northeastern Africa that, for all practical purposes, human life and human activity in exploiting nature were almost the same. For this reason we shall find it necessary, when dealing with vegetation and surface changes, whether due to natural or to human agencies, to keep in mind the very close connection and correlation between the two sides of the Red Sea or, rather, between the desert of the Sahara and Libya, on the one hand, and Arabia, on the other. We shall in this short treatise, however, concentrate chiefly on the African side of this belt.

The importance of the Saharo-Arabian belt may be attributed to more than one geographical factor. There is, perhaps first and foremost, the unique geographical situation between different zones and lands. It lies between the Mediterranean and western European climatic zones on the north, and the Sudanese and semimonsoonal zones on the south. But it may be noted that the dividing line between the Saharo-Arabian belt and the zones flanking it on both sides was never clearly demarcated, either in climate or in vegetation. This is true not only of the present day but also of the past climates and vegetation. The case, however, was not one of regular and fixed transition but rather one of oscillating and vibrating relation. There was always an encroachment either of the desert on its bordering lands or vice versa. This oscillation, which started with climatic conditions and changes in vegetation and surface, was finally reflected in, and in some cases affected by, human life and human adjustments. In this process it will be found difficult to separate data from the Saharo-Arabian belt and from its adjoining areas. But the importance of the geographical situation of this belt is manifold. To the northwest of it lay western Europe, connected with Africa through the Iberian Peninsula and across Gibraltar. Human migrations in this direction go deep into Paleolithic times and were affected both by climatic oscillations and by changes in vegetational and animal life. Migrations were in both directions, and, in turn, they had their effect upon the natural

milieu in northwestern Africa and in Iberia. The Mediterranean represented no real barrier between its African and its European coasts. It has become abundantly clear, however, that no land bridge ever existed between the two continents during human times. The straits of Gibraltar and of Sicily have always been covered with water, at least since late Pliocene times. Evidence is being accumulated that the eastern Mediterranean was connected with the Atlantic and that the Mediterranean never really formed one or two lakes within the Pleistocene. It is true that some of its islands such as Malta, or some of the Cyclades, were connected with the European mainland; but the Mediterranean was never completely bridged over. Not only do we find high raised beaches practically all around the Mediterranean but we also find molluscans and water fauna migrating both from Lusitania and the Senegal coast into the Mediterranean. Human connections during Paleolithic times, however, were maintained either across Gibraltar or through Asia Minor and over Caucasia and the Balkans.

To the east, land connections were maintained between the Saharo-Arabian belt and the Iranian Plateau and east into innermost Asia. This connection had its effect upon the early migration of fauna and flora as well as that of man. In the domain of culture the land connections with the east fanned out in different directions—toward Caucasia and the Russian mainland, Turkestan and beyond, as well as toward the Indian peninsula. To the southeast of the Saharo-Arabian belt, connections were maintained over the waters of the Arabian Sea and the Indian Ocean. It is to be noted that, singularly enough, the southern seas of the tropics extend two arms toward the Mediterranean, namely, the Persian Gulf and the Red Sea. Various areas along the coasts of Arabia and northeastern Africa served as bases for sea connections. Natural conditions along the coasts of southern Arabia and northeastern Africa affected human activity and human expansion by sea toward the east. In some parts, arid or subarid conditions forced men to depend more on the sea and sea trade for their livelihood. In other parts, vegetational wealth was of such a kind as to provide a basis for a special type of trade, such as that of incense from the ancient coastal plateau of Hadhramaut. In other cases, the existence of semimonsoonal plateaus fringed by desert coastal plains gave a special pattern of life and activity, as in the case of the ancient lands of Punt, which covered Abyssinia, Somaliland, and Yemen. Human connections and human expansion in this part of the fringe area of the Saharo-Arabian belt, however, were not limited to its own population which spread actively toward southern Asia and eastern Africa. Both Indian and African elements spread northward and occupied parts of the coasts of southern Arabia. We have here, therefore, another example of the difficulty of demarcating the limits of the Saharo-Arabian belt either on natural or on human and historical grounds.

To the south of the Saharan belt, in the direction of Sudanese and subequatorial Africa, the border is even more loosely demarcated. We can never focus on a line which limits the desert in this direction either in the past or in the present. The shift was constant and was marked not only by major oscillations, owing to principal and radical climatic changes, but also by microchanges in climate and vegetation during short cycles or from year to year. The border area was also traversed in certain parts by high ridges which had their effect upon local rainfall and vegetation and led to curves and interlocking in vegetational zones. This is clear in the highlands of Urdi, Ennedi, Tibesti, and Hoggar in the central and western Sahara and in the highlands on both sides of the Red Sea. The border area is also complicated by the existence of two types of river valleys, the one represented in streams running in an east-west direction, such as the Senegal and other rivers of the western Sudan, and the other represented in the great river Nile, which runs persistently from south to north. It is remarkable indeed that the Nile, whose headwaters lie a few hundred kilometers from both the Indian Ocean and the Red Sea, persists on heading northward for more than 6,000 kilometers to reach the Mediterranean across the great desert. Strictly speaking, this is not what one would have expected under regular and normal conditions of river drainage. But the Nile had such a complicated story of physiographic evolution that it had no alternative but to collect the waters of the equatorial and the Abyssinian plateaus and drain them northward across the plains of the Sudan and the Libyan Desert toward the Mediterranean. In doing so, it acquired the somewhat paradoxical achievement of running parallel to one of the arms of the Indian Ocean (the Red Sea), separated from it by the tilted edge of the so-called "Red Sea ranges." In doing so, it also complicated the story of vegetational distribution as well as that of human adjustment and human life. Not only did it represent the cradleland of settled life along its course in Egypt and the Sudan, but it also represented the highway of expanding tribal elements which fanned out, once they were able to cross the desert belt, into the savanna plains of the Sudan. This was particularly true of the Arab expansion in the Sudan during the Islamic phase. The effects of human movement, in one direction or the other during various phases of human history along the Nile Valley and across the desert belt, upon vegetational and animal life in the borders of the desert belt are still very little known. But we shall attempt to review some of them at a later stage in this treatise.

We may well see from this general review of the geographical situation of the Saharo-Arabian belt in the Old World that the story of its space relationships in different directions is a complicated one. It derives its complexity from both natural conditions in the belt and the instability of its climate and vegetation through the ages. This is perhaps why we find it essential, in order to have a proper perspective and a proper retrospect of man's tenure of this part of the earth through the corridors of time, to go into some of the details of the past climates and vegetation of the Saharo-Arabian belt.

A PALEOGEOGRAPHIC RETROSPECT: PAST CLIMATE, VEGETATION, AND HUMAN ACTIVITY

The study of prehistoric activity of man over a region like the Saharo-Arabian area can best be approached through a geographical treatment which brings in climatic changes (in the past) and their relation to plant, animal, and human life. Such a study would aim at treating the culture complexes of the past in their proper geographical setting. In trying to reconstruct the geographical stage of human activity in past times, however, we are usually forced to employ biogeographical observations for inferring changes of climate. But, unfortunately, data relating to past climates and drawn from various sources are not always compatible with each other; and the methods of their interpretation by experts are again less coherent. There is also the constant danger of generalizations and of drawing the same conclusions from sets of data which may be comparable only in appearance. For example, the existence of sandstones and similar formations and that of salts and gypsum may not necessarily all correspond to the existence of desert conditions in the climatic sense. This is why it is not always easy

to draw a picture of the climatic conditions as may be inferred from formations of the past. Yet we have to depend very largely upon physiographic data in order to infer the climates of the past in this desert region. These data may be represented either in the formations themselves, their nature and their kind, or in the shape which they take. Formations existing in these desert areas may be indicative either of dry conditions by the presence of sand dunes and sand seas or of wet ones, represented by wadi terraces, lacustrine beds, or travertines and tufas. The shape which these formations may take can also shed light upon past climatic features. The orientation of a fossil dune chain may indicate direction of prevailing wind different from that of the present day. Also, the length and extension of dry wadis now dissecting the surface of the desert, such as Wadi Tefezzezat in the western Sahara or Wadi Tilemsi north of the Niger or such as the many *wādis bi'lama* (waterless wadis) in the deserts of Egypt and Arabia, should give a picture of rainfall and vegetation entirely different from that of the present day. There are also wind-excavated depressions in the desert, such as those of Biskra and Faiyûm, whose extension and shape may be useful as indications of the character and strength of the wind which excavated them, or at least was partly responsible for their present outline and shape. But, apart from these physiographic data of paleoclimatology, we have to depend, in the study of past geographical conditions in the Sahara and Arabia, upon biogeographical evidence—namely, flora and fauna. The evidence from flora may be either fossil or of the present day. Fossil plants or seeds have been collected from various formations and beds in many different parts of the Sahara and its fringes. It will suffice for our present purpose to give a few examples in order to show the problems they may raise for the investigator. In the Oasis of Khârga, for example, some plant remains were discovered in the second part of the past century and were identified as belonging to the evergreen oak (*Quercus ilex*), now living in the northern Mediterranean. It was then inferred that the Oasis of Khârga must have received rainfall equivalent to that of the habitat of the evergreen oak. New discoveries and more recent identifications of these plant remains of the Pleistocene of Khârga, however, have shown them to belong to three varieties of *Ficus*, which need much less rainfall. Another plant discovered in Khârga is a seed of a variety of date (*Phoenix*) now living in tropical Africa between the Senegal and Kenya. Of course one has to allow for the migration of this variety across what is now forbidding desert. But evidence from flora is not limited to fossil species. The study of present-day vegetation also offers immense possibilities as well as problems for the research worker. Let us take but one example. The high mountains of Hoggar in the western Sahara are covered with vegetation of mixed origin. There are a few subequatorial or equatorial types, a larger number of Sudano-Ethiopian varieties, and a number of Algerian and Mediterranean plants. The slopes of these mountains may be divided into three zones:

1. *The* so-called "*subequatorial*" *zone.* —Up to 1,700–1,800 meters, with no permanent vegetation except in the bottom of the valleys and on alluvial fans. The flora is chiefly Sudano-Ethiopian, with some subequatorial types. There are also some Saharan species with Mediterranean affinities.

2. *The lower Mediterranean zone.* — Between 1,700–1,800 and 2,300–2,400 meters, with only a few Sudano-Ethiopian types and an increasing number of species from the Mediterranean, or having Mediterranean affinities.

3. *The high Mediterranean zone.* — From 2,300 to 2,400 meters to the summits (3,000 meters), with no Sudano-Ethiopian types, and having a number of typically Mediterranean plants. This zone also has a permanent vegetation of steppe (outside the watered areas) similar to that on some of the Algerian plateaus.

All this indicates that the interior of the Sahara must have had a higher precipitation at some recent geological period. It was this precipitation which made possible the migration of species of plants both from the Mediterranean southward and from the subequatorial belt northward. But we must remember that the migration of northern types would need a relative lowering of the temperature, while that of the southern ones would need temperatures either similar to those of the present day or at least less fluctuating. In other words, the researcher in past climates is here faced with a problem which touches not only upon the past rainfall in this now desert area but also upon past temperatures—their degree and their range of variation.

Faunal evidences from the Sahara and Arabia are perhaps somewhat more complex in nature and more diversified in the problems which they set before the research worker. There are not only land and fresh-water molluscans but also fishes and land animals. The molluscans may be much disputed, but their evidence, as it stands, is very helpful. They not only indicate differences in climatic conditions but they also throw light upon possibilities of wide migrations across what are now desert stretches. It is true that some of them may have migrated through somewhat special agencies (such as birds), but most of them must have needed a certain amount of rainfall and vegetation in order to spread over the desert. Evidence from truly aquatic species is somewhat more conclusive. The study of these species in North Africa and in many oasis areas has brought forth interesting results. They show the wide spread of distinctly palearctic types. At the same time, however, these molluscans were capable of survival in certain favored spots, like oases, in spite of oscillations in water supply. Thus, from a study of them, we cannot get sufficient detailed evidence of violent extinctions or migrations during the successive phases of the Pleistocene. This, however, may not represent more than a negative piece of evidence. In other words, phases of such extinctions may have existed, though they are difficult for us to trace. Indeed, the study of other types of faunal evidence makes it imperative to assume the existence of such phases of extinction or migration. In this respect, mammalian and other fauna offer interesting and valuable evidence.

Animal remains from the so-called "Pluvial Period" (Upper Pliocene and Pleistocene) point to definitely better climatic conditions. Although the abundance of ostrich eggs would indicate the extension of grasslands, the appearance of the elephant, the waterbuck, and the hippopotamus must have coincided with the existence of running streams and fresh-water pools. This is also corroborated by the wide migration of various types of fishes and crocodiles, some of which survived during long periods and even to the present day. The migration of all these fauna across the desert must have been made possible only through better conditions of rainfall and running water. The fossil fauna of North Africa and the Sahara, however, are particularly mixed. There are both Eurasiatic and Ethiopian types. The research worker must therefore assume that migrations of animals into the Sahara, either from Eurasia via Palestine and Sinai or from Sudanese and subequatorial Africa, must have taken place during varying conditions of climate, especially in temperature. It is also noted that in North Africa certain types are found in formations belonging to two different stages of the Pleistocene, but not in those belonging to an intervening stage. For example, a

number of animals requiring a fairly abundant supply of rainfall, and which appear earlier in the Pleistocene, skip over the Upper Paleolithic phase (Uppermost Pleistocene) and reappear in the Neolithic, to disappear again in the post-Neolithic and historical phase. These include the serval panther, hippopotamus, buffalo, and reedbuck. But the history of fauna in North Africa is still far from being completely known. Complementary evidence has been forthcoming from Palestine, especially from caves. But the evidence of Palestine is again limited chiefly to the Upper Pleistocene; and identifications have shown that the fauna of this part of southwestern Asia were less diversified than those of northwestern Africa and the Sahara. The interior of Arabia is still almost a blank for us in its faunal history during Pleistocene and recent times. Also, the Nile Valley, which could have been expected to give us valuable data in this respect, has been proving singularly poor in well-preserved faunal remains. It is thought that calcification of the formations and beds may have been responsible for the destruction of such remains and of their evidence. Only from the Faiyûm depression do we have valuable material; but even in this area most of the evidence relates to the Uppermost Pleistocene and later phases.

The gist of evidence from faunal remains from different parts of the Saharo-Arabian belt indicates the very great and real need that exists for the co-ordination and correlation of data to be drawn from fauna, flora, and physiographic evidence. This means that we are still in great need of teams of workers collaborating with one another and trying to check and cross-check evidence.

But there is still another type of evidence with which the paleogeographer of this area has to deal, namely, that of human stone industries and antiquities. During various stages of the Stone Age the Saharo-Arabian belt played a particularly important role in the development of early human civilization. The remains left by man over practically all the desert are a clear indication to this effect. During the Stone Age, man was not only affected by the prevailing geographical conditions but he also worked as a positive agency in transforming certain aspects of his milieu. He roamed in groups, in what was at that time open and relatively poor grasslands, hunting animals and collecting plants. During phases of aridity his existence must have helped toward the extinction of other species of fauna as well as the cutting-down and burning of scrubs and scattered trees for fire. During such phases of aridity he also had to limit his activity to relatively small areas around springs or pools of water. During other phases of greater rainfall he must have expanded and spread in scattering groups. Later, when he knew how to cultivate plants and to tame animals, he was able to settle in oases and riverine areas and to contribute through his civilized and constructive actions toward the transformation of certain spots on the face of the desert.

But the study of human relics in desert areas during the Stone Age is important not only for the tracing of the story of human civilization and its development or for the study of man's destructive or constructive activity on the face of the earth but also for the study of climatic oscillations during the Pleistocene and later times. The very fact that we find stone implements in areas where there is now no possibility of livelihood for man indicates different climatic and vegetational conditions from those of the present day. The flourishing of stone industry during one phase of the Paleolithic and the degeneration of that industry during a following phase may well be taken as an indication of the deterioration of living conditions as a whole. Also, the wide spread of a certain industry over large

areas of the desert indicates the facility of movement which could be afforded only under favorable conditions of rainfall and vegetation, while the concentration of stone industries around segregated favorable spots may well be taken as an indication in the opposite direction. A comparative study of successive human cultures over the Saharo-Arabian area may therefore represent a particularly useful source of information for anyone who desires to follow the history of changes and transformations in the face of this part of the earth as a living stage for man. In this respect, the desert represents an area of study much richer and more remunerative in results than perhaps any other type of environment.

Let us, for example, compare the Saharan belt, on the one hand, with the plateau of Kenya and eastern Africa, on the other. The Sahara was so situated as to represent an area of effective oscillation and fluctuation in rainfall during the whole of the Pluvial period. It lay between the northern latitudes and the Mediterranean, affected by the westerlies and their winter rainfall, on the one hand, and the Sudan and subequatorial latitudes, affected by the summer winds and the rainy semimonsoons, on the other. The Pluvial period coincided with the Ice Age, during which there were shifts in climatic zones. These shifts were most marked and effective along the Saharan belt. The zone of the northern latitudes, for example, was either expanded southward or contracted toward the north. The subequatorial and Sudanese zone was either expanded at the expense of the desert belt or compressed between this latter and the truly equatorial zone. But the desert belt was invaded and affected on both sides by different agencies of climate and different types of flora and fauna. The question does not seem to have been simply one of expansion or contraction of the desert belt, but rather one of penetration of either

Mediterranean or Sudanese and sub-equatorial conditions. We may recall in this respect that the prevailing winds at present are the dry northerly winds. In the western Sahara they shut off the southwest semimonsoons coming from the Atlantic and prevent them from taking rainfall beyond the Sudanese belt. The south fringes of the desert represent an area of contest between the dry northerlies and the wet winds penetrating from the south and southwest. It is possible to visualize conditions during pluvial phases of the Pleistocene. During such phases the depressions of the Mediterranean moving from west to east must have been more frequent and must have traveled along a more southerly course than they do at present. Their more frequent passage along the southern border of the Mediterranean and the northern edges of the desert belt must have cut the dry trade winds from their roots in the center of high pressure over inner Eurasia. The resulting weakening of the dry northerlies of the Sahara would lead to an increase in the penetrating power of the southerly semimonsoons, which could, in that case, reach the central massifs of the Sahara more frequently and more effectively than they do today. At the same time one must assume that the temperature of the northerly winds of the Saharan belt during glacial episodes must have been lower than that of the present day. This would make them carry cold air masses, which, on confronting the warm and moist masses of the southerly semimonsoons, would help promote condensation and precipitation over the southern parts of the desert belt. Thus we may well imagine that during pluvial phases the desert belt was invaded by moisture and rainfall from both sides.

This double climatic invasion and encroachment were followed by a similar double penetration of fauna, flora, and man from both directions. It is true that the invasion was never an excessive one and that the increase in precipitation and the enrichment of vegetation and animal life were always moderate in extent. However, the fact that this was a truly desert belt made any slight change in precipitation and vegetation a particularly effective one. The increase in rainfall in a spot like that of the Oasis of Khârga in the Libyan Desert of Egypt may not have exceeded 20 or 25 centimeters per year, but this was enough to alter the face of the desert and change the geographical milieu to make it possible for man to live and act as a positive agency. On the other hand, the change from wet to dry conditions could very easily be brought about by any small change in rainfall toward aridity. A drop in precipitation of 10 or 15 centimeters per year would have disastrous and far-reaching effects upon vegetation and animal life and would thus lead to large-scale migrations of human groups. In certain cases when it would not lead to such migrations, it would certainly lead either to degeneration of culture or to the concentration of human societies in small and more favorable spots such as near-by streams or springs.

Such changes and fluctuations in the geographical milieu during the Pluvial period in the Saharo-Arabian belt led to constantly changing conditions for man. Phases of prosperity and rainfall would make the desert an open paradise for man, where he could roam and develop his stone industries and widen his contacts. Migrating elements from the north could mix freely with migrating elements from the south. The desert became like a great sponge, seeping peoples and cultures from north and from south. Later on, when dry conditions began to prevail and the vegetational cover of the desert began to be destroyed by nature as well as by animals and man, the desert became powerless to support its peoples. They either degenerated or tried desperately to adapt themselves to the new conditions. Some of their communities relapsed into degeneration or were eaten away by hunger and deficiency of resources; but some of them would succeed through adaptations and innovations to meet varying and unfavorable conditions. This would finally lead to technological developments in stone industries, which would mean the appearance of a new phase in technological sequence. Other groups from the desert would perhaps prefer to disperse and migrate to adjoining areas such as Iberia and western Europe in the north, the Sudan, Eritrea, and eastern Africa in the south, or the more favorable riverine spots like the Nile Valley or the plains of Iraq in the east. There they would mix with older communities and would promote culture and civilization through the new contacts. Thus, we may well see how the changing geographical conditions in the Saharo-Arabian belt, even during the remote Pluvial period, gave a valuable impetus for change and development in the human occupation of the face of the earth.

This was quite different from conditions prevailing in an area like the high plateau of Kenya and eastern Africa. This latter area was a high one and was so situated as to receive a more constant and regular supply of rainfall. It is true that in eastern Africa the study of Pleistocene climatology has revealed the existence of a Pluvial period with more than one maximum of rainfall. That Pluvial period was divided into two pluvial phases with a dry interval in between. Each of the two pluvial phases had an oscillating crest of maximum rainfall. The Pluvial period as a whole was followed by increasingly dry conditions, which were interrupted by a wetter phase during Neolithic times. But, in spite of all these oscillations, there can be no doubt that the fluctuations were never so great as to affect vegetational, animal, and human life to the same extent as they did along the desert belt. During phases of relative aridity, plants, animals, and men could easily take refuge and find protection and means of survival in the many favorable spots, such as the tops of mountain blocks or the borders of wide lakes and water surfaces. Thus the change of geographical pattern on the plateau of eastern Africa as a whole was never deep enough to lead to far-reaching change in human life and industries. This is perhaps why the technological evolution of stone industries during all that phase was more regular in eastern Africa perhaps than in any other part of the world. The desert, on the other hand, was the land of constant change and constant need for adaptation.

IMPLICATIONS OF THE CHANGES IN
MILIEU FOR THE RESEARCH WORKER

The implications for the research worker of these changes in the Saharo-Arabian area are even more complicated than may appear at firsthand. The complex sequence of culture and stone industries is but a reflection of the complex nature of changes in geographical environment. There is, therefore, the constant need for correlation of changes in climate, in vegetation, in physiography, and in human adaptations. No one specialist can claim on his own to be able to grasp mastery of all these different fields of study. The desert belt, therefore, is an arena where teams of workers and specialists must co-operate if the story of human life on the changing face of the desert is to be clearly discerned. Such a co-operation needs not only training in the field but also the special gift on the part of each worker to appreciate the value of evidence which others can afford. A sense of wide judgment and of balance would have to be promoted if any group of workers were to achieve any coherent results. There have, so far, been certain results achieved by co-operation of small groups of workers in missions sent to different parts of the desert belt. But the need is still very great for such missions to explore not only the fringes of the desert but also remote parts in its heart. Two types of research work are needed in this area. There is first the field work to be carried out by missions sent to still-unexplored areas. Then there is the need for studies of correlation with material obtained from areas already better known, such as the European latitudes or even parts of the tropics. In the first type of research a number of missions have already carried out most useful work in parts of Little Africa, Egyptian oases, and the Nile Valley. But the remainder of the Sahara is still very little known. What is really needed are not those quick-moving expeditions which carry out general exploration work, collect stone implements, or make tracings and photographs of rock drawings in remote areas. Rather do we need more of that kind of expedition which would include specialists in Pleistocene geology, physiography, paleontology, prehistoric archeology, and such studies as may contribute to the emergence of a coherent picture of past human activity in this area. These expeditions should settle down in limited areas and carry out intensive, systematic work. Only through such a method can we obtain that type of reliable and comparable data that would help discern the story of man, his activities, and his civilizations. As for research in correlation with other areas to the north and to the south, we shall have to depend mostly on theoretical studies. It is true that, in certain cases, one may be able to carry out practical field work in correlation. This may be possible, for instance, in the Nile Valley, where one could follow events of climatic oscillations in Ethiopia or in eastern Africa and link them directly with physiographic events in

the lower Nile Valley. But this is a very special case, in which research work has started, though it remains incomplete. It was found that at one time the river Nile was made up of three distinct and independent river systems—one in Nubia and Egypt, the second in Ethiopia, and the third in the Equatorial Plateau. The linking-up of these three systems and the formation of the river Nile in its present shape, however, do not seem to go further than the Middle Pleistocene. Thus the possibility of a direct link in events is limited chiefly to the latter part of the Pluvial period. For any correlation covering the whole of the period of human occupation of the Saharan belt with events in northern and equatorial latitudes, one would have to depend almost entirely on theoretical studies and comparisons. Some effort has already been made in this respect, and it may be useful to make a brief review of the conclusions already reached. This would help bring out the lacunae in our knowledge and the gaps still to be filled by future research.

CORRELATIONS OF CHANGES IN CLIMATE, VEGETATION, AND SURFACE IN HUMAN TIMES

If we compare evidences drawn from physiographic data, flora, fauna, and archeological material, we can draw the following picture of climatic oscillations in the Saharo-Arabian belt during human times. The Pluvial period started in the Upper Pliocene and continued to the end of the Pleistocene. It was divided into two major pluvial phases. The First Pluvial was a very long one, marked chiefly with the cutting of large wadis in the rocks of the surface of the deserts, followed in places by the sedimentation of huge river terraces. In these latter, some early, Lower Paleolithic implements were discovered *in situ*. The details of this First Pluvial are not known, though it is almost certain that it must have had more than one submaximum. During part of it the climate was marked with a rise in temperature as well as in precipitation.

This First Pluvial continued to the end of the Lower Pleistocene and was followed by a phase of aridity, marked also by crustal movements. The interpluvial was a short one, but it was very effective, not only in extinctions and emigrations of plants, animals, and human groups, but also in the remodeling of large areas of the surface of the desert. Wind activity and sand abrasion became very strong and effective. Also, thermal weathering helped in the same direction. As a result, many of the former features of desert physiognomy became obliterated. Evidence has been increasingly forthcoming that many of the features in the present-day physiognomy of the Saharan deserts may have had their origin during this interval. We believe, for example, that such depressions as that of Faiyûm (and perhaps that of Biskra) may not have acquired their final shape until this dry interval, during which further excavation and widening of such depressions seem to have taken place. But this is still one of the main points in which complementary research is needed. There even may be a possibility of comparing the sequence of events in some of the desert depressions in Africa with that of similar depressions in other continents.

After the interpluvial came the Second Pluvial phase, which corresponded to the Upper Pleistocene. It also coincided with both Middle and Upper Paleolithic cultures. The Second Pluvial was much less intensive in precipitation than the First. It was also much shorter but had at least two, or perhaps three, submaxima. It was also characterized chiefly by a relative drop in temperature, and during this phase there was a clear immigration of Asiatic fauna through the Isthmus of Suez. It is also very likely that it was during this Second Pluvial that Mediterranean flora penetrated furthermost into the Sahara.

The Second Pluvial was followed by progressive aridity at the close of the Pleistocene. This aridity was also marked by a continuation of the relatively low temperature which characterized the previous phase. The condition of aridity, however, was interrupted during what we call the "wet phase" of Neolithic and later times. But the story of this latter phase is of special interest, and we shall come back to it a little later.

Thus we may see that the sequence of climatic oscillations and of vegetational changes connected with it in the Saharo-Arabian belt is a fairly simple one. To compare it, however, with the more complex story that we know from western Europe is not at all an easy task. In the northern latitudes, where the Ice Age existed and coincided with the Pluvial period, we know that there have been three or four glacial phases—namely, those of Günz, Mindel, Riss, and Würm in the Alps. They were separated from one another by interglacial phases, of which the one between Mindel and Riss was very long and was characterized by warm conditions. There have been various attempts to draw up correlations between the glacial episodes in Europe and the pluvial ones in Africa. Difficulties arose from the fact that the number of glacials is larger than that of pluvials. There is good reason at present, however, to correlate the First Pluvial with most of the glacial period until the end of the Riss phase. If this be accepted, the Second Pluvial would correspond to Würm, which, in Europe, also had two submaxima followed by further oscillations during the melting of the icecaps. This correlation is based on the fact that a glacial phase in Europe should lead to a southward shift of the climatic zones and consequently to pluvial conditions in North Africa and the Sahara. On the other hand, an interglacial in Europe could coincide with either pluvial or dry conditions in middle latitudes. If the interglacial is marked with a rise in temperature, this would increase evaporation from the seas, would accelerate wind circulation and activity, would foster the formation of storms due to excess of latent heat in the air, and then would lead generally to an increase of precipitation in all climatic zones. We know that the Mindel-Riss interglacial was marked by a rise in temperature, not only in the air, but also in the waters of the Atlantic and Mediterranean. This would mean that such an interglacial could well have coincided with pluvial conditions in the Saharo-Arabian belt. On the other hand, the Riss-Würm interglacial was marked, at least in its middle part, with cool conditions during which there was less evaporation, a relaxation in air circulation, and a general drop in precipitation. As for the earliest interglacial, that which separated Günz from Mindel, there was little evidence available, though on the whole it may have been relatively warm. The last interglacial (Mindel-Riss) is therefore the only one likely to have coincided with a dry interpluvial in the Saharo-Arabian belt. But the whole of the question of correlation of past climates still remains a primarily theoretical one; and added research is still to be looked for.

POST-PLEISTOCENE CHANGES IN GEO-GRAPHICAL ENVIRONMENT AND HUMAN ADAPTATIONS

If we may now pass on from the Pleistocene phase in the Saharo-Arabian belt to the Recent geological phase, we find the story of changes in geographical environment and human adaptations largely preserving the same character that we have been trying to trace in the Pleistocene. The desert belt remained as the scene of intense changes and wide repercussions in the relation of man to his milieu. As usual, changes always started with the climatic cycle, had their direct effect in the general physiognomy and vegetational cover of the desert, and finished in human adjustments to the new conditions. In some cases, however, man was instrumental in the change. He destroyed vegetation and was, in turn, responsible for the onset of denudation and aridity. Until recent years it was generally assumed that the Neolithic stage in human civilization was marked by desiccation and aridity. It was assumed that this desiccation forced both animals and men to migrate from the open desert to settle down in riverine plains and oases. This led to a *rapprochement* between man and animal, which finally ended in the domestication of the relatively tame types of animals. It is also suggested that, when man was forced to concentrate upon and settle down in the well-watered spots, he gradually learned how to plant cereals. In other words, this gave rise to agriculture. More recent research, however, threw increasing doubt upon this relatively simple sequence of events. Evidence has been forthcoming that the dry interval which followed upon the Upper Paleolithic at the close of the Pluvial period was interrupted by the renewal of relatively wet conditions in the very early Neolithic. In other words, it was the Mesolithic stage which was characterized by aridity and degeneration in the stone industry. The pre-Neolithic and the Neolithic were characterized, on the other hand, not by the onset of the crisis, but rather by its relaxation and the renewal of relatively wet, though not truly pluvial, conditions.

Traces of the Neolithic occupation by man of many widely dispersed areas and spots in the Saharo-Arabian belt have been forthcoming during the last thirty years or more. By the sides of rivers and around springs and water-spots in oases, man cultivated the land, raised the domesticated animals, and settled down in small groups of huts and, in some cases, in villages proper. The date of such occupation may be difficult to fix, though in Egypt, for example, it has been fixed at about 5200 B.C. or a little after. The changes in environment as a result of this occupation were far-reaching, especially in areas where cultivation depended mostly on irrigation. The increase in precipitation was enough for cultivation only in limited areas, such as the slopes of mountains or favorably located areas, either near the coast of the Mediterranean or on the borders of Ethiopia and Sudanese Africa. More than one theory has been put forward as to how and where cultivation started. It would be superfluous to go into the details of these theories, though it may be useful to mention a few points about the lower Nile Valley, on the one hand, and the slopes of Ethiopia and Mount Hermon in Syria, on the other. We know that man cultivated both barley and wheat in Egypt as early as the close of the sixth millennium B.C. The variety of barley cultivated at that time was not much different from that of the present day. This may indicate that it was probably growing in the wild state in northeastern Africa, where it had been already domesticated for some time, and under similar conditions. It may, indeed, be inferred that man may have started domesticating barley even earlier than the 5200 B.C. date suggested above. As to wheat, it was probably introduced from without, most likely from southwestern Asia.

The question of how cultivation became known in the lower Nile Valley is also interesting to discuss. Some of the ideas put forward seem fantastic. It is very likely, however, that cultivation became known in this valley in a very normal and gradual way. We know that the Nile flood reaches Egypt in late summer and early autumn. It covers the flood plain and enriches it with silt, propitious for the cultivation of winter plants. The waters of the Nile subside exactly at the time suitable for the planting and growth of winter plants such as barley and wheat, and we may imagine that seeds could easily have been blown by wind from the adjoining plateau—at that time receiving slightly higher winter rainfall. All sorts of vegetable growth would cover the edges of the valley and delta immediately after the subsidence of the floods, and fishing and hunting groups may have marked and guarded them until the reaping season. This was admittedly not cultivation in the strict sense; but it represented a spontaneous and evolutionary progress toward cultivation proper. Such a suggestion would appeal more to reason because it averts the necessity of a sudden "invention" of agriculture as may be assumed by most current theories on the subject of how cultivation was first known. We may add that nature itself was very propitious for the growth of winter plants in the lower Nile Valley. After the subsidence of the floods the season of winter rainfall begins, which at that time was enough to foster the growth and maturing of both barley and wheat. Both these plants reach maturity with the close of spring, when the winter rainfall begins to cease. The role of man during the early stages of the development of agriculture may have been rather to take a complementary part in the natural process of wild growth, especially by guarding the maturing plant against wild game and birds. Gradually, through the observation of nature, man learned that he could take a more positive part in this process. In the same way we prefer to think that most of the domesticated animals may have been first kept in captivity before the idea of domestication proper was evolved. Gradually man became the tamer, in this desert area and its borders in Asia and Africa, of such animals as cattle, sheep, and asses.

Ethiopia and the horn of eastern Africa together with the borders of the Sudan may have been another area of easy cultivation and domestication. We have mentioned already that barley may have originally been a northeastern African plant; but we may also add that certain varieties of millet must have been first domesticated and cultivated either in Sudanese Africa or on the borders of Ethiopia. It is possible also that the zebu variety of cattle may have first been domesticated in eastern Africa. All these points, however, still require further research.

As for the cultivation of wheat, it is very likely that it first started in western Asia. The plateau extending from Anatolia to Afghanistan must have been the scene of selection of wild wheat plants from which man made his first domestications. The region of Mount Hermon and its vicinity must have played a particularly important role in the development of early cultivation. In these parts of Syria there are areas where soil derived from disintegrating volcanic material, such as in the region of Hauran, was particularly propitious for the growth of wheat. This soil keeps the moisture derived from winter rains and feeds the wheat grasses right through their season of growth. But the story of early cultivation in the Middle East is too wide for us to deal with in any detail.

In the African Sahara a relatively wet phase relieved the crisis of aridity which marked the Mesolithic stage of culture. The so-called "Neolithic wet phase" started about the middle of the sixth millennium B.C. and continued for about three thousand years before it gave way to gradual desiccation during the historic phase. Rainfall over the Saharan belt was certainly not consistent, but there were more frequent storms to provide vegetational life enough for roaming animals and migrating groups of men. Traces of Neolithic culture have

been found in scattered spots in the Sudanese Sahara, on the borders of the deserts of Morocco and Algeria, in some spots on the tops of the high mountains of the central Sahara, as well as even in certain spots and oases of the relatively dry Libyan deserts of Egypt. The pattern of the desert Neolithic culture was relatively poor and less coherent than we find in the Nile Valley itself. But there is sufficient evidence to show that the desert was not a forbidding area for cultural contacts to take place. We even have evidence of such contacts between the desert borders of the western Sudan and some of the oases of Egypt. These relations were partly coincident with early Chalcolithic cultures in Egypt.

One aspect which would be interesting for us to trace, and which would throw light upon the changes that took place in the fauna and flora of the desert during this phase of human occupation, is represented in the rock drawings and paintings of the desert. These have been discovered in a large number of localities, mostly rock shelters in the central Sahara, the Uweinat massif, and other blocks in both the Saharan and the Egyptian deserts. Unfortunately, the question of dating these drawings is not easy to settle, as they have never been found in undoubted association with stone implements or other remains that may help to date them. Apart, however, from the historic drawings, the fauna include a wide variety of elephant, rhinoceros, lion, panther, giraffe, antelope, African cattle, African ram, ostrich, etc. In certain cases there are signs either of domestication or of semidomestication, which give indication of the Neolithic or even post-Neolithic date of these rock drawings. Accurate dating still needs further research, but it may be rightly inferred from the wide distribution of this culture and the variety of animal groups it represents that the desert must have enjoyed at that time a richer covering of vegetation. It was this which made it possible for human groups to roam about the deserts extending between the hills of the Red Sea and the slopes of the Atlas and to draw pictures of animals which they hunted or attempted to domesticate. The vegetational growth must have continued through the early historic phase, because we know that, later on, pharaonic influences seem to have become marked in some of the drawings of the Algerian Sahara—an indication of continued movements and contacts across what were still unforbidding tracts of desert. The Neolithic and early historic phase, therefore, was a period of relatively wet conditions and renewal in the vegetation and fauna of the Saharan belt. There are indirect evidences from Egypt that this phase was also marked in its earlier parts by a relative rise in temperature. In a limited way, therefore, it reminds us of what happened during the warm interglacial which took place between the Mindel and the Riss glacial phases. The small rise in temperature increased evaporation, fostered storm activity due to more latent heat in the air, and also accelerated air circulation on the whole. The desert belt, therefore, may have received more moisture and torrential storms (though varying in intensity from one place to another). It is interesting to note that this so-called "Neolithic wet phase" had its equivalent in Abyssinia and East Africa, where it is called the "Makalian wet phase." During this phase the Nile was characterized by exceptionally high floods which took place immediately before the beginning of the Neolithic and continued for some time, though subsiding gradually during the predynastic phase. It is very likely that this warm-wet phase may have coincided with the so-called "climatic optimum phase" of northwestern Europe. But the story of the so-called "Neolithic wet phase" of the Saharan belt, starting from about the middle of the sixth millennium B.C. and continuing for some time, is still one of the interesting subjects for students of paleoclimatology and ancient fauna and flora of the deserts. The changes which took place in the vegetational cover of the deserts, first due to the rather sudden onset of this wet phase, and later due to its gradual and oscillating ending, should be of particular interest to paleogeographers. They affected not only the aspect of the natural environment but also the activity of man during this very interesting phase of the human cultural development.

CHANGES DURING HISTORICAL TIMES

Mention must be made of the changes in climate and vegetation and their effect upon human activity in the Saharo-Arabian belt during historical times. Evidence has been forthcoming that the onset of aridity after the so-called "Neolithic wet phase" was a very gradual one. This is manifested by the presence and activity of man in many parts of desert areas during early historic times. The general tendency among students of past historical climates is to assume that aridity in its present form and extent does not go much beyond the early centuries of the Christian Era. It is even thought that the desert belt in Africa and Asia did not reach its present-day aridity until about the third or even the sixth century A.D. The question of climatic desiccation in historic times, however, remains still a very vexing one. The dispute between the two schools of changeability and non-changeability of climate during historic times becomes more complicated when we think of the fact that, even if we admit the gradual desiccation, it is always necessary to assume the existence of oscillations leading to more and more dry conditions. Also, such changes must have been very minute in their extent; and evidence relating directly to a decrease and oscillation in rainfall was often perplexed by evidence of migrations of tribal elements due to purely political reasons. Furthermore, we must remember that in certain areas like northern Arabia or the mountain blocks of the interior Sahara, the cutting of woodlands and the destruction of vegetational cover must have been in itself an important factor in promoting aridity and aggravating its aftereffect. There is always the danger, however, of running into a vicious circle by considering the gradual disappearance of the vegetational cover and of many of the wild animals in Arabia and the Sahara as an indication of the onset of drier conditions while at the same time attributing the aggravation of aridity to deforestation by cutting woodlands and scrubs for fuel and other purposes.

In dealing with this still unsettled question of relatively recent climatic changes, archeological evidence may be of particular value. Roman cisterns found on the Mediterranean coast of Egypt west of Alexandria and in several places on the edge of the Syrian Desert are not fully examined or even properly known. Their abundance and the large capacity of some of them may be taken as a sign of greater precipitation of rainfall at that time. In the desert east of the Jordan there is some evidence that the underground water level, which is ultimately affected by the supply of rainfall, has fallen by 2 meters since Roman times. Other and perhaps more conclusive evidence comes from such remote parts of Arabia as the highlands of Yemen. There we know that the earlier historic civilizations were established on the lower step of the table land, that of the Yemen Jauf, lying at about 1,000 meters elevation. Gradually, the ancient Minaeans and Sabaeans shifted their capitals to the higher slopes of Yemen until, finally, the capital was transferred to San'a at some 2,200 meters. Also, if we trace the an-

cient cisterns of the Sabaeans and Himyarites in Yemen, we find that invariably they were situated on the crests of hills rather than in collecting basins, where we find the present-day cisterns. At present, the ancient cisterns are never more than partly filled with water, while the low-lying new ones are usually filled to the rim. It is evident, however, that precipitation and runoff on the crests of hills must have at one time been enough to fill these Sabaean and Himyarite cisterns (*ca.* 1000 B.C.–A.D. 500) with water. In North Africa and the interior of the Sahara archeological evidence is still lacking, but the abundance of remains in many of the desolate areas may be taken as an indication of the somewhat more favorable climate lasting until Roman times. There is still, however, a very clear need for research on those ruins of the western Sahara as well as on traces of early and undated habitations on the Sudanese border of the western Sahara.

The story of climatic oscillations is still of some interest even in the study of present-day conditions. Certain studies have been carried out in the desert border of Nigeria, where it is thought that there is an encroachment of the desert upon the scrubland. Such an encroachment has also been studied in the case of oases, where cultivated areas have been either abandoned or covered by sand. In the region of Lake Mariut in Egypt, statistical data within the last sixty or eighty years has shown an oscillation of rainfall with what may perhaps give a slight indication of progressive aridity. Such studies, however, remain very inconclusive, and it is difficult to say whether this very recent aridity represents a steady factor or whether it is but an ebb in the oscillation of rainfall, to be followed by a new increase. The frequent annual changes shown by the records from Mariut make it difficult to draw any definite conclusions from them. As for inland oases, it has been found that the digging of new wells often leads to the seeping of water from the old wells to the new ones. Thus, with the increase of wells in the same oasis, old wells may even dry up, and the fields around them would be abandoned. This has been noted not only in Egypt but also in parts of southern Algeria. The question of present-day progressive aridity, therefore, cannot be easily settled. The likelihood is that the desert borders in the north and in the south are exposed to oscillating encroachment of truly desert conditions due to cyclic and temporary oscillations in rainfall. The nature of these cycles remains to be studied in the future.

CONCLUDING REMARKS

From this broad study of the changes in climate, vegetation, surface, and human adjustments in the Saharo-Arabian belt, with special reference to Africa, the following broad conclusions may be drawn.

1. The Saharo-Arabian belt of desert and semidesert represents an area of very special value for the students of past changes in climate, vegetation, and human activity and adjustment. Perhaps in no other area of the world have such changes been so violent, far-reaching, or effective. The amount of change in actual precipitation during the so-called "Pluvial Period" and down to the present day was not very great. But the fact that this region is a desert makes any perceptible change in precipitation most effective upon both vegetation and animal life.

2. The reflection of this change upon the story of man in this area was a very pronounced one. We must imagine that, even during the phases of maxima of rainfall, climatic conditions in this area must always have been unstable in character. In other words, micro-oscillations in pluviosity must have had their ef-

fects upon the milieu in which man lived and acted. The need was constant, therefore, for changes in human adjustment to the ever changing scene of human activity. Consequently, the Saharo-Arabian belt was never the scene for any stagnant industry or civilization during the whole of the Stone Age. If we remember that this latter covered by far the greatest portion of human history upon the earth, we would easily realize and appreciate the role of this Saharan belt in the evolution of human civilization. This was the scene of constant change and development.

3. The story of man in this belt was always closely connected with his story in the bordering margins. During the whole of Pleistocene times, the Saharan belt was like a big sponge, which during phases of rainfall attracted groups of migrating people both from Eurasia and from Sudanese and eastern Africa. During phases of aridity the big sponge squeezed its population out in both directions.

4. The question of space relationships between the desert belt and its bordering areas to the north, to the east, and to the south should also be a particularly interesting one to students of paleogeography. It is true that evidence is no longer tenable of the existence of land bridges across Gibraltar or the strait of Sicily since late Pliocene times; but water was no real obstacle in the face of expanding men, especially across Gibraltar. The Isthmus of Suez was fitted with natural conditions which made migrations easy between Asia and Africa. Bab el Mandeb was never really an effective obstacle. The borders of the Sahara to the south were open ones. Thus space relationships on all sides fostered interaction and contacts. Co-operation must, therefore, be complete between research workers studying the desert core and those working upon changes and adjustments in bordering areas.

REFERENCES

ADAMETZ, L.
1920 "Herkfunt und Wanderungen der Hamiten erschlossen aus ihren Haustierrassen," *Osten und Orient*, 1st ser., II, 7–10. Vienna.

ALIMEN, H.
1955 *Préhistoire de l'Afrique*. Paris: Éditions Boubée. 578 pp.

ANGSTROM, A.
1936 "Teleconnections of Climatic Changes in Present Time," *Geografiska Annaler*, XVII, 242–58.

ANTEVS, E.
1928 *The Last Glaciation: With Special Reference to the Ice Retreat in Northeast North America*. ("American Geographical Society Research Series," No. 17; Shaler Memorial Series.) New York: American Geographical Society. 292 pp.

ARKELL, A. J.
1948 *Early Khartoum*. London: Oxford University Press. 145 pp.

AUFRÈRE, L.
1932 "Morphologie dunaire et météorologie saharienne," *Extrait du Bulletin Association Géographes Français*, No. 56 (February), pp. 34–48.

BAGNOLD, R. A.; MYERS, O. H.; PEEL, R. F.; and WINKLER, H. A.
1939 "An Expedition to the Gilf Kebir and Uweinat," *Geographical Journal*, XCIII, 281–312.

BALL, J.
1939 *Contributions to the Geography of Egypt*. (Survey and Mines Department.) Cairo: Government Press. 308 pp.

BARTHOUX, J.
1925 "Paléogéographie de l'Égypte," *Comptes-rendus Congrès International de Géographie, Le Caire, 1925*, III, 68–100.

BEADNELL, H. J. L.
1905 *The Topography and Geology of the Fayum Province of Egypt*. (Survey Department.) Cairo: National Printing Department. 101 pp.

BERMANN, R. A.
1934 "Historic Problems of the Libyan Desert," *Geographical Journal*, LXXXIII, No. 6, 456–70.

BLANCKENHORN, M.
1921 "Aegypten," *Handbuch der regionalen Geologie*, VII, Abstract 9, 1–244. Heidelberg: Carl Winter.

BOURCART, J.
1937 "Géologie et archéologie quaternaires du Maroc: Extrait d'une conférence," *L'Anthropologie*, XLVII, Nos. 3–4, 437–39.

BREUIL, H.
1930 "L'Afrique préhistorique (extrait)," *Cahiers d'art*, Nos. 8–9, pp. 61–122, 440–500. Paris.
1934 "Peintures rupestres préhistoriques du Harar (Abyssinie)," *L'Anthropologie*, XLIV, Nos. 5–6, 473–83.

BROOKS, C. E. P.
1932 "Le Climat du Sahara et de l'Arabie," pp. 25–105 in *Le Sahara*, Vol. I. (Published under the Direction of MASAUJI HASCHISUKA.) Paris: Société des Editions Géographiques, Maritimes et Coloniales. 167 pp.

CATON-THOMPSON, G.
1946 "The Aterian Industry: Its Place and Significance in the Palaeolithic World," *Journal of the Royal Anthropological Institute of Great Britain and Ireland*, LXXVI, Part II (Huxley Memorial Lecture), 87–130.
1952 *Kharga Oasis in Prehistory*. With a Physiographic Introduction by E. W. GARDNER. London: University of London (The Athlone Press). 213 pp.

CATON-THOMPSON, G., and GARDNER, E. W.
1934 *The Desert Fayum*. 2 vols. London: Royal Anthropological Institute of Great Britain and Ireland.

CHUDEAU, R.
1931 "L'Hydrographie ancienne du Sahara," *Revue scientifique*, April 23, p. 194.

DALLONI, M.
1935 *Mission au Tibesti (1930–31)*, dirigée par M. Dalloni, Vol. II. (Mémoires de l'Académie des Sciences de l'Institut de France," Vol. LXII.) Paris. 449 pp.

DALLONI, M., and MONOD, TH.
1948 *Missions scientifiques au Fezzan*,

géologie et préhistoire. ("Institut de Recherches Sahariennes," Vol. VI.) Université d'Alger. 156 pp. and 49 pls.

DESIO, A.

1932 "Osservazioni geografiche e geologiche compiute dalla Spedizione della Reale Academia d'Italia nel Deserto Libico e nel Fezzan orientale (1931) (estratto)," *Memorie geologiche e geografiche di Giotto Dainelli,* III, 111–49. Florence.

FLEURE, H. J.

1928 *The Races of Mankind: The Races of England and Wales.* 2d ed. London: Benn Bros.; Garden City, N.Y.: Doubleday, Doran & Co. 78 pp.

1937 "Racial Evolution and Archaeology," *Journal of the Royal Anthropological Institute of Great Britain and Ireland,* LXVII, 205–29.

GARDNER, E. W.

1932 "Some Problems of the Pleistocene Hydrography of the Kharga Oasis, Egypt," *Geological Magazine,* LXIX, No. 819 (September), 386–421.

GARROD, D. A. E., and BATE, D. A. M.

1937 *The Stone Age of Mount Carmel,* Vol. I: *Excavations at the Wady el-Mughara.* Oxford: Clarendon Press. 240 pp.

GAUTHIER, E. F.

1923 *Le Sahara.* Paris: Payot. 174 pp.

GRAZIOZI, P.

1941 *L'Arte rupestre della Libia.* 2 vols. Naples: Edizioni della Mostra d'Oltremare. 322 pp.

HELLESTROM, B.

1940 "The Subterranean Water in the Libyan Desert," *Geografiska Annaler,* XXII, Nos. 3–4, 206–39.

HUME, W. F.

1925 *Geology of Egypt,* Vol. I: *The Surface Features of Egypt, Their Determining Causes and Relation to Geological Structure.* Cairo: Government Press. 408 pp.

HUNTINGTON, E., and VISHER, S. S.

1922 *Climatic Changes, Their Nature and Causes.* New Haven, Conn.: Yale University Press. 329 pp.

HUZAYYIN, S. A.

1935 "Changement historique du cli-

mat et du paysage de l'Arabie du Sud," *Bulletin of the Faculty of Arts, Cairo University,* III, Part II, 19–23.

1936 "Glacial and Pluvial Episodes of the Diluvium of the Old World: A Review and Tentative Correlation," *Man,* XXXVI, No. 20 (February), 19–22 (and correction in No. 115 [May], p. 88).

1941 *The Place of Egypt in Prehistory.* ("Mémoires de l'Institut d'Égypte," Vol. XLIII.) Cairo. 474 pp.

1942 *Arabia and the Far East.* Cairo: Geographical Society of Egypt. 319 pp.

1953 "Physiographic History of the River Nile" (in Arabic), *Risalat-al-Ilm,* IV, 184–202. Cairo.

LEAKEY, L. S. B.

1931 *The Stone Age Cultures of Kenya Colony.* Cambridge: Cambridge University Press. 287 pp.

MCBURNEY, C. B. M.

1947 "The Stone Age of the Libyan Littoral," *Proceedings of the Prehistoric Society of East Anglia* (N.S.), XIII, 56–84.

MAIRE, R.

1928 "La Végétation et la flore du Hoggar," *Comptes-rendus de l'Académie des Sciences,* CLXXXVI, 1680–82. Paris.

NILSSON, E.

1931 "Quaternary Glaciations and Pluvial Lakes in British East Africa," *Geografiska Annaler,* XIII, No. 4, 249–349.

1935 *Traces of Ancient Changes of Climate in East Africa.* ("Meddelanden fran Stockholms Högskolas Geologiska Institut," No. 36; Särtryck ur *Geografiska Annaler,* Nos. 1–2.) 21 pp.

1938 "Pluvial Lakes in East Africa," *Geologiska Foreningens i Stockholm Forhandlingar,* LX, No. 3, 423–33.

1953 "Contributions to the History of the Blue Nile," *Bulletin de la Société de Géographie d'Égypte,* XXV, 29–47.

PEAKE, H.

1928 *The Origins of Agriculture.* London: E. Benn, Ltd. 78 pp.

PEDRALS, D. P. DE
1950 *Archeologie de l'Afrique noire.* Paris: Payot. 233 pp.

PICARD, L.
1937 "Inferences on the Problem of the Pleistocene Climate of Palestine and Syria Drawn from Flora, Fauna and Stratigraphy," *Proceedings of the Prehistoric Society of East Anglia* (N.S.), III, Part I, No. 5, 58–70.

ROMER, A. S.
1928 "Pleistocene Mammals of Algeria: Fauna of the Paleolithic Station of Mechta-el-Arbi," in "A Contribution to the Study of Prehistoric Man in Algeria, North Africa," *Beloit College Bulletin,* XXIX, No. 5, 79–163.

RUHLMANN, A.
1938 *Les Recherches préhistoriques dans l'Extrème-Sud-Marocain.* ("Publications du Service des Antiquités du Marocain," No. 5.) Rabat. 107 pp.

SANDFORD, K. S.
1934 *Prehistoric Survey of Egypt and Western Asia,* Vol. III: *Paleolithic Man and the Nile Valley in Upper and Middle Egypt.* ("Oriental Institute Publications," Vol. XVIII.) Chicago: University of Chicago Press. 152 pp.

SANDFORD, K. S., and ARKELL, W. J.
1939 *Prehistoric Survey of Egypt and Western Asia,* Vol. IV: *Paleolithic Man and the Nile Valley in Lower Egypt with Some Notes upon a Part of the Red Sea Littoral.* ("Oriental Institute Publications," Vol. XLVI.) Chicago: University of Chicago Press. 124 pp.

TOTHILL, J. D. (ed.)
1948 *Agriculture in the Sudan.* London: Oxford University Press. 974 pp.

URVOY, Y.
1933 "Les Formes dunaires à l'ouest du Tchad," *Annales de géographie,* XLII, No. 239 (September 15), 506–15.

VAUFREY, R.
1929 "La Question des isthmes mediterranéens Pleistocenes" (extrait), *Revue de géographie physique et de géologie dynamique,* II, No. 4, 325–42. Paris.
1939 *L'Art rupestre nord-africain.* ("Archives de l'Institut de Paléontologie Humaine," Mémoire 20.) Paris. 127 pp.

WALTHER, J.
1924 *Das Gesetz der Wünstenbildung in Gegenwart und Vorzeit.* Leipzig: Verlag von Quelle & Meyer. 421 pp.

WAYLAND, E. J.
1934 "Rifts, Rivers, Rains and Early Man in Uganda," *Journal of the Royal Anthropological Institute of Great Britain and Ireland,* LXIV, 333–52.

WINKLER, H.
1938–39 *Rock Drawings of Southern Upper Egypt, Sir Robert Mond Desert Expedition.* 2 vols. London: Humphrey Milford.

WOLDSTEDT, P.
1929 *Das Eiszeitalter: Grundlinien einer Geologie des Diluviums.* Stuttgart: Ferdinand Enke. 406 pp.

WRIGHT, W. B.
1937 *The Quaternary Ice Age.* 2d ed. London: Macmillan & Co. 478 pp.

ZEUNER, F.
1945 *The Pleistocene Period.* London: B. Quaritch, Ltd. 322 pp.

Introduction to the Subsistence Economy of India

E. K. JANAKI AMMAL*

THE INDIAN SUBCONTINENT

To examine the subsistence economy of India, it is first necessary to know the background history of the peoples who constitute the population of India and the relationship of these peoples with one another and with their environment. To do this, let us recall the physical aspect of India.

The subcontinent of India is composed of three well-defined regions: Peninsular India, the Himalayas, and the Indo-Gangetic Plain.

Peninsular India is geologically a very old land, being, perhaps, a pla-

* Dr. Janaki Ammal is Director of the Central Botanical Laboratory of the Government of India, at present located in Lucknow. After graduating in Honors at the University of Madras, she continued her postgraduate studies at the University of Michigan and received the Doctor of Science degree in 1931. On returning to India, she was appointed a professor of botany at the University of Madras. Her career has been devoted to genetical studies. She was the sugar-cane geneticist of the Central Agricultural Department of India and contributed to the understanding of the breeding behavior of sugar cane. Later she extended her work on the origin and evolution of cultivated plants. The *Chromosome Atlas of Cultivated Plants*, which she co-authored with Dr. C. D. Darlington, has become one of the great sources for cytological work on the economic plants of the world. She is a Fellow of the Linnaean Society of London, the Royal Geographical Society, the Asiatic Society of Bengal and London, and the Indian Academy of Sciences. An honorary *Legum Doctoris* was bestowed on her in 1955 by the University of Michigan.

teau fragment of the ancient continent of Gondwana, the breaking-up of which may have given rise to Australia, South America, and Africa. This disintegration having occurred after flowering plants had evolved on the earth, the flora of India has many genera in common with Africa, South America, and, to a lesser extent, Australia. Among common plants of economic value may be mentioned rice, cotton, sorghum, amaranthus, yams, and many species of the smaller millets. In this breaking-up of a mighty continent, fissures were formed through which series of lava flows reached thicknesses of up to 10,-000 feet and covered an area of over 200,000 square miles. The region in which this occurred, known as the Deccan trap, covers Kathiawar, Cutch, Madhya Bharat, Gujarat, and Hyderabad. It is characterized by its fertile, black, cotton soil, rich in calcium, magnesium carbonates, potash, and phosphates.

The Himalayas arose from the bed of the great Mesozoic sea Tethys, which once separated Gondwana from Eurasia and through which the warm currents of the Indian Ocean had found their way to western Europe. Along the shores of Tethys the palm *Nipa* grew at a period when species of *Magnolia*, *Artocarpus*, and *Cinnamomum* were flourishing in Greenland and Spitzbergen.

The Himalayan thrust, from north to south, resulted in the formation of a trough 15,000 feet deep, in which the alluvium of the great rivers has been accumulating. From this has developed the third major landform region of India, the Indo-Gangetic Plain, comprising 300,000 square miles of fertile land into which have poured from the north and northwest, in spite of the barrier of the lofty Himalayas, wave upon wave of human migrations. It is difficult to say what the original flora of the Gangetic Plain was like. Quite probably it never supported a dense forest flora but grew from swamp and grasslands which could support both pastoral and agricultural economies. The flora of the Gangetic Plain today is mainly composed of plants that have been introduced from surrounding areas. The plain has been the seat of human activity for such a long time that it is impossible today to see any vestige of virgin vegetation.

From this brief description we can see that India became part of Asia as a result of the Himalayan uplift. Like Arabia, it was an annexation to Asia. It is possible that the evolution of man will be found to be very closely linked with this annexation. The close affinity between the flora and fauna of Sind and that of Africa and Arabia, the continuation of the Sahara into India as the Great Rajputana Desert, and the movement of this desert from west to east are factors that have to be taken into consideration when studying the movement of primitive man into India and within India.

The Ice Age of Europe and northern Asia has been studied very exhaustively in its relation to the evolution of man. In India the changes between interglacial and glacial periods have not been well examined. It is known that, while the ice was confined to the glaciers of the high mountains, Peninsular India was undergoing several pluvial periods corresponding to the advance and receding of ice in the north. The presence of temperate Himalayan plants on isolated hill ranges of southern India is indicative of their migration during periods when the climate of southern India was cooler and wetter than it is today. A most remarkable feature was noted by Blanford (1879) —"the occurrence on the Nilgiris and Anamalai ranges of a wild goat, *Capra Hypocrius*, belonging to a subgenus of which the only known species, *Capra Jeemlaica*, inhabits temperate regions of the Himalayas from Kashmir to Bhutan." *Viburnum* and *Rhododendrons* species of the Nilgiris examined by me are identical with those of the Himalayas (Janaki Ammal, 1952).

MAN IN INDIA

Man, being a naked animal, must have arisen in a tropical or subtropical country. It is impossible to say when men first appeared on the subcontinent of India.

Northwestern India was a great breeding place of anthropoid apes during the Tertiary period, judging from the great numbers of fossils reported from the Siwalik formation. According to Wadia (1953), at least fifteen genera have been found.

Australoids are found today in the Andamans, Madagascar, Indochina, Formosa, Philippines, and Ceylon. They are also found scattered over Peninsular India, where, as food-gatherers, they derive their subsistence by hunting and by the digging of roots. According to Majumdar (1947), Paleolithic people occupied Peninsular India first and then drifted north to the Schan Valley of the Punjab.

The proto-Dravidians must have evolved in India as segregates from the Australoid type. This southern element is to be found not only in India but also as far west as Baluchistan and southern Arabia (Coon, 1939).

The megalithic culture of India is very similar to that of the Mediterranean. The Indus civilization of the third millennium, typified in Mohenjo-Daro culture, is probably pure Dravidian. After the Indus culture came the Aryan invasion, believed to have originated from southern Russia, perhaps from a temporary invasion center near Lake Aral, beginning between 1500 and 1400 B.C. The Bronze Age Aryans brought with them their dairy and cattle culture, which gradually fused with the mainly agricultural culture of pre-Aryan India.

The ancient Aryans, who were practically patriarchal, met the strongly matriarchal Dravidian peoples of India somewhere in the Punjab, and intermingling of the two peoples resulted in the present hybrid Aryo-Dravidian population of the Indo-Gangetic Valley. This process of fusion is still in progress farther south, where the vedic Nambudiri Brahman, supposedly of Aryan stock, takes a Dravidian wife from the matriarchal people of Malabar. The children born from such a union belong to the matriarchal family of the mother. A pure line of Nambudiris is maintained by the eldest son's marrying a Nambudiri woman.

The highly developed Dravidian culture, together with its gods, Shiva and Vishnu, and the cult of the mother-goddess, was assimilated into the simple nature and clan cults of the Aryans to result in what is known as Hindu culture. This is a synthesis of all types of thought which have originated or have been introduced since man existed in India.

The main social feature of Hinduism is its acceptance of caste, or color (*varna*). Caste was at first a genetic classification by the Aryans of the hybrid progeny of Aryans and Dravidians. The Aryans before their invasion had only three castes which were functional—the Priests, the Fighters, and the Artisans. The Sudras, or Dasyus, who formed the fourth class in Aryan nomenclature, were generally the Dravidian people.

In India today, caste is neither functional nor genetic. It essentially defines a mating and eating group, chiefly the latter. Having been a fluid institution, it became rigid during the British occupation. The tendency during the last century has been toward multiplication of caste divisions, so much so that anyone who disbelieved in caste created a new caste. Except the peoples of northwestern India and the vedic Nambudiris of Malabar, who have rigidly kept to their mating systems, there are no pure Indo-Aryans in India today: the bulk of the population of northern India is Aryo-Dravidian; Mongoloid types are found in Bengal, Assam, and Bihar; and Dravidians, proto-Dravidians, and Asio-Australoids form the bulk of the population of Peninsular India. The latter is the best region for analysis of the subsistence economy of the many primitive tribes of India, for Paleolithic and Neolithic cultures still are to be found there.

GENESIS OF TRIBAL ECONOMIES

Of India's total population of 360,-000,000, tribal people number about 25,000,000 (see Fig. 90). Many of them inhabit the fringe of civilized areas and are now being gradually assimilated into the populations of Hindu culture.

Tribal peoples must have formed a considerable part of the population of India during ancient and medieval times, yet the jungle tribes now found scattered over southern India can never have been very numerous, and it was only the first efforts of food production that paved the way to a settled life and resulted in gradual increase of population.

Qualities of Primitives

Primitive man must have devoted more time and expended more energy in securing a food supply than does civilized man. To understand the economics of primitive people, we must understand that, in their minds, all aspects of life are harmonized into a whole. This is due to the long mutual adaptation of mental and institutional life. Primitive economy is nearly static and remains so unless it comes into contact with a different culture, whereupon there first is conflict, then disintegration or assimilation. For the aborigine, every natural process is a manifestation of magical power. He tries to insure success through the exercise of certain ritual acts by which this magical power is evoked. Magic is thus a way of organizing intensive economic results; it is a way of concentration. For example, in Malabar, the man who sows seed has to remain celibate during the period of sowing. Most religious fasts among Hindus have a similar agricultural motivation.

Just as the origin of new forms in plants and animals is brought about by hybridization, resulting in new combinations of parental characters (as

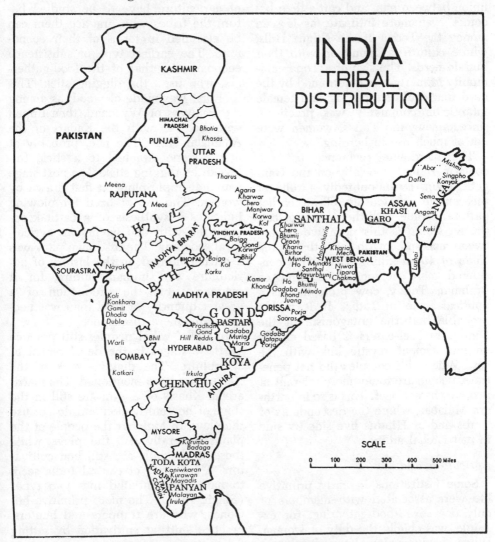

FIG. 90.—India: tribal distribution

well as by isolation in which mutational changes may occur), so also different peoples and cultures arise out of the old by contact and fusion. For example, cattle-keeping evolved from hunting. In North America, whole communities used to follow a particular herd of buffalo upon which they owed their dependence and with which they felt themselves mystically united (Thurnwald, 1932). Once a measure of control over the herd is secured, the herd gradually becomes domesticated. The union between man and cattle then becomes even more intimate, as is seen among the Todas of the Nilgiri Hills, whose culture is bound up with their buffalo herds. The size of a Toda community formerly was determined by the herd that could support it, and female infanticide commonly was practiced, since, among the Todas, women were not of much use in herding.

The inordinate reverence paid to cows in India, especially on the Gangetic Plain, is undoubtedly a relic of this mystic relationship of an earlier pastoral people with their herds of cattle. So strong is this primitive tie between man and cow in India that in the *Code of Manu* killing a cow was considered more heinous than killing a Brahman. Today, cow protection is a political issue in India. It is highly probable that the antagonism of the Hindus to beef-eaters is based chiefly on this ancient mystic link with the cow. Where this complex did not penetrate, people are today more tolerant of people who eat beef. This is so in northern Malabar, where the descendants of Arabs and of Hindus live side by side in matriarchal amity.

Agriculture and Sex

Some institutions in early primitive life were associated with members of only one sex. Food-gathering, for example, was chiefly the duty of women. When food-growing later developed, this was also done by women. Where women regularly provided food, descent is mainly matrilineal, as among the Khasis of Assam, while in pastoral communities, where the herds are tended and kept by men and woman's part is secondary, descent is patrilineal, as with the Todas. In understanding economic patterns this has to be taken into account.

TYPES OF PRIMITIVE AGRICULTURE

Different stages in the development of agriculture have to be studied before the tribes who practice them can be classified in terms of their economies. The earliest type of subsistence economy was that of the food-gatherers, who used the digging stick. This tool first was made of wood, as among the Paniyars of Wyanaad, then tipped with iron, as with the Kadars of the Anamalai Hills. The hoe, probably at first a stone attached to a stick, followed the digging stick. The next stage was the simple plow, at first drawn by women. The use of oxen for plowing indicates a synthesis of a cattle-keeping tribe with one having an agricultural economy. The ox-drawn plow was a great landmark in the history of agriculture and human culture, for it made possible the production of a greater quantity of food than was necessary for mere subsistence.

In India, tribal peoples still practice all these stages in the development of agriculture. The digging stick of the Kadars has been mentioned. The matriarchal Khasis of Assam are still in the stage of hoe cultivation and do not use the plow. In Malabar the people of the plains generally use the plow, while those of the hills are still hoe cultivators. The Gonds of central India seem to have differentiated into two types (Singh, 1944). The more primitive hill Gonds, who are trappers and hunters, practice shifting cultivation by setting fire to the forest and scattering seeds in the ashes, while the Gonds of the plains are agriculturists who have mixed with Hindus and learned to use the ox-drawn plow. It is said that, when rain fails, the latter "harness nude girls to the plough that they draw bleeding under the spur of the goad" (Mukerjee, 1944). Such a reversion during times of stress to an ancient practice identifies the fertility of the soil with the fertility of women. Today, for example, the Khasis transfer women's fertility to the fields by a slow-moving dance (*Nongkrem*) by young girls who perform annually in the open fields. The sanctity of the cow among plow agriculturists derives from its replacing women as drawers of the plow; in India the cow is still designated as "Mother." By extension, cattle are considered holy in India among both pastoral and agricultural peoples.

Increase of population can make one tribe impinge on another's reserve and can thus lead to conflict and disaster. The upland migration of the fast-multiplying and aggressive Syrian Christians of Travancore and Cochin into Wyanaad has had a profound effect on the tribal people there. The Paniyars find their jungles under the plow of new settlers, and a tribe that once was independent in its habitat has now become "depressed," and its whole economy has been changed. The Kadars of Cochin, who once roamed the forests in search of honey, yams, and roots, are now under the care of the Forest Department and are paid in rice for collecting minor forest products. Their women, who were once food-hunters, have ceased to dig for roots, have taken to a life of idleness, and are fast becoming degenerate. Thus the "noble savage" in contact with civilization generally finds himself in an awkward state.

The changing subsistence economies of tribes have been well described by one of India's leading anthropologists, Dr. D. N. Majumdar (1950), with reference to the Hos:

Primitive social groups are aptly called food groups, for the size of the groups depends to a large extent on the mode of food supply. Each stage of culture has its peculiar solution of the problem of numbers in relation to food supply, the mode of subsistence determining the social organisation of the group. Any increase in numbers must keep pace with the improvements in the technique of food production, as otherwise, there is every chance of destroying the social stability which is the pivot of economic progress. There has been a tremendous change in the economic environment of primitive tribes in India. Hunting tribes have given up hunting. The semi-nomadic tribes who lived on fruits and roots and occasional jhuming of their forest clad environment, have become permanent cultivators. Some have no land and are eking out their miserable existence as labourers in the village, and in the neighbouring industrial centres. Consequently many of the customs and practises that were necessary at an earlier stage have become useless, and therefore meaningless to their cultural life. With the restriction of the large areas of forest, over which the Hos were used to roam, and the resulting diminution in the supply of food, a change in diet among the Hos was called for. But they have yet failed to respond to the needs of the hour, as we shall find below.

The gradual increase in number among the Hos without any corresponding increase in the food resources, or improvement in the technique of food production, has lowered the standard of comfort, and many of their present troubles are traceable to this deficiency. Their vitality and the splendid co-operative organisation for exploiting the natural resources of their physical environment (to which competent authorities have given unstinted testimony) have suffered much.

There are many factors that restrict the life of primitive peoples. Since wild products collected by women do not provide suitable food for children, the time of nursing is prolonged, and the interval between births is thus greater in India among primitive people than among urban dwellers. One of the chief causes for the great rise in India's population is the urbanization of its rural population. The effects of a nomadic life, the hunting of dangerous animals, and fishing in the ocean also are great checks on the growth of tribal population.

AGRICULTURE IN RELATION TO CLIMATE

India is part of the monsoon region of the world, and its vegetation is very much influenced by the amount and seasonal distribution of rainfall received. These factors again are reflected in the type of agricultural economies of the peoples occupying the region. The vegetative climax of India is the dense and tall tropical evergreen forest, found on the Western Ghats and in Assam, where the total annual rainfall averages well over 100 inches. Semi-evergreen forests, adjacent to the evergreen forests, are of lesser density, and there man has had a better chance of subduing the vegetation. Food-gatherers are found living in little groups in open places. Here, also, primitive agriculture in the tropics must have evolved. *Jhuming*, or shifting cultivation, by burning and by scattering seeds in the ash, is the only type of agriculture practiced in the region.

The most highly evolved type of *jhuming* is seen in Assam, where a regular rotation of forest clearing takes place once every eight years, so that sufficient time elapses for regeneration of the forest. It is apparent that this continual cutting has its effect, for the flora that come up after clearance are not always the same as those previously destroyed.

The practice of declaring part of the forests sacred has done a great deal to keep the vegetation unchanged. The sacred forests belong to local chiefs or tribal village communities and repre-

sent what may be called nature's primeval forests. People do not dare to cut the trees for fear of disturbing spirits. Hence these forests comprise rich stores of botanical specimens which have become extinct in other parts of Assam. Sacred forests are also a feature of Malabar, where they are known as *kavus*. They serve as sanctuaries for snakes and wild life and often become the nuclei of sylvan temples.

Shifting cultivation is generally practiced in hilly tracts where the rainfall is fairly high. As man becomes more sedentary, he reaches an equilibrium with his environment. This is best seen in Malabar, where mixed plantings (*paramba*) follow *jhuming*. Clearing is only partial, and useful trees are preserved either for timber or firewood or for the growing of pepper and other vines. Among trees kept uncut are species of *Artocarpus* and the wild mango, nutmeg, *Strychnos*, and *Cycas*. Ginger, turmeric, yams, bananas, and tapioca are grown between trees which are pruned annually. Around the houses garden vegetables are also grown. Lowlands are set aside for rice cultivation. This *paramba* form of cultivation is characteristic of the west coast of India. It does not upset the ecological balance of the natural vegetation, and a variety of useful plants is grown simultaneously the year round. Each *paramba* is a self-contained economic unit.

In the Gangetic Valley the type of agriculture varies with the annual rains. This area is the great grain belt of India, where rice, wheat, and barley are grown (Figs. 91–93). Wheat and barley are confined to the northern part, while rice is intensively grown chiefly in Bengal, Assam, Bihar, and on the deltas of Peninsular India. There are two well-marked cropping seasons known as *kharif,* or summer-rain season, and *rabi,* or winter-rain season. *Kharif* crops, sown at the commencement of the southwest, or summer, monsoon and harvested in autumn, are rice, maize, millets, cotton, hemp, sugar cane, tobacco, groundnuts, jute, castor seed, and sesamum. The principal *rabi* crops are wheat, barley, grams, peas, beans, potatoes, linseed, and mustard; they are sown in autumn and harvested in spring. Together these form the cash crops of India. As more and more land is being given to these crops, the subsistence economy of the inhabitants changes.

Low productivity has been the most serious deficiency in India's agricultural practices. One of the chief causes of low production is the uncertainty of rainfall. A weak monsoon results in famine; a too heavy one, in flood. The control of river waters for irrigation and the storage of excess water in tanks have been features of agriculture in India from ancient times. Though the acreage under crops is great, the yield per acre is very low. With an expanding population, more and more land yielding less and less comes under the

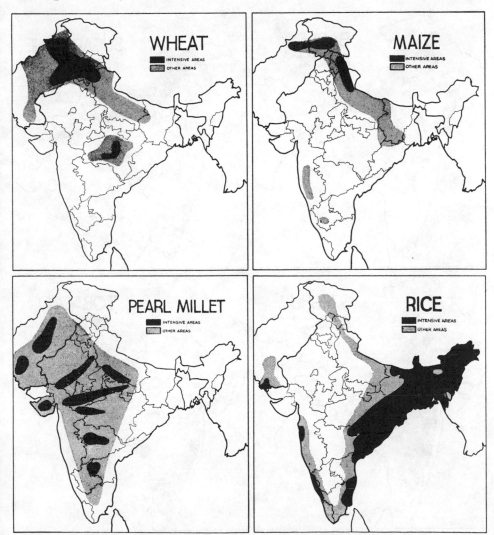

Fig. 91.—Important crops of India: wheat, maize, pearl millet, rice

plow. Independent India is making great strides to increase productivity of land already under cultivation; the first five-year plan made India self-sufficient in food supply.

PLANTS AND MAN IN INDIA

The region including India, Pakistan, and the surrounding countries of Afghanistan and Iran has been the center of origin of many cultivated plants (Vavilov, 1935). Among these, the following are classed as typically of Indian origin: *Oryza sativa*, rice; *Cajanus cajan*, dhall; *Phaseolus aconitifolius*, moth bean; *Phaseolus calcaratus*, rice bean; *Dolichos biflorus*, horse gram; *Vigna sinensis*, asparagus bean; *Amaranthus paniculatus*, amaranth; *Solanum melongena*, eggplant; *Raphanus caudatus*, rat-tailed radish; *Colocasia antiquorum*, taro yam; *Cucumis sativus*, cucumber; *Mangifera indica*, mango; *Gossypium arboreum*, tree cotton; *Corchorus olitorius*, jute; *Cannabis indica*, hemp; *Piper nigrum*, pepper; *Acacia arabica*, gum

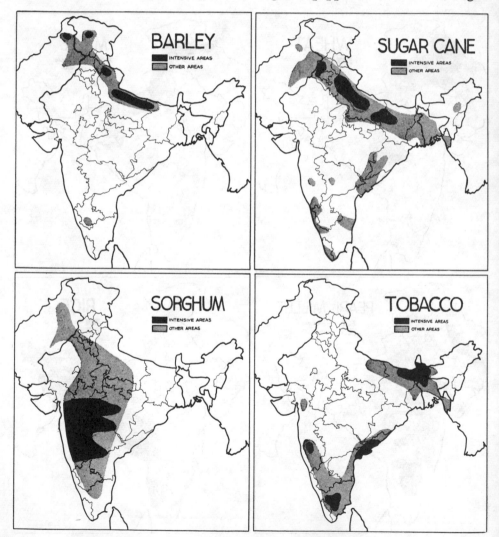

Fig. 92.—Important crops of India: barley, sugar cane, sorghum, tobacco

arabic; *Indigofera tinctoria,* indigo
(Darlington and Janaki Ammal, 1945).

Many economic plants, like banana
and rice, were domesticated simultaneously at various places in Southeast
Asia, where many species are recorded.
The wild banana with its stony fruit
must have attracted, as it still attracts,
primitive tribes. Evolution of the wild
banana into cultivated forms has been
been through the chance development
of sterile forms produced either by hy-
bridity or by triploidy. The occurrence

of sterile and consequently stoneless
forms is immediately noted by wild
tribes which collect and grow them
near their huts. In Assam it is possible
to see the gradation from seed to seed-
less varieties in the local wild form.

Cultivation of the world's food crops
has centered around the great cereals—
wheat, rice, and maize. Combining with
one or more of these are plants of
great local or regional importance. For
example, the coconut is the predominant tree along the west coast of India,

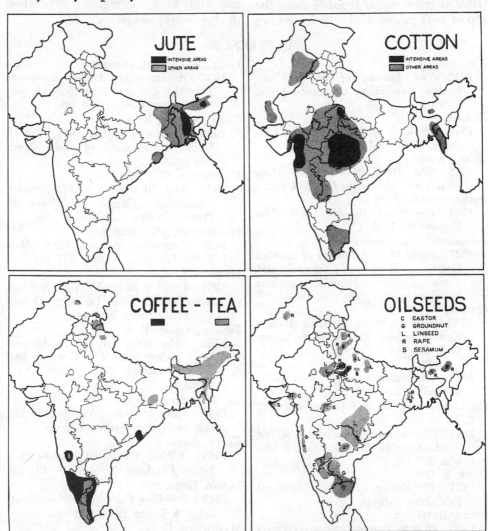

Fig. 93.—Important crops of India: jute, cotton, coffee–tea, oilseeds

and all parts of the tree are used by man as food or for domestic uses and rituals.

Primitive tribes make considerable use of the *Caryota* palm, found scattered in the forests; they use the leaves for thatching and the starch in the pith as food. The digging sticks of the Paniyars in Wyanaad are made of the outer hard rind of *Caryota urens.* Two other palms, *Borassus* and the wild date *Phoenix sylvestris,* also play an important part in the subsistence economy of tribal peoples. Sugar is made from the sap of both palms, while the leaves are used for thatching and for basketmaking. A plant of great significance to the tribals of Peninsular India is the mahua tree, *Madhuca latifoba,* the flowers of which are collected by Gonds, Hos, and other Munda tribes and eaten dried or fermented into a liquor. The seeds contain oil which is used for lamps. The fruit of *Cycas circinalis,* which is rich in starch, is eaten by both the tribal and the peasant population of Malabar. Its leaves are used for thatching and as an evergreen decoration during festive occasions.

REFERENCES

ANDERSON, J. D.
    1913 *The Peoples of India.* Cambridge: Cambridge University Press. 118 pp.
BLANFORD, W. T.
    1879 *Geology of India.* 4 vols. Calcutta: Geological Survey Office.
BOAS, FRANZ
    1938 *The Mind of Primitive Man.* New York: Macmillan Co. 285 pp.
BODENHEIMER, F. S.
    1951 *Insects as Human Food.* The Hague: W. Junk. 352 pp.
BRODERICK, ALAN HOUGHTON
    1947 *Early Man: A Survey of Human Origins.* ("Hutchinson's Scientific and Technical Publications.") London: Hutchinson. 288 pp.
CHILDE, V. GORDON
    1952 *New Light on the Most Ancient East.* London: Routledge & Kegan Paul. 255 pp.
COON, C. S.
    1939 *The Races of Europe.* New York: Macmillan Co. 399 pp.
DARLINGTON, C. D., and JANAKI AMMAL, E. K.
    1945 *Chromosome Atlas of Cultivated Plants.* London: George Allen & Unwin. 397 pp.
DUBE, S. C.
    1951 *The Kamar.* Lucknow: Universal Publishers. 216 pp.
FIRTH, RAYMOND
    1938 *Human Types.* London: Thomas Nelson & Sons. 211 pp.

GOLDENWEISER, ALEXANDER
    1937 *Anthropology: An Introduction to Primitive Culture.* New York: Appleton-Century-Crofts. 550 pp.
GOPALASWAMI, R. A.
    1953 *Census of India, 1951,* Vol. I. Delhi: Government of India Press. 234 pp.
HADDON, A. C.
    1927 *The Wanderings of Peoples.* Cambridge: Cambridge University Press. 124 pp.
HERSKOVITS, MELVILLE J.
    1952 *Economic Anthropology.* New York: Alfred A. Knopf. 547 pp.
HUTTON, J. H.
    1951 *Caste in India: Its Nature, Function and Origins.* London: Oxford University Press. 315 pp.
JANAKI AMMAL, E. K.
    1952 "The Race History of Magnolias," *Indian Journal of Genetics and Plant Breeding,* XII, 82–92. New Delhi.
KANJILAL and DAS
    1954 *Flora of Assam,* Vol. I. Shillong: Government of Assam. 182 pp.
KEITH, ARTHUR
    1948 *A New Theory of Human Evolution.* London: Watts & Co. 451 pp.
LOWIE, ROBERT H.
    1949 *Primitive Society.* London: Routledge & Kegan Paul. 453 pp.
MAJUMDAR, D. N.
    1947 *The Matrix of Indian Culture.*

Lucknow: Universal Publishers. 242 pp.

1950   *The Affairs of a Tribe.* Lucknow: Universal Publishers. 362 pp.

MASANI, MINOC
1945   *Picture of a Plan.* London: Oxford University Press. 63 pp.

MINISTRY OF INFORMATION AND BROADCASTING
1952   *First Five Year Plan.* Delhi: Publication Division, Ministry of Information and Broadcasting, Government of India. 263 pp.

MUKERJEE, RADHAKAMAL
1944   Foreword (pp. i–iv) in SINGH, INDRAJIT, *The Gondwana and the Gonds.* Lucknow: Universal Publishers. 200 pp.

SINGH, INDRAJIT
1944   *The Gondwana and the Gonds.* Lucknow: Universal Publishers. 200 pp.

THURNWALD, RICHARD
1932   *Economics in Primitive Commu-*

nities. London: Oxford University Press. 314 pp.

VAN LOON, HENDRIK WILLEM
1933   *The Home of Mankind.* London: George G. Harrap & Co. 506 pp.

VAVILOV, N. I. (ed.)
1935   *Theoretical Bases of Plant Breeding.* (The Lenin Academy of Agricultural Sciences, Institute of Plant Industry.) Moscow and Leningrad: State Agricultural Publishing House. (In Russian.) (See also English translation of selected writings of N. I. VAVILOV by CHESTER, K. STARR: *The Origin, Variation, Immunity and Breeding of Cultivated Plants.* [*Chronica botanica,* Vol. XIII, Nos. 1–6.] Waltham, Mass.: Chronica Botanica Co. 364 pp. Volume XIII bears the date 1949–50, but it was issued in spring, 1951.)

WADIA, D. N.
1953   *Geology of India.* 3d ed. London: Macmillan & Co. 531 pp.

The Quality of Land Use of Tropical Cultivators

PIERRE GOUROU[*]

INTRODUCTION

What are the limits of our domain, the warm and rainy tropics? The average of the coldest month does not descend below 18° C.; the yearly total of rainfall is greater than 750 millimeters; agriculture is possible without irrigation. These limits are quite controversial, and we are not disposed to insist that they are the best. They seem reasonably good and differ little from other limits that could be proposed.

The continental area within the above limits is about 38,000,000 square kilometers—a notable portion of the emerged continents and an even more notable portion of the valuable area of these continents if we think of how much is cold desert and dry. The tropical rainy world covers a little more than one-third of the non-desert areas of the emerged earth. At first sight, it seems that the rainy tropical world is poorly utilized and that the intensity of tropical land use is below the world average. It seems that the rainy tropical world offers great possibilities of agricultural expansion and that minds disturbed by

the quick increase of the world's population may therefore rest easy (Gourou, 1947b).

There are many approaches to the quality of land use of tropical cultivators: the extent of cultivated areas in the tropical world, physical conditions of tropical agriculture, outputs of the tropical fields, productivity of the individual tropical cultivator, density of the agricultural population in the total area, density of the agricultural population in the effectively cultivated area, various agricultural techniques, and length of fallowing. One approach, however, must be forbidden: to explain tropical agriculture (or tropical agricultures) by a simple determinism, in defiance of the results of observation.

The agricultural potentiality of an area whose climate is not hostile to agriculture stems only in part from the physical conditions of this area; it depends, too, and most importantly, on the techniques used, the number of inhabitants, the level of consumption, the duration of the soil's occupancy, and the nearness and the accessibility of markets. Unavoidably, there are many different kinds of tropical agriculture.

Is it useful to present general views on agriculture in the tropical world as a whole? Tropical Asia counts 8,000,000 square kilometers and 650,000,000 people. The remainder of the tropical world, however, has only 190,000,000 inhabitants for 30,000,000 square kilometers. It is clear that populations of such dif-

[*] Dr. Gourou is Professor of Tropical Geography in the Collège de France, Paris, and Director of the Institute of Geography of the University of Brussels, Belgium. He has conducted extensive field work in Indochina, central Africa, Madagascar, and Brazil. His principal publications include: Les Paysans du Delta tonkinois, 1936; L'Utilisation du sol en Indochine française, 1940; Les Pays tropicaux, 1947; and L'Asie, 1953.

ferent densities cannot receive the same treatment. Within tropical Africa there is a remarkable unevenness of density. Large areas of the Sudan, the Congo Basin, and the Congo-Zambezi plateaus have from 2 to 3 inhabitants per square kilometer. On the other hand, dense concentrations of population appear in Hausaland, in Mossiland, in Iboland, in Ruanda-Urundi (and most generally in the area between the lakes Tanganyika, Albert, and Victoria), and on the southern slopes of Mount Kilimanjaro. It is impossible to explain this unevenness by hasty reference to the "soil's fertility" or to the "altitude's healthfulness"; for example, the Ibo of Nigeria live in a lowland not especially fertile. The same observations apply to the Mossi and the Hausa. A deeper explanation gives first importance to production techniques (especially to the agricultural techniques) and to the systems of organization of space (social and political organization) making possible control of long duration over large and expanding areas. The human geography of the tropical world is not simple even in Africa!

SMALLNESS OF THE CULTIVATED AREAS AND HEAVINESS OF THE AGRICULTURAL DENSITIES

One fact is striking: the areas actually under cultivation are small in the tropical world. By "areas actually under cultivation," we mean those which bear cultivated plants in the course of the year; fallows are excluded. Official statistics may be employed, though they are difficult to use. Brazil has 188,000 square kilometers actually cultivated out of a total area of 8,500,000 square kilometers; that is, 2 per cent of the total area. The agricultural density of Brazil (total number of inhabitants, urban and rural, reported for the cultivated area) is 250 inhabitants on a cultivated square kilometer. The Belgian Congo has an actually cultivated area

of 25,000 square kilometers (1 per cent of its total area); the agricultural density is about 400 persons on a cultivated square kilometer (Gourou, 1951). India has an actually cultivated area of 930,000 square kilometers (30 per cent of its total area); the agricultural density is 360 (Gourou, 1953a, pp. 392–403).

These few examples, which we could easily multiply, teach some important facts. Large differences exist in the percentages of cultivation of the total areas, yet in a country as highly populated as India the actually cultivated area rises only to the modest limit of 30 per cent of the total area—a very low percentage for a country evidently affected by a hunger for cultivated fields. Three things require explanation: the unevenness of the percentages of cultivation, the general smallness of the cultivation percentages, and the heaviness of the agricultural densities. Since, in the three countries examined, rural population is predominant, heaviness of agricultural density is a heaviness of peasant density on the area actually cultivated.

The general smallness of the percentages of cultivation is explained partly by physical conditions. For example, we may assume that in India 30 per cent of the total area is a maximum for the total cultivable area; in a country of ancient history, high civilization, and high density of population (general, agricultural, peasant densities), it is probable that all the cultivable land is actually under plow. Present efforts of Indian authorities are oriented not toward a large extension of the cultivated area but toward an intensification of agricultural processes (first by the transformation of dry fields into irrigated fields). But why this low cultivation of 30 per cent? The answer lies not with a respect on the part of Indian peasants for forests or in the necessity of great pastures for large herds (in fact, Indian oxen and buffaloes are pastured only on the strictly unarable areas). The answer is a physical one: Indian agriculture has reached the maximum of cultivated area. Seventy per cent of India is uncultivable because of the dryness of climate, the steepness of slopes, and the outcropping of rocks or laterite.

But what a difference among the actually cultivated areas in India (30 per cent), Brazil (2 per cent), and the Belgian Congo (1 per cent)! True, natural conditions partially explain this difference. Recent alluvial plains cover a far larger part of the total area in India than in Brazil or in the Belgian Congo. But the natural advantages of India are not large enough to account for the whole difference. We must consider the general densities of population: 6 inhabitants on a square kilometer of total area in Brazil, 5 in the Belgian Congo, and 130 in India. Inequalities in general densities of population mean differences in agricultural techniques, in the organization of space, and in history. India for a long time has been a country of high civilization; the agricultural techniques, especially that of inundating rice fields, and the social and political organization allowed an increase in population (and the capitalization of the increases) and an extension of the permanently cultivated area (and the consolidation of the expansion in cultivated areas).

Heaviness of agricultural densities (250 per square kilometer in Brazil, 400 in the Belgian Congo, and 360 in India) and heaviness of peasant density mean a low individual productivity and low levels of consumption for the peasant population. These facts result from human factors and express the economic value of the agricultural techniques. Hence we understand why the differences among the general densities in Brazil, the Belgian Congo, and India are bound not to substantial differences in the agricultural (and peasant) densi-ties but to differences in the percentages of the actually cultivated areas.

THE "LADANG"

In Africa, America, and New Guinea, shifting cultivation (*ladang*) is the primary source of vegetal foods; agriculturalists clear a portion of forest or savanna, burn the dried vegetation, make holes with a stick and put in various grains, weed or do not weed, protect the cultivated plants from wild animals, and reap. The cleared field may be abandoned after a single harvest or after two or three. Then it is permitted to lie fallow long enough for vegetation to increase so as to restore the soil's humus content and to produce a good quantity of ashes. A fallow of fifteen to twenty-five years appears rational. The *ladang* gives only a weak basis to human societies; such agriculture precludes a high density of population, since only a small part of the arable area is productive at any one time. An increasing population necessitates an extension of the cultivated area, a shortening of the fallow period, then the progressive ruin of the soils, and, after some delay, the inability of the population to continue to subsist in its ancestral home. Without technical innovations (manuring, irrigation, etc.), fields will not be able to support the increase of population; disasters surely will occur. It is often supposed that some process of this sort would explain some of the migrations and the decay of Mayan civilization. The Maya, endowed with the attributes of a superior civilization in respect to intellectual and political matters, had no agricultural technique other than the "milpa," that is to say, *ladang*. Such an agriculture in the end could not support the increasing population correlative with remarkable social and political institutions.

Are physical conditions responsible for the *ladang*, so widely practiced throughout the tropical world? More precisely, does the poverty of tropical soils (or of a very great percentage of tropical soils), owing to their weak resistance to leaching and erosion, favor *ladang* more than other agricultural systems?

In order to understand this problem, we propose to give examples which prove that there is nothing that requires *ladang* to be *the* agricultural technique in the tropical world. As with all agricultural techniques, *ladang* is the expression of a civilizational level and not the result of any inescapable physical constraint. Our first example concerns the Lala of Northern Rhodesia (Peeters, 1950). This tribe practices a particular system of *ladang*, the *chitemene* system, which for the Lala is even more elementary than the same practice of the neighboring Bemba (Richards, 1939). The Northern Rhodesian plateau has a very poor sandy soil, which bears a light forest of sparse and low trees. A Lala family clears each year about 7 hectares of this forest; the trees are chopped down, and then all the vegetal material is piled up in round heaps and the whole is burned. The area covered by the ashes is 50 ares (of the 7 hectares cleared). Eleusine, the cereal comprising the essential part of the food supply, is sown exclusively on these 50 ares. Since the eleusine harvested is able to feed 6.7 persons during one year; since the total area utilized under the *chitemene* system is only 60 per cent of the total area of the country (40 per cent being too steep, of rocky outcrops, or of fluvial beds); since the field cleared is cultivated only one year; and, since the fallow lasts twenty-two years, the agricultural system of the Lala is able to support, durably, some 2.6 persons per square kilometer.

Here is a well-linked whole, it seems: (1) very poor tropical soils, compelling the gathering onto a small part of the cleared area of the woody products of the entire clearing; (2) an elementary agricultural technique, which utilizes no tool except the ax; (3) very low density of population; and (4) a low level of consumption. However, nothing in this harmony is inevitable. The *chitemene* system utilizes only the soils of the plateau, which are very poor and often suffer from dryness. The swampy depressions, which have richer soils and are better supplied with water, are unused or very weakly used. The Lala do not possess agricultural techniques permitting them to benefit from these *dambo,* probably the best parts of their land, and the most valuable as the basis of a permanent and intensive agriculture. The *dambo* comprise 5 per cent of the total area and would assure a cultivated area more extensive than the minute fields of the *chitemene* system.

MADAGASCAR

A part of the population of Madagascar still practices *ladang,* here termed *tavy* (pronounced "tav"). The cultivators clear secondary vegetation (*savoka,* pronounced "savouk"), harvest once or twice, then allow the field to return to secondary vegetation. The *tavy* system has destroyed nearly all the forests of the island. *Tavy* supports only a scattered population, unstable, of low economic level. In contrast, other inhabitants of Madagascar make inundated rice fields. Why so large a difference in agricultural techniques? To answer this question, we shall rapidly describe the Merina and Betsileo lands. These are the most densely inhabited parts of Madagascar; population densities vary between 30 and 100 inhabitants per square kilometer, while the general average of Madagascar is only 6.5 per square kilometer.

Do the Merina and Betsileo regions have exceptionally beneficial natural conditions? Not at all. A visit there and an examination of the excellent maps available, covering a large part of the Merina and Betsileo homelands,[1] show that roughly 90–95 per cent is occupied by hills and plateaus bearing a very poor lateritic clay. On this clay grows a sparse steppe of scattered tufts of *Aristida,* which fire ravishes annually. Agriculture is impossible on the poor soils of the steppe—very poor lands, it would seem at first glance. However, these regions contain the most numerous populations of Madagascar. Merina and Betsileo peasants make inundated rice fields, evidently of Asiatic inspiration (but of *ancient* Asiatic inspiration, since until the twentieth century they ignored the plow and tilled the rice fields only by hoeing and by the stamping of oxen). The surface able to support inundated rice fields is very minute; on several maps[2] it is shown not to exceed 3 or 4 per cent of the total area. The crystalline pre-Cambrian rocks which constitute the high plateaus of Madagascar are dissected by a network of narrow valleys with flat bottoms. The waters filtering through the thick weathered soils covering the crystalline rocks reappear in the valley bottoms and cause the formation of narrow ribbons of swamps, sometimes not exceeding 20 meters in width. If the peat developed in the swamps is destroyed by drainage and fire, the valley bottoms are favorable to the creation of inundated rice fields. The bright green of the young plants in the narrow strips of inundated rice fields contrasts with the

1. Service Géographique de Madagascar publishes excellent maps on the scale of 1:100,000 with precise indications of the human occupation.

2. E.g., Map No. R.43 (Amparafaravola) shows only 1 per cent of the area effectively under inundated rice fields and 1.4 per cent cultivable (but non-utilized) by inundated rice fields. The same values for Map. No. O.51 (Ambositra) are 2.2 and 1.4 per cent; for Map No. P.47 (Tananarive), 13 and 10 per cent.

mournful solitude of the steppes. In addition, peasants sometimes cut watered rice terraces on the lowest slopes. Since the peasant density is at least 4 persons per hectare of inundated riceland, it suffices that 4 per cent of a square kilometer (i.e., 4 hectares) be cultivated in inundated rice to give to this square kilometer a peasant density of 16 inhabitants per square kilometer. If the area of the rice field, in exceptional topographical conditions, reaches 10 per cent of the square kilometer, the peasant density rises to 40.

Thus, although the crystalline plateaus of Madagascar bear soils as poor as the soils of Lala country in Northern Rhodesia, the inundated rice-field technique feeds in Madagascar a much more numerous population. From the same point of view, Mysore, India, shows, on some parts of its ancient crystalline plateaus, populations which exceed 100 inhabitants per square kilometer of total area. Large rice fields are inundated from a remarkable network of artificial tanks or reservoirs.

THE LAND OF BELÉM

The land of Belém is situated in Brazil, to the east of the Pará River and to the north of the Guama River (Gourou, 1949). This area of 21,000 square kilometers is notable for its relatively high density of population. The average density was 14.4 inhabitants per square kilometer in 1940, excluding the town of Belém do Pará. The average density of both the remainder of the state of Pará and all the state of Amazonas was 0.28 inhabitant per square kilometer. In Amazonia one may find many areas of several thousand square kilometers each altogether without inhabitants.

On the low terraces which occupy the largest part of the land of Belém, the rural population practices an agriculture of a traditional kind which finds its origin in the Indian past. But today this agriculture is not only a subsistence agriculture but also a commercial agriculture, producing all the products necessary to the market of the city of Belém. The cassava (Portuguese *mandioca*), which is the basis for *farinha,* the principal food, is cultivated under the *roça* system, the same technique as *ladang.* Since the rural population is relatively large, and since it has to supply the great market of the city of Belém (with *farinha* and also with charcoal), the land of Belém has been entirely cleared of its primary forest, and all the vegetation is secondary. Frequently the fallow is not prolonged beyond five years. Moreover, Portuguese colonization began in the seventeenth century, taking on a more intensive rhythm in the eighteenth century (with immigration of Azorians). Then in the nineteenth century the rubber boom and catastrophic droughts in northeastern Brazil resulted in a heavy colonization by Cearenses.

Under such conditions, and without fertilizer, soils rapidly wear out. It is conceivable that the output of cassava will be so reduced within a few decades that the food supply of town and country will present a problem. However, the remedy lies near at hand. Experiments by the Instituto Agronomico do Norte in the vicinity of the city of Belém reveal that the flooded areas of the *igarapé* (valleys with flat bottoms, dissecting the terraces of the land of Belém) of the experimental station produce without manure, on 1 hectare, 4,000 kilograms of paddy, or 1,500 kilograms of jute fibers. The future of the land of Belém resides in the soils now being flooded by the tides (which, on the southern shore, move only fresh waters). The necessary condition of progress lies in the shifting of fields from the valley-top terraces to the bottom of the valleys and in the adoption of hydraulic techniques and collective works allowing for the utilization of the best soils, neglected until now. The higher soils will not be useless; they will have a commercial value as tree plantations producing rubber, cacao, oil palm, and so on.

It is interesting to compare the land of Belém and the island of Marajó, which is to the west of the Pará River. Marajó, largely similar to the land of Belém, is not an expansion of modern deltaic alluvium. It has large terraces of leached soils. Today these terraces are utilized as pastures for cattle. The density of population on Marajó Island is 3 inhabitants per square kilometer. Archeological evidence reveals that before European discovery Marajó Island was as notable for its relatively high level of civilization as for its large number of inhabitants. Great mounds give evidence of large public works and of an elaborate social and political organization. Fine pieces of pottery indicate that the Marajó people were socially stratified. It is logical (though hypothetical) to imagine that the Marajó people were too numerous for their agricultural technique; practicing only shifting cultivation, the Marajó people were unable to insure a permanent food production for the long run. Deterioration of the people and of their civilization was the end of the disharmony among the political, demographic, and artistic aspects and the agricultural technique of the Marajó civilization. Such decline was not an unavoidable result of poor soils. With inundated cultivation and with manuring, the Marajó people would not have been the victims of soil exhaustion (if such a cause was responsible for the decadence of the Marajó people).

RUANDA-URUNDI

Ruanda-Urundi, with agricultural techniques less refined than those of Asia, has a demographic evolution that generates problems similar to those in India or Java. A surface of 21,000 square kilometers has an average density of 135 inhabitants per square kilometer, and in the "Territoire" of Ruhengeri, for example, the general density reaches 166 inhabitants per square kilometer of total area. The agricultural density is 393 inhabitants per cultivated square kilometer (Gourou, 1953*b*). Of the total area, 42 per cent is effectively cultivated. This percentage is remarkably high, given the greatly incised relief of the country, where differences of 1,000 meters frequently occur between summits and valley floors. Several *collines* ("hills")—as the townships are called—have a general density higher than 400 inhabitants per square kilometer. The high general density has been possible by extension of the cultivated area. The agricultural techniques are, unfortunately, only a little better than *ladang*. The production per hectare and per cultivator is very low, though men and women devote a great deal of work to the fields. The high density of population of Ruanda-Urundi is consequently not the result of advanced techniques; it results from local political circumstances and from history. From the sixteenth or seventeenth century, the Ruanda and the Urundi had a strong system of government; hereditary monarchies with relatively efficient administrations gave to Ruanda-Urundi a protection against external dangers and the possibility of capitalizing on the annual increase of population.

The situation suggests a population stage intermediate between the human geographies of Negro Africa and tropical Asia. Such a development is full of dangers, as we saw for the land of Belém. One possible partial remedy would be inundated rice fields, as in Madagascar. Such a technique is not unthinkable in the Ruanda-Urundi, where so many valley bottoms are swampy. However, it is evident that the area of possible rice fields is not enough for the increasing demand of a growing population (birth rate, 52 per thousand; death rate, 27).

ASIAN TROPICAL CULTIVATORS

In many parts of tropical Asia the valuable area is totally utilized. In the case of the delta of Tonkin (Gourou, 1936, 1940*a*, 1940*b*), the entire alluvial plain—15,000 square kilometers—is effectively cultivated every year (with the exception of roads, rivers, houses, graveyards), and one-half of the cultivated area yields two harvests a year. Such intensive agriculture is the result of fertile alluvial soils, of dikes and irrigation canals assuring protection against river floods and against dryness, and of a skilful agriculture paying a great deal of attention to the manure problem. The peasant population averages 500 persons per square kilometer of total area and 600 persons per square kilometer of cultivated area (areas harvested twice in a year are taken only for their topographical, cartographical value).

The agriculture of the Tonkinese Delta is highly expensive in terms of human labor. One harvest of paddy requires up to 200 days of work for 1 hectare, so that, if this harvest produces 2,000 kilograms of paddy, a day's work has produced only 10 kilograms of paddy; a field with two annual harvests requires as much as 400 man-days of work per year. It is certainly feasible to reduce the quantity of agricultural work without reduction of the output; the problem is to find employment for the unemployed agriculturalists in a country with an annual surplus of births over deaths not lower than 25 per thousand. The annual increase of the peasant population of the delta must be on the order of 150,000 persons, already a large group to be added each year to the people employed in industrial and tertiary activities. Yet the reduction of agricultural work (with the corollary increased productivity) would certainly induce a great exodus from the countryside. If the expenditure of human agricultural labor be only a quarter of the present expenditure, if a rice field twice harvested requires only 100 days of work instead of 400, will it be possible to find employment for the three-quarters of the peasantry deprived of work? Is it not possible to say that intensive agricultural techniques (and vegetarian food habits) have led the Tonkinese peasants into a blind alley? The same situation is found in all countries with high peasant-population densities per cultivated area. It is not too disturbing when the cultivated area is only a modest percentage of the total area, but it becomes terribly disturbing if the cultivated area extends to the entire valuable part of the total area.

To repeat, natural conditions do play a role in such an evolution but not in a decisive fashion. For example, the island of Madura, with a total area of 5,971 square kilometers, had in 1940 an average density of 313 inhabitants per square kilometer. Yet Madura does not benefit from volcanic soils (too often held to be determinant of the high densities of some parts of Indonesia), and only 740 square kilometers of the 4,460 cultivated are irrigated.[3] Madura, with its low hills and its soils of medium grade at best, has a remarkably high percentage of the total area in permanent fields, or *tegalan*. The peasants of Madura have set off elaborate techniques of permanent dry agriculture—artificial terracing, rotation, manuring, etc.—which demand much work but which every year produce remunerative crops (remunerative, that is, relative to the economy of the peasant of Madura). The quality of land use in the Asiatic tropics is not fundamentally different from that in the Asiatic temperate plains; it derives from a civiliza-

tional complex and not particularly from tropical conditions.

PROSPECTS

In the largest part of the tropical world (keeping in mind that the majority of tropical cultivators are concentrated in a small part of the tropical world), the peasants practice extensive techniques as poor when measured by output (harvest per hectare) as when measured by productivity (harvest per day of work). The quality of land use is very low; such a situation is primarily the result of techniques (and of the civilizations in a broader sense) and not the direct result of unfavorable physical conditions. Surely large areas of tropical soils are very poor. But, except in Asia and in some other places like Madagascar, tropical cultivators have not employed the techniques which would allow them to make the best of the richest soils, of the soils well watered. Thus tropical cultivators, circumscribed by their techniques, have limited themselves to the use of poor soils (selecting, from the large category of poor tropical soils, the less poor and the physically arable soils). The *ladang* permits one harvest on very bad soils, the extreme example being the Lala of Northern Rhodesia, who sow only on the patches of ashes and neglect the remainder of the cleared area. Numerous tropical cultivators, knowing only extensive techniques, have cultivated just the areas best adapted to these techniques—areas with light soils on the terraces and the plateaus. They have neglected the swampy and heavy soils of the valley bottoms, which are endowed with the greater agricultural potentialities but are less easily utilizable by means of *ladang*. On the contrary, the cultivators of the Asiatic tropics have applied their intensive techniques on the lowest soils. To the various "levels" of the agricultural techniques correspond various

3. Gourou, 1953*a*, pp. 350–52; some observations on the relations between density of population and soils in Indonesia.

topographic levels of application of these techniques. The simplest techniques apply to the lighter soils, whose clearing is rather easy. The intensive techniques apply to heavy soils, whose clearing is less easy. Human choices have been influenced much more by the level of techniques than by physical conditions.

A true "inversion" of the cultivated areas is necessary if tropical agriculture is to become more intensive, more productive, and able to support increasing populations. Given the conditions of soil fertility and the need for water for the plants, the tropical agriculturalist has to concentrate his efforts on the lowest topographic levels, generally the richest and the wettest. Mastery over water is the first necessary condition of agricultural progress in the tropical world, particularly in the dry fields of food plants. By descending the slopes, abandoning the fallows, and limiting itself to the most fertile areas, tropical agriculture will increase the output per hectare, the productivity per man-hour, and the total mass of food delivered to a mankind expanding in numbers. Tropical agriculture has a bright and considerable future if it concentrates on the very soils able to reward intensive techniques and if it is not reluctant to improve dry and poor soils.

The confining of tropical agriculture on the best soils would ease the introduction of motorized implements and, incidentally, increase the productivity of the cultivators. Let us keep in mind that one hour of work of a tropical peasant produces no more than 4 or 5 kilograms of grain (De Schlippe, 1948). Among the obstacles to mechanical tropical agriculture, first place must be given to the present necessity for fallowing; the careful and expensive work required for perfect mechanical clearing is justified if the clearing is definitive, but it is less justified (and less re-warded) if a new clearing must be made after a long fallow. Mechanized clearing must be associated with intensive and permanent agriculture. Another obstacle to clearing by machines is the extreme hardness of the plateau soils in dry seasons. Because of this hardness, the land is cleared only in the rainy season, and this delay in beginning the planting means that the period of cultivation is dangerously short and that the employment of mechanical implements is correlatively expensive. These various inconveniences have been underlined by the "groundnut scheme" of Tanganyika (Wood, 1950).[4]

In tropical agriculture intensive production of food products must replace extensive production; the more favorable situation for intensive production of food products is in the bottom of the valleys; and the slopes and the plateaus must be utilized for tree plantations (*Hevea, Elaeis,* etc.) and for scientific silviculture. I do think that tropical cultivators will have a brilliant economic future with a balanced agriculture: irrigated and inundated fields in the valley bottoms, animal husbandry (not by extensive pasture but by cultivation of food for animals on fields intensively cultivated), and tree plantations.

I must say that other views have been published. In an interesting paper (Vine, 1955) a specialist on Nigeria says that the soils on the Nigerian low plateaus are able to support for an in-

4. This interesting experiment, made between 1947 and 1952 in three parts of Tanganyika Territory—Kongwa, Urambo, and Nachingwea—was intended to produce enormous quantities of groundnuts (peanuts). It was abandoned, after an expenditure of £36,000,000, because of the scarceness of the yields. The failure was explained as due to uniform clearing of very different soils and to very expensive methods of clearing. It was found very difficult to clear the soils of all the woody roots, which were obstacles against the use of mechanical implements.

definite time native agriculture with short fallows (three to four years) and that prospects of integrating modern techniques into the native agriculture of the plateaus (green manure, chemical manuring, selection, etc.) are good. The soils of Nigeria are very different from one field to the next; it is incautious to generalize about them.

It is easier to talk about means of improvement than to carry them out. The first step must be acceptance by tropical cultivators of the necessity for a re-evaluation of their techniques. Will the new methods give the peasants a greater productivity? Within a framework of premechanical techniques, the passage from *ladang* to intensively cultivated, permanent fields does not necessarily carry with it an increase of productivity—not if the available arable area is so spacious as to permit suitable fallows and thus evade the risk of soil exhaustion. Tropical cultivators are aware of this. Thus, the peoples of some mountains of West Africa (Atacora Mountains, Bauchi Plateau, Mandara Mountains, Adamawa, etc.) learned relatively intensive agricultural techniques, such as artificial terracing and manuring, in response to a crisis: they had retreated into the mountains primarily for defense against external dangers, particularly against the raids of slavers. The establishment of peace and the suppression of slavery allowed these peoples to abandon their mountains and to clear the surrounding plains where arable areas were plentiful. In the new environment they are forgetting these techniques and returning to *ladang*, in which they find a greater productivity. In the same way, all the efforts made between 1920 and 1940 to lead the Moi Rhade (Annamite Cordillera of Indochina) to utilize the plow and to till inundated rice fields have been wasted. Since administrative pressure has been relaxed in keeping

with political events affecting eastern Indochina, the Rhade have returned to *ladang*. They have rediscovered cherished habits (we must not underestimate the strength of custom), and they obey also the lessons of experience; they have observed that permanent rice fields, without manure, gave a lesser output per day of work than *ladang*. To be sure, this point applies only with reference to a rather sparse population, *ladang* on unexhausted soils, suitable fallows, and annual rice fields without manure. In the same way, the Mnong Rlam of Darlac, Indochina, forced by the authorities to use the plow and to replant rice, have reverted to stamping by buffaloes and to direct sowing. Still worse, the Vietnamese colonists of Ban Methuot, Darlac, have turned for the first time to *ladang* and have abandoned the ancestral plow.

The passage from extensive to intensive techniques does not appear to the tropical peasant to be necessarily advantageous. Such an evolution is likely to be realized only where the following conditions prevail: exhaustion of the soils because of short fallows, reasonably high intellectual level of the population, introduction of techniques enhancing the productivity of intensive agriculture (motorization, manure, etc.), opening of markets, and development of commercial agriculture.

CONCLUSIONS

I have intended to explain by some examples the quality of land use by tropical cultivators; I have made some comments about the renovation of tropical agriculture. It seems certain to me that the tropical world is able to produce larger and larger quantities of agricultural products and to give the cultivators a higher level of consumption. Good roads and railways to destroy the isolation and enlarge the markets and the rational use of water, manure, and machines will allow immense progress. The comparison of cultivated areas in diverse tropical countries underlines the magnitude of the possible progress.

However, nothing very valuable will be realized if all the elements of the present situation are not clearly understood. It is not less indispensable to study the relations between the elements of a part of the earth's surface than to analyze each of those elements.

Perhaps it will be useful to indicate that such an intellectual position is exactly the position of human geography. Human geography is a synthetic discipline, aiming at the description and explanation of the relations between man and his environment. But what is the "natural environment"? The geographer would be wrong if he considered the natural environment as independent from man. The natural environment in two ways depends on man: first, man has transformed profoundly the environment (savanna substituted for forest, fields substituted for forest, secondary forest substituted for primary forest, etc.); second, man has interpreted the environment in terms of his techniques. The same natural environment will result in different human landscapes when interpreted (and transformed) by traditional European peasant civilization, by Chinese civilization, and by modern American civilization. The Merina of Madagascar and the Bemba of Rhodesia have created very different human landscapes in similar physical environments.

Density of population is a good basis for the study of human geography. A detailed map of the density of the population asks many questions: Why so few inhabitants here? Why so many there? Answers may be given by climate, physiography, soils, diseases, history, or techniques (of production and of spatial organization). Each particular question may be the field of specialists. But the weight of a population over a particular area is not explained by the juxtaposition of specialized studies; it must be explained by geographical appreciation of the interdependence of multiple factors.

No progress in the understanding of the human aspects of the landscape is possible if these aspects are simply considered to react to the physical elements of the landscape. The relations between the two are not direct; they are obliged to cross the prism of a civilization. Explanation does not progress if the human groups are considered to be compelled by the natural environment to adopt such-and-such techniques. Nor does the explanation make better progress if we consider that a human group examines a natural environment, evaluates the "possibilities," and chooses the more attractive. "Determinism" (physical determinism) and "possibilism" are unable to give a total explanation. The "possibilities" are in man much more than in nature; they are given to man by the civilization. Civilization is not a product of the physical environment, nor is it a product of a choice oriented by a finality. If a human group selected a certain type of exploitation of some resources, the choice was undetermined. Man has made himself, without knowing where he was willing to go. He has made himself by the making of himself. There was no physical determination, finalistic predestination, or conscious decision; there was a necessity for an undetermined choice and, consequently, a departure into a future. This geographical interpretation of the position of man on earth and in history is full of hope. The future, good or bad, will be the work of man and not the result of physical constraints.

REFERENCES

ADRIAENS, E. L.
  1951 "Recherches sur l'alimentation des populations au Kwango," *Bulletin agricole du Congo belge*, XLII, No. 2, 227–69, 473–550.

ALLOUARD, P.
  1936 "Pratique de la lutte contre les feux de brousse," *Bulletin économique de l'Indochine*, XXXIX, 991–1009.

ANONYMOUS
  1954–55 *Comptes-rendus de la 2e Conférence interafricaine des sols, Leopoldville*. 2 vols. Brussels: Ministère des Colonies.

AUBRÉVILLE, A.
  1949 *Climats, forêts et desertification de l'Afrique tropicale*. Paris: Société d'Editions Géographique, Maritime et Coloniale. 352 pp.

BEARD, J. S.
  1946 *The Natural Vegetation of Trinidad*. ("Oxford Forestry Memoirs," No. 20.) Oxford: Clarendon Press. 152 pp.

BECKETT, W. H.
  1943 *Akokoazo: A Survey of a Gold Coast Village*. ("London School of Economics Monographs on Social Anthropology," No. 10.) 96 pp.

BENNETT, H. H.
  1928 "Some Geographic Aspects of Cuban Soils," *Geographical Review*, XVIII, No. 1, 62–82.

BRIGGS, G. W. G.
  1941 "Soil Deterioration in the Southern District of the Tiv Division, Benue Province," *Farm and Forest*, June, pp. 8–12. Ibadan.

BROWN, W. H.
  1919 *Vegetation of Philippine Mountains*. Manila: Bureau of Printing. 434 pp.

CHEVALIER, A.
  1935 "Les Îles du Cap-Vert," *Revue de botanique appliquée et d'agriculture tropicale*, XV, Nos. 170–71, 734–1090.

COOK, O. F.
  1921 "Milpa Agriculture," *Annual Report of the Smithsonian Institution for 1919*, pp. 307–26. Washington, D.C.: Government Printing Office.

CRAENE, A. DE
  1955 "La Fertilité des latosols du nord-est du Congo belge et des relations avec la morphologie des profils pédologiques: La Latérisation," pp. 309–29 in *Comptes-rendus de la 2e Conférence interafricaine des sols, Leopoldville*. 2 vols. Brussels: Ministère des Colonies.

CRIST, R. W.
  1935 "Le Llanero," *Revue de géographie alpine*, XXIII, No. 1, 97–114. Grenoble.
  1944 "Cultural Crosscurrents in the Valley of the Rio São Francisco," *Geographical Review*, XXXIV, No. 4, 587–612.

FALKNER, F. R.
  1938 "Die Trockengrense des Regenfeldbaus in Afrika," *Petermanns geographische Mitteilungen*, LXXXIV, Nos. 7–8, 210–14.

FARMER, B. H.
  1954 "Problems of Land Use in the Dry Zone of Ceylon," *Geographical Journal*, CXX, 21–33.

FORDE, C. DARYLL
  1937 "Land and Labour in a Cross River Village," *Geographical Journal*, LXXXIX, No. 1, 24–51.

FÜRER-HAIMENDORF, C. VON
  1943 *The Aboriginal Tribes of Hyderabad*, Vol. I: *The Chenchus*. London: Macmillan & Co. 391 pp.

GOUROU, PIERRE
  1936 *Les Paysans du Delta tonkinois*. ("Publications de l'École Française d'Extrême-Orient," Vol. XXVI.) Paris: L'Éditions d'Art et d'Histoire. 666 pp.
  1940a *L'Utilisation du sol en Indochine française*. Paris: Centre d'Études de Politique Étrangère. 466 pp.
  1940b *La Terre et l'homme en Extrême-Orient*. Paris: Librairie Armand Colin. 224 pp.
  1947a "Geographie du peuplement en Nigérie méridionale," *Bulletin de la*

Société Belge d'Études Géographiques, XVII, Nos. 1–2, 58–64. (After C. DARYLL FORDE and C. SCOTT, *The Native Economies of Nigeria*. London, 1946.)

1947b *Les Pays tropicaux*. Paris: Presses Universitaires. 196 pp. (Translated into English as: *The Tropical World: Its Social and Economic Conditions and Its Future Status*. London, 1953. 156 pp.)

1948 "Problèmes du monde tropical," *Les Cahiers d'Outre-Mer*, I, No. 1, 4–13. Bordeaux.

1949 "Le Pays de Belém," *Bulletin de la Société Belge d'Études Géographiques*, XVIII, No. 1, 19–36.

1951 "Carte de la densité de la population au Congo belge et au Ruanda-Urundi," *Atlas général du Congo*. Brussels: Académie Royale des Sciences Colonials. (Seven-page separate for *Atlas* in course of publication.)

1953a *L'Asie*. Paris: Hachette. 542 pp.

1953b *La Densité de la population au Ruanda-Urundi; esquisse d'une étude géographique*. ("Institut Royal Colonial Belge, Section des Sciences Naturelles et Médicales," Vol. XXI, No. 6.) Brussels. 239 pp.

1955 *La Densité de la population rurale au Congo belge*. ("Académie Royale des Sciences Coloniales, Classe des Sciences Naturelles et Médicales" [N.S.], Vol. I, No. 2.) Brussels. 168 pp.

HARDY, F.
1939 "Soils and Soil Erosion in St. Vincent," *Tropical Agriculturist*, XVI, No. 3, 58–65.

JONES, G. L.
1943 "The Human Factor in Land Planning," *Farm and Forest*, December, pp. 161–66.

KEESING, F. M.
1938 "Population and Land Utilization among the Lepanto," pp. 458–64 in *Comptes-rendus du Congrès International de Géographie, Amsterdam*, Vol. II. Leiden: E. J. Brill. 615 pp.

KOPP, A.
1932 "La Vanille dans l'assolement de la canne à sucre à La Réunion," *Revue de botanique appliquée et d'agri-*

culture tropicale, XII, No. 125, 32–47.

KUHNHOLTZ-LORDAT, G.
1939 *La Terre incendiée: Essai d'agronomie comparée*. Nîmes: Éditions de la Maison Carrée. 362 pp.

LAL, R. B., and SEAL, S. C.
1949 *General Health Survey, Lingur Health Center, 1944*. Calcutta: All India Institute of Hygiene and Public Health. 323 pp.

LAMAL, R. P. F.
1949 *Essai d'étude demographique d'une population du Kwango: Les Basuku du territoire de Feshi*. ("Institut Royal Colonial Belge, Section des Sciences Morales et Politiques," Vol. XV, No. 4.) Brussels. 189 pp.

LEHMANN, H.
1938 "Die Bevölkerung der Insel Sumatra," *Petermanns geographische Mitteilungen*, LXXXIV, No. 1, 3–15.

LÉVI-STRAUSS, C.
1948 "La Vie familiale et sociale des Indiens Nambikwars," *Journal de la Société des Americanistes* (N.S.), XXXVII, 1–132.

McBRIDE, G. M. and M. A.
1942 "Highland Guatemala and Its Maya Communities," *Geographical Review*, XXXII, No. 2, 252–68.

MAURAND, P.
1938 "L'Indochine forestière," *Bulletin économique de l'Indochine*, XLI, No. 4, 801–29.

MAURICE, A., and PROUX, G. M.
1954 "L'Âme du Riz," *Bulletin de la Société des Études Indochinois*, XXIX, Nos. 2–3, 125–258.

MENDES DA SILVEIRA, RENATO
1948 "Paisagens culturais da Baixada Fluminense." Doctoral dissertation, Faculdade de Filosofia, Ciencias e Letras, Universidade de São Paulo.

MURPHY, R. C.
1939 "The Littoral of Pacific Colombia and Ecuador," *Geographical Review*, XXXII, No. 1, 1–33.

NICOLAÏ, H., and JACQUES, J.
1954 *La Transformation des paysages congolais par le chemin de fer: L'Exemple du B.C.K.* ("Institut Royal Colonial Belge, Section des Sciences Na-

turelles et Médicales," Vol. XXIV,
No. 1.) Brussels. 208 pp.

PEETERS, D. U.
1950 *Land Usage in Serenje District.*
("Rhodes-Livingstone Institute Paper," No. 19.) London: Oxford University Press. 100 pp.

PELZER, K. J.
1945 *Pioneer Settlement in the Asiatic Tropics.* (Special Publication No. 29.) New York: American Geographical Society. 290 pp.

PENDLETON, R. L.
1941 "Laterite and Its Structural Uses in Thailand and Cambodia," *Geographical Review,* XXXI, No. 2, 177–202.
1942 "Land Utilization and Agriculture in Mindanao," *ibid.,* XXXII, No. 2, 180–210.

PITTIER, H.
1936 "Consideraciones acerca de la destrucción de los bosques y del incendio de las sabanas," *Boletín Sociedad Venezolana de Ciencias Naturales,* III, No. 26, 1–12.

RICHARDS, A. I.
1939 *Land, Labour and Diet in Northern Rhodesia.* London: Oxford University Press. 423 pp.

RODHAIN, J.
1950 "Documents pour servir à l'histoire de la maladie du sommeil au Congo belge: La Trypanosomiase humaine au Katanga," *Institut Royal Colonial Belge, Bulletin des Séances,* XXI, No. 3, 692–707. Brussels.

SCAETTA, H.
1936 "Les Pâturages de haute montagne en Afrique centrale," *Bulletin agricole du Congo belge,* XXVII, No. 3, 323–78.

SCHLIPPE, G. P. DE
1948 "Sous-station d'essai de l'INEAC à Kurukureta: extraits du premier rapport annuel," *Bulletin agricole du Congo belge,* XXXIX, No. 2, 361–402.

SHAH, V. and S.
1949 *Bhuvel: Socio-economic Survey of a Village.* Bombay: Indian Society of Agricultural Economics. 154 pp.

SPURR, A. M. M.
1955 "A Basis of Classification of the Soils of Areas of Composite Topography in Central Africa, with Special Reference to the Soils of the Southern Highlands of Tanganyika," pp. 175–90 in *Comptes-rendus 2e Conférence interafricaine des sols, Leopoldville.* 2 vols. Brussels: Ministère des Colonies.

STAMP, L. DUDLEY
1938 "Land Utilization and Soil Erosion in Nigeria," *Geographical Review,* XXVIII, No. 1, 32–45.

TOTHILL, J. D.
1940 *Agriculture in Uganda.* London: Oxford University Press. 551 pp.

VINE, H.
1955 "Is the Lack of Fertility of Tropical African Soils Exaggerated?" pp. 389–406 in *Comptes-rendus 2e Conférence interafricaine des sols, Leopoldville.* 2 vols. Brussels: Ministère des Colonies.

WAIBEL, L.
1948 "Vegetation and Land Use in the Planalto Central of Brazil," *Geographical Review,* XXXVIII, No. 4, 529–54.

WHITE, S.
1941 "Notes on Mixed Farming as Practised by Some Shuwa Arabs in Parts of Dikwa Emirate," *Farm and Forest,* June, pp. 24–25.
1944 "Agricultural Economy of the Hill Pagans of Dikwa Emirate, Cameroons (British Mandate)," *ibid.,* September, pp. 130–34.

WISER, W. H. and C. V.
1946 *Behind Mud Walls.* New York: Friendship Press. 180 pp.

WOOD, A.
1950 *The Groundnut Affair.* London: Bodley Head. 264 pp.

The Grassland of North America: Its Occupance and the Challenge of Continuous Reappraisals

JAMES C. MALIN*

THE PROBLEM OF DEFINITION

Any attempt at regional definition of a portion of earth space involves time as one of the determining criteria. Also, in view of the fact that the term "grassland" has been designated as the term descriptive of the region proposed for study, that selection implies that the definition is in terms of vegetational cover. As plant growth varies with total prevailing conditions, both temporary and long term, every vegetational map has to be dated. For some areas conditions have been so decisive that over long periods of time no major variation has occurred. In transition zones between such relatively stabilized nuclear areas, the vegetational cover has fluctuated to a greater or lesser degree with the prevailing variability of environment. Extremes of moisture and temperature operated differently upon each type of vegetation as well as upon particular species. As between trees and grass, trees may expand their coverage over a period favorable to their growth

and then suffer a severe setback, or even destruction, by an extreme of drought and heat or extreme cold; such weakened woody growth as may have survived may be finished off by disease or insect enemies. In addition, we know that destruction from fire caused by lightning took its toll.[1] Added to these

1. Two examples of reported lightning-ignited prairie fires in the High Plains are cited. The location was Cheyenne County, Kansas, near the intersection of 40° north latitude and 102° west longitude at an altitude of nearly 4,000 feet. The number of such examples might be multiplied indefinitely. In using newspaper sources as evidence, not all references to lightning as a cause of fires would be acceptable. These particular instances possess characteristics that contribute to credibility: the specific location is given; the community turned out to fight the fire; the area burned was specified; and the record was printed within the week. The point to be emphasized is that such discriminative details would seem to differentiate these reports from the rumor category and, in making the record specific, would justify the use of these cases and many other similar ones that might be cited in the High Plains newspapers and would constitute proof of lightning as a cause of prairie fires.

St. Francis (Kan.) Herald, July 13, 1911, Bird City Department: "Not every year will the prairie grass burn in July, but such is the case now. During one of our electrical storms last week lightning struck a little ways southwest of W. D. Kyle's place burning over quite a territory before the flames were extinguished."

St. Francis (Kan.) Herald, August 3, 1911: "Last Thursday a bad prairie fire destroyed the winter range of Henry Weaver. Sunday

* Dr. Malin has been in the Department of History at the University of Kansas since 1921. He was president of the Agricultural History Society in 1943–44. His books include: *Winter Wheat in the Golden Belt of Kansas*, 1944; *The Grassland of North America: Prolegomena to Its History*, 1947; *The Nebraska Question*, 1954; and *The Contriving Brain and the Skillful Hand in the United States*, 1955.

hazards were those introduced by man, primitive and modern, particularly the use of fire. The factor of fire has been little understood and has been subject to much exaggeration as well as lack of discrimination. Generalization is always dangerous and nowhere more so than on the matter of fire and vegetation. The variables are too numerous: time and method of using fire, hot or cold, variations in response to fire of different types of vegetation, the several species of grasses and of woody growth.

These matters are not merely theoretical, although they strike at the very foundations of the ecologists' concepts of succession and climax. They raise an honest doubt as to whether the idea of climax vegetation is even legitimate or of practical value. At any rate, the idea needs restatement based upon fresh thinking. Possibly the term "steady state" recently introduced into soil-science literature might be open to less objection because it is not yet freighted with so many unwarranted overtones, implications, and inferences.

Gilpin (1860) compared the European and the North American continents to a bowl: Europe, a bowl turned upside down, therefore high in the middle and sloping to the sea in all directions; North America, a bowl turned right side up, a rim around the outside and great valleys in the interior, closed off from free atmospheric circulation from the seas. North America had in fact a double rim on the west and on the south of 49° north latitude. This double rim encompassed the Great Basin area, mostly moist desert; at the north the Palouse prairie, in the middle the sagebrush desert, and at the south the Larrea Desert. The moist desert permitted some grasses, and this, therefore, in a limited sense made it a grassland.

The Rocky Mountains continental divide, however, was the major physical feature of the interior. It formed a barrier separating all west of it from the great interior valleys whose rivers emptied northward into the Arctic waters, eastward into the Atlantic through the St. Lawrence gap in the eastern rim, and southward into the Gulf of Mexico. The high point of the three watersheds was the nearly level plain of the Dakotas and Minnesota, modified by the glaciation of the Pleistocene.

Geologically speaking, all this was the work of comparatively recent time. The Appalachian Revolution formed the mountains of that name, the eastern rim of the American bowl, during Permian time. The Rocky Mountains were formed by the Laramide Revolution of late and post-Cretaceous time, but the Cascadian Revolution of Pleistocene time completed the Pacific coastal rim. The Mississippi Valley proper was largely Pennsylvanian (Later Carboniferous); parts of east-central Kansas, much of Oklahoma, and northern Texas were Permian; and the northwest of these areas were Cretaceous and Tertiary formations. However, much of the entire surface was reworked during the Pleistocene by glaciation, combined with winds and water.[2] Cut off from ocean moisture on the west by the double rim of mountains, the moisture of this area east of the continental divide is derived from warm, moist air masses moving northward from the Gulf of Mexico to meet cold, dry air masses

---

another big fire raged off southwest of Asa Cress's place. It burned a place 2½ miles long and 1½ miles wide. It was set by lightning and required the most heroic efforts on the part of the settlers to extinguish it and save some winter pasture. This year when feed is scarce the loss of the grass will be sorely felt."

2. Any clear realization of the role of glaciation dates from slightly more than a century ago. An intensive investigation of Pleistocene times, especially accompanied by a realization of the interplay of geological processes and primitive man, dates particularly from the Folsom discoveries of the second quarter of the twentieth century.

from the Canadian plain; the whole moves eastward. Thus, close to the mountain barrier the annual rainfall is scanty, increasing somewhat to the eastward, but highly variable within the unique continental interior (Borchert, 1950).

The geologists who dealt with the rocks of later geological time represented in the central part of this grassland commented upon their relative softness, which meant that, where exposed, they were subject to rapid erosion; most of them were covered by unconsolidated Pleistocene deposits. Few of the streams but were turbid. Hayden recorded that water in the several tributaries of the Missouri River began to clear only above the meridian of the mouth of the Musselshell (1863, chap. xii). The high country received an annual average rainfall of 10–25 inches. A rhetorical question that may be worth pondering is what would happen in the way of erosion if the Great Plains area should be visited with an annual average rainfall of 40–50 inches. The fact is that the scanty rainfall of the area constitutes its major value to the occupying human culture.

The "natural" properties of the vegetation of the Mississippi Valley east of the river itself were long a subject of disagreement mixed with a degree of mystery (Adams, 1902a, 1902b; Transeau, 1935). Shaler (1889, 1891) considered the prairie condition of much of the country to be the consequence of fire used after about A.D. 1000. Interested particularly in Kentucky history, he suggested that, if European intervention had been delayed another five hundred years, the prairie might have extended as far east as the Appalachian Mountains. He had been impressed particularly by the excavations he had made around the salt springs at Big Bone Lick, Boone County, Kentucky, which revealed a succession of deposits from glacial times to the date of his

work. In Mississippi, Hilgard (1860, pp. 349, 361–62) contrasted the vegetational status of parts of that area as the white man had received it from the hands of the Indians with its condition in 1860: a well-grassed, longleaf-pine savanna versus a country denuded of both trees and grass.

In the northern Ozark country west of the Mississippi River, Beilman and Brenner (1951) emphasized "the recent intrusion of forests in the Ozarks" during historic time. The invasion of trees dated from the time that the use of fire by the natives was curtailed and virtually eliminated. The rapid spread of woody growth in eastern Kansas and Nebraska during the first decade under white settlement was the subject of particular comment in 1867 by Bayard Taylor. So far as he described what he saw of the spread of woody growth at the expense of grass, his account was a significant document. A syllogistic conclusion from these last two examples is to be avoided, however. Only in some of the terrain most favorable to trees could timber have grown to maturity for marketable lumber, especially in eastern Kansas and Nebraska. Even in the stream bottoms, the oak-hickory-walnut combination disappeared west of 97° west longitude (Fort Riley and Council Grove), or at about the western boundary of the tall-grass country.

In the mid-latitudes west of the hundredth meridian the short grasses, the buffalo (*Buchloë dactyloides*) and the blue gramma (*Bouteloua gracilis*), were characteristic. Between 97° and 100° west longitude in this area the vegetation was conspicuously mixed and represented species from both the tall-grass and the short-grass areas. There was wide variation in accord with topography and soil. Two strips of sandy outcrops in Oklahoma and northern Texas produced the Cross Timbers which ran generally north and south. Sand-dune country along the Cimarron, south of the Arkansas and north of the Platte rivers, grew bunch grasses. At the extreme north the needle grasses (*Stipa*) predominated, and at the south the mesquite grasses (*Hilaria*) were characteristic. Variety was more conspicuous than were the uniformities emphasized by some of the plant ecologists.

The soils formed in the tall-grass area were mostly on the acid side, while those west of about 97° or 98° west longitude were alkaline, a characteristic of so-called "arid soils" first explained by Hilgard (1892). The scanty rainfall and the absence of leaching, which accounted for alkalinity, also contributed to the explanation of the phenomenal fertility of these grassland and desert soils.

ON THE NATURE OF GRASSLAND INSTABILITY: PROBLEM OF CONCEPTUAL ORIENTATION

Whenever and wherever a discussion is proposed of man-earth relations, or of man-food relations, certain fundamental conceptual barriers usually tend to block a free and effectual meeting of minds about even the nature of the problem. One of these is the assumption, tacit or explicit, that, as differentiated from plants and other animals, man's relations with the earth and all its properties are always destructive. A second barrier, which is really a corollary of the first, is that the imperative responsibility of any student of these matters is to provide the bases for restoring what man, especially "civilized" man, has supposedly destroyed. The overtones, if not the explicit assumption, are those of urgency of decision and of action to forestall disaster. The time scale of the geologist and the anthropologist is essential to maintain perspective on the area in question which has been "destroyed" repeatedly, both before and since the appearance of man, and is now the abode of man. The grassland of North America is conspicuously the product of destruction, and, as applied to this problem, destruction and creation are merely different aspects of the same thing. All areas of the earth's surface present a similar process to challenge the curiosity and understanding of men, but possibly a grassland reveals to the observation of contemporary men a more direct opportunity to study certain of the forces actively at work than do some other areas.

As the first draft of this paper was being written, March 11, 1955, a thermonuclear bomb had just been exploded in the Nevada desert. Afterward, red dust, falling over Baltimore, Maryland, some 2,200 miles eastward, aroused fear of radioactive fall-out from the explosion. In undertaking to allay that alarm by assuring the public that the red particles were nothing more dangerous than red dust blown from the Texas range country, the Weather Bureau inadvertently created another alarm about the destruction of the Great Plains by dust storms, supposedly caused by overgrazing and by plowing up the grass for wheat, cotton, and sorghum. Man is not happy unless he is worrying about something.

The Great Plains dust storms are a case in point that illustrate the problem and its overtones—the immediate push-button reaction in terms of a supposed solution to dust storms—to restore the Great Plains to their "original" grassland equilibrium as supposedly enjoyed in the state of nature. According to this stereotype, aboriginal man was a superior being, endowed with the wisdom of nature and of nature's God of the so-called "Enlightenment" of the eighteenth century—only civilized man was evil. Of course, not everyone reacted to the Weather Bureau's explanation in this manner, but this generalized response was more inclusive than it should have been, even among people in possession of some specialized knowledge about the subject.

The red dust that fell over Baltimore had its determinable origin in Permian time, hot and dry, during which beds of gypsum and salt were deposited, along with the materials from which the red soils of northern Texas and western Oklahoma were derived. The restoration philosophy does not propose to restore Permian conditions or those more favorable to prolific growth of vegetation which laid down the Pennsylvanian, Cretaceous, or Tertiary coal fields. There is no intent here merely to be facetious. If some past condition must be restored, why not choose that most favorable to present desires? Is it any more possible to restore less remote than more remote time conditions? Are not all such changes in space and time irreversible? Each space-time situation is the product of a unique combination of factors which never can be brought together again.

Early interpretations of the geological history of Pleistocene time as applied to the area east of the Rocky Mountains were oversimplified generalizations. Johnson's monograph (1901, 1902) was the most influential and, from the standpoint of geological history, represented the Great Plains as having been formed from debris washed out from the Rocky Mountains and thereafter undisturbed, except as it was eroded on either side and cut through from west to east at its northern end by such rivers as the Platte, the Republican, the Arkansas, the Canadian, and the Red. But that oversimplified view of the stability of the area has been disproved conclusively by Pleistocene research and archeological excavation, separately and in co-operation, during the second quarter of the present century. Instead of having been cut once, it was found that a large part of the Great Plains had been eroded and redeposited several times. Aboriginal village sites were excavated which revealed a succession of occupations of identical spots, separated by varying thicknesses of wind-blown material. Also, even on the high ridges of eastern Kansas south of the glaciated area, a large portion of the current soils are derived from loessal materials.

The stereotyped formula for soil formation pictured by Marbut, in the Department of Agriculture's *Atlas of American Agriculture* (1935), divided the soil body into four horizons: A, B, C, and D—the D horizon being unweathered rock. A stabilized, soil-forming process was represented as being found in the weathering of rock at the bottom as fast as erosion removed top soil. Thus, soil was supposedly formed normally from the bottom up. Whatever the degree of validity of that formula as a generalization, it has comparatively little applicability to the grassland, where the soils are derived so extensively from material transported by wind, water, and glacier. The soil material is added at the top as well as being eroded from the top. More often than is realized, the additions are in excess of the subtractions. The red dust that worried Baltimore in March, 1955, was only a demonstration of the continuance of Pleistocene geological and soil-forming processes actively at work in unbroken sequence. Mature soils in the sense of Marbut's soil stereotype can scarcely be expected. The same observations apply to the plant ecologists' stereotype of plant succession and climax. They are constructs of the mind, not realities, and never have been realities.

A further emphasis upon the absence of a stabilized condition in the grassland must be focused upon the period of about three centuries between the first arrival of Europeans into the interior of America and the middle of the nineteenth century, when the actual displacement of the Indians by white men began. Two changes of conditions occurred during that interval that were revolutionary in their effects upon Indian culture: the introduction of the horse and the change of location of many tribes. The Sioux, in part at least a forest people, were pushed southwestward into the northern grassland, the last stage in that process being completed after the New Ulm, Minnesota, massacre of 1862. Both of these revolutionary changes in the cultural pattern of what are usually called "Plains" Indians were too recent and too sudden to represent a stabilized culture in equilibrium with environment.

The question does not appear to occur to historians that the Indian culture might have been headed for a major crisis, possibly disaster, even if displacement by white culture had not intervened to give disaster a different form as well as to provide the Indian with a good alibi. In fact, there is reason to assert that these Indian cultures were already off-balance and were running into trouble prior to any definite "pressure" being placed upon them by the actual invasion of the area and their displacement by white men. Proof of such an assertion would be difficult, and, in a strict sense, possibly it is not subject to proof. But at the same time the opposite, which is the orthodox assumption upon which most history has been written, presents even greater difficulties. A mere unquestioned acceptance of an unproved assumption does not constitute proof, regardless of the penalties imposed upon those who refuse to conform to the requirements of orthodoxy. In any case, the conditions prevailing in the grassland interior during the century from 1750 to 1850 were anything but the eighteenth-century ideal "state of nature."

Proof is yet forthcoming that imitation of the Indian culture would have been a safe course. But under no circumstances could such a course have

prevented dust storms in this grassland. No more vivid description of a dust storm has been recorded than that of Isaac McCoy, written on the spot in what is now north-central Kansas during the fall of 1830 (not 1930),[3] when

3. "Had a little rain last night—the country is exceedingly parched with drought. When we got on to the prairies, the ashes from the recently burned prairies, and the dust and sand raised so by the wind that it annoyed us much, the wind raising, I found that the dust was so scattered that it became impossible to perceive the trail of the surveyors, who had gone a few hours ahead of the horses. While conversing with Calvin about the course we should go, we discovered the atmosphere ahead darkening, and as it had become cloudy, we fancied that a misting rain was coming upon us, and made some inquiry respecting the security of our packs. A few minutes taught us that what we had fancied to be rain, was an increase of the rising dust, sand, and ashes of the burnt grass, rising so much and so generally that the air was much darkened, and it appeared on the open prairies as though the clouds had united with the earth. Our eyes were so distressed that we could scarcely see to proceed. . . . The wind blew incessantly and excessively severe. . . . Was about to select a camping ground, when we met a man whom the Doctor [sent] to inform me that he could not proceed with his work, and that they waited for us in a wood a mile ahead. It being very difficult for me to look at my pocket compass I told the soldier . . . to lead us back. He set off with great confidence that he could find his way back and in a few minutes was leading us north instead of west. . . . On finding the surveyors, we encamped for the residue of the day. Even in this wood, and after the wind had somewhat abated, the black ashes fell on us considerably" (Barnes, 1936, p. 365).

Wind and dust accompanied the expedition farther west, and on October 26 the Republican Valley was reached: "Wind very high, scarcely allowing us to pass" (*ibid.*, p. 368). October 27: ". . . Today we reached the Republican, . . . and to our great disappointment we found it more destitute of grass than any place we had seen where wood was to be found. The river runs over a bed of sand —the banks low, and all the bottom lands are a bed of sand white and fine, and now as dry as powder ought to be. I never saw a river along which we might not find some rich alluvial moist bottoms, on which, at this

the so-called "native Plains Indians" were still in full possession. And dust storms in Kansas (1850–1900) have been described from contemporary records by the present writer. No more brazen falsehood was ever perpetrated upon a gullible public than the allegation that the dust storms of the 1930's were *caused* by "the plow that broke the Plains."

RAILROADS AND LAND-MASS POWER

The United States completed legal possession of the mid-latitude grassland

season of the year, could not be found green grass. But here there is in a manner none. "We examined along the river for grass until satisfied that none could be found and then turned back to a creek we had passed five miles back. . . . The scarcity of wood on the river and the sandiness and poverty of the bottoms, greatly discourage me as to the country—While the great scarcity of food for our horses made us fear that we should not be able to proceed much further" (*ibid.*, pp. 368–69).

The entry of November 5 represents the country about the ninety-eighth meridian and reads: "Completed the line of the outlet to 150 miles, and stopped. For some days we have discovered that our horses were failing so fast, that we must soon return, or lose them all. . . . We are beyond all Indian villages, and 50 miles, or more, into the country of Buffaloes. . . .

"After we completed our survey, we turned on to a creek, and were looking for an encampment—the day calm and fair—when suddenly the atmosphere became darkened by a cloud of dust and ashes from the recently burnt Prairies occasioned by a sudden wind from the north! It was not three minutes after I had discovered its approach, before the sun was concealed, and the darkness so great, that I could not distinguish objects more than three or four times the length of my horse. The dust, sand, and ashes, were so dense than one appeared in danger of suffocation. The wind driving into one's eyes seemed like destroying them. . . .

"The storm commenced, sun three quarters of an hour high in the evening, and blew tremendously all night. It had abated a little by morning. The dust was most annoying at the commencement. There was no clouds over us" (*ibid.*, pp. 371–72).

of North America (between the forty-ninth parallel and the Rio Grande) during the late 1840's. This made of the United States a two-front nation, facing both the Atlantic and the Pacific oceans, and laid the basis for a claim of right to a voice in the affairs of both the Atlantic and the Pacific systems. At that particular time in modern history the possession of the mid-latitude portion of the land mass of North America was fraught with a peculiar significance and one that has not been adequately interpreted. The power lent to this geographical position, and to the United States as its possessor, was for a duration of but one hundred years, since which the whole situation has changed. The greater part of that century was the century of world peace (1814–1914) and a century in which steam railroads virtually monopolized the communication systems of land-mass interiors.

The new series of world wars since 1914, air communication, and atomic bombs have changed basic relationships. The point is stressed here that the power vested in geographical position is held only on temporary loan and is not inherent in geographical position per se. The power wielded by a geographical site changes with the cultural technology that uses it. It is not the purpose of this paper to explore the ramifications of these facts from the standpoint of world history, but what is said here about the grassland of North America must be envisioned in such a world perspective in order to have any particular meaning (Malin, 1955*b*).

Down through the centuries, when the Western world faced the Mediterranean Sea and, after 1492, the North Atlantic Ocean, power was wielded through water communications. So long as land communications were dependent upon the muscle power of men and animals, costs of interior transport of heavy commodities were prohibitive. Economies of water transport did not extend to upstream navigation of the great rivers that drained continental interiors. The steam locomotive operating on iron railroads changed all this, because even the steamboat operating against the current of great rivers could reach only limited interior parts.

Prior to the steam railroad, penetration of the interior of the North American continent had followed water-communication systems. Penetration of the interior country from any water-based point was limited by the prohibitive costs of muscle power. The exceptions only tend to highlight the rule. Large areas not served by water were bypassed in the settlement process. Conspicuously, there was no connected frontier line in the Turner tradition; instead, scattered water-based diffusion centers served the land-mass interior areas. This applied particularly to the country east of the Mississippi River. West of that stream the diminished rainfall and the number and navigability of streams rendered water-based penetration of the grassland relatively unimportant for the area as a whole. By the early 1850's, in the state of Missouri, the argument was made that the available land accessible by water was already virtually taken up. To occupy and to develop the remainder of Missouri, railroads would have to be built. In Kansas, where there were no navigable rivers, and which was organized and opened to settlement in 1854, the issue was explained explicitly by Robinson (1859). Without railroads, corn at Lawrence, thirty to forty miles from the Missouri River, was worth nothing for sale on the Missouri River markets, because the cost of carriage by animal power equaled the normal market price. The steam railroad not only made the grassland a grain-growing area but also provided a structure for its livestock economy. It made possible also the marketing of the Pacific Coast fruits of California and the Northwest at the population centers of the East. So much for the grassland and its occupance in its own right. Comparatively, however, during the period of nearly a century of steam-railroad dominance of communication in continental interiors, by coincidence, the United States was the only great land-mass state that was in a position to capitalize fully upon this unique advantage (Malin, 1947, chap. xii; 1954a, pp. 56–71, 320–27, 408–16, 446–48; 1955a, 1955b).

COMMERCIAL ECONOMIES

In approaching the study of the history of the commercial economies of the grassland, certain prerequisites are imperative. Because the grassland possessed environmental peculiarities quite unlike the conditions of the forest, European-American culture with its forest background approached it with an unconscious ecological outlook quite foreign to the requirements of life under the strange conditions that had produced a grassland. Regardless of what the origin of the grassland may have been, the fact remained that conditions had produced grass there and not forest. Again, regardless of origins, occupance must be effected in terms of grass, not of forest. Still again, regardless of origins, the potential capacities of the grassland had to be tested by the new occupants to determine what they were. There were no precedents for European-American culture, which was derived predominantly from the British Isles and northern Europe. The first obligation of the historian in studying this particular stage of occupance is to determine the total body of knowledge and the ecological outlook these people possessed at the outset of the invasion of the grassland, regardless of whether it be called "science" or "folk thought." Next on this theme of knowledge and attitudes must be traced the growth and accumulation of the total fund of information and the transformation of atti-

tudes. The record is not in the nature
of a straight-line growth but is one of
highly irregular pattern, if pattern there
be, and of many false starts and by-
paths. Only in large perspective can it
appear to represent anything like a consistent and reasoned structure of
thought about man and the earth. Too
often the tendency appeared to insist
upon simple answers and to create
stereotypes, and nowhere more conspicuously than in the sciences, theoretical and applied; and stereotypes interfere with understanding.

An approach to the grassland from
the standpoint of the history of agricultural economies must necessarily emphasize the range-livestock industry
and field-crop production. The tall-grass
area to the eastward presented relatively little difficulty to the westward extension of traditional forest man's livestock and crops: cattle, hogs, sheep,
corn, oats, and soft wheats. West of the
strictly tall-grass area the issues were
increasingly challenging. Westward toward the Rocky Mountains, rainfall diminished and elevation increased. Also,
the north-south latitudinal range was
greater and imposed wider variability
in temperature and photoperiodicity.
Domesticated livestock and field crops
introduced into the area could scarcely
be expected to possess equally the
capacity to exhibit their full potentials,
or even to survive, in all parts of so extended a geographical space. Livestock
presented lesser difficulties in these matters than field crops, but, with more
extensive and sounder scientific information, greater emphasis was being
placed upon specialized breeds of livestock for each area and purpose.

The history of the livestock industry
in the North American grassland has
never been told in a comprehensive
manner or with objectivity and perspective. Besides the bias of a particular
frame of reference which vitiates the
standard accounts, the basic research

for much, if not most, of a comprehensive history is yet to be done. The past
of the livestock industry in all its aspects needs to be written as a whole
without pretense of telling the whole of
the past.

The particular frame of reference
which distorts the history of the range-
livestock industry is the result of undue
emphasis upon the Texas influence and
upon cattle. Of course, Texas has never
been noted for modesty. According to
United States history, the United States
annexed Texas, but, according to Texas
history, Texas annexed the United
States. That is the Texas contribution
to the generalized theory of relativity.

When Texas "brags," of course it is
done facetiously, and each "brag," bigger than its predecessor, is expected to
bring a hearty laugh. Nevertheless,
there is a serious side to the Texas
exaggeration that has left an indelible
impress upon the writing of the history
of the whole western area of the United
States and especially upon the history
of the livestock industry and upon land-
utilization policies. Webb's *The Great
Plains* (1931) brought those elements
together within the covers of one book
in such a form as to give them a wide
currency, if not influence. It incorporated the Johnson geological interpretations of the High Plains (see pp. 10–17,
419–22) with the combined views of
the Powell report on arid lands and the
Johnson High Plains report on land
utilization. All this fitted neatly into
the "big cattleman's" view of the type
of society that should monopolize the
area and keep it in grass. The erroneous view of Johnson on Pleistocene geological history of the Plains is no
longer a matter of doubt. Unfortunately for accurate thinking, the social phi-
losophies of both Powell and Johnson,
especially the former, have gained an
acceptance that is remarkably uncritical
of geographical determinism and its
consequential regimentation of society.

Among the merits of the Powell report on arid lands was the fact that he did recognize that the limited area with which he dealt possessed a unique character that justified a special treatment. Yet, in spite of the fact that he was both a geologist and an ethnologist, his social philosophy for the area was essentially a prescription of social statics. Landholding in large lots, except for limited irrigation communities, would have afforded opportunity for only a favored few; and this view committed him to a social structure so rigid and static as to be without capacity to absorb even a normal population increase. At the same time, by creating a powerful vested interest, the plan would not necessarily have insured constructive, long-term utilization policies. Quite certainly it could not have prevented either the physical or the economic disasters of the 1930's.

Powell was notably blind to soil science and was in no sense abreast of the status of the subject even in his own day and in the environment for which his system was designed. At the time of the arid lands report in 1878, Hilgard had not yet published much of his basic ideas leading to a new soil science; but, as those contributions were issued, Powell failed to understand their significance. He never realized what the soil problem was that needed to be understood.

This emphasis upon Powell, Johnson, and Webb is not intended to leave the impression that the Powell plan was adopted as the policy for the original occupation of the arid region for which it was designed. But it did have some bearing upon more recent policies and still possesses an unfortunate propaganda influence.

Besides cattle from Texas, the northern ranges were stocked from the Pacific Coast (Oliphant, 1932, 193?, 1946, 1948) as well as from the farms of the eastern states. The most important influence of all, however, for reconstruction of the history of the cattle industry as a whole has been the contribution of pure-bred animals from Great Britain, the European continent, and India and the creation of new hybrid breeds (Malin, 1947; Hazelton, 1939; Rhoad, 1949). The story of sheep likewise is in the process of being reconstructed on a more meaningful basis (Wentworth, 1942, 1948, 1954).

The first English colonists to settle in what is now the United States brought with them the seed for traditional English crops: wheat, oats, barley, rye, etc., and the tillage methods of the homeland. For various reasons, their labor achieved no great success. The Indians taught them the culture and uses of the maize, the Indian staple. One of the most remarkable aspects of European adaptation to America was the manner in which corn (Indian maize), especially the dent type, became an integral part of American culture. When Americans reached the western extent of the tall-grass prairie where corn could not be depended upon because of the hazards of climate, they stubbornly persisted in growing corn because they could not, or would not, adjust to an agricultural system without it. A large part of the excessive hardships in the grass country of the late nineteenth century was the result of this failure in adjustment. The soft wheats, spring and winter types, according to latitude, were likewise subject to a high casualty rate. The belated introduction to and reluctant schooling in the uses of hard wheat provided a remarkably reliable grain crop for bread. After the opening of the twentieth century came durum, a spring wheat suitable for macaroni flour. The hard spring wheats dominate the northern grassland and the hard winter wheats the central portion (Malin, 1942; 1947, pp. 327–30; Ball, 1930; Clark *et al.*, 1923).

For the central part of the grassland

the sorghums became a major crop, affording a reliable substitute for corn. Introduced first, after the middle of the nineteenth century, were the saccharine varieties, used for syrup, but which became more widely grown as a forage substitute for corn. Kaffir and milo, etc., were introduced near the end of the century. In their mid-twentieth-century forms, as developed by plant-breeders, the grain sorghums afford a reliable feed for livestock as a substitute for corn and thus have become an integral part of the range-livestock economy where corn could not be grown. This facet of the whole situation must be stressed as one of several which demonstrate that the range-livestock industry could not survive on grass alone.

Fibers, both cotton and wool, were produced extensively. Texas and Oklahoma were the leading short-staple cotton states but were challenged after World War II by California, which developed the growth of irrigated, long-staple cotton under a highly mechanized regime. Historically, the range-sheep industry was identified almost exclusively with wool production, using the fine-wool breeds, especially the Merino. The shift to the dual-purpose English breeds for meat and wool came late. The interregional aspects of lamb production will be noted later.

REGIONAL INTERRELATIONS

No summary of commercial economies of the grassland, however sketchy, can forego reference to the mineral resources of the region and their peculiar relation to the necessities of such an area. Without forests, the grassland was dependent largely upon outside areas for the building materials and fuel traditional to American culture. The search for substitutes for wood was persistent and not immediately or fully successful. This introduces one of the most conspicuous aspects of the occupance of the grassland—regional interdepend-

ence. Not only the steam railroad but industrialization in all its aspects contributed what were essentials to the grassland economy. Capital and consumption goods furnished by the industrialized regions had to be paid for in money derived from cash crops. A degree of subsistence economy, such as had been the resort of the pioneer in the forest, was virtually impossible on natural grounds, and this imperative demand for money emphasized the necessity of specialized cash crops. Railroads made possible the import of sawed lumber, which was put together with machine-made nails. The grassland was characteristically a "sawed house," not a "sod house," country and still remains so (Malin, 1944, 1950, 1954b, 1954c). Coal for fuel was shipped in largely to supplement the lower-grade bituminous or lignite coals produced in some parts of the region (Malin, 1944, pp. 102–4; 1950a, chaps. i–iv, xvi, xix). The opening of the mid-continent oil and gas fields on a large scale after the beginning of the twentieth century afforded for the first time an efficient fuel, not only for use in the grassland, but eventually for large-scale export to other regions. The industrial minerals existed only in the mountain areas, but the accent on uranium during the last decade opened unknown possibilities.

Regional interdependency of another sort evolved out of the Texas cattle drives of song and story. First driven northward to market, the animals were found to fatten on the way, or were held on northern range to fatten on grass, before shipment by rail to Corn Belt feed lots or to market for slaughter. In 1887 the Santa Fe Railroad built southward into the Texas range country, and others followed. Soon afterward the controls for Texas fever were worked out. On the basis of these developments a stabilized procedure evolved to ship southwestern cattle to the Kansas-Oklahoma bluestem pastures to be grass-fattened for slaughter or to be fattened and matured for Corn Belt feed lots. Out of these practices a favorable rail-rate structure emerged: billing, with pasture stopover privileges, and standard pasture contracts from April 1 to October 1. According to the estimates of the United States Department of Agriculture's Agricultural Marketing Service, an annual average of 360,000 head of cattle was received in these pastures over the period 1943–52. Not only was this a larger number of animals but it represented a far larger potential of high-quality beef than was ever marketed from the southwestern range during the most fabulous days of the notorious Texas cattle drives, when grass, cattle, and Texans were supposed to be close to a "state of nature." This simple statement of facts suggests many more challenging questions about grass, soil, conservation, and cattle than can be considered here (Malin, 1942).

The chain of established services just described, that is, breeding on the range, maturing, and grass-fattening in transit on the bluestem pastures, full-feed finishing in the Corn Belt feed lots, and slaughter at the packing centers of Kansas City, St. Louis, and Chicago, represented, among other things, the pull of the great population centers of northeastern United States and Europe. It was an intricately woven pattern stretching diagonally across the United States, virtually from one corner to the other, and was the product of a complex of forces operating through a century of time. Like Topsy, it "just growed" and was not planned, although, after it had taken shape, interested parties at various points and times did consciously perfect details. In the sheep industry, although on a less permanent basis and in less volume, a somewhat comparable procedure also operated to move Idaho and Arizona lambs to feed lots near the major packing centers for finishing or to the winter-wheat pastures of the hard winter-wheat belt for maturing and fattening.

The first challenge to these systems came from the Pacific Coast, especially from southern California, which was sustaining a phenomenal population growth (Buechel, 1933). The bid of the Pacific Coast for food supplies became conspicuous during the depression decade of the 1930's and mounted to all but revolutionary proportions during and after the World War II boom. The economic continental divide had been located some distance west of the physical continental divide. Before the end of World War II the economic divide had moved eastward to such an extent as to draw much business to the southern Pacific Coast from western Nebraska, Kansas, Oklahoma, and a large part of Texas (Haystead, 1945; Malin, 1947, pp. 318–22). Thus far, the Pacific Northwest has not generated a comparable drawing power from the northern end of the grassland (Freeman and Martin, 1942). Great oil and gas developments and hydroelectric power may operate similarly in that area, but on the eve of atomic industrial power the historian must refrain from prophecy.

The interrelationships that have become effective between or among regions have not been the consequence of any preconceived plan, but that does not mean that no planning was undertaken. During the winter of 1876–77, and while the controversy was pending over the outcome of the disputed presidential election of 1876, a conciliation program was proposed. According to this plan, a through railroad was to be assembled and/or constructed from Philadelphia through the southern states to connect with the Texas and Pacific Railroad and southern California (Woodward, 1951). Had this over-all project been executed together with a favorable rate structure, the effects upon the Old South and upon the southern grassland would have been momentous.

Possibly the Texas–Kansas–bluestem pasture–Corn Belt–Chicago system previously described might not have emerged.

At the outbreak of World War II a similar plan was before the Interstate Commerce Commission, with a view of making Richmond, Virginia, a packing center and of diverting southwestern livestock through the Gulf states to be fed on their way east. World War II blocked the plan, but it was fought by all the interests in the Texas–Kansas–Corn Belt–Chicago system already in being, as well as by southern California, just then drawing heavily upon the same source for supplies of meat. One observation at least about the proposed Richmond plan is in order. Like much social planning of such magnitude, there was little, if anything, that was positive in the system for the country as a whole; its conspicuous characteristic was a proposal to benefit one region at the expense of others without any certainty of benefiting anybody on a long-term basis.

STRATEGIC STATUS

The regional interdependence just described was the product of railroads, supplemented by internal combustion engines on land wheels, whether tractors, trucks, or automobiles. New forces of air communications were at work on a reorientation and a redistribution of power. Already the fact has been pointed out that, for the first time in history, the potential of land-mass power had been implemented by steam railroads, dating from the mid-nineteenth century. The internal combustion engine in its several applications to surface movement in space supplemented and extended what steam railroads had begun. The effect of air power was not necessarily to withdraw the loan of power from geographical positions intrusted with power under the rail regime. But the strategic significance of every site underwent a re-evaluation in terms of air power. Significantly, in a north circumpolar system, the North American grassland interior again rated a new loan of power, but subject to a substantial reassessment of relationships —among them a north-south orientation in addition to, rather than instead of, the exclusive east-west orientation of surface communication systems. Besides being called upon to provide bread, meat, fibers, coal, oil, gas, and uranium, the North American grassland served other functions at the mid-point of the twentieth century.

At the center of the North American continental land mass, this grassland contained the nerve centers of the military communication systems that defend or strike in its behalf. In such a perspective would anyone be so naïve as to insist that the problem of the grassland could be solved by turning it back to the Indian or to the cattleman? Instead of a return to the simplicity of a grazing country, the challenges of atomic power indicate a further incorporation into the complex network of areal and cultural interdependence. Much more, indeed, has become involved than the exclusive interests of the United States as an individual nation. This grassland region of North America, the interior of the United States and Canada, occupies one of the key geographical positions in the north circumpolar system of political power actually in being. Intrusted with such a loan of power, a heavy responsibility rests upon its holders for the use that is made of the opportunities committed to its charge.

REFERENCES

Something of the extent of the present writer's deviation from orthodoxy in the writing of history may be gathered by comparison of the essay offered here with an article by

Earl Pomeroy, "Toward a Reorientation of Western History: Continuity and Environment," *Mississippi Valley Historical Review,* XVI (1930), 579–600. Books that also represent conventional treatments are Billington, Briggs, Caughey, Richardson and Rister, and Winther. Thus far, little has been done toward a synthesis of the newer point of view presented here. Such an over-all revision awaits research representative of a wider range of areas and topics, together with fresh interpretations of old and of new facts. Regions are not superior, inferior, or equal to one another. Each region is unique as well as are all the parts of which it is composed. The historian's emphasis is upon uniqueness; the social scientist's emphasis is upon likenesses subject to classification.

ADAMS, C. C.
1902a "Postglacial Origin and Migrations of the Life of the Northeastern United States," *Journal of Geography,* I, 303–10, 352–57.
1902b "The Southeastern United States as a Center of Geographical Distribution of Flora and Fauna," *Biological Bulletin,* III, 115–31.

BALL, CARLETON R.
1930 "A History of American Wheat Improvement," *Agricultural History,* IV, 48–71.

BARNES, LELA (ed.)
1936 "Journal of Isaac McCoy for the Exploring Expedition of 1830," *Kansas Historical Quarterly,* V, 339–77.

BEILMAN, A. P., and BRENNER, L. G.
1951 "The Recent Intrusion of Forests in the Ozarks," *Annals of the Missouri Botanical Gardens,* XXXVIII, 261–82.

BILLINGTON, RAY A.
1949 *Westward Expansion: A History of the American Frontier.* New York: Macmillan Co. 873 pp.

BORCHERT, JOHN R.
1950 "The Climate of the Central North American Grassland," *Annals of the Association of American Geographers,* XL, 1–39.
1953 "Regional Differences in the World Atmospheric Circulation," *ibid.,* XLIII, 14–26.

BRIGGS, HAROLD E.
1940 *Frontiers of the Northwest: A History of the Upper Missouri Valley.* New York: D. Appleton–Century Co. 629 pp.

BRYAN, KIRK
1940 "Erosion in the Valleys of the Southwest," *New Mexico Quarterly,* X, 227–32.
1941 "Pre-Columbian Agriculture in the Southwest, as Conditioned by Periods of Alluviation," *Annals of the Association of American Geographers,* XXXI, 219–42.

BUECHEL, F. A.
1933 *Eight Years of Livestock Shipments in Texas, 1924–1932,* Part I: *Cattle and Calves.* . . . (Bureau of Business Research Monograph No. 10.) Austin: University of Texas. 131 pp.

BYRON, LEONARD A., and FRYE, JOHN C.
1954 "Ecological Conditions Accompanying Loess Deposition in the Great Plains Region of the United States," *Journal of Geology,* LXII, 399–404.

CAUGHEY, JOHN W.
1938 *History of the Pacific Coast of North America.* New York: Prentice-Hall, Inc. 429 pp.

CLARK, JACOB A., *et al.*
1923 *Classification of American Wheat Varieties.* (U.S. Department of Agriculture Bulletin No. 1074.) Washington, D.C.: Government Printing Office. 238 pp.

CLEMENTS, F. E., and SHELFORD, V. E.
1933 *Bio-ecology.* New York: John Wiley & Sons. 425 pp.

COLBERT, EDWIN H. (ed.)
1948 "Pleistocene of the Great Plains (A Symposium)," *Bulletin of the Geological Society of America,* LIX, 541–630.

CONDRA, G. E., and REED, E. C.
1943 *The Geological Section of Nebraska.* (Nebraska Geological Survey Bulletin No. 14.) 2d ed. Lincoln, Neb. 82 pp.
1948 *Correlation of the Pleistocene Deposits of Nebraska.* (Nebraska Geological Survey Bulletin No. 15.) Lincoln, Neb. 73 pp.

EGLER, FRANK E.
1951 "A Commentary on American Plant Ecology, Based on the Textbooks of 1947–1949," *Ecology,* XXXII, 673–

94. (This is a must for anyone dealing with ecology in the United States.)

ELIAS, M. K. (ed.)
1945 "Symposium on Loess," *American Journal of Science.* CCXLIII, 225–303.

FLINT, RICHARD F.
1947 *Glacial Geology and the Pleistocene Epoch.* New York: John Wiley & Sons. 589 pp.

FLINT, RICHARD F., *et al.*
1949 "Pleistocene Research: A Review by the Members of the Committee on Interrelations of Pleistocene Research, National Research Council," *Bulletin of the Geological Society of America,* LX, 1305–1525.

FREEMAN, O. W., and MARTIN, H. W. (eds.)
1942 *The Pacific Northwest.* New York: John Wiley & Sons. 542 pp.

FRYE, JOHN C.
1945 "Problems of Pleistocene Stratigraphy in Central and Western Kansas," *Journal of Geology,* LIII, 73–93.
1946a "Review of Studies of Pleistocene Deposits in Kansas," *American Journal of Science,* CCXLIV, 403–516.
1946b "The High Plains Surface in Kansas," *Transactions of the Kansas Academy of Science,* XLIX, 71–86.
1951 "Soil Forming Intervals Evidenced in Kansas Pleistocene," *Soil Science,* LXXI, 403–8.
1955 "Erosion History of the Flint Hills," *Transactions of the Kansas Academy of Science,* LVIII, 79–86.

FRYE, JOHN C., and BYRON, LEONARD A.
1951 "Stratigraphy of the Late Pleistocene Loesses in Kansas," *Journal of Geology,* LIX, 287–305.
1952 *Pleistocene Geology of Kansas.* (State Geological Survey of Kansas Bulletin No. 99.) Lawrence, Kan. 230 pp.

GILPIN, WILLIAM
1860 *The Central Gold Region: The Grain, Pastoral and Gold Region of North America.* Philadelphia: Somer, Barnes & Co. 194 pp.

GLEASON, H. A.
1926 "The Individualistic Concept of the Plant Association," *Bulletin of the Torrey Botanical Club,* LIII, 7–26.

1939 "The Individualistic Concept of the Plant Association," pp. 92–108 in JUST, THEODORE (ed.), *Plant and Animal Communities.* Notre Dame: Notre Dame University. 255 pp.

HAYDEN, F. V.
1863 "On the Geological and Natural History of the Upper Missouri [Expedition of 1857]," *Transactions of the American Philosophical Society* (N.S.), Vol. XII, chap. xii: "Quaternary Deposits."

HAYSTEAD, LADD
1945 *If the Prospect Pleases: The West the Guide Books Never Mention.* Norman: Oklahoma University Press. 208 pp.

HAZELTON, JOHN M.
1939 *A History of Linebred Anxiety 4th Herefords of Straight Gudgell & Simpson Breeding.* Kansas City: Missouri Associated Breeders of Anxiety 4th Herefords. 569 pp.

HILGARD, E. W.
1860 *Report on the Geology and Agriculture of the State of Mississippi.* Jackson: Mississippi State Printer. 391 pp.
1892 *A Report on the Relations of Soil and Climate.* (U.S. Department of Agriculture, Weather Bureau Bulletin No. 3.) Washington, D.C.: Government Printing Office. 59 pp.

JOHNSON, W. D.
1901 "The High Plains and Their Utilization," pp. 601–768 in *Twenty-first Annual Report, United States Geological Survey,* Part IV: *Hydrology.* Washington, D.C.: Government Printing Office. 768 pp.
1902 "The High Plains and Their Utilization," pp. 631–69 in *Twenty-second Annual Report, United States Geological Survey,* Part IV: *Hydrology.* Washington, D.C.: Government Printing Office. 671 pp.

KOLLMORGEN, WALTER M., and JENKS, GEORGE F.
1951–52 "A Geographic Study of Population and Settlement Changes in Sherman County, Kansas," *Transactions of the Kansas Academy of Science,* LIV, 449–94; LV, 1–37.

LAUTENSACH, HERMANN
1953 *Das Mormonenland als Beispiel sozialgeographischen Raumes.* ("Bonner Geographische Abhandlungen," No. 11.) Bonn: The Author and the Geographischen Instituts der Universität. Bonn. 46 pp.

MALIN, JAMES C.
1935 "The Turnover of Farm Population in Kansas," *Kansas Historical Quarterly,* IV, 339–72.
1942 "An Introduction to the History of the Bluestem Pastures," *ibid.,* XI, 3–28.
1944 *Winter Wheat in the Golden Belt of Kansas.* Lawrence: University of Kansas Press. 290 pp.
1946a "Dust Storms, 1850–1900," *Kansas Historical Quarterly,* XIV, 129–44, 265–96, 391–413.
1946b *Essays on Historiography.* Lawrence, Kan.: The Author. 188 pp.
1947 *The Grassland of North America: Prolegomena to Its History.* Lawrence, Kan.: The Author. 398 pp. (Contains an extensive bibliography.)
1950a *Grassland Historical Studies: Natural Resources Utilization in a Background of Science and Technology,* Vol. I: *Geology and Geography.* Lawrence, Kan.: The Author. 377 pp.
1950b "Ecology and History," *Scientific Monthly,* LXX, 295–98.
1952 "Man, the State of Nature, and Climax: As Illustrated by Some Problems of the North American Grassland," *ibid.,* LXXIV, 29–37.
1953 "Soil, Animal, and Plant Relations of the Grassland, Historically Reconsidered," *ibid.,* LXXVI, 207–20.
1954a *The Nebraska Question, 1852–1854.* Lawrence, Kan.: The Author. 455 pp.
1954b "Emergency Housing at Lawrence, 1854," *Kansas Historical Quarterly,* XXI, 34–49.
1954c "Housing Experiments in the Lawrence Community," *ibid.,* pp. 95–121.
1954d Review of SAUER, CARL O., *Agricultural Origins and Dispersals,* in *Agricultural History,* XXVIII, 34–35.
1955a "Notes on the Writing of General Histories of Kansas, Part Three:

The Historical and Philosophical Societies; Repositories of the Material of History and of Science," *Kansas Historical Quarterly,* XXI, 331–78.
1955b *The Contriving Brain and the Skillful Hand in the United States: Something about History and Philosophy of History.* Lawrence, Kan.: The Author. 436 pp. (This book undertakes to deal with the issues raised in the third section of the present paper, "Railroads and Land-Mass Power," but in a much larger setting, with special reference to the nineteenth century and to cultural technology.)

MARBUT, C. F.
1935 *Soils of the United States,* Part III: *Atlas of American Agriculture.* Washington, D.C.: Government Printing Office. 98 pp.

MARTIN, PAUL S., *et al.*
1947 *Indians before Columbus: Twenty Thousand Years of North American History Revealed in Archeology.* Chicago: University of Chicago Press. 582 pp.

OLIPHANT, J. ORIN
1932 "The Cattle Trade from the Far Northwest to Montana," *Agricultural History,* VI, 69–83.
1933 "The Cattle Trade of Puget Sound, 1858–1890," *ibid.,* VII, 129–49.
1946 "The Eastward Movement of Cattle from the Oregon Country," *ibid.,* XX, 19–43.
1948 "History of the Livestock Industry in the Pacific Northwest," *Oregon Historical Quarterly,* XLIX, 1–29.

PHILLIPS, RALPH W.
1944 "The Cattle of India," *Journal of Heredity,* XXXV, 273–88.

POWELL, J. W.
1878 *Report on the Lands of the Arid Region of the United States, with a More Detailed Account of the Lands of Utah.* (House Executive Document No. 73; 45th Cong., 2d sess.) Washington, D.C.: Government Printing Office. 208 pp.

PRICE, EDWARD T.
1955 "Values and Concepts in Conservation," *Annals of the Association of American Geographers,* XLV, 64–84.

RHOAD, A. O.
1949 "The Santa Gertrudis Breed," *Journal of Heredity*, XL, 115–26.

RICHARDSON, RUPERT N., and RISTER, CARL C.
1935 *The Greater Southwest.* Glendale, Calif.: Arthur H. Clark Co. 506 pp.

ROBINSON, CHARLES
1859 "Letter to the Editor," *Lawrence* (Kan.) *Herald of Freedom*, May 7.

SAUER, CARL O.
1952 *Agricultural Origins and Dispersals.* (Bowman Memorial Lectures, Series Two.) New York: American Geographical Society. 110 pp.

SCHOEWE, WALTER H.
1948–53 "The Geography of Kansas," Part I: "Political Geography"; Part II: "Physical Geography"; Part III: "Hydrogeography," *Transactions of the Kansas Academy of Science*, LI, 253–88; LII, 261–333; LIV, 263–329; LVI, 131–90.

SHALER, N. S.
1889 *Aspects of the Earth.* New York: Charles Scribner's. 344 pp.
1891 *Nature and Man in America.* New York: Charles Scribner's. 290 pp.

SHANNON, FRED A.
1940 *Critiques of Research in the Social Sciences. III. An Appraisal of Walter Prescott Webb's "The Great Plains: A Study in Institutions and Environments."* (With a panel discussion.) New York: Social Science Research Council. 254 pp.

TAYLOR, BAYARD
1867 *Colorado, a Summer Trip.* New York: G. P. Putnam's. 185 pp.

THORP, JAMES, *et al.*
1950 "Some Post-Pliocene Buried Soils of Central United States," *Journal of Soil Science*, Vol. II, Part I.

TRANSEAU, E. N.
1935 "The Prairie Peninsula," *Ecology*. XVI, 423–37.

WEATHERWAX, PAUL
1954 *Indian Corn in Old America.* New York: Macmillan Co. 253 pp.

WEAVER, JOHN E.
1954 *The North American Prairie.* Lincoln, Neb.: Johnsen Publishing Co. 384 pp.

WEAVER, J. E., and CLEMENTS, F. E.
1938 *Plant Ecology.* 2d ed. New York: McGraw-Hill Book Co. 601 pp.

WEBB, W. P.
1931 *The Great Plains.* Boston: Ginn & Co. 525 pp.

WENTWORTH, EDWARD N.
1942 "Eastward Sheep Drives from California and Oregon," *Mississippi Valley Historical Review*, XXVIII, 507–38.
1948 *America's Sheep Trails.* Ames, Iowa: Iowa State College Press. 667 pp.
1954 "Trailing Sheep from California to Idaho in 1865: The Journal of Gorham Gates Kimball," *Agricultural History*, XXVIII, 49–83.

WILLHAM, OLIVER S.
1937 "A Genetic History of Hereford Cattle in the United States," *Journal of Heredity*, XXVIII, 283–94.

WINTHER, OSCAR O.
1947 *The Great Northwest: A History.* New York: A. A. Knopf. 383 pp.

WOODWARD, C. VANN
1951 *Reunion and Reaction: The Compromise of 1877 and the End of Reconstruction.* Boston: Little, Brown & Co. 263 pp.

The Age of Fossil Fuels

EUGENE AYRES[*]

Significant changes in man's way of life have often come about with almost inconceivable slowness. The characteristics of an age do not dawn suddenly upon our consciousness but are likely to be fully realized only when we have gone so far upon the long new path that the end of the path is almost in sight. Is the so-called "atomic age" an exception? I do not think so. The very readiness with which we have accepted nuclear energy and have woven intricate scientific fancies about it seems to strike a false historical note. Almost the only thing we can say with assurance about the future is that it will bear little resemblance to preconceptions of it.

REMOTE BEGINNINGS

No one can say when the age of fossil fuels began. We might set the date before 6000 B.C., when the forests in the

* Mr. Ayres is consultant to the Gulf Research & Development Company, Pittsburgh, Pennsylvania. In 1934 he became associated with this company to undertake the organization and direction of research concerned with the refining of petroleum and refined petroleum products, later becoming Technical Assistant to the Executive Vice-President of the Gulf Laboratories. During the past few years, Mr. Ayres has devoted most of his time to the study of national and international energy resources—production, use, and economy—and is consultant to several government agencies and petroleum industry organizations. Holder of more than fifty patents on a wide variety of inventions, he also is the author of numerous articles in various technical fields and is co-author, with C. A. Scarlott, of *Energy Sources: The Wealth of the World*, 1952.

Garden of Eden had almost disappeared and when the fertile valleys had become desert. Or when the Babylonians began to use pools of native asphalt. Or when ancient Persian kings (according to Aristotle) had their food cooked in caves where seepages of natural gas were continuously aflame. Or when the Chinese, about two thousand years ago, were mining coal and using it in considerable volume. Or perhaps a little later when the Chinese drilled laborious wells through solid rock to tap great reservoirs of natural gas. Or when the Burmese, beginning before the tenth century, similarly drilled wells to tap, abundantly, the reservoirs of liquid oil.

The real beginning of the fossil fuel age may be more properly regarded, I believe, not as a matter of production but as a matter of effective utilization, and this came much later.

An understanding of the present age requires that we see how it came into being. As Becker (1932, p. 19) has said, "We can identify a thing only by pointing to what it was before it became the thing that it will presently cease to be."

By the thirteenth century, England's forests had been seriously depleted and people were cold. King Henry III gave his grudging consent to the inhabitants of Newcastle to mine coal. This was about a thousand years after the Roman invaders had burned coal in England and more than a thousand years after the beginning of Chinese coal production, but Henry's act made an official beginning in England. Henry's son, Edward I, found it necessary to propitiate the barons, and he signed a decree prescribing the death penalty for the burning of coal in London while Parliament was in session, "lest the health of the Knights of the Shire should suffer during their residence in London." At least one man was executed for this crime. Later, Queen Elizabeth I also signed a decree against the use of coal. France in earlier centuries had legislated against the use of coal, but in 1600 Henry IV of France exempted coal from the ground rent of the one-tenth due the sovereign by virtue of his royal right and prerogative. The French had already perceived the utility of encouraging the production and use of fossil fuels. Unfortunately, this perception was to become dull in later years, and France, like England, was to become prematurely deprived of its magnificent forests.

By the fifteenth century the forests of Scotland were already largely a thing of the past. Pope Pius II, whose writings are said to have influenced Christopher Columbus, told how he had seen at the doors of churches in Scotland mendicants in rags who "received for alms pieces of black stone with which they went away contented. This species of stone they burn in place of wood of which their country is destitute" (Taylor, 1845, p. 211).

SEVENTEENTH CENTURY

In the early part of the seventeenth century a Franciscan missionary traveled through what is now Upper New York State and reported "some very good oil" there issuing from the ground. The item aroused no particular interest. Petroleum was already well known but was of no importance anywhere. In particular, America was a vast wooded wilderness, and no one knew or cared about the stores of coal, oil, and gas beneath the forest floor.

By 1650 a fair start had been made at coal utilization in England, Scotland, Belgium, and France. Two sailing vessels were constantly employed in carrying coal from Newcastle to London, and England's export trade in coal was under way. Most of the coal then burned in Paris was from Newcastle. The price of coal on board ship at Newcastle was about a dollar a ton (10s. for a chaldron of 53 cwt.). But Oliver Cromwell's Parliament was petitioned by the people of London against two nuisances—hops and coal—because "they spoyle the taste of drinck and endanger the people" (*ibid.*, p. 320). Gas at this time was described by the Chinese as being applied very advantageously to economic uses. These uses were not understood by contemporary European reporters—in no sense technologists—who said, in effect: "We have wells of water in Europe, but the Chinese have wells of fire. Beneath the surface of the earth are mines of sulfur which are already lighted. They have only to make a small opening whence issues heat enough to cook whatever they wish." We know now that the Chinese at this time were carrying out certain industrial operations with the heat of burning natural gas. About a century later the Western world learned some of the details—how gas was being distributed in bamboo pipe lines with clay terminals to homes and industrial establishments. Streets of some towns and many homes were lighted with gas, and gas was being used to heat buildings and to evaporate brine. Central heating with gas and coal had been widely practiced for many centuries, although not continuously. Such arts were used for a few generations, lost because of some economic or military cataclysm, and then rediscovered. (One period of rediscovery of central heating in China came about A.D. 900.)

Coal was common in China. The mountains west of Peiping contained "coal in such abundance that a space of half a league cannot be traversed without meeting with rich strata." Coal in Peiping was abundant and was sold at a moderate price. The provinces of Shansi and Chihli were supplying large quantities of coal. Many boats were being used continuously for transportation of anthracite from Liaotung to Tientsin. Both anthracite and bituminous coal were in the Nanking and other Chinese markets—also coal briquettes for the fires of the poor. Coal brought into Canton was high in sulfur and ash and was used for the manufacture of green vitriol. Iron ore was being smelted with anthracite. This was in the seventeenth century, when the utilization of coal in England was much more primitive and when coal in America was still unknown.

The earliest notice of the presence of coal in America came in 1665, when a French missionary marked "houille" on a map of the country then occupied by Indians at Pimitoui (now Peoria, Illinois). This was almost a century before coal was known to exist in Pennsylvania. Purchases of land from the Indians by William Penn and his family, and later by the proprietaries, did not include any portion of the coal land of Pennsylvania until 1749. In that year the 3,750 square miles embracing the whole anthracite region were acquired for £500 ($2,000)! And acquisition of bituminous coal lands came even later.

Before 1700, European technologists were finding new things to do with coal. British patent No. 214 was for distillation of coal to obtain coal tar. J. J. Becher, a German "chemist" who had been trying to transmute Danubian sand into gold, published a report on coal gas. An English patent was granted for "a way to extract and make great quantities of pitch, tar, and oil out of a sort of stone." This stone was oil shale. The idea was to be used on a limited scale in England about a century and a

half later. Its general use is still in the future.

EIGHTEENTH CENTURY

The use of coal in England grew rapidly. By 1700 about six hundred sailing vessels were engaged in the London coal trade, and coal was selling in London for the equivalent of about four dollars a ton. Some unknown English inventor tried the smelting of iron ore with coke instead of wood charcoal, but this use of coke (from bituminous coal) was not to become general in England for a century, and an additional half-century was to pass before coke superseded charcoal in America. In both places the Chinese process of anthracite smelting was rediscovered and used before coke.

In 1715 France began commercial mining of coal (Anzin); England started, in a small way, to smelt iron ore with coke (Colebrookdale); and the first blast furnace was erected in America (eastern Virginia)—but here charcoal was the fuel, for it was not until 1735 that coal-mining started in America. Local wood near Richmond, Virginia, had, at last, become scarce, and transportation of wood was impractical. By this time steam-engine pumps were in quite general use in England to drain water from deep mines, and now this operation began in France. This was the small beginning of the conversion of heat to power.

In the 1750's Samuel Johnson completed his famous *Dictionary of the English Language*. "Coal" was well defined, and so was "petroleum," but a "mill" was "in general an engine in which any operation is performed by means of wind or water; sometimes it is used of engines turned by hand, or by animal force." No mention was made of steam as a motive force. It was also about this time that the presence of petroleum in northwestern Pennsylvania was noted on a map of the "Middle

British Colonies in America." The word "petroleum" was printed close to the present site of Titusville and Oil City —the very area that was to have the first wild American oil boom a century later. Thus the occurrence of oil in Pennsylvania was recorded several years before the occurrence of coal there was reported. But petroleum at this time was already being produced on a small scale in Rumania, and production was now started also in Galicia.

By 1760 a few tons of bituminous may have been dug up and used locally in western Pennsylvania. But this is by no means certain, for Pennsylvania coal was not known east of the Alleghenies for about a half-century, and up to this time there was probably not a white man living within the limits of the present Allegheny County.

In 1766 anthracite coal was reported in eastern Pennsylvania, and a few tons were consumed in a local blacksmith's forge. At this time the proprietaries made their last purchase of land from the Indians. This purchase embraced the whole great area of bituminous land in Pennsylvania, and the purchase price was about $10,000. The land was valued, of course, not for its coal but for its vast resource of timber. At this time petroleum was also in the news. Since moderate importation of Burmese petroleum for a century was beginning to pique the curiosity of London, the governor-general of India sent Major Michael Symes of the British army as ambassador to the Burmese king. Symes reported that the annual petroleum production of Burma was about 400,000 hogsheads. He counted 520 oil wells in a small area bordering Petroleum Creek, a tributary of the Irrawaddy. Somehow Britain was unimpressed. The British waited until a half-century later to make a more detailed report of the phenomenon.

The indifference of Western nations is odd, considering the fact that the suitability of petroleum as a fuel was then well known in Europe. And David Zeisberger, famous Moravian missionary to the Indians, reported in 1769 that the oil being collected in Forest County, Pennsylvania, "can be used in lamps" (Egle, 1877, p. 613). But America had no real need at this time for any fuel except wood. This was pointed up when the Provincial Convention held in Philadelphia in 1775 adopted a lengthy and detailed resolution covering all the items of agriculture and manufacture that the authors considered important to the defense of the Colonies. Fuel was not mentioned.

Immediately after the American Revolution the first American coal-mining company was organized at Pottsville, Pennsylvania. The first few tons of coal (anthracite) were sent down the Susquehanna River from Wilkes-Barre to the armory at Carlisle, Pennsylvania, probably for use in blacksmith forges. This was the tiny beginning of the great coal production in America. On the other side of the earth, in India, 73 tons of coal were sent down from Burdwan to the armory at Calcutta. Burdwan coal was to become of minor importance later on, but Indian production has not even yet fulfilled its potentialities.

At long last coal was recognized in America as a resource of consequence. The first sale of land purchased because of its coal was recorded in 1785 at Clearfield, Pennsylvania, but the first load of coal from this land was not shipped for nineteen years! In the meantime Russia was employing English miners to dig coal along the Donets River. At this time France produced about 213,000 tons of coal and imported much more than this amount from England. The United States imported 3,850 tons of coal and produced almost none. The price of coal in London had risen to $10.00 a ton. American petroleum was selling for $16.00 a gallon, but as a medicine rather than as a fuel.

The discovery of coal in the Lehigh Valley came in 1791. A sample of the hard anthracite was taken to Philadelphia, where a group of adventurous men thought that something profitable could be done with it. So they formed the Lehigh Coal Mine Company. Their hopes were doomed, for nobody would buy or use such coal at this time. The company was succeeded some years later by the Lehigh Coal and Lehigh Navigation Companies, which prospered mightily.

1800 TO 1850

The story of the battle to win acceptance for coal in America is interesting. In 1800 the only American concern with coal of any sort was on the Atlantic Seaboard, where a little bituminous was being imported from England. Commercial use of coke for ironmaking was still far in the future for America but was in some use in Europe (e.g., in Upper Silesia), and coal tar was in commercial production in England. More than 99 per cent of the heat produced in America was from the burning of wood.

In 1804 the first coal of any sort reached the interior villages of the American East. A little bituminous was floated down the Susquehanna River to Columbia. This was a great surprise to the inhabitants of Lancaster County, Pennsylvania, who had never seen coal before.

In 1808, for the first time in America, a grate was constructed for the use of anthracite for domestic heat. The grate was made for Judge Jesse Fell of Wilkes-Barre, Pennsylvania, who wrote: "Made the experiment of burning the common stone coal of the valley in a grate, in a fireplace in my house, and found it will answer the purpose of a fuel, making a cleaner and better fire at less expense than burning wood in the common way" (*ibid.*, p. 876).

News of this sensational discovery spread over the countryside, and people came to witness the phenomenon that had been so familiar to the Chinese about two millenniums earlier. Soon, similar grates had been constructed by Judge Fell's neighbors. In the same year, John and Obigah Smith loaded two arks with anthracite in Ronson's Creek and floated them down the Susquehanna to Columbia. The people of Columbia had seen bituminous a few years before, but never anthracite, and no one could be induced to buy. The "black stones" had to be left behind in a dump heap. Not discouraged, the Smith brothers took two more arks of coal down the river the next year, but this time they took along one of Judge Fell's grates. The practicability of using the "black stones" as domestic fuel was convincingly demonstrated, and the coal was sold. Thereafter the market was grudgingly assured.

While this first primitive appreciation of coal was being developed in the United States, coal-gas lighting was spreading in London. Street lighting with gas did not start until 1810 in London. World street lighting was limited to a few whale-oil lamps in London and to a few petroleum-distillate lamps in Genoa and Parma. The distillate was obtained from petroleum flowing from a well in Modena, Italy. Added to this were lamps in India supplied with oil from Burma—but this had been going on for many centuries. Because the demand was so meager, the cost of petroleum in America dropped to $1.50 a gallon.

The periods from 1780 to 1820 in America and from 1800 to 1820 in England saw intensive development of power uses for the steam engine, but this had no effect on fossil fuel consumption, for wood was used almost entirely as fuel for steam-raising, and wood charcoal was the preferred fuel for iron manufacture. The impetus toward large-scale substitution of heat power for animate power was beginning to be felt in the Western world, but it was not to become really important until the twentieth century, when generation of electric power (from coal) and the internal combustion engine (for petroleum) were well launched.

During the first decade of the nineteenth century the Chinese are said to have had about ten thousand wells at the foot of the high mountains of the Tibetan chains (Taylor, 1845, p. 402). Many individual Chinese personally owned hundreds of wells producing brine and natural gas and averaging about twelve barrels a day of oil. The wells were through rock, with walls as polished as glass. In general, they were almost 2,000 feet deep (sometimes 3,000) and 5 or 6 inches in diameter. They had been drilled without power machinery, but so was the famous Drake well that came forty-seven years later.

While anthracite had been used in China for centuries, it was having a rough time not only in America but in England. Bakewell, in the first edition of his *Geology* (1813, p. 47), remarked: "It is true that a considerable part of the coal in South Wales is of an inferior quality [anthracite] and is not at present burned for domestic use; but in proportion as coal becomes scarce, improved methods of burning it will assuredly be discovered."

By 1815 bituminous coal was being used in Pittsburgh to operate steam engines for generation of about 150 horsepower. This meant that industrial consumption of coal in Pittsburgh was about 700 tons a year, and this was probably not far from the total United States industrial consumption of domestic coal. Industrial use of anthracite was about nil. Tried at the Philadelphia

Water Works, it was rejected because it "put the fire out." One of the principal manufacturers in Philadelphia, a Mr. Wetherill, buried the coal that had been consigned to him. Others crushed the coal and used it like gravel. Intensive sales effort was employed, including the printing of directions for burning, provision of certificates of approval from blacksmiths, and even bribery of foremen. A handicap to development was the relatively high price ($14.00 a ton) because of cost of transportation. But the price of English coal in New York was about $17.00 a ton (duty was $2.75). Wood and wood charcoal were soon to become even more costly. France, in 1815, produced 870,000 tons of coal and imported 230,000 tons from England. No figures were yet available on English production.

By 1820 the first consignment of coal from Wilkes-Barre reached Philadelphia. The total production of anthracite in the United States was estimated by Taylor (1845, p. 217) as not over 365 tons.[1] But the use of anthracite was to grow very rapidly, for, six years later, Philadelphia brought in 16,000 tons. A writer expressed his opinion that anthracite would some day become the principal fuel not only of Philadelphia but of some other cities. He was talking about domestic use, for even in 1830 almost no anthracite was being used industrially. And even for domestic heat, coal was of minor consequence. France was in about the same stage as America except that its records were much more precise. Charcoal was used all over the world, except in China and Wales, for the smelting of iron ore.

The first use of anthracite in America to raise steam for operating a steam engine came in 1830 in Pottsville, Pennsylvania. Abraham Pott used special grate bars that could resist the high heat of combustion. Thus, iron, made

1. I believe that some recent estimates of about ten times this amount are in error.

with wood charcoal, in turn made possible the burning of coal to provide steam for an engine used to saw wood.

In the 1830's wood was still king, but coal was growing. Annual consumption of domestic fuel in New York City was valued at $616,000 for wood, $100,000 for wood charcoal, and $613,000 for coal. Most of the coal was anthracite, but some was bituminous from Virginia. Philadelphia spent $740,000 for wood and $404,000 for coal (all anthracite). These figures do not include imported fuel. Vienna, with a much larger population than New York City, spent the equivalent of $300,000 for wood, $100,000 for wood charcoal, and only $30,000 for coal.

During the 1830's oil wells were beginning to appear in the United States. One, in Burksville, Kentucky, gushed oil 12 feet into the air before subsiding to a more moderate flow. We were doing what the Chinese had been doing for many centuries—drilling wells for brine and often finding oil or gas instead. And people began to notice oil seepages all over the world. In western Iran, where so much oil is being produced today, exudant liquid bitumen was being collected in the way described by Herodotus about twenty-four hundred years ago. Productive springs of naphtha were in operation on the borders of the Persian Gulf. Oil from the provinces of Fars and Azerbaijan was being used in lamps and to coat the bottoms of vessels on the Tigris and Euphrates rivers. In fact, oil was noted in the majority of places where modern production has been successful—Baku, Venezuela, California, Mexico, Texas. Men began to wonder what the eventual importance of oil might be. Someone said: "It surely was not placed there in vain" (Taylor, 1845, p. 218).

In 1840 an official attempt was made through the Census Act to determine the production of bituminous coal in the United States, but the attempt was a failure. It was thought by many that "this species of investigation savors too much of scrutiny into the private affairs of men, and is unsuited to the spirit of republican institutions." The statisticians of the period concluded that the extent of the bituminous coal fields was so large that "it seems futile to hazard even the roughest calculation." This uncertainty was to continue for a decade, but it was assumed that production of bituminous was somewhat less than production of anthracite, the amount of which could be estimated with reasonable accuracy because so much of it was shipped by common carrier.

A guess was made in 1840 that about a million tons of bituminous were produced in Pennsylvania and perhaps an additional half-million tons in West Virginia and Kentucky. These figures do not agree with actual census returns for the year, but, in my opinion, they are probably more accurate. France kept good records: its production of coal was nearly three million tons. But in spite of the fact that Britain was the oldest coal-producing nation, its records were as indefinite as ours. Not even a good guess could be made of Britain's production in 1840 except that it was probably larger than that of France and the United States combined. Belgium was in second place. Any statistics prior to 1850 (except for France) must be regarded with suspicion.

An increasing proportion of the iron of the world was being produced with coal, but in the United States all blast furnaces except six were still using charcoal.

Much of the coal in the middle of the nineteenth century was being mined by actual, or virtual, slaves. But laws were being passed in France, the Netherlands, Belgium, and the United States for the regulation of mining. Britain was the last to establish a system of humane, judicial interference. In spite of laws, miners were being poorly treated everywhere. In the United States the wage in Pennsylvania was 87.5 cents a day. In England and Scotland thousands of females were being used as beasts of burden to carry coal from the mines, the ordinary load for a woman being 230 pounds. The report of the Midland Commission was characterized by sickening and almost incredible details of such coal-mining practices in Britain. Long after the Civil War had freed our Negro slaves, England was still regarding its white mining force as a part of capital investment. Denmark was using convict labor.

Contemporary estimates of the life of coal reserves of the United States and the world are interesting today, because they were so fearfully wrong. It was thought then that Pennsylvania had as much coal as we now believe can be produced ultimately by the entire nation. United States coal was expected to be adequate for a great many thousand years. This fallacious conception lasted a full century. We believe now that our peak of coal production (all grades) will come within a hundred years if some of the higher coal-consumption estimates can be relied upon. United States anthracite reached its peak of production in 1915. The peak of production of "cheap coal"—coal that can be mined at anything like present costs—is likely to be around 1975. It was thought that coal fields in Britain could produce 116 billion tons, "or more than 5,500 years of supply for consumption and exportation." But Britain's coal production has already passed its peak. The coal future belongs not to Britain but to the rest of the world.

1850 TO 1900

Figures for 1850 are the first that can be relied upon. Total coal production of the world was about 50 million tons, with Britain supplying 62 per cent. Belgium, the United States, and France each supplied about 11 per cent. We had 540 blast furnaces, of which only 43 were not using wood charcoal. These 43 were using anthracite coal, but anthracite was to be promptly supplanted by coke from bituminous coal—already common in England.

Transportation of bituminous was a problem. This is highlighted by the fact that, while Pittsburgh was consuming three-quarters of a million tons, only 40,000 tons were finding their way east of the Allegheny Mountains. The railroad systems were soon to take care of this.

By 1850 the great deposits of sub-bituminous coal and lignite on the eastern flank of the Rocky Mountains had been roughly located. This coal area had been described (Taylor, 1845, p. 575) as exceeding "all others on the present surface of our planet." More than a century later we are looking forward to extensive use of this store of energy.

The 1850's saw the awakening of world-wide interest of Western nations in liquid fuel. James Young, in England, took out his patent for obtaining oil by distillation of cannel coal and oil shale. Two Boston chemists started to make lubricating oil from coal tar. A Canadian geologist developed a process for making oil from coal and founded the New York Kerosene Oil Company. Large plants were built in Boston and Portland for making liquid fuel from coal and oil shale, and some fifty smaller plants appeared at various inland points. Oil wells were not uncommon. At least a dozen men owned wells with moderate production, and oil was having a ready sale. But synthetic oil from coal was being produced twenty times as fast as natural petroleum. Smart men of the time thought that we were entering upon a synthetic-oil period, but they were wrong.

The famous Drake well, drilled in 1859, was not the first well for petroleum and by no means the largest. The well was drilled in about the same way that the Chinese and Burmese had drilled their wells a thousand years earlier. But, for some strange reason, the Drake well aroused the imagination of speculators. People with a little money flocked to the wilderness of Pennsylvania to try their luck without benefit of technology. Some made fortunes, while others became bankrupt. The net result of eight years of violent confusion was proof that petroleum and natural gas could be produced in the United States in abundance, as it had been produced in Burma in abundance for many centuries. We had been ranging the seven seas for whale oil, and our whale oil "take" for 1859 was two hundred times our oil production, but it seemed to occur to no one to import Burmese petroleum. Perhaps this is because such importation would have involved so much less physical danger and hardship than whaling or, indeed, than oil production in Pennsylvania in those initial years. Until recently, Americans have been a romantic and speculative people.

At the end of eight years of violent turmoil, the oil boom subsided in Pennsylvania. The drop of oil production in those early wells to a mere trickle had a sobering effect. Drunken audiences no longer threw five-hundred-dollar bills on the stage in appreciation of cheap shows. Men no longer threw fireballs into oil tanks. Locomotives no longer fixed chains about oil pipe lines to uproot them. Personal degradation, dishonesty, and murder were no longer accepted as normal. The oil business was about to mature.

Smart people (John D. Rockefeller, for example) thought we were entering a period when petroleum was to light the lamps of the world. There was no other known use for petroleum at that time. But, of course, these people were wrong. Electric lighting had already appeared above the horizon and was destined soon to supplant kerosene. Unsuspected by petroleum pioneers, the internal combustion engine was ready to take the load of production in the twentieth century, after smart people (in Wall Street, for example) thought we were entering a period of steam motorcars and, later, electric motorcars. They, too, were wrong. When the internal combustion engine was established, smart people (Henry Ford, for example) thought that we were entering a period of expensive cars for the few. Later, Ford and others discovered that the trend was toward relatively inexpensive cars for the many.

Literally no one has foreseen the present universality of American motorcar use. Now that the highways are almost saturated with gasoline-burning vehicles, we call this a motorcar age, but recorded predictions make incredible reading. They came from automotive companies, oil companies, investment bankers, and economists. They were all wrong—even predictions as recent as 1950. This is no reflection on their intelligence. But I believe it is a reflection on present intelligence when we presume to know what the next age will be like.

But we are ahead of our story.

By 1870, when both coal and petroleum had been launched in the world, no country was yet mechanized with mobile power except for the locomotive. We had more than half the railroad mileage of the world, and steam locomotives had finally supplanted horses and mules; but railroads had all been built without benefit of tractors, bulldozers, or power equipment of any sort. Our system, and all other systems, had been built by the sweat of men and horses—as the ancient pyramids had been built by the sweat of the Egyptians. Smart people thought that railroads were the most conservative of all investments, but they were wrong. By the time power equipment was available (in the twentieth century), railway systems had reached their peak and were thereafter to decline, because power equipment has been used to build competitive highway systems for cars, busses, and trucks.

Steamships were common, but they still all had sails. Sails were beginning to be considered auxiliary to steam power instead of the other way around. But England had only two naval steamers. The rest depended entirely upon sails. McCormick reapers were multiplying on the farms, but they were all horse-operated. Most mining was still done with wood as fuel, and many thousands of acres of woodland were being denuded to supply fuel for steam boilers.

But the foundations for power equipment had been laid. Everywhere wood was becoming scarce and expensive, and coal and oil were becoming plentiful and cheap. The small high-pressure steam engine was in production, and the steam turbine was just around the corner. Men had made workable mobile vehicles (as early as 1800). Generation of electric power had been developed, and various forms of electric lighting had been demonstrated. The telegraph was in operation, and the telephone was about to come. (The Western Union Telegraph Company mistakenly thought we were entering a period of telegraphic communication and turned down Bell's offer to sell them the rights to the telephone for $100,000.) Wireless communication and the motion picture were in embryo. The stage was all set for the rapid industrial development that has taken place within the last fifty years.

TWENTIETH CENTURY

All industrial operations require power (and fuel), but the two outstanding circumstances that have skyrocketed fuel demand during the last fifty years have been electric power and the internal combustion engine. Each one has advanced more rapidly than had been thought possible. The drain on the world's finite supply of fossil fuels is becoming fantastic and shows every sign of continuing acceleration. Today, day in and day out, we are consuming in the United States over a quarter of a million barrels of petroleum, nearly 45,000 tons of coal, and a billion cubic feet of natural gas *every hour*. No wonder we think of this as the fossil fuel age. But these overwhelming rates of depletion of finite resources have come only recently. In 1900 the petroleum production of the world was about 400,000 barrels a day, and more than half of this was in Russia. Thus, our daily production in 1900 was much less than our hourly consumption is now. The rest of the world is moving forward nearly four times as rapidly as the United States. The reasons for more rapid increase in consumption abroad are (1) that we already have our tens of millions of motorcars, while automotive development in many other nations is just beginning, and (2) that the rest of the world has about ten times as much potential oil land as we have. We have developed our oil production energetically and effectively, while other nations have not. Most of the oil production outside the United States has been accomplished with American technology and American money. We have drilled about 150,000 wells in this country, and current rate of drilling is about 10,000 wells a year. We are spending several billion dollars a year for exploration and drilling. Other countries have not been able to afford such rapid dissipation of fossil fuel resources. So the petroleum future naturally belongs not to the United States but to the rest of the world.

What can be said about the petroleum future? Smart prophets have been consistently wrong in the past. It would be presumptuous to assume any supe-

Fig. 94a.—Coal-crushing plant by river and railroad. Modern coal-crushing plants are not so unsightly as two decades ago.

Fig. 94b.—Strip mining for coal. For strip mining of coal, power shovels are many times as large as those used for digging the Panama Canal.

FIG. 95a.—Early oil derricks. In 1925, oil wells were closely spaced above oil pools. Today this wasteful practice has been largely eliminated. Now, modern steel derricks are widely spaced.

FIG. 95b.—Modern oil refinery and storage tanks. Modern oil refineries are largely automatic with huge capacity and few operators.

rior clairvoyance today. But certain conditional statements are quite safe to make. If we have a 100-gallon tank of water and start to drain the tank at the rate of 1 gallon an hour, it is safe to say that the tank will be empty in 100 hours if the rate of outgo remains constant. Economists have applied this simple reasoning to petroleum with absurd results. The hypothetical 100-gallon supply has had the awkward habit of growing to 500 or 1,000 gallons by discovery of more oil. The rate of outflow has not remained constant but has increased rapidly. Under these complicating conditions it is not possible to determine how long it will take to empty the tank. In the case of oil the tank is not likely to be empty for several thousand years, because much of the oil will not be *found* for a long, long time. But it *is* possible to draw a curve of production rates for the future, and the curve is not a prediction. It is a definite thing *if* the assumptions upon which it is based are correct. The assumptions are (1) that geologists are reasonably correct in their present estimates of the total remaining oil to be discovered and (2) that demand for oil will keep on rising for a few years. Both of these assumptions may be wrong.

Studies along this line have been made for United States and world petroleum and for natural gas and coal in the United States. According to these studies, we are likely to reach the peak of petroleum production in the United States about 1965, the peak of world petroleum production about 1985, the peak of United States gas production about 1965, and the peak of United States production of coal of all grades about 2025. After these dates production will decline. Some technologists believe that the dates are too early, because they have little faith in the order of magnitude of estimates of ultimate reserves. Some others believe that the dates are too early, because they expect future demand for energy to be less lively. Some others believe that the dates are too early, because it will not be practical to increase production during the next few decades at the predicated rates. These men may all be right, but if ample allowances are made—if present estimates of recoverable reserves prove to be only half of what they should be, if the demand curves rise only half as steeply as they have in the past, if we are destined to put only half as much effort in exploration and drilling and mining as demands would justify—the cold mathematics of the problem shows only moderate postponement of peaks of production: perhaps 1970 for United States oil production, 1975 for gas, 2000 for world petroleum, and 2050 for United States coal.

The United States and the world have other fossil fuels to fall back upon —oil shale and tar sands. Oil shale is undoubtedly abundant in the United States. Ample supplies of shale oil can be obtained at an indeterminate average cost, and an undetermined amount can be obtained at moderate cost. These are about the only safe statements that can be made at this time. Most of the oil shale is in Colorado, Utah, and Wyoming, where water for processing is scarce. The consensus of technologists is that we may expect not more than seven billion barrels of shale-oil production during the first twenty years of operation. Since we are consuming more than two billion barrels of petroleum a year, the shale-oil figures are not impressive. But, to produce even this amount, we would need a mining force five times as large as that employed by the entire United States iron-ore-mining industry, extensive intermountain water-storage reservoirs would have to be created, and seven billion dollars would have to be invested. Any increase in shale-oil production would depend upon the rates at which labor, money, and water can be provided and, of course, upon the location and quality of oil shale. Oil shale will provide another chapter in the fossil fuel story, but it will be a small one unless present technical studies of underground retorting of oil shale should lead to a practicable process.

As far as the United States is concerned, tar sands will provide not a chapter but a sentence, for our reserves of tar sands are small. Canadian reserves are great but are not economically accessible. A little oil will be produced there in the course of time.

Petroleum, natural gas, coal, oil shale, and tar sands are believed to be continually forming in the earth, but they are of no use to us as fuels until they accumulate in massive deposits from which they may be produced. When they are gone, we shall have to wait for hundreds of millions of years and for unpredictable geologic shifts in the earth's crust before the present fossil fuel age could be repeated. In a practi-

cal sense, fossil fuels, after this century, will cease to exist except as raw materials for chemical synthesis.

If one might hazard a guess, the next age might well be one in which power is obtained from chemical and nuclear reactions without the intermediate generation of heat with attendant losses. This would be in contrast with the present age, in which nearly all power is obtained from heat. But this will require inventions of high order, and few are even thinking about the problem now.

Only now that we can see what has been called the "climactic approach to exhaustion" are we fully conscious of the importance of the fossil fuel age. We cannot name the next age before it has even begun. Technology has not failed us in the past, and I am confident that it will not fail us in the future. But what its solutions will be to the world's energy problem lies in Thomas Carlyle's "continents of darkness."

REFERENCES

ANONYMOUS

1935–54 *Drilling and Production Practice, 1934–1953.* New York: American Petroleum Institute, Division of Production. (Annual.)

1949 *Petroleum: The Story of an American Industry.* New York: American Petroleum Institute. 95 pp.

1952 *Bituminous Coal Annual, 1952.* Washington, D.C.: Bituminous Coal Institute. 176 pp.

1953a *Gasification and Liquefaction of Coal.* New York: American Institute of Mining and Metallurgical Engineers. 621 pp.

1953b *Oil for Today—and for Tomorrow.* Oklahoma City: Interstate Oil Compact Commission. 83 pp.

1954 *Technology of Lignitic Coals,* Parts I and II. (Bureau of Mines Information Circulars Nos. 7691 and 7692.) Washington, D.C.: U.S. Department of the Interior. 142 and 120 pp.

ASHTON, T. S., and SYKES, JOSEPH

1929 *Coal Industry of the Eighteenth Century.* Manchester: Manchester University Press. 268 pp.

AYRES, EUGENE

1953 "U.S. Oil Outlook: How Coal Fits In," *Coal Age,* LVIII, No. 8, 70–73.

1954 "Raw Materials for Organic Chemicals," *Chemical and Engineering News,* XXXII, No. 29, 2876–82.

AYRES, EUGENE, and SCARLOTT, C. A.

1952 *Energy Sources: The Wealth of the World.* New York: McGraw-Hill Book Co. 344 pp.

BAKEWELL, GEORGE

1813 *Geology of the Earth.* London. 212 pp.

BALL, M. W.

1950 "Oil and Human Welfare," *Quarterly of the Colorado School of Mines,* XLV, No. 1A, 29–37.

BECKER, CARL

1932 *The Heavenly City of the Eight-*

eenth-Century Philosophers. New Haven, Conn.: Yale University Press. 168 pp.

CHARLES, J. M.
1950 "Coal and Its Future," Quarterly of the Colorado School of Mines, XLV, No. 2B, 67–75.

DONATH, E. E.
1954 "Fuels and Chemicals from Coal Hydrogenation," Industrial and Engineering Chemistry, XLVI, No. 10, 2032–35.

DUNSTAN, A. E., et al. (eds.)
1938–53 The Science of Petroleum, Vols. I–VI. New York: Oxford University Press.

EAVENSON, H. N.
1939 Coal through the Ages. New York: American Institute of Mining and Metallurgical Engineers. 123 pp.
1942 First Century and a Quarter of American Coal Industry. Pittsburgh, Pa.: The Author. 701 pp.

EGLE, W. H.
1877 An Illustrated History of the Commonwealth of Pennsylvania. Harrisburg, Pa.: De Witt C. Goodrich. 1,204 pp.

ELLIS, CARLETON
1934–37 Chemistry of Petroleum Derivatives, Vols. I–II. New York: Reinhold Publishing Corp. 1,464 pp.

FANNING, L. M.
1948 Rise of American Oil. Rev. ed. New York: Harper & Bros. 178 pp.

LOWRY, H. H. (ed.)
1945 Chemistry of Coal Utilization, Vols. I–II. New York: John Wiley & Sons. 1,868 pp.

POPE, P. C. (ed.)
1953 Coal: Production, Distribution, Utilization. New York: Anglobooks. 236 pp.

SACHANEN, A. N.
1948 Conversion of Petroleum. 2d ed. New York: Reinhold Publishing Corp. 602 pp.

SALL, G. W.
1954 "Short History of Coal Mining," Mining Congress Journal, XL, No. 4, 36–39.

STRUTH, H. J. (ed.)
1954 World Petroleum Statistical Yearbook. New York: Mona Palmer. 454 pp.

TAYLOR, R. C.
1845 Statistics on Coal. Philadelphia: J. W. Moore. 754 pp.

WHITESHOT, C. A.
1905 The Oil-Well Driller: History of the Oil Industry of the World. Mannington, W.Va.: The Author. 895 pp.

WILSON, P. J., and WELLS, J. H.
1950 Coal, Coke and Coal Chemicals. New York: McGraw-Hill Book Co. 509 pp.

The Natural History of Urbanization

LEWIS MUMFORD[*]

[*] Mr. Mumford since 1952 has been Professor of City Planning at the University of Pennsylvania, Philadelphia. He is a fellow of the American Academy of Arts and Sciences, a member of the American Philosophical Society, an honorary associate of the Royal Institute of British Architects, and an honorary fellow of Stanford University. His publications include: *Technics and Civilization*, 1934; *The Culture of Cities*, 1938; and *The Conduct of Life*, 1951.

THE EMERGENCE OF THE CITY

The natural history of urbanization has not yet been written, for only a small part of the preliminary work has been done. The literature of the city itself, until a half-century ago, was barren to the point of nonexistence; and even now the ecologists of the city, dealing too largely with a late and limited aspect of urbanism, have hardly staked out the ground that is to be covered. Our present purpose, accordingly, is to make use of such studies as have so far been made in order to ask more pointed questions and so, incidentally, to indicate further fields of profitable study.

Whether one looks at the city morphologically or functionally, one cannot understand its development without taking in its relationship to earlier forms of cohabitation that go back to non-human species. One must remember not only the obvious homologies of the anthill and the beehive but also the nature of fixed seasonal habitations in protected sites, like the breeding grounds of many species of birds.

Though permanent villages date only from Neolithic times, the habit of resorting to caves for the collective performance of magical ceremonies seems to date back to an earlier period; and whole communities, living in caves and hollowed-out walls of rock, have survived in widely scattered areas down to the present. The outline of the city as both an outward form and an inward pattern of life might be found in such ancient assemblages. Whatever the aboriginal impetus, the tendency toward formal cohabitation and fixed residence gave rise, in Neolithic times, to the ancestral form of the city: the village, a collective utility brought forth by the new agricultural economy. Lacking the size and complexity of the city, the village nevertheless exhibits its essential features: the encircling mound or palisade, setting it off from the fields; permanent shelters; storage pits and bins, with refuse dumps and burial grounds recording silently past time and spent energy. At this early stage, at least, Mark Jefferson's observation (1931) holds true: urban and rural, city and country, are one thing, not two things.

Though the number of families per acre in a village is greater than the number per square mile under a pastoral economy, such settlements bring with them no serious disturbance in the natural environment; indeed, the relation may even be favorable for building up the soil and increasing its natural productivity. Archeological explor-

382

ers in Alaska have been able to detect early settlements by noting the greenness of the vegetation around the otherwise submerged village sites, probably due to the enrichment of the soil from the nitrogenous human and animal waste accumulated near by. Early cities, as we find them in Mesopotamia and Egypt, maintain the symbiotic relation with agriculture that we find in the village. In countries like China, still governed by the principles of village economy, even contemporary cities with high population density, such as Keyes describes (1951), exhibit the same reciprocal relations: "The most concentrated highly developed agriculture is just outside the walls of cities." King estimated (1927) that each million city dwellers in China account for more than 13,000 pounds of nitrogen, 2,700 pounds of phosphorous, and almost 4,500 pounds of potassium in the daily night soil returned to the land. Brunhes' description (1920) of cities under "unproductive occupation of the soil" does not altogether hold for the earliest types or, as I shall show, for the latest types of city.

The emergence of the city from the village was made possible by the improvements in plant cultivation and stock-breeding that came with Neolithic culture; in particular, the cultivation of the hard grains that could be produced in abundance and kept over from year to year without spoiling. This new form of food not merely offered insurance against starvation in the lean years, as was recorded in the famous story of Joseph in Egypt, but likewise made it possible to breed and support a bigger population not committed to food-raising. From the standpoint of their basic nutrition, one may speak of wheat cities, rye cities, rice cities, and maize cities, to characterize their chief source of energy; and it should be remembered that no other source was so important until the coal

seams of Saxony and England were opened. With the surplus of manpower available as Neolithic man escaped from a subsistence economy, it was possible to draw a larger number of people into other forms of work and service: administration, the mechanical arts, warfare, systematic thought, and religion. So the once-scattered population of Neolithic times, dwelling in hamlets of from ten to fifty houses (Childe, 1954), was concentrated into "cities," ruled and regimented on a different plan. These early cities bore many marks of their village origins, for they were still in essence agricultural towns: the main source of their food supply was in the land around them; and, until the means of transport had greatly improved and a system of centralized control had developed, they could not grow beyond the limit of their local water supply and their local food sources.

This early association of urban growth with food production governed the relation of the city to its neighboring land far longer than many observers now realize. Though grains were transported long distances (even as special food accessories like salt had circulated in earlier times), cities like Rome, which drew mainly on the distant granaries of Africa and the Near East—to say nothing of the oyster beds of Colchester in England—were exceptions down to the nineteenth century. As late as fifty years ago large portions of the fruits and vegetables consumed in New York and Paris came from nearby market gardens, sometimes on soils greatly enriched, if not almost manufactured, with urban refuse, as Kropotkin pointed out in *Fields, Factories, and Workshops* (1899). This means that one of the chief determinants of large-scale urbanization has been nearness to fertile agricultural land; yet, paradoxically, the growth of most cities has been achieved by covering over and removing from cultivation the very land—often, indeed, the richest alluvial soils—whose existence at the beginning made their growth possible. The tendency of cities to grow along rivers or near accessible harbors was furthered not alone by the need for easy transportation but by the need to draw on aquatic sources of food to supplement those produced by the soil. This rich and varied diet may itself have contributed to the vital energy of city dwellers as contrasted with the more sluggish ways of hinterlanders and perhaps may also have partly offset the bad effect of close quarters in spreading communicable diseases. While modern means of transport have equalized these advantages, they have not yet hastened the migration of urban populations to upland sites on poorer soils, though often these present more salubrious climates and better living conditions.

The village and the small country town are historic constants. One of the outstanding facts about urbanization is that, while the urban population of the globe in 1930 numbered around 415,-000,000 souls, or about a fifth of the total population, the remaining four-fifths still lived under conditions approximating that of the Neolithic economy (Sorre, 1952). In countries as densely peopled as India, as late as 1939, according to the *Statesman's Yearbook,* less than 10 per cent of the total population lived in cities. These "Neolithic" conditions include the utilization of organic sources of energy, vegetable and animal, the use of a local supply of drinking water, the continuous cultivation of land within walking distance of the village, the partial use of human dung along with that of animals for fertilizer, a low concentration of inorganic refuse, like glass and metals, and an absence of air pollution. In many parts of the world, village settlements, far from encroaching on ara-

ble land, occupy barren hill sites of little use for agriculture; the stony outcrop of an Italian hill town involves only a slightly more symmetrical arrangement of the original rock strata. The chief weakness of these settlements, particularly in parts of the world long cultivated, notably in Spain, Greece, or China, is due to the peasant's begrudging the land needed for forest cover; he thus tends, by overtillage, to promote erosion and to create a further imbalance among the bird, insect, and plant populations. But, just as the early village economy was indebted to the astronomical calendar produced in the temple cities for the timely planting of their crops, so the present development of ecological knowledge, which has led to increasing concern and care for the woodland preserves in highly urbanized countries, may in time counteract the otherwise destructive effects of earlier stages in urban settlement.

URBAN SYMBIOSIS AND DOMINANCE

With the first growth of urban populations in ancient Mesopotamia, the symbiotic relations that originally held between village and land were not greatly altered. "The city," as Childe (1942, p. 94) describes its earliest manifestations, "is girt with a brick wall and a fosse, within the shelter of which man found for the first time a world of his own, relatively secure from the immediate pressure of raw, external nature. It stands out in an artificial landscape of gardens, fields, and pastures, created out of reed swamp and desert by the collective activity of preceding generations in building dykes and digging canals." Though these cities represented "a new magnitude in human settlement," the populations of Lagash, Umma, and Khafaje are "reliably estimated to have been 19,000, 16,000, and 12,000 respectively during the third millennium." The Levitical cities described in the Bible, confirmed by modern excavations of Gezer, had a town area of about 22 acres, with pasture land, permanently reserved, amounting to about 300 acres (Osborn, 1946). More than four thousand years later, as late as the sixteenth century, the characteristic size of the city in western Europe ranged from 2,000 to 20,000 people; it was only in the seventeenth century that cities of more than 100,000 began to multiply. In both the Near East in ancient times and in western Europe in the Middle Ages, cities prudently retained some portion of the land within their walls for gardens and the harboring of animals for food in case of military siege. Even the vast domains of Babylon must not mislead us into looking upon it as comparable in density to modern London. A map drawn in 1895 by Arthur Schneider, and republished by Hassert (1907), shows that Babylon covered an area big enough to contain Rome, Tarentum, Syracuse, Athens, Ephesus, Thebes, Jerusalem, Carthage, Sparta, Alexandria, and Tyre, together with almost as much open space between these cities as they occupied in their own right. Even in Herodotus' time, Babylon had many of the aspects of an overgrown village.

The Neolithic economy appears to have been a co-operative one. The concentration upon plant cultivation in small neighborly communities, never with a sufficient surplus of food or power to promote too much arrogance in man's relation with other men or with nature, established a natural balance between fields and settlements. In Europe, as Élisée Reclus long ago noted, country towns and villages tended to spread evenly, as far as topography allowed, about the space of a day's walk apart. With the introduction of metallurgy, during the succeeding period of urbanization, came technological specialization, caste differentiation, and heightened temptations to aggression; and with this began a dis-

regard for the welfare of the community as a whole and, in particular, a tendency to ignore the city's dependence upon its local resources. Excess of manpower abetted an excessive belief in the power of man—a belief deepened, no doubt, by the efficacy of the new edged weapons and armor in giving control to aggressive minorities who took the law into their own hands. With the development of long-distance trading, numerical calculation, and coinage, this urban civilization tended to throw off its original sense of limits and to regard all forms of wealth as purchasable by trade or procurable by a demonstration of military power. What could not be grown or produced in the local region could be, by theft or exchange, obtained elsewhere. In time this urban economy made the mistake of applying the pragmatic standards of the market place to the environment itself: the process began of building over the interior open spaces and building out over the surrounding land.

Until modern times the extension of a city's walls marked its growth as surely as does each additional ring of a tree. The wall had perhaps a formative role in the transformation of the village into the city; when made of heavy, permanent materials, surrounded by a moat, it gave the city a means of protection the little village could not afford. Not merely was it capable of military defense, but the city, through its surplus population, could muster enough manpower to hold against a large army of attackers. The earliest meaning of "town" is an inclosed or fortified place. The village that, because of its defensible site, offered protection against predators of all kinds would in times of peril attract families from more exposed areas and so, with a larger, mixed population, would turn into a city. Thus the temple citadel would add to its original population and, even after the danger had passed, would retain some of those who sought shelter and so become a city. In Greece, at least, the city comes into existence, historically, as such a synoecism.

But the morphological difference between the village and the city is not simply the result of the latter's superior site or of the fact that its geographic situation enables it to draw on a wider area for resources, foods, and men and in turn to export their products to a larger market, though both are facts conducive to population growth and economic expansion. What distinguish city from village are mainly two facts. The first of these is the presence of an organized social core, around which the whole structure of the community coheres. If this nucleation may begin in the village stage, as remains of temples seem to indicate, there is a general shift of household occupations and rituals into specialized collective institutions, part of the intensified social division of labor brought in with civilization itself. But, from the standpoint of the city's relation to the earth, the important point to notice is that, in this social core or nucleus, the sharpest departures from the daily habits and the physical structure of the village take place. Thus the temple, unlike the hut, will be built of permanent materials, with solid stone walls, often plated with precious stones or roofed with rare timber taken from a distant quarry or forest, all conceived on a colossal scale, while the majority of dwelling houses will still be built of clay and reed, or wattle and daub, on the old village pattern. While the temple area will be paved, the streets and alleys of the rest of the city will remain unpaved. As late as imperial Rome, pavement will be introduced first into the Forum, while most of the arteries remain uncovered, to become sloughs of mud in rainy weather. Here too, in the urban palace, as early as Akkad, such technological innovations as baths,

toilets, and drains will appear—innovations that remain far beyond the reach of the urban populations-at-large until modern times.

Along with this bold aesthetic transformation of the outward environment, another tendency distinguishes the city from the village—a tendency to loosen the bonds that connect its inhabitants with nature and to transform, eliminate, or replace its earth-bound aspects, covering the natural site with an artificial environment that enhances the dominance of man and encourages an illusion of complete independence from nature. The first age of the "urban revolution," to use Childe's term, had little extrahuman power and few machines. Its technological heritage, once it had learned to smelt copper and iron, was in every sense a static one; and its major skills, weaving aside, were concentrated on fashioning utensils and utilities (pots, jars, vats, bins) and on building great collective works (dams, irrigation systems, buildings, roads, baths) and, finally, cities themselves. Having learned to employ fire of relatively high intensity to glaze and smelt ores, these early civilizations offset its danger by creating a fireproof environment. The importance of this fact, once papyrus and paper were in use, can hardly be overestimated. In this general transformation from the transient to the fixed, from fragile and temporary structures to durable buildings, proof against wind, weather, and fire, early man emancipated himself likewise from the fluctuations and irregularities of nature. Each of the utilities that characterized the new urban form—the wall, the durable shelter, the arcade, the paved way, the reservoir, the aqueduct, the sewer—lessened the impact of nature and increased the dominance of man. That fact was revealed in the very silhouette of the city, as the traveler beheld it from a distance. Standing out in the vegetation-clad landscape, the city became an inverted oasis of stone or clay. The paved road, a man-made desert that speeds traffic and makes it largely independent of the weather and the seasons; the irrigation ditch, a man-made river system that releases the farmer from irregularities of seasonal rainfall; the water main, an artificial brook that turns the parched environment of the city into an oasis; the pyramid, an artificial mountain that serves as symbolic reminder of man's desire for permanence and continuity—all these inventions record the displacement of natural conditions with a collective artifact of urban origin.

Physical security and social continuity were the two great contributions of the city. Under those conditions every kind of conflict and challenge became possible without disrupting the social order, and part of this new animus was directed into a struggle with the forces of nature. By serving as a secure base of operations, a seat of law and government, a repository of deeds and contracts, and a marshaling yard for manpower, the city was able to engage in long-distance activities. Operating through trade, taxation, mining, military assault, and road-building, which made it possible to organize and deploy thousands of men, the city proceeded to make large-scale transformations of the environment, impossible for groups of smaller size to achieve. Through its storage, canalization, and irrigation, the city, from its earliest emergence in the Near East, justified its existence, for it freed the community from the caprices and violences of nature—though no little part of that gift was nullified by the further effect of subjecting the community more abjectly to the caprices and violences of men.

URBAN DISPLACEMENT OF NATURE

Unfortunately, as the disintegration of one civilization after another reminds us, the displacement of nature in the city rested, in part, upon an illusion—or, indeed, a series of illusions—as to the nature of man and his institutions: the illusions of self-sufficiency and independence and of the possibility of physical continuity without conscious renewal. Under the protective mantle of the city, seemingly so permanent, these illusions encouraged habits of predation or parasitism that eventually undermined the whole social and economic structure, after having worked ruin in the surrounding landscape and even in far-distant regions. Many elements supplied by nature, necessary for both health and mental balance, were lacking in the city. Medicine, as practiced by the Hippocratic School in the great retreats, like that at Kos, concerned with airs, waters, and places, seems at an early age to have employed in therapy natural elements that were depleted or out of balance even in the relatively small Aegean cities of the fifth century B.C., though their ruling classes spent no small part of their leisure in the exercise of the body. Through the ages the standard prescription for most urban illnesses— and perhaps as effective as more specific remedies—is retreat to some little village by seacoast or mountain—that is, restoration to a pre-urban natural environment. In times of plague the retreat repeatedly has taken on the aspects of a rout. Though man has become the dominant species in every region where the city has taken hold, partly because of the knowledge and the system of public controls over both man and nature he exercises there, he has yet to safeguard that position by acknowledging his sustained and inescapable dependence upon all his biological partners. With the ecological implications of this fact, I shall deal later.

Probably no city in antiquity had a population of much more than a million inhabitants, not even Rome; and, except in China, there were no later Romes until the nineteenth century. But, long before a million population is reached, most cities come to a critical point in their development. That occurs when the city is no longer in symbiotic relationship with its surrounding land; when further growth overtaxes local resources, like water, and makes them precarious; when, in order to continue its growth, a city must reach beyond its immediate limits for water, for fuel, for building materials, and for raw materials used in manufacture; and, above all, when its internal birth rate becomes inadequate to provide enough manpower to replace, if not to augment, its population. This stage has been reached in different civilizations at different periods. Up to this point, when the city has come to the limits of sustenance in its own territory, growth takes place by colonization, as in a beehive. After this point, growth takes place, in defiance of natural limitations, by a more intensive occupation of the land and by encroachment into the surrounding areas, with the subjugation by law or naked force of rival growing cities bidding for the same resources.

Most of the characteristics of this second form of urban growth can be observed in the history of Rome. Here the facts are better documented than they are for most ancient cities; and the effects upon the landscape have remained so visible that they suggested to George Perkins Marsh (1864, 1874) the principal lines of his investigation of *The Earth as Modified by Human Action*. Rome of the Seven Hills is an acropolis type of city, formed by a cluster of villages united for defense; and the plain of the Tiber was the original seat of their agriculture. The surplus population of this region conquered first the neighboring territories of the Etruscans and then those of more distant lands. By systematic expropriation, Rome brought wheat, olive oil, dried fish, and pottery back to the original site to sustain its growing population. To facilitate the movement of its legions and speed up the processes of administration, it carved roads through the landscape with triumphant disregard of the nature of the terrain. These roads and viaducts went hand in hand with similar works of engineering, the aqueducts and reservoirs necessary to bring water to Rome. By short-circuiting the flow of water from mountainside to sea, the city monopolized for its special uses a considerable amount of the runoff; and, to offset some of the effects of metropolitan overcrowding, it created a cult of the public bath that in turn imposed a heavy drain upon the fuel supplied by the near-by forest areas. The advance of technology, with central hot-air heating, characteristically hastened the process of deforestation, as was later to happen in the glass- and ironmaking and shipbuilding industries of northern Europe and to be repeated today in the heavy industrial demand for cellulose. Meanwhile, the sewers of Rome, connected to public toilets, polluted the Tiber without returning the precious mineral contents to the soil, though even in imperial Rome dung farmers still collected most of the night soil from the great tenements of the proletariat. At this stage the symbiotic relation turns into a parasitic one; the cycle of imbalance begins, and the mere massing of the demand in a single center results in denudations and desiccations elsewhere. The more complete the urbanization, the more definite is the release from natural limitations; the more highly the city seems developed as an independent entity, the more fatal are the consequences for the territory it dominates. This series of changes characterizes the growth of cities in every civilization: the transformation of eopolis into megalopolis. If the process wrought damage to the earth even in the ancient world, when cities as big as Rome, Carthage, and Alexandria were the exception rather than the rule, we have good reason to examine carefully the probable consequences of the present wave of urbanization.

MODERN FORCES OF EXPANSION

Let me sum up the observations so far made with respect to the natural history of cities. In the first stage of urbanization the number and size of cities varied with the amount and productivity of the agricultural land available. Cities were confined mainly to the valleys and flood plains, like the Nile, the Fertile Crescent, the Indus, and the Hwang Ho. Increase of population in any one city was therefore limited. The second stage of urbanization began with the development of large-scale river and sea transport and the introduction of roads for chariots and carts. In this new economy the village and the country town maintained the environmental balance of the first stage; but, with the production of grain and oil in surpluses that permitted export, a specialization in agriculture set in and, along with this, a specialization in trade and industry, supplementing the religious and political specialization that dominated the first stage. Both these forms of specialization enabled the city to expand in population beyond the limits of its agricultural hinterland; and, in certain cases, notably in the Greek city of Megalopolis, the population in smaller centers was deliberately removed to a single big center—a conscious reproduction of a process that was taking place less deliberately in other cities. At this stage the city grew by draining away its resources and manpower from the countryside without returning any equivalent goods. Along with this went a de-structive use of natural resources for industrial purposes, with increased concentration on mining and smelting.

The third stage of urbanization does not make its appearance until the nineteenth century, and it is only now beginning to reach its full expansion, performance, and influence. If the first stage is one of urban balance and cooperation, and the second is one of partial urban dominance within a still mainly agricultural framework, behind both is an economy that was forced to address the largest part of its manpower toward cultivating the land and improving the whole landscape for human use. The actual amount of land dedicated to urban uses was limited, if only because the population was also limited. This entire situation has altered radically during the last three centuries by reason of a series of related changes. The first is that world population has been growing steadily since the seventeenth century, when the beginnings of reasonable statistical estimates, or at least tolerable guesses, can first be made. According to the Woytinskys (1953), the average rate of population increase appears to have gone up steadily: 2.7 per cent from 1650 to 1700; 3.2 per cent in the first half of the eighteenth century and 4.5 per cent in the second half; 5.3 per cent from 1800 to 1850; 6.5 per cent from 1850 to 1900; and 8.3 per cent from 1900 to 1950. As the Woytinskys themselves remark, these averages should not be taken too seriously; yet there is a high probability that an acceleration has taken place and hardly any doubt whatever that the world population has doubled during the last century, while the manpower needed to maintain agricultural productivity in mechanized countries has decreased.

By itself this expansion might mean no more than that the less populated parts of the earth would presently acquire densities comparable to those of

India and China, with a great part of the increase forced to undertake intensive cultivation of the land. But this increase did not take place by itself; it was accompanied by a series of profound technological changes which transformed the classic "age of utilities" into the present "age of the machine" and a predominantly agricultural civilization into an urban one—or possibly a suburban one. These two factors, technical improvement and population growth, have been interacting since at least the sixteenth century, for it was the improvement in the sailing ship and the art of navigation that opened up the almost virginal territory of the New World. The resulting increase of food supply, in terms of added tillage, was further augmented by New World crops like maize and the potato. Meanwhile, the increased production of energy foods—vegetable oils, animal fats, and sugar cane and sugar beet—not merely helped support a larger population but in turn, through the supply of fat, turned soap from a courtly luxury to a household necessity; and this major contribution to hygiene—public and personal—probably did more to lower the death rate than any other single factor. From the beginning of the nineteenth century the surplus population made it possible for old cities to expand and new cities to be founded. As Webber long ago pointed out (1899), the rate was even faster in Germany in the second half of the nineteenth century than it was in the United States.

This wave of urbanization was not, as is sometimes thought, chiefly dependent upon the steam engine or upon improvements in local transportation. The fact is that the number of cities above the 100,000 mark had increased in the seventeenth century, well before the steam engine or the power loom had been invented. London passed the million mark in population by 1810, before it had a mechanical means of transportation or the beginning of an adequate water supply (in parts of London piped water was turned on only twice a week). But a marked change, nevertheless, took place in urban growth during the nineteenth century.

At this moment the four natural limits on the growth of cities were thrown off: the nutritional limit of an adequate food and water supply; the military limit of protective walls and fortifications; the traffic limit set by slow-moving agents of reliable transportation like the canalboat; and the power limit to regular production imposed by the limited number of water-power sites and the feebleness of the other prime movers—horse and wind power. In the new industrial city these limits ceased to hold. While up to this time growth was confined to commercial cities favorably situated at the merging point of two or more diverse regions with complementary resources and skills, urban development now went on in places that had easy access to the coal measures, the iron-ore beds, and the limestone quarries. Pottery towns, cotton towns, woolen towns, and steel towns, no longer held down in size, flourished wherever the tracks for steam locomotives could be laid and the steam engine established as a source of power. The only limitation on the spread and multiplication of towns under this regime was the disability of the steam locomotive to operate efficiently on grades of more than 2 per cent. Whereas the water power and wind power of the eotechnic period had tended to distribute industry in the coastal cities of high winds or along fast-running upland streams, coal power tended to group industry in the valleys near the mine pits or along the railroad lines that constituted a continuation of the mine and the mining environment (Mumford, 1934). Industry, like agriculture, competes for the heavy lowland soils. As for the railroad itself, it is one of the greatest devourers of land and transformers of landscape. The marshaling yards of its great urban terminals put large areas out of urban or agricultural use.

GROWTH OF THE CONURBATION

Up to the middle of the nineteenth century, water-power sites, the seats of earlier industrial improvements, continued to attract industries into mill villages; but, with the coming of the railroad, industries grouped together in cities in order to take advantage of the surplus labor that accumulated there. From this time on, whole districts, such as Elberfeld-Barmen, Lille-Roubaix, the Black Country, and the Delaware Valley, become urbanized, and the limits of city growth are reached only when one city, by its conversion of farmland into building lots, coalesces with another city engaged in the same process. Growth of this kind, automatic and unregulated, a result of the railroad and the factory, had never been possible before; but now the agents of mechanization not merely created their own environment but set a new pattern for the growth of already existing great cities. Looking at Bartholomew's population map of Britain early in the present century, Patrick Geddes discovered (1915) that urbanization had taken a new form: urban areas, hitherto distinct, both as political units and as topographic features, had in fact flowed together and formed dense population masses on a scale far greater than any of the big cities of the past, forming a new configuration as different as the city itself was from its rural prototypes. He called this new kind of urban grouping the "conurbation." This new urban tissue was less differentiated than the old. It presented an impoverished institutional life; it showed fewer signs of social nucleation; and it tended to increase in size, block by block, avenue by avenue, "develop-

ment" by "development," without any individuality of form and, most remarkable of all, without any quantitative limits (West Midland Group, 1948).

This concentration of industry had marked effects upon the entire environment. The new source of power—coal; the new industrial processes, massed in the new steelworks and coke ovens; the new chemical plants for manufacturing chlorine, sulfuric acid, and hundreds of other potentially noxious compounds —all poured their waste products into the air and waters on a scale that made it impossible for the local environment to absorb them as it might have absorbed the effluvia of a village industry or the organic waste of a tannery or a slaughter-house. Streams hitherto well stocked with fish, salubrious for bathing, and even potable became poisonous sewers; while the fall of soot, chemical dust, silica, and steel particles choked vegetation in what open ground remained and left their deposits in human lungs. The effects of this pollution, and the possibility of more radical and irretrievable pollution to come through the use of atomic reactors, are dealt with in chapters that follow. Here the point to mark is that it was a natural penalty of overconcentration. The very ubiquity of the new type of city, coupled with its density, increases, for example, the threat of a lethal fog from chemicals normally in the air, such as wiped out over five thousand lives in a single week in London in 1952; a mass exodus by cars, at the low speed imposed by a heavy fog, would itself add to the deadly gases already in the air.

The extension of the industrial conurbation not merely brings with it the obliteration of the life-sustaining natural environment but actually creates, as substitute, a definitely antiorganic environment; and even where, in the interstices of this urban development, land remains unoccupied, it progressively ceases to be of use for either agriculture or recreation. The removal of the topsoil, or its effacement by buildings and slag piles, brings on no temporary denudation; it results in deserts that, even if every effort suggested by science were made, might take centuries to redeem for human occupancy, to say nothing of more organic forms of cultivation. Though the conurbation came into existence through the dense industrial occupation of a whole region rather than through the overgrowth of a single dominant city, the two types overlap. In England, Birmingham itself, though the center of congeries of smaller towns, has passed the million mark, to become the second city in Britain. By offering a big local market, the great conurbations, in addition to attracting the consumption trades and industries, have brought in petroleum refineries, chemical plants, and steelworks, which gravitate to the cheaper land on the edge of metropolitan areas. This tends to create industrial defilement at the point where Sir John Evelyn, in 1661 in his pamphlet *Fumifugium* (1933), proposed to create a protective green belt, filled with aromatic shrubs, to purify the already noisome air of London. This extension of the area of industrial pollution into the very land that the overgrown city needs for mass recreation—accessible to sunlight, to usable ocean, river front, and woodland—likewise lessens the advantage of the only form of temporary escape left: retreat to the suburb.

From the very nature of the city as a market, a workshop, and a place of civic assemblage, there is a direct relation between its growth and the growth of transportation systems, though, in the case of seaways and airways, the latter may be visible only in the increase of harbor facilities and storehouses. In general, one may say that, the heavier the urbanization, the heavier the transportation network, not merely within but without. From ancient Rome to recent times, the fifteen-foot roadway remained the outsize. But, with the eighteenth century, land transportation takes a new turn. In 1861, Wilhelm Heinrich Riehl noted it (1935) in the change from the rural highroads of the old town economy to the new *Landstrasse*, planned in more systematic fashion by the new bureaucracy—wider by three feet, more heavily paved, and often lined with trees, as in the beautiful highway lined with ancient lindens between Lübeck and Travemunde. With the coming of railroad transportation, the width of the new kind of permanent way again increased; the railroad made fresh demands for large areas of flat, low-lying land to serve as marshaling yards, adjacent to the city or even cutting a great wedge through it. The economy of the water-level route again turned to a non-agricultural use of precisely the land that was often the most fertile available and spoiled even its recreational value. With the introduction of the motorcar, even secondary roads demanded pavement, and arterial roads both widened and multiplied, with the result that around great metropolises six-, seven-, and eight-lane highways with two-hundred-foot rights of way have become increasingly common. They are further complicated by great traffic circles or clover-leaf patterns of overpass and underpass to permit the continuous flow of traffic at intersections, however wasteful of land these junctions may be. In the case of parkways planned to follow the ridges, like the Taconic State Parkway in New York State, the land given over to the road may be of minor value either for agricultural or for civic use; but where the highway engineer ignores the contours, follows the valleys, and cuts through hills to maintain his level, the motorway may be an active agent both in eroding the soil and in disrupting the habitat. The yielding of water navigation to land transport has aggravated this damage; and every further congestion of population leads to still more highway-building of a permanent and costly kind to accommodate the mass week-end exit of motorists. Thus the city, by its incontinent and uncontrolled growth, not merely sterilizes the land it immediately needs but vastly increases the total area of sterilization far beyond its boundaries.

THE SUBURBAN OVERSPILL

At this point we are confronted with two special phenomena known only in embryonic form in other urban cultures: the production of a new kind of urban tissue, in the open pattern of the suburb, and the further development of a mass transportation by means of self-propelled, individual vehicles, trucks, and motorcars. The first change, the result of seeking an environment free from noise, dirt, and overcrowding of the city, actually antedated the means that made it possible on a mass scale. In London this suburban movement began as early as Elizabethan times as a reaction against the overbuilding and overcrowding that had then taken place in the center of the city; and at the end of the eighteenth century a similar exodus occurred among merchants who could afford a private coach to take them into the city. With increased facilities of transportation offered by the public coach and the railroad, this suburban movement became more common through the nineteenth century, as witness the growth of St. John's Wood, Richmond, and Hampstead in London, of Chestnut Hill and Germantown in Philadelphia, and of the Hudson River suburbs in New York. But, up to 1920, it was mainly the upper-income groups that could afford the luxury of sunlight, fresh air, gardens, open spaces, and access to the open country. The new open-type plan, with houses set in gardens, at densities of from two houses to ten or twelve per acre, had long been characteristic of American country towns, most notably those of New England; indeed, this open pattern dominated west of the Alleghenies. But this standard now became universalized in the upper-class suburb, though its economic base lay outside the area the suburb occupied and from the beginning demanded a heavy sacrifice of man-hours in commuting to the distant metropolis. The low cost of suburban land and the possibility of economizing on local utilities like roads and sewers encouraged luxurious standards of space and gave those who could afford to escape a superior biological environment and perhaps, if Thorndyke is correct (1939), a superior social one. The initiative of a few farsighted industrialists, like Lever (Port Sunlight, 1887) and Cadbury (Bournville, 1895), proved that similar standards could be applied to building working-class quarters when land was sufficiently cheap.

Since 1920 the spread of private motor vehicles has completed the work of enlarging potential suburban territory, an expansion already well begun in the 1900's by interurban electric transit. The exodus to suburbia has taken in wave after wave of city dwellers, at lower and lower income levels, seeking to escape the congested and disordered environment of the big city. This removal from the city has not been accompanied by any equivalent decentralization of industry; rather it has served to sustain an antiquated pattern of concentration. The pattern of population distribution around great cities has been the product, not of social foresight for public ends, but mainly of private initiative for private profit, though it could not have taken place on its present scale in America without a vast public investment in highways, expressways, bridges, and tunnels. The result of this uncontrolled spread of the suburb has been to nullify the very purposes that brought the movement into existence.

But suburban agglomeration cannot be treated as a fact in itself; it carries with it, through the demands of the motorcar, both for private transportation and for the movement of goods, an enormous increase in paved roads, which eat into the surviving agricultural and wilderness areas and permanently sterilize ever larger quantities of land. The filling-up of marshes, the coverage of rich soils with buildings, the felling of woodlands, the clogging of local brooks and streams, and the abandonment of local springs and wells were all secondary disturbances of the early type of metropolis, even when it reached a population of a million people. When Rome was surrounded by the Aurelian wall in A.D. 274, it covered, according to Carcopino (1940), a little more than 5 square miles. The present area of Greater London is about a hundred and thirty times as great as this, while it is roughly six hundred and fifty times as great as the area, namely, 677 acres, surrounded by its wall in the Middle Ages. The metropolitan area of New York is even more widespread; it covers something like 2,514 square miles; and already a good case could be made out for treating a wide coastal strip from Boston to Washington as one continuous conurbation, geographically speaking (see Fig. 43, pp. 38–39). This difference in magnitude between every earlier type of urban development and that characterizing our own age is critical. What is more, as population increases, the percentage of the population in cities increases, too, and the ratio of those going into metropolitan areas is even higher. Even in England, though the amount of land occupied by cities, "built-over land," is low (2.2 per cent) in proportion to the

entire land area of the British Isles, this is more than half the area of "first-class" land available for agriculture and is a tenth of the "good land" available, according to Sir L. Dudley Stamp's classification (1952). Since requirements for manufacture and urban development are for accessible, graded land, these demands conflict with the needs of the farmer; they compete for the same good soils, and only government intervention in England, since 1932, has saved this misuse of valuable agricultural land.

Under modern technical conditions the open pattern of the residential suburb is not confined to domestic needs alone. The demand for large land areas characterizes modern factory organization, with its horizontally ordered assembly lines, housed in spreading one-story structures, and, above all, airports for long-distance flights, whose demand for landing lanes and approaches on the order of miles has increased with the size and speed of planes. In addition, the noise of planes, especially jets, sterilizes even larger areas of land for residential use as both hazardous to life and dangerous to health. There are many urban regions, like that tapped by the main-line railroads from Newark, New Jersey, to Wilmington, Delaware, where urban tissue has either displaced the land or so completely modified its rural uses as to give the whole area the character of a semi-urban desert. Add to this, in every conurbation, the ever larger quantity of land needed for collective reservoir systems, sewage works, and garbage-disposal plants as dispersed local facilities fall out of use.

As a result of population increase and urban centralization, one further demand for land, unfortunately a cumulative one, must be noted: the expansion of urban cemeteries in all cultures that maintain, as most "Christian" nations do, the Paleolithic habit of earth burial. This has resulted in the migration of the burying ground from the center to the outskirts of metropolitan areas, where vast cemeteries serve, indeed, as temporary suburban parks, until they become a wilderness of stone monuments. Unless the custom of periodically emptying out these cemeteries, as was done in London and Paris with the bones in old churchyards, takes hold, or until cremation replaces burial, the demand for open spaces for the dead threatens to crowd the quarters of the living on a scale impossible to conceive in earlier urban cultures.

URBAN-RURAL BALANCE

Whereas the area of the biggest cities, before the nineteenth century, could be measured in hundreds of acres, the areas of our new conurbations must now be measured in thousands of square miles. This is a new fact in the history of human settlement. Within a century the economy of the Western world has shifted from a rural base, harboring a few big cities and thousands of villages and small towns, to a metropolitan base whose urban spread not merely has engulfed and assimilated the small units, once isolated and self-contained, as the amoeba engulfs its particles of food, but is fast absorbing the rural hinterland and threatening to wipe out many natural elements favorable to life which in earlier stages balanced off against depletions in the urban environment. From this, even more critical results follow. Already, New York and Philadelphia, which are fast coalescing into a single conurbation along the main-line railroads and the New Jersey Turnpike, find themselves competing for the same water supply, as Los Angeles competes with the whole state of Arizona. Thus, though modern technology has escaped from the limitations of a purely local supply of water, the massing of population makes demands that, even apart

from excessive costs (which rise steadily as distance increases), put a definable limit to the possibilities of further urbanization. Water shortages may indeed limit the present distribution long before food shortages bring population growth to an end.

This situation calls for a new approach to the whole problem of urban settlement. Having thrown off natural controls and limitations, modern man must replace them with an at least equally effective man-made pattern. Though alternative proposals may be left to that portion of this volume dealing with the future, one new approach has fifty years of experience behind it and may properly be dealt with under the head of history. In the last decade of the nineteenth century two projects came forth relating to the need, already visible by then, to achieve a different balance among cities, industries, and natural regions from that which had been created by either the old rural economy, the free town economy, or the new metropolitan economy. The first of these suggestions was the work of the geographer Peter Kropotkin. His book *Fields, Factories, and Workshops* (1899) dealt with the alteration in the scale of technically efficient enterprise made possible by the invention of the electric motor. The other book, *Tomorrow,* published in 1898 by Howard, embodied a proposal to counteract the centralization of the great metropolis by reintroducing the method of colonization to take care of its further growth. Howard proposed to build relatively self-contained, balanced communities, supported by their local industry, with a permanent population, of limited number and density, on land surrounded by a swath of open country dedicated to agriculture, recreation, and rural occupation. Howard's proposal recognized the biological and social grounds, along with the psychological pressures, that underlay the current movement to suburbia. It recognized the social needs that were causing an exodus from rural regions or drab, one-industry towns into the big city. Without disparaging such real advantages as the concentrated activities and institutions of the city offered, Howard proposed to bring about a marriage between town and country. The new kind of city he called the "garden city," not so much because of its internal open spaces, which would approach a sound suburban standard, but more because it was set in a permanent rural environment.

Besides invoking the Aristotelian ideas of balance and limits, Howard's greatest contribution in conceiving this new garden city was provision for making the surrounding agricultural area an integral part of the city's form. His invention of a horizontal retaining wall, or green belt, immune to urban building, was a public device for limiting lateral growth and maintaining the urban-rural balance. In the course of twenty years two such balanced communities, Letchworth (1903) and Welwyn (1919), were experimentally founded by private enterprise in England. The soundness of the garden-city principle was recognized in the Barlow report (1940) on the decentralization of industry. Thanks to World War II, the idea of building such towns on a great scale, to drain off population from the overcrowded urban centers, took hold. This resulted in the New Towns Act of 1947, which provided for the creation of a series of new towns, fourteen in all, in Britain. This open pattern of town-building, with the towns themselves dispersed through the countryside and surrounded by permanent rural reserves, does a minimum damage to the basic ecological fabric. To the extent that their low residential density, of twelve to fourteen houses per acre, gives individual small gardens to

almost every family, these towns not merely maintain a balanced micro-environment but actually grow garden produce whose value is higher than that produced when the land was used for extensive farming or grazing (Block, 1954).

On the basis of the garden-city principle, Stein (1951) and others have put forth the possibility of establishing a new type of city by integrating a group of communities into an organized design that would have the facilities of a metropolis without its congestion and loss of form. The basis for this kind of grouping was laid down in the survey of the state of New York made by the Commission of Housing and Regional Planning, of which Stein was chairman, and was published with Henry Wright in 1926. Wright, the planning adviser, here pointed out that the area of settlement was no longer the crowded terminal metropolitan areas of the railroad period but that electric power and motor transportation had opened up a wide belt on each side of the railroad trunk lines, equally favorable for industry, agriculture, and urban settlement. The most fertile soil and the most valuable geological deposits were almost entirely in the areas below the thousand-foot level; and, in planning for new urban settlement, the reservation of forest areas for water catchment and recreation, for lumber, and for electric power was important. Instead of treating the city as an intrusive element in a landscape that would finally be defaced or obliterated by the city's growth, this new approach suggested the necessity of creating a permanent rural-urban balance. In the regional city, as Stein conceived it, organization would take the place of mere agglomeration and, in doing so, would create a reciprocal relation between city and country that would not be overthrown by further population growth (Mumford, 1925, 1938; MacKaye, 1928; Stein, 1951).

With this statement of the problems raised for us today by the natural history of urbanization, our survey comes to an end. The blind forces of urbanization, flowing along the lines of least resistance, show no aptitude for creating an urban and industrial pattern that will be stable, self-sustaining, and self-renewing. On the contrary, as congestion thickens and expansion widens, both the urban and the rural landscape undergo defacement and degradation, while unprofitable investments in the remedies for congestion, such as more superhighways and more distant reservoirs of water, increase the economic burden and serve only to promote more of the blight and disorder they seek to palliate. But however difficult it is to reverse unsound procedures that offer a temporary answer and immediate—

often excessive—financial rewards, we now have a prospect of concrete alternatives already in existence in England and partly established in a different fashion by the regional planning authority for the highly urbanized Ruhr Valley in Germany. With these examples before us, we have at least a hint of the future task of urbanization: the re-establishment, in a more complex unity, with a full use of the resources of modern science and techniques, of the ecological balance that originally prevailed between city and country in the primitive stages of urbanization. Neither the blotting-out of the landscape nor the disappearance of the city is the climax stage of urbanization. Rather, it is the farsighted and provident balancing of city populations and regional resources so as to maintain in a state of high development all the elements—social, economic, and agricultural—necessary for their common life.

REFERENCES

BARLOW, ANTHONY M.
  1940 *Royal Commission on Distribution of Industrial Population Report.* London: H.M. Stationery Office. 320 pp.
BLOCK, GEOFFREY D. M.
  1954 *The Spread of Towns.* London: Conservative Political Centre. 57 pp.
BRUNHES, JEAN
  1920 *Human Geography, an Attempt at a Positive Classification: Principles and Examples.* 2d ed. Chicago: Rand McNally & Co. 648 pp.
CARCOPINO, JEROME
  1940 *Daily Life in Ancient Rome: The People and the City at the Height of the Empire.* New Haven, Conn.: Yale University Press. 342 pp.
CHILDE, V. GORDON
  1942 *What Happened in History.* Harmondsworth: Penguin Books. 288 pp.
  1954 "Early Forms of Society," pp. 38–57 in SINGER, CHARLES; HOLMYARD, E. J.; and HALL, A. R. (eds.),

A History of Technology. Oxford: Clarendon Press. 827 pp.
EVELYN, JOHN
  1933 *Fumifugium: Or the Inconvenience of the Aer and Smoake of London Dissipated.* Reprint of 1661 pamphlet. London: Oxford University Press. 49 pp.
GEDDES, PATRICK
  1915 *Cities in Evolution: An Introduction to the Town Planning Movement and to the Study of Civics.* London: Williams & Norgate. 409 pp. (Rev. ed. by JAQUELINE TYRWHITT and ARTHUR GEDDES. London: Williams & Norgate, 1949. 241 pp.)
HASSERT, KURT
  1907 *Die Städte: Geographisch Betrachtet.* Leipzig: B. G. Teubner. 137 pp.
HOWARD, EBENEZER
  1898 *To-morrow: A Peaceful Path to Real Reform.* London: Swann, Sonnenschein & Co. 176 pp.

1902   *Garden Cities of To-morrow.* London: Swann, Sonnenschein & Co. 167 pp.

1945   *Garden Cities of To-morrow.* With a Preface by F. J. OSBORN and an Introduction by LEWIS MUMFORD. London: Faber & Faber. 168 pp.

JEFFERSON, MARK

1931   "Distribution of the World's City Folks: A Study in Comparative Civilization," *Geographical Review*, XXI, No. 3, 446–65.

KEYES, FENTON

1951   "Urbanism and Population Distribution in China," *American Journal of Sociology*, LVI, No. 6, 519–27.

KING, F. H.

1927   *Farmers of Forty Centuries.* New York: Harcourt, Brace & Co. 379 pp.

KROPOTKIN, PETER

1899   *Fields, Factories, and Workshops.* New York: G. P. Putnam & Sons. 477 pp.

MACKAYE, BENTON

1928   *The New Exploration: A Philosophy of Regional Planning.* New York: Harcourt, Brace & Co. 235 pp.

MARSH, GEORGE P.

1864   *Man and Nature.* London: Sampson, Low & Son. 577 pp.

1874   *The Earth as Modified by Human Action: A New Edition of "Man and Nature."* New York: Scribner, Armstrong & Co. 656 pp.

1885   *The Earth as Modified by Human Action: A Last Revision of "Man and Nature."* New York: Charles Scribner's Sons. 629 pp. (Note that in this last edition of *Man and Nature*, Marsh refers for the first time, in a long footnote [p. 473], under the heading "Inundations and Torrents," to the influence of large urban masses on climate, particularly heat and precipitation—an anticipation of present-day studies.) Last printing in 1907.

MUMFORD, LEWIS

1934   *Technics and Civilization.* New York: Harcourt, Brace & Co. 495 pp.

1938   *The Culture of Cities.* New York: Harcourt, Brace & Co. 586 pp.

MUMFORD, LEWIS (ed.)

1925   "Regional Planning Number," *Survey Graphic*, LIV, No. 3, 128–208.

OSBORN, F. J.

1946   *Green-Belt Cities: The British Contribution.* London: Faber & Faber. 191 pp.

RIEHL, WILHELM HEINRICH

1935   *Die Naturgeschichte des Deutschen Volkes.* Reprint of 1861 edition. Leipzig: Alfred Kröner Verlag. 407 pp.

SCHNEIDER, ARTHUR

1895   "Stadtumfänge in Altertum und Gegenwart," *Geographische Zeitschrift*, I, 676–79.

SORRE, MAX

1952   *Les Fondements de la géographie humaine.* 3 vols. Paris: Librairie Armand Colin.

STAMP, L. DUDLEY

1948   *The Land of Britain: Its Use and Misuse.* London: Longman's Green. 570 pp.

1952   *Land for Tomorrow.* New York: American Geographical Society; Bloomington, Ind.: Indiana University Press. 230 pp.

STEIN, CLARENCE S.

1951   *Toward New Towns for America.* Chicago: Public Administration Service. 245 pp.

STEIN, CLARENCE S., and WRIGHT, HENRY

1926   *Report of the Commission of Housing and Regional Planning to Governor Alfred E. Smith, May 7, 1926.* (New York State Document.) Albany. 82 pp.

THORNDYKE, EDWARD LEE

1939   *Your City.* New York: Harcourt, Brace & Co. 204 pp.

WEBBER, ADNA FERRIN

1899   *The Growth of Cities in the Nineteenth Century: A Study in Statistics.* New York: Macmillan Co. 495 pp.

WEST MIDLAND GROUP

1948   *Conurbation: A Planning Survey of Birmingham and the Black Country.* London: Architectural Press. 288 pp.

WOYTINSKY, W. S. and E. C.

1953   *World Population and Production.* New York: Twentieth Century Fund. 1,268 pp.

Symposium Discussion: Retrospect

Symposium Discussion: Retrospect

Man's Tenure of the Earth

The Impress of Primitives on Environment

The Classical Period—East and West

The Modern Era of Exchange Economy

Man's Attitudes toward Nature

Unstable Equilibrium and Constant Change

Dr. F. FRASER DARLING, who chaired the first of the discussion sessions, called attention in his introductory remarks to Sauer's expression, "Man's deformation of the pristine." If man is to civilize, he must *de*form; yet many are concerned at how man has de*formed* the pristine—and this is the central theme of the symposium.

As man reached consciousness and changed from the hunting and food-gathering state of existence, he began in some measure to dig into the accumulated organic and inorganic wealth of the world. The tapping of this wealth of resources provided man with the leisure and the time to think, to play, and to create.

Western civilization has been markedly influenced by the idea of man's dominion over the earth put to him in Genesis. Western man has tended to set himself apart from the rest of animate nature, while other and older civilizations and systems of religion have regarded man as being a part of nature. Though very different from the nineteenth-century approach, nevertheless there is today a very real movement in science toward resolution of this dualism through studies of the association of mankind with nature.

THE IMPRESS OF PRIMITIVES ON ENVIRONMENT

STEWART emphasized that man has influenced the face of the earth for a million years or so. Before agriculture and herding, there were the effects during the long reaches of prehistory of man's use of fire and tools. Setting fire to the landscape has been a universal cultural trait. All peoples apparently did it in all places, so that burning has been effective in producing the first landscape of which man has record. Early human activity influenced vegetation, and, in turn, vegetation has had a very great influence on changes in soil.

BANKS asked how small numbers of men associated in primitive tribes and having very short life-spans really could have been effective modifiers of the surface of the earth. What meaningful lessons are to be drawn from early times, when now we are facing times when few die young and many live to maturity—when there is a clear difference in scale of populations? SPOEHR, in reply, stressed the broad framework in space and time of man's activities. By at least 10000 B.C., if not by 20000 B.C., man had penetrated into every major land area of the world as we know it today; the effects of small societies are not to be gauged by their size but rather through their wide and early distribution and the great time span of thousands of years through which they have acted.

SAUER cited examples from Lower California and the lower Mixteca area of Mexico. The southern end of the former, a quite arid area, contains peoples who are among the most primitive in skills that the New World knows. Yet, without fire, they have driven back palms and other useful vegetation. Primitive agriculture, too, has produced some very significant deteriorations of soils on slopes. The field studies of Sherburne Cook have shown that man's cultivation of slopes, even where the general system of agriculture was benign, has led to losses which culminated in catastrophes of considerable duration. The lower Mixteca today comprises hundreds of square miles of limestone hill country with apparently little else but palmetto growths. Yet all through the area there are remains of early settlement. The pottery fragments, for example, point to the period of Monte Albán I, but further studies are necessary combining knowledge of physiography, archeology, and plant composition. SEARS pointed out that Cook's work substantiates a guess made many years before by Vaillant that the pyramid-builders of Teotihuacán, who flourished from about 500 B.C. to A.D. 800, must have cleared the forests extensively for the burning of lime. Cook found evidence of very heavy erosion concomitant with the period of active occupation of Teotihuacán.

DAVIS described another example of the work of early man—the building of shell mounds or refuse heaps, of which some in Florida are as long as 3 miles, 30 feet in height, and about 150 yards wide. To build these obviously required a very long time or a considerable population.

NARR, in writing, called attention to the book of Kraft[1] as one of the most important works in the field of prehistory that has appeared in recent years. WISSMANN, also in writing, summarized the point of his chapter that plants and animals were first domesticated by man in the moist tropics, then adapted to the margins of the steppes and oases of the deserts, where the first civilizations were formed, and then spread from the deserts and steppes into the forests. More recently, the European occupation of North America went from the moist east to the dry west.

THE CLASSICAL PERIOD—EAST AND WEST

In India, Southeast Asia, and central and southern China something distinctly different from the westward trend of civilization developed. WITTFOGEL pointed out that many civilizations were greatly concerned about water control for the sake of combating floods and creating a standardized, artificial environment in which standardized irrigated crops could be grown. With the emphasis placed on intensive agricultural production, there was not much space for labor animals. Man in horticulture-fashion and with the simplest tools did most of the work. By the time of Confucius, China worshiped three great culture heroes, Yao, Shu, and Yu, all of whom worked to regulate water. From the beginnings of settled life, man, in the North China plain, had to tame the rivers and dig irrigation canals. This effort has been perpetuated through the ages and has transformed the swampy North China plain into a man-made landscape.

Arab sources, too, provide useful indications of conditions of the past, though such sources, as HUZAYYIN pointed out, are not very well known,

1. Georg Kraft, *Der Urmensch als Schöpfer: Die geistige Welt des Eiszeitmenschen* (2d ed.; Tübingen: M. Matthiesen & Co., 1948).

since they exist mostly in manuscripts not fully studied. Masoudi, writing in the tenth century, mentioned changes in northern Arabia, especially in the southern part of the Syrian Desert. In about the sixth century there were wells and oases sufficient to enable a woman to travel alone across the desert, passing from one watering area to another in safety and with an abundance of water and of food along the way. Perhaps there is a tendency by writers of the East to glorify the past, yet the archeological evidence bears out this point. In late Roman times wells in the Syrian Desert region of Azraq had a level of water about 6 feet higher than at present.

Explanations of such phenomena are complex rather than simple: there were natural reasons, perhaps changes of climate, and there were human reasons, such as the cutting-down of vegetation, which had a secondary effect on water sources and the increase of evaporation. Also involved were indirect effects of human activities; for example, the development of the Arabian horse, a subject requiring further study. The horse was introduced into Arabia in lieu of the camel, which is rather a peaceful animal, not one for expansion or trouble. But the horse was different, and the Arabian species made expansion possible. The importance attached to the development of the particularly Arabian horse is reflected in pre-Islamic mythology: one of the most important intertribal wars was named after two mares—the War of Dahis and Ghabraa.

HEICHELHEIM cited the examples of French colonization measures in North Africa and the recent colonization in Israel as showing clearly that the potential fertility of the soil had not been destroyed to any measurable degree in the regions of Numidia, Mauretania, and Cyrenaica. He also pointed out that Plato, when speaking of Attica, is a second- or third-hand source, for he could not possibly have known about the deforestation of Attica in the seventh century B.C. or before, about which he wrote in his *Critias*. Referring to the recent monograph by Kahrstedt, HEICHELHEIM brought out that in Greece during Roman imperial times there were more forest estates than in classical times. Similarly, in Italy, air photos taken by the Royal Air Force during World War II, and studied by Bradford, revealed many ancient structures and farm estates from the prehistoric period to the early Middle Ages. In Italy it was only with the introduction of Spanish sheep-breeding and other more recent changes that destruction of fertility resulted.

Both GLACKEN and OSBORN questioned Heichelheim's views. GLACKEN made note that in his chapter he neither accepted nor rejected Plato's arguments but had cited his work as a landmark in the history of an idea. Plato had grasped the notion that man could change his environment, that a remnant of soil might be representative of a former fertile soil, and that a certain patch of forest might suggest a past condition. OSBORN referred to the works of Columella and others—contemporary Romans—which were filled with observations made by them during their lifetimes on what might be called the "degradation of the Italian peninsula"—that the capacity of the soil to grow wheat and other crops constantly declined. Also, Vladimir Simkhovitch, in an essay called "Hay and History," expounded the thesis that the causes for the decline of the Roman Empire were twofold: the falling-apart of family life and the inability of wheat production to support the population.[2]

DARLING agreed that we do need to

2. Vladimir Gregorievitch Simkhovitch, *Toward the Understanding of Jesus, and Two Additional Historical Studies: Rome's Fall Reconsidered; Hay and History* (New York: Macmillan Co., 1933).

examine the sources of the general historical view of latifundia. The large estate means some measure of conservation, and conservation goes when, under a money economy or an export-import situation, the estate is broken into small peasant holdings.

To DARWIN's query, "How did the cedars of Lebanon, of biblical record, survive longer than the forests of Italy?" HEICHELHEIM replied that the forests of Italy in Roman times were, over all, really not depleted, while in Lebanon there was a gradual decline, because the trees were extremely valuable.

In summarizing, at the end of the session, DARLING felt that Heichelheim spoke not as a biologist but primarily as a classicist, though with a certain chemical awareness. In considering that potential fertility in the Mediterranean lands and Arabia was not impaired, what perhaps had been lost sight of was the biologic complex, which makes use of the potential mineral wealth in the soil. With the loss of that biologic complex, only a desert results, though a satisfactory chemical analysis may remain.

DARBY introduced a concrete example from England to illustrate the effects upon the contemporary landscape of the works of a small number of people in ancient times. The Anglo-Saxons who invaded England during the fifth and sixth centuries were very small in total numbers. As small bands of practical-minded immigrant farmers, they experimented and finally settled at various places. But these settlements fixed for all later time the pattern of the geography of England. For instance, where men named "Redder" and "Wals" settled in the sixth century, there stand the towns of Reading and Walsingham today. While a great deal had gone on in the Roman and earlier periods, this relatively small group effected a "re-start" in the history of the landscape. Through all the later changes in techniques and methods and all the quickening and slowing of economic life, this pattern of settlement persisted until the industrial revolution. And even today the main network of population dates from the efforts of that small group of people in the fifth and sixth centuries. DARLING added the thought that the Anglo-Saxons, possibly more than any earlier people in Britain, used animals as a means of achieving their desired landscape—in this case, the use of swine to clear the forest floor, followed by sheep-grazing on the soil, which then grew grass.

THE MODERN ERA OF EXCHANGE ECONOMY

The idea of population growth is a very ancient one, GLACKEN commented—the notion that there is a niche for things and that these niches in the universe will gradually be filled up. This "principle of plenitude," though very deep in Western thinking, really did not emerge until the eighteenth and nineteenth centuries, when such writers as Süssmilch and, later, Malthus, expressed the notion of a gradual filling-up of the earth. And so in the modern era, as BANKS pointed out, we must take into account the changing age pattern and the changing numbers of the population, for we are facing a time when few die young and many live to maturity.

Adding to Banks's remarks, GREGG remembered that once in inland Brazil he had met a *caboclo*, a peasant, who said about his clearing: "When my sons were here and before they married, we had a good *roça*, but they wanted to have farms of their own; they left me, and soon came the 'green wave,' and I lost it all." This suggested that the capacity to fight the battle against the growing forest involved the use by a farmer of his sons. In the Connecticut River Valley of the United States a man who had plenty of sons could settle and manage the land; but, when families became smaller, the management of farms was lost to Italian immigrants, who took up the land again and made a go of it because they had sons to work cost-free to keep the thing going. A culture in which many children are born but in which many die early offers very different opportunities for the management of the land from one in which all the sons grow to maturity and in which the law of primogeniture, together with the increased span of life, means that a man will not turn over his farm to his son until his son is nearly forty years old or more. Nobody develops a wild enthusiasm for property by having to wait until he is over forty to get it.

JANAKI AMMAL introduced the problem of the population of India—four hundred million people being quite a large percentage of the world's population. In India the industrial revolution meant the clearing of land used chiefly for a subsistence economy of village farming, cattle-grazing, and hunting and the shifting to a money economy, using the land for the growing of cotton, oilseeds, and other export crops. The result has been that for the last one hundred and, fifty years the Indians have lived hedged in, as it were, by an artificial environment, with all the necessary facilities of security and safety to increase their population. Any kind of medical aid only makes them live longer and increases demands on food supply; any method of curtailing population must deal with people who have not yet assimilated the scientific attitude.

GOUROU provided an example from India of the impact of a commercial economy. At the end of the sixteenth century, Goa was a great Portuguese city of three hundred thousand people, a considerable market for the consumption of produce. Transport was not well developed, and it was necessary to buy from the immediate surroundings. The result was destruction of the soil on the lateritic plateau of the interior, which today is without trees, fields, houses, or even much grass. In Travancore, to the south, the plateau soils have been used only since the beginning of the twentieth century. Fifty years ago there were no fields on the plateau; now the cassava produced there by poor, low-caste Christians is beginning to be of importance for the food supply of the growing population of Travancore.

The question was raised by KLIMM of whether there is going to be less communication in the future between parts of the world, and smaller markets, less exchange, and fewer people in an exchange economy, or whether the exchange economy is going to become more nearly universal, with more people entering into an exchange relationship. If the world market as a whole is going to increase, then we must not put too much emphasis on locally closed environments but must realize that man's habitat is actually the world and that pieces of the world compete with each other. However, if there are going to be fewer people in the world exchange economy, if regions like India and China are not going to become commercialized and compete for production and consumption, then we are able to take another view of man's relation to his habitat.

GUTKIND felt that there is already a settled answer to the question of whether the world will be more unified in the future than it is today. It will be one because it is one. If the world is one, we can get our food from anywhere; there is no fear that population increase will outrun food supply.

OSBORN brought out that at least three-fifths of all the people of the world are at a virtual minimum diet and below the standard of a desirable diet. Even if the United States were to, and could physically, export its entire

surplus of food to one country only—
India—it would but barely meet the
minimum requirements of the objective
of the Indian government's five-year
plan. GUTKIND in reply suggested that
the problem is one of proper distribution of settlements but that for the next
two or three generations there is nothing else but to do what we can to develop natural resources.

In summarizing, DARLING expressed
the thought that the replacement of
subsistence economies by money economies is a central point in the effect of
man on the planet. But, where there is
export of produce, almost everywhere
there is a very considerable deterioration of habitat. A subsistence economy
maintains itself for a very long time and
engenders its own conservation ethos,
but an export economy spells deterioration. With an increasing and expanding
economy, we may, indeed, without very
great knowledge and without very great
thought, be heading for disaster. This
is not inevitable, but a much greater
knowledge is required than we have at
the moment.

JONES, in writing, questioned Darling's thesis that subsistence societies
reach a harmony with their habitat in
all cases, while an export economy leads
to deterioration. A Pacific atoll, completely under subsistence in past times,
could become overpopulated, unless a
hurricane or other disaster took place,
and bring about migration. An exchange economy *might* have made migration unnecessary.

MAN'S ATTITUDES TOWARD NATURE

The influence that environment has
on a culture and the contrasting notion
—much more difficult and confused—of
man as a changer of the environment
are both very old ideas, but, as
GLACKEN pointed out, they are more
notable for the frequency of observation than for systematic study. Related
to them is the notion of the unity of

nature and man's interrelationships with
nature. The history of the idea of nature must include the history not only
of biology but also of aesthetics, of religion, and of philosophy, because teleology must be taken into account: Is
the earth designed for man; is the earth
designed for use with man at the top of
the scale; or is there another relationship of man to the earth? Many seventeenth-century scientists were very
strongly concerned with looking into
nature to see there the proofs of a living God. One of the most frequently
quoted Psalms was the One Hundred
and Fourth: "How wondrous are Thy
works, O Lord! In wisdom hast Thou
made them all." The concept of a balance or harmony in nature goes back
fundamentally to the seventeenth-century idea of a sort of primordial harmony in the world with which man has
interfered. The feeling we have in reading the background papers is not only
that man was no passive instrument in
the past but also that he not always
quite knew what he was up to—a sort
of clash between the conscious controls
of science and the great unintended
effects of man's activity.

SEARS provided several examples of
man's attitude toward the landscape,
what kind of thing he thinks it is, what
it means to him in terms of his fundamental concepts—all of which determine how he treats it. In the valley of
Mexico it was not simply that the Spaniards had found a use for timber and
needed the space it occupied. Their action, according to contemporary testimony, was influenced by their values.
They were homesick for the treeless
plains of Castile. They preferred the
type of landscape in which they had
grown up and which had been produced by the activities of the Mesta,
that great grazing syndicate that operated over the Spanish peninsula and effectively denuded it. In another example, communities have been observed

that have practiced good land use over several generations, some for as much as two centuries. So far as known, these have been communities which have been united by some common religious bond, and it does not make too much difference what religion it was. Whether these communities are in Texas, eastern Pennsylvania, Ohio, or Iowa, their system of ethics is fundamental to the way they treat the land.

ANDERSON reported on the attitude toward nature which the botanist Bor observed during his collections in the forests of Upper Burma and of Assam. Since unrecorded time the peoples there have had a simple nature worship; although they had a *Brandwirtschaft*—they burned and moved on—their hilltops were not burned over. The hilltops were sacred; as places of worship, they were not cut over or pastured. Therefore, in this back country, in a place where man has been the longest in a state similar to what he must have been in the Stone Age, an attitude toward nature has preserved inviolate a very considerable proportion of the landscape.

SEIDENBERG, in writing, drew by analogy a moral from this primitive example. The recent "conquest" of Mount Everest, universally acclaimed as a triumph and culmination of mountain-climbing, was in fact a profane act which denuded man of the last symbol left on earth of unconquerable nature. The ascent of Everest, which represented a kind of psychological, if not spiritual, peak, resulted in what can only be termed a belittling of our world. It would have been singularly appropriate to have preserved it inviolate, if only as a universal symbol of man's place in the infinity of nature.

In his summary DARLING brought out another example of the importance of social behavior to land-use practices. In Scotland, rod-and-line fishing of salmon would never fish out a river, while continued bag-netting at the coasts would certainly do so. But, especially in the highland areas of Scotland, where bag-netting is done, there is a strong Sabbatarian feeling, and the bag nets are taken up at six o'clock on Saturday evening and not put down again until six o'clock Monday morning. That piece of socioreligious behavior is quite sufficient to act as a conservation measure on the salmon stocks, since for 21 per cent of the time fish can go up the river unhindered.

For GALDSTON a crucial philosophical or cultural question was whether man looks upon himself as within or without nature. In science generally, but in the medical sciences in particular, man regards himself as quite without nature, in that he assumes he can manipulate nature freely and without suffering any untoward consequences. This is very clearly reflected in the history of medicine. There was a time when the microcosm and the macrocosm and the relationship of the two were deliberated on seriously, as, for example, by Hippocrates and later by Paracelsus. Today, except to a few ecologists, this is looked upon as a rather silly concern; and we have grandiose enterprises to "wipe out" infantile paralysis, tuberculosis, and a host of other diseases, based on the very serious assumption that, once they are wiped out, they stay wiped out and that there are no equilibration upsets.

DARLING disagreed with Galdston's contention that any definition of ecology takes its line of departure from some value system which is essentially homocentric. The ecologist is not concerned with what man considers desirable or not but rather with what is most fitting to any particular environment. In any habitat there is an ecological situation which is the most efficient in the circulation of energy. This situation, or particular association of plants and animals, for every environment in which there is life is termed "climax." It is that ideal situation that ecologists consider—what it is that a particular habitat can produce without the presence of man at all and what efficiency is lost in certain situations due to man's activities.

The concern of most preliterate peoples, at least philosophically, has not been so much with natural resources as with habitat. Philosophically, too, ancient man felt himself to be a part of nature; only in the last two or three centuries has man set himself apart from nature. For these reasons, SPOEHR felt that a consideration of "natural resources" could not be held at any time except the present, for it is a term which is culturally defined and which has grown out of our world-wide preoccupation with how the millions of people today are to live.

Darwin the naturalist had a sensitive insight, SPOEHR added, into the interrelationships within nature, a point of view that was represented by preliterate peoples, except that he was dealing with observed reality rather than with created reality. On the other hand, the achievements of the physical sciences and their practical applications have led us to a very practical concern with controlling nature. In SEARS's observation biologists, geologists, and geographers are all concerned with the question of natural resources. On the other hand, there are many who are intimately concerned with technology and its application and who tend to play down the concern about man's relation to natural resources. This very serious cleavage of opinion or attitude within the ranks of science is to be found in other groups of thought. For example, we frequently hear talk of an expanding economy as though it were the dream of the American people. Yet the term is used without qualification and without saying for how long the economy is to expand or by how much. It is assumed to be the basic concept of our civilization.

UNSTABLE EQUILIBRIUM AND CONSTANT CHANGE

DARLING, in his introductory remarks, emphasized that Sears's paper has an important passage on "niche" and "role." The occupation of a niche and its maintenance thereafter mean, in our civilization, having a regard for, or obligation to, the environment in which our niche is located. Developing from that is the new ethic of conservation which ultimately may have a great deal more religious consequence than it has had up to the present. Respect for habitat is fundamental in some of the other past and present religions of the world, but in our own it has been foreign to our idea that we have dominion over the earth.

CLARK thought that one of the reasons why the world sometimes does not listen to conservationists as keenly as it ought is that different datum lines are assumed from which deformation may be said to begin; each person has his own "Garden of Eden," his own "Golden Age," and tends to measure what is going on in the world, or what is bad with what is going on, in terms of his own conception of what would be perfect. This is partly implied in any concept of niche: that plants, animals, and particular cultural groups have a special niche in the world and that, somehow or other, things must be fitted so that the niche is properly occupied. The difficulty is that niches are not stable but constantly changing. They have been appearing and disappearing for countless thousands of years. It is a prehistorical and historical viewpoint that provides the framework for the idea of a constantly changing world. If less were said about deformation and more thought given to living in a constantly changing world, then some of the difficulties continually brought out by those who seem opposed to the conservationists might be surmounted.

SEARS replied that, as a student of vegetation history, he thought himself to be sufficiently aware of the constancy of change. The main point with which the ecologist is concerned is that there is in the landscape a system of energy and material transformation whose trend—whether or not it is at climax—is very easily disrupted. Any landscape involves a multitude of organisms, all very closely integrated and interrelated, and each more or less helping to sustain the system. There is a tendency or a trend toward relatively efficient use of the energy which impinges and of the material which is present and toward minimizing the destructive action of the forces of climate and weather and toward regulation of the flow of water. It is this process that makes possible man's occupation of the earth and provides relatively efficient returns. And whether man maintains it or substitutes something else which performs the same function is immaterial.

JONES, in writing, suggested that, since ecologists are recognizing that the environment is not a constant but is unstable, for both natural and human reasons, a need is created for studies of "the topography of environmental instability," using "topography" in its classical sense.

Subsistence Economies

In his introductory statement Chairman ALEXANDER SPOEHR referred to the time scale of human history, during most of which subsistence economies have been dominant. This kind of life was general throughout the world before 5000 B.C. and common to considerable parts of the world almost to modern times. What have been the relations of such societies to the earth's surface?

THE TIME ASPECT

It seemed to BLUMENSTOCK that the climatic upheavals of the Pleistocene interposed a very important kind of semipermeable screen through which only certain kinds of things resulting from the influence of man could move. Ninety-nine per cent of human history lies within the pale of the archeologist. By ten to twenty thousand years ago man had pushed his way, except for a few islands, to the remote corners of the earth. HAURY felt that we need to ask ourselves what this long and widely based tenure has meant. The archeologist has not yet supplied adequate information of a sort that the ecologist and others perhaps want. The framework within which the archeologist operates has broad dimensions in space and time. Change comes as a response to continual adjustment to changing environmental conditions; out of the continual adjustments man has made, new things have emerged. From an early hunting condition in the Americas there was change to a gathering type of economy incident to the extinction of some of the large game animals. Correlated with that change were certain cultural losses and gains which then led to the nuclear developments in South America, Central America, Mexico, and, to a lesser degree, North America.

HUZAYYIN stressed the importance of having a true perspective of the time scale in the evolution of human culture. The Paleolithic represents by far the longest chapter in human activity compared with the Neolithic and later stages. In some areas, such as the mid-latitude deserts, the importance of the Paleolithic unfortunately has been overshadowed by stress on the Neolithic phase of human settlement. As compared to the historic phase with its documents and descriptions left by man, our study of the tools and stone implements of prehistoric man is not prejudiced. Among the Lower Paleolithic industries (Chellean-Acheulean complex, etc.) there was no significant difference between one world area and another, except for South Africa and perhaps Southeast Asia. Not until the Upper Paleolithic was there a significant change in human life: different kinds of stone industries localized in certain areas—Aurignacian, etc., in Europe, Capsian in North Africa, Aterian in the Sahara, Badarian in Egypt, etc. This localization of industry for the first time in human history can be interpreted as being due to a clearer adjustment of human activity to natural environmental conditions. It was in the Upper Paleolithic, too, that art began as a result of sufficient leisure for development of spiritual aspects of human life. Co-operative efforts of archeologists, paleogeographers, paleobotanists, and paleoclimatologists are called for to shed light on this first phase of human settlement in which groups of men began to differentiate local patterns of culture.

FIRE

Omitting consideration of energy of the human body, the first chapter in a history of energy technology would treat of man's use of fire and of the unanticipated side effects that occurred with its use, such as the role it played in creating new environments for human habitation. SAUER's field work in Mexico was largely in the mountains during the warm season. The difficulty of obtaining landscape photographs irritated him; it was annoying that good pictures could not be had until the rains hit heavily. Gradually he realized that fire was the most important step that the people had for preparing land for cultivation or in improving pastures. Out of this experience came further thoughts on the universality and longevity of man's use of fire.

NARR, though he did not attend the symposium, submitted the following written statement about the oldest evidence for the use of fire by man:

I think that the doubt which has persisted about the "hearths" discovered near Ipswich cannot be diminished by the "rostrocarinates" and other pretended "artifacts" of the "crag series." As far as I see, S. H. Warren[1] in 1923 was the first who denied the artificial origin of those flints. Further arguments were brought forth by statistical inquiries of A. S. Barnes[2] in 1938. This opposition against the "artifacts" was shared by most participants at the International Geological Congress in 1948 (see *Man*, LXIX [1949], 58). Also, the abbé Breuil has modified his former views,[3] though he still regards "traces of fire" and "a certain number of flakes" as "possible," simultaneously admitting that "their flaking angle is generally unfavorable." A 1954 study by K. P. Oakley on "Evidence of Fire in South African Cave Deposits" (*Nature*, CLXXIV, 261–64) shows that the vitreous material in question probably has been due to fires. But the cave deposits consist largely of bat guano, which could have easily been ignited at the cave entrance by a natural grass fire. The oldest evidence for the human use of fire thus seems to be the hearths of Peking man. Nevertheless, this cannot be taken as proof that man learned the use of fire only in the mid-Pleistocene. In my opinion the use of fire is, beneath language and manufactured tools, a criterion which distinguishes mankind from other primates.

1. "Sub-soil Pressure-flaking," *Proceedings of the Geological Association*, XXXIV, 153 ff., and "Sub-soil Flint-flaking Sites at Grays," *ibid.*, pp. 38 ff.

2. "Les Outils de l'homme tertiaire en Angleterre: Étude critique," *Anthropologie*, LXVIII, 217 ff.

3. See H. Breuil and H. Lantier, 1951, p. 63 (cited by Sauer, p. 69 above).

Therefore, if there should turn up evidence that the "Australopithecinae" were true men (in the psychologic and philosophic sense), I shall not hesitate to ascribe to them the ability of having used fire, whether the latter can be proved or not.[4] I think that in this respect I am in full accord with Dr. Stewart.

Man is cutting into the wealth of ecological climaxes, but very few men (certainly not civilized men) lived in forests under climax conditions. DARLING commented that fire has been man's instrument for setting back succession in creating his habitats. There are extensive habitats in stages of succession well below climax which, through loss of organic natural wealth, must be considered as deteriorated by factors other than the occurrence of natural fire only.

In Ireland, and probably in much of northwestern Europe, EVANS observed, the use of fire as a major force in altering the environment would seem to have depended upon climatic change. Scandinavian students of the history of technology and agriculture claim that the extensive use of fire began with subsistence economy and could not have been effective under the old hunting economy. The sub-boreal climate which followed the Atlantic phase was a factor in the establishment of subsistence economies which have been fossilized to a certain extent ever since and whose last remnants in Europe are only now passing away.

It was the contention of STEWART that fire has always been an environmental factor in areas such as the Great Plains. On the other hand, where there is adequate moisture, a tremendous amount of burning will not produce a pure grassland. The best example is found in the southeastern United States, where the longleaf pine forest is the re-

4. See also Narr's short 1954 paper on "Australopithicinen und älteste Geröllindustrien," *Germania*, XXXII, 315–18.

sult of burning. Without fire the forest simply will not reproduce itself. A related question, difficult to answer, is the distinction between man's production of fire and fire produced from natural causes, such as lightning. Frequently, assertions are made that lightning has caused fires on the prairies, yet Stewart had found no record of lightning-ignited prairie fires.

DAVIS considered the southern longleaf pine (*Pinus palustris*) to have evolved over many hundreds of thousands of years, with fire sufficiently prevalent to produce the species. A fire every ten years is even better than one every other year. He saw no difficulty in postulating lightning as the origin for a fire every fifteen to twenty years in any forest in Florida without human beings necessarily ever having been there. EGLER granted that fire is of extraordinary importance, but he felt that we should be very careful in considering whether fire (of whatever origin) produced a species or a vegetation type. There is an important difference. Most weed species, like the red birch in the northeastern United States, undoubtedly existed for a long time, but as a community the red birch has come into existence with a different regime. In dealing with a system—a holistic unit—we cannot isolate fire as a causal factor and hold to that alone.

In all his personal experience in tropical grasslands (Indochina, central Africa, Madagascar), GOUROU, in writing, stated that he had never seen a fire produced by lightning, in spite of numerous thunderstorms. While personal experience is not a proof, it nevertheless explains his strong skepticism about lightning fires in grass or forest. Also, he cautioned against "observations." In some "protected parks" of tropical Africa, some fires officially attributed to lightning are perhaps man-made fires. In effect, cessation of fires produces a diminution of the land occupied by grasses and a progress of trees. The result is a diminution of herbivores (antelopes, zebras, etc.) and, in consequence, of lions. Yet, great herbivores and lions are the principal attraction and interest of these parks. Without fires the vegetation would return to forest. Fire is a means—perhaps the only means—of maintaining the vegetation in a static situation. Officially, the use of fire is not allowed, but it is providential that responsibility for fire may be attributed to lightning.

MALIN read into the record quotations from two newspaper articles, later inserted as footnotes (see pp. 350–51) to his chapter in this volume. His point was that considerable evidence of first-hand observations of lightning-set prairie fires may be obtained from country newspapers which report the week-by-week activities in a neighborhood. In Kansas, for example, the State Historical Society has a virtually complete file of every newspaper, weekly or daily, printed in the state since 1876 as well as earlier ones. The evidence that meets reasonable tests of accuracy and validity is there for the collecting in newspaper reports. Malin was stimulated to introduce this comment because Sauer, in 1944 (pp. 553–54 of "A Sketch of Early Man in America," *Geographical Review*, XXXIV, 529–73), and Stewart, in his present chapter (see p. 128), had stated that they knew of no documentation of lightning-set fires for the plains.

To BARTLETT, newspaper reports of the kindling of grass fires seemed entirely credible. In a United States National Park Service report on the Florida Everglades, Robertson (1955) states that lightning-started fires in that subtropical area actually have been seen by trained fire-prevention observers (see the full reference to Robertson, p. 718).

World wide, approximately ten thousand thunderstorms occur daily, with roughly a hundred thousand lightning strokes per day to the ground, LANDSBERG remarked. Lightning should not be underestimated as a source of fire. In Florida, for example, there are at least ninety days per year with thunderstorms. From the amount of lightning, there is no doubt whatsoever of its ability to start fires.

The large problem is not the effect of fire on grass, ANDERSON commented, but the effect of fire on vegetation. Grass is a special and dramatic example, but what of the subtler effects, where forest or savanna did not change to grass?

ALBRECHT thought it would be helpful to look at fire on the land in terms of soil. Fire is more detrimental for the survival of forests than for grasslands, because forest residues burn very handily, while grass is an annual which dies, with its roots adding organic matter to the soil where fire does not destroy it. Fire converts vegetation residues into the more soluble form of ash. The result of fire is equivalent to a fertilizer treatment to the soil. If the ratio of nutrient elements is suited to a particular physiological performance, then certain plants are given a boost toward species dominance. Species should be viewed in terms of physiological requirements from the soil rather than taxonomically.

TAX, in writing, thought that we should think of the influence of man as the extinguisher of fires as well as the maker of them.

In the wooded Northeast of the United States there were various patches of grasslands known as "plains." The White Plains in Westchester County, New York, gave their name to the modern city. MURPHY, in writing, pointed out that on Long Island the more extensive Hempstead Plains (250 square miles in area), as described by Daniel Denton (1670), were certainly sustained by fire set by Indians. It is likely that annual burning was carried out in late summer, so that the Indians might snare great numbers of Eskimo curlew and golden plover on their southward migration. At any rate, the Hempstead Plains remained grassland well toward the opening of the twentieth century. As recently as 1893, Long Island folklore held that trees would not grow on Hempstead Plains. About this date residential development began, and, within two decades, Garden City became a sylvan community. Today, the Hempstead Plains are a region of wood lot and copse. The reversion to forest was, in short, concomitant with the cessation of fire.

DOMESTICATION AND MIGRATION

SPOEHR, as Chairman, shifted the discussion from fire to plants and animals. Wherever man has gone he has been the center of a biotic assemblage of plants, both cultivated and wild, of insects and terrestrial arthropods, and of microörganisms, some of which are parasitic on man himself. In the time scale of human history these factors occurred early.

BATES called attention to the phenomenon of pre-adaptation with respect to plants and animals. When change is brought into a situation, many adaptations among the organisms for some other purpose will switch over and protect them against this new change. For example, many groups of insects, such as ants, have resisted the insecticide DDT. Other populations have rapidly shifted, so that certain elements within them which were resistant are able to take over as dominants. The same is true of resistance to fire. Certain plants, such as the pines, might have been extremely rare, but, because of their adaptation to fire, they became the ecological dominant under conditions where fire was an important element. The organisms associated with man perhaps belong in this category of organisms with very odd characteristics

which made them rather unsuited to the world before man started to mess it up but which enabled them to join in and reinforce man's activities in remolding the landscape. There is a general tendency for biologists, as natural scientists, to ignore man and his crop plants in their search for something in which man has not interfered, so that they can study "natural" processes. In so doing, they overlook the possibility of studying man as a part of nature; in studying human modifications, we are studying nature as well as man.

ANDERSON pointed out that there is mounting evidence that evolution proceeds very rapidly when there are new niches for things to flow into. Hybridization, for instance, may have been going on for a long time. It may not have been getting anywhere; but, when a new niche is formed into which the products of hybridization flow, something new is created very quickly. Therefore, it would be one thing to have the longleaf pines. But if there were an increased use of fire, so that longleaf pines and things like them which can withstand fire come together, a new association is formed. With new niches, there is a place for the product of hybridization which had been previously ignored by natural selection. There is a place for something new and something different. Therefore, as soon as early man created new associations —not new species—such as a longleaf pine forest, there was change from an occasional pine here and there among hardwoods to great stands of pine. This kind of thing must have happened in various ways throughout the world as soon as man arrived bringing fire with him. In this way a rapid evolution of new kinds of things followed in man's track.

NARR, in writing, contributed the following discussion on the origins of pastoralism and on the beginning of important sheep-breeding in Europe:

That domestication of sheep and goats began somewhere among tribes of the Indo-Iranian border ranges, probably stimulated from early plant-cultivating populations, is a view favored by Wissmann and his collaborators. However, an assumption that pastoralism had an independent origin somewhere farther north and thence (perhaps in the still primitive form of "companionship") spread to the south would require no severe modification of the other views expressed by Wissmann. If we admit, furthermore, that an early plant cultivation was already in existence between 13000 and 9000 B.C. or, more cautiously, before the beginning of the fifth millennium B.C., though it cannot be proved archeologically,[5] we wonder whether the same possibility also should not be conceded to pastoralism.

The theory that pastoralism rose independently is by no means contradictory to the assumption that plant cultivation originated rather early in southern Asia. It should be remembered in this respect that the very partisans of the theory of a separate origin of pastoralism, namely, the older generation of the ethnological school of Vienna and, among prehistorians in particular, O. Menghin (1931), also favored the view that agriculture began in southern Asia, probably as a kind of tuber-planting. Furthermore, that does not exclude the possibility that those early southern Asiatic plant-cultivators domesticated some animals, in particular, the pig. This domestication may have originated from "taming" (*Zähmen*) in the sense given that word by H. Pohlhausen (1954). "Taming" consists of accustoming animals to the neighbor-hood of men, so that the beasts no longer shrink from them, remain close to human settlements, and accept additional food from men. Similar "taming" can be observed especially in southeastern Asia and Melanesia.[6] According to Pohlhausen, "taming" was developed by "territorially fixed hunters"; this statement is in agreement with the assumption that tuber-planting originated among sedentary hunter-fishers and food-gatherers. I think that it would be wise not to stress too much one specified theory about the origin of pastoralism, for it seems that on the evidence available today there is no possibility for a definite, objective, and really conclusive decision.

The material on sheep in prehistoric Europe, used by J. G. D. Clark (1952), comes from full Neolithic and from late Bronze Age and early Iron Age sites. The late Neolithic and, in particular, the early and middle Bronze Age are virtually unrepresented. Therefore, the statements of Clark cannot mean more than that sheep were unimportant in the economy of the full Neolithic of Europe, as far as this could be ascertained, whereas they were really of great importance in the closing Bronze Age and the early Iron Age. The regrettable lack of evidence from the early and middle Bronze Age leaves open the question whether and when sheep-breeding became more important during that time. But there is direct evidence from the late Neolithic Pontic, and similar inferences can be made for late Neolithic Middle Europe, that sheep-breeding had grown more important in this period and probably was introduced on a greater scale by a distinct culture group, namely, the Battle-ax civilization.

EVANS added this anecdote: With regard to the movement of plants with man, there is a delightful essay by Lord Acton, who must have been one of the first to look into this question with the eye of a historian and with an aesthetic sense. He has an essay in his studies in history on the commerce of thought, with a wonderful section about a sol-

5. On the unlikelihood of archeological evidence for nomadic pastoralism see in particular M. Hermanns, 1949, pp. 160, 180–81, as quoted by Narr and by Wissmann (pp. 148 and 301 above). Indeed, we may modify the statement of G. Smolla (quoted by Wissmann, p. 284 above) as follows: "The lack of archeological proof for these earliest planter tribes [pastoralists] does not, therefore, speak against their former existence. . . . The archeologist can maintain only that no discoveries are against such an argument [see Narr, 1953, pp. 69, 73] and that, by using it, several phenomena become understandable which before were inexplicable."

6. See also p. 754 of K. Jettmar, 1952, "Zu den Anfängen der Rentierzucht," *Anthropos*, XLVII, Nos. 5–6, 737–66, and Narr, 1953, p. 89.

dier in Vespasian's army invading England. The soldier's great tramping boot wore out, and, with it, the seed lodged in the dirt picked up in Gaul was discarded in Kent. From it, he says, "Next year England gained another wild flower." And he goes on in assessing, no doubt in a prescientific way, the long list of plants which the Romans brought; and he has, I remember, this very delightful phrase: "We owe to the Roman"—then he lists a succession of plants and adds—"green peas. God bless him."

DARLING pointed to the impoverishment of the flora of wild lands under the intentional pastoralism of domesticated stock. He put it as a fundamental that domestication cuts down the mobility of animals. Having got them where they are wanted when they are wanted, they are on the spot for a longer time than under natural conditions. Pastoralization puts wild land under pressure which, in general, it is unable to withstand for an indefinite period. The result is an impoverishment of the flora, which is, in turn, an impoverishment of the organic circulation within the particular habitat.

In the islands of the French West Indies the lowland plains and foothills differ from the hill lands in soil types and, in a way, in local climatic types. The vegetation type of the flatlands is all savanna—isolated thorny trees and grassland; that of the hills is scrub. Usually these vegetation differences are interpreted in terms of climate and soil, yet the real explanation, EGLER found, lay in the form of grazing. The key to it was located where fence lines ran no longer between slopes but up them. Goats, almost omnivorous and keeping to the higher rocky slopes, did not eat certain scrub plants; the result was croton thickets. Cattle ate almost anything except thorny leguminous trees and stayed mostly on the lowlands; the result was the savanna cattle country.

The marked division correlated with soil and climate differences but not in a cause-and-effect relationship.

DEFORESTATION

The clearing of woodlands was important in Europe and America and in various parts of Asia. WITTFOGEL spoke of the avoidance of woodland in early China. China's culture originated in the Yellow River Valley, whose loesslands were not densely wooded. The more heavily wooded areas of central and southern China were only gradually opened up to Chinese culture. Records of the Han dynasty (about the time of Christ) describe the Yangtze area as still backward agronomically. In the T'ang dynasty (A.D. 618–906) the great majority of the Chinese still lived in the north, only two million Chinese then residing south of the Yangtze. Thus, it took the Chinese a long time to conquer the woodlands and to create the artificial landscape of terraced paddy fields which characterizes central and southern China.

It was PFEIFER's impression that the 27 per cent of area in Germany preserved in forest is rather exceptional. In England, for example, only 3–4 per cent remains in forest cover. Riehl, the nineteenth-century sociologist, always spoke of the forests in Germany as the autocratic feature of the landscape: during revolutions, the peasantry, taking advantage of their freedom, reduced the forests by their cuttings. Thus are the changing relations of man and nature linked to social conditions of particular times.

SEARS reported that Enrico Martínez, an engineer who attempted the drainage of the valley of Mexico, wrote in 1609 that at the time of the conquest, which was less than a hundred years before his birth, the hills were densely forested. It was not until the Spaniards came and tackled the forests with steel tools and fire and turned what he called

"Christian cattle" loose on the hills that the erosion cycle once more was resumed. Martínez described very vividly the consequent flow of mud and water down into Mexico City. That is not conjecture but the testimony of a trained observer at the time.

The modern world, since the sixteenth century and especially since the mid-nineteenth century, has become alarmed over a shortage of suitable timber. DARBY mentioned that the woods, their destruction and its consequences, and the need for some policy of conservation were one of the main themes of George P. Marsh's *Man and Nature* in 1864. "The Woods" was the title of his very long third chapter.

The large surfaces still remaining in forest (about 20 per cent) in present-day France, GOUROU, in writing, accounted for by the facts that (1) large areas of forests are in state lands or *terres communales,* which are collective lands with special forest legislation; (2) on marginal lands forest is the best economic system; (3) a rural exodus has occurred (economically justified); and (4) sheep have regressed.

GRAHAM commented upon the relationship between clearing of land and subsistence economy as illustrated in northeastern North America. By the late eighteenth century much of the land in New England had been cleared. In north-central Massachusetts, which we know very well in terms of its land-use history, there was essentially a subsistence economy—not in a primitive sense but certainly in comparison with the present day. By 1850 the land which had been cleared and brought into cultivation was largely abandoned due to the opening of new lands in the prairie states, where it was economically much easier to produce food crops, or (as TUKEY pointed out) because of migration to the California gold fields. Today, that land in north-central Massachusetts is practically all

forest. Thus a reverse generalization is true here, for the disappearance of a subsistence economy has resulted in the rapid appearance of a heavy forest growth.

PLOW AGRICULTURE

Following the Paleolithic, special types of agriculture arose: digging-stick and hoe cultivation, the clearing of woodland, and the eventual development of plow agriculture. EVANS thought that an important topic to be looked into was the introduction of and various modifications of the plow. He asked for advice from technologists on the exact differences in purpose and function between the chill plow and the steel plow and between the left-handed and the right-handed plow. PFEIFER reiterated that in his chapter he emphasized the importance of plow agriculture as a stabilizing factor. Central Europe has been cultivated since the fourth century B.C. without very detrimental effects. There is hardly anything by way of soil erosion to compare with what happened in the New World under colonial European agriculture. It is possible that plow agriculture was adaptable to different conditions by the shift of emphasis between animal-raising and crop tillage.

FROM TECHNIQUES TO SOCIAL ORDERS

SPOEHR made reference to Gourou's statement, in his chapter on tropical agriculture, that human choices have been influenced much more by the level of techniques than by physical conditions alone.

SAUER suggested that Gourou's paper was interesting because it emphasized the significance of wet-land crops, of drainage, and of their possibilities. Wet-land plants made into crop plants apparently was an exclusively Old World set of techniques. The establishment of modern contacts was a means of invitation to admission of a large number of crops.

Brazil provided an example where modern man has reverted to more primitive types of agriculture. PFEIFER pointed out how German agricultural colonists in the state of Espíritu Santo took over *caboclo* ways, using fire and shifting fields in forest clearings. But the colonists could not move around fully like the *caboclo;* restricted to colonies of limited areas, the colonists had to rotate their fields so fast that there was incomplete recovery of vegetation and of soil productivity. EVANS, in his discussion of the Danish fields of the "Celtic Iron Age," mentioned that in many open-field systems, especially in regions of difficulty, plots changed hands periodically. This type of tenure in which land was periodically redistributed seemed to GLACKEN to be of great antiquity and to have existed in many parts of Eurasia. He first became acquainted with it in studying Ryukyuan history. In Okinawa, village lands were communally held by a village and were periodically redistributed. The system, which apparently existed in early China and Japan, was abolished by the Japanese around the turn of the century. At present it is found in the Near East, where it is known as *mashá;* here, pastoral lands are periodically redistributed. A criticism made of both types was that the system led to land deterioration because of neglect and carelessness in its use toward the end of the allotment period. Periodic redistributions also were characteristic of old Russian village communities. Ancient land-tenure systems, of which this periodic reallotment is an illustration, are of great importance in studying the mechanisms through which changes of the earth have occurred in the past.

Several speakers, among them PFEIFER and WITTFOGEL, directed attention toward the social and cultural circumstances which had to develop before certain techniques of land use could be employed on a wide scale.

In Central Europe the sociological structure of peasant society was of importance. State authority, directing settlement and political economy, developed at the end of the fifteenth century. Forests were to be preserved. Emphasis in housebuilding shifted to bricks; hedges and walls replaced movable fences to shut off pastures. Peasant wars of the early sixteenth century had the effect of canceling out the forest conservation acts of the government.

Before the modern industrial period, between 60 and 70 per cent of all mankind during the last three to four thousand years lived under conditions shaped by hydraulic civilizations. This cultural development, with its complex technological, economic, and governmental institutions, required large communities for its development.

In the retreat from the imperial Roman social organization, the cities of Western Europe shrank, and the countrysides became more populous. HEICHELHEIM suggested that there might be something of a law: that a subsistence economy populates the countryside, while market economies produce much more but empty the countryside. He posed the question: Was the retreat from urban centers of civilization to church monasteries, royal courts, aristocratic estates, and humble villages really a catastrophe? There is a good deal of evidence that in Egypt, in the eastern Mediterranean, and in the West the late Roman time was not a period of decline. For example, comparing the evidence of what the population of Helvetia knew of Roman order and civilization under Roman rule with what was known in Alemannic time, the Swiss actually knew considerably more Latin literature in the later period than they had known under Roman rule. In the south of France the Greco-Roman survival was even more marked. Thus, such a retreat, to something near a subsistence economy, does not necessarily destroy civilization.

THE FIFTEENTH-CENTURY DEPOPULATION

At the time white men came to the northeastern United States there were very extensive stretches of white pine, EGLER explained. We know today that white pine is a one-generation type; it does not reproduce itself without disturbance, nor does it become a dominant type except after disturbance. It would seem that a disturbance occurred—or an otherwise different situation prevailed—about A.D. 1400, approximately two hundred years before white men arrived. Did an epidemic possibly wipe out a very large Indian population, and did pines enter into areas that formerly had been grasslands? With great changes in Indian populations, there were enormous changes in vegetation. White men arrived at a very unstable moment.

Archeology reveals that during the period from A.D. 1400 to 1500 there was a very marked change in Iroquois population, or at least in Iroquois culture, SCHAEFER reported. About 1450 there was a gathering-together of small villages into very large ones. Around 1500, these suddenly disappeared, to be followed by scattered, smaller villages.

A further coincidence concerning the 1450 period was pointed up by CURTIS, in writing. Extensive pine forests around the upper Great Lakes and the pine forests that preceded hemlock forests in Pennsylvania both date back to 1450. Though not the only possible explanation, this may be correlated with a temporary decrease in Indian pressure.

DARBY indicated that the great and fairly continuous expansive movement of the clearing of woodland did not continue uninterruptedly into modern times. Only recently has it been appreciated that a very great economic recession took place between A.D. 1300 and 1500. Causes are obscure—perhaps plague, perhaps warfare, perhaps a crisis resulting from something else. But abandoned holdings and deserted villages are dated from this period. In England alone, thirteen hundred deserted villages date from the period 1400–1550, and the number is increasing with further discoveries. Over many of their cleared fields, the woods spread again. Jäger has recently shown that many tracts of woodland in Germany came into being during the fifteenth century and have remained as woodland ever since.

BANKS drew attention to the obvious coincidence between the period of A.D. 1400 (mentioned by Egler, Darby, and others) and the Black Death, which was a world-wide pandemic in 1346. The death rate in Europe was one in two or one in four. The plague spread slowly from Asia to Europe, but how would it have gotten to the New World? MALIN pointed out that there was a Scandinavian connection with North America to about the mid-fourteenth century. Then there was a break, and connection between Scandinavia and North America was not resumed until the 1480's, before the time of Columbus. This gap in the record has never been satisfactorily explained.

DARBY then made the point that in Europe the Black Death must have been, and certainly was, a considerable factor, yet it is quite clear that the recession was well under way *before* the Black Death. While the matter is controversial, to pin the recession entirely on the Black Death would be a mistake.

PFEIFER agreed that the Black Death, while a known phenomenon, must not be held fully responsible. What about climatic change? Floehn has pointed out that in the mid-fifteenth century there was a definite change for the worse in climate, which might have accounted for certain retreats in the less favorable uplands of central Germany. For this area an apparent climatic optimum in the thirteenth century coincided with the spread of colonization; the fifteenth century saw the retreat. Again this is too simple an explanation. The abandonment of land began much earlier—and in different sections. It was very early in the best areas of old settlement; there was a redistribution of population and a consolidation of smaller settlements into larger ones. Mortensen holds that the datum level for the modern development of the landscape is at just this point which marks the end of the medieval period.

HEICHELHEIM thought that behind the recession of about 1400 was an economic catastrophe in Islam, the leading economic center of the time, which led to an enormously high price for silver. The resultant upheaval in all medieval market economies was made good only by the discovery of America.

THE QUALITY OF PEASANT LIVING

With the thought that perhaps a clearer conception of how man's social order is related to his environment and to his quality of life ought to be striven for, Chairman SPOEHR turned to TAX for the session's closing comments.

TAX again posed the question: Is man conceived as a part of nature? Man certainly is a different kind of animal in nature. He mediates his relationship through a set of values which are thought of as basic to the culture, and he has what some think of as free will. In other words, man knows what he wants sometimes and goes out to get it, and in this respect he is different from other animals. Man must not be thought of as something which is only being used or is using. It is man and the human element that must be brought in when different kinds of cul-

tures are characterized. The peasant way of life is to be contrasted, on the one side, with the way of life of the tribe and, on the other side, with the commercial way of life, whether in the city or elsewhere.

The tribal way of life presumably was characteristic of that long, long Paleolithic period right into the Neolithic. A peasant way of life can be spoken of only in the Neolithic (food-producing, hydraulic civilizations, and all the rest), which, of course, is very recent. To speak of a commercial way of life or an urban way of life is to be concerned with only the most recent movement in world perspective.

The way of life in the innumerable "savage" tribes, to use the old evolutionary terminology, is a kind of web of meaning in which man achieves a satisfactory relationship to the universe, including the ecology around him, and which for a long time can slowly change, but change only within a limited area. By the end of the Paleolithic there were a great number of these tribes who achieved a level of culture where they could fairly well control the environment as they found it. They were confidently able to move into new environments, and culture change was very rapid before the period of the Neolithic. This was the period during which man explored and spread out over the world even more than before, for he rapidly invaded the New World in a relatively short space of time and adapted himself to the thousand different physical-biological environments that were there.

Tribal man, or whatever he is called, never is, or was, unchanging or unchangeable or conservative. The history of humanity would not be what it is if man had not adapted very quickly and adjusted to change wherever necessary.

What happened next was that, in numerous places, for numerous reasons in different places, and for some common reasons in all places, a group of small societies became one large society. This is what Childe called the "urban revolution," from which are derived civilizations. This second stage was based on agriculture and the domestication of animals wherever it occurred and on such things as irrigation. But then there exist side by side what Redfield terms both a large tradition, based on literature, held by an elite class, so to speak, and carried on by that class, and small peasant traditions. Always in this stage of human society there is the peasantry as well as towns and cities and commerce. We have to think of a peasant way of life as part of a large way of life—a civilization—including some commerce and some division of labor. The tribal way of life continues in some, but not all, respects.

Three ways in which peasants seem to differ from tribes are:

1. Landownership and inheritance become very important. With property comes the whole notion of savings and investment and the notion of "a rainy day." In other words, property—animals, plants, barns, houses, land, land boundaries, and all the rest—becomes a terribly important concern for man, and, consequently, so does the next generation.

2. Where there are domestic animals with full agriculture rather than simple tillage, time becomes terribly important, and a heavy sense of responsibility is felt. The animals have to be fed; man cannot leave them. He has to "make hay while the sun shines." The whole notion of time makes man not only a slave to property—this is the true story of the Garden of Eden—but a slave to time as well.

3. Individual motivation and competition begin. There arises a conflict of values between the individual's life-ambition and what he thinks of as saving for his children and his grandchil-dren. The conflict between an individual's values and the values of society as a whole arises, generally, only within the peasant state of life. In the tribal state of life as it is lived at the present time among North American Indians, this conflict is not important. It is won by the community or society; individual competition just does not have a prominent place, and people are able to adjust to one another. The great value is the characteristic harmony in the society. Competition and individual initiative have to take second place to the notion of the harmonious whole. This is important, because the harmonious whole in the tribal society relates to nature as well. And this value of harmony is certainly not entirely lost by peasants. There is a feeling of the harmony of the universe and a proper relation with nature, with God, with one's fellow-men, and with the whole web of human culture which is important in tribal life, which remains important in peasant life, but which undoubtedly becomes lost in some degree with the development of commerce and of urbanization.

Neither is evolution inevitable nor must all people proceed through the same stages. An important historical or archeological point to be made is that differences persist. Peoples do have different ways of life on any level, and one of the ways in which they do tend to differ is in the basic value judgment of harmony versus competition. Did man ever universally give up the notion of the harmony of society as contrasted with what he could get for himself? Does it necessarily follow that man ever will in all places or that this will become widespread throughout the world?

This becomes exceedingly important, because many people believe that, in order to get economic development in the underdeveloped areas of the world, it is necessary to make people over into the kind of people that Europe developed at the time of the commercial and industrial revolutions. But, Tax asked, are there not many roads, not simply one, to development of better lives for different peoples in different cultures? Westerners take a very narrow view if they assume that their way of getting a better life is either transportable or should be transported to groups with very fundamentally different cultures and, with respect to many human values that are shared, better cultures than their own.

Commercial Economies

Forest Regions outside the Tropics
Grasslands
Arid Lands
Humid Tropics
Capital and Surplus

Dr. PAUL B. SEARS, as Chairman, began the session by putting on the blackboard the notation

$$\frac{R}{P} = f(C) ,$$

with R representing resources, environment, or land; P, human population; and C, culture. The sum total of resources and the population among which the resources have to be divided are a function of the pattern of culture.

There is a definite connection between the culture pattern and the resources which are considered useful. The flint ridges in northern Wyoming or in eastern Ohio which were tremendously important centers for the Indian are today negligible for us. The great deposits of coal, petroleum, and ore which lay under the surface near by meant nothing to the Indian but mean everything to our own way of life.

The pressure of population on resources also is a function of culture. Some populations maintain themselves by cultural means in fairly stable equilibrium with available resources. On the other hand, American culture is inclined to value continual expansion: some is good; more is better; more and more are both bigger and better. This is a cultural value which seems to be inherent in the system.

In considering the interrelationships among resources, population, and culture, we must remember that each is a complex of many factors. Much discussion of correlations or cause and effect seems beside the point because of the multiple impact of the great number of factors involved. The key factor may be conspicuous and overabundant or scarce and limiting.

The distinctions among subsistence economies, commercial economies, and technological civilizations seem flexible; we can expand or contract the distinctions in relation to others even at the present time. For example, during the depression of the 1930's many unemployed in the cities returned to simple hill farms such as those in the Ozarks. Such hill farmers made the quickest adjustment to the economic depression; they shot a few more squirrels, picked a few more blackberries, and got along very well. Though some of their tools were of metal, they had essentially a Neolithic culture which was cushioned against the impact of what was regarded as a great tragedy in most of the country.

Something of this flexible arrangement is reflected in our patterns of land use. In an area put under commercial pressure to obtain maximum revenue, a definite sequence often occurs. The three common types of land use in western Europe and eastern North America are forest, pasture, and cropland. Under pressure of a commercial economy, the tendency is to plow up everything that possibly can be plowed, to pasture everything that cannot be plowed, and, if there is anything left, to leave it in forest or other wild vegetation. The paradox is that to attempt maintenance of a permanent commercial economy destroys capital in the long run. Much of the conservation movement as it has evolved in the United States has been able to reverse this trend.

An economy partly commercial and partly subsistence which, after several hundred years, is still operating on a very solid basis is that of the Amish of eastern Pennsylvania. Hilltops remain forested; the pastures on the hillsides are grass-covered and cross-fenced, so that one part may rest while another is grazed; and the plowland or cropland is confined to the rich valley-floor alluvium. This prudent, permanent, successful pattern maintains the value of its capital in the midst of a commercial civilization.

Discussion turned to the presentation of case histories of specific instances of man's relation to his environment in connection with commercial economies and the effects of that relationship.

FOREST REGIONS OUTSIDE THE TROPICS

Sears began the discussion by citing such a case history. The state of Ohio at the time of European invasion was 95 per cent forested. Its Indian population was between twelve and fifteen thousand; but, even if it had been twenty thousand, the average density would have been but one-half person per square mile. On a partly agricultural subsistence economy, though there were some exchange goods brought in from the outside, such as copper, obsidian, and shells, the people, as far as we can tell, were crowded at the end of the fifteenth century. The Indian population in North America at the time of European discovery was in a condition of very delicate balance; the effect of the first encroachment of Europeans on the Atlantic coast was like the snipping of the outer connecting strands on a spider web. Repercussions which were felt across the continent brought on profound readjustments, so that true pre-Columbian conditions in the interior were never known to the whites except by inference. Some years ago the locations of Indian settlement were plotted on a map in correlation to the distribution of original vegetation. It was hoped that relationships could be found between Indian settlement and vegetation types. Instead, the result was that settlements were grouped along the rivers, regardless of the type of forest, because rivers were more important than vegetation differences.

New England in the 1830's was from 80 to 90 per cent in farms. Most of these clearings reverted to forest, for 60 per cent of modern New England is in forests, which produce less than 10 per cent of the rural income. The ancient fields now covered with forest were divided by stone walls. On the upper slopes the bases of these walls are exposed; at the bottoms of slopes these bases are buried under transported soil. Land abandonment was due not solely to the competition of cheap land to the west but was aided by a faulty relation of land use and management to the economic base—a faulty relation of culture to resources.

Thornthwaite was asked to speak of his experience at Seabrook Farms in disposing of waste water as an example of the difference between forest land and cropland. Seabrook Farms is a huge commercial agricultural enterprise devoted to raising vegetables and to harvesting, processing, freezing, storing, and distributing them. In preparing the vegetables for freezing, a large amount of water is used for washing, fluming, and other operations. Polluted with dirt and organic matter, this water, for lack of dissolved oxygen, cannot be discharged into near-by creeks without destroying the fish. In attempting to use the water for irrigation, it was discovered that the plowed land had a very low infiltration rate, for, after receiving an inch of water, the soil became soupy. Then a woodland was sprayed with the waste water, and it seemed that there was no limit to the amount that could be applied. In preliminary experiments, 5 inches an hour for ten hours were absorbed, whereas, only 600 feet away, forest-cleared, cultivated land of the same soil type could not take over an inch. As a result of this astonishing experiment, ten million gallons of waste water have been disposed of daily in this forest since 1950. This is equivalent to 600 inches of water a year for the last five years. And weeds and other vegetation flourish.

In central southern New Jersey there is an empty area of some two million acres known as the "barrens" and considered to be essentially useless, except as an area for storage of water supplies for peripheral cities and towns. Apparently it was once heavily forested, but, owing to a sandy soil incapable of holding much water, it suffers tremendously from drought and in rain-deficient periods is very subject to fire. At present the area is covered with woody growth only a few feet in height, but, where fire has been kept out, trees are 20 feet or more high. From the experiments at Seabrook, it seems clear that what is wrong with the "barrens" is its lack of water. Water is there, only 10 feet beneath the surface. Here is an opportunity for a reclamation project

that would outstrip the controversial one on the Colorado River.

Sears emphasized that the principle back of Thornthwaite's remarks is that a great deal of agricultural practice tends to lessen the capacity of the soil to absorb water. A commercial enterprise sometimes can be too smart for its own good; in the interest of increasing production, it can destroy an asset essential to its continuance. This principle is in the same category as urbanization, which has the effect of waterproofing the land surface while at the same time raising the per capita consumption of water. As Thornthwaite summarized: Here is one powerful way man has modified the earth. By clearing the forests and cultivating the soil, he has reduced the infiltration capacity of the soil by a phenomenal amount.

Smith asked Thornthwaite whether the New Jersey "barrens" has a layer of hardpan under it, while Evans, in writing, asked whether there is hardpan under the arable land which does not absorb water or if the lack of absorption is due to change of soil structure without leaching. Evans' question bears closely on the problem of water-logging of early cultivated lands (forest-cleared) in northwestern Europe and the subsequent accumulation of peats. Thornthwaite replied that the area has no hardpan under it. In drilling ground-water observation wells throughout the "barrens" in Lebanon State Forest, no hardpan was found, only clean white sand: fine grains interspersed with coarse, from the surface down to 70 or 80 feet. Hardpan sometimes develops in areas where there is excessive water. At Seabrook Farms a battery of evapotranspirometers has been in operation for eight years. This is a series of identical tanks, about 7 feet in diameter and 3 feet deep, filled with soil in which crops are raised; for the last five or six years the crop has been grass. It is possible to irrigate the soil in the tanks by a pipe from beneath and to keep track of the amount of water used, so that the rate of evapotranspiration can be determined by the amount of water applied and the amount used. This was the purpose of the installation. Four years ago the method of applying water to three of the tanks was modified. While three were irrigated from below, as before, three others were supplied by water from the surface by sprinkling. On these latter three, slightly more water was put on in the morning than would be evaporated and transpired during the day. There would be a slight amount of percolation through the soil; this was caught and the amount subtracted from that applied; this gave the amount of evapotranspiration. In early June, 1955, efforts were made to determine the effect of the difference in watering on the permeability of the soil in the tanks to see how it compared with the soil permeability in the surrounding cultivated fields. On three tanks, water was poured on. Amazingly, the one that had been watered from above for four years took water at a rate more than five times as great as the irrigated tanks, which, themselves, took water at about twenty-five times the rate of the cultivated soil.

That the "barrens" had porous soil that did not hold water and that the plants suffered from drought indicated to THOMAS that such conditions were not true of the usual forest or grassland. Rather, such conditions are typical of the places for the best ground-water recharge, such as the mouth of the Lost River in Idaho or some of the beach gravels around Lake Bonneville. But these areas that contribute to prolific and perennial ground-water reservoirs comprise only a very small proportion of the earth's surface.

BLUMENSTOCK wondered whether if water were raised from beneath the "barrens" for agricultural purposes there would be further underground invasion of salt water, which is now a problem at Atlantic City. THOMAS replied that with modern pumps it is certainly possible to bring on salt-water encroachment but that, being aware of the problem, it should be possible to maintain a balance and not overdraw by pumping to excess.

LEOPOLD thought the discussion was getting dangerously close to the conclusion that the way to control floods was merely to allow wasteland to revert to forest under as ideal conditions as civilization would allow. There are two complicating factors in flood control. First, one of the most important principles to emerge from study of the effects of different kinds of vegetation on floods has been contributed by the United States Forest Service. At Coweeta Experiment Station it was demonstrated that floods in that part of the Appalachian Mountains were formed by water, none of which had been surface flow. Water that had infiltrated into the forest soil reappeared in the stream channel from underflow. This is just a warning that reforestation will not necessarily be a primary means of controlling floods. Second, in most soils there is a tendency for infiltration rates to be reduced with increased application of water. The rate decreases with time, even under natural vegetative conditions. Floods generally occur during times when flood-producing rainfalls immediately follow a period of moisture sufficient to reduce the infiltration rate to a minimal value. That there have been floods throughout all time, long before the existence of civilization, must be recognized.

HEICHELHEIM asked whether libertarian administration of forests is especially difficult. Is it a matter of chance, or do forests to be administered well require organization collectively for the common interest. Even the otherwise most libertarian Hellenistic and Roman societies tended to be administered as large collective units in accord with a unified plan. Athens tried to administer collectively the forests of Macedonia for naval and peacetime needs. The Ptolemies established a monopoly for all forests in their territories. For Rome, forests at first were public property, then later were taken care of by large latifundia, and, finally, there were great imperial forest estates throughout the Empire. In the medieval period, forests were very often exclusively in the hands of the king.

The classic sequence of what happens to forest when commercial activities are introduced is that the land is cleared, leaving the forest only in a few relict areas, and that the forest does not return to the land unless something disastrous happens to the economy. KLIMM brought out that field study and aerial photo interpretation had revealed the opposite for the northeastern United States. With increasing commercial intensification of agriculture and competition with the western states, the tendency has been for crop acreage to shrink. Crops are produced only on the best land. There has been a shrinking downhill of the cropland, with increased abandonment of hill farms and an increase of forest. Competition has restricted agriculture to the better lands, the poorer lands have gone out of production, and the forests have come downhill. Every state in the Northeast, except Delaware, has had an increase in forest area and, correspondingly, a decrease in cropland. But the cropland, however, has increased in per acre yield. Most of the abandoned land was originally owned in farms. As it gets to the debit side of the tax rolls, the states buy it up for protected hunting land. One might argue that commercialization of agriculture is the way to bring about conservation of the landscape.

GRASSLANDS

Regardless of whether fire was started by man or by lightning, its prevention was of some consequence to the commercial range-cattle industry, MALIN remarked. In the early twentieth century, after pastures were fenced, conservation of grassland became even more important, because cattle owners could not move from place to place but had to depend upon what lay within their fenced land. Another point to be kept in mind when discussing the Great Plains was that dust storms have always been a regular part of the phenomena of the area. Archeologists have supplied evidence for repeated occupations of the same prehistoric site— the levels of successive occupation being separated by dust or other windblown material. Dust storms were present before commercial livestock ranged the prairies; they arose when winds blew over the plains after denudation of vegetation, whatever the cause. In an article in *Scientific Monthly*, early in 1953, Malin raised questions on the significance of dust storms not only to the areas from which dust was blown but also to the areas on which it fell. He pleaded for soil scientists to publish their views on whether the chernozem soils of the grasslands are maintained, at present, by dust-fall. And what effect would stoppage of dust storms have on all the eastern areas that regularly receive falling dust.

SEARS remarked that there are three sources of dust: the wide river valleys, perennially full of fine material; dried lake beds, full of fine silt; and the plowed fields. Resource men not only do not deny the importance of wind-transported source material for soil but recognize it as a very important factor. JONES, in writing, thought Malin's use of accounts in local newspapers as evidence for dust storms to be a good idea if the accounts were evaluated with care. The evidence, however, is likely to be qualitative rather than quantitative. For instance, we would learn of dust storms in the Great Plains prior to agriculture but not of how they compared, in quantity of soil removal, with the dust storms of the 1930's, for it would not be reported what land types (dry lakes or potentially arable land) were being eroded.

We attach a value to grassland, AL-BRECHT pointed out, because the vegetation cover is a forage for livestock. But this necessitates a soil that makes a forage worth a cow's time to eat. Much of our food has come out of the grasslands by a type of extensive agriculture that is more speculation than production, because we depend upon the cow to supply something capable of being fattened. The pressure for beef supply from the grasslands is very rapidly depleting the potential for protein. Where the plow went ahead of the cow, we have been able to measure the reduction in soil capabilities. The protein content of the wheat now grown on the eastern edge of the grassland area has been dropping decidedly. Where once it ranged from 19 to 11 per cent, it is now 14–9 per cent.

GRAHAM pointed out that the wheat yield in the Nile Delta is something like 30 bushels per acre, while the wheat yield in the United States under commercialized farming is only 17 bushels per acre. Commercial agriculture forces us to utilize a great deal of land which probably never should have been utilized for agricultural production and, as a result, forces an exploitation of our soil resources. KLIMM replied that economists and other social scientists for a long time have been critical of comparison of yields per acre as an index of the value or efficiency of agriculture. For the comparison depends on what is produced and what is conserved. Peasant agriculture in Egypt does manage to produce more bushels to the acre, but many more people are engaged in pro-

duction per unit area than in the United States. Are we interested in producing the most per acre or the most per man? If land "should not" have been plowed, what is it that so determines? That it will blow away or wash away? Is this a value superior to the backbreaking labor of peasant agriculture that produces so much more from so little land on very small per capita yields? The meeting of these two concepts is perhaps one of the better things that can arise from this symposium.

STEWART drew attention to an example of a complete change from grassland to virtual forest land by commercial overgrazing. In Texas millions of acres of prairie have been converted into mesquite jungle, a process accelerated by the cessation of burning. Under conditions of wild-game grazing and in the early years of open-range grazing, these Texas prairies were burned by Indians and later by the stockmen. But they were overgrazed, especially after fencing, so that not sufficient fuel remained to carry fire and burn off the mesquite seedlings that soon spread over the ground. Ancient prairie flora is still preserved in experimental plots along railroad rights of way that were fenced but also burned.

CLARK could not feel that those bits of prairie have the same ecological situation as in the days prior to the coming of the railroad or of commercial economy. In a discussion of "Retrospect" the contrast of precommercial and postcommercial economy has been missed. In writing, he asked whether we were not talking about processes of change before we have had any serious discussion of the kind and dimensions of change which have taken place? He could not speak about very extensive areas, but, with regard to the New World unplowed grasslands, he hoped his chapter had raised some doubts as to fairly widespread assumptions about change. This did not involve very much of the earth's surface or very many people; the point is that it is hopeless to talk about processes of change anywhere at any time unless the change itself can be established, at least as to probability, in its general outlines. The changes of nature involved in the establishment of hydraulic civilizations are in certain respects clear; in many others they deserve much more searching analysis if we are to know what the establishment of a great irrigation network really has meant in this or that place or time. Again, we recurrently lose our focus on man's role in changing the face of the earth if we talk too closely to the point of what commercial economies have done to primitive cultures and unless we compare more closely than we have the contrast of the two in changing vegetation and soils. But this, too, involves at least a reasonable guess at a "before and after" picture. We are concerned always with a changing and not a static picture, or, to express it perhaps more precisely, we are concerned with comparative rates of change. But we must, surely, first be reasonably definite as to what we are talking about.

ARID LANDS

In evaluating the historical importance of commerce in promoting and upsetting institutions and ways of life, WITTFOGEL desired to place on record some facts in connection with hydraulic societies operating in arid and semi-arid lands. The primitive and supposedly harmonious relation between man and nature had been disturbed long before professionalized trade became a major feature of civilization. A system of class distinctions, with one group controlling the mass of the population, existed long before the development of a merchant class. The records of pharaonic Egypt indicate no development of an important group of professional merchants before the beginning of the New

Kingdom. Scholars, such as Breasted and Kees, have shown that trade expeditions were carried on by the governments of the Old and Middle Kingdoms, but professional merchants played no role. Means and others claim that in the Inca Empire there were no professional merchants. The empire was operated essentially on a non-commercial basis. But it certainly was no classless society. A similar situation prevailed in China up to the middle of the Chou dynasty. There was a strong development of a ruling bureaucratic-military elite and a peasantry, but there were virtually no merchants. In all simpler Oriental ("hydraulic") civilizations, societal stratification occurred under conditions having nothing to do with commercial economies.

At the end of the first millennium B.C., the Chinese system of village agriculture was destroyed; the peasants who had lived in regulated village communities became owners of land. A contemporary statement noted, in effect, that, whereas on the public fields the peasants showed no zeal, on their private land they worked "their heads off." China, by spreading private property, introduced more competition among peasants than did most other great hydraulic civilizations. For two thousand years China maintained a very intensive peasant agriculture, based on private landownership and tenancy. Until the end of the Chiang Kai-shek regime, peasants cultivated their land intensively. Yet today the government has to exhort the peasants to till their fields with care. Today the Chinese Communist newspapers *Jen Min Jih Pao* and *Ta Kung Pao* implore the peasants not to sell or slaughter their work animals, because they will be needed later. Today the peasant lands are being pooled (collectivized) throughout China. This is a development similar to the tragic experience in Russia in 1929 and 1930, when the peasants killed their work animals for food rather than pool them in collectives. Generally speaking, private ownership of land has been a great stimulus for the peasant economy.

HUZAYYIN brought in the significance of geographical situation for an area. The arid zone of northern Africa and southwestern Asia lies between the tropics and subtropics and the Mediterranean, where the seas do not meet. In this land interruption to the seas, man had the camel as a beast of burden suitable for caravan travel. A middle area developed for exchange of products between different zones. The spirit of an intermediary or middle man is reflected in the cultural thought and mental and spiritual attitudes of the people. Trading is almost a sacred profession. Commercial economies, however, are not necessarily based upon the production of surplus. The Arabs, for example, had no surplus except in a few oases, and their commercial activity was based not upon local subsistence economies but on surpluses from other regions.

There is at present an increasing pressure to make more intensive use of the arid lands of the world, SEARS remarked. But in practically all places, over millenniums, or at least for centuries, there have been going economies which would be jeopardized by further use. Engineers who have worked in the Near East report that, in trying to locate irrigation works, they can do no better than to relocate old systems in use during prehistoric times. Empirical experience over long periods has been very effective in the Old World. Any increased pressure on such arid-land regions is fraught with certain danger.

ALBRECHT added the point that arid-land economies are based upon the buying and selling of water. Crop plants are grown more by a kind of hydroponic procedure, with water being poured onto lithic deposits, rather than in true soils, because arid soils have not been able to break down into the fine clay particles required for their absorption and exchange of nutrients to plant roots.

Having been in the Middle East just prior to coming to the symposium, BANKS called attention to Iraq as an arid land to watch for future development under a commercial economy. In that country there are now five million people when once there were thirty million. It has the rivers and the ancient irrigation system but, in addition, now has an income of £70,000,000 from oil.

HUMID TROPICS

BARTLETT, characterizing himself as a "Neolithic" man, spoke of his experiences many years ago in the east coast of Sumatra, where he was concerned with establishing vast rubber plantations for the United States Rubber Company and became appalled at the contrast between the manner of European life on the plantations and that of the natives in the adjoining jungle and grassland. Going south from Medan through the great cultivated belt, one passes first through the Deli tobacco country. Then comes a much more sterile region covered with great fields of lalang, a tropical grass of very little usefulness to man except for the grazing of cattle or water buffalo on its very young shoots that appear after annual burning. Finally, one enters the country planted to rubber. In 1917, when Bartlett arrived, only one tiny patch of primary forest remained. All the rest of the great expanse of rain forest had been cut and burned, for it was easier to convert forest into rubber culture than to subdue the relatively useless grassland.

An almost Neolithic culture existed alongside of the most highly developed commercial agricultural enterprise in the East Indies. The two reacted upon one another in a most interesting way.

There is nothing more admirable, theoretically, for the utilization of tropical lands than the growing of rubber trees. Nothing is actually removed from the land except carbon, hydrogen, and oxygen, derived ultimately from air and water. There is no loss of combined nitrogen or fertilizer salts. The plantations had a population of twenty-five thousand, including laborers' families. The trees were all planted in beautiful rows on land cultivated absolutely clean by an army of workers who went forth each morning and, after the rubber had been tapped, scraped off every vestige of a weed.

At the edge of the plantation stood an abrupt wall of the old secondary forest in which the Pardembanan Batak lived. The agriculture of these people consisted of cutting down successive, small areas of forest, waiting until the debris had dried sufficiently to burn, and then burning as completely as possible. However, to plant at the right time, the large logs not yet entirely dry would be left helter-skelter, only the areas between being completely burned. The ash that coated the land represented a tremendously valuable asset, for it contained all of the useful soluble fertilizer salts that the trees had brought up from beneath the ground. Although the first season's cultivation did not completely exhaust this resource, it nearly did so. The burning which followed a season or two later consumed what remained of the fallen logs. Planting in these fields was based upon long experience; it had been learned which crops were shade-tolerant and which were not. In addition to upland rice, a mixture of crops was grown, so that a field was covered with different crops having a wide range of utility. Seemingly abandoned after two or three years to secondary growth, the former clearings still contained fruit trees and sugar palms. This manner of living was exceedingly important to those who practiced it.

The local forest dwellers refused to work for the plantations, for they did not want their way of life destroyed; instead, laborers had to be obtained from Java, a region of surplus population.

SMITH emphasized how plantation agriculture, by bringing in mid-latitude techniques of the plow, fallow, and clean cultivation, had contributed to soil erosion in the tropics. Most of present tropical plantation agriculture is in trees: coconuts, oil palm, rubber, tea, coffee, etc. Fertility is found not on the heavily leached lowlands but on the hillsides. It is on the hillslopes that the tropical farmer seeks a place to plant if he can. Can there be developed a hill tropical agriculture which will preserve the forest? We should be able to apply to the tropic hillside the idea of unplowed orchards as developed over the last thirty years by apple-growers in the eastern United States. The grass cover is mowed, the soil is fertilized, and the grass mat keeps the soil in place while the trees produce the crop. SMITH called for the creation of tropical experiment stations to pool information with existing research stations and to work out a tropical agriculture that would keep the forest cover on the valley floor and develop hill crops above it.

While Smith had just advocated tropical hillside tree crops, GLACKEN recalled that Gourou's chapter urged commercial agriculture of wet-land crops in swampy valley bottoms. A further comment originated from the thesis of Richards (*The Tropical Rain Forest*, 1954) that the tropical rain forest is a great gene reservoir for future plant evolution throughout the world but that it might very well be eradicated by commercial agriculture during the next century.

CAPITAL AND SURPLUS

BOULDING could not help feeling that the study of ecology did not fit one to speak about commercial economies. The significance of the rise of world-wide trade is that it makes man into a single organism, and hence the conclusions derived from study of small parts of man's habitat are not wholly relevant. He had the feeling that ecologists want us to go back to the Neolithic, but he was not going, for it was a very uncomfortable and disagreeable time to have lived. Why assume that soil should not be mined? We mine coal; then why not mine soil under certain circumstances, in certain places, at certain times? If it is assumed, implicitly, that nothing should be exported from any piece of land, does that mean every piece of land has a natural, moral right to be what it was, if it ever was? But we *are* going to mine certain soils; we *are* going to turn certain areas into deserts; we *are* going to have shifting populations. Because commercial economy makes man a single unity rather than a multitude of disparate self-supporting population groups, we can afford to do this. Is the population of Greece today larger or smaller than it was at the time of the flowering of classical civilization? Considerably larger—in spite of all the awful things man has done to the earth. He has been able to multiply practically everywhere over the last two thousand years because of a commercial economy. If man had not mined the soil and cut down the forests, he would still be in the Neolithic. This is not to deny the existence of real conservation problems.

GALDSTON asked to play the tail to this comet. He mentioned that in epidemiology there is a category known as *civilisations sociales*, which includes the miserable epidemic diseases known as tuberculosis, scarlet fever, diphtheria, cholera, typhoid, and sclerosis, which were in part produced by the concentration of man in the cities made possible by commercial agriculture. Whose ecology is being discussed? If man's, then these factors are to be included.

The thought expressed by Darling, that man gains his leisure and builds up his civilization by "breaking into the stored wealth of the . . . natural ecological climaxes," was considered rather pessimistic by GLIKSON, in writing. Though greatly true for our time, he asked whether this is the only way for man to develop higher activities. Are not biological as well as socioeconomic processes of production and reproduction ruled by a natural principle of surplus production which makes possible a peaceful development of higher activities and living conditions? Animal life in nature subsists on a surplus growth of vegetation apparently not needed for the survival and annual renewal of plants. Moreover, it is essential for the very existence of vegetation that its surpluses be consumed by other species. The same relation of mutual dependence exists with respect to the surplus in animal life on which predatory animals and man partly subsist. Somewhat similarly, economic and social organization and division of labor are possible when a well-balanced family farm can produce a quantity of foodstuffs sufficient to nourish an additional number of non-farm families. Such a surplus production, based upon the biologic capabilities of the land, represents a sufficiently reliable basis for the development of civilization. Industrial development has been possible by the forceful concentration, by combined technological and political means, of large surpluses of food and raw materials into specialized regions. If such concentrations of surpluses create scarcity and deterioration in the areas of their production, they are neither true surpluses nor reliable bases for civilization. Surpluses are dynamic factors which initiate natural and social development. But man has often been misled to believe that there are no limits to nature's capability to produce a surplus. Only when he transgresses these limits does man begin to break into the "stored wealth" of the earth.

HEICHELHEIM added to Sears's notation with which the Chairman began this discussion session by stating that capital is the most important factor in commercial societies—even more important than resources or population.

In conclusion, SEARS expressed the thought that mankind's relation to environment *can* be analyzed in terms of accounting if so desired. The main problem is not to confuse two items in the accounting budget: (1) income and (2) depreciation. What is done to maintain the value of the capital structure is good; what is done that destroys it is bad. And that, it seems, is all we have been trying to say.

Industrial Revolution and Urban Dominance

The Rise of Cities

Influence of the City on Exploitation of the Earth

Is the Industrial World Community a Permanent Civilization?

Why Change?

Differences in Approach to Man and Environment

Dr. KENNETH BOULDING, as session Chairman, spent the first several minutes in developing an agenda for discussion. Additional topics suggested from the floor were added to an outline previously distributed by the Chairman. The final roster of topics was as follows:

1. What is the relative importance, in explaining the rise of cities, of the following?
   a) Agricultural techniques; fisheries
   b) Transportation techniques
   c) Industrial techniques (capital, trade, resources such as fossil fuels)
   d) Political techniques
   e) Demand for gregariousness; sociability; vanity and gossip; playfulness
   f) Ownership
   g) Cultural facilities
   h) Religion
   i) Protection (defense)
2. What part is played in cultural dynamics by the *contrast* between urban and rural cultures, and what is the significance of this contrast in modern society?

BOULDING suggested that the most important and inevitable consequence of the present urban revolution is the disappearance of differentiation between urban and rural life in the United States outside the South.

THE RISE OF CITIES

ANDERSON suggested that many people like cities because people like to get together. Man is an animal, and animals come together. Early man, when he could not afford to get together permanently, did so for temporary periods.

The biological basis for this togetherness is reproduction. The very sexual conjugation is a getting-togetherness. As DARLING pointed out, there could be no continuance in a bisexual species without a coming-together. It is a social need of the species. Cities come to be by allowing people to rest together in numbers which, in early hunting and food-gathering systems, they could not do in an environment of relatively poor yields. For example, the Indian settlement of Council Bluffs on the Missouri River was based upon this intense social desire to get together, although technologically the settlement was unable to maintain itself permanently. Even today the Eskimos get together in summer, which is not their busy hunting period, but their environment and technological development do not allow the social amenities to achieve permanence.

STEWART added that non-agricultural peoples gather together whenever the opportunity arises. Even the Australians or the natives of Lower California, when the food supply was sufficient, congregated to eat the surplus food and then dispersed again. The Kwakiutl of

434

the Northwest Coast, merely by having enough salmon, were able to live together in towns.

HEICHELHEIM thought that the urge in man to congregate is not so much for reproduction as simply for the sake of congregating, which is a distinct characteristic of man. MUMFORD, on the other hand, characterized the city as primarily a protected human breeding place. The element of protection brings together a larger number of people within a small area and increases the opportunity for people from quite different biological stocks to intermingle and to produce more combinations than would be possible in a more widespread community.

But KNIGHT pointed out that the city is antibiological. He asked: How and in what stages of human history do cities universally fail to maintain themselves without recruitment from outside? BROWN wondered whether the failure to maintain itself is a phenomenon of the city or of the economy with which it is associated. In India, for example, age-specific birth rates of Calcutta and Bombay are equal to those of the smallest villages.

BATES cautioned that getting-togetherness underlies the whole phenomenon of human society; the discussion should strive to emerge from that into the particulars. EVANS, in writing, warned that it should not be forgotten that society is older than man, is inherited from prehuman ancestors, and is not a human invention. STEINBACH, in writing, considered the discussion of gregariousness on a biological basis to have confused two issues: (1) the basic tendency to aggregation, which is reversible, accounts for *initial* formation of groups and is a biological factor; and (2), once aggregation takes place in organisms or communities, the setting-in of *differentiation,* which is irreversible, applies to communities following the formation of groups and is a cultural factor.

HUZAYYIN preferred to start from space relations rather than from human activity to explain the rise of cities. The social need of man to come together may be perfectly true, but what of the natural forces which compel man to agglomerate? About 7500 B.C. there came a phase of aridity in the Middle East that forced man and animal to come together in small, limited watering areas. About 5500 B.C. more rainfall, a phase of relaxation, allowed space relationships to be established among these areas of concentration.

It seemed to MAYER that biological factors account for the village but not for the city and that a distinction between the city and the village was necessary. BROWN agreed and pointed out that plotting a frequency-distribution curve of sizes of living units gave a continuum, whether for India or for the United States.

GUTKIND did not feel that size meant anything. The big village towns of Hungary, which are miles apart and contain up to thirty thousand people, are not cities, because everyone in them, save a few artisans, is engaged in agriculture. He suggested the real distinction between city and country to be based on function. Another distinction is that in villages a person may have a close group of many relatives, while in a city he is freer to form elective affinities, which has led to an atomization of society.

Among those who could not accept the distinction between town and village based upon function was HUZAYYIN. As far back as we can go in Egypt and the Middle East, where villages and cities began, the two can never be distinguished in their functions. Villages are not always agricultural; some are based on industry, others on trade. Rather the criterion is space relations —the village limited to the surrounding subsistence area, the town having a wider hinterland and wider space relationships. GUTKIND replied that the very large village towns of Hungary have enormous areas around them, yet they remain villages, because everyone is engaged in agriculture. He could not see any possible distinction between town and village other than the functional activities of men living in either place.

GLIKSON found that the size of villages is ordinarily limited by the distance from the house of the farmer to the land on which he has to work. There is a certain maximum limit to this distance and a certain minimum size for the area of land on which the villager has to do his work. Exceptions to this occur, such as in Bavaria, Italy, and Hungary, for reasons of security; villagers concentrate in rural towns, but even today they suffer the handicap of the distance which must be traveled from home to fields.

The meaning of the terms "city" and "town" has fundamentally changed, WISSMANN added, in writing. Until the nineteenth century and in some parts of the world to a later time, a town in most countries was a *fortified* settlement, generally founded by the government and having governmental functions. This was especially true in China, in ancient and medieval Europe, and in the Near and Middle East. In all these regions the development of cities was different, but fortification, except perhaps in Egypt, and government centralization were present.

The classic area for the study of the industrial revolution is nineteenth-century Britain; but, despite a great deal of work on many aspects of the movement, little has been done to show how cities came into being. DARBY asked: What really happened when Manchester grew or Birmingham came about? What were the mechanics of the movement that produced these "million" cities by the end of the nineteenth century? Based upon census information that from about 1841 included data on birthplaces, Arthur Redford, in a pioneer study published in 1926, showed that the movement to any growing center was essentially short term. People came into Manchester from the surrounding countryside, which, in turn, was replenished from the more remote countryside; that, in turn, was replenished from adjacent regions until the coast was reached. This was true of every growing center; the whole island was one mobile mass of population. Later in the century a long-term movement obviously became more important, but exactly how, when, and which areas were most closely affected are not known, because material about birthplaces has not been worked out. If we knew the how, perhaps we would be better equipped to answer the why.

It was suggested by LANDSBERG, in writing, that some valuable information could be gathered by studying the rebuilding of cities after catastrophes in a scientific, objective manner. There are many of these in all lands and all ages. A few come directly to mind from recent history: Chicago after the fire (1871); San Francisco after the earthquake and fire (1906); Messina after an earthquake (1908); the destruction wrought by Mount Pelée on Martinique (1902); the destruction of Tokyo and Yokohama by earthquake (1923), with a repeat performance for the former city by fire bombs (1945); the destruction of World Wars I and II, in particular during the last war in such different habitats as Coventry, Plymouth, London, Berlin, Hamburg, Frankfurt, Warsaw, Hiroshima, Nagasaki, Agaña, Manila, etc.

What patterns did reconstruction take? Why did people go back to the old places? What improvements were made? Did the people make "choices"? Were there notable differences in different nations? How do reconstruction practices differ with time? How does the further development of reconstructed cities compare with untouched towns in the same area? Answers to these and similar questions seem to contain "ecological" information comparable in value to that obtained for plants after prairie and forest fires.

Jones, in writing, referred to Boulding's list of factors of importance to explain the rise of cities and pointed out that we must differentiate among (1) the *requirements* for a city; (2) the *functions* of cities; and (3) the *developmental history* of specific cities or of cities in specific societies. Among the requirements for a city are means of subsistence, transportation, government (for reasonable internal order and protection), and site. The functions of cities are many, and the hierarchy is different in different cities. Washington, D.C., is governmental but has recreational functions. Atlantic City is recreational but, of course, has its government. And, as Darby properly stressed, there is need for developmental histories of cities, since the present city may be structurally and functionally different from what it was in earlier periods.

Boulding proposed that cities are the products of agriculture and exploitation. That is, without agriculture there is no surplus to feed the cities, and without exploitation there is no way of gathering the surplus together.

It seemed to Thompson that there was a very marked change in the agriculture of Europe during the seventeenth century. The industrial revolution was preceded and accompanied by an agricultural revolution. This latter was not so obvious; it did not attract attention. The improvement in techniques effectively increased the productivity per hour of labor bestowed on a particular type of work. When the industrial revolution began, probably not more than 20 per cent of the people of any country lived in what would be called "cities," as characterized by differentiations in occupations of their in-

habitants. With the growing efficiency in agriculture (introductions of new crops and improvements in animal breeding), the proportion of people who could be spared to live in communities and carry on non-agricultural occupations slowly increased. As the industrial revolution grew in its use of power and as more labor was needed, people moved from the country to the city. The modern growth of cities has been based fundamentally upon changes in agriculture. These changes have taken place gradually but continuously, so that in a country like the United States only about 13½ per cent of the population now resides on farms. Basically, the growth of modern cities has depended upon moving along *pari passu* with improvements in techniques and knowledge of agricultural production, though this does not altogether answer the question why. As agriculture became more efficient in modern times, other countries, such as Japan, were able to make the industrial transition much more quickly.

The influx of population to towns depended on the state of agriculture only to a certain degree, Gutkind countered. There is an old saying in Germany that "town air sets people free." People came to towns desiring to escape the feudal powers which were then stronger in the countryside. The towns were not able to absorb them all, and, in consequence, a sort of unemployed proletariat arose in many European medieval towns.

Gourou, in writing, observed that a diminution in density of rural population was possible in the United States and in Western Europe, because rural densities were not very high. In Japan, however, the rural density in 1868, before the industrial revolution, was 600 per square mile, and it has continued at that level until today. Growth of Japanese cities has not resulted in rural exodus but has been possible only by demographic excedents of rural population. When the rural population is very heavy at the onset of industrialization, the role of cities and industrialization is very different. Therein lies a great difference between East and West.

Again, in writing, GOUROU presented an obverse example. In central Africa the cities are in a somewhat difficult situation with regard to their food supply. For example, Leopoldville (300,000 Africans) finds difficulty in obtaining enough food. Yet the average density of population in the Belgian Congo is only 5 per square kilometer, and 85 per cent of the inhabitants are rural. The explanation is found in the disparity between the two civilizations. European civilization is responsible for the creation of the city; the traditional African civilization is responsible for the scarcity of salable foods. Today it is easier and cheaper to import wheat flour to make bread for consumption by Africans in Leopoldville than to find in the countryside sufficient quantities of *chikwangues* (cassava paste).

GALDSTON inquired whether the agricultural population under conditions of agricultural surplus automatically reduced itself through exodus in inverse proportion to the quantity produced. BOULDING then modified his original proposition that cities are the products of agriculture and exploitation. A surplus from agriculture is necessary but is not a sufficient condition to account for the formation of cities.

GOUROU, in writing, said that, for him, the discussion of the city had been most confused. Is it necessary to ask why there are cities and what are their characteristics? The only point that appeared to him important was whether the development of cities in modern civilization was dangerous, profitable, or indifferent for the future of humanity.

At this point in the discussion, BLU-

MENSTOCK rose to voice his objection that the discussion had strayed too far from the theme and that consideration should be given to the influence of the industrial revolution on the ability of man to change the face of the earth. Cities do change the face of the earth, but, while a fascinating subject, their modes of origin do not.

INFLUENCE OF THE CITY ON EXPLOITATION OF THE EARTH

MUMFORD thought it must be realized that the cities of the nineteenth century and, very largely, the present day were successful in a commercial sense because they were parasitic on a subsistence economy. The assumption was that the farmer should not be able to make a normal commercial living from his work and the rent of his land; that he would not be a good bookkeeper and find out whether it was worthwhile to supply food to the city. As long as that condition prevailed and as long as a colonial population—an external or internal proletariat, to use Toynbee's terms—was available, cities were able to flourish at a great rate. Now, subsistence economies are in rebellion. In the United States the farmer, through the influence of education in agricultural colleges, keeps books and demands profits on his farm labor and farm investment comparable to those made on industrial investments. This becomes a limiting factor in the growth of cities. For example, cities are now obliged to offer subsidies to dairy farmers in order to obtain a sufficient amount of milk, and that is true of such other products as cotton and tobacco. We have reached the point where the fundamental relationship of the city to the land is being changed through the very success of the commercial economy in invading agriculture. This, in the long run, MUMFORD thought, is going to have very serious, and perhaps beneficial, results both on the spread of cities and on the exploitation of the land.

HARRIS objected to Mumford's use of the term "parasitic" for cities. Cities are no more parasitic on the land than farmers are parasitic on the cities. Who is paying the subsidies now, for example? Cities exist because they perform important economic functions. They are the most efficient areal technique yet devised by man for most types of production. For most of the things that people want, production can be organized more efficiently in urban agglomerations than by any other means. Cities also transform agriculture. That farmers have learned to do bookkeeping is part of the urban transformation of rural society. It has been said that only in the South is there still a genuine rural society. The commercially oriented farmer of the Middle West has become to a certain extent urbanized. His places of work are dispersed, but his attitudes are urban. The most atrocious waste of resources on earth today is rural underemployment. The technique of improving the utilization of this resource probably lies through industrialization and urbanization.

Far from ruining the countryside, cities are perhaps its salvation, ULLMAN suggested. Tractors made in the city have enabled individual men to handle more than they could before; agriculture thereby has made enormous strides in productivity.

BOULDING asked whether cities today are not utterly different from those even of three hundred years ago. Though agricultural incomes are lower than industrial income—and this is doubtfully true in the Middle West—this is a temporary result of the difficulties caused by migration from agriculture. Actually, cities can produce enough to pay the agricultural population almost anything it wants—almost too much.

In the modern era a great change has taken place in the relation between town and village. WITTFOGEL suggested that the term "parasitic" was used perhaps with the thought that parasitism did not occur in the early days but came into existence with the development of commerce. Assuming that function is the basis for the rise of cities, two conditions have to exist, that is, surplus and the transport of surplus. What do people in cities have that people in the countryside do not? Thought of trade focuses upon the *things* that are exchanged. People of the cities, ever since the time of early Egypt have provided *services*. They kept peace and order, administered the regulation of the waterworks, and so on, albeit, WITTFOGEL added, he preferred the present service relationship with Washington, D.C., over that in existence at the time of the Pyramids. One of the great revolutions is the democratic revolution that in the United States involved considerable influence over the cities, enabling the farmers, although a minority, to wield considerable political power. A completely new city-village relationship has arisen.

There is a difference between the large nations and the small. BANKS pointed out that the United States in the last decade had experienced the largest peacetime migration in the history of the world—ten million people moved to the West Coast. Such a phenomenon, little noticed and certainly not disruptive of internal affairs of a large country, is to some extent incomparable with conditions in small countries such as Israel, in which, as GLIKSON expressed it, the nearness and importance of what may be termed the biological-ecological equilibrium existence is felt very well. HISLOP was reminded that England, too, is small, though it has a large population. At one time it could feed itself, but today it cannot, and so it has developed industrially. It has large cities and conurbations composed of cities and their gradually merging adjoining towns, for example, Tyneside. The Tyne, a little river toward the north of England near the Scottish border, had various towns along its banks, north and south as far as the coast, about ten miles distant. But now these towns are gradually approaching one another until there is almost a continuous city stretching from the coast to Newcastle and the west. These conurbations are necessary, because England must manufacture goods and export them to feed itself. It cannot carry on solely through inward and outward traffic between the cities and their adjacent rural countrysides.

MALIN, in writing, discussed the significance to the industrial revolution and to the English Midlands cities of the development of interior communications *within* the landmass during the second quarter of the nineteenth century. Historically, water transport had served to carry bulky commodities, but muscle power for that purpose was too expensive in energy expenditure. The rise of England's Midlands cities during the late eighteenth century had been based in large part upon canals which were designed to introduce economies of water transport into the interior of the landmass. They served remarkably well up to a certain point. But canals soon reached their maximum capacity to serve their purpose and gave way to a new order of magnitude in interior communication. Canals could be built only in a few places because of limitations of topography, water, etc. The steam railroad and locomotive were tested by Richard Trevithick in 1804 in the all-but-inaccessible country of southwestern England. The steam railroad introduced cheap interior communication into the landmass. Its great significance lay in opening up interiors hitherto unavailable, together with their mineral wealth. Thus the railroad enlarged the limits of natural resources. It also provided access to

new markets and enlarged existing ones, affording outlets for surpluses and inducements to enlarging production of surplus products. Furthermore, interiors could be supplied from the abundance of the outside world with commodities new to them or scarce. Socially, railroads spread intelligence and cultural amenities throughout England. The railroad as a mode of interior communication exerted a revolutionary influence upon international competition. In his book on railroads (1825, 1831), Nicholas Wood argued that the nation first to acquire this new technology would lead the world into a new era. The most remarkable aspect of this dictum was that Britain's leadership has been attributed usually to sea power. The implication of Wood's argument was that, even in a small country like England, landmass was critical to Britain's international position—even to Britain's sea power. The sea was equally available, theoretically, to all nations as a highway to states fronting on oceans. Landmass was different. It was unique to each state, and the effectiveness of its use was the responsibility of each state and its *opportunity* to wield this uniqueness as an advantage over rivals. During the nineteenth century England's industrial system capitalized upon that fact in a big way. Later, of course, large, continental, landmass countries were to challenge Britain, but Britain, as Wood had predicted, held the lead for quite some time. Railroads were the basis of the rise of Britain's rivals later in the nineteenth century, which partly neutralized Britain's sea power. Still later, air power, another new order of magnitude in communication, largely neutralized both sea power and landmass power per se.

Improvements in transportation were an obvious part of the industrial transformation, ULLMAN thought. The main effect was to enable areas to specialize in what they could do best. The scale of the earth's regions thus has been changed by the developments in transportation.

The last century or so, probably, was one of the first times in which man had almost unlimited choice as to what the configuration of a country should be as among big cities, small cities, and towns. On this point, MAYER introduced the subject of choice. Probably in established countries, but certainly in underdeveloped countries, no one questions organization, gregariousness, agriculture, and the other absolutely true things that have here been discussed. But are we choosing the kind of configuration that is most efficient? If we want to exercise choice, we can do so, because we now command the technology. Rural underemployment can be remedied. Certain areas of India are being developed in ways that do not involve huge cities; many consumer industries can be handled in very small cities. In discussing choice and the configuration to be chosen, we are confronted by certain problems. What is the effect on people of the size of the city in which they live? What kinds of relationship can or cannot exist in cities of different sizes? Are the cultural values in the very big cities outweighed by the passivity with regard to participation?

ULLMAN granted that technology now permits the choice of picking the size of the city desired, but who makes the choice? In our society is it not the factory-builder? And where does he build? For footloose industries, where he can get labor. Formerly this meant the cities; now, the favored spot is the satellite-suburb, where, by compromising, he can be close to labor and other urban aspects yet have a good site on cheaper land with access to good roads and better living conditions for his labor. Such are the growing places which have experienced the greatest shift in population over the last two decades in the United States. But this does not mean a dispersed population in small towns scattered over the countryside. North Carolina, for example, is almost a truly dispersed industrial area, with a few large cities of about 100,000 and many tiny towns. Labor in the rural population was dispersed to begin with, and industry has dispersed to reach its labor supply. But the industries, such as textiles, pay relatively low wages, for skilled specialists are not found among dispersed populations. The dilemma of North Carolina is its low per capita income. Does man have the power for change? Is it real or only apparent?

SMITH spoke of recent changes in the Philadelphia suburbs. It depressed him to travel the ten miles from his home into the city. What was last year a field is now row after row of little houses, only a few feet apart, with nothing between, in front, or behind them but a slight touch of green and several little trees. These accursed rows of houses are the action of an individual who happens to own a farm or to buy a field and wants to jam as many houses as possible onto his pasture to sell at from $14,000 to $20,000. About sixty years ago an English shorthand reporter, Ebenezer Howard, wrote a little book with a plan called *Garden Cities of Tomorrow* (1903). Based on a concentric-circle concept, with two or three great circular streets, the plan included business buildings in the center, residences all around, and the fields beyond reserved as fields. Lots were big enough to have a little garden, and in the fields beyond a larger garden could be had by those who wanted it. Such cities have been brought into existence in England, as described in Mumford's chapter (pp. 395–96). Here has been a true revolution—a place for people to live, where they can dig, have fresh air, have more sunshine, and have a place to play and which will not be turned into a slum by the next real estate operation. MUMFORD added that fourteen garden cities are in existence, some just coming into completion. All are of limited size, none proposed numbers over 90,000, and all have green belts of varying amounts around them.

MAYER mentioned that something much more revolutionary had happened in England in the last several years. A new law permits big cities to buy land beyond their own limits to set up satellite towns. These subtowns are being built around certain existing small communities as nuclei. This is done by covenant with communities which are willing and ready to accept this planned expansion. For the first time in Western civilization over the last century, a city (London) has decided that it is too big and is going to resettle some of its population, not in a suburb a few miles away, but way beyond, in new settlements. BANKS added the comment that it has been recognized that, in making such a new town, there must be included a mixture of types of people with different interests—not all slum dwellers or all professional people. GUTKIND spoke of physical planning. These developments in Britain were achieved not by planning single towns or a single county but by planning on a regional or sometimes national scale. Ten satellite towns are being built around London, almost like the earlier garden cities. Most of these towns have mixed populations, but a problem that arises is that up to 60 or 70 per cent of the people have to work elsewhere. Thus it is also important to decentralize industry. A garden city was originally conceived as an independent, almost self-contained unit, but the final result of physical decentralization without cultural decentralization is that all these very nice cities, planned with the best intentions, will be new, stuffy small towns with small-town folk, because the cultural amenities, save the cinema and a few others, do not exist. BANKS did

not entirely agree that there would be lack of culture in the satellite towns. Television, radio, improved education, and transportation have opened new vistas, giving access to incredible beauty and knowledge to persons wherever they may live. As he put it, "When I buy my cigarettes every morning in Cambridge, I learn more archeology than I myself know from the lady who serves me who has witnessed Glyn Daniel the night before describing the beautiful things on television. She has seen things which I have not seen."

Most of the discussion had been spent on the additions that cities have made to the face of the earth and very little about the losses that have taken place, CLARK remarked. There are very important losses, culturally, of many satisfactory folkways. And there are also the tremendous losses in the organization of biological communities—in the soil and in vegetation. He was not at all sure that we are very much better off for having so many more people or for extending cities in such fashion. In an inventory of what cities have done to the face of the earth, it is peculiar that thought should have been given only to additions and not to subtractions in the long historical record.

ALBRECHT personally did not like the lining-up of city versus country, because both contribute to food production. The city man makes machines for the farmer to produce more food. It is not antithesis; everybody is hungry, and everybody must be fed if he is to survive. Man has done a good deal to populate the face of the earth in regions where he could not have survived if forced to depend on what was produced there. Transportation, industry, and politics have enabled people to reach back into "oasis" areas where surplus foods or tools are produced. The specializations of certain men have extended resources to other world areas. But biological man is a manifestation of certain forces; there must be energy behind him. The high level of energy in the United States has been based on the tremendous fertility of resources that could be mined, converted into food, and started flowing toward the oceans by means of sanitary sewage disposal. The energy stream of China and Japan does not run to the ocean; part of what goes to the cities is carried back. That reversal of the energy differential slows down the congestion of cities. The United States has been mining its resources; and now conservation is a kind of post mortem. The protein content of wheat is dropping; crops have been substituted that neglect protein, but they fill and fool and bring on degenerative diseases; and it has not yet been seen that cities are merely the concentration of "flies collecting around the honey jar." Soil fertility, the agricultural capital of food production, is not perpetuated in the United States. City values can be transformed into a common unit—the dollar —but the pounds of calcium, potassium, magnesium, copper, zinc, and cobalt in the soil cannot be so readily transformed. A farm is bought for its fertility capital, but it is assessed in terms of such utilities as highway frontage, not fertility, its real value. Commercial agriculture liquidates capital assets and calls it "taking a profit." Fertility capital has not yet been put into monetary values and reduced to the level with which other resources are viewed.

IS THE INDUSTRIAL WORLD COMMUNITY A PERMANENT CIVILIZATION?

STEWART proposed that the industrial revolution be thought of in terms of villages. Almost every village in Switzerland has its factory. Is Switzerland one town—an urban center as a whole —or has industrialization so spread to the villages that the "industrial" city versus "rural" village distinction is not really proper? Industrial villages have

so developed in the United States that there is even the phenomenon of a watch-crystal factory being built on an Indian reservation.

Industrialization has erased the distinction between cities and non-cities, TAX suggested. Industrialized societies appear to be a kind of integrated whole to those from other societies. For example, the Indians of highland Guatemala are organized into villages each practicing agriculture but each, also, having economic specialization, such as pottery-making in one village, basketry in another. When Tax told them where he was from, he was told, "Well, if you're from the United States, then you know how to make an airplane." This naïveté is significant; the important difference between them and us is not geographical location but organization— economic, social, political. What the industrial revolution meant was not simply some technological advances but organizational changes.

It seemed to BOULDING that the present industrial civilization is completely unprecedented. If a map of the world could be drawn on which all distances were in proportion to cost of transport, then the oceans would disappear, and it would be clear that there is one world city—that all cities are suburbs of one another. All previous civilizations also have rested on the differentiation of rural and urban, whereas the industrial civilization does not. Both the Swiss villager and the Iowa farmer are signs of this. If past civilizations have been unstable because they were made in cities and overthrown in the country, the establishment of a modern rural-urban identity has profound implications for cultural dynamics. Human history has consisted of the long Paleolithic, then the Neolithic, followed by the rise and fall of civilizations based on agriculture and exploitation. Now, if we do not blow ourselves to pieces, there is a long chance that the next stage of man will be a permanent high-level civilization.

HEICHELHEIM accepted this as a plausible hypothesis. He submitted that the decisive factors behind all earlier urban developments were environment and a new organization of capital. Behind the industrial revolution were the religious changes in Protestantism, Catholicism, and Judaism to what is called a "capitalist mentality." As an illustration, the farmer no longer looked upon his cow as an animal to be loved, petted, or maltreated but as a piece of capital to be used as well as he could for the betterment of himself and of mankind. New money structures brought cities into stronger relationships to the countryside than they had had before. For example, active investment banking of the nineteenth century completely changed the agricultural-urban structure of the United States.

BROWN noticed that agricultural and transportation revolutions had been suggested as responsible agents for the industrial revolution, and an economist had just spoken of capital formation. A geologist would refer to coal fields, and a technologist would speak of Abraham Darby, who first linked coal with iron. BROWN preferred to look upon the industrial revolution as a mesh—to see it in the same way that one looks upon an ecological assemblage, in which everything interacts on everything else. The net result is that feedback is encountered, which enormously accelerates everything. The industrial revolution is not one thing but the interaction of a vast complex of things.

GRAHAM reminded everyone that in all interrelationships there is a limiting factor. For example, one of the limiting factors today in the location of many large industrial developments is water. Lacking this single factor, many find it impossible to settle where they wish to settle.

The reference to capital led to GLIKSON's recall of the analysis by G. T. Wrench in his 1946 volume, *Reconstruction by Way of the Soil*, which compared the capital of the farmer with that of the nomad. Man's attitudes to the environment and to life are expressed in his various ideas of capital. According to Wrench, land is the basic capital of the farmer. All care is given to maintenance of soil fertility as a preservation of capital not only for the present but also for future generations. Domestic animals are the capital of the nomad. As movable property, they can be transferred from one land area to another, exhausting a maximum of land fertility in a minimum of time, then moving on (with the wealth of the land stored in the animals) to another region for another period of exploitation. Though clashes between farmers and nomads today have become rare, the basic controversy in attitudes remains. The economic values prevailing among the majority of city populations (and often among modern farmers, too) are very close to the idea of the nomad: land and its products are valued in terms of money. In the past, nomad actions endangered and destroyed land as a permanent source of livelihood; with the development of techniques, transportation, and markets, the "nomadic" values today represent an even greater danger. On the other hand, the work by the Dutch of reclaiming agricultural land from the sea expresses the farmer's values: an increase of fertile land is an increase of the basic capital of the country.

This question of the measure of value, BOULDING felt, was critical for the symposium. There is a strong feeling that the dollar is not the perfect measure—that there are other values which are not conserved under a banking civilization. On the other hand, no simple physical measures are satisfactory—neither phosphorus nor protein.

There is no escape from the psychological nature of utility.

LEOPOLD took up the question of values. Continual development of the urban community during the industrial revolution has been directed presumably toward, we can say, more and better bathtubs. What will happen in the future depends on what people consider to be the values to be obtained or achieved. In California, for example, urbanization has continued to the point where cities have become so large that there has been a very surprising and rapid movement of people not only to the suburbs but actually to the desert. So great is the desire, apparently, for certain aesthetic and perhaps ethical values not obtainable in the city that people, in their movement to the desert, have built homes to which they actually haul water. What happens next to man will depend upon the rapidity and nature of change in values, influenced more and more by a desire for improved ethical and aesthetic standards beyond the limit of what can be achieved through industrialization and urbanization.

WHY CHANGE?

BOULDING was interested in the theoretical background of the dynamics of change. What is the model underlying the extraordinary phenomenon of development and change in society? He suggested the mutation-selection model and asked whether it could be applied to changes in technology and organization. If so: (a) What factors affect the rate of *mutation* (new "ideas")? (b) What is the relation between the rate of mutation and the over-all rate of "development," however measured? (c) Why is there such a strong relation between religious nonconformity and technical change? (d) What are the factors in society which *prevent* development? (e) The weakness of the mutation-selection model in explaining

technical development is that mutations in "ideas" are *not* random. How can this "un-randomness" be expressed in a theoretical model?

All evolution falls into periods of relative stability, which leave records, interspersed with periods of rapid development, of which very little is known. In the history of man there have been perhaps three periods of rapid development: (1) the development of *Homo sapiens* himself; (2) the great transition from the Paleolithic, with the invention of civilization (agriculture, cities); and (3) the present period—the second great transition. Can a mutation in society, in ideas, in institutions, be identified? Is there such a thing as a rate of mutation in social institutions? What is the relation of this to development? In a stable society all mutations are strangled at birth; in an equilibrium society selection cancels out all mutations, and the society reproduces itself. In the process of biological evolution partial isolation is important. Is it important in social change? Obviously, social change is not the same as biological change. What are the important differences that can be identified?

The great problem to BOULDING was why change occurred at all. There is something in human society which will not permit rest. If men are to understand change, let alone dream of controlling it, they must understand the processes of change. Almost the only theoretical scheme which has an account of change is that of biological evolution. This theory is certainly shaky and highly dubious, but it is the only theory that can offer any kind of explanation of the processes of change. There are what might be called "social species" in the shape of ideas, organizations, customs, types, and ways of doing things. Mutations occur occasionally—new ideas, new ways of doing things—and there is obviously a selective process of society which enables some mutations to survive and not others. The difficulty when studying the basic empirical problem is that things which do not survive are not there to study. We talk about survival of the fittest—not the fittest for what, but the fittest for survival. Evolution, then, is the survival of the surviving, but do we know what makes for survival?

GREGG suggested that man's inborn curiosity, when reasonably actively employed, is more nearly responsible for such changes as are known than many other factors. He thought also of age-group pressures. It is almost certain that, after a certain set of values persist for a reasonable time, the next generation will come along inclined to challenge it. "I always liked the account of Mussolini having a meeting in Bologna. The triumph of his speech was, 'The man to succeed me is not born.' And the next line in the newspaper was, 'At this moment the band struck up "Giovanezza, Giovanezza."'"

Innovators belong to a different class, suggested GALDSTON. How the biological sport arises among humans we do not know. He granted that the technologies of agriculture, fisheries, transport, and industry are the instruments by which certain end results are actually realized; only an idiot would deny the cardinal importance and historic potency of those factors. But what he wanted to know was: Who creates a Da Vinci? Who inspires a Darwin? Who gives us a Pasteur? A Wagner? Do we really pretend that by the study of technologic factors we can ever assess how they come into being? Can we ever gauge what such people have done in order to produce the instrumentalities that have led to cities and all?

Take, for example, three important things related to the industrial revolution—steam, internal combustion, and the electric motor. We have had copper; we knew about electricity—Volta long antedated Watt. But why was it,

GALDSTON wondered, that the electric motor and the dynamo were not created before the steam engine? Also, what of significance preceded the Renaissance? Long before inclosures were started, there were such things as the vulgar languages, the cult of the Virgin, the troubadours, and many cultural factors contributing to the rise of cities and of agriculture. Human beings have certain cultural and intellectual impulsions. And these must be included in any ecological assessment.

GLACKEN took the Chairman to task for importing a biological scheme to the neglect of human history. During the session various speakers had brought up important historical details very troublesome to makers of theoretical systems. Many European colleagues have a far greater sense of the tremendous value of the historical experience of mankind and the events that have determined it. To import biological analogies, no matter with how many qualifications, is to repeat a system which began with the Greeks and ended with the fanciful theories of nineteenth-century German political thought and sociology. GLACKEN, in writing, suggested, too, that the chapters dealing with the early history of man's modifications of the earth are an excellent corrective to the view—widely expressed in contemporary literature—that the greatest and most significant changes in the earth's surface have come as a consequence of the industrial revolution. These chapters show how extensive were the modifications by non-industrial peoples. Notable, too, was that a large part of Marsh's work dealt with changes brought about in ancient and medieval times and in the preindustrial era.

DIFFERENCES IN APPROACH TO MAN AND ENVIRONMENT

BOULDING pointed up what seemed to him the fundamental issue which had arisen in the symposium and which probably would continue in all subsequent sessions. Quite obviously within the group present there was a sharp division between the "biological-ecological" point of view and the "socioeconomic" viewpoint.

The biological-ecological view is expressed in terms of equilibrium systems and of movements toward equilibrium, that is, systems in which there is circulation and conservation. The form of something is changed, but everything eventually returns, and the cycle is repeated. Biologists and conservationists feel that man has to find his place with-

EGLER felt extremely enlightened by at last being able to comprehend the extraordinary references to ecology that he had found in various parts of the literature on economics. But ecologists no longer think that, when white men came to America, everything was in a stable equilibrium or in a fixed balance of nature; that white men knocked it down; and that, if left alone, nature would rise up again to a certain productive point and stay there, moving along at a balance. To the contrary, the past was an extraordinary series of irregular upheavals, not little cycles. Present cultures produce additional

Stage of Life	Organisms	Communities
Aggregation	Cleavage of eggs, movement of slime-mold cells, etc.	Formation of original communities
Morphogenetic Movements (slowly reversible sluggish movements)	Cell orientations, etc.	Organization of technology and government
Differentiation (practically irreversible)	Tissue and organ formation (obligatory interaction)	Specialization of function, including obligatory interaction within community and environment
Variable Growth and/or Differentiation		
Adult?		
Senility and Death?		

in a cycle of this 'kind; if he violates it, he is heading for trouble.

On the other hand, all history, geological as well as human, is not the repetition of a cycle. It is an irreversible process of curiously decreasing entropy —that is, of increasing complexity of organization. This process of agricultural improvement, urbanization, and industrialization has just been discussed. The development of surplus from agriculture permits the establishment of towns. Also, the towns develop the skills and techniques of science and industry, and these feed back on the agricultural countryside. This is a cumulative process in which the critical element is not the conservation of materials or of energy but information.

imbalances through which they move on to new irregularities, not inscribed in the finite world of traditional ecology. Ecologists should not be blamed for what is no longer ecology. STEINBACH, in writing, supported Egler's contention that biologists do *not* assume equilibrium systems. He felt rather that the most relevant area of biology was *not* field ecology, which he considered largely sterile and archaic, but developmental biology. The "curious" nonadditive, locally irreversible, entropy decrease is fundamental and destructive for biological (including sociological) existence. The accompanying diagram was presented.

SAUER asked the Chairman to expand his remarks on the deficiency of the biological group in its lack of knowledge of an antientropic system. BOULDING explained that organization was introduced into human evolution through man's consciousness, his learning capacity, and the development of such cultural factors as language, communication, and information transfer. Man is a problem-solving animal. Antientropy refers to the extraordinary process of rapid increase of organizational complexity. Culture builds up entropy instead of tearing it down, and this has to be taken into account in ecological systems. Biological systems are subsystems with which we should not rest. There must be taken into account the process of communication and information among human beings, which is antientropic. For example, a class when taught knows more, and the instructor does not know any less. This is the key to life, which is a process for diminishing entropy, and civilization is its extension.

DARWIN asked whether increasing organization and increasing complication are not themselves increasing the entropy of the world. He thought quite confidently that this had been very rapidly increased by all that has been going on in the last fifty years. Putnam, in his *The Future of Energy*, states that half the coal which has been burned in the whole history of the world has been burned in the United States in the last thirty years. In this sense, then, the United States in the last thirty years has done as much to increase the entropy of the world as the whole of the human race in the whole of the past. This is not a boast!